ANNUAL EDITIONS

Drugs, Society, and Behavior 13/14
Twenty-Eighth Edition

EDITORS

Mary H. Maguire
California State University—Sacramento

Dr. Mary Maguire is an Associate Professor of Criminal Justice at California State University Sacramento, one of the largest Criminal Justice programs in the United States. She teaches Criminology, Research Methods, and Contemporary Issues in Criminal Justice. She has an MA in Psychology, an MSW, and a PhD. in Social Work and Social Research. Dr. Maguire has fifteen years of professional experience in behavioral health. She has twelve years of research experience measuring clinical models and behaviors of high-risk populations, including best practices for those with mental illness and co-occurring substance abuse. Dr. Maguire is the recent past President of the Western Society of Criminology and the recipient of the J.D. Lohman Award for Outstanding Service to the Society. She is published in the area of policing, corrections, and criminal justice policy.

Clifford Garoupa
Fresno City College

Mr. Garoupa received his Bachelor of Arts degree from California State University—Fresno in Sociology, his Master's degree in Sociology from The Ohio State University, and his Juris Doctor degree from The San Joaquin College of Law. He worked for many years in the criminal justice system, both in law enforcement and criminal defense, primarily as an investigator but also as a consultant, particularly in homicide and serious drug cases. During his academic career, he has not only served in an advisory capacity to members of Congress, but also was appointed to the Fresno County Drug and Alcohol Advisory Board, acting for five years as that Board's Chairman. He has been interviewed on National Public Radio concerning European Harm Reduction Policy and Practice, particularly the implementation and effect of drug decriminalization in Portugal. He is the former Program Coordinator for the Drug and Alcohol Counseling program at Fresno City College, which is one of the largest such educational programs in California. He currently teaches both Sociology and Drug Studies.

McGraw Hill

*Connect
Learn
Succeed*™

ANNUAL EDITIONS: DRUGS, SOCIETY, AND BEHAVIOR, TWENTY-EIGHTH EDITION

Published by McGraw-Hill, a business unit of The McGraw-Hill Companies, Inc., 1221 Avenue
of the Americas, New York, NY 10020. Copyright © 2014 by The McGraw-Hill Companies, Inc.
All rights reserved. Printed in the United States of America. Previous edition(s) 2013, 2012, 2009.

Some ancillaries, including electronic and print components, may not be available to customers
outside the United States.

This book is printed on acid-free paper.

Annual Editions® is a registered trademark of The McGraw-Hill Companies, Inc.

Annual Editions is published by the **Contemporary Learning Series** group within the
McGraw-Hill Higher Education division.

1 2 3 4 5 6 7 8 9 0 QDB/QDB 1 0 9 8 7 6 5 4 3

ISBN 978-0-07-813610-8
MHID 0-07-813610-5
ISSN 1091-9945 (print)
ISSN 2158-8856 (online)

Acquisitions Editor: *Joan L. McNamara*
Marketing Director: *Adam Kloza*
Marketing Manager: *Nathan Edwards*
Developmental Editor: *Dave Welsh*
Senior Content Licensing Specialist: *Beth Thole*
Senior Project Manager: *Melissa Leick*
Cover Graphics: *Studio Montage, St. Louis, MO*
Buyer: *Nichole Birkenholz*
Media Project Manager: *Sridevi Palani*

Compositor: Laserwords Private Limited
Cover Images: © Stockbyte/PunchStock [background]; © Royalty-Free/Corbis [inset]

www.mhhe.com

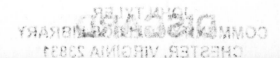

Editors/Academic Advisory Board

Members of the Academic Advisory Board are instrumental in the final selection of articles for each edition of ANNUAL EDITIONS. Their review of articles for content, level, and appropriateness provides critical direction to the editors and staff. We think that you will find their careful consideration well reflected in this volume.

ANNUAL EDITIONS: Drugs, Society, and Behavior 13/14
28th Edition

EDITORS

Mary H. Maguire
California State University—Sacramento

Clifford Garoupa
Fresno City College

ACADEMIC ADVISORY BOARD MEMBERS

Editors/Academic Advisory Board continued

Preface

In publishing ANNUAL EDITIONS we recognize the enormous role played by the magazines, newspapers, and journals of the public press in providing current, first-rate educational information in a broad spectrum of interest areas. Many of these articles are appropriate for students, researchers, and professionals seeking accurate, current material to help bridge the gap between principles and theories and the real world. These articles, however, become more useful for study when those of lasting value are carefully collected, organized, indexed, and reproduced in a low-cost format, which provides easy and permanent access when the material is needed. That is the role played by ANNUAL EDITIONS.

Humanity has developed an ambiguous relationship with substances we have come to define as drugs, particularly those drugs that alter human consciousness and behavior, psychoactive drugs. The use of such substances has resulted in a social circumstance whereby societies struggle to control human behaviors motivated and altered by their use. Although we consider modern society to function based upon logic, science, and reason, closer scrutiny of policy, regulation, and control belies this belief. In effect, such attempts at regulation face an enormous biological and psychological challenge: we humans are designed to alter our consciousness, or to use another term familiar to drug use, to "get high." As a result, to a significant degree, our societies face a seemingly insurmountable challenge: to control and/or manipulate human behavior with regard to drug using or consciousness-altering behaviors. To this end, societies have, presumably in an attempt to protect their members, developed what they perceive to be rational control mechanisms to protect people from themselves.

Unfortunately the historical foundations upon which drug regulation and control are based, especially in the United States, have their roots in racism and discrimination. This further complicates society's attempts to address, in a logical and coherent sense, what type of role or relationship humans should have with these substances. The reality of our modern world concerning drugs is unequivocal. Despite repeated resolutions by the United State's government in an attempt to achieve a "Drug Free America," and the staggering amount of money spent in the attempt to achieve that end, drugs are ubiquitous in American society; they are here to stay. What has come to be defined as deviant and antisocial behaviors in our attempts to "denormalize" drug use has, in fact, resulted in these activities becoming testimony to people's inherent creativity in their never-ending pursuit of states of altered consciousness. When this penchant to "get high" is combined with the precociousness inherent in our species, one ends up with the current circumstance: new substances are discovered regularly, either by scientific research or common curiosity, and the ritual of consciousness alteration begins anew. We currently find ourselves in a conundrum concerning drugs. For whatever reason, none of which are based upon science or rationality, some drugs are considered to be acceptable and appropriate, while others are seen to be highly

dangerous and a threat. One does not need to be a psychopharmacologist or toxicologist to realize that there is very little difference, for instance, between ethyl alcohol and heroin. As a result, we readily accept and condone the use of one (alcohol) while declaring "war" against the other (heroin). The same situation exists with regard to tobacco, a compound that is among the most toxic and highly addictive known. For these reasons, oftentimes it is in fact impossible to make sense of how modern societies have come to view and address drug using behavior. We hope that the materials presented in this book offer the reader some insight and perspective with regard to understanding the role that drugs play in today's world and how we have come to our current situation concerning drugs and drug use.

The articles contained in Annual Editions: Drugs, Society, and Behavior 13/14 are a collection of issues and perspectives designed to provide the reader with a framework for examining current drug-related issues of facts. The book is designed to offer students something to think about and something with which to think. It is a unique collection of materials of interest to the casual as well as the serious student of drug-related social phenomena. Unit 1 addresses the significance that drugs have in affecting diverse aspects of American life. It emphasizes the often-overlooked reality that drugs—legal and illegal—have remained a pervasive dimension of past as well as present American history. The unit begins with examples of the multiple ways in which Americans have been and continue to be affected by both legal and illegal drugs. Unit 2 examines the ways drugs affect the mind and body that result in dependence and addiction. Unit 3 examines the major drugs of use and abuse, along with issues relative to understanding the individual impacts of these drugs on society. It addresses the impacts produced by the use of legal and illegal drugs and emphasizes the alarming nature of widespread prescription drug abuse. Unit 4 reviews the dynamic nature of drugs as it relates to changing patterns and trends of use. It gives special attention this year to drug trends among youth, particularly those related to prescription drug abuse. Unit 5 focuses on the social costs of drug abuse and why the costs overwhelm many American institutions. Unit 6 illustrates the complexity in creating and implementing drug policy, such as that associated with medical marijuana and that associated with foreign drug control policy. Unit 7 concludes the book with discussions of current strategies for preventing and treating drug abuse. Can we deter people from harming themselves with drugs, and can we cure people addicted to drugs? What works and what does not work? Special attention is given to programs that address at-risk youth and programs that reduce criminal offender rehabilitation and recidivism. Annual Editions: Drugs, Society, and Behavior 13/14 contains a number of features that are designed to make the volume user-friendly. These include a table of contents with abstracts that summarize each article and key concepts in boldface, a topic guide to help locate articles on specific individuals or subjects, Internet References that can be used to further explore the topics, and Critical Thinking study questions at the end of each article to help students better understand what they have read.

Clifford Garoupa, Mary Maguire
Editors

The Annual Editions Series

VOLUMES AVAILABLE

Adolescent Psychology

Aging

American Foreign Policy

American Government

Anthropology

Archaeology

Assessment and Evaluation

Business Ethics

Child Growth and Development

Comparative Politics

Criminal Justice

Developing World

Drugs, Society, and Behavior

Dying, Death, and Bereavement

Early Childhood Education

Economics

Educating Children with Exceptionalities

Education

Educational Psychology

Entrepreneurship

Environment

The Family

Gender

Geography

Global Issues

Health

Homeland Security

Human Development

Human Resources

Human Sexualities

International Business

Management

Marketing

Mass Media

Microbiology

Multicultural Education

Nursing

Nutrition

Physical Anthropology

Psychology

Race and Ethnic Relations

Social Problems

Sociology

State and Local Government

Sustainability

Technologies, Social Media, and Society

United States History, Volume 1

United States History, Volume 2

Urban Society

Violence and Terrorism

Western Civilization, Volume 1

World History, Volume 1

World History, Volume 2

World Politics

Contents

Preface   v

Series   vii

Correlation Guide   xiv

Topic Guide   xvi

Internet References   xviii

UNIT 1
Living with Drugs

Unit Overview   xxii

1. **History of Alcohol and Drinking around the World,** David J. Hanson,
    adapted from David J. Hanson, *Preventing Alcohol Abuse: Alcohol,
    Culture and Control,* Westport, CT: Praeger, 1995
    Alcohol use by humans, probably tens of thousands of years old, has both comforted
    and plagued almost every society. In this discussion author David Hanson describes the
    drug's journey through time.   3

2. **How Latin America Is Reinventing the War on Drugs,** Sarah Miller Llana
    and Sara Shahriari, *The Christian Science Monitor,* July 30, 2012
    Latin American countries are fundamentally rethinking their drug control policies, which
    have, over time, been largely influenced by the U.S.   10

3. **Police Officers Find That Dissent on Drug Laws May Come With a Price,**
    Marc Lacey, *The New York Times,* December 2, 2011
    Law enforcement officers risk the loss of their jobs if they disagree with the govern-
    ment's War on Drugs.   14

4. **Tackling Top Teen Problem—Prescription Drugs,** George Lauby and
    Kamie Wheelock, *North Platte Bulletin,* April 11, 2009
    The illegal use of prescription drugs looms larger than problem drinking or marijuana
    use. This article examines the lives of a group of teens who currently use prescription
    drugs.   16

5. **When Booze Was Banned but Pot Was Not,** Jacob Sullum, *Reason
    Magazine,* February 2011
    The Eighteenth Amendment to the U.S. Constitution established a legal prohibition on
    alcohol. Was it successful?   20

6. **Scientists Are High on Idea That Marijuana Reduces Memory
    Impairment,** Emily Caldwell, *Ohio State University Research Publications,*
    November 2008
    Certain compounds in marijuana may be beneficial to the aging brain and may delay or
    prevent Alzheimer's disease.   24

The concepts in bold italics are developed in the article. For further expansion, please refer to the Topic Guide.

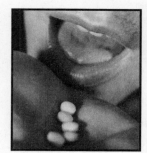

UNIT 2
Understanding How Drugs Work—Use, Dependency, and Addiction

Unit Overview 26

7. **Family History of Alcohol Abuse Associated with Problematic Drinking among College Students,** Joseph W. LaBrie, et al., *Addictive Behaviors,* 35(7), 2010

Studies examining family history of alcohol abuse among college students are conflicting and suffer from research limitations. This report investigates family history of alcohol abuse and its potential for predicting future alcohol-related problems. 30

8. **A Longitudinal Examination of the Relationships between Childhood Maltreatment and Patterns of Adolescent Substance Use among High-Risk Adolescents,** Sunny Hyucksun Shin, *American Journal on Addictions,* 21(5), 2012

Childhood maltreatment is known to be a risk factor for substance abuse. This study uses a sample of over 900 adolescents who are receiving public services to examine how childhood experiences affect changes in substance use patterns. 36

9. **Medical Marijuana and the Mind: More Is Known about the Psychiatric Risks than the Benefits,** *Harvard Mental Health Letter,* vol. 26, no. 10, April 2010

More is known about the risks of medical use of marijuana than the benefits. Most of the research is based on the study of those who have smoked the drug for recreational, not medical, purposes. The movement to legalize marijuana in the U.S. has renewed the discussion about how this drug affects the brain, and whether it might be useful in treating psychiatric disorders. 45

10. **The Genetics of Alcohol and Other Drug Dependence,** Danielle M. Dick and Arpana Agrawal, *Alcohol Research and Health,* vol. 31, no. 2, 2008

This article explores the hypothesis that certain genetic factors increase a person's risk for both alcohol and drug abuse. 48

11. **Understanding Recreational Ecstasy Use in the United States: A Qualitative Inquiry,** Masuma Bahora, Claire E. Sterk, and Kirk W. Elifson, *International Journal of Drug Policy,* vol. 20(1), January 2009

This study explores the perceptions of ecstasy by its users. In particular, it examines the role of Normalization of ecstasy in its increased use. 54

12. **Examination of Over-the-Counter Drug Misuse Among Youth,** Erin J. Farley and Daniel J. O'Connell, *Sociation Today,* vol. 8(2) 2010

Over the counter drug misuse by adolescents is on the rise. This article examines the prevalence of over the counter drug misuse by adolescents and the relationship between OTC drug misuse and misuse of other substances. 62

13. **Self-Control, Opportunity, and Substance Use,** Scott A. Desmond, Alan S. Bruce, and Melissa J. Stacer, *Deviant Behavior,* 33(6), 2012

To what extent does self-control, or lack thereof, have on substance abuse? This study uses data from the National Longitudinal Study of Adolescent Health to examine the relationships between perceived sanctions, availability of substances and self-control on decisions to smoke tobacco or use marijuana or alcohol. 69

The concepts in bold italics are developed in the article. For further expansion, please refer to the Topic Guide.

UNIT 3
The Major Drugs of Use and Abuse

Unit Overview   84

14. **Marijuana and Medical Marijuana,** John Birchard, *The New York Times,*
February 11, 2011
This article provides a thorough discussion of the ongoing debate of legalizing marijuana and the benefits of medical marijuana. It highlights the complexity of the debate
when federal drug laws do not mirror state drug laws.   87

15. **'Bath Salt' Poisonings Rise as Legislative Ban Tied Up,** Donna Leinwand
Leger, *USA Today,* April 12, 2012
Sold under the names Ivory Wave, Bliss, Hurricane Charlie, and White Lightning, these
drugs are not yet regulated by the Drug Enforcement Administration, but they are
coming to the attention of Federal Authorities as calls to Emergency Rooms and law
Enforcement increase. This article discusses the chemical Compound and patterns of
use of this drug fast becoming a community problem.   89

16. **Inhalant Abuse,** *National Institute on Drug Abuse Report,* Published
May 1999. Revised July 2012
Evidence suggests that a number of inhalants have a similar effect on the central nervous system as alcohol and other sedatives, but inhalants are much more readily available to young people. Shoe shine spray, gases, solvents and aerosols are all popular
options for what is commonly known as "huffing." This report provides a thorough overview of the current state of inhalant use in the United States.   91

17. **"Spice" and "K2" Herbal Highs: A Case Series and Systematic Review
of the Clinical Effects and Biopsychosocial Implications of Synthetic
Cannabinoid Use in Humans,** Erik W. Gunderson, et al., *American Journal
on Addictions,* 21(4), 2012
There is a growing public health concern over synthetic herbal mixtures that resemble
marijuana but legally marketed as incense. These substances, sometimes known as
"K2" or "Spice", can have deleterious effects on users such as unusual levels of anxiety
or psychosis. This study examines and discusses all available clinical literature related
to the synthetic marijuana.   97

18. **Monitoring the Future: National Results on Adolescent Drug Use,
Overview of Key Findings 2011,** Lloyd D. Johnston, et al., University of
Michigan, Institute for Social Research, February 2012
Monitoring the Future is a long-term study that examines substance use of people rang-
ing in age from adolescent to 50 years old. This report is a comprehensive discussion of
substance use and abuse patterns in 2011.   103

19. **Transcending the Medical Frontiers: Exploring the Future of
Psychedelic Drug Research,** David Jay Brown, *Multidisciplinary
Association for Psychedelic Studies,* June 2011
There has been a renewed scientific interest in the pharmacology of psychedelics. This
article points to the recent research and discusses the benefits of psychedelics as a
class of drugs.   121

The concepts in bold italics are developed in the article. For further expansion, please refer to the Topic Guide.

UNIT 4
Other Trends in Drug Use

Unit Overview   **126**

20. **Adolescent Painkiller Use May Increase Risk of Addiction, Heroin Use,** *Alcoholism & Drug Abuse Weekly,* September 22, 2008

    A recent study found that oxycodone produced different effects in adolescents than in adults. Adolescents who use opiates may be more likely to become addicts as adults. This article suggests that prescription opiates are gateway drugs to heroin.   **128**

21. **'Legal Highs' Prevalence Makes Ban Policy 'Ridiculous',** Mark Townsend, *The Guardian,* September 3, 2011

    The increasing discovery of new psychoactive substances, which now averages about one a week, makes regulation and control virtually impossible.   **130**

22. **Alcoholism Isn't What It Used To Be,** *NIAA Spectrum,* vol. 4, issue 2, June 2012

    According to the National Institute of Alcoholism and Alcohol Abuse, there are serious new questions about alcoholism and alcohol abuse.   **132**

UNIT 5
Measuring the Social Costs of Drugs

Unit Overview   **134**

23. **Drugs 'R' Us,** Stanton Peele, *Psychology Today,* June 11, 2012

    Drug use is so ubiquitous in society today that the author believes that our drug control policies are ineffective.   **137**

24. **OxyContin Abuse Spreads from Appalachia across United States,** Bill Estep, Dori Hjalmarson, and Halimah Abdullah, *McClatchy Tribune Information Services,* March 13, 2011

    The abuse of OxyContin, which initially hit the Appalachian region of the United States hard, is now spreading across the country.   **139**

25. **My Mother-in-Law's One High Day,** Marie Myung-Ok Lee, *The New York Times,* October 9, 2011

    The author discusses the beneficial effect that medical marijuana had on her terminally ill mother-in-law.   **141**

The concepts in bold italics are developed in the article. For further expansion, please refer to the Topic Guide.

UNIT 6
Creating and Sustaining Effective Drug Control Policy

Unit Overview   **142**

26. **Do the United States and Mexico Really Want the Drug War To Succeed?,** Robert Joe Stout, *Monthly Review,* 63. 8 34–44, January 2012

    The United States and Mexico both have long histories of drug policy that precede the current state of violence and drug trafficking between the two countries. This article puts the current narco-war waging at the United States-Mexico border in historical context and discusses the implications of legalization or harsher drug policy.   **145**

27. **Engaging Communities to Prevent Underage Drinking,** Abigail A. Fagan, J. David Hawkins, and Richard F. Catalano, *Alcohol Research and Health,* 34(2), 2011

    What makes the greatest impact for reduction of under-age drinking? There are many community programs to reduce drunk driving and underage substance use. This article examines the most salient and robust factors in community level interventions for preventing underage drinking.   **150**

28. **Do No Harm: Sensible Goals for International Drug Policy,** Peter Reuter, October 2011

    This article discusses the problems nations—specifically the United States—encounter in the pursuit of a sensible and diplomatic drug policy.   **158**

29. **Convergence or Divergence? Recent Developments in Drug Policies in Canada and the United States,** Clayton J. Mosher, *American Review of Canadian Studies,* vol. 41, issue 4, Winter 2011

    This article discusses the history of both American and Canadian drug policy and compares the similarities and differences. Is it possible that the United States has learned some more lenient and effective drug policies from its neighbor to the north?   **163**

30. **Legalize Drugs—all of Them!,** Vanessa Baird, *New Internationalist,* (455), 2012

    With an international context, this article presents the differences between decriminalization and legalization. Implications for legalization of drugs are discussed.   **174**

31. **Former ONDCP Senior Advisor on Marijuana and Harm Reduction,** *Alcoholism & Drug Abuse Weekly,* 23(38), 2011

    When compared to recent developments in opiate use and the dangers of synthetic mixtures such as "K2" or "bath salts", marijuana appears more innocuous. This report highlights the dangers of marijuana addiction and the possible negative effects of marijuana.   **179**

32. **Portugal's Drug Policy Pays Off; US Eyes Lessons,** Barry Hatton and Martha Mendoza, *The Seattle Times,* May 14, 2011

    Ten years ago, Portugal had the worst injection drug use rate in Europe. Then they decriminalized drug use.   **180**

The concepts in bold italics are developed in the article. For further expansion, please refer to the Topic Guide.

UNIT 7
Prevention, Treatment, and Education

Unit Overview   **182**

33. **Old Habits Die Hard for Ageing Addicts,** Matthew Ford, *The Guardian,*
    January 25, 2011
    The Netherlands, as part of their harm reduction philosophy, has established retirement
    homes for aging drug addicts.   **185**

34. **Fetal Alcohol Spectrum Disorders: When Science, Medicine, Public
    Policy, and Laws Collide,** Kenneth R. Warren and Brenda G. Hewitt,
    Developmental Disabilities Research Reviews, 2009
    This article provides an overview of the inherent confusion that happens when new
    scientific findings confront prevailing medical practice.   **187**

35. **Addiction Diagnoses May Rise Under Guideline Changes,** Ian Urbina,
    The New York Times, May 11, 2012
    The Diagnostic and Statistical Manual of Mental Disorders, considered to be the "bible"
    of addictive and psychological disorders, has a new edition coming out in 2013 that will
    significantly increase what are recognized as addictive behaviors.   **193**

36. **An Addiction Vaccine, Tantalizingly Close,** Robert Benson, *The New York
    Times,* October 4, 2011
    What if an addict could get a shot that would block the desired feeling from drug of
    choice? This article discusses just such a vaccine, and it's on the way. **195**

37. **Understanding Recovery Barriers: Youth Perceptions about Substance
    Use Relapse,** Rachel Gonzales, et al., *American Journal of Health Behavior,*
    36(5), 2012
    This study uses data from 118 youth in substance abuse treatment programs to measure
    youth perception of relapse. What do you think leads to youth relapse during recovery? **197**

38. **High-Risk Offenders Participating in Court-Supervised Substance
    Abuse Treatment: Characteristics, Treatment Received, and Factors
    Associated with Recidivism,** Elizabeth Evans, David Huang, and Yih-Ing
    Hser, *The Journal of Behavioral Health Services & Research,* vol. 38(4), 2011
    The risk of relapse for court mandated drug offenders is high, but what contributes to
    success for these high-risk offenders? This article uses data from high and low risk
    offenders to examine the variables that might predict greater treatment success for
    court-supervised treatment.   **207**

Test-Your-Knowledge Form   **218**

The concepts in bold italics are developed in the article. For further expansion, please refer to the Topic Guide.

Correlation Guide

The *Annual Editions* series provides students with convenient, inexpensive access to current, carefully selected articles from the public press. **Annual Editions: Drugs, Society, and Behavior 13/14** is an easy-to-use reader that presents articles on important topics such as *drug lifestyle, drug types, drug-use trends, drug policy,* and many more. For more information on *Annual Editions* and other *McGraw-Hill Contemporary Learning Series* titles, visit www.mhhe.com/cls.

This convenient guide matches the units in **Annual Editions: Drugs, Society, and Behavior 13/14** with the corresponding chapters in three of our best-selling McGraw-Hill Health textbooks by Hart et al., Goode, and Fields.

Annual Editions: Drugs, Society, and Behavior 13/14	Drugs, Society, and Human Behavior, 15/e by Hart et al.	Drugs in American Society, 8/e by Goode	Drugs in Perspective, 8/e by Fields
Unit 1: Living with Drugs	**Chapter 1:** Drug Use: An Overview **Chapter 2:** Drug Use as a Social Problem	**Chapter 1:** Drug Use: A Sociological Perspective	**Chapter 1:** Putting Drugs in Perspective
Unit 2: Understanding How Drugs Work—Use, Dependency, and Addiction	**Chapter 4:** The Nervous System **Chapter 5:** The Actions of Drugs	**Chapter 2:** Drug Use: A Pharmacological Perspective	**Chapter 3:** Drug-Specific Information **Chapter 4:** Assessment of Substance Abuse, Dependence, and Addiction
Unit 3: The Major Drugs of Use and Abuse	**Chapter 6:** Stimulants **Chapter 7:** Depressants and Inhalants **Chapter 9:** Alcohol **Chapter 10:** Tobacco **Chapter 11:** Caffeine **Chapter 12:** Dietary Supplements and Over-the-Counter Drugs **Chapter 13:** Opioids **Chapter 14:** Hallucinogens **Chapter 15:** Marijuana **Chapter 16:** Performance-Enhancing Drugs	**Chapter 3:** Drugs in the News Media **Chapter 7:** Alcohol and Tobacco **Chapter 8:** Marijuana, LSD, and Club Drugs **Chapter 9:** Stimulants: Amphetamine, Methamphetamine, Cocaine, and Crack **Chapter 10:** Heroin and Narcotics **Chapter 11:** The Pharmaceutical Neuroleptics: Sedatives, Hypnotics, Tranquilizers, Antipsychotics, and Antidepressants	**Chapter 3:** Drug-Specific Information
Unit 4: Other Trends in Drug Use	**Chapter 1:** Drug Use: An Overview **Chapter 2:** Drug Use as a Social Problem **Chapter 3:** Drug Policy	**Chapter 1:** Drug Use: A Sociological Perspective **Chapter 3:** Drugs in the News Media **Chapter 5:** Historical Trends in Drug Consumption **Chapter 12:** Controlling Drug Use: The Historical Context	**Chapter 1:** Putting Drugs in Perspective **Chapter 2:** Why Do People Abuse Drugs?
Unit 5: Measuring the Social Costs of Drugs	**Chapter 2:** Drug Use as a Social Problem	**Chapter 1:** Drug Use: A Sociological Perspective **Chapter 12:** Controlling Drug Use: The Historical Context **Chapter 13:** Drugs and Crime: What's the Connection? **Chapter 14:** The Illicit Drug Industry **Chapter 15:** Law Enforcement, Drug Courts, Drug Treatment **Chapter 16:** Legalization, Decriminalization, and Harm Reduction	**Chapter 1:** Putting Drugs in Perspective **Chapter 2:** Why Do People Abuse Drugs? **Chapter 5:** Substance Abuse and Family Systems **Chapter 10:** Prevention of Substance Abuse Problems **Chapter 11:** Disorders Co-occurring with Substance Abuse **Chapter 12:** Alcohol/Drug Recovery and Relapse Prevention

Correlation Guide

Unit 6: Creating and Sustaining Effective Drug Control Policy	**Chapter 3:** Drug Products and Their Regulations **Chapter 17:** Preventing Substance Abuse	**Chapter 15:** Law Enforcement, Drug Courts, Drug Treatment **Chapter 16:** Legalization, Decriminalization, and Harm Reduction	**Chapter 10:** Prevention of Substance Abuse Problems **Chapter 12:** Alcohol/Drug Recovery and Relapse Prevention
Unit 7: Prevention, Treatment, and Education	**Chapter 17:** Preventing Substance Abuse **Chapter 18:** Treating Substance Abuse Disorders	**Chapter 15:** Law Enforcement, Drug Courts, Drug Treatment **Chapter 16:** Legalization, Decriminalization, and Harm Reduction	**Chapter 10:** Prevention of Substance Abuse Problems **Chapter 12:** Alcohol/Drug Recovery and Relapse Prevention

Topic Guide

This topic guide suggests how the selections in this book relate to the subjects covered in your course. You may want to use the topics listed on these pages to search the Web more easily.

On the following pages a number of websites have been gathered specifically for this book. They are arranged to reflect the units of this Annual Editions reader. You can link to these sites by going to www.mhhe.com/cls

All the articles that relate to each topic are listed below the bold-faced term.

Addiction

10. The Genetics of Alcohol and Other Drug Dependence
16. Inhalant Abuse
18. Monitoring the Future: National Results on Adolescent Drug Use, Overview of Key Findings 2011
20. Adolescent Painkiller Use May Increase Risk of Addiction, Heroin Use
33. Old Habits Die Hard for Ageing Addicts
35. Addiction Diagnoses May Rise Under Guideline Changes
36. An Addiction Vaccine, Tantalizingly Close

Alcohol

1. History of Alcohol and Drinking around the World
5. When Booze Was Banned but Pot Was Not
7. Family History of Alcohol Abuse Associated with Problematic Drinking among College Students
10. The Genetics of Alcohol and Other Drug Dependence
22. Alcoholism Isn't What It Used To Be
27. Engaging Communities to Prevent Underage Drinking
34. Fetal Alcohol Spectrum Disorders: When Science, Medicine, Public Policy, and Laws Collide

Amphetamines

11. Understanding Recreational Ecstasy Use in the United States: A Qualitative Inquiry

College

7. Family History of Alcohol Abuse Associated with Problematic Drinking among College Students
23. Drugs 'R' Us

Drug economy

2. How Latin America Is Reinventing the War on Drugs
3. Police Officers Find that Dissent on Drug Laws May Come With a Price
26. Do the United States and Mexico Really Want the Drug War To Succeed?
30. Legalize Drugs—all of Them!

Epidemiology

1. History of Alcohol and Drinking around the World
7. Family History of Alcohol Abuse Associated with Problematic Drinking among College Students

Drinking among college students

8. A Longitudinal Examination of the Relationships between Childhood Maltreatment and Patterns of Adolescent Substance Use among High-Risk Adolescents
9. Medical Marijuana and the Mind
10. The Genetics of Alcohol and Other Drug Dependence
13. Self-Control, Opportunity, and Substance Use
22. Alcoholism Isn't What It Used To Be
35. Addiction Diagnoses May Rise Under Guideline Changes

Hallucinogens

11. Understanding Recreational Ecstasy Use in the United States: A Qualitative Inquiry
15. 'Bath Salt' Poisonings Rise as Legislative Ban Tied Up

19. Transcending the Medical Frontiers: Exploring the Future of Psychedelic Drug Research
20. Adolescent Painkiller Use May Increase Risk of Addiction, Heroin Use

Heroin use

4. Tackling Top Teen Problem—Prescription Drugs
27. Engaging Communities to Prevent Underage Drinking
33. Old Habits Die Hard for Ageing Addicts
36. An Addiction Vaccine, Tantalizingly Close
37. Understanding Recovery Barriers: Youth Perceptions about Substance Use Relapse

Law enforcement

2. How Latin America Is Reinventing the War on Drugs
3. Police Officers Find that Dissent on Drug Laws May Come With a Price

Legalization

2. How Latin America Is Reinventing the War on Drugs
5. When Booze Was Banned but Pot Was Not
14. Marijuana and Medical Marijuana
21. 'Legal Highs' Prevalence Makes Ban Policy 'Ridiculous'
23. Drugs 'R' Us
30. Legalize Drugs—all of Them!

Marijuana

6. Scientists Are High on Idea That Marijuana Reduces Memory Impairment
9. Medical Marijuana and the Mind
14. Marijuana and Medical Marijuana
17. "Spice" and "K2" Herbal Highs: A Case Series and Systematic Review of the Clinical Effects and Biopsychosocial Implications of Synthetic Cannabinoid Use in Humans
25. My Mother-in Law's One High Day
31. Former ONDCP Senior Advisor on Marijuana and Harm Reduction
4. Tackling Top Teen Problem—Prescription Drugs
12. Examination of Over-the-Counter Drug Misuse Among Youth

Policy

2. How Latin America Is Reinventing the War on Drugs
3. Police Officers Find That Dissent on Drug Laws May Come With a Price
5. When Booze was Banned but Pot Was Not
14. Marijuana and Medical Marijuana
15. 'Bath Salt' Poisonings Rise as Legislative Ban Tied Up
21. 'Legal Highs' Prevalence Makes Ban Policy 'Ridiculous'
23. Drugs 'R' Us
25. My Mother-in-Law's One High Day
26. Do the United States and Mexico Really Want the Drug War to Succeed?
28. Do No Harm
29. Convergence or Divergence? Recent Developments in Drug Policies in Canada and the United States

Prescription drug abuse

4. Tackling Top Teen Problem—Prescription Drugs
12. Examination of Over-the-Counter Drug Misuse Among Youth

Research

6. Scientists Are High on Idea That Marijuana Reduces Memory Impairment

Impairment

7. Family History of Alcohol Abuse Associated with Problematic Drinking among College Students
8. A Longitudinal Examination of the Relationships between Childhood Maltreatment and Patterns of Adolescent Substance Use Among High-Risk Adolescents

10. The Genetics of Alcohol and Other Drug Dependence
13. Self-Control, Opportunity, and Substance Use
18. Monitoring the Future: National Results on Adolescent Drug Use, Overview of Key Findings 2011

Treatment

20. Adolescent Painkiller Use May Increase Risk of Addiction, Heroin Use

Internet References

The following Internet sites have been selected to support the articles found in this reader. These sites were available at the time of publication. However, because websites often change their structure and content, the information listed may no longer be available. We invite you to visit www.mhhe.com/cls for easy access to these sites.

Annual Editions: Drugs, Society, and Behavior 13/14

General Sources

Higher Education Center for Alcohol and Other Drug Prevention
www.edc.org/hec

The U.S. Department of Education established the Higher Education Center for Alcohol and Other Drug Prevention to provide nationwide support for campus alcohol and other drug prevention efforts. The Center is working with colleges, universities, and preparatory schools throughout the country to develop strategies for changing campus culture, to foster environments that promote healthy lifestyles, and to prevent illegal alcohol and other drug use among students.

Mind for Better Health
www.mind.org.uk/help/diagnoses_and_conditions

This site provides information on a wide range of subjects from addiction and dependency to mental health problems. It also has information on legislation.

Narconon
www.youthaddiction.com

This site contains drug information, information on addiction, rehab information, online consultations, and other related resources.

National Clearinghouse for Alcohol and Drug Information
www.ncadi.samhsa.gov

This site provides information to teens about the problems and ramifications of drug use and abuse. There are numerous links to drug-related informational sites.

NSW Office of Drug Policy Home Page
www.druginfo.nsw.gov.au

This is an Australian government-based website with a great deal of drug-related information. The site includes information about illicit drugs (amphetamines, pseudoephedrine, GHB, heroin, ketamine, rohypnol, marijuana, paramethoxyamphetamines [PMA], steroids, cocaine, hallucinogens, inhalants, ecstasy, ritalin, and psychostimulants), information and resources, treatment services, law and justice, illicit drug diversion, and medical cannabis. It also includes statistics on drug use in Australia.

ONDCP (Office of National Drug Control Policy)
www.whitehousedrugpolicy.gov

This site contains a vast amount of drug-related information, resources, and links. Included is information about drug policy, drug facts, publications, related links, prevention, treatment, science and technology, enforcement, state and local along with international facts, and policies, and programs. The site is easy to use and understand.

U.S. Department of Health and Human Services
http://ncadi.samhsa.gov/research

This site contains links and resources on various topics that include, but are not limited to, substance abuse and Mental Health Data Archive, OAS Short Reports (on such drugs as marijuana, crack cocaine, inhalants, club drugs, heroin, alcohol, and tobacco). Also included are government studies and an online library and databases.

United Nations Office on Drugs and Crime
www.unodc.org/unodc/index.html

This site includes information on the following drug-related topics, in addition to many other topics: treatment and addiction and illicit drug facts. Also available on this site are recent and archive press releases and multimedia presentations.

UNIT 1: Living with Drugs

Freevibe Drug Facts
www.freevibe.com/Drug_Facts/why_drugs.asp#1

This website contains information on drug facts with links on drug information, why people take drugs, the physical effects and drug-related behavior, drug recognition, and discussions of addiction. The site also includes personal accounts by addicts.

Guide4Living Independent Health Information Online
www.guide4living.com/drugabuse

This site examines the use and abuse of a wide range of substances. It also provides personal stories, information on rehabilitation facilities, and a place for feedback.

Harm Reduction Coalition
www.harmreduction.org

This site provides valuable information about various harm reduction programs operating within the United States. Needle exchange programs, methadone maintenance, and also information about how harm reduction differs from criminalization of drug using behavior.

National Council on Alcoholism and Drug Dependence, Inc.
www.ncadd.org

According to its website, the National Council on Alcoholism and Drug Dependence provides education, information, help, and hope in the fight against the chronic, and sometimes fatal, disease of alcoholism and other drug addictions.

Parents. The Anti-Drug
www.theantidrug.com

Tips and links for helping children avoid drugs can be found at this site. Also provided is help in parenting with drug-related issues such as how to advise young persons about the drug-related influences of peer pressure.

Internet References

UNIT 2: Understanding How Drugs Work—Use, Dependency, and Addiction

AddictionSearch.com
www.addictionsearch.com

Check this site out for information on addiction and rehabilitation. Some of the other features of this site are the use of statistics, identification of social issues, resources for treatment, facility listings for the United States, and analysis of types of addictions by race, sex, and age of human populations.

Addiction Treatment Forum
www.atforum.com

News on addiction research and reports on substance abuse are available here.

American Psychological Association's Addiction Related Publications
http://search.apa.org/search?query=&facet=classification:Addictions&limited=true&section=pubs

This site is a good resource with several articles and information mostly on alcohol.

British Broadcasting Company Understanding Drugs
www.bbc.co.uk/health/conditions/mental_health/drugs_use.shtml

This is a good reference for information about drug use, addiction, and dependence. Includes links.

Centre for Addiction and Mental Health (CAMH)
www.camh.net

One of the largest addictions facilities in Canada, CAMH advances an understanding of addiction and translates this knowledge into resources that can be used to prevent problems and to provide effective treatments.

Dealing with Addictions
http://kidshealth.org/teen/your_mind/problems/addictions.html

This site contains information on addictions and includes a quiz on substance abuse. Categories are entitled Your Mind, Your Body, Sexual Health, Food and Fitness, Drugs and Alcohol, Diseases and Conditions, Infections, School and Jobs, Staying Safe, and questions and answers. Much of this site is available in Spanish.

Drugs and the Body: How Drugs Work
www.doitnow.org/pdfs/223.pdf

This site pinpoints some basic but critical points in a straightforward manner. It explains how drugs can be administered, the processes through the body, effects, and changes over time. Included are drug-related information resources and links.

National Alcoholism Drug Information Center
http://addictioncareoptions.com

Get help and information about drug addition, alcoholism abuse, and top-rated addiction treatment centers.

The National Center on Addiction and Substance Abuse at Columbia University
www.casacolumbia.org

The National Center on Addiction and Substance Abuse at Columbia University is a unique think/action tank that brings together all of the professional disciplines (health policy, medicine and nursing, communications, economics, sociology and anthropology, law and law enforcement, business, religion, and education) needed to study and combat all forms of substance abuse—illegal drugs, pills, alcohol, and tobacco—as they affect all aspects of society.

National Institute on Drug Abuse (NIDA)
www.nida.nih.gov

NIDA's mission is to lead the nation in bringing the power of science to bear on drug abuse and addiction.

Public Agenda
www.publicagenda.org/articles/illegal-drugs

A guide on illegal drugs has links that include understanding the issues, public opinions, and additional resources. Includes several links for each of these groups.

Understanding Addiction—Regret, Addiction and Death
http://teenadvice.about.com/library/weekly/aa011501a.htm

This site has several resources and articles related to drug use by young persons.

UNIT 3: The Major Drugs of Use and Abuse

The American Journal of Psychiatry
http://ajp.psychiatryonline.org/cgi/content/abstract/155/8/1016

This site contains a study on female twins and cannabis.

Multidisciplinary Association for Psychedelic Studies (MAPS)
www.maps.org

This site discusses current research into the possible medical uses of some psychedlic drugs and marijuana.

National Institute on Drug Abuse
www.drugabuse.gov

This is the National Institute on Drug Abuse website that identifies the major drugs of use and abuse. It provides resources and information for students, parents, and teachers, as well as reports on drug trends.

Office of Applied Studies
www.oas.samhsa.gov

Data and statistics on the major drugs of use and abuse along with reports on the effects of these drugs focusing on the emotional, social, psychological, and physical aspects are contained at this site. Also available are extensive survey findings on drug use related to evolving patterns of drug abuse.

QuitNet
www.quitnet.org

The QuitNet helps smokers control their nicotine addiction. This site operates in association with the Boston University School of Public Health.

Streetdrugs.org
www.streetdrugs.org

This site provides a great deal of information on street drugs. It is designed to target different audiences—teachers, parents, students, and law enforcement. On this site one can find information on the top ten most misused drugs in the world today, a comprehensive drug index, and information on signs of a drug abuser.

Internet References

UNIT 4: Other Trends in Drug Use

Drug Story.org
www.drugstory.org/drug_stats/druguse_stats.asp

This site contains lots of information—"Hard Facts, Real Stories, Informed Experts"; information on drugs and their effects. Also covered are prevention and treatment, drugs and crime, drug trafficking, drug use statistics.

Marijuana as a Medicine
http://mojo.calyx.net/~olsen

Monitoring the Future
www.monitoringthefuture.org

Located at this site is a collaboration of drug trend data tables from 2005 focusing on students in the eighth, tenth, and twelfth grades; also described are trends in the availability of drugs, the attitudes of users, and the use of major drugs.

Prescription Drug Abuse
www.prescription-drug-abuse.org

This is a website designed to provide information on where and when to get help for drug abuse. It also has a decent amount of information outlining what prescription drug abuse is and the particular ones that are abused, links to additional articles, and information on who is abusing the drugs.

Prescriptions Drug Use and Abuse
www.fda.gov/fdac/features/2001/501_drug.htm

This site contains lots of resources and links related to prescription drug use and abuse.

SAMHSA
www.drugabusestatistics.samhsa.gov/trends.htm

This link is to the office of applied studies, where you can link to numerous drug-related resources. It includes the latest and most comprehensive drug survey information in the United States.

United States Drug Trends
www.usdrugtrends.com

Provided at this site are drug trends for each state in the United States, such as information where each drug is most likely to be used in each state, cost of the drug, and where the drug supply is coming from.

UNIT 5: Measuring the Social Costs of Drugs

BMJ.com a publishing group
http://bmj.bmjjournals.com/cgi/content/abridged/326/7383/242/a

Drug Enforcement Administration
www.usdoj.gov/dea

The mission of the Drug Enforcement Administration is to enforce the controlled substances laws and regulations

Drug Policy Alliance
www.drugpolicy.org/database/index.html

News about drug policies and articles critiquing the real social and economic costs associated with drug abuse versus the cost of the drug war policies can be found here.

Drug Use Cost to the Economy
www.ccm-drugtest.com/ntl_effcts1.htm

European Monitoring Center for Drugs and Addiction
www.emcdda.europa.eu/html.cfm/index1357EN.html

A collection of research studies, based out of the European Union, on how much governments spend to tackle their drug problem.

National Drug Control Policy
www.ncjrs.org/ondcppubs/publications/policy/ndcs00/chap2_10.html

This site contains information about the consequences of illegal drug use, including economic loss, drug-related death, drug related medical emergencies, spreading of infectious diseases, homelessness, and drug use in the workplace.

The November Coalition
www.november.org

The November Coalition is a growing body of citizens whose lives have been gravely affected by the present drug policy. This group represents convicted prisoners, their loved ones, and others who believe that United States drug policies are unfair and unjust.

TRAC DEA Site
http://trac.syr.edu/tracdea/index.html

The Transactional Records Access Clearinghouse (TRAC) is a data gathering, data research, and data distribution organization associated with Syracuse University. According to its website, the purpose of TRAC is to provide the American people—and institutions of oversight such as Congress, news organizations, public interest groups, businesses, scholars, and lawyers—with comprehensive information about the activities of federal enforcement and regulatory agencies and the communities in which they take place.

United Nations Chronicle—online edition
www.un.org/Pubs/chronicle/1998/issue2/0298p7.html

This site contains information about the global nature of drugs.

UNIT 6: Creating and Sustaining Effective Drug Control Policy

Drug Policy Alliance
www.drugpolicy.org

This site explores and evaluates drug policy in the United States and around the world.

DrugText
www.drugtext.org

The DrugText library consists of individual drug-related libraries with independent search capabilities.

Effective Drug Policy: Why Journey's End Is Legalisations
www.drugscope.org.uk

This site contains the drug scope policy and public affairs in the United Kingdom.

Harm Reduction Coalition
www.harmreduction.org

The Higher Education Center for Alcohol and Other Drug Prevention
www.edc.org/hec/pubs/policy.htm

Setting and Improving Policies for Reducing Alcohol and Other Drug Problems on Campus: A Guide for School Administrators.

The National Organization on Fetal Alcohol Syndrome (NOFAS)
www.nofas.org

NOFAS is a nonprofit organization founded in 1990 dedicated to eliminating birth defects caused by alcohol consumption during pregnancy and improving the quality of life for those individuals and families affected. NOFAS is the only national organization focusing solely on fetal alcohol syndrome (FAS), the leading known cause of mental retardation.

Internet References

National NORML Homepage
www.norml.org

This is the home page for the National Organization for the Reform of Marijuana Laws.

Transform Drug Policy Foundation
www.tdpf.org.uk

Transform Drug Policy Foundation exists to promote sustainable health and well-being by bringing about a just, effective, and humane system to regulate and control drugs at local, national, and international levels. Available on the website are media news articles—both recent and archived—links to other websites related to drug policy, and many other resources.

UNIT 7: Prevention, Treatment, and Education

American Council for Drug Education
www.acde.org

This site educates employers, parents, teachers, and health professionals about drugs and includes information on recognizing the signs and symptoms of drug use.

D.A.R.E.
www.dare-america.com

This year 33 million schoolchildren around the world—25 million in the United States—will benefit from D.A.R.E. (Drug Abuse Resistance Education), the highly acclaimed program that gives kids the skills they need to avoid involvement in drugs, gangs, or violence. D.A.R.E. was founded in 1983 in Los Angeles.

The Drug Reform Coordination Network (DRC)
www.drcnet.org

According to its home page, the DRC Network is committed to reforming current drug laws in the United States.

Drug Watch International
www.drugwatch.org

Drug Watch International is a volunteer nonprofit information network and advocacy organization that promotes the creation of healthy drug-free cultures in the world and opposes the legalization of drugs. The organization upholds a comprehensive approach to drug issues involving prevention, education, intervention/treatment, and law enforcement/interdiction.

Hazelden
www.hazelden.org

Hazelden is a nonprofit organization providing high-quality, affordable rehabilitation, education, prevention, and professional services and publications in chemical dependency and related disorders.

Join Together
www.jointogether.org

Contained here are multiple types of resources and web links regarding youth drug prevention for parents, teachers, community members, public officials, and faith leaders.

KCI (Koch Crime Institute) The Anti-Meth Site
www.kci.org/meth_info/faq_meth.htm

This site contains Frequently Asked Questions on methamphetamine. Very interesting.

Marijuana Policy Project
www.mpp.org

The purpose of the Marijuana Policy Project is to develop and promote policies to minimize the harm associated with marijuana.

National Institute on Drug Abuse
www.nida.nih.gov/Infofacts/TreatMeth.html

Information on effective drug treatment approaches, costs for treating drug addiction, and the different treatment options (inpatient, outpatient, group, etc.) can all be found at this site.

Office of National Drug Control Policy (ONDCP)
www.whitehousedrugpolicy.gov

The principal purpose of ONDCP is to establish policies, priorities, and objectives for the nation's drug control program, the goals of which are to reduce illicit drug use, manufacturing, and trafficking; drug-related crime and violence; and drug-related health consequences.

The Partnership for Drug-Free America
www.drugfree.org/#

The Partnership for a Drug-Free America is a private, nonprofit organization that unites communications professionals, renowned scientists, and parents in the mission to reduce illicit drug abuse in America. Drugfree.org is a drug abuse prevention and treatment resource, existing to help parents and caregivers effectively address alcohol and drug abuse with their children. This website gives families the tools, information, and support they need to help their children lead healthy, drug-free lives.

United Nations International Drug Control Program (UNDCP)
www.undcp.org

The mission of UNDCP is to work with the nations and the people of the world to tackle the global drug problem and its consequences.

UNIT 1

Living with Drugs

Unit Selections

1. **History of Alcohol and Drinking around the World,** David J. Hanson
2. **How Latin America Is Reinventing the War on Drugs,** Sarah Miller Llana and Sara Shahriari
3. **Police Officers Find That Dissent on Drug Laws May Come With a Price,** Marc Lacey
4. **Tackling Top Teen Problem—Prescription Drugs,** George Lauby and Kamie Wheelock
5. **When Booze Was Banned but Pot Was Not,** Jacob Sullum
6. **Scientists Are High on Idea That Marijuana Reduces Memory Impairment,** Emily Caldwell

Learning Outcomes

After reading this Unit, you should be able to:

- Explain why history is important when attempting to understand contemporary drug-related events.

- Compare how the U.S. response to drug-related issues compares to those occurring in other countries.

- Describe what role the media plays in U.S. society's perception of drug-related events.

- Explain how Central and South American countries are changing their drug policies.

- Determine what use marijuana may have in treating age-related diseases.

Student Website

www.mhhe.com/cls

Internet References

Freevibe Drug Facts
www.freevibe.com/Drug_Facts/why_drugs.asp#1

Guide4Living Independent Health Information Online
www.guide4living.com/drugabuse

Harm Reduction Coalition
www.harmreduction.org

National Council on Alcoholism and Drug Dependence, Inc.
www.ncadd.org

Parents. The Anti-Drug
www.theantidrug.com

When attempting to define the U.S. drug experience, one must examine the past as well as the present. Very often, drug use and its associated phenomena are viewed through a contemporary looking glass relative to our personal views, biases, and perspectives. Although today's drug scene is definitely a product of recent historical trends such as the crack trade of the 1980s, the methamphetamine problem, and the turn toward the expanded non-medical use of prescription drugs, it is also a product of the distant past. This past and the lessons it has generated, although largely unknown, forgotten, or ignored, provide one important perspective from which to assess our current status and to guide our future in terms of optimizing our efforts to manage the benefits and control the harm from legal and illegal drugs.

The U.S. drug experience is often defined in terms of a million individual realities, all meaningful and all different. In fact, these realities often originated as pieces of our historical, cultural, political, and personal past that combine to influence present-day drug-related phenomena significantly. The contemporary U.S. drug experience is the product of centuries of human attempts to alter or sustain consciousness through the use of mind-altering drugs. Early American history is replete with accounts of the exorbitant use of alcohol, opium, morphine, and cocaine. Further review of this history clearly suggests the precedents for Americans' continuing pursuit of a vast variety of stimulant, depressant, and hallucinogenic drugs. Drug wars, drug epidemics, drug prohibitions, and escalating trends of alarming drug use patterns were present throughout the early history of the United States. During this period, the addictive properties of most drugs were largely unknown. Today, the addictive properties of almost all drugs are known. So why is it that so many drug-related lessons of the past repeat themselves in the face of such powerful new knowledge? Why does Fetal Alcohol Syndrome remain as the leading cause of mental retardation in infants? How is it that the abuse of drugs continues to defy the lessons of history? How big is the U.S. drug problem and how is it measured?

One important way of answering questions about drug abuse is by conducting research and analyzing data recovered through numerous reporting instruments. These data are in turn used to assess historical trends and make policy decisions in response to what has been learned. For example, one leading source of information about drug use in America is the annual federal Substance Abuse and Mental Health Services Administration's National Survey on Drug Use and Health. It currently reports that there continues to be more than 19 million Americans over 12 years of age who are current users of illicit drugs. The most widely used illicit drug is marijuana with approximately 14 million users—a figure that has remained constant for the past five years. Approximately 51 percent of Americans over 12 are drinkers of alcohol; over 43 percent of full-time enrolled college students are binge drinkers (defined as consuming five or more drinks during a single drinking occasion). Approximately 29 percent of Americans over 12 use tobacco. Almost 23 million people are believed to be drug-dependent on alcohol or illicit drugs. There are approximately five million people using

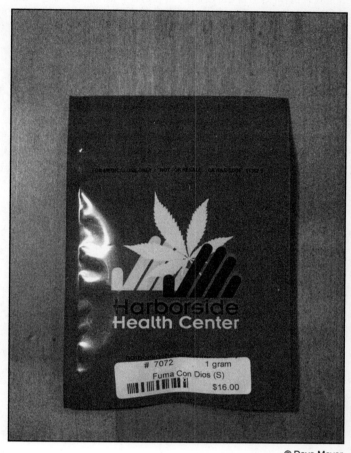

© Dave Moyer

prescription painkillers for nonmedical reasons—an alarming trend. The size of the economy associated with drug use is staggering; Americans continue to spend more than $70 billion a year on illegal drugs alone.

Drugs impact our most powerful public institutions on many fronts. Drugs are the business of our criminal justice system, and drugs compete with terrorism, war, and other major national security concerns as demanding military issues. Over $3 billion per year is committed to the Department of Homeland Security to strengthen drug-related land and maritime border interdictions. The cost of illegal street drugs is up, and the post-9/11 national security infrastructure is impacting historical patterns of trafficking. And the relationship between drug trafficking and terrorism has focused added military emphasis on drug fighting. As the war in Iraq, Afghanistan, and Pakistan continues, U.S. drug agents in those countries are increasing efforts to contain the expanding heroin trade, a major source of funding for the Taliban. As you read through the pages of this book, the pervasive nature of drug-related influences on everyday life will become more apparent.

The lessons of our drug legacy are harsh, whether they are the subjects of public health or public policy. Methamphetamine is now recognized as having produced consequences equal to or surpassing those of crack. The entire dynamic of illicit drug use is changing. Once quiet rural towns, counties, and states have reported epidemics of methamphetamine abuse over the past 10 years, and these suggest comparisons to the inner-urban crack epidemics of the 1980s. The current level of drug-related violence in Mexico is out of control and is firmly in control of the U.S. drug market. This issue is the most dangerous emerging drug problem.

Families, schools, and workplaces continue to be impacted by the many facets of drug abuse. One in three Americans has a close relationship to someone who abuses drugs. It is only because of war, terrorism, and a struggling economy that more public attention toward drug problems has been diverted. The articles and graphics contained in this unit illustrate the evolving nature of issues influenced by the historical evolution of legal and illegal drug use in America. The changing historical evolution of drug-related phenomena is reflected within the character of all issues and controversies addressed by this book. Unit 1 presents examples of the contemporary and diverse nature of current problems, issues, and concerns about drugs and how they continue to impact all aspects of public and private life. The drug-related events of today continue to forecast the drug-related events of tomorrow. The areas of public health, public policy, controlling crime, and education exist as good examples for discussion. As you read this and other literature on drug-related events, the dynamics of past and present drug-related linkages will become apparent.

History of Alcohol and Drinking around the World

Davıd J. Hanson, PhD

Alcohol is a product that has provided a variety of functions for people throughout all history. From the earliest times to the present, alcohol has played an important role in religion and worship. Historically, alcoholic beverages have served as sources of needed nutrients and have been widely used for their medicinal, antiseptic, and analgesic properties. The role of such beverages as thirst quenchers is obvious and they play an important role in enhancing the enjoyment and quality of life. They can be a social lubricant, can facilitate relaxation, can provide pharmacological pleasure, and can increase the pleasure of eating. Thus, while alcohol has always been misused by a minority of drinkers, it has proved to be beneficial to most.

Ancient Period

While no one knows when beverage alcohol was first used, it was presumably the result of a fortuitous accident that occurred at least tens of thousands of years ago. However, the discovery of late Stone Age beer jugs has established the fact that intentionally fermented beverages existed at least as early as the Neolithic period (cir. 10,000 B.C.) (Patrick, 1952, pp. 12–13), and it has been suggested that beer may have preceded bread as a staple (Braidwood et al, 1953; Katz and Voigt, 1987); wine clearly appeared as a finished product in Egyptian pictographs around 4,000 B.C (Lucia, 1963a, p. 216).

The earliest alcoholic beverages may have been made from berries or honey (Blum *et al,* 1969, p. 25; Rouech, 1960, p. 8; French, 1890, p. 3) and winemaking may have originated in the wild grape regions of the Middle East. Oral tradition recorded in the Old Testament (Genesis 9:20) asserts that Noah planted a vineyard on Mt. Ararat in what is now eastern Turkey. In Sumer, beer and wine were used for medicinal purposes as early as 2,000 B.C (Babor, 1986, p. 1).

Brewing dates from the beginning of civilization in ancient Egypt (Cherrington, 1925, v. 1, p. 404) and alcoholic beverages were very important in that country. Symbolic of this is the fact that while many gods were local or familial, Osiris,

the god of wine, was worshiped throughout the entire country (Lucia, 1963b, p. 152). The Egyptians believed that this important god also invented beer (King, 1947, p. 11), a beverage that was considered a necessity of life; it was brewed in the home "on an everyday basis" (Marciniak, 1992, p. 2).

Both beer and wine were deified and offered to gods. Cellars and winepresses even had a god whose hieroglyph was a winepress (Ghaliounqui, 1979, p. 5). The ancient Egyptians made at least seventeen varieties of beer and at least 24 varieties of wine (Ghaliounqui, 1979, pp. 8 and 11). Alcoholic beverages were used for pleasure, nutrition, medicine, ritual, remuneration (Cherrington, 1925, v. 1, p. 405) and funerary purposes. The latter involved storing the beverages in tombs of the deceased for their use in the after-life (King, 1947, p. 11; Darby, 1977, p. 576).

Numerous accounts of the period stressed the importance of moderation, and these norms were both secular and religious (Darby, 1977, p. 58). While Egyptians did not generally appear to define inebriety as a problem, they warned against taverns (which were often houses of prostitution) and excessive drinking (Lutz, 1922, pp. 97, 105–108). After reviewing extensive evidence regarding the widespread but generally moderate use of alcoholic beverage, the historian Darby makes a most important observation: all these accounts are warped by the fact that moderate users "were overshadowed by their more boisterous counterparts who added 'color' to history" (Darby, 1977, p. 590). Thus, the intemperate use of alcohol throughout history receives a disproportionate amount of attention. Those who abuse alcohol cause problems, draw attention to themselves, are highly visible and cause legislation to be enacted. The vast majority of drinkers, who neither experience nor cause difficulties, are not noteworthy. Consequently, observers and writers largely ignore moderation.

Beer was the major beverage among the Babylonians, and as early as 2,700 B.C. they worshiped a wine goddess and other wine deities (Hyams, 1965, pp. 38–39). Babylonians regularly used both beer and wine as offerings to their gods (Lutz, 1922, pp. 125–126). Around 1,750 B.C, the famous Code of Hammurabi devoted attention to alcohol. However, there were no penalties for drunkenness; in fact, it was not even mentioned. The concern was fair commerce in alcohol (Popham, 1978, pp. 232–233). Nevertheless, although it was not a crime, it would appear that the Babylonians were critical of drunkenness (Lutz, 1922, pp. 115–116).[1]

A variety of alcoholic beverages have been used in China since prehistoric times (Granet, 1957, p. 144). Alcohol was considered a spiritual (mental) food rather than a material (physical) food, and extensive documentary evidence attests to the important role it played in the religious life (Hucker, 1975, p. 28; Fei-Peng, 1982, p. 13). "In ancient times people always drank when holding a memorial ceremony, offering sacrifices to gods or their ancestors, pledging resolution before going into battle, celebrating victory, before feuding and official executions, for taking an oath of allegiance, while attending the ceremonies of birth, marriage, reunions, departures, death, and festival banquets" (Fei-Peng, 1982, p. 13).

A Chinese imperial edict of about 1,116 B.C. makes it clear that the use of alcohol in moderation was believed to be prescribed by heaven. Whether or not it was prescribed by heaven, it was clearly beneficial to the treasury. At the time of Marco Polo (1254–1324) it was drunk daily (Gernet, 1962, p. 139) and was one of the treasury's biggest sources of income (Balazs, 1964, p. 97).

Alcoholic beverages were widely used in all segments of Chinese society, were used as a source of inspiration, were important for hospitality, were an antidote for fatigue, and were sometimes misused (Samuelson, 1878, pp. 19–20, 22, 26–27; Fei-Peng, 1982, p. 137; Simons, 1991, pp. 448–459). Laws against making wine were enacted and repealed forty-one times between 1,100 B.C. and A.D. 1,400. (Alcoholism and Drug Addiction Research Foundation of Ontario, 1961, p. 5). However, a commentator writing around 650 B.C. asserted that people "will not do without beer. To prohibit it and secure total abstinence from it is beyond the power even of sages. Hence, therefore, we have warnings on the abuse of it" (quoted in Rouecbe, 1963, p. 179; similar translation quoted in Samuelson, 1878, p. 20).

While the art of wine making reached the Hellenic peninsula by about 2,000 B.C. (Younger, 1966, p. 79), the first alcoholic beverage to obtain widespread popularity in what is now Greece was mead, a fermented beverage made from honey and water. However, by 1,700 B.C., wine making was commonplace, and during the next thousand years wine drinking assumed the same function so commonly found around the world: It was incorporated into religious rituals, it became important in hospitality, it was used for medicinal purposes and it became an integral part of daily meals (Babor, 1986, pp. 2–3). As a beverage, it was drunk in many ways: warm and chilled, pure and mixed with water, plain and spiced (Raymond, 1927, p. 53).

Contemporary writers observed that the Greeks were among the most temperate of ancient peoples. This appears to result from their rules stressing moderate drinking, their praise of temperance, their practice of diluting wine with water, and their avoidance of excess in general (Austin, 1985, p. 11). An exception to this ideal of moderation was the cult of Dionysus, in which intoxication was believed to bring people closer to their deity (Sournia, 1990, pp. 5–6; Raymond, 1927, p. 55).

While habitual drunkenness was rare, intoxication at banquets and festivals was not unusual (Austin, 1985, p. 11). In fact, the symposium, a gathering of men for an evening of conversation, entertainment and drinking typically ended in intoxication (Babor, 1986, p. 4). However, while there are no references in ancient Greek literature to mass drunkenness among the Greeks, there are references to it among foreign peoples (Patrick, 1952, p. 18). By 425 B.C., warnings against intemperance, especially at symposia, appear to become more frequent (Austin, 1985, pp. 21–22).

Xenophon (431–351 B.C.) and Plato (429–347 B.C.) both praised the moderate use of wine as beneficial to health and happiness, but both were critical of drunkenness, which appears to have become a problem. Hippocrates (cir. 460–370 B.C.) identified numerous medicinal properties of wine, which had long been used for its therapeutic value (Lucia, 1963a, pp. 36–40). Later, both Aristode (384–322 B.C.) and Zeno (cir. 336–264 B.C.) were very critical of drunkenness (Austin, 1985, pp. 23, 25, and 27).

Among Greeks, the Macedonians viewed intemperance as a sign of masculinity and were well known for their drunkenness. Their king, Alexander the Great (336–323 B.C.), whose mother adhered to the Dionysian cult, developed a reputation for inebriety (Souria, 1990, pp. 8–9; Babor, 1986, p. 5).

The Hebrews were reportedly introduced to wine during their captivity in Egypt. When Moses led them to Canaan (Palestine) around 1,200 B.C., they are reported to have regretted leaving behind the wines of Egypt (Numbers 20:5); however, they found vineyards to be plentiful in their new land (Lutz, 1922, p. 25). Around 850 B.C., the use of wine was criticized by the Rechabites and Nazarites,[2] two conservative nomadic groups who practiced abstinence from alcohol (Lutz, 1922, p. 133; Samuelson, 1878, pp. 62–63).

In 586 B.C., the Hebrews were conquered by the Babylonians and deported to Babylon. However, in 539 B.C., the Persians captured the city and released the Hebrews from their Exile (Daniel 5:1–4). Following the Exile, the Hebrews developed Judaism as it is now known, and they can be said to have become Jews. During the next 200 years, sobriety increased and pockets of antagonism to wine disappeared. It became a common beverage for all classes and ages, including the very young; an important source of nourishment; a prominent part in the festivities of the people; a widely appreciated medicine; an essential provision for any fortress; and an important commodity. In short, it came to be seen as a necessary element in the life of the Hebrews (Raymond, 1927, p. 23).

While there was still opposition to excessive drinking, it was no longer assumed that drinking inevitably led to drunkenness. Wine came to be seen as a blessing from God and a symbol of joy (Psalms 104; Zachariah 10:7). These changes in beliefs and behaviors appear to be related to a rejection of belief in pagan gods, a new emphasis on individual morality, and the integration of secular drinking behaviors into religious ceremonies and their subsequent modification (Austin, 1985, pp. 18–19; Patai, 1980, pp. 61–73; Keller, 1970, pp. 290–294). Around 525 B.C., it was ruled that the Kiddush (pronouncement of the Sabbath) should be recited over a blessed cup of wine. This established the regular drinking of wine in Jewish ceremonies outside the Temple (Austin, 1985, p. 19).

King Cyrus of Persia frequently praised the virtue of the moderate consumption of alcohol (cir. 525 B.C.). However, ritual intoxication appears to have been used as an adjunct to decision making and, at least after his death, drunkenness was not uncommon (Austin, 1985, p. 19).

Between the founding of Rome in 753 B.C. until the third century B.C., there is consensus among historians that the Romans practiced great moderation in drinking (Austin, 1985, p. 17). After the Roman conquest of the Italian peninsula and the rest of the Mediterranean basin (509 to 133 B.C.), the traditional Roman values of temperance, frugality and simplicity were gradually replaced by heavy drinking, ambition, degeneracy and corruption (Babor, 1986, p. 7; Wallbank & Taylor, 1954, p. 163). The Dionysian rites (Bacchanalia, in Latin) spread to Italy during this period and were subsequently outlawed by the Senate (Lausanne, 1969, p. 4; Cherrington, 1925, v. 1, pp. 251–252).

Practices that encouraged excessive drinking included drinking before meals on an empty stomach, inducing vomiting to permit the consumption of more food and wine, and drinking games. The latter included, for example, rapidly consuming as many cups as indicated by a throw of the dice (Babor, 1986, p. 10).

By the second and first centuries B.C., intoxication was no longer a rarity, and most prominent men of affairs (for example, Cato the Elder and Julius Caesar) were praised for their moderation in drinking. This would appear to be in response to growing misuse of alcohol in society, because before that time temperance was not singled out for praise as exemplary behavior. As the republic continued to decay, excessive drinking spread and some, such as Marc Antony (d. 30 B.C.), even took pride in their destructive drinking behavior (Austin, 1985, pp. 28 and 32–33).

Early Christian Period

With the dawn of Christianity and its gradual displacement of the previously dominant religions, the drinking attitudes and behaviors of Europe began to be influenced by the New Testament (Babor, 1986, p. 11). The earliest biblical writings after the death of Jesus (cir. A.D. 30) contain few references to alcohol. This may have reflected the fact that drunkenness was largely an upper-status vice with which Jesus had

little contact (Raymond, 1927, pp. 81–82). Austin (1985, p. 35) has pointed out that Jesus used wine (Matthew 15:11; Luke 7:33–35) and approved of its moderate consumption (Matthew 15:11). On the other hand, he severely attacked drunkenness (Luke 21:34, 12:42; Matthew 24:45–51). The later writings of St. Paul (d. 64?) deal with alcohol in detail and are important to Christian doctrine on the subject. He considered wine to be a creation of God and therefore inherently good (1 Timothy 4:4), recommended its use for medicinal purposes (1 Timothy 5:23), but consistently condemned drunkenness (1 Corinthians 3:16–17, 5:11, 6:10; Galatians 5:19–21; Romans 13:3) and recommended abstinence for those who could not control their drinking.[3]

However, late in the second century, several heretical sects rejected alcohol and called for abstinence. By the late fourth and early fifth centuries, the Church responded by asserting that wine was an inherently good gift of God to be used and enjoyed. While individuals may choose not to drink, to despise wine was heresy. The Church advocated its moderate use but rejected excessive or abusive use as a sin. Those individuals who could not drink in moderation were urged to abstain (Austin, 1985, pp. 44 and 47–48).

It is clear that both the Old and New Testaments are clear and consistent in their condemnation of drunkenness. However, some Christians today argue that whenever "wine" was used by Jesus or praised as a gift of God, it was really grape juice; only when it caused drunkenness was it wine. Thus, they interpret the Bible as asserting that grape juice is good and that drinking it is acceptable to God but that wine is bad and that drinking it is unacceptable. This reasoning appears to be incorrect for at least two reasons. First, neither the Hebrew nor Biblical Greek word for wine can be translated or interpreted as referring to grape juice. Secondly, grape juice would quickly ferment into wine in the warm climate of the Mediterranean region without refrigeration or modern methods of preservation (Royce, 1986, pp. 55–56; Raymond, 1927, pp. 18–22; Hewitt, 1980, pp. 11–12).

The spread of Christianity and of viticulture in Western Europe occurred simultaneously (Lausanne, 1969, p. 367; Sournia, 1990, p. 12). Interestingly, St. Martin of Tours (316–397) was actively engaged in both spreading the Gospel and planting vineyards (Patrick, 1952, pp. 26–27).

In an effort to maintain traditional Jewish culture against the rise of Christianity, which was converting numerous Jews (Wallbank & Taylor, 1954, p. 227), detailed rules concerning the use of wine were incorporated into the Talmud. Importantly, wine was integrated into many religious ceremonies in limited quantity (Spiegel, 1979, pp. 20–29; Raymond, 1927, 45–47). In the social and political upheavals that rose as the fall of Rome approached in the fifth century, concern grew among rabbis that Judaism and its culture were in increasing danger.[4] Consequently, more Talmudic rules were laid down concerning the use of wine. These included the amount of wine that could be drunk on the Sabbath, the way in which wine was to be drunk, the legal status of wine in any way connected with idolatry, and the extent of personal responsibility for behavior while intoxicated (Austin, 1985, pp. 36 and 50).

Roman abuse of alcohol appears to have peaked around mid-first century (Jellinek, 1976, pp. 1,736–1,739). Wine had become the most popular beverage, and as Rome attracted a large influx of displaced persons, it was distributed free or at cost (Babor, 1986, pp. 7–8). This led to occasional excesses at festivals, victory triumphs and other celebrations, as described by contemporaries. The four emperors who ruled from A.D. 37 to A.D. 69 were all known for their abusive drinking. However, the emperors who followed were known for their temperance, and literary sources suggest that problem drinking decreased substantially in the Empire. Although there continued to be some criticisms of abusive drinking over the next several hundred years, most evidence indicates a decline of such behavior (Austin, 1985, pp. 37–44, p. 46, pp. 48–50). The fall of Rome and the Western Roman Empire occurred in 476 (Wallbank & Taylor, 1954, pp. 220–221).

Around A.D. 230, the Greek scholar Athenaeus wrote extensively on drinking and advocated moderation. The extensive attention to drinking, famous drinks, and drinking cups (of which he described 100) reflected the importance of wine to the Greeks (Austin, 1985, pp. 45–46).

The Middle Ages

The Middle Ages, that period of approximately one thousand years between the fall of Rome and the beginning of the High Renaissance (cir. 1500), saw numerous developments in life in general and in drinking in particular. In the early Middle Ages, mead, rustic beers, and wild fruit wines became increasingly popular, especially among Celts, Anglo-Saxons, Germans, and Scandinavians. However, wines remained the beverage of preference in the Romance countries (what is now Italy, Spain and France) (Babor, 1986, p. 11).

With the collapse of the Roman Empire and decline of urban life, religious institutions, particularly monasteries, became the repositories of the brewing and winemaking techniques that had been earlier developed (Babor, 1986, p. 11). While rustic beers continued to be produced in homes, the art of brewing essentially became the province of monks, who carefully guarded their knowledge (Cherrington, 1925, v. 1, p. 405). Monks brewed virtually all beer of good quality until the twelfth century. Around the thirteenth century, hops (which both flavors and preserves) became a common ingredient in some beers, especially in northern Europe (Wilson, 1991, p. 375).[5] Ale, often a thick and nutritious soupy beverage, soured quickly and was made for local consumption (Austin, 1985, p. 54, pp. 87–88).

Not surprisingly, the monasteries also maintained viticulture. Importantly, they had the resources, security, and stability in that often-turbulent time to improve the quality of their

vines slowly over 1986, (p. 11). While most wine was made and consumed locally, some wine trade did continue in spite of the deteriorating roads (Hyams, 1965, p. 151; Wilson, 1991, p. 371).

By the millennium, the most popular form of festivities in England were known as "ales," and both ale and beer were at the top of lists of products to be given to lords for rent. As towns were established in twelfth-century Germany, they were granted the privilege of brewing and selling beer in their immediate localities. A flourishing artisan brewing industry developed in many towns, about which there was strong civic pride (Cherrington, 1925, v. 1, p. 405; Austin 1985, pp. 68, 74, 82–83).

The most important development regarding alcohol throughout the Middle Ages was probably that of distillation. Interestingly, considerable disagreement exists concerning who discovered distillation and when the discovery was made.[6] However, it was Albertus Magnus (1193–1280) who first clearly described the process which made possible the manufacture of distilled spirits (Patrick, 1952, p. 29). Knowledge of the process began to spread slowly among monks, physicians and alchemists, who were interested in distilled alcohol as a cure for ailments. At that time it was called aqua vitae, "water of life,"[7] but was later known as brandy. The latter term was derived from the Dutch brandewijn, meaning burnt (or distilled) wine (Seward, 1979, p. 151; Roueche, 1963, pp. 172–173).

The Black Death and subsequent plagues, which began in the mid-fourteenth century, dramatically changed people's perception of their lives and place in the cosmos. With no understanding or control of the plagues that reduced the population by as much as 82% in some villages, "processions of flagellants mobbed city and village streets, hoping, by the pains they inflicted on themselves and each other, to take the edge off the plagues they attributed to God's wrath over human folly" (Slavin, 1973, pp. 12–16).

Some dramatically increased their consumption of alcohol in the belief that this might protect them from the mysterious disease, while others thought that through moderation in all things, including alcohol, they could be saved. It would appear that, on balance, consumption of alcohol was high. For example, in Bavaria, beer consumption was probably about 300 liters per capita a year (compared to 150 liters today) and in Florence wine consumption was about ten barrels per capita a year. Understandably, the consumption of distilled spirits, which was exclusively for medicinal purposes, increased in popularity (Austin, 1985, pp. 104–105, 107–108).

As the end of the Middle Ages approached, the popularity of beer spread to England, France and Scotland (Austin, pp. 118–119). Beer brewers were recognized officially as a guild in England (Monckton, 1966, pp. 69–70), and the adulteration of beer or wine became punishable by death in Scotland (Cherrington, 1929, vol. 5, p. 2,383). Importantly, the consumption of spirits as a beverage began to occur (Braudel, 1974, p. 171).

Early Modern Period

The early modern period was generally characterized by increasing prosperity and wealth. Towns and cities grew in size and number, foreign lands were discovered and colonized, and trade expanded. Perhaps more importantly, there developed a new view of the world. The medieval emphasis on other-worldliness—the belief that life in this world is only a preparation for heaven—slowly gave way, especially among the wealthy and well educated, to an interest in life in the here and now (Wallbank & Taylor, 1954, p. 513).

The Protestant Reformation and rise of aggressive national states destroyed the ideal of a universal Church overseeing a Holy Roman Empire. Rationality, individualism, and science heavily impacted the prevalent emotional idealism, communalism, and traditional religion (Wallbank & Taylor, 1954, pp. 513–518; Slavin, 1973, ch. 5–7).

However, the Protestant leaders such as Luther, Calvin, the leaders of the Anglican Church and even the Puritans did not differ substantially from the teachings of the Catholic Church: alcohol was a gift of God and created to be used in moderation for pleasure, enjoyment and health; drunkenness was viewed as a sin (Austin, 1985, p. 194).

From this period through at least the beginning of the eighteenth century, attitudes toward drinking were characterized by a continued recognition of the positive nature of moderate consumption and an increased concern over the negative effects of drunkenness. The latter, which was generally viewed as arising out of the increased self-indulgence of the time, was seen as a threat to spiritual salvation and societal well being. Intoxication was also inconsistent with the emerging emphasis on rational mastery of self and world and on work and efficiency (Austin, 1985, pp. 129–130).

However, consumption of alcohol was often high. In the sixteenth century, alcohol beverage consumption reached 100 liters per person per year in Valladolid, Spain, and Polish peasants consumed up to three liters of beer per day (Braudel, 1974, pp. 236–238). In Coventry, the average amount of beer and ale consumed was about 17 pints per person per week, compared to about three pints today (Monckton, 1966, p. 95); nationwide, consumption was about one pint per day per capita. Swedish beer consumption may have been 40 times higher than in modern Sweden. English sailors received a ration of a gallon of beer per day, while soldiers received two-thirds of a gallon. In Denmark, the usual consumption of beer appears to have been a gallon per day for adult laborers and sailors (Austin, 1985, pp. 170, 186, 192).

However, the production and distribution of spirits spread slowly. Spirit drinking was still largely for medicinal purposes throughout most of the sixteenth century. It has been said of distilled alcohol that "the sixteenth century created it; the seventeenth century consolidated it; the eighteenth popularized it" (Braudel, 1967, p. 170).

A beverage that clearly made its debut during the seventeenth century was sparkling champagne. The credit for that development goes primarily to Dom Perignon, the wine-master in a French abbey. Around 1668, he used strong bottles, invented a more efficient cork (and one that could contain the effervescence in those strong bottles), and began developing the technique of blending the contents. However, another century would pass before problems, especially bursting bottles, would be solved and sparkling champagne would become popular (Younger, 1966, pp. 345–346; Doxat, 1971, p. 54; Seward, 1979, pp. 139–143).

The original grain spirit, whiskey, appears to have first been distilled in Ireland. While its specific origins are unknown (Magee, 1980, p. 7; Wilson, 1973, p. 7) there is evidence that by the sixteenth century it was widely consumed in some parts of Scotland (Roueche, 1963, pp. 175–176). It was also during the seventeenth century that Franciscus Sylvius (or Franz de la Boe), a professor of medicine at the University of Leyden, distilled spirits from grain.

Distilled spirit was generally flavored with juniper berries. The resulting beverage was known as junever, the Dutch word for "juniper." The French changed the name to genievre, which the English changed to "geneva" and then modified to "gin"[8] (Roueche, 1963, pp. 173–174). Originally used for medicinal purposes, the use of gin as a social drink did not grow rapidly at first (Doxat, 1972, p. 98; Watney, 1976, p. 10). However, in 1690, England passed "An Act for the Encouraging of the Distillation of Brandy and Spirits from Corn" and within four years the annual production of distilled spirits, most of which was gin, reached nearly one million gallons (Roueche, 1963, p. 174).

The seventeenth century also saw the Virginia colonists continue the traditional belief that alcoholic beverages are a natural food and are good when used in moderation. In fact, beer arrived with the first colonists, who considered it essential to their well being (Baron, 1962, pp. 3–8). The Puritan minister Increase Mather preached in favor of alcohol but against its abuse: "Drink is in itself a good creature of God, and to be received with thankfulness, but the abuse of drink is from Satan; the wine is from God, but the Drunkard is from the Devil" (quoted in Rorabaugh, 1979, p. 30). During that century the first distillery was established in the colonies on what is now Staten Island (Roueche, 1963, p. 178), cultivation of hops began in Massachusetts, and both brewing and distilling were legislatively encouraged in Maryland (Austin, 1985, pp. 230 and 249).

Rum is produced by distilling fermented molasses, which is the residue left after sugar has been made from sugar cane. Although it was introduced to the world, and presumably invented, by the first European settlers in the West Indies, no one knows when it was first produced or by what individual. But by 1657, a rum distillery was operating in Boston. It was highly successful and within a generation the manufacture of rum would become colonial New England's largest and most prosperous industry (Roueche, 1963, p. 178).

The dawn of the eighteenth century saw Parliament pass legislation designed to encourage the use of grain for distilling spirits. In 1685, consumption of gin had been slightly over one-half million gallons (Souria, 1990, p. 20). By 1714, gin production stood at two million gallons (Roueche, 1963, p. 174). In 1727, official (declared and taxed) production reached five million gallons; six years later the London area alone produced eleven million gallons of gin (French, 1890, p. 271; Samuelson, 1878, pp. 160–161; Watney, 1976, p. 16).

The English government actively promoted gin production to utilize surplus grain and to raise revenue. Encouraged by public policy, very cheap spirits flooded the market at a time when there was little stigma attached to drunkenness and when the growing urban poor in London sought relief from the newfound insecurities and harsh realities of urban life (Watney, 1976, p. 17; Austin, 1985, pp. xxi–xxii). Thus developed the so-called Gin Epidemic.

While the negative effects of that phenomenon may have been exaggerated[9] (Sournia, 1990, p. 21; Mathias, 1959, p. xxv), Parliament passed legislation in 1736 to discourage consumption by prohibiting the sale of gin in quantities of less than two gallons and raising the tax on it dramatically.[10] However, the peak in consumption was reached seven years later, when the nation of six and one-half million people drank over 18 million gallons of gin. And most was consumed by the small minority of the population then living in London and other cities; people in the countryside largely remained loyal to beer, ale and cider (Doxat, 1972, pp. 98–100; Watney, 1976, p.17).

After its dramatic peak, gin consumption rapidly declined. From 18 million gallons in 1743, it dropped to just over seven million gallons in 1751 and to less than two million by 1758, and generally declined to the end of the century (Ashton, 1955, p. 243). A number of factors appear to have converged to discourage consumption of gin. These include the production of higher quality beer of lower price, rising corn prices and taxes which eroded the price advantage of gin, a temporary ban on distilling, a stigmatization of drinking gin, an increasing criticism of drunkenness, a newer standard of behavior that criticized coarseness and excess, increased tea and coffee consumption, an increase in piety and increasing industrialization with a consequent emphasis on sobriety and labor efficiency (Sournia, 1990, p. 22; King, 1947, p. 117; Austin, 1985, pp. xxiii–xxiv, 324–325, 351; Younger, 1966, p. 341).

While drunkenness was still an accepted part of life in the eighteenth century (Austin, 1985, p. xxv), the nineteenth century would bring a change in attitudes as a result of increasing industrialization and the need for a reliable and punctual work force (Porter, 1990, p. xii). Self-discipline was needed in place of self-expression, and task orientation had to replace

relaxed conviviality. Drunkenness would come to be defined as a threat to industrial efficiency and growth.

Problems commonly associated with industrialization and rapid urbanization were also attributed to alcohol. Thus, problems such as urban crime, poverty and high infant mortality rates were blamed on alcohol, although "it is likely that gross overcrowding and unemployment had much to do with these problems" (Soumia, 1990, p. 21). Over time, more and more personal, social and religious/moral problems would be blamed on alcohol. And not only would it be enough to prevent drunkenness; any consumption of alcohol would come to be seen as unacceptable. Groups that began by promoting temperance—the moderate use of alcohol—would ultimately become abolitionist and press for the complete and total prohibition of the production and distribution of beverage alcohol. Unfortunately, this would not eliminate social problems but would compound the situation by creating additional problems.

Summary and Conclusion

It is clear that alcohol has been highly valued and in continuous use by peoples throughout history. Reflecting its vital role, consumption of alcohol in moderation has rarely been questioned throughout most of recorded time. To the contrary, "Fermented dietary beverage . . . was so common an element in the various cultures that it was taken for granted as one of the basic elements of survival and self-preservation" (Lucia, 1963b, p. 165). Indicative of its value is the fact that it has frequently been acceptable as a medium of exchange. For example, in Medieval England, ale was often used to pay toll, rent or debts (Watney, 1974, p. 16).

From the earliest times alcohol has played an important role in religion,"[11] typically seen as a gift of deities and closely associated with their worship. Religious rejection of alcohol appears to be a rare phenomenon. When it does occur, such rejection may be unrelated to alcohol per se but reflect other considerations. For example, the nomadic Rechabites rejected wine because they associated it with an unacceptable agricultural life style. Nazarites abstained only during the period of their probation, after which they returned to drinking (Sournia, 1990, p. 5; Samuelson, 1878, pp. 62–63). Among other reasons, Mohammed may have forbidden alcohol in order to further distinguish his followers from those of other religions (Royce, 1986, p. 57).

Alcoholic beverages have also been an important source of nutrients and calories (Braudel, 1974, p. 175). In ancient Egypt, the phrase "bread and beer" stood for all food and was also a common greeting. Many alcoholic beverages, such as Egyptian bouza and Sudanese merissa, contain high levels of protein, fat and carbohydrates, a fact that helps explain the frequent lack of nutritional deficiencies in some populations whose diets are generally poor. Importantly, the levels of amino acids and vitamins increase during fermentation

(Ghaliounqui, 1979, pp. 8–9). While modern food technology uses enrichment or fortification to improve the nutrition of foods, it is possible to achieve nutritional enrichment naturally through fermentation (Steinkraus, 1979, p. 36).

Alcoholic beverages have long served as thirst quenchers. Water pollution is far from new; to the contrary, supplies have generally been either unhealthful or questionable at best. Ancient writers rarely wrote about water, except as a warning (Ghaliounqui, 1979, p. 3). Travelers crossing what is now Zaire in 1648 reported having to drink water that resembled horse's urine. In the late eighteenth century most Parisians drank water from a very muddy and often chemically polluted Seine (Braudel, 1967, pp. 159–161). Coffee and tea were not introduced into Europe until the mid-seventeenth century, and it was another hundred or more years before they were commonly consumed on a daily basis (Austin, 1985, pp. 251, 254, 351, 359, 366).

Another important function of alcohol has been therapeutic or medicinal. Current research suggests that the moderate consumption of alcohol is preferable to abstinence. It appears to reduce the incidence of coronary heart disease (e.g., Razay, 1992; Jackson *et al.*, 1991; Klatsky *et al.*, 1990, p. 745; Rimm *et al.*, 1991; Miller *et al.*, 1990), cancer (e.g., Bofetta & Garfinkel, 1990) and osteoporosis (e.g., Gavaler & Van Thiel, 1992), among many other diseases and conditions, and to increase longevity (e.g., DeLabry *et al.*, 1992). It has clearly been a major analgesic, and one widely available to people in pain. Relatedly, it has provided relief from the fatigue of hard labor.

Not to be underestimated is the important role alcohol has served in enhancing the enjoyment and quality of life. It can serve as a social lubricant, can provide entertainment, can facilitate relaxation, can provide pharmacological pleasure and can enhance the flavors of food (Gastineau *et al.*, 1979).

While alcohol has always been misused by a minority of drinkers, it has clearly proved to be beneficial to most. In the words of the founding Director of the National Institute on Alcohol Abuse and Alcoholism, ". . . alcohol has existed longer than all human memory. It has outlived generations, nations, epochs and ages. It is a part of us, and that is fortunate indeed. For although alcohol will always be the master of some, for most of us it will continue to be the servant of man" (Chafetz, 1965, p. 223).

References

Hanson, David J. *Preventing Alcohol Abuse: Alcohol, Culture and Control.* Wesport, CT: Praeger, 1995. www2.potsdam.edu/hansondj/controversies/1114796842.html. Retrieved May 2, 2008

Marley, David. *Chemical Addiction, Drug Use, and Treatment.* MedScape Today 2001 www.medscape.com/viewarticle/418525. Retrieved May 2, 2008

Critical Thinking

1. Why have patterns related to alcohol use remained consistent around the world for centuries?
2. Consider the theme(s) of alcohol use throughout history as presented in this article and describe how alcohol use today relates to those themes.

Adapted from **DAVID J. HANSON,** PhD *Preventing Alcohol Abuse: Alcohol, Culture and Control.* Westport, CT: Praeger, 1995.

How Latin America Is Reinventing the War on Drugs

Frustrated with US dictates, countries across the region are floating new ideas to curb drug trafficking, from 'soft' enforcement to legalization.

SARAH MILLER LLANA AND SARA SHAHRIARI

Like thousands of other Bolivians, Marcela Lopez Vasquez's parents migrated to the Chapare region, in the Andean tropics, desperate to make a living after waves of economic and environmental upheaval hit farming and mining communities in the 1970s and '80s.

The new migrants, who spread across the undulating green hills here, planted bananas. They planted yucca and orange trees. But it was in the coca leaf that thrives in this climate that they found the salvation of a steady cash crop—and themselves at the nexus of the American "war on drugs."

The coca leaf has been sacred in Andean society for 4,000 years and is a mainstay of Bolivian culture. It is chewed by farmers and miners, enlisted in religious ceremonies, and used for medicinal purposes. "The only resource for maintaining our families is the coca leaf," says Ms. Lopez Vasquez. "With coca we maintain our families: We dress ourselves, take care of our health, and educate our kids."

Coca is also used to make cocaine. To American society, from White House officials to worried parents, the nation's drug problems start in places like the back fields of the Chapare, where neat rows of coca's spindly bushes, bursting with bright green leaves, stand head high. Bolivia is the world's third largest grower of coca, behind Colombia and Peru.

For decades the coca growers here, Lopez Vasquez among them, resisted US-backed forced eradication in a long simmering protest that defined US-Bolivian relations and often turned violent. Growers in the Chapare scored a victory in 2004 when they were granted the right to grow a small plot of coca per family. But a turning point came with the 2006 election of Bolivian President Evo Morales, a former coca grower from the Chapare and still the head of its unions, who promised an end to the old US-Bolivian paradigm. Within three years of his presidency, Mr. Morales kicked out the United States Drug Enforcement Administration (DEA), as well as the US ambassador, accusing both of fomenting opposition. Last year Bolivia became the first country ever to withdraw from the United Nations 1961 Single Convention on Narcotic Drugs for the charter's failure to recognize the traditional use of the coca leaf.

Now the Chapare is once again a nexus—but this time for a new government experiment markedly different from former US drug policy. Today, farmers unions partner with government agencies to control coca production, reducing the amount of the leaf cultivated across Bolivia, as well as the quantities destined for illegal uses. This cooperation is new, and the very acceptance of coca crops in the Chapare defies US wishes.

The US, in fact, has voiced deep skepticism about Bolivia's commitment to the international fight against narcotics, condemning La Paz in a 2012 report for "failing demonstrably" in its antinarcotic obligations.

For the residents of the Chapare, however, the "nationalization" of Bolivia's drug fight means the preservation of a lifestyle and a basic income without the threat of constant conflict.

"I am a coca producer, and they made us take out our crops so cocaine would disappear and narcotraffic would disappear," says Felipe Martinez, who heads a state entity in charge of monitoring and eradicating coca that exceeds legal limits in the Chapare. "But that didn't bring results. It brought blood, sorrow, orphans. We lost the right to be people."

Bolivia's more go-it-alone approach symbolizes a fundamental shift in the drug war in Latin America—one that is creating a tense new relationship between the US and its southern neighbors and could help determine how many drugs ultimately end up on urban streets.

Countries across the region are adopting a more autonomous, sometimes nationalistic, response to narcotics control that increasingly questions Washington's priorities and prescriptions. From Bolivia, where drugs are produced, to Mexico and Guatemala, where they transit through, to Brazil, where they are increasingly consumed, officials are forging new policies or floating ideas to deal with a problem they believe 40 years of US-dictated solutions hasn't curbed.

The relationship between Latin America and the US has always been at its most fraught over the war on drugs, ever since Richard Nixon launched the initiative in the 1970s. Nowhere has Washington's scolding finger been more in the face of its Latin American counterparts. Nowhere has Latin America felt it has fewer options than to just acquiesce, dependent as it is on US aid and military might to overcome the cartels that control narcotics trafficking.

But in the past five years, frustration has mounted. Gruesome drug crimes have brought record levels of violence to swaths of Mexico and Central America, despite the billions that the US has poured into the antinarcotics fight.

Leaders in the region are pleading for new alternatives—some are even discussing legalized drug markets—no matter how much those ideas might alienate the US.

The restiveness reflects a growing political assertiveness in the region. While Latin America has always been weary of the heavy hand of the US, Bolivia and Venezuela have taken their indignation to a new level, refusing to cooperate with the DEA and other US officials. Many countries also seem less inclined to genuflect toward Washington on other issues, from trade to foreign policy.

Yet it is the drug issue that will most define US relations with the hemisphere—and have the most impact around the world. Latin America remains the world's No. 1 supplier of cocaine, and how various countries deal with their coca tracts will not only affect the flow of narcotics, but might lead to new strategies in the drug fight.

For now, the range of ideas and possible routes of action vary widely. Leaders in the most vociferous countries even concede that their ideas might not work. But what seems certain is that the days of policy dictated so heavily from Washington are vanishing.

"There is a desperate call from Latin America for peace, which includes a new model for drug policies," says Milton Romani, Uruguay's ambassador to the Organization of American States (OAS).

Otto Perez Molina is hardly a squeamish liberal. The president of Guatemala, who took office in January, is a retired military general who once served in the country's brutish special forces (Kaibiles). The day after his inauguration, the silver-thatched leader fulfilled a campaign promise to bring an "iron fist" to lawlessness by militarizing the drug fight in Guatemala.

So it stunned the region when the Guatemalan president, in March, floated a provocative initiative to deal with the violence spiraling out of control in another way: He called for an entire rethink of the war on drugs, including the option of the state running a legally regulated drug market.

The idea of pursuing more liberalized drug policies rather than harsher punishments is hardly novel in Latin America. But such notions are usually championed by intellectuals and academics on the left. They have rarely been promoted by sitting presidents.

Yet 2009 marked a hinge moment: A Latin American commission on drug policy headed by three former presidents, from Mexico, Brazil, and Colombia, published a report declaring the war on drugs a failure—one that desperately needed to shift from repression to prevention. Two years later, the group pulled former officials and business leaders from around the world into the Global Commission on Drug Policy, which went further, rallying nations to consider ways to regulate drugs rather than just crack down on their use.

Amid this growing consensus, Mr. Perez Molina, and perhaps even more significant, President Juan Manuel Santos of Colombia, began floating similar ideas. At a talk in London in late 2011, Mr. Santos, a former defense minister, said the war on drugs was stuck on a "stationary bike."

Other leaders rallied to their side, including Laura Chinchilla, the president of Costa Rica. Mexico's conservative president, Felipe Calderón, while not siding with legalization, has said in moments of exasperation that if US consumption cannot be controlled, the hemisphere should consider "market solutions," meaning some kind of regulated legal exchange.

Drug policy became a centerpiece of the OAS Summit held in Cartagena in April, too. The organization set a mandate to study drug policy alternatives and deliver a review in a year's time—what many consider a significant step.

Since then, in the boldest proposal to date, President José Mujica of Uruguay announced the possibility of establishing a legal marijuana market, in which the drug would be produced and distributed under state control. It would be the first market of its kind in the world.

Yet many drug policy experts in the region question whether a state-run exchange could work. Santos in Colombia criticized Mr. Mujica's plan, saying "unilateral" action is not the way forward. Others say corruption—in Guatemala, for instance—would only empower drug traffickers if there were a legal market. Still others note that talk of legalization, which focuses on marijuana, misses the point since cocaine is the big concern and no one is suggesting legalizing it.

But the debate, which has evolved from one led by activists to former presidents to current heads of state in Latin America, suggests that some kind of fundamental change is inevitable.

"For former presidents, it is easy to say 'let's have a debate' on a topic that they cannot do anything about," says Daniel Mejia, who runs a drug policy research center at the University of los Andes in Bogotá. "But having sitting presidents [say that] is a completely new thing that we've seen during the past five years."

While legalization is the buzz word that always draws media attention—and virulent US protests—Latin America is leading the way today in considering a whole range of alternative policy options. It is beginning to focus on drug use as a public health issue, and not a crime, through judicial rulings and legislation, following in the footsteps of Western Europe in the past two decades. Several countries have already introduced decriminalization of possession of small amounts of drugs, mainly marijuana, and are proposing lighter sentences for minor trafficking offenses.

In Argentina, for instance, the Supreme Court ruled in 2009 that it is unconstitutional to punish someone for possessing drugs for personal consumption. Mexico decriminalized personal use that same year, although only for minute quantities. Colombia's Constitutional Court in June upheld an earlier law that decriminalized personal consumption of marijuana and cocaine, while lawmakers in Brazil are debating whether to make possessing small quantities a noncriminal offense as well.

The moves mark a swing back from harsher sentences and an escalation of the war on drugs that have been a hallmark of US influence in the region since the 1980s, according to Martin Jelsma, a drug policy expert at the Transnational Institute in the Netherlands.

Bolivia's changes have been dramatic in their own way. On a recent morning, the Chapare, a New Hampshire-size province in the middle of the country, lies under a heavy mist. Wooden houses propped up on stilts sit among plots of banana trees.

Women in bright velvet skirts and brimmed hats, characteristic of the area's Quechua Indians, shop at local markets. Chickens scour dirt yards and dogs wander the roads. It's a peaceful tableau.

Yet the quietude has only come here recently, residents say. Rosa Montaño, who migrated to the Chapare as a young woman, still farms her legally allotted coca field, called a cato, which helps her maintain her home, a small unpainted wooden room. She lives there with her daughter, Irma Cornejo, who grew up in the height of the coca grower conflict, and her grandchildren. Both say dramatic changes have occurred since Bolivian rural police units, backed by the US, stopped coming in and forcing the eradication of coca.

"They brought my brother here and beat him," Ms. Cornejo says. "Now that doesn't happen. . . . It's calmer now. The kids don't see those beatings that I've seen; and the abuse, it isn't here anymore."

Under the current system, the responsibility for inspecting the size of the coca crops lies with the coca-growing unions and a government-monitoring body. It includes satellite surveillance. The Bolivians are backed in the program, called "social control," with funding from the European Union.

Farmers who consistently grow more than the allotted amount of coca, or who produce it outside designated areas, are subject to forced eradication. Bolivia's anti-narcotics forces also still search out cocaine labs and confiscate illegal drug shipments.

"[Bolivia] challenged the United States, and it turned out the United States was not the omnipotent force in drug war policy that it seemed to be," says Kathryn Ledebur, director of the Andean Information Network, a Bolivia-based advocacy group. "And it was important to establish that for everyone in Latin America."

The US isn't completely divorced from the process. It continues to fund the antinarcotics effort in Bolivia through the US embassy, but the aid has dropped from about $40 million in 2006 to $10 million in 2012, according to US State Department figures.

Instead, Bolivia has increasingly been partnering with both the EU and Brazil, with whom it shares a long, porous border. Brazil, which is now the second-largest consumer of cocaine in the world, plans to use drones and other technology to help patrol the Amazonian area that the two countries share.

Brazil's ambassador to Bolivia, Marcel Biato, says the countries have been cooperating more closely since 2010, at the request of La Paz. "I think this link has to do with various internal elements, but also a clear distancing from the US and perhaps greater confidence that Brazil can develop an alternative to all of the historic problems," he says.

As part of the social control program, the coca unions educate local growers about the importance of keeping cultivation at legally accepted limits, which markedly increased during the early years of the Morales administration. When the US government was heavily involved in the eradication effort, before 2004, Bolivia was allowed to plant 46 square miles of coca a year for traditional uses. Since then, the Bolivian government has boosted that amount to 77 square miles.

To further aid growers, Morales is trying to find more legal international markets for the leaf, something the UN charter on narcotics prohibits. In Bolivia, coca is widely used in teas and chewed (bags of leaves are sold on street corners) as well as incorporated into consumer items such as candy, cookies, granola bars, and toothpaste.

The leaf acts as a mild stimulant—it produces no major high like purified cocaine—but can help overcome fatigue, hunger, and thirst. For these reasons, it has long been used as a medicine—something Bolivians have turned to for everything from nosebleeds to indigestion to dealing with childbirth.

The question is how much of it gets made into cocaine. Growers like Lopez Vasquez say there are always people who want to produce more coca than the state allows, or who turn it into cocaine and ship it off to Brazil and as far away as Africa and Europe. But as she stands in a coca field in her hometown, Lopez Vasquez is confident that coca cultivation will decline in the Chapare because the powerful unions are committed to working with, instead of fighting, the government to manage cultivation.

Mr. Martinez, the state official and coca grower, agrees. "More than ever we have applied ourselves to agree on mechanisms between the state and the coca producers so we have positive results," he says in his Chapare office, where he pulls out some coca leaves from his drawer and slips them in his cheek. "We haven't had any deaths. We haven't had any injuries. There has been no blood spilled and no conflicts."

Yet not everyone is convinced the situation is under control. Even though coca leaf cultivation has stabilized in recent years, the US believes that Bolivia is producing far more than even the limits La Paz has set—and thus the potential for cocaine production remains dangerously high.

According to the US's annual International Narcotics Control Strategy Report, the country cultivated 133 square miles of coca in 2010, down slightly from 2009's 135 square mile estimate. From this, the US estimates that the pure cocaine potential remains at 195 metric tons, or 70 percent higher than in 2006.

Further, the US believes Bolivia's ability to arrest major traffickers has eroded since the DEA was kicked out in 2008. "Expelling DEA has seriously harmed Bolivia's counternarcotics capability, especially in regard to interdiction," the report says.

Bolivia has certainly seen setbacks. In 2011, an ex-commander of the nation's antidrug police and current head of a drug intelligence agency was arrested by the DEA in Panama and subsequently pleaded guilty to trafficking. While no reliable evidence has surfaced linking other top Bolivians to the drug trade, accusations swirl that the links go beyond the one official.

"The highest levels of governance in those countries [Bolivia and Venezuela] are complicit in the global drug trade now," says Michael Braun, the former chief of operations for the DEA.

Bolivia represents one of the most extreme examples of countries diverging with the US over drug policy. But others are starting to question elements of America's priorities as well—some of them surprising.

When Mexican President Calderón was elected in 2006 and made fighting the scourge of drug cartels the cornerstone of his presidency, he was feted in American circles. A new era of "co-responsibility" was ushered in as the US signed off on a $1.6 billion aid package to help Mexico fight trafficking.

But as the years wore on and the toll mounted—including more than 50,000 dead in six years, even as top traffickers were caught and extradited to the US—so did public criticism of the strategy. It ultimately cost Calderón's conservative National Action Party the presidency in July elections. The incoming president, Enrique Peña Nieto, who takes office in December, has promised to "reduce violence" instead of focusing single-mindedly on netting traffickers and stanching the flow of drugs.

What that means exactly isn't clear. But ideas are being floated that would make American officials grimace, according to Alejandro Hope, a security analyst and former official in Mexico's intelligence agency.

He argues that Mexico should go after the most violent criminals, not the ones that move the most drugs. He says the country should quietly end eradication efforts, calling it a "pointless exercise." "What Mexico can't do and should not attempt to do is stop the flow of drugs into the US," says Mr. Hope.

US priorities are also under assault in Central America, where violence and trafficking have migrated after crackdowns in Mexico. In Honduras, DEA squadrons have been involved in three fatal shootouts in less than three months. The teams, called Foreign-deployed Advisory and Support Teams (FAST), have been accompanying local forces throughout Honduras and other countries in Central America.

But the program, which was begun quietly in Afghanistan and expanded into Central America, exploded onto the front pages in May after a group of Hondurans, who claim to be innocent victims, were shot at by Honduran forces, accompanied by the DEA, as they plied the waters of the Mosquito Coast in canoes. Four were killed. Since then, the DEA has been involved in two more fatal incidents.

The US and Honduras have defended the raids, and so does Mr. Braun, an architect of the program. "The government of Honduras is asking for more DEA resources, rather than backing away from the incidents. That is pretty telling," says Braun.

A US official echoes those sentiments. He says the success so far of Operation Anvil, under which the FAST teams were dispatched in April, is clear: Honduran forces, with DEA support, have interdicted 2,300 kilograms of cocaine from smuggling flights, mostly coming from Venezuela. "It showed us there is unchallenged illicit air traffic going through Honduras, and Honduras has not been able to control it until now," he says.

More broadly, he notes that the US has put more resources into the "soft" side of the drug fight, not just eradication and hardware but in institution-building and anti-corruption measures. "The old paradigm, the idea of a war on drugs, is long past," he says. "We realize there are a lot of other pieces of it that go well beyond eradicating a coca field."

Still, the incidents in Honduras and the perception of a continued militarization of the fight has provoked an outcry from human rights workers and others in Honduras and beyond. "The use of the military has just caused violence to spiral to levels we have never seen," says Sandino Asturias, head of the Center for Guatemalan Studies.

How far all this change in Latin America, whether in Lopez Vasquez's backyard or in the presidential palace in Bogotá, will go remains uncertain. But the days of Washington dictation seem to be diminishing. As John Walsh at the Washington Office on Latin America puts it: "No one is taking marching orders from the US anymore."

Critical Thinking

1. How long has coca leaf been used in Andean societies?
2. What do the indigenous Andean peoples use coca leaf for traditionally?
3. What exactly do Central and South American countries mean when they say that they want to establish legally regulated drug?

From *The Christian Science Monitor* by Sara Miller Llana and Sara Shahriari, July 30, 2012. Copyright © 2012 by Christian Science Monitor. Reprinted by permission. www.CSMonitor.com

Police Officers Find That Dissent on Drug Laws May Come With a Price

Marc Lacey

PHOENIX—*Border Patrol* agents pursue smugglers one moment and sit around in boredom the next. It was during one of the lulls that Bryan Gonzalez, a young agent, made some comments to a colleague that cost him his career.

Stationed in Deming, N.M., Mr. Gonzalez was in his green-and-white Border Patrol vehicle just a few feet from the international boundary when he pulled up next to a fellow agent to chat about the frustrations of the job. If *marijuana* were legalized, Mr. Gonzalez acknowledges saying, the drug-related violence across the border in Mexico would cease. He then brought up an organization called Law Enforcement Against Prohibition that favors ending the war on drugs.

Those remarks, along with others expressing sympathy for illegal immigrants from Mexico, were passed along to the Border Patrol headquarters in Washington. After an investigation, a termination letter arrived that said Mr. Gonzalez held "personal views that were contrary to core characteristics of Border Patrol Agents, which are patriotism, dedication and esprit de corps."

After his dismissal, Mr. Gonzalez joined a group even more exclusive than the Border Patrol: law enforcement officials who have lost their jobs for questioning the war on drugs and are fighting back in the courts.

In Arizona, Joe Miller, a probation officer in Mohave County, near the California border, filed suit last month in Federal District Court after he was dismissed for adding his name to a letter by *Law Enforcement Against Prohibition,* which is based in Medford, Mass., and known as LEAP, expressing support for the decriminalization of marijuana.

"More and more members of the law enforcement community are speaking out against failed drug policies, and they don't give up their right to share their insight and engage in this important debate simply because they receive government paychecks," said Daniel Pochoda, the legal director for the *American Civil Liberties Union of Arizona,* which is handling the Miller case.

Mr. Miller was one of 32 members of LEAP who signed the letter, which expressed support for a California ballot measure that failed last year that would have permitted recreational marijuana use. Most of the signers were retired members of law enforcement agencies, who can speak their minds without

fear of action by their bosses. But Mr. Miller and a handful of others who were still on the job—including the district attorney for Humboldt County in California and the Oakland city attorney—signed, too.

LEAP has seen its membership increase significantly from the time it was founded in 2002 by five disillusioned officers. It now has an e-mail list of 48,000, and its members include 145 judges, prosecutors, police officers, prison guards and other law enforcement officials, most of them retired, who speak on the group's behalf.

"No one wants to be fired and have to fight for their job in court," said Neill Franklin, a retired police officer who is LEAP's executive director. "So most officers are reluctant to sign on board. But we do have some brave souls."

Mr. Miller was accused of not making clear that he was speaking for himself and not the probation department while advocating the decriminalization of cannabis. His lawsuit, though, points out that the letter he signed said at the bottom, "All agency affiliations are listed for identification purposes only."

He was also accused of dishonesty for denying that he had given approval for his name to appear on the LEAP letter. In the lawsuit, Mr. Miller said that his wife had given approval without his knowledge, using his e-mail address, but that he had later supported her.

Kip Anderson, the court administrator for the Superior Court in Mohave County, said there was no desire to limit Mr. Miller's political views.

"This isn't about legalization," Mr. Anderson said. "We're not taking a stand on that. We just didn't want people to think he was speaking on behalf of the probation department."

Mr. Miller, who is also a retired police officer and Marine, lost an appeal of his dismissal before a hearing officer. But when his application for unemployment benefits was turned down, he appealed that and won. An administrative law judge found that Mr. Miller had not been dishonest with his bosses and that the disclaimer on the letter was sufficient.

In the case of Mr. Gonzalez, the fired Border Patrol agent, he had not joined LEAP but had expressed sympathy with the group's cause. "It didn't make sense to me why marijuana is illegal," he said. "To see that thousands of people are dying, some of whom I know, makes you want to look for a change."

Since his firing, Mr. Gonzalez, who filed suit in federal court in Texas in January, has worked as a construction worker, a bouncer and a yard worker. He has also gone back to school, where he is considering a law degree.

"I don't want to work at a place that says I can't think," said Mr. Gonzalez, who grew up in El Paso, just across the border from Ciudad Juárez, which has experienced some of the worst bloodshed in Mexico.

The Justice Department, which is defending the Border Patrol, has sought to have the case thrown out. Mr. Gonzalez lost a discrimination complaint filed with the Equal Employment Opportunity Commission, which sided with his supervisors' view that they had lost trust that he would uphold the law.

Those challenging their dismissals are buoyed by the case of Jonathan Wender, who was fired as a police sergeant in Mountlake Terrace, Wash., in 2005, partly as a result of his support for the decriminalization of marijuana. Mr. Wender won a settlement of $815,000 as well as his old job back. But he retired from the department and took up teaching at the University of Washington, where one of his courses is "Drugs and Society."

Among those not yet ready to publicly urge the legalization of drugs is a veteran Texas police officer who quietly supports LEAP and spoke on the condition that he not be identified.

"We all know the drug war is a bad joke," he said in a telephone interview. "But we also know that you'll never get promoted if you're seen as soft on drugs."

Mr. Franklin, the LEAP official, said it was natural that those on the front lines of enforcing drug laws would have strong views on them, either way. It was the death of a colleague at the hands of a drug dealer in 2000 that prompted Mr. Franklin, a veteran officer, to begin questioning the nation's drug policies. Some of his colleagues, though, hit the streets even more aggressively, he said.

Mr. Franklin said he got calls all the time from colleagues skeptical about the drug laws as they are written but unwilling to speak out—yet.

"I was speaking to a guy with the Maryland State Police this past Saturday, and he's about to retire in January and he's still reluctant to join us until he leaves," Mr. Franklin said. "He wants to have a good last couple of months, without any hassle."

Critical Thinking

1. What happens to law enforcement officers who disagree with the U.S. governments' "War on Drugs"?

2. What is LEAP? Who founded it?

3. Who are the members of LEAP?

Tackling Top Teen Problem— Prescription Drugs

Taking prescription drugs makes you feel 'chill'; a teenager recently told the Bulletin, "and nothing worries you.

GEORGE LAUBY AND KAMIE WHEELOCK

Many people ages 11 to 18 routinely take pills such as Vicodin, Percocet, Xanax, Klonopin, Adderal, Concerta, Ritalin or generic knockoffs of the same.

The illegal use of prescription drugs looms larger than problem drinking or marijuana use, North Platte High School Principal Jim Whitney said.

The drugs are stolen from medicine cabinets, parents' or grandparents' medicine cabinets, or from a friend's house, or even bought off the Internet.

Drugs are passed to friends, either for free or for money. Some pills are reportedly taken by the handful at so-called "pharma parties" where pills are reportedly dumped in a bowl for anyone and everyone, and chased down with beers.

"You are just messed up," a student said of the effects. "You don't even want to move. You just want to lay there and stare off into space."

"Prescription drug abuse has been around in different forms for a long time," Whitney said, "but in the last year and a half it has probably become more popular than alcohol."

In a 2007 Lincoln County survey, 12–14 percent of high school students said they had abused prescription drugs. The same survey found more than 3 percent of sixth graders abused the drugs, and more than 5 percent of eighth graders.

The number who get caught is much lower. Only 12 students have been caught with illegal prescription drugs this year at the high school, Whitney said. Nearly all of them were suspended.

Kids steal drugs not just to chill, but to sell. Many pills bring from $2–5 each. Oxycontin can bring $40 each, according to a high school user who asked to remain anonymous.

"Have you ever attended a pharma or pill party?" we asked the student.

"I wouldn't call them pill parties," she said, "but at pretty much any party there's someone who has pills, or is on pills. Recently a couple of people had some Adderal and we were snorting it. Adderal is popular because it makes it so you can drink more and you can stay up all night long."

Adderal is an amphetamine usually prescribed to treat attention deficit hyperactivity.

Taking the Call

The growing problem prompted a group of North Platte residents to fight back. Listeners are hearing hundreds of radio announcements on virtually every North Platte radio station, alerting the public to the problem.

The group has distributed thousands of pamphlets, bundles of posters and dozens of banners.

They have set a day—April 25—aside to collect prescription drugs, including syringes and over-the-counter drugs. They will set up a drive-up drop point at the high school.

The drugs will ultimately be incinerated.

They have lined up a team of powerful speakers who will talk about the danger, the self-destruction that comes with drug abuse.

The group of residents joined together during the Leadership Lincoln County program, wherein 20 people spend a year learning about major businesses and public services so they can get good things done.

In one part of the leadership program, the 20 split into groups of 5–6 people. Each group was challenged to develop a public project that will continue into the future.

The group–Wendy Thompson, Wanda Cooper, Sandy Ross, Bob Lantis, Patrick O'Neil and Connie Cook— kicked around ideas. After a visit with law enforcement officials they agreed to tackle the prescription drug problem at the urging of Capt. Jim Parish of the Nebraska State Patrol.

"The more we learned, the more we got involved," said Cook, a driving force in the project. "The information was riveting—and motivating. We learned about some kids at high school who got in trouble. Their parents were completely shocked. We were shocked. We had no idea."

"Now, we're passionate to do something constructive," Cook said. "It's amazing; every day we learn more and more."

"Have you taken other drugs?" the Bulletin asked another student.

"Yeah. I smoke weed like every day and used ecstasy once and I dabbled in coke for a couple of months last year and still do it every once in awhile," he said.

"I tried meth twice, but it made me crazy. I don't want to ever do very much of it; it's bad stuff. I've done mushrooms a couple times too, and of course alcohol is a drug too."

"I'm out of my alcoholic phase but I still drink on the weekends," he said. "I won't buy any drug except weed or alcohol but if someone's offering, I'll do pretty much anything. I'll never do heroin though, but I want to try acid in a few years just to see what it's like."

"Do a lot of your friends take pills?"

"Yeah, pretty much all of them. I have five friends that always have them. They take them pretty much every day."

"What do they think of it?"

"It's not considered a bad thing to do. Pills are the equivalent of smoking weed for people who can't smoke because they are on probation or just don't like pot. Like, the preppy kids do it because their parents would know if they smoked pot because they'd smell it. But most parents have no idea that their kids are getting messed up on pills."

Leadership Is Learning

The leadership group recently dropped posters and flyers at all of Lincoln County's schools, plus Stapleton.

At North Platte's middle schools, they asked the principals if they have caught kids using prescription drugs.

"They told us, 'As far as catching them, no, we've not caught them yet, but we know there are kids here who are stealing drugs so they can sell them to other kids," Cook said.

"We want this information out to the public," she said. "We know there is a need to educate those who are all the way from 101 years old to 10 years old. They need to know it's happening and how bad it is for kids, and the environment."

Cook said kids don't understand the dangers.

"What do you take the most?" we asked a North Platte high school student.

"I started out taking Xanax because I got as many as I wanted, for free. Then I had some Percocet. I loved those but they're too addictive to take for a long time. Most people take pain pills (Vicodin/Percocet), anxiety pills (Xanax/Klonopin), or attention deficit disorder pills (Adderal/Concerta/Ritalin)."

"How much would a kid spend on drugs in an average week?"

"People always gave them to me for free, but the average pill popper could probably spend $50–100 a week. The preppies can spend a lot from their lunch-gas-pocket money."

Harm to Creatures Large and Small

Even when the drugs are thrown away, they are usually flushed down the toilet.

Even when drugs are taken properly, traces enter the waste stream that eventually empties into nature, according to the Environmental Protection Agency.

The EPA is becoming more concerned. A study in Boulder, Colo. found female sucker fish outnumber males 5 to 1, and 50 percent of the males have female sex indicators, apparently from estrogen traces from pills for women.

Near Dallas, tiny amounts of Prozac have been found in the livers and brain cells of channel catfish and crappie.

Lots of Help

As part of the leadership project, Cook addressed the Lincoln County noon Rotary in mid-March. She cited national reports that the use of Oxycontin increased by 30 percent in one year—2007—among high school seniors. And she said one out of 10 high school seniors that year used Vicodin illegally.

Eighty-one percent of teens who abuse prescription or over-the-counter drugs combine them with alcohol, the national study said.

Hospital emergency room visits involving such drugs increased 21 percent in 2008. Nearly half of those visits were from patients 12 to 20 years old.

The number of teens going into drug treatment has increased 300 percent in the last 10 years.

As Cook painted the alarming picture of abuse and incapacitation, community members offered to help. So far, 24 individuals and businesses have stepped up to sponsor the local education and collection effort.

"The support is overwhelming," Cook said.

The Language of Pharming

Big boys, cotton, kicker–Various slang for prescription pain relievers.

Chill pills, french fries, tranqs–Various slang for prescription sedatives and tranquilizers.

Pharming (pronounced "farming")–From the word pharmaceutical. It means kids getting high by raiding their parents' medicine cabinets for prescription drugs.

Pharm parties–Parties where teens bring prescription drugs from home, mix them together into a big bowl (see 'trail mix'), and grab a handful. Not surprisingly, pharm parties are usually arranged while parents are out.

Pilz (pronounced pills)–A popular term used to describe prescription medications. Can also include over-the-counter medications.

Recipe–Prescription drugs mixed with alcoholic or other beverages.

Trail mix–A mixture of various prescription drugs, usually served in a big bag or bowl at pharm parties.

"We heard you got into serious medical trouble once from taking too many drugs. Why didn't that stop you from taking more?" we asked a student.

"Well, I know I won't ever take that many again, and it did stop me for the most part. I was getting messed up every day. After that I didn't touch a pill for months. I switched to coke for a couple months, then pot when the person that always gave me coke got sent to rehab."

Featured Speaker—Former Abuser

Former Husker football All-American Jason Peter will speak to the public at the end of the drug collection day, April 25.

Peter, one of the nation's best defensive linemen in 1997, graduated from Nebraska and went to the NFL, where he earned $6.5 million from the Carolina Panthers. But he blew most of the money on illegal drugs, taking up to 80 pain killers a day.

Jason Peter's life finally crashed. A series of injuries took him off the NFL roster.

He managed to clean up and wrote a book, "Heros of the Underground" and now hosts an ESPN talk show from his hometown of Lincoln. He spends his spare time traveling, talking about the dangers of drug abuse.

"Prescription drugs are a lot more addictive than people realize," another North Platte student told the Bulletin.

"You can get into big-time trouble," he said. "Possession of a controlled substance is a felony. They can even charge you for each pill in your possession. If they think you're selling them you get possession of a controlled substance with intent to distribute, which is prison time."

National Obsession

"Our national pastime—self-destruction," writer Jerry Stahl said in a review of Jason Peter's book.

"We are a nation obsessed with pharmaceuticals," Cook said as she addressed the Rotary. "We spend vast sums to manage our health, and we pop pills to address every conceivable symptom. In this nation, we abuse prescription drugs . . . daily."

Persons 65 and older take one-third of all prescribed medications even though they comprise 13 percent of the population, Cook said. Older patients are more likely to have multiple prescriptions, which can lead to unintentional misuse, more drugs stored in medicine cabinets for kids to steal.

The leadership group advises to keep medicine containers closed, even locked. Keep a record of prescriptions and the amount on hand. Reinforce a message of caution and restraint to your children. Start early, long before adolescence. Build a solid foundation for resisting temptations and outside influences.

North Platte Therapist: Most Clients Abuse Prescriptions

Young people steal grandma's pills and distribute them at school. Senior citizens falsify prescriptions for more pain medication. Babysitters take pills from cabinets.

An Ohio real estate agent lost her license for pilfering pills from bathrooms at open houses.

The appeal is obvious—the drugs can be legally obtained, the stigma of going to a street pusher can be avoided, and the price isn't steep.

There are an estimated 800,000 websites which sell prescription drugs on the Internet and will ship them to households no questions asked.

Today, about one-third of all U.S. drug abuse is prescription drug abuse.

Approximately 1.9 million persons age 12 or older have used Oxycontin (pain reliever, like morphine) nonmedically at least once in their lifetime, according to Columbia University's National Center on Addiction and Substance Abuse.

Vicki Dugger, a therapist with New Beginnings Therapy Associates in North Platte, said about 75 percent of the patients she treats admitted abusing prescription drugs.

Dugger said many more people are aware of it today than in the 1980s and 1990s. Still, much more awareness is needed.

"There's a misconception that abusing prescription medication is not harmful," Dugger said. "The fact is, it can have deadly results."

Dugger said. kids have died after attending pharming parties. She has some tips for parents to help keep their teenagers safe:

- Consider your own drug behavior and the message you are sending.
- Do a drug inventory. Forgotten or expired prescriptions or leftover over-the-counter meds could be appealing to kids, so get rid of them. Put new drugs away.
- Reach out and have a discussion. Dugger said research showed that kids who learn a lot about drug risks from their parents are up to half as likely to use drugs as kids who haven't had that conversation from mom and dad.
- Look on the computer. Try conducting your own web search to see how easily one can buy prescription meds without a prescription.
- Watch for warning signs. These may include unexplained disappearance of meds from medicine cabinets, declining grades, loss of interest in activities, changes in friends and behaviors, disrupted sleeping or eating patterns and more.

Dugger said she recently had a mother of a teen ask her about all the Musinex boxes around her house.

Musinex is a medication that is used for temporary relief of coughs caused by certain respiratory tract infections but teens have been known to abuse it by taking more than the recommended amounts to get high.

Dugger said she advised the mother to have a conversation with her teen immediately.

Critical Thinking

1. Do you see an abuse of prescription drugs among your friends or fellow classmates? How will you know when abuse exists?

2. What, in your opinion, needs to take place in the wider society to lessen dependency and prevent the abuse of prescription drugs?

The entire Bulletin staff contributed to this report. It was first published April 1 in the Bulletin print edition.

When Booze Was Banned but Pot Was Not

What can today's antiprohibitionists learn from their predecessors?

Jacob Sullum

Of the 27 amendments to the U.S. Constitution, the 18th is the only one explicitly aimed at restricting people's freedom. It is also the only one that has ever been repealed. Maybe that's encouraging, especially for those of us who recognize the parallels between that amendment, which ushered in the nationwide prohibition of alcohol, and current bans on other drugs.

But given the manifest failure and unpleasant side effects of Prohibition, its elimination after 14 years is not terribly surprising, despite the arduous process required to undo a constitutional amendment. The real puzzle, as the journalist Daniel Okrent argues in his masterful new history of the period, is how a nation that never had a teetotaling majority, let alone one committed to forcibly imposing its lifestyle on others, embarked upon such a doomed experiment to begin with. How did a country consisting mostly of drinkers agree to forbid drinking?

The short answer is that it didn't. As a reveler accurately protests during a Treasury Department raid on a private banquet in the HBO series *Boardwalk Empire,* neither the 18th Amendment nor the Volstead Act, which implemented it, prohibited mere possession or consumption of alcohol. The amendment took effect a full year after ratification, and those who could afford it were free in the meantime to stock up on wine and liquor, which they were permitted to consume until the supplies ran out. The law also included exceptions that were important for those without well-stocked wine cellars or the means to buy the entire inventory of a liquor store (as the actress Mary Pickford did). Home production of cider, beer, and wine was permitted, as was commercial production of alcohol for religious, medicinal, and industrial use (three loopholes that were widely abused). In these respects Prohibition was much less onerous than our current drug laws. Indeed, the legal situation was akin to what today would be called "decriminalization" or even a form of "legalization."

After Prohibition took effect, Okrent shows, attempts to punish bootleggers with anything more than a slap on the wrist provoked public outrage and invited jury nullification. One can imagine what would have happened if the Anti-Saloon League and the Woman's Christian Temperance Union had demanded a legal regime in which possessing, say, five milliliters of whiskey triggered a mandatory five-year prison sentence (as possessing five grams of crack cocaine did until recently). The lack of penalties for consumption helped reassure drinkers who voted for Prohibition as legislators and supported it (or did not vigorously resist it) as citizens. Some of these "dry wets" sincerely believed that the barriers to drinking erected by Prohibition, while unnecessary for moderate imbibers like themselves, would save working-class saloon patrons from their own excesses. Pauline Morton Sabin, the well-heeled, martini-drinking Republican activist who went from supporting the 18th Amendment to heading the Women's Organization for National Prohibition Reform, one of the most influential pro-repeal groups, apparently had such an attitude.

In addition to paternalism, the longstanding American ambivalence toward pleasure in general and alcohol-fueled pleasure in particular helped pave the way to Prohibition. The Puritans were not dour teetotalers, but they were anxious about excess, and a similar discomfort may have discouraged drinkers from actively resisting dry demands. But by far the most important factor, Okrent persuasively argues, was the political maneuvering of the Anti-Saloon League (ASL) and its master strategist, Wayne Wheeler, who turned a minority position into the supreme law of the land by mobilizing a highly motivated bloc of swing voters.

Defining itself as "the Church in Action Against the Saloon," the clergy-led ASL reached dry sympathizers through churches (mostly Methodist and Baptist) across the country. Okrent says the group typically could deliver something like 10 percent of voters to whichever candidate sounded driest (regardless of his private behavior). This power was enough to change the outcome of elections, putting the fear of the ASL, which Okrent calls "the mightiest pressure group in the nation's history," into the state and federal legislators who would vote to approve the 18th Amendment. That doesn't mean none of the legislators who voted dry were sincere; many of them—including Richmond Hobson of Alabama and Morris Sheppard of Texas, the 18th Amendment's chief sponsors in the House and Senate, respectively—were deadly serious about reforming their fellow citizens by regulating their liquid diets. But even the most ardent drys depended on ASL-energized supporters for their political survival.

The ASL strategy worked because wet voters did not have the same passion and unity, while the affected business interests feuded among themselves until the day their industry was abolished. Americans who objected to Prohibition generally did not feel strongly enough to make that issue decisive in their choice of candidates, although they did make themselves heard when the issue itself was put to a vote. Californians, for example, defeated four successive ballot measures that would have established statewide prohibition before their legislature approved the 18th Amendment in 1919.

As Prohibition wore on, its unintended consequences provided the fire that wets had lacked before it was enacted. They were appalled by rampant corruption, black market violence, newly empowered criminals, invasions of privacy, and deaths linked to alcohol poisoned under government order to discourage diversion (a policy that Sen. Edward Edwards of New Jersey denounced as "legalized murder"). These burdens seemed all the more intolerable because Prohibition was so conspicuously ineffective. As a common saying of the time put it, the drys had their law and the wets had their liquor, thanks to myriad quasi-legal and illicit businesses that Okrent colorfully describes.

Entrepreneurs taking advantage of legal loopholes included operators of "booze cruises" to international waters, travel agents selling trips to Cuba (which became a popular tourist destination on the strength of its proximity and wetness), "medicinal" alcohol distributors whose brochures ("for physician permittees only") resembled bar menus, priests and rabbis who obtained allegedly sacramental wine for their congregations (which grew

dramatically after Prohibition was enacted), breweries that turned to selling "malt syrup" for home beer production, vintners who delivered fermentable juice directly into San Francisco cellars through chutes connected to grape-crushing trucks, and the marketers of the Vino-Sano Grape Brick, which "came in a printed wrapper instructing the purchaser to add water to make grape juice, but to be sure *not* to add yeast or sugar, or leave it in a dark place, or let it sit too long before drinking it because 'it might ferment and become wine.'" The outright lawbreakers included speakeasy proprietors such as the Stork Club's Sherman Billingsley, gangsters such as Al Capone, rum runners such as Bill McCoy, and big-time bootleggers such as Sam Bronfman, the Canadian distiller who made a fortune shipping illicit liquor to thirsty Americans under the cover of false paperwork. Their stories, as related by Okrent, are illuminating as well as engaging, vividly showing how prohibition warps everything it touches, transforming ordinary business transactions into tales of intrigue.

The plain fact that the government could not stop the flow of booze, but merely divert it into new channels at great cost, led disillusioned drys to join angry wets in a coalition that achieved an unprecedented and never-repeated feat. As late as 1930, just three years before repeal, Morris Sheppard confidently asserted, "There is as much chance of repealing the Eighteenth Amendment as there is for a hummingbird to fly to the planet Mars with the Washington Monument tied to its tail."

That hummingbird was lifted partly by a rising tide of wet immigrants and urbanites. During the first few decades of the 20th century, the country became steadily less rural and less WASPy, a trend that ultimately made Prohibition democratically unsustainable. Understanding this demographic reality, dry members of Congress desperately delayed the constitutionally required reapportionment of legislative districts for nearly a decade after the 1920 census. "The dry refusal to allow Congress to recalculate state-by-state representation in the House during the 1920s is one of those political maneuvers in American history so audacious it's hard to believe it happened," Okrent writes. "The episode is all the more remarkable for never having established itself in the national consciousness."

Other Prohibition-driven assaults on the Constitution are likewise little remembered today. In 1922 the Court reinforced a dangerous exception to the Fifth Amendment's Double Jeopardy Clause by declaring that the "dual sovereignty" doctrine allowed prosecution of Prohibition violators in both state and federal courts for the same offense. In 1927 the Court ruled that requiring a bootlegger to declare his illegal earnings for tax purposes did not violate the Fifth Amendment's guarantee against compelled self-incrimination. And "in twenty separate cases between 1920 and 1933," Okrent notes, the Court carried out "a broad-strokes rewriting" of the case law concerning the Fourth Amendment's prohibition of "unreasonable searches and seizures." Among other things, the Court declared that a warrant was not needed to search a car suspected of carrying contraband liquor or to eavesdrop on telephone conversations between bootleggers (a precedent that was not overturned until 1967). Because of Prohibition's demands, Okrent writes, "long-honored restraints on police authority soon gave way."

That tendency has a familiar ring to anyone who follows Supreme Court cases growing out of the war on drugs, which have steadily whittled away at the Fourth Amendment during the last few decades. But unlike today, the incursions required to enforce Prohibition elicited widespread dismay. Here is how *The New York Times* summarized the Anti-Saloon League's response to the wiretap decision: "It is feared by the dry forces that Prohibition will fall into 'disrepute' and suffer 'irreparable harm' if the American public concludes that 'universal snooping' is favored for enforcing the Eighteenth Amendment."

The fear of a popular backlash was well-founded. From the beginning, Prohibition was resisted in the wetter provinces of America, where the authorities often declined to enforce it. Maryland never passed its own version of the Volstead Act, while New York repealed its alcohol prohibition law in 1923. Eleven other states eliminated their statutes by referendum in November 1932, months before Congress presented the 21st Amendment (which repealed the 18th) and more than a year before it was ratified.

This history of noncooperation is instructive in considering an argument that was often made by opponents of Proposition 19, the marijuana legalization initiative that California voters rejected in November. The measure's detractors claimed legalizing marijuana at the state level would run afoul of the Supremacy Clause, which says "this Constitution, and the laws of the United States which shall be made in pursuance thereof . . . shall be the supreme law of the land." Yet even under a prohibition system that, unlike the current one, was explicitly authorized by the Constitution, states had no obligation to ban what Congress banned or punish what Congress punished. In fact, state and local resistance to alcohol prohibition led the way to national repeal.

That precedent, while encouraging to antiprohibitionists who hope that federalism can help end the war on drugs, should be viewed with caution. For one thing, federalism isn't what it used to be. Alcohol prohibition was enacted and repealed before the Supreme Court transformed the Commerce Clause into an all-purpose license to meddle, when it was taken for granted that the federal government could not ban an intoxicant unless the Constitution was amended to provide such a power. While the feds may not have the resources to wage the war on drugs without state assistance, under existing precedents they clearly have the legal authority to try.

Another barrier to emulating the antiprohibitionists of the 1920s is that none of the currently banned drugs is (or ever was) as widely consumed in this country as alcohol. That fact is crucial in understanding the contrast between the outrage that led to the repeal of alcohol prohibition and Americans' general indifference to the damage done by the war on drugs today. The illegal drug that comes closest to alcohol in popularity is marijuana, which survey data indicate most Americans born after World War II have at least tried. That experience is reflected in rising public support for legalizing marijuana, which hit a record 46 percent in a nationwide Gallup poll conducted the week before Proposition 19 was defeated.

A third problem for today's antiprohibitionists is the deep roots of the status quo. Alcohol prohibition came and went in 14 years, which made it easy to distinguish between the bad effects of drinking and the bad effects of trying to stop it. By contrast, the government has been waging war on cocaine and opiates since 1914 and on marijuana since 1937 (initially under the guise of enforcing revenue measures). Few people living today have clear memories of a different legal regime. That is one reason why histories like Okrent's, which bring to life a period when booze was banned but pot was not, are so valuable.

Reflecting on the long-term impact of the vain attempt to get between Americans and their liquor, Okrent writes: "In 1920 could anyone have believed that the Eighteenth Amendment, ostensibly addressing the single subject of intoxicating beverages, would set off an avalanche of change in areas as diverse as international trade, speedboat design, tourism practices, soft-drink marketing, and the English language itself? Or that it would provoke the establishment of the first nationwide criminal syndicate, the idea of home dinner parties, the deep engagement of women in political issues other than suffrage, and the creation of Las Vegas?" Nearly a century after the war on other drugs was launched, Americans are only beginning to recognize its far-reaching consequences, most of which are considerably less fun than a dinner party or a trip to Vegas.

Critical Thinking

1. What exactly did the Eighteenth Amendment prohibit?
2. Describe the similarities and differences between alcohol prohibition and the current prohibition of illegal drugs.

3. Do you think that Prohibition was effective? Why or why not?

Senior editor **JACOB SULLUM** (jsullum@reason.com) is a nationally syndicated columnist and the author of *Saying Yes: In Defense of Drug Use* (Tarcher/Penguin).

From *Reason Magazine*, February 2011, pp. 56–59. Copyright © 2011 by Reason Foundation, 3415 S. Sepulveda Blvd., Suite 400, Los Angeles, CA 90034. www.reason.com

Scientists Are High on Idea That Marijuana Reduces Memory Impairment

Emily Caldwell

Columbus, Ohio—The more research they do, the more evidence Ohio State University scientists find that specific elements of marijuana can be good for the aging brain by reducing inflammation there and possibly even stimulating the formation of new brain cells.

The research suggests that the development of a legal drug that contains certain properties similar to those in marijuana might help prevent or delay the onset of Alzheimer's disease. Though the exact cause of Alzheimer's remains unknown, chronic inflammation in the brain is believed to contribute to memory impairment.

Any new drug's properties would resemble those of tetrahydrocannabinol, or THC, the main psychoactive substance in the cannabis plant, but would not share its high-producing effects. THC joins nicotine, alcohol and caffeine as agents that, in moderation, have shown some protection against inflammation in the brain that might translate to better memory late in life.

"It's not that everything immoral is good for the brain. It's just that there are some substances that millions of people for thousands of years have used in billions of doses, and we're noticing there's a little signal above all the noise," said Gary Wenk, professor of psychology at Ohio State and principal investigator on the research.

Wenk's work has already shown that a THC-like synthetic drug can improve memory in animals. Now his team is trying to find out exactly how it works in the brain.

The most recent research on rats indicates that at least three receptors in the brain are activated by the synthetic drug, which is similar to marijuana. These receptors are proteins within the brain's endocannabinoid system, which is involved in memory as well as physiological processes associated with appetite, mood and pain response.

This research is also showing that receptors in this system can influence brain inflammation and the production of new neurons, or brain cells.

"When we're young, we reproduce neurons and our memory works fine. When we age, the process slows down, so we have a decrease in new cell formation in normal aging. You need those cells to come back and help form new memories, and we found that this THC-like agent can influence creation of those cells," said Yannick Marchalant, a study coauthor and research assistant professor of psychology at Ohio State.

> **Could people smoke marijuana to prevent Alzheimer's disease if the disease is in their family? We're not saying that, but it might actually work. What we are saying is it appears that a safe, legal substance that mimics those important properties of marijuana can work on receptors in the brain to prevent memory impairments in aging. So that's really hopeful, Wenk said.**

Marchalant described the research in a poster presentation Wednesday (11/19/08) at the Society for Neuroscience meeting in Washington, D.C.

Knowing exactly how any of these compounds work in the brain can make it easier for drug designers to target specific systems with agents that will offer the most effective anti-aging benefits, said Wenk, who is also a professor of neuroscience and molecular virology, immunology and medical genetics.

"Could people smoke marijuana to prevent Alzheimer's disease if the disease is in their family? We're not saying that, but it might actually work. What we are saying is it appears that a safe, legal substance that mimics those important properties of marijuana can work on receptors in the brain to prevent memory impairments in aging. So that's really hopeful," Wenk said.

One thing is clear from the studies: Once memory impairment is evident, the treatment is not effective. Reducing inflammation and preserving or generating neurons must occur before the memory loss is obvious, Wenk said.

Marchalant led a study on old rats using the synthetic drug, called WIN-55212-2 (WIN), which is not used in humans because of its high potency to induce psychoactive effects.

The researchers used a pump under the skin to give the rats a constant dose of WIN for three weeks—a dose low enough to induce no psychoactive effects on the animals. A control group of rats received no intervention. In follow-up memory tests, in which rats were placed in a small swimming pool to determine how well they use visual cues to find a platform hidden under the surface of the water, the treated rats did better than the control rats in learning and remembering how to find the hidden platform.

"Old rats are not very good at that task. They can learn, but it takes them more time to find the platform. When we gave them the drug, it made them a little better at that task," Marchalant said.

In some rats, Marchalant combined the WIN with compounds that are known to block specific receptors, which then offers hints at which receptors WIN is activating. The results indicated the WIN lowered the rats' brain inflammation in the hippocampus by acting on what is called the TRPV1 receptor. The hippocampus is responsible for short-term memory.

With the same intervention technique, the researchers also determined that WIN acts on receptors known as CB1 and CB2, leading to the generation of new brain cells—a process known as neurogenesis. Those results led the scientists to speculate that the combination of lowered inflammation and

neurogenesis is the reason the rats' memory improved after treatment with WIN.

The researchers are continuing to study the endocannabinoid system's role in regulating inflammation and neuron development. They are trying to zero in on the receptors that must be activated to produce the most benefits from any newly developed drug.

What they already know is THC alone isn't the answer.

"The end goal is not to recommend the use of THC in humans to reduce Alzheimer's," Marchalant said. "We need to find exactly which receptors are most crucial, and ideally lead to the development of drugs that specifically activate those receptors. We hope a compound can be found that can target both inflammation and neurogenesis, which would be the most efficient way to produce the best effects."

References

The National Institutes of Health supported this work.

Coauthors on the presentation are Holly Brothers and Lauren Burgess, both of Ohio State's Department of Psychology.

Critical Thinking

1. What role does chronic inflammation in the brain play in Alzheimer's disease?
2. What is THC and how does it affect the brain?
3. What is the endocannabinoid system? What is it responsible for in the brain?

UNIT 2

Understanding How Drugs Work—Use, Dependency, and Addiction

Unit Selections

7. **Family History of Alcohol Abuse Associated with Problematic Drinking among College Students,** Joseph W. LaBrie, et al.
8. **A Longitudinal Examination of the Relationships Between Childhood Maltreatment and Patterns of Adolescent Substance Use Among High-Risk Adolescents,** Sunny Hyucksun Shin
9. **Medical Marijuana and the Mind: More Is Known about the Psychiatric Risks than the Benefits,** Harvard Mental Health Letter
10. **The Genetics of Alcohol and Other Drug Dependence,** Danielle M. Dick and Arpana Agrawal
11. **Understanding Recreational Ecstasy Use in the United States: A Qualitative Inquiry,** Masuma Bahora, Claire E. Sterk, and Kirk W. Elifson
12. **Examination of Over-the-Counter Drug Misuse Among Youth,** Erin J. Farley and Daniel J. O'Connell
13. **Self-Control, Opportunity, and Substance Use,** Scott A. Desmond, Alan S. Bruce and Melissa J. Stacer

Learning Outcomes

After reading this Unit, you should be able to:

- Explain why some people become dependent on certain drugs far sooner than other people.

- Describe how is it possible to predict one's own liability for becoming drug dependent.

- Describe multiple processes by which a person becomes addicted to alcohol and/or drugs.

- Outline and support an argument for which influences most predict addictive behavior.

Understanding how drugs act upon the human mind and body is a critical component to the resolution of issues concerning drug use and abuse. An understanding of basic pharmacology is requisite for informed discussion on practically every drug-related issue and controversy. One does not have to look far to find misinformed debate, much of which surrounds the basic lack of knowledge about how drugs work.

Different drugs produce different bodily effects and consequences. All psychoactive drugs influence the central nervous system, which, in turn, sits at the center of how we physiologically and psychologically interpret and react to the world around us. Some drugs, such as methamphetamine and LSD, have great, immediate influence on the nervous system, while others, such as tobacco and marijuana, elicit less-pronounced reactions. Almost all psychoactive drug effects on the body are mitigated by the dosage level of the drug taken, the manner in which it is ingested, and the physiological and emotional state of the user. For example, cocaine smoked in the form of crack versus snorted as powder produces profoundly different physical and emotional effects on the user.

Even though illegal drugs often provide the most sensational perspective from which to view drug effects, the abuse of prescription drugs is being reported as an exploding new component of the addiction problem. Currently, the non-medical use of pain relievers such as oxycodone and hydrocodone is continuing at alarming rates. This trend has been increasing steadily since 1994, and it currently competes with methamphetamine abuse as the most alarming national trend of drug abuse. Currently, more than 5 million Americans use prescription pain medications for non-medical reasons. Molecular properties of certain drugs allow them to imitate and artificially reproduce certain naturally occurring brain chemicals that provide the basis for the drugs' influence.

The continued use of certain drugs and their repeated alteration of the body's biochemical structure provide one explanation for the physiological consequences of drug use. The human brain is the quintessential master pharmacist and repeatedly altering its chemical functions by drug use is risky. Doing such things may produce profound implications for becoming addicted. For example, heroin use replicates the natural brain chemical endorphin, which supports the body's biochemical defense to pain and stress. The continued use of heroin is believed to deplete natural endorphins, causing the nervous system to produce a painful physical and emotional reaction when heroin is withdrawn. Subsequently, one significant motivation for continued use is realized.

A word of caution is in order, however, when proceeding through the various explanations for what drugs do and why they do it. Many people, because of an emotional and/or political relationship to the world of drugs, assert a subjective predisposition when interpreting certain drugs' effects and consequences. One person is an alcoholic while another is a social drinker. People often argue, rationalize, and explain the perceived nature of drugs' effects based upon an extremely superficial understanding of diverse pharmacological properties of different drugs. A detached and scientifically sophisticated awareness of drug

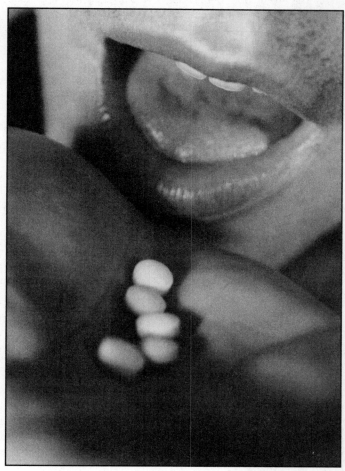

© Royalty-Free/CORBIS

pharmacology may help strengthen the platform from which to interpret the various consequences of drug use. Drug addiction results as a continuum comprised of experimentation, recreational use, regular use, and abuse. The process is influenced by a plethora of physiological, psychological, and environmental factors. Although some still argue that drug dependence is largely a matter of individual behavior—something to be chosen or rejected—most experts agree that new scientific discoveries clearly define the roots of addiction to live within molecular levels of the brain. Powerful drugs, upon repeated administration, easily compromise the brain's ability to make decisions about its best interests.

One theory used to describe specific drugs as more addictive or less addictive explains a process referred to as "reinforcement." Simply explained, reinforcement is a form of psychological conditioning that results from a drug's influence on a person's brain. Reinforcement is the term used to describe a person's behavior that expresses the uncontrollable need to repeatedly introduce the drug to the body. Powerful drugs such as the stimulant cocaine and the depressant oxycodone influence the brain's reward pathway and promote behavior in which drug seeking is recognized by the brain as actions necessary for survival. Persons addicted to drugs known to be strongly reinforcing typically report that they care more about getting the drug than about anything else—even in the face of self-destruction. Drug addiction and the rate at which it occurs must compete with certain physiological and psychological, as well as environmental, variables that are unique to individuals. A drug user with a greater number of biological markers known to be associated with drug addiction, such as mental illness, alcoholism, and poor physical health, may encourage drug dependency sooner than a person with fewer biological markers. Similarly, a person's positive environmental associations, or "natural reinforcers," such as a strong family structure and healthy personal and professional relationships may not only make experimentation unappealing, it may delay a user's developing drug addiction. Subsequently, one's liability for drug addiction is closely associated with genetics, environment, and the use of psychoactive drugs. Understanding the concept of addiction requires an awareness of these factors. For many people, drug addiction and the reasons that contribute to it are murky concepts.

The articles in Unit 2 illustrate some of the current research and viewpoints on the ways that drugs act upon the human body. New science is suggesting that a new era has begun relative to understanding drugs and their pharmacological influence on the human body. This new science is critical to understanding the assorted consequences of drug use and abuse. Science has taken us closer to understanding that acute drug use changes brain function profoundly and that these changes may remain with the user long after the drug has left the system. New research investigating the liabilities produced by adolescents smoking tobacco suggests that even small amounts produce a remarkable susceptibility for addiction. Subsequently, many new issues have emerged for drug and health-related public policy. Increasingly, drug abuse competes with other social maladies as public enemy number one. Further, the need for a combined biological, behavioral, and social response to this problem becomes more evident. Many healthcare professionals and healthcare educators, in addition to those from other diverse backgrounds, argue that research dollars spent on drug abuse and addiction should approach that spent on heart disease, cancer, and AIDS. The articles in Unit 2 provide examples of how some new discoveries have influenced our thinking about addiction. They also provide examples of how, even in light of new knowledge, breaking addictions is so very hard to do.

Student Website

Internet References

AddictionSearch. com
www.addictionsearch.com

Addiction Treatment Forum
www.atforum.com

American Psychological Association's Addiction Related Publications
http://search.apa.org/search?query=&facet=classification:
Addictions&limited=true&section=pubs

British Broadcasting Company Understanding Drugs
www.bbc.co.uk/health/conditions/mental_health drugsuse.shtml

Centre for Addiction and Mental Health (CAMH)
www.camh.net

Dealing with Addictions
http://kidshealth.org/teen/your_mind/problems/addictions.html

Drugs and the Body: How Drugs Work
www.doitnow.org/pdfs/223.pdf

National Alcoholism Drug Information Center
http://addictioncareoptions.com

The National Center on Addiction and Substance Abuse at Columbia University
www.casacolumbia.org

National Institute on Drug Abuse (NIDA)
www.nida.nih.gov

Public Agenda
www.publicagenda.org/articles/illegal-drugs

Understanding Addiction—Regret, Addiction and Death
http://teenadvice.about.com/library/weekly/aa011501a.htm

Family History of Alcohol Abuse Associated with Problematic Drinking among College Students

JOSEPH W. LABRIE, ET AL.

1. Introduction

Risky drinking among college students is of particular concern for university administrators and health professionals. Researchers have attempted to isolate correlates of risky drinking. A family history of alcohol abuse (FH+) is a well-documented risk factor for heavy alcohol use and alcohol-related problems (Chalder, Elgar, & Bennett, 2006; Cotton, 1979; Hussong, Curran, & Chassin, 1998; Kuntsche Rehm, & Gmel, 2004; Pullen, 1994; Turnbull, 1994; Warner, White, & Johnson., 2007). About 20% of college students are FH+ (Perkins, 2002) and the college environment may be more harmful for those students predisposed to alcohol problems. A few studies have revealed considerably higher rates of alcohol use (Kushner & Sher, 1993; LaBrie, Kenney, Lac, & Migliuri, 2009; Pullen, 1994) and alcohol-related problems (Leeman, Fenton, & Volpicelli, 2007) among FH+ compared with FH– college students. In contrast, other studies have found no relationship between family history and problematic alcohol use among college students (Engs, 1990; MacDonald, Fleming, & Barry, 1991; Harrell, Slane, & Klump, 2009). Further, there have been conflicting results on the role gender plays among FH+ college students. Some have found FH+ males to be more susceptible to risky drinking and consequences than FH+ females (e.g. Andersson, Johnsson, Berglund, & Öjehagen, 2007; Jackson, Sher, Gotham, & Wood, 2001; Sher, Walitzer, Wood, & Brent, 1991), while Hartford, Parker and Grant (1992) found no such gender difference. Inconsistencies in existing research highlight the need to explicate how family history status may impact drinking behaviors and problems in collegiate populations.

Alcohol expectancies, the specific beliefs about the behavioral, emotional, and cognitive effects of alcohol (Leigh, 1987), are a potential psychosocial motivator of risky drinking. Stronger positive alcohol expectancies are associated with problem drinking (e.g. Anderson, Schweinsburg, Paulus, Brown, & Tapert, 2005; Brown, Goldman, & Christiansen, 1985).

Alcohol-outcome expectancies result from both personal experience with alcohol and from mirroring drinking behavior of individuals (Lundahl et al, 1997), and have thus been shown to differ by family history status in that FH+ individuals have endorsed stronger alcohol-related expectancies, particularly overall positive expectancies (Morean et al, 2009; Pastor & Evans, 2003). Further, FH+ individuals with stronger overall positive expectancies are most likely to experience alcohol-related problems (Conway, Swendsen, & Merikangas, 2003; VanVoorst & Quirk, 2003).

Much of the previous research on family history of alcohol abuse has focused on COAs (children of alcohols) during adolescence (Barnow, Schuckit, Lucht, John, & Freyberger, 2002; Brown, Creamer, & Stetson, 1987; Chalder et al., 2006; Nash, McQueen, & Bray, 2005; Sher et al., 1991) and middle–late adulthood (Beaudoin, Murray, Bond, & Barnes, 1997; Cloninger, Sigvardsson, & Bohman, 1996; Curran et al., 1999). Moreover, family history studies involving college students have suffered from various limitations, such as a relatively small sample size (e.g. Leeman et al., 2007; Pullen, 1994), single-sex samples (e.g. LaBrie et al., 2009; Harrell et al., 2009), or first-year student samples (e.g. Andersson et al., 2007, Gotham, Sher, & Wood, 2003; Jackson et al., 2001). The present study broadens previous research by offering unique insight into family history of alcohol abuse, alcohol-related behaviors and problems, and further examines the moderating effect of gender in family history status on alcohol consumption, alcohol expectancies, and alcohol-related consequences among a large, multisite, ethnically diverse sample of male and female college students.

2. Methods
2.1 Participants

Participants were recruited from two west-coast universities, a large, public institution with 30,000 undergraduates and a mid-sized private institution with approximately 5500 undergraduates. Of a randomly selected pool of 7000 students, 3753 (53.6%) consented to participate. Representative of the makeup of the corresponding institutions, participants' mean age was 19.88 (SD = 1.36) and the majority of the participants were female (61%). The sample consisted of 18.9% first-year students, 24.5% sophomores, 27.4% juniors, and 29.2% seniors. Racial representation was as follows: 57.4% Caucasian, 18.7% Asian, 10.7% Multiracial, 3.2% African American, and 10.0% reported other racial/ethnic groups. On average, participants consumed 6.04 (SD = 8.58) drinks over 1.59 (SD = 1.53) drinking days per week. Among the 67.5% of students who drank, they consumed an average of 8.94 (SD = 9.11) drinks per week and averaged 2.36 (SD = 1.30) drinking days.

2.2. Design and Procedure

At the start of the fall semester, 7000 students (3500 from each campus), received letters inviting them to participate in a study about alcohol use and perceptions of college-student drinking. The students were directed to a link for an online survey. After students clicked on the link and entered their individual pin, they were presented with a local IRB-approved consent form. Participants then completed a 20 min survey, for which they received a $20 compensation.

2.3 Measures

2.3.1. Demographics

Participants indicated their gender, age, most recent GPA, and race.

2.3.2. Family History

Participants indicated whether they had a biological relative that "has or has had a significant drinking problem—one that should or did lead to treatment." This measure was previously developed and successfully used by Miller & Marlatt (1984).

2.3.3. Alcohol Consumption

The Daily Drinking Questionnaire (DDQ: Collins, Parks, & Marlan, 1985; Kivlahan, Marlatt, Fromme, & Coppel, 1990) asked students to report, from the past 30 days, the typical number of drinks they consumed each day of the week. Responses were summed to form a total drinks per week variable used in this analysis.

2.3.4. Negative Consequences

The 25-item Rutgers Alcohol Problem Index (RAPI, White & Labouvie, 1989) (α = .925) assessed alcohol-related consequences. Using a 0 (*never*) to 4 (*more than 10 times*) scale, participants indicated how many times in the past three months they had experienced each stated circumstance (e.g., "Caused shame or embarrassment to someone," "Passed out or fainted suddenly," or "Felt that you had a problem with school.").

2.3.5. Alcohol Expectancies and Evaluations

The Comprehensive Effects of Alcohol (CEOA; Fromme, Stroot, & Kaplan, 1993) is a two-part questionnaire consisting of 76 items. In Part 1, representing items tapping expectancies, participants indicated expectations concerning how he or she may act or feel under the influence of alcohol (e.g., "I would enjoy sex more," "I would act sociable"; 1 = "disagree" 4 = "agree"). In Part 2, representing evaluations, participants subjectively evaluated the effects of alcohol with the same 38 items as Part 1 of the questionnaire (e.g., "Enjoying sex more," "Feeling sociable"; 1 = "bad" 3 = "neutral" 5 = "good"). Each of the expectancies and evaluations components may be further divided into positive factors (sociability, tension reduction, liquid courage, and sexuality) and negative factors (cognitive behavioral impairment, risk and aggression, and self-perception).

3. Results

A family history of alcohol abuse was reported by 35.0% of the total sample, and FH+ participants were more likely to have drank in the past year than their FH– peers (81% vs. 74%; χ^2 = 9.63, p <.001). Independent sample t-tests, separately conducted for males and females, revealed several systematic differences between FH+ and FH– respondents (Table 1). Among males, FH+ respondents averaged significantly higher than their FH– counterparts on drinks per week, negative consequences, overall positive expectancies, positive expectancies concerned with tension reduction and liquid courage, as well as positive evaluations concerned with tension reduction. Among females, FH+ respondents reported significantly higher drinks per week, negative consequences, overall positive expectancies, as well as positive expectancies concerned with sociability, tension reduction, and sexuality in comparison to the FH– participants. Typically, FH+ females reported negative evaluations (risk and aggression, and self-perception) to be worse than did FH– females.

Additional analyses show that, among males, FH+ participants drank 45.7% more drinks per week and experienced 43.6% more negative consequences than those classified as FH–. Among females, however, FH+ individuals consumed 14.4% more drinks and experienced 23.6% more negative consequences than their FH– counterparts. Such results, taken together, suggest that a family history of alcohol abuse may adversely impact males more than females in the college environment.

An ANCOVA model, controlling for age, GPA, race, overall positive and negative expectancies, and overall positive and negative evaluations, was performed to predict drinks per week. Family history status (FH+ or FH–) and respondent gender (male or female) served as the independent factors. After ruling out the statistical contribution of the covariates, main effects were found for both family history and gender, and their interaction also emerged (Table 2). This statistical interaction, presented in Figure 1, revealed that the difference between FH+ and FH– on drinking was more pronounced in males than females, and that FH+ males were especially vulnerable to higher levels of alcohol consumption.

A second ANCOVA model was conducted to predict alcohol negative consequences. Age, GPA, race, and drinks per week were entered as covariates, and family history and gender served

Table 1 Mean Difference on Drinking Variable by Family History, for Males and Females

Measure	Males					Females				
	FH+ (n = 435)		FH– (n = 1008)			FH+ (n = 875)		FH– (n = 1420)		
	M	(SD)	M	(SD)	t-test	M	(SD)	M	(SD)	t-test
Drinks per week	10.75	(12.83)	7.38	(10.43)	5.21***	4.94	(6.04)	4.32	(5.68)	2.48*
Negative consequences	6.72	(9.10)	4.68	(8.77)	5.21***	4.55	(6.64)	3.68	(6.03)	3.11**
Overall positive expectancies	2.55	(0.55)	2.47	(0.58)	2.16*	2.42	(0.58)	2.35	(0.59)	2.73**
Sociability	2.94	(0.68)	2.88	(0.70)	1.50	2.96	(0.73)	2.87	(0.73)	2.74**
Tension reduction	2.63	(0.71)	2.53	(0.74)	2.39*	2.32	(0.72)	2.24	(0.72)	2.53*
Liquid courage	2.48	(0.69)	2.39	(0.72)	2.14*	2.29	(0.71)	2.25	(0.73)	1.18
Sexuality	2.13	(0.73)	2.09	(0.73)	0.93	2.12	(0.76)	2.05	(0.75)	2.11*
Overall negative expectancies	2.28	(0.52)	2.28	(0.59)	0.07	2.20	(0.56)	2.20	(0.58)	0.21
Cognitive behavioral imp.	2.64	(0.60)	2.63	(0.65)	0.32	2.64	(0.65)	2.62	(0.68)	0.73
Risk and aggression	2.31	(0.71)	2.26	(0.73)	1.21	2.10	(0.74)	2.11	(0.74)	−0.40
Self-perception	1.89	(0.64)	1.95	(0.72)	−1.34	1.87	(0.69)	1.87	(0.69)	0.25
Overall positive evaluations	3.48	(0.84)	3.40	(0.83)	1.75	3.18	(0.85)	3.19	(0.86)	−0.39
Sociability	3.84	(0.93)	3.80	(0.92)	0.85	3.66	(0.94)	3.65	(0.95)	0.27
Tension reduction	3.82	(1.00)	3.67	(0.97)	2.55*	3.41	(0.99)	3.40	(1.00)	0.26
Liquid courage	2.95	(0.91)	2.90	(0.90)	0.98	2.72	(0.90)	2.79	(0.91)	−1.79
Sexuality	3.32	(1.07)	3.21	(1.02)	1.69	2.92	(1.08)	2.92	(1.05)	−0.20
Overall negative evaluations	1.89	(0.57)	1.92	(0.62)	−0.89	1.68	(0.50)	1.76	(0.55)	−3.45***
Cognitive behavioral imp.	1.82	(0.64)	1.82	(0.68)	0.04	1.62	(0.56)	1.63	(0.58)	−0.19
Risk and aggression	2.13	(0.83)	2.15	(0.84)	−0.39	1.92	(0.76)	2.07	(0.81)	−4.25***
Self-perception	1.71	(0.64)	1.79	(0.71)	−1.85	1.49	(0.55)	1.58	(0.61)	−3.49***

*$p<.05$. **$p<.01$. ***$p<.001$.

as the independent variables. After the variance attributed to the covariates were accounted for in the model, family history remained statistically significant, but no gender main effect or interaction was discovered (Table 2).

4. Discussion

The present investigation uses a large multisite sample and corroborates extant literature by identifying family history as a significant risk factor for alcohol misuse and related consequences among male and female college students (Kushner & Sher, 1993; Leeman et al., 2007; LaBrie et al., 2009; Pullen, 1994). More specifically, this study extends previous research by finding that, whether attributable to genetics or environmental upbringing, familial ties to alcoholism were considerably more hazardous for males than females in regard to excessive alcohol consumption. Compared to FH− same-sex peers, FH+ males drank 41% more drinks per week and FH+ females drank 14% more drinks per week. Notably, results covaried out other important predictors

of drinking (e.g. age, GPA, race) to better assess how FH status and gender may be related to drinking in college, over and above such variables. By highlighting family history positive college students' heightened susceptibility to risky drinking and consequences, and male FH+ students' enhanced risk for alcohol misuse, the current results may help college personnel identify and target prevention efforts to at-risk students. Preventative interventions taking place early in college with FH+ students might help them better understand their heightened alcohol-related vulnerabilities and provide them with tools and motivation to reduce potential harm.

In addition, findings both confirm and extend relevant research examining the role that alcohol expectancies play in FH+ college students' alcohol behaviors and outcomes. Not only did students reporting familial alcohol abuse endorse significantly greater overall positive expectancies than same-sex FH− counterparts, but FH+ female respondents evaluated the negative effects of alcohol to be substantially "more bad" than FH− females. This paradoxical finding, in which women exposed to familial alcohol

Table 2 ANCOVA Models Predicting Drinks Per Week and Negative Consequences

Variable	df	MS	F test
DV: drinks per week			
Covariates			
Age	1	137.51	2.29
GPA	1	209.84	3.49
Race	1	5207.62	86.57***
Overall positive expectancies	1	10,846.35	108.31***
Overall negative expectancies	1	6536.75	108.67***
Overall positive evaluations	1	6.15	0.10
Overall negative evaluations	1	2833.10	47.10***
Family history	1	1032.70	17.17***
Gender	1	8485.34	141.06***
Family history × gender	1	1025.75	17.05***
DV: negative consequences			
Covariates			
Age	1	95.33	2.34
GPA	1	452.91	11.09***
Race	1	423.66	10.39**
Drinks per week	1	43,439.92	1063.97***
Family history	1	460.67	11.28
Gender	1	130.98	3.21
Family history × gender	1	2.71	0.07

Note: race (1 = Caucasian, 0 = non-Caucasian).
* $p < .05$. ** $p < .01$. *** $p < .001$.

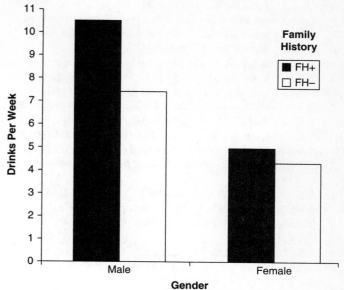

Figure 1 Family history status × gender interaction on drinks per week

abuse judged alcohol's negative evaluations to be worse, yet were more likely to agree that drinking personally yielded positive effects (i.e., expectancies) may suggest that FH+ women may not equate their own drinking with that of alcoholic family members and thus may feel immune to the negative evaluations they themselves associate with alcohol. More concerning, however, is the possibility that these findings may be indicative of cognitive dissonance, whereby highly endorsed positive expectancies contribute to continued drinking, often heavy drinking, in students even though they have been exposed to, and thus recognize, the negative aspects of drinking. By rationalizing alcohol misuse through heightened expectancies, FH+ college females may be able to reduce dissonance and fulfill strong, possibly genetically predisposed desires to imbibe. Regardless, FH+ students' apparent awareness of the negative effects of alcohol use through their own familial experience may be a promising avenue for intervening. Intervention with these students should allow them to reflect on and be mindful of their experiences with these negative effects, thereby building motivation to avoid these same consequences while challenging positive alcohol expectancies.

The present findings are limited in that they do not account for environmental risk factors known to co-occur with FH+ status (e.g., histories of physical or sexual abuse or attraction to high-risk student groups) and that may confound the relationship between FH+ status and both alcohol expectancies and misuse. Future studies assessing such risk factors may be warranted. Another limitation of the current study is the use of one, nonspecific classification of FH+ status. Future research may benefit from distinguishing first, second, and third degree affiliation to alcohol abuse (e.g. parent vs. grandparent or aunt/uncle), gender of the relative with alcohol problems (e.g. mother vs. father), or familial history density (i.e., whether an individual has more than one family member with an alcohol problem). A more defined classification of FH status may also reveal environmental risk factors; for instance, the extent to which residential exposure to alcoholism may heighten risk.

The current study reveals that FH+ students make up a substantial percentage (35%) of the college population and that these students are at increased risk for problematic drinking and consequences as compared to their FH− peers. Despite this and previous research in concert with the current findings, preventative interventions targeting FH+ students are lacking. Both researchers and college health personnel may wish to invest resources in targeting these individuals.

References

Anderson, K. G., Schweinsburg, A., Paulus, M., Brown, S. A., & Tapert, S. (2005). Examining personality and alcohol expectancies using functional magnetic resonance imaging (fMRI) with adolescents. *Journal of Studies on Alcohol, 66,* 323–331.

Andersson, C., Johnsson, K., Berglund, M., & Öjehagen, A. (2007). Alcohol involvement in Swedish university freshmen related to gender, age, serious relationship and family history of alcohol problems. *Alcohol and Alcoholism, 42*(5), 448–455.

Barnow, S., Schuckit, M., Lucht, M., John, U., & Freyberger, H. J. (2002). The importance of positive family history of alcoholism, parental rejection and emotional warmth, behavioral problems and peer substance use for alcohol problems in teenagers: a path analysis. *Journal of Studies on Alcohol, 63,* 305–315.

Beaudoin, C. M., Murray, R. P., Bond, J., Jr., & Barnes, G. E. (1997). Personality characteristics of depressed or alcoholic adult children of alcoholics. *Personality and Individual Differences, 23,* 559–567.

Brown, S. A., Creamer, V. A., & Stetson, B. A. (1987). Adolescent alcohol expectancies in relation to personal and parental drinking patterns. *Journal of Abnormal Psychology, 96,* 117–121.

Brown, S., Goldman, M., & Christiansen, B. (1985). Do alcohol expectancies mediate drinking patterns of adults? *Journal of Consulting and Clinical Psychology, 53*(4), 512–519.

Chalder, M., Elgar, F. J., & Bennett, P. (2006). Drinking and motivations to drink among adolescent children of parents with alcohol problems. *Alcohol & Alcoholism, 41*(1), 107–113.

Cloninger, C. R., Sigvardsson, S., & Bohman, M. (1996). Type I and Type II Alcoholism: an update. *Alcohol Health and Research World, 20,* 18–23.

Collins, R. L., Parks, G. A., & Marlett, A. (1985). Social determinants of alcohol consumption: the effects of social interaction and model status on self-administration of alcohol. *Journal of Consulting and Clinical Psychology, 53*(2), 189–200.

Conway, K. P., Swendsen, J. D., & Merikangas, K. R. (2003). Alcohol expectancies, alcohol consumption, and problem drinking. *The moderating role of family history. Addictive Behaviors, 28,* 823–836.

Cotton, N. S. (1979). The familial incidence of alcoholism: a review. *Journal of Studies on Alcohol, 40*(1), 89–116.

Curran, G. M., Stoltenberg, S. F., Hill, E. M., Mudd, S. A., Blow, F. C., & Zucker, R. A. (1999). Gender differences in the relationship among SES, family history of alcohol disorders and alcohol dependence. *Journal of Studies on Alcohol, 60,* 825–832.

Engs, R. (1990). Family background of alcohol abuse and its relationship to alcohol consumption among college students: an unexpected finding. *Journal of Studies on Alcohol, 51*(6), 542–547.

Fromme, K., Stroot, E., & Kaplan, D. (1993). Comprehensive effects of alcohol: development and psychometric assessment of a new expectancy questionnaire. *Psychological Assessment, 5*(1), 19–26.

Gotham, H. J., Sher, K. J., & Wood, P. K. (2003). Alcohol involvement and development task completion during young adulthood. *Journal of Studies on Alcohol, 64,* 32–42.

Harford, T., Parker, D., & Grant, B. (1992). Family history, alcohol use and dependence symptoms among young adults in the United States. *Alcoholism: Clinical and Experimental Research, 16*(6), 1042–1046.

Harrell, Z., Slane, J., & Klump, K. (2009). Predictors of alcohol problems in college women: the role of depressive symptoms, disordered eating, and family history of alcoholism. *Addictive Behaviors, 34*(3), 252–257.

Hussong, A. M., Curran, P. J., & Chassin, L. (1998). Pathways of risk for accelerated heavy alcohol use among adolescent children of alcohol parents. *Journal of Abnormal Child Psychology, 26*(6), 453.

Kivlahan, D. R., Marlatt, G. A., Fromme, K., & Coppel, D. B. (1990). Secondary prevention with college drinkers: evaluation of an alcohol skills training program. *Journal of Consulting and Clinical Psychology, 58,* 805–810.

Kuntsche, E., Rehm, J., & Gmel, G. (2004). Characteristics of binge drinkers in Europe. *Social Science & Medicine, 59,* 113–127.

Kushner, M. G., & Sher, K. J. (1993). Comorbidity of alcohol and anxiety disorders among college students: effects of gender and family history of alcoholism. *Addictive Behaviors, 18,* 543–552.

Jackson, K. M., Sher, K. J., Gotham, H. J., & Wood, P. K. (2001). Transition into and out of large-effect drinking in young adulthood. *Journal of Abnormal Psychology, 110*(3), 378–391.

LaBrie, J. W., Kenney, S. R., Lac, A., & Migliuri, S. M. (2009). Differential drinking patterns of family history positive and family history negative first semester college females. *Addictive Behaviors, 34,* 190–196.

Leeman, R., Fenton, M., & Volpicelli, J. (2007). Impaired control and undergraduate problem drinking. *Alcohol & Alcoholism, 42*(1), 42–48.

Leigh, B. C. (1987). Evaluations of alcohol expectancies: do they add to prediction of drinking patterns? *Psychology of Addictive Behaviors, 1*(3), 135–139.

Lundahl, L., Davis, T., Adesso, V., & Lukas, S. (1997). Alcohol expectancies: effects of gender, age, and family history of alcoholism. *Addictive Behaviors, 22*(1), 115–125.

MacDonald, R., Fleming, M., & Barry, K. (1991). Risk factors associated with alcohol abuse in college students. *American Journal of Drug and Alcohol Abuse, 17*(4), 439–449.

Miller, W. R., & Marlatt, G. A. (1984). Brief drinking profile. Odessa, FL: Psychological Assessment Resources.

Morean, M. E., Corbin, W. R., Sinha, R., & O'Malley, S. S. (2009). Parental history of anxiety and alcohol-use disorders and alcohol expectancies as predictors of alcohol-related problems. *Journal of Studies on Alcohol and Drugs, 70,* 227–236.

Nash, S. G., McQueen, A., & Bray, J. H. (2005). Pathways to adolescent alcohol use: family environment, peer influence, and parental expectations. *Journal of Adolescent Health, 37,* 19–28.

Pastor, A. D., & Evans, S. M. (2003). Alcohol outcome expectancies and risk for alcohol use problems in women with and without a family history of alcoholism. *Drug and Alcohol Dependence, 70,* 201–214.

Perkins, H. W. (2002). Surveying the damage: a review of research on consequences of alcohol misuse in college populations. *Journal of Studies on Alcohol, 14,* 91–100.

Pullen, L. M. (1994). The relationship among alcohol abuse in college students and selected psychological/demographic variables. *Journal of Alcohol and Drug Education, 40*(1), 36–50.

Sher, K. J., Walitzer, K. S., Wood, P. K., & Brent, E. E. (1991). Characteristics of children of alcoholics: putative risk factors, substance use and abuse, and psychopathology. *Journal of Abnormal Psychology, 100,* 427–448.

Turnbull, J. E. (1994). Early background variables as predictors of adult alcohol problems in women. *International Journal of the Addictions, 29,* 707–728.

VanVoorst, W. A., & Quirk, S. W. (2003). Are relations between parental history of alcohol problems and changes in drinking moderated by positive expectancies? *Alcoholism: Clinical and Experimental Research, 26,* 25–30.

White, H., & Labouvie, E. (1989). Towards the assessment of adolescent problem drinking. *Journal of Studies on Alcohol, 50*(1), 30–37.

Warner, L. A., White, H. R., & Johnson, V. (2007). Alcohol initiation experiences and family history of alcoholism as predictors of problem-drinking trajectories. *Journal of Studies on Alcohol and Drugs, 68,* 56–65.

Critical Thinking

1. Explain why FH+ women may experience cognitive dissonance regarding their own use of alcohol.

2. Would having this information available influence college student's behavior?

Acknowledgment—Support for this research was provided by National Institute of Alcohol Abuse and Alcoholism grant R01-AA012547.

A Longitudinal Examination of the Relationships between Childhood Maltreatment and Patterns of Adolescent Substance Use among High-Risk Adolescents

Background: Childhood maltreatment has been linked to adolescent substance use in cross-sectional studies but the studies were unable to test the associations between childhood maltreatment and changes in substance use patterns during adolescence. The present study investigated the linkages between exposure to childhood maltreatment and developmental trends of alcohol, cannabis, cocaine, opioid, and hallucinogen use among high-risk adolescents.

Methods: We used a sample of 937 adolescents (mean age: 15.9 years; range: 13–18), who were selected from five publicly-funded service systems, to examine the extent to which childhood maltreatment may influence changes in patterns of adolescent substance use over time.

Results: The present study identified a 3-class model of adolescent substance use. Mover-stayer latent transition analyses (LTA) indicated that progression toward heavy polysubstance use increased with experience of childhood maltreatment. Findings also suggested that older male adolescents (ages 15–18) who are involved with public service systems are at high risk for developing and maintaining multiple-substance use in adolescence.

Conclusions: Experience of childhood maltreatment is associated with problematic patterns of adolescent substance use and may shape the longitudinal course of substance use during adolescence. (Am J Addict 2012;21:453–461)

SUNNY HYUCKSUN SHIN, MSW, PhD

Introduction

In the United States, a large number of children suffer from childhood maltreatment (eg, sexual abuse, physical abuse, emotional abuse, neglect) and its damaging effects on emotional and behavioral health. Nearly 6 million referrals were made to local CPS for investigation, and over 888,000 children were known childhood maltreatment victims in 2008.[1] Children who have exposure to childhood maltreatment are at particular risk for using illicit substances in adolescence.[2–9] Nationally representative data show that exposure to childhood maltreatment is associated with a 3.44-fold increase in the relative risk of using illicit substances in the past 30 days among 5,513 adolescents in grades 7 through 12.[10] Although much of the past research on the associations between childhood maltreatment

and adolescent substance use problems has found that exposure to childhood maltreatment increases an individual's risk for developing substance use in adolescence, the research pointing to these associations has been mainly cross-sectional. Relatively little research has addressed the longitudinal course of substance use among maltreated adolescents. As a consequence, an understanding of the developmental unfolding of the associations between childhood maltreatment and adolescent substance use is lacking.

During adolescence, experimentation with illicit substances is relatively common, and patterns of substance use rapidly change.[11–13] Recent variable-centered longitudinal studies have captured such developmental changes in substance use patterns. For example, using 363 adolescents 10.5–15.5 years old, and interviewed at three time points, Curran[14] found that there are substantial individual differences in the average starting point and average rate of change over time in adolescent substance use, and that male adolescents have higher growth rates of substance use than female adolescents. Although variability in intraindividual differences in the developmental growth trajectories of adolescent substance use is well modeled in variable-centered approaches, contemporary theories of adolescent substance use patterns such as the gateway hypothesis, the common liability model, and the route of administration model[15-17] emphasize that in testing theories of adolescent substance use, it is critical to understand the change to a qualitatively different status over time (eg, moving from abstainers to heavy polysubstance users).

Recent person-centered analyses have characterized patterns of substance use among adolescent populations in both cross-sectional and longitudinal studies. For example, in a cross-sectional analysis of 4,708 adolescents in grades 7 through 12, Dierker et al.[18] identified five subgroups of adolescent substance users based on levels of experience with alcohol, cigarettes, cannabis, and other illicit substances (eg, cocaine, inhalants, LSD), including low users, alcohol-only users, alcohol–cannabis users, cigarette users, and polysubstance users. In addition, among 8,879 high school students, six subgroups of adolescent substance users were identified based on alcohol, cigarettes, and cannabis use.[19] These subgroups include abstainers, alcohol experimenters, alcohol–cigarettes–other drug experimenters, current smokers, binge drinkers, and heavy polysubstance users.

Furthermore, research that characterizes patterns of adolescent substance use and examines change in substance use patterns over time among adolescent populations is emerging. For example, using latent transition analysis (LTA), a stage-sequential latent variable model for longitudinal data, Maldonado-Molina et al.[20] longitudinally compared the patterns of substance use among Hispanic adolescents in the United States and Puerto Rico. These patterns include abstainers, alcohol only, alcohol and cigarettes, heavy drinking without smoking, heavy drinking and smoking, and polysubstance use. They found that Hispanic adolescents in Puerto Rico transitioned out of the abstainer group faster than abstainers in the United States. Furthermore, using a sample of 3,356 female adolescents (ages 12–15), Chung et al.[21] classified five subgroups of adolescent substance users (ie, abstainer, alcohol-only users, cigarette-only users, alcohol and cigarette users, and heavy-drinking and cigarette users), and found that adolescents who experienced puberty were more likely to transition into more problematic substance use patterns than those who never experienced puberty.

Few studies have characterized the variations in patterns of substance use among adolescents who are at high risk for substance use problems, particularly adolescents who are involved in publicly funded service systems (eg, mental health, child welfare, juvenile justice). Furthermore, fewer studies have explored how common risk factors (eg, being male, being older) and population-specific risk factors (eg, childhood maltreatment) influence transitions from one substance use pattern (eg, alcohol-only) to another substance use pattern (eg, heavy polysubstance) across time among high-risk adolescents. In

particular, given that the relationship between childhood maltreatment and adolescent polysubstance use was found in cross-sectional data,[2,4–6,9,22] it is important to study how patterns of substance use change over time and how exposure to childhood maltreatment relates to such change. Such knowledge could inform prevention and treatment efforts aimed at young victims of childhood maltreatment who exhibit risky patterns of substance use during adolescence. In this study, an attempt was made to extend previous work by classifying at-risk youth based on their experience of illicit substance use over 2 years, examining transitions in substance use patterns across time, and exploring how childhood maltreatment, age, and gender relate to such change in substance use patterns over time. We hypothesized that childhood maltreatment, being older, and being male were associated with transition into more severe patterns of substance use (eg, moving from abstainers to heavy substance users) over time.

Methods
Design and Sample
Using a longitudinal study design, the Patterns of Youth Mental Health Care in Public Service Systems Study (POC) interviewed 1,642 children (6–18 years of age) who were active in one or more of the following publicly funded service systems during 1996–1997 fiscal year in a large metropolitan area: alcohol and drug treatment, child welfare, juvenile justice, mental health, and public school-based mental health. The POC sample was stratified by race and ethnicity, and service sectors. The Year 1 interviews ($N = 1,642$) were conducted in 1997–1999, and 92 percent of the first respondents were followed up 2 years later (Year 2). Institutional review board (IRB) approval and informed consent were obtained before data collection.

Since our interest is to investigate transitions in substance use patterns across time during adolescence, this study used 937 adolescents (ages 13–18) who were older than 12 years of age at Year 1. The sample included 308 female and 629 male adolescents. Among the 937 adolescents, 31 percent were Caucasian, 21 percent African American, 32 percent Latino, 9 percent Asian/Pacific Islander, and 7 percent other. An estimated 50 percent reported experiencing childhood maltreatment: 17 percent reported sexual abuse, and slightly over a quarter reported child physical abuse (26.0 percent) and child neglect (25.1 percent).

Measures
Childhood maltreatment was measured by the 34-item Childhood Trauma Questionnaire (CTQ).[23] The CTQ assesses the five types of childhood maltreatment. The respondent was asked to indicate how often each item was experienced using a 5-point scale ranging from never true to very often true (eg, "I was punished with a belt, a board, a cord, or some other hard object"). Scores were computed for a total childhood maltreatment scale. Previously established cut-off scores for the total childhood maltreatment scale were used in this study: a dichotomous variable of childhood maltreatment (Yes/No) derived from the total childhood maltreatment score was used.[23] The

CTQ has good reliabilities ($\alpha = .73 - .80$), and validity supported by significant associations of the CTQ with official records such as court records and child protective service agency records.[23,24] Internal consistency of the CTQ for the current sample was .79.

This study examined rates of use of the five most frequently used illicit substances by adolescents in the sample county over the past year, including alcohol, cannabis, cocaine, opioids, and hallucinogens. Adolescent substance use was measured by the Personal Experience Inventory (PEI), which was developed to examine the onset, degree, and duration of substance use in adolescent populations (ages 12–18).[25] The PEI has shown high internal consistency reliabilities, ranging between .87 and .97, and good criterion validity that was supported by significant associations of the PEI with substance abuse treatment histories.[25,26] In this sample, internal consistency was .80 for the five illicit substances. Adolescent past-year substance use was dichotomized for analysis. Finally, respondents were asked about their gender and age. Age was further dichotomized to reflect early (ages 13–14 at Year 1) and late adolescence (ages 15–18 at Year 1).

Analysis

This study specified a mover–stayer LTA model based on past-year use of five illicit substances over 2 years. A mover–stayer LTA is a special case of LTA. Although traditional LTA models are well suited to examine change in substance use patterns over time, LTA assumes that a single model fits the population from which the sample was drawn. Specifically, in LTA, a subgroup that does not move around over time (eg, abstainers at Year 1 and 2) and another subgroup that does move around over time (eg, an abstainer at Year 1 who transitions to a moderate drinker at Year 2) are analyzed in a single model, which might lead to less accurate estimations of transition probabilities. To address this limitation, a mover–stayer LTA model was developed, which uses a second-order latent class variable that characterizes respondents as "mover" (eg, respondents who are in an abstainer class at Year 1 and move to a moderate drinker class at Year 2) or "stayer" (eg, respondents who remain in the same substance use class across time).[27]

The current analyses involved four latent variable modeling steps: (1) cross-sectional latent class analyses (LCA) to explore measurement models for each time point for the full sample, (2) exploration of unconditional probability of membership in each latent class at each year for the full sample, (3) exploration of a mover–stayer LTA model for the full sample, and (4) cross-group comparisons of a mover–stayer LTA model for childhood maltreatment, gender status, and age group. First, LCA performed to examine measurement models for each time point for the full sample is characterized by two parameters: (1) probabilities of class membership assignment for individuals, and (2) the prevalence of each class. Once the most parsimonious latent class model was determined for each year, mover–stayer LTA were conducted to examine transitions among substance use classes across time. Mover–stayer LTA uses two parameters: (1) the prevalence of movers and stayers in the full sample and (2) transitional probabilities.

This study used a variety of statistical indicators and information criteria to determine relative model fit. First, for LCA and mover–stayer LTA, the Bayesian information criterion (BIC) statistics were used to determine relative model fit. Lower values of the BIC indicate a better fitting model.[28] Since the chi-square distribution is not well estimated when large numbers of sparse cells exist, neither Pearson nor likelihood ratio-based chi-square statistics are recommended for mover–stayer LTA modeling.[29] This study also used the Lo–Mendell–Rubin adjusted likelihood ratio test (LMR)[30] and a bootstrap likelihood ratio test (BLRT)[31] to select the number of latent classes that adequately described our data. The LMR provides testing of $k-1$ versus k classes where k is a number of latent classes. A better fitting model has non-significant ($p > .05$) LMR and BLRT at $k + 1$ class.

Because of the nature of the complex survey design used in the POC study, data were weighted using sampling weights in all analyses, and clustering in primary sampling units (PSUs) was used to adjust the standard errors. In all analyses, a combination of statistical and substantive consideration is used to specify a model. Both LCA and mover–stayer LTA models were estimated with Mplus, Version 6.0[32] using maximum likelihood estimation, which allows for missing data under missing at random.[33] This study used random start values to avoid convergence on local, rather than global, solutions which is common in any mixture model.[29]

Results
Cross-sectional LCA Results

Cross-sectional LCA identified a 3-class model of past-year substance use at each year, which demonstrated the most parsimonious description of our data by BIC, LMR, and BLRT. Probabilities of past-year substance use for 3-class models for Year 1 and 2 are depicted in Figures 1 and 2, respectively. Although a 2-class model had the lowest BIC (Year 1 BICs: two classes = 2,456.24, three classes = 2,483.16, four classes = 2,518.27, five classes = 2,554.89/Year 2 BICs: two classes = 1,289.61, three classes = 1,313.24, four classes = 1,348.02, five classes = 1,385.89), both LMR (Year 1 LMR: four classes (p) = .29, five classes (p) = .24/Year 2 LMR: four classes (p) = .04, five classes (p) = .29), and BLRT (Year 1 BLRT: four classes (p) = .67, five classes (p) = .38/Year 2 BLRT: four classes (p) = .24, five classes (p) = .67) suggested three classes for each year. The measurement parameter estimates for the final model is shown in Table 1. The three classes included (a) moderate alcohol, low cannabis, and no hard drug (ie, cocaine, opioids, hallucinogens) users (Class 1), (b) high alcohol/cannabis and moderate hard drug users (Class 2), and (c) heavy polysubstance users (Class 3). It is important to note that we subjectively chose these names based on the probabilities of positive responses to substance use items.

Mover–Stayer Model Results

Nearly 92 percent of the sample, the movers, transitioned across stages whereas the stayers represented about 8 percent

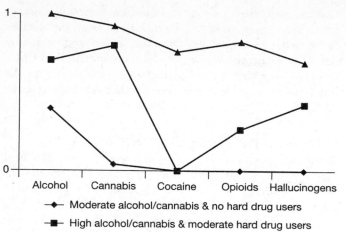

Figure 1 Probability of past-year substance use for a 3-class model at Year 1.

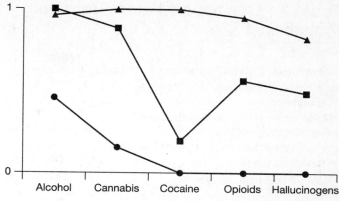

Figure 2 Probability of past-year substance use for a 3-class model at Year 2.

of the sample ($N = 71$). The transition probabilities conditional on initial latent classes (Year 1) are presented in Table 2, which demonstrated the specific transition patterns over time. Among the six different patterns of movers, many reflected movement toward a more polysubstance use class, except two probabilities of the heavy polysubstance user class. The most frequent patterns of movers were those adolescents who started in less polysubstance use classes and then transitioned into classes with more polysubstance use (eg, the moderate alcohol, low cannabis, and no hard drug user class (Class 1) to the high alcohol/cannabis and moderate hard drug user class (Class 2), or from the high alcohol/cannabis and moderate hard drug user class (Class 2) to the heavy polysubstance user class (Class 3)). Movers who started from more polysubstance use classes to

less polysubstance use classes represented only 13 percent of the sample (not shown in Table 2).

Childhood Maltreatment and Transition Patterns

The next modeling steps included cross-group analyses in which the initial classes and transition probabilities were compared across childhood maltreatment status. We constrain unconditional measurement parameters for each substance use item to be identical across subgroup (ie, childhood maltreatment and no-childhood maltreatment groups) as well as across time. Table 3 showed the transition probabilities for the childhood maltreatment group (CM+; those who have been maltreated) and the no-childhood maltreatment group (CM−), respectively.

Table 1   Measurement Parameter Estimates for the Final Model and Standard Errors

	Latent class		
Indicator	Moderate Alcohol, Low Cannabis and No Hard Drug Users (SE)	High Alcohol/Cannabis and Moderate Hard Drug Users (SE)	Heavy Polysubstance Users (SE)
Y1 Alcohol	.398 (.057)	.706 (.216)	1.000 (.000)
Y1 Cannabis	.037 (.215)	.805 (.244)	.925 (.024)
Y1 Cocaine	.000 (.000)	.000 (.000)	.760 (.125)
Y1 Opioids	.006 (.045)	.263 (.265)	.828 (.043)
Y1 Hallucinogens	.003 (.078)	.423 (.167)	.692 (.054)
Y2 Alcohol	.456 (.128)	1.000 (.000)	.964 (.016)
Y2 Cannabis	.148 (.112)	.883 (.060)	1.000 (.000)
Y2 Cocaine	.000 (.000)	.195 (.257)	1.000 (.000)
Y2 Opioids	.000 (.000)	.564(.080)	.952 (.088)
Y2 Hallucinogens	.000 (.000)	.485 (.091)	.824 (.077)

Y1 = Year 1; Y2 = Year 2.

Table 2 Conditional Latent Transition Probability Estimates for the Full Sample.

Conditional Latent Transition Probability Estimates

Year 1 classes (rows) by Year 2 classes (columns)

Moderate alcohol, low cannabis, and no hard drug users	.34	.38	.28
High alcohol/cannabis and moderate hard drug users	.08	.40	.52
Heavy polysubstance users	.42	.58	.00

Bayesian information criterion (BIC) = 3,386.27

Some interesting patterns of substance use between the CM+ and CM− individuals emerged. The majority (69 percent) of maltreated adolescents were already in the heavy polysubstance user class at Year 1 whereas only 14 percent of nonmaltreated adolescents belonged to the heavy polysubstance user class at Year 1 (not shown in Table 3). In addition, the stability of the heavy polysubstance user class was higher in the CM+ group (.92) than the CM− group (.72), indicating that compared to the CM− group, fewer adolescents in the CM+ group moved away from the most severe substance user class to the less severe substance user classes (ie, Class 1 or 2). In contrast, the stability of the moderate alcohol, low cannabis, and no hard drugs user class (Class 1) was lower in the CM+ group (.10) than CM− group (.40), which suggested that more adolescents in the CM+ group moved to the more severe substance user classes (ie, Class 2 or 3) in the Year 1 to 2 transition.

Gender and Transition Patterns

Given that gender differences were reported in adolescent substance use, we conducted a mover–stayer LTA across gender. The results of this mover–stayer model were presented in Table 4, which showed the transition probabilities for female and male adolescents, respectively. For the Year 1 to 2 transition, probabilities of progressing from the moderate alcohol, low cannabis, and no hard drug user class (Class 1) toward the heavy polysubstance user class were much higher among male adolescents (.74) than among female adolescents (.00). However, the probabilities of moving from the heavy polysubstance user class to the moderate alcohol, low cannabis, and no hard drug user class (Class 1) were much higher in female adolescents (.19) than in male adolescents (.00), indicating that female adolescents, compared to male adolescents, were more likely to transition out of heavy polysubstance use over time.

Table 3 Conditional Latent Transition Probability Estimates for the CM+ and CM− Samples.

Conditional Latent Transition Probability Estimates				BIC
Year 1 classes (rows) by Year 2 classes (columns)				
CM+ (468)* Moderate alcohol, low cannabis, and no hard drug users	.10	.90	.00	
High alcohol/cannabis and moderate hard drug users	.00	.20	.80	2,050.14
Heavy polysubstance users	.00	.08	.92	
CM− (469)* Moderate alcohol, low cannabis, and no hard drug users	.40	.00	.64	
High alcohol/cannabis and moderate hard drug users	.05	.00	.95	1,498.90
Heavy polysubstance users	.28	.00	.72	

*Sample size; BIC = Bayesian information criterion.

Table 4 Conditional Latent Transition Probability Estimates for the Female and Male Samples.

Conditional Latent Transition Probability Estimates				BIC
Year 1 classes (rows) by Year 2 classes (columns)				
Female (308)* Moderate alcohol, low cannabis, and no hard drug users	.17	.83	.00	
High alcohol/cannabis and moderate hard drug users	.20	.00	.80	2,498.53
Heavy polysubstance users	.19	.00	.81	
Male (629)* Moderate alcohol, low cannabis, and no hard drug users	.26	.00	.74	
High alcohol/cannabis and moderate hard drug users	.35	.03	.62	1,209.09
Heavy polysubstance users	.00	.17	.83	

*Sample size; BIC = Bayesian information criterion.

Table 5 Conditional Latent Transition Probability Estimates for Two Age Groups

	Conditional Latent Transition Probability Estimates			BIC
Year 1 classes (rows) by Year 2 classes (columns)				
Ages 13–14 (306)*	Moderate alcohol, low cannabis, and no hard drug users	.43	.00	.58
	High alcohol/cannabis and moderate hard drug users	.00	.28	.72	574.38
	Heavy polysubstance users	.27	.73	.00
Ages 15–18 (631)*	Moderate alcohol, low cannabis, and no hard drug users	.28	.10	.62
	High alcohol/cannabis and moderate hard drug users	.46	.03	.51	1,952.45
	Heavy polysubstance users	.00	.81	.19

*Sample size; BIC = Bayesian information criterion.

Age and Transition Patterns

Given the relatively broad range of ages (13–18) used in this study, we also conducted a mover–stayer LTA across two age groups. Table 5 showed the transition probabilities for the younger (13–14) and older adolescents (15–18), respectively. Comparing the Year 1 to 2 transitions between two age groups, probabilities of staying in the moderate alcohol, low cannabis, and no hard drug user class (Class 1) over time were much higher among younger adolescents (.43) than among older adolescents (.28). In contrast, probabilities of progressing from the high alcohol/cannabis and moderate hard drug user class (Class 2) to the heavy poly-substance user class were much lower in older adolescents (.51) than in younger adolescents (.72).

Discussion

Using self-reports of past-year use of five illicit substances among a sample of high-risk adolescents recruited from five publicly funded services systems, we identified three qualitatively different patterns of substance use in adolescence: moderate alcohol, low cannabis, and no hard drug users; high alcohol/cannabis and moderate hard drug users; and heavy polysubstance users. The results of this study also supported prior research documenting remarkable changes in patterns of substance use during adolescence and high rates of substance use among adolescents involved in public service systems.[12,13,34,35] Furthermore, we found that adolescents who had been abused and/or neglected in childhood were more likely to transition into more severe substance user classes and less likely to transition out of heavy polysubstance use than those with-out a history of childhood maltreatment. Finally, we found differences in the course of adolescent substance use associated with gender and age groups.

Our mover–stayer LTA of past-year illicit substance use in adolescence suggested rapid changes in patterns of substance use during adolescence. We found that the majority of adolescents (92 percent) do change patterns of substance use during the developmental period spanning 13–20 years of age. Prior research has documented that adolescent substance use is a developmental phenomenon, which increases from early adolescence to late adolescence.[36–41] Consistent with this developmental perspective, many adolescents in this study tended to transition from less severe patterns of substance use

(eg, moderate alcohol, low cannabis, and no hard drug use) to heavy polysubstance use. The transition probabilities showed that more adolescents progressed to a more severe class than regressed to a less severe class. The periods over which these changes in patterns of substance use occurred represented times of heightened vulnerability to the onset and escalation of substance use.

Numerous developmental changes occur during adolescence, including ontogenic changes related to puberty, changes in the adolescent brain, and changes in family and peer relationships.[42–45] Although the timing of and variations in developmental changes differ across individuals, these interrelated cognitive, biological, and social changes influence an individual's risk of illicit substance use. A consistent body of research has shown that the onset and escalation of substance use in adolescence have their roots in biological, behavioral, and social development in earlier life stages. Since adolescents are more vulnerable than adults to the adverse effects of substance use on biological and social functioning, future research is warranted to consider all dimensions of childhood and early adolescent development (ie, genetic, biological, affective, cognitive, and social) that might decrease or increase adolescent involvement in multiple-substance use. Normative developmental tasks in adolescence, changes in psychological and environmental contexts, and person–environment transactions all play critical roles in the development of adolescent resilience and/or vulnerability to substance use. From transactional and developmental perspectives, future longitudinal studies are required to examine how developmental challenges from infancy to early adolescence, and complex multilevel changes in environmental contexts, influence individuals' adaptive capacities to protect themselves from the future allure of illicit substance use.

Current evidence supporting the linkage between childhood maltreatment and adolescent substance use is primarily cross-sectional. Thus, this study reporting the associations between childhood maltreatment and transitional probabilities of adolescent substance use represents an advance in understanding the associations between experiences of childhood maltreatment and the escalation of adolescent substance use over time. The latent transition perspective used in this study allows us to examine the relationship between childhood maltreatment and potential differences in the course of adolescent substance use. Our findings suggest that childhood maltreatment not only influences the onset but also shapes the longitudinal course of adolescent substance use. In this study, adolescents with a history of childhood maltreatment are more likely to progress from the less severe to the more severe substance user classes than adolescents without such a maltreatment history. In addition, adolescents who were abused and/or neglected were less likely to regress from the more severe to the less severe substance user classes.

We also found that childhood maltreatment relates to the initial status of adolescent substance use. Furthermore, the current work also suggests that experience of childhood maltreatment relates to the persistence of more risky patterns of adolescent substance use over time. Heavy poly-substance users with a history of childhood maltreatment were less likely to transition out of risky patterns of illicit substance use than their counterparts with no history of childhood maltreatment. As suggested in several theoretical and empirical articles, childhood maltreatment is related to deviations in several developmental processes related to optimal childhood development, which make maltreated children vulnerable to the initiation of substance use during adolescence.[3,46-48] These deviations include increased expression of negative emotion,[49,50] poor emotion management skills,[51] behavioral dysregulation,[52,53] and internalizing symptoms like depression and anxiety.[54] Such compromised developmental competencies experienced by maltreated adolescents might also contribute to steeper increases in multiple-substance use and perpetuation of problematic patterns of multiple-substance use in adolescence. It is possible that the same developmental sequelae of childhood maltreatment that increase the likelihood of initiating substance use in adolescence might also harm individuals' resilience to recover and mature out of risky patterns of adolescent substance use. Further examination of the mechanisms through which maltreated children's behavioral and psychological maladaptation links to adolescent onset of illicit substance use also needs to delineate the processes through which childhood maltreatment sequentially influences the velocity and acceleration of progression to problematic multiple-substance use in adolescence and eventuate in substance abuse and dependence in adulthood.

The current investigation focused on adolescents who were involved in public service systems, including alcohol and drug treatment. It is clearly beyond the scope of this study to examine the effects of the involvement in public service systems on the course of adolescent substance use and recovery. However, the extent to which drug prevention and treatment targeting these at-risk adolescents are sufficiently available and accessible is a cause for great concern. Since we have greater consensus on the conceptualization of adolescent substance use as a developmental phenomenon, the roles of publicly funded services in preventing developmental trends in multiple-substance use during adolescence should be addressed in future research.

Age-related trends in adolescent substance use were found in this study: younger adolescents were more likely to begin their transitions from the least severe substance user class (ie, moderate alcohol, low cannabis, and no hard drug user class) than were older adolescents. In addition, the stability of staying in the least severe substance user class was higher in the younger sample than in the older sample. Adolescent substance use is a developmental phenomenon, which shows systematic age-related trends with first incidents of substance use usually occurring between ages 13 and 18, peaking in "emerging adulthood" (ages 18–25), and declining thereafter.[12,55,56] This study suggested that velocity of progression to problematic multiple-substance use during adolescence may be much faster among high-risk populations, including adolescents involved in publicly funded service systems than in the general population. Given that 31 percent of our sample at Year 1 was at high risk for progressing into heavy polysubstance users, further intervention efforts should target to preventing initiation of hard drug use and delaying age of progression to heavy polysubstance use among adolescents in contact with public services.

Research investigating gender differences in the course of adolescent substance use has reported that age-related changes in adolescent substance use closely interact with gender.[13,38,56] In this study, we found that male adolescents were more likely to start from a multiple-substance use typology than were female adolescents, which supports the findings from a recent national study. According to the 2009 National Survey on Drug Use and Health, male adolescents (ages 12–17) had higher rates than females for current use of cannabis, cocaine, opioids, and hallucinogens.[57] Consistent with previous work on gender effects on substance use trajectories, we also found that being male was associated with elevated probabilities to transition to more severe substance user classes. Gender differences in individuals' adoption of traditional "adult" roles (eg, marriage, job, education) may explain different age-related changes in adolescent substance use. For example, females may assume adult roles such as marriage earlier than males. Married young people showed greater decreases in substance use, specifically hard drug use, than their counterparts who were not married, lived with partners, or were divorced.[58,59] Furthermore, adoption of adult roles may constrain females' substance use more than males' substance use because new adult roles such as marriage and parenthood situate domestic responsibilities more on females than males. In addition, female adolescents may suffer more from substance use-related adverse consequences such as victimization and pregnancy, which might alter substance use patterns over time.

Limitations

Although to the best of our knowledge, this study is the first LTA that examined the associations between childhood maltreatment and the course of adolescent substance use, we note several limitations of our study. Our sample consisted of adolescents involved in urban public service systems including public drug treatment, who are at high risk of illicit substance use. For example, 67 percent and 55 percent of the current sample (ages 13–18) reported past-year cannabis and hallucinogen use, respectively, whereas only 7.3 percent and .9 percent of the 2009 National Survey on Drug Use and Health sample (ages 12–17) reported the same substance use in the past year.[57] Given the unique characteristics of our sample, the initial and transitional patterns of adolescent substance use found in this study should not be generalized to adolescents in the general population. In addition, our findings need to be corroborated through future LTA using the general adolescent populations who might not be involved in public service systems or not live in an urban setting. Second, our sample included those adolescents involved in child welfare systems whose experiences of childhood maltreatment were severe enough to be involved in child welfare systems. Such sample characteristics might inflate the associations between childhood maltreatment and the course of adolescent substance use. In this connection, a complete history of childhood maltreatment (eg, frequency, duration, and types of maltreatment, types of perpetrators, developmental timing of the episodes) was not available in our study; it might have helped us determine which child maltreatment victims were at greatest risk for problematic multiple-substance use in adolescence. Finally, we used self-report measures for childhood maltreatment and past-year substance use, and these measures are subject to certain limitations including recall bias, social desirability, and response acquiescence.

Conclusions

Past studies highlight the associations between childhood maltreatment and adolescent substance use. However, change in patterns of substance use over time has been less well characterized. This study examined the patterns of transitions in adolescent substance use among three substance use classes and documented childhood maltreatment-, gender-, and age-related differences in these patterns of adolescent substance use. Adolescents in public service systems who have exposure to childhood maltreatment are the most likely group to develop substance abuse and dependence in adulthood. Future work should focus on identifying developmental mechanisms through which childhood maltreatment influences risky patterns of adolescent substance use, which might provide malleable targets for intervention and prevention of substance use among maltreated children.

The Patterns of Youth Mental Health Care in Public Service Systems Study was supported by grant U01-MH55282 from the National Institute of Mental Health, Bethesda, MD (Dr. Shin).

Thanks to Richard L. Hough, PhD and John Landsverk, PhD for their support during the data preparation.

Declaration of Interest

The authors report no conflicts of interest. The authors alone are responsible for the content and writing of the paper.

References

1. U.S. Department of Health and Human Services. *Child Maltreatment 2008*. Washington, DC: Government Printing Office; 2010.
2. Shin SH, Hong HG, Hazen AL. Childhood sexual abuse and adolescent substance use: A latent class analysis. *Drug Alcohol Depend*. 2010;109:226–235.
3. Rogosch AF, Oshri A, Cicchetti D. From child maltreatment to adolescent cannabis abuse and dependence: A developmental cascade model. *Dev Psychopathol*. 2010;22:883–897.
4. Kilpatrick DG, Acierno R, Saunders B, et al. Risk factors for adolescent substance abuse and dependence: Data from a national sample. *J Counsel Clin Psychol*. 2000;68:19–30.
5. Dube SR, Miller JW, Brown DW, et al. Adverse childhood experiences and the association with ever using alcohol and initiating alcohol use during adolescence. *J Adoles Health*. 2006;38:1–44.
6. Hamburger ME, Leeb RT, Swahn MH. Childhood maltreatment and early alcohol use among high-risk adolescents. *J Stud Alcohol Drugs*. 2008;69:291–295.
7. Shin SH, Edwards E, Heeren T. Child abuse and neglect: Relations to adolescent binge drinking in the National Longitudinal Study of Adolescent Health (AddHealth) Study. *Addict Behav*. 2009;34:277–280. PMCID: PMC2656346.
8. Fergusson DM, Horwood LJ, Lynskey MT. Childhood sexual abuse and psychiatric disorder in young adulthood: II. Psychiatric outcomes of childhood sexual abuse. *J Am Acad Child Adoles Psychiatry*. 1996;35:1365–1374.
9. Clark DB, De Bellis MD, Lynch KG, et al. Physical and sexual abuse, depression and alcohol use disorders in adolescents: Onsets and outcomes. *Drug Alcohol Depend*. Jan 24 2003;69:51–60.
10. Diaz A, Simantov E, Rickert V. Effect of abuse on health: Results of a national survey. *Arch Pediatr Adolesc Med*. 2002;156:811–817.
11. Duncan SC, Duncan TE, Hops H. Progressions of alcohol, cigarette, and marijuana use in adolescence. *J Behav Med*. 1998;21:375–388.
12. Johnston LD, O'Malley PM, Bachman JG, et al. *Monitoring the Future: National Survey Results on Drug Use, 1975–2008: Volume 1, Secondary school students*. Bethesda, MD: National Institute on Drug Abuse; 2009. NIH 09–7402.
13. Chassin L, Flora DB, King KM. Trajectories of alcohol and drug use and dependence from adolescence to adulthood: The effects of familial alcoholism and personality. *J Abnorm Psychol*. 2004;113:483–498.
14. Curran PJ. A latent curve framework for studying developmental trajectories of adolescent substance use. In: Rose J, Chassin L, Presson C, Sherman J, eds. *Multivariate Applications in Substance Use Research*. Hillsdale, NJ: Erlbaum; 2000:1–42.
15. Agrawal A, Lynskey MT. Tobacco and cannabis co-occurrence: Does route of administration matter? *Drug Alcohol Depend*. 2009;99:240–247.
16. Kandel DB, Yamaguchi K, Klein LC. Testing the gateway hypothesis. *Addiction*. 2006;101:470–472.
17. Vanyukov MM, Tarter RE, Kirisci L, et al. Liability to substance use disorders: 1. Common mechanisms and manifestations. *Neurosci Biobehav Rev*. 2003;27:507–515.
18. Dierker LC, Vesel F, Sledjeski EM, et al. Testing the dual pathway hypothesis to substance use in adolescence and young adulthood. *Drug Alcohol Depend*. 2007;87:83–93.
19. Cleveland MJ, Collins LM, Lanza ST, et al. Does individual risk moderate the effect of contextual-level protective factors? A latent class analysis of substance use. *J Prev Interv Community*. 2010;38:213–228.
20. Maldonado-Molina MM, Collins LM, Lanza ST, et al. Patterns of substance use onset among Hispanics in Puerto Rico and the United States. *Addict Behav*. 2007;32:2432–2437.
21. Chung H, Park Y, Lanza ST. Latent transition analysis with covariates: Pubertal timing and substance use behaviours in adolescent females. *Stat Med*. 2005;24:2895–2910.
22. Moran PB, Vuchinich S, Hall NK. Associations between types of maltreatment and substance use during adolescence. *Child Abuse Neglect*. 2004;28:565–574.
23. Bernstein DP, Fink L. *Childhood Trauma Questionnaire: A Retrospective Self-Report*. San Antonio, TX: Harcourt Brace, Psychological Corporation; 1998.
24. Bernstein DP, Ahluvalia T, Pogge D, et al. Validity of the childhood trauma questionnaire in an adolescent psychiatric population. *J Am Acad Child Adoles Psychiatry*. 1997;36:340–348.
25. Winters KC, Henly GA. *Personal Experience Inventory (PEI) Manual*. Los Angeles: Western Psychological Services; 1994.

26. Winters KC, Stinchfield R, Henly RA. Convergent and predictive validity of scales measuring adolescent substance abuse. *J Child Adoles Subst.* 1996;5:37–55.

27. Langeheine R, Van de Pol F. Discrete-time mixed Markov latent class models. In: Dale A, Davies RB, eds. *Analyzing Social and Political Change: A Casebook of Methods.* London: Sage Publications; 1994:171–197.

28. Raftery AE. Bayesian model selection in social research. In: Mars-den PV, ed. *Sociological methodology.* Cambridge: Basil Blackwell; 1995:111–163.

29. McLachlan G, Peel D. *Finite Mixture Models.* New York: Wiley; 2000.

30. Lo Y, Mendell N, Rubin D. Testing the number of components in a normal mixture. *Biometrika.* 2001;88:767–778.

31. Nylund KL, Asparouhov T, Muthen BO. Deciding on the number of classes in latent class analysis and growth mixture modeling: A Monte Carlo simulation study. *Struc Equ Modeling.* 2007;14:535–569.

32. Muthén L, Muthén B. *Mplus User's Guide.* Los Angeles: Muthén and Muthén; 2010.

33. Little R, Rubin D. *Statistical Analysis with Missing Data.* New York: Wiley; 1987.

34. Palmer RH, Young SE, Hopfer CJ, et al. Developmental epidemiology of drug use and abuse in adolescence and young adulthood: Evidence of generalized risk. *Drug Alcohol Depend.* 2009;102:78–87.

35. Orton HD, Riggs PD, Libby AM. Prevalence and characteristics of depression and substance use in a U.S. child welfare sample. *Child Youth Serv Rev.* 2009;31:649–653.

36. Brown SA, McGue M, Maggs J, et al. A developmental perspective on alcohol and youths 16 to 20 years of age. *Pediatrics.* 2008;121:S290–310.

37. White HR, Pandina RJ, Chen PH. Developmental trajectories of cigarette use from early adolescence into young adulthood. *Drug Alcohol Depend.* Jan 2002;65:167–178.

38. Windle M, Mun EY, Windle RC. Adolescent-to-young adulthood heavy drinking trajectories and their prospective predictors. *J Stud Alcohol.* May 2005 2005;66:313–322.

39. Zucker RA, Donovan JE, Masten AS, et al. Early developmental processes and the continuity of risk for underage drinking and problem drinking. *Pediatrics.* 2008;121:S252–S272.

40. Masten AS, Faden VB, Zucker RA, et al. Underage drinking: A developmental framework. *Pediatrics.* 2008;121:S235–S251.

41. Schulenberg JE, Maggs JL, O'Malley PM. How and why the understanding of developmental continuity and discontinuity is important: The sample case of long-term consequences of adolescent substance use. In: Mortimer JT, Shanahan MJ, eds. *Handbook of the Life Course.* New York: Kluwer Academic/ Plenum Publishers; 2003:413–436.

42. Blakemore SJ, Choudhury S. Development of the adolescent brain: Implications for executive function and social cognition. *J Child Psychol Psychiatry.* 2006;47:296–312.

43. Cicchetti D, Rogosch FA. A developmental psychopathology perspective on adolescence. *J Consult Clin Psychol.* Feb 2002;70:6–20.

44. Heard HE. The family structure and trajectory and adolescent school performance: Differential effects by race and ethnicity. *J Fam Issues.* 2007;28:319–354.

45. Oh W, Rubin KH, Bowker JC, et al. Trajectories of social withdrawal from middle childhood to early adolescence. *J Abnorm Child Psychol.* 2008;36:553–566.

46. Ellis WE, Wolfe DA. Understanding the association between maltreatment history and adolescent risk behavior by examining popularity motivations and peer group control. *J Youth Adolesc.* 2009;38:1253–1263.

47. Taussig HN, Culhane SE. Impact of a mentoring and skills group program on mental health outcomes for maltreated children in foster care. *Arch Pediatr Adolesc Med.* 2010;164:739–746.

48. Clark DB, Thatcher DL, Martin CS. Child abuse and other traumatic experiences, alcohol use disorders, and health problems in adolescence and young adulthood. *J Pediatr Psychol.* 2010;35:499–510.

49. Bennett DS, Sullivan MW, Lewis M. Young children's adjustment as a function of maltreatment, shame and anger. *J Am Profess Soc Abuse Child.* 2005;10:311–323. PMCID: PMC1828211.

50. Gaensbauer TJ. The relationship between infant play with inanimate objects and social interest in mother. *J Am Acad Child Adolesc Psychiatry.* 1982;37:29–66.

51. Shipman KL, Zeman J, Penza S, et al. Emotion management skills in sexually maltreated and nonmaltreated girls: A developmental psychopathology perspective. *Dev Psychopathol.* 2000;12:47–62.

52. Shields A, Cicchetti D. Parental maltreatment and emotion dysregulation as risk factors for bullying and victmization in middle childhood. *J Clin Child Psychol.* 2001;30:349–363.

53. Briere J, Rickards S. Self-awareness, affect regulation, and relatedness: Differential sequels of childhood versus adult victimization experiences. *J Nerv Ment Dis.* 2007;195:497–503.

54. Widom CS, DuMont K, Czaja SJ. A prospective investigation of major depressive disorder and comorbidity in abuse and neglected children grown up. *Arch Gen Psychiatry.* 2007;64:49–56.

55. Chassin L, Pitts SC, Prost J. Binge drinking trajectories from adolescence to emerging adulthood in a high-risk sample: Predictors and substance abuse outcomes. *J Consult Clin Psychol.* 2002;70:67–78.

56. Jackson KM, Sher KJ, Gotham HJ, et al. Transitioning into and out of large-effect drinking in young adulthood. *J Abnorm Psychol.* 2001;110:378–391.

57. Substance Abuse and Mental Health Services Administration OoAS. *Results from the 2009 National Survey on Drug Use and Health: National Findings.* Rockville, MD: Substance Abuse and Mental Health Services Administration; 2010.

58. Bachman JG, Wadsworth KN, O'Malley PM, et al. *Smoking, Drinking, and Drug Use in Young Adulthood: The Impacts of New Freedoms and New Responsibilities.* Mahwah, NJ: Lawrence Erlbaum Associates; 1997.

59. Flora DB, Chassin L. Changes in drug use during young adulthood: The effects of parent alcoholism and transition into marriage. *Psychol Addict Behav.* 2005;19:352–362.

Critical Thinking

1. Describe two variables correlated with high rates of substance use in adolescence.

2. Discuss what might lead adolescents to change their substance abuse patterns.

3. Discuss the role of person-environment transactions in adolescent substance abuse.

Received May 23, 2011; revised July 6, 2011; accepted July 19, 2011.

Address correspondence to **Dr. Shin,** Boston University School of Social Work, 264 Bay State Road, Boston, MA 02215. E-mail: hshin@bu.edu.

Medical Marijuana and the Mind

More Is Known about the Psychiatric Risks than the Benefits

The movement to legalize marijuana for medical use in the United States has renewed discussion about how this drug affects the brain, and whether it might be useful in treating psychiatric disorders.

Unfortunately, most of the research on marijuana is based on people who smoked the drug for recreational rather than medical purposes. A review by researchers in Canada (where medical marijuana is legal) identified only 31 studies (23 randomized controlled trials and 8 observational studies) specifically focused on medical benefits of the drug.

A separate review by the American Medical Association (AMA) also concluded that the research base remains sparse. This was one reason that the AMA recently urged the federal government to reconsider its classification of marijuana as a Schedule 1 controlled substance (prohibiting both medical and recreational use), so that researchers could more easily conduct clinical trials.

Consensus exists that marijuana may be helpful in treating certain carefully defined medical conditions. In its comprehensive 1999 review, for example, the Institute of Medicine (IOM) concluded that marijuana may be modestly effective for pain relief (particularly nerve pain), appetite stimulation for people with AIDS wasting syndrome, and control of chemotherapy-related nausea and vomiting.

Given the availability of FDA-approved medications for these conditions, however, the IOM advised that marijuana be considered as a treatment only when patients don't get enough relief from currently available drugs. Additional research since then has confirmed the IOM's core findings and recommendations.

Although anecdotal reports abound, few randomized controlled studies support the use of medical marijuana for psychiatric conditions. The meager evidence for benefits must be weighed against the much better documented risks, particularly for young people who use marijuana.

Challenges in Drug Delivery

Marijuana is derived from the hemp plant, *Cannabis*. Although marijuana contains more than 400 chemicals, researchers best understand the actions of two: THC (delta-9-tetrahydrocannabinol) and cannabidiol.

THC is the chemical in marijuana primarily responsible for its effects on the central nervous system. It stimulates cannabinoid receptors in the brain, triggering other chemical reactions that underlie marijuana's psychological and physical effects—both good and bad.

Less is known about cannabidiol, although the research suggests that it interacts with THC to produce sedation. It may independently have anti-inflammatory, neuroprotective, or antipsychotic effects, although the research is too preliminary to be applied clinically.

Drug delivery remains a major challenge for medical marijuana. The FDA has approved two pills containing synthetic THC. Dronabinol (Marinol) combines synthetic THC with sesame oil. Most of the active ingredient is metabolized during digestion, so that only 10% to 20% of the original dose reaches the bloodstream. Nabilone (Cesamet) uses a slightly different preparation of synthetic THC that is absorbed more completely into the bloodstream. Among the concerns about both of these drugs, however, are that they do not work rapidly, and the amount of medication that reaches the bloodstream varies from person to person.

Another medication under investigation in the United States (and already approved for sale in Canada) combines THC and

---

Key Points

- Medical marijuana may be an option for treating certain conditions, such as nerve pain or chemotherapy-related nausea.
- There is not enough evidence to recommend medical marijuana as a treatment for any psychiatric disorder.
- The psychiatric risks are well documented, and include addiction, anxiety, and psychosis.

cannabidiol. In Canada, it is marketed as Sativex. This drug is sometimes referred to as "liquid cannabis" because it is sprayed under the tongue or elsewhere in the mouth, using a small handheld device. However, it takes time to notice any effects, as the drug has to be absorbed through tissues lining the mouth before it can reach the bloodstream.

Inhalation is the fastest way to deliver THC to the bloodstream, which is why patients may prefer smoking an herbal preparation. But while this method of drug delivery works fast, smoking marijuana exposes the lungs to multiple chemicals and poses many of the same respiratory health risks as smoking cigarettes. Limited research suggests that vaporizers may reduce the amount of harmful chemicals delivered to the lungs during inhalation.

More Psychiatric Risk than Benefit

Part of the reason marijuana works to relieve pain and quell nausea is that, in some people, it reduces anxiety, improves mood, and acts as a sedative. But so far the few studies evaluating the use of marijuana as a treatment for psychiatric disorders are inconclusive, partly because this drug may have contradictory effects in the brain depending on the dose of the drug and inborn genetic vulnerability.

Much more is known about the psychiatric risks of marijuana (whether used for recreational or medical purposes) than its benefits.

Addiction

Observational studies suggest that one in nine people who smokes marijuana regularly becomes dependent on it. Research both in animals and in people provides evidence that marijuana is an addictive substance, especially when used for prolonged periods.

Addiction specialists note with concern that THC concentration has been increasing in the herbal form of marijuana. In the United States, THC concentrations in marijuana sold on the street used to range from 1 to 4% of the total product; by 2003, average THC concentration had risen to 7%. Similar trends are reported in Europe. This increased potency might also accelerate development of dependence.

Less conclusive is the notion that marijuana is a "gateway drug" that leads people to experiment with "hard" drugs such as cocaine. The research is conflicting.

Anxiety

Although many recreational users say that smoking marijuana calms them down, for others it has the opposite effect. In fact, the most commonly reported side effects of smoking marijuana are intense anxiety and panic attacks. Studies report that about 20–30% of recreational users experience such problems after smoking marijuana. The people most vulnerable are those who have never used marijuana before.

Dose of THC also matters. At low doses, THC can be sedating. At higher doses, however, this substance can induce intense episodes of anxiety.

It is not yet known whether marijuana increases the risk of developing a persistent anxiety disorder. Observational studies have produced conflicting findings. Studies of recreational users suggest that many suffer from anxiety, and it is difficult to know what underlies this association. Possibilities include selection bias (e.g., that anxious people are more likely to use marijuana), a rebound phenomenon (e.g., that marijuana smokers feel worse when withdrawing from the substance), and other reasons (e.g., genetic vulnerability).

Mood Disorders

Little controlled research has been done about how marijuana use affects patients with bipolar disorder. Many patients with bipolar disorder use marijuana, and the drug appears to induce manic episodes and increases rapid cycling between manic and depressive moods. But it is not yet clear whether people who use marijuana are at increased risk of developing bipolar disorder.

The small amount of research available on depression is also muddied. In line with what studies report about anxiety, many marijuana users describe an improvement in mood. Animal studies have suggested that components of marijuana may have antidepressant effects. Yet several observational studies have suggested that daily marijuana use may, in some users, actually increase symptoms of depression or promote the development of this disorder.

For example, an Australian study that followed the outcomes of 1,601 students found that those who used marijuana at least once a week at ages 14 or 15 were twice as likely to develop depression seven years later as those who never smoked the substance—even after adjusting for other factors. Young women who smoked marijuana daily were five times as likely to develop depression seven years later as their nonsmoking peers. Although such studies do not prove cause and effect, the dose-outcomes relationship is particularly worrisome.

Psychosis

Marijuana exacerbates psychotic symptoms and worsens outcomes in patients already diagnosed with schizophrenia or other psychotic disorders. Several large observational studies also strongly suggest that using marijuana—particularly in the early teenage years—can increase risk of developing psychosis.

An often-cited study of more than 50,000 young Swedish soldiers, for example, found that those who had smoked marijuana at least once were more than twice as likely to develop schizophrenia as those who had not smoked marijuana. The heaviest users (who said they had used the drug more than 50 times) were six times as likely to develop schizophrenia as the nonsmokers.

Until recently, the consensus view was that this reflected selection bias: Individuals who were already vulnerable to developing psychosis or in the early stages (the prodrome) might be more likely to smoke marijuana to quell voices and disturbing thoughts. But further analyses of the Swedish study, and other observational studies, have found that marijuana use increases the risk of psychosis, even after adjusting for possible confounding factors.

Although cause and effect are hard to prove, evidence is accumulating that early or heavy marijuana use might not only trigger psychosis in people who are already vulnerable, but might also cause psychosis in some people who might not otherwise have developed it.

Certainly genetic profile mediates the effect of marijuana. People born with a variation of the gene COMT are more vulnerable to developing psychosis, for example. Because there is as yet no reliable way for clinicians to identify vulnerable young people in advance, however, it is safest to restrict use of medical marijuana to adults.

Other Effects

A review of side effects caused by medical marijuana found that most were mild. When compared with controls, people who used medical marijuana were more likely to develop pneumonia and other respiratory problems, and experience vomiting, and diarrhea.

There's no question that recreational use of marijuana produces short-term problems with thinking, working memory, and executive function (the ability to focus and integrate different types of information). Although little research exists on medical marijuana, anecdotal reports indicate that some patients take the drug at night to avoid these types of problems.

The real debate is about whether long-term use of marijuana (either for medical or recreational purposes) produces persistent cognitive problems. Although early studies of recreational users reported such difficulties, the studies had key design problems. Typically, they compared long-term marijuana smokers with people who had never used the drug, for example, without controlling for baseline characteristics (such as education or

cognitive functioning) that might determine who continues to smoke the drug and who might be most at risk for thinking and memory problems later on.

Recent studies suggest that although overall cognitive ability remains intact, long-term use of marijuana may cause subtle but lasting impairments in executive function. There is no consensus, however, about whether this affects real-world functioning.

Additional research, focused on the benefits and consequences of medical marijuana use for specific disorders, may help to clarify some issues. In the meantime, there is not enough evidence to recommend marijuana as a medical treatment for any psychiatric disorder.

References

Crippa JA, et al. "Cannabis and Anxiety: A Critical Review of the Evidence," *Human Psychopharmacology* (Oct. 2009): Vol. 24, No. 7, pp. 515–23.

Grinspoon L, et al. *Marijuana: The Forbidden Medicine* (Yale University, 1997).

Iversen LL. *The Science of Marijuana, Second Edition* (Oxford University Press, 2008).

Wang T, et al. "Adverse Effects of Medical Cannabinoids: A Systematic Review," *Canadian Medical Association Journal* (June 17, 2008): Vol. 178, No. 13, pp. 1669–78.

Critical Thinking

1. Fifteen states all permit the use of medical marijuana. Why have these states chosen to allow marijuana for pain relief?

2. Provide a discussion of the primary issues inherent in states' legalization of marijuana.

The Genetics of Alcohol and Other Drug Dependence

DANIELLE M. DICK AND ARPANA AGRAWAL

This article explores the hypothesis that certain genetic factors increase a person's risk of both alcohol abuse and dependence and other drug abuse and dependence. It first reviews the evidence suggesting that certain genetic factors contribute to the development of alcohol and other drug (AOD) use disorders, as well as to the development of a variety of forms of externalizing psychopathology—that is, psychiatric disorders characterized by disinhibited behavior, such as antisocial personality disorder, attention deficit/hyperactivity disorder, and conduct disorder. After summarizing the difficulties associated with, and recent progress made in, the identification of specific genes associated with AOD dependence, the article then discusses evidence that implicates several genes in a person's risk for dependence on both alcohol and illicit drugs.

Genetic Epidemiology of AOD Dependence

Alcohol dependence frequently co-occurs with dependence on illicit drugs (Hasin et al. 2007). Both alcohol use disorders (i.e., alcohol abuse and alcohol dependence) and drug use disorders (drug abuse and drug dependence) are influenced by several factors. For example, family, twin, and adoption studies have convincingly demonstrated that genes contribute to the development of alcohol dependence, with heritability estimates ranging from 50 to 60 percent for both men and women (McGue 1999). Dependence on illicit drugs only more recently has been investigated in twin samples, but several studies now suggest that illicit drug abuse and dependence also are under significant genetic influence. In these studies of adult samples, heritability estimates ranged from 45 to 79 percent (for reviews, see Agrawal and Lynskey 2006; etc. Kendler et al. 2003a; Tsuang et al. 2001).

Twin studies also can be used to assess the extent to which the *co-occurrence* of disorders is influenced by genetic and/or environmental factors. Thus, a finding that the correlation between alcohol dependence in twin 1 and drug dependence in twin 2 is higher for identical (i.e., monozygotic) twins, who share 100 percent of their genes, than for fraternal (i.e., dizygotic) twins, who share on average only 50 percent of their genes, indicates that shared genes influence the risk of both alcohol and drug dependence. The twin studies conducted to date support the role of such shared genetic factors. For example, in the largest twin study of the factors underlying psychiatric disorders, Kendler and colleagues (2003b) analyzed data from the Virginia Twin Registry and found that a common genetic factor contributed to the total variance in alcohol dependence, illicit drug abuse and dependence, conduct disorder, and adult antisocial behavior. This pattern also has been identified in several other independent twin studies (Krueger et al. 2002; Young et al. 2000). Taken together, these findings suggest that a significant portion of the genetic influence on alcohol dependence and drug dependence is through a general predisposition toward externalizing disorders, which may manifest in different ways (e.g., different forms of AOD dependence and/or antisocial behavior) (see Figure). However, some evidence also suggests that disorder-specific genetic influences contribute to AOD dependence (Kendler et al. 2003b). These specific influences likely reflect the actions of genes that are involved in the metabolism of individual drugs.

The idea that alcohol and drug dependence share a genetic liability with each other, as well as with other forms of externalizing psychopathology, is further supported by electrophysiological studies recording the brain's electrical activity. These studies, which are conducted using electrodes placed on the person's scalp, provide a noninvasive, sensitive method of measuring brain function in humans. They generate a predictable pattern in the height (i.e., amplitude) and rate (i.e., frequency) of brain waves that can show characteristic abnormalities in people with certain types of brain dysfunction. For example, electrophysiological abnormalities have been observed in people with a variety of externalizing disorders as well as in unaffected children of these people. These findings suggest that electrophysiological measurements can be used as markers of a genetic vulnerability to externalizing disorders.

One commonly measured electrophysiological characteristic is the so-called P3 component of an event-related potential—that is, a spike in brain activity that occurs about 300 milliseconds after a person is exposed to a sudden stimulus (e.g., a sound or light). Researchers have observed that the amplitude of the P3 component is reduced in alcohol-dependent people and their children, suggesting that this abnormality is a marker for a genetic predisposition to alcohol dependence (Porjesz et al. 1995). However, the abnormal P3 response is not specific to alcohol dependence but appears to be associated with a variety of disinhibitory disorders, including other forms of drug dependence, childhood externalizing disorders, and adult antisocial personality disorder, again suggesting a shared underlying predisposition to multiple forms of AOD dependence and other externalizing problems (Hicks et al. 2007).[1]

Interestingly, electrophysiological abnormalities are most pronounced in alcohol-dependent people who also have a diagnosis of illicit drug abuse or dependence (Malone et al. 2001). This observation is consistent with data from twin and family studies suggesting that co-morbid dependence on alcohol and another drug represents a more severe disorder with higher heritability than dependence on one drug alone (Johnson et al. 1996; Pickens et al. 1995). This conclusion also appears to be supported by new studies exploring the roles of specific genes, which are discussed later in this article.

Identifying Specific Genes Related to AOD Dependence

With robust evidence indicating that genes influence both alcohol dependence and dependence on illicit drugs, efforts now are underway to identify specific genes involved in the development of these disorders. This identification, however, is complicated by many factors. For example, numerous genes are thought to contribute to a person's susceptibility to alcohol and/or drug dependence, and affected people may carry different combinations of those genes. Additionally, environmental influences have an impact on substance use, as does gene–environment interaction (Heath et al. 2002). Finally, the manifestation of AOD dependence varies greatly among affected people, for example, with respect to age of onset of problems, types of symptoms exhibited (i.e., symptomatic profile), substance use history, and presence of co-morbid disorders.

Despite the complications mentioned above, the rapid growth in research technologies for gene identification in recent years has led to a concomitant increase in exciting results. After suffering many disappointments in early attempts to identify genes involved in complex behavioral outcomes (i.e., phenotypes), researchers now are frequently succeeding in identifying genes that help determine a variety of clinical phenotypes. These advances have been made possible by several factors. First, advances in technologies to identify a person's genetic makeup (i.e., genotyping technology) have dramatically lowered the cost of genotyping, allowing for high-throughput analyses of the entire genome. Second, the completion of several large-scale research endeavors, such as the Human Genome Project, the International HapMap Project,[2] and other government and privately funded efforts,

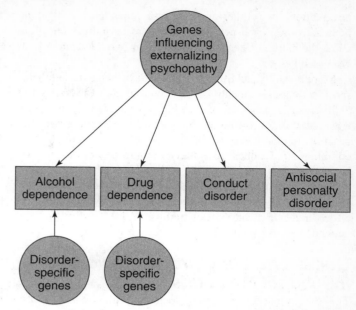

Figure Schematic representation of a model to illustrate the influence of genetic factors on the development of alcohol dependence, dependence on other drugs, and other externalizing disorders (e.g., conduct disorder or antisocial personality disorder). Some of the proposed genetic factors are thought to have a general influence on all types of externalizing conditions, whereas others are thought to have a disorder-specific influence.

have made a wealth of information on variations in the human genome publicly available. Third, these developments have been complemented by advances in the statistical analysis of genetic data.

Several large collaborative projects that strive to identify genes involved in AOD dependence currently are underway. The first large-scale project aimed at identifying genes contributing to alcohol dependence was the National Institute on Alcohol Abuse and Alcoholism (NIAAA)-sponsored Collaborative Study on the Genetics of Alcoholism (COGA), which was initiated in 1989. This study, which involves collaboration of investigators at several sites in the United States, examines families with several alcohol-dependent members who were recruited from treatment centers across the United States. This study has been joined by several other gene identification studies focusing on families affected with alcohol dependence, including the following:

- A sample of Southwestern American Indians (Long et al. 1998);
- The Irish Affected Sib Pair Study of Alcohol Dependence (Prescott et al. 2005a);
- A population of Mission Indians (Ehlers et al. 2004);
- A sample of densely affected families collected in the Pittsburgh area (Hill et al. 2004); and
- An ongoing data collection from alcohol-dependent individuals in Australia.

Importantly, most of these projects include comprehensive psychiatric interviews that focus not only on alcohol use and alcohol use disorders but which also allow researchers to collect information about other drug use and dependence. This comprehensive approach permits researchers to address questions about the nature of genetic influences on AOD dependence, as discussed below.

More recently, additional studies have been initiated that specifically seek to identify genes contributing to various forms of illicit drug dependence as well as general drug use problems (for more information, see www.nida.nih.gov/about/organization/Genetics/consortium/index.html). Through these combined approaches, researchers should be able to identify both genes with drug-specific effects and genes with more general effects on drug use. The following sections focus on several groups of genes that have been identified by these research efforts and which have been implicated in affecting risk for dependence on both alcohol and illicit drugs.

Genes Encoding Proteins Involved in Alcohol Metabolism

The genes that have been associated with alcohol dependence most consistently are those encoding the enzymes that metabolize alcohol (chemically known as ethanol). The main pathway of alcohol metabolism involves two steps. In the first step, ethanol is converted into the toxic intermediate acetaldehyde; this step is mediated by the alcohol dehydrogenase (ADH) enzymes. In a second step, the acetaldehyde is further broken down into acetate and water by the actions of aldehyde dehydrogenase (ALDH) enzymes. The genes that encode the ADH and ALDH enzymes exist in several variants (i.e., alleles) that are characterized by variations (i.e., polymorphisms) in the sequence of the DNA building blocks. One important group of ADH enzymes are the ADH class I isozymes ADH1A, ADH1B, and ADH1C. For both the genes encoding ADH1B and those encoding ADH1C, several alleles resulting in altered proteins have been identified, and the proteins encoded by some of these alleles exhibit particularly high enzymatic activity in laboratory experiments (i.e., in vitro) (Edenberg 2007). This suggests that in people carrying these alleles, ethanol is more rapidly converted to acetaldehyde.[3] Several studies have reported lower frequencies of both the *ADH1B*2* and *ADH1C*1* alleles, which encode some of the more active proteins, among alcoholics than among non-alcoholics in a variety of East Asian populations (e.g., Shen et al. 1997) and, more recently, in European populations (Neumark et al. 1998; Whitfield et al. 1998).

In addition, genome-wide screens to identify genes linked to alcoholism and alcohol-related traits have been conducted in three independent samples consisting largely of people of European descent—the COGA study (Saccone et al. 2000), the Irish Affected Sib Pair Study of Alcohol Dependence (Prescott et al. 2005*a*), and an Australian sample (Birley et al. 2005). These studies have found evidence that a region on chromosome 4 containing the ADH gene cluster shows linkage to the phenotypes studied. This cluster contains, in addition to the genes encoding ADH class I isozymes, the genes *ADH4, ADH5, ADH6,* and *ADH7,* which encode other ADH enzymes. Polymorphisms exist for each of these genes, some of which also have been associated with alcohol dependence (Edenberg et al. 2006; Luo et al. 2006*a,b;* Prescott et al. 2005*b*).

Interestingly, the effects of these genes do not appear to be limited to alcohol dependence. One study compared the frequency of alleles that differed in only one DNA building block (i.e., single nucleotide polymorphisms [SNPs]) throughout the genome between people with histories of illicit drug use and/or dependence and unrelated control participants. This study detected a significant difference for a SNP located near the ADH gene cluster (Uhl et al. 2001). More recent evidence suggests that genetic variants in the *ADH1A, ADH1B, ADH1C, ADH5, ADH6,* and *ADH7* genes are associated with illicit drug dependence and that this association is not purely attributable to co-morbid alcohol dependence (Luo et al. 2007). The mechanism by which these genes may affect risk for illicit drug dependence is not entirely clear. However, other observations[4] also indicate that enzymes involved in alcohol metabolism may contribute to illicit drug dependence via pathways that currently are unknown but independent of alcohol metabolism (Luo et al. 2007).

Genes Encoding Proteins Involved in Neurotransmission

AODs exert their behavioral effects in part by altering the transmission of signals among nerve cells (i.e., neurons) in the brain. This transmission is mediated by chemical messengers (i.e., neurotransmitters) that are released by the signal-emitting neuron and bind to specific proteins (i.e., receptors) on the signal-receiving neuron. AODs influence the activities of several neurotransmitter systems, including those involving the neurotransmitters γ-aminobutyric acid (GABA), dopamine, and acetylcholine, as well as naturally produced compounds that structurally resemble opioids and cannabinoids. Accordingly, certain genes encoding components of these neurotransmitter systems may contribute to the risk of both alcohol dependence and illicit drug dependence.

Genes Encoding the GABA$_A$ Receptor

GABA is the major inhibitory neurotransmitter in the human central nervous system—that is, it affects neurons in a way that reduces their activity. Several lines of evidence suggest that GABA is involved in many of the behavioral effects of alcohol, including motor incoordination, anxiety reduction (i.e., anxiolysis), sedation, withdrawal signs, and preference for alcohol (Grobin et al. 1998). GABA interacts with several receptors, and much of the research on alcohol's interactions with the GABA system has focused on the GABA$_A$ receptor. This receptor also is the site of action for several medications that frequently are misused and have high addictive potential, such as benzodiazepines, barbiturates, opiates, α-hydroxybutyrates, and other sedative–hypnotic compounds. Accordingly, this receptor likely is involved in dependence on these drugs as well (Orser 2006).

The GABA$_A$ receptor is composed of five subunits that are encoded by numerous genes, most of which are located in clusters. Thus, chromosome 4 contains a cluster comprising the genes *GABRA2, GABRA4, GABRB1,* and *GABRG1;* chromosome 5 contains *GABRA1, GABRA6, GABRB2,* and *GABRG2;* and chromosome 15 contains *GABRA5, GABRB3,* and *GABRG3* (see www.ncbi.nlm.nih.gov/sites/entrez?db=gene).

Interest in the GABA$_A$ receptor genes on chromosome 4 grew when this region consistently was identified in genome-wide scans looking for linkage with alcohol dependence (Long et al. 1998; Williams et al. 1999). Subsequently, COGA investigators systematically evaluated short DNA segments of known location (i.e., genetic markers) that were situated in the GABA$_A$ receptor gene cluster on chromosome 4. These studies found that a significant association existed between multiple SNPs in the *GABRA2* gene and alcohol dependence (Edenberg et al. 2004). This association has been replicated in multiple independent samples (Covault et al. 2004; Fehr et al. 2006; Lappalainen et al. 2005; Soyka 2007). In addition, the same SNPs in the *GABRA2* gene have been shown to be associated with drug dependence in both adults and adolescents (Dick et al. 2006*a*), as well as with the use of multiple drugs in another independent sample (Drgon et al. 2006).

Variations in the *GABRA2* gene are associated not only with AOD dependence but also with certain electrophysiological characteristics (i.e., endophenotypes) in the COGA sample (Edenberg et al. 2004). As reviewed above, these electrophysiological characteristics are not unique to alcohol dependence but also are found in individuals with other forms of externalizing psychopathology. This association supports the hypothesis that the *GABRA2* gene generally is involved in AOD use and/or externalizing problems. Interestingly, subsequent analyses investigating the role of *GABRA2* in drug dependence (Agrawal et al. 2006) found that the association with *GABRA2* was strongest in people with co-morbid AOD dependence, with no evidence of association in people who were only alcohol dependent. This observation supports the assertion that co-morbid AOD dependence may represent a more severe, genetically influenced form of the disorder.

Several other GABA$_A$ receptor genes have yielded more modest evidence of association with different aspects of AOD dependence. Thus, *GABRB3* (Noble et al. 1998) and *GABRG3* (Dick et al. 2004) are modestly associated with alcohol dependence, *GABRA1* (Dick et al. 2006*b*) is associated with alcohol-related phenotypes (e.g., history of alcohol-induced blackouts and age at first drunkenness), and *GABRG2* (Loh et al. 2007) is associated with aspects of drug dependence. These findings await confirmation in independent samples.

Genes Involved in the Cholinergic System

The cholinergic system includes neurons that either release the neurotransmitter acetylcholine or respond to it. Acetylcholine generally has excitatory effects in the human central nervous system—that is, it affects neurons in a way that enhances their activity. It is thought to be involved in such processes as arousal, reward, learning, and short-term memory. One of the receptors through which acetylcholine acts is encoded by a gene called *CHRM2*. In the COGA sample, linkage was observed between a region on chromosome 7 that contains the *CHRM2* gene and alcohol dependence, and subsequent experiments confirmed that an association existed between alcohol dependence and the *CHRM2* gene (Wang et al. 2004). This association has been replicated in a large independent study (Luo et al. 2005) that also found evidence that the gene was associated with drug dependence.

As with the *GABRA2* gene described above, the association between *CHRM2* and alcohol dependence in the COGA sample was strongest in people who had co-morbid AOD dependence (Dick et al. 2007). Additional analyses in the COGA sample have suggested that *CHRM2* is associated with a generally increased risk of externalizing disorders, including symptoms of alcohol dependence and drug dependence (Dick et al. 2008). This potential role of *CHRM2* in contributing to the general liability of AOD use and externalizing disorders is further supported by findings that *CHRM2,* like *GABRA2,* also is associated with certain electrophysiological endophenotypes (Jones et al. 2004).

Genes Involved in the Endogenous Opioid System

Endogenous opioids are small molecules naturally produced in the body that have similar effects as the opiates (e.g., morphine and heroin) and which, among other functions, modulate the actions of other neurotransmitters. The endogenous opioid system has been implicated in contributing to the reinforcing effects of several drugs of abuse, including alcohol, opiates, and cocaine. This is supported by the finding that the medication naltrexone, which prevents the normal actions of endogenous opioids (i.e., is an opioid antagonist), is useful in the treatment of alcohol dependence and can reduce the number of drinking days, amount of alcohol consumed, and risk of relapse.

Research on the role of the endogenous opioids in AOD dependence has centered mainly on a gene called *OPRM1*, which encodes one type of opioid receptor (i.e., the μ-opioid receptor), although the results so far have been equivocal. This gene contains a polymorphism resulting in a different protein product (i.e., a non-synonymous polymorphism) that in one study was found to bind one of the endogenous opioids (i.e., β-endorphin) three times as strongly as the main variant of the gene (Bond et al. 1998); other studies, however, could not confirm this finding (Befort et al. 2001; Beyer et al. 2004).

Laboratory studies have suggested that *OPRM1* is associated with sensitivity to the effects of alcohol (Ray and Hutchison 2004). In addition, several studies have reported evidence of an association between *OPRM1* and drug dependence (e.g., Bart et al. 2005). Other studies, however, have failed to find such an association (e.g., Bergen et al. 1997), and a combined analysis of several studies (i.e., a meta-analysis) concluded that no association exists between the most commonly studied *OPRM1* polymorphism and drug dependence (Arias et al. 2006). However, this finding does not preclude the possibility that other genetic variants in *OPRM1* and/or other genes related to the endogenous opioid system are involved in risk for drug dependence. For example, a recent study determining the genotypes of multiple genetic variants across the gene uncovered evidence of association with *OPRM1* and AOD dependence (Zhang et al. 2006).

Researchers also have investigated genetic variations in other opioid receptors and other components of the endogenous opioid system; however, the results have been mixed. One study

(Zhang et al. 2007) found modest support that the genes *OPRK1* and *OPRD1*—which encode the κ- and δ-opioid receptors, respectively—are associated with some aspects of drug dependence. Other researchers (Xuei et al. 2007) reported evidence that the genes *PDYN, PENK,* and *POMC*—which encode small molecules (i.e., peptides) that also bind to opioid receptors—may be associated with various aspects of drug dependence.

Genes Involved in the Endogenous Cannabinoid System

Endogenous cannabinoids are compounds naturally produced in the body that have a similar structure to the psychoactive compounds found in the cannabis plant and which bind cannabinoid receptors. The endogenous cannabinoid system is thought to regulate brain circuits using the neurotransmitter dopamine, which likely helps mediate the rewarding experiences associated with addictive substances. The main cannabinoid receptor in the brain is called CB1 and is encoded by the *CNR1* gene, which is located on chromosome 6. This gene is an excellent candidate gene for being associated with AOD dependence because the receptor encoded by this gene is crucial for generating the rewarding effects of the compound responsible for the psychoactive effects associated with cannabis use (i.e., Δ9-tetrahydrocannabinol). However, the findings regarding the association between *CNR1* and AOD dependence to date have been equivocal, with some studies producing positive results (e.g., Zhang et al. 2004) and others producing negative results (e.g., Herman et al. 2006). Most recently, Hopfer and colleagues (2006) found that a SNP in the *CNR1* gene was associated with cannabis dependence symptoms. Moreover, this SNP was part of several sets of multiple alleles that are transmitted jointly (i.e., haplotypes), some of which are associated with developing fewer dependence symptoms, whereas others are associated with an increased risk for cannabis dependence. Finally, a recent case–control study found that multiple genetic variants in *CNR1* were significantly associated with alcohol dependence and/or drug dependence (Zuo et al. 2007).

Conclusions

For both alcohol dependence and drug dependence, considerable evidence suggests that genetic factors influence the risk of these disorders, with heritability estimates of 50 percent and higher. Moreover, twin studies and studies of electrophysiological characteristics indicate that the risk of developing AOD dependence, as well as other disinhibitory disorders (e.g., antisocial behavior), is determined at least in part by shared genetic factors. These observations suggest that some of a person's liability for AOD dependence will result from a general externalizing factor and some will result from genetic factors that are more disorder specific.

Several genes have been identified that confer risk to AOD dependence. Some of these genes—such as *GABRA2* and *CHRM2*—apparently act through a general externalizing phenotype. For other genes that appear to confer risk of AOD dependence—such as genes involved in alcohol metabolism and in the endogenous opioid and cannabinoid systems—however, the pathways through which they affect risk remain to be elucidated. Most of the genes reviewed in this article originally were found to be associated with alcohol dependence and only subsequently was their association with risk for dependence on other illicit drugs discovered as well. Furthermore, studies that primarily aim to identify genes involved in dependence on certain types of drugs may identify different variants affecting risk, underscoring the challenge of understanding genetic susceptibility to different classes of drugs.

This review does not exhaustively cover all genes that to date have been implicated in alcohol and illicit drug dependence. For example, several genes encoding receptors for the neurotransmitter dopamine have been suggested to determine at least in part a person's susceptibility to various forms of drug dependence. In particular, the *DRD2* gene has been associated with alcohol dependence (Blum et al. 1990) and, more broadly, with various forms of addiction (Blum et al. 1996). This association remains controversial, however, and more recent studies suggest that the observed association actually may not involve variants in the *DRD2* gene but variants in a neighboring gene called *ANKK1* (Dick et al. 2007*b*). Studies to identify candidate genes that influence dependence on illicit drugs, but not on alcohol, are particularly challenging because of the high co-morbidity between alcohol dependence and dependence on illicit drugs. Therefore, meaningful studies require large sample sizes to include enough drug-dependent people with no prior history of alcohol dependence.

The increasingly rapid pace of genetic discovery also has resulted in the identification of several genes encoding other types of proteins that appear to be associated with alcohol use and/or dependence. These include, for example, two genes encoding taste receptors (i.e., the *TAS2R16* gene [Hinrichs et al. 2006] and the *TAS2R38* gene [Wang et al. 2007]) and a human gene labeled *ZNF699* (Riley et al. 2006) that is related to a gene previously identified in the fruit fly *Drosophila* as contributing to the development of tolerance to alcohol in the flies. Future research will be necessary to elucidate the pathways by which these genes influence alcohol dependence and/or whether they are more broadly involved in other forms of drug dependence.

Notes

1. Abnormalities in the P3 response also have been associated with risk for other psychiatric disorders, such as schizophrenia (van der Stelt et al. 2004).

2. The International HapMap Project is a multicountry effort to identify and catalog genetic similarities and differences in human beings by comparing the genetic sequences of different individuals in order to identify chromosomal regions where genetic variants are shared. Using the information obtained in the HapMap Project, researchers will be able to find genes that affect health, disease, and individual responses to medications and environmental factors.

3. Rapid acetaldehyde production can lead to acetaldehyde accumulation in the body, which results in highly unpleasant effects, such as nausea, flushing, and rapid heartbeat, that may deter people from drinking more alcohol.

4. For example, the medication disulfiram, which inhibits another enzyme involved in alcohol metabolism called aldehyde dehydrogenase 2 (ALDH2) and is used for treatment of alcoholism, has demonstrated a treatment effect in cocaine dependence (Luo et al. 2007).

5. The SNP was not located in one of those gene regions that encode the actual receptor (i.e., in an exon) but in a region that is part of the gene but is eliminated during the process of converting the genetic information into a protein product (i.e., in an intron).

Critical Thinking

1. Why are electrophysiological abnormalities most pronounced in alcohol-dependent people who also have a diagnosis of illicit drug abuse or dependence?

2. What are risk factors for cannabis dependence? Explain.

DANIELLE M. DICK, PhD, is an assistant professor of psychiatry, psychology, and human genetics at the Virginia Institute for Psychiatric and Behavioral Genetics, Virginia Commonwealth University, Richmond, Virginia. **ARPANA AGRAWAL,** PhD, is a research assistant professor in the Department of Psychiatry, Washington University, St. Louis, Missouri.

Acknowledgments—Danielle M. Dick is supported by NIAAA grant AA–15416 and Arpana Agrawal is supported by National Institute on Drug Abuse (NIDA) grant DA–023668. The COGA project is supported by grant U10–AA–08401 from NIAAA and NIDA.

Understanding Recreational Ecstasy Use in the United States: A Qualitative Inquiry

Masuma Bahora, Claire E. Sterk, and Kirk W. Elifson

Introduction

Ecstasy and its users began receiving media attention in the United States in the mid-1990s. During the 1970s and 1980s it was used in some psychotherapy as a means to assist people to cope with past traumatic past experiences (Beck & Rosenbaum, 1994; Millman & Beeder, 1994). The increase in the use of ecstasy among young adults in the 1990s triggered attention and a renewed interest among policymakers, service providers, researchers, and the general public (Beck & Rosenbaum, 1994). By the year 2003, in the United States ecstasy became a Schedule I drug under the Controlled Substance Act (Drug Enforcement Administration, 2003).

During the 1980s, at least a decade earlier than in the United States, ecstasy use already was being noticed in other parts of the world, most notably in the United Kingdom and in Australia. Its use frequently was associated with raves (Diemel & Blanken, 1999; Forsyth, Barnard, & McKeganey, 1997; Hammersley, Ditton, Smith, & Short, 1999; Hammersley, Khan, & Ditton, 2002; Hitzler, 2002; Measham, Parker, & Aldridge, 1998; Schwartz & Miller, 1997; Riley, Gregory, Dingle, & Cadger, 2001; Spruit, 1999). In the 1990s, the rave rage blew over to North America (Gross, Barrett, Shestowsky, & Pihl, 2002; Sloan, 2000). Ravers (those attending raves) tended to be young and white, and predominantly from a middle class background in the United States (Johnston, O'Malley, & Bachman, 2001). Subsequent studies among ecstasy users revealed an increased representation of non-white and non-middle class individuals. For example, this trend was reported in the United Kingdom (Measham et al., 1998), the Netherlands (Spruit, 1999), and the United States (Boeri, Sterk, & Elifson, 2004).

To date, ecstasy remains easily available on the drug market in the United States (Byrnes, 2003; Chang, 2001; Schensul, Diamond, Disch, Bermudez, & Eiserman, 2005), which may explain the spread of its use into wider groups and more diverse settings (Boeri, Sterk, & Elifson, 2004; Eiserman, Diamond, & Schensul, 2005). Increasingly, U.S. studies conducted by social science and public health researchers began focusing on the potential negative consequences of ecstasy use, including inquiries with a focus on the need for effective prevention and health education about ecstasy (Baggott, 2002; Carlson et al., 2004; Dew, Elifson, & Sterk, 2006; Gamma, Jerome, Liechti, & Sumnall, 2005; McElrath & McEvoy, 2002; Reid, Elifson, & Sterk, 2007; Riley & Hayward, 2004; Scholey et al., 2004; Theall, Elifson, & Sterk, 2006). Findings from these and other studies reveal that ecstasy is typically viewed as a relatively safe drug with minimal health consequences. In terms of its social consequences, the main risk was being detected as using an illegal substance and subsequent criminal justice involvement. Among those users who did express some awareness or concerns of health risks associated with ecstasy use, their positive use experiences tended to overwrite their worries (Boys et al., 2000; Gamma et al., 2005; Hansen, Maycock, & Lower, 2001; Lenton, Boys, & Norcross, 1997; Shewan, Dalgarno, & Reith, 2000; Topp, Hando, Dillon, Roche, & Solowij, 1999). Ecstasy, despite its illegal nature, was viewed as a substance that did not interfere with leading a normal life in mainstream society. Parker and his colleagues introduced the notion of a possible "normalisation" of ecstasy and other club drugs in the United Kingdom, especially among recreational users (Measham, Newcombe, & Parker, 1994; Parker, 2005; Parker, Williams, & Aldridge, 2002). They defined recreational use as "the occasional use of certain substances in certain settings and in a controlled way" (Parker, 2005, p. 206) with a recognition of such use as "perceived and sometimes tolerated as an embedded social practice" (Duff, 2005, p. 162). The normalisation of club drugs was supported by the reality that young British drug users included "well-adjusted and successful goal-oriented, non-risk taking young persons who see drug taking as part of their repertoire of life" (Parker, 1997, p. 25). Parker and colleagues distinguished five dimensions of normalisation, including access/availability, drug-trying rates, rates of recent/regular drug use, social accommodation of sensible recreational drug use, and cultural acceptance. In this paper, we explore the insider's perspective that of active young adult ecstasy users, on recreational ecstasy use. Their views largely have been ignored in the literature. In addition, we explore their views on the access and availability of ecstasy and the extent to which social circumstances accommodate its use.

Methods
Study Procedures

The data presented in this paper are part of a larger project, Project X, an investigation of the ecstasy scene in Atlanta, Georgia. Between September 2002 and October 2007, we conducted 112 face-to-face open-ended interviews with young adult ecstasy users. During that period, we also tracked possible changes in the local ecstasy scene. The only major shift we noted was an expansion of its use at raves, which made it more widely available. As is common in qualitative studies, we have a convenience sample. Our initial recruitment was based on information from our own previous research, that of other local drug researchers and information from local social and health service providers. Using ethnographic mapping we identified additional locations for recruitment (Boeri et al., 2004; Sterk, Theall, & Elifson, 2006, 2007). We employed targeted sampling (Watters & Biernacki, 1989) and theoretical sampling (Glaser & Strauss, 1967; Strauss & Corbin, 1998).

A team of ethnographers and interviewers, including three white, one African American and one Asian American woman and two African-American and one Hispanic men conducted the recruitment and interviewing. Potential participants were screened in or near the setting where they were recruited such as at coffee shops, bars, clubs, parks, college dorms and off-campus student housing. Passive recruitment, involving the posting of flyers in local music venues and areas with greater concentrations of young adults, was also utilised. Individuals who called the project phone line listed on the flyers were screened over the phone using the same short form recruiters presented. The screening consisted of a number of socio-demographic questions and questions about past and current drug use.

To be eligible for participation in Project X, the participants had to be between 18 and 25 years and be an active ecstasy user, which was defined as having used ecstasy at least four times in the past 90 days prior to the interview. Exclusion criteria included being in drug treatment or any other institutional setting, being unable to conduct the interview in English, and being intoxicated at the time of the interview.

Once a potential respondent was identified as meeting the study's criteria, interviews were scheduled for interested individuals. The interviews were held at mutually agreed upon central locations and included such venues as the project offices, the participant's home, a local restaurant or cafeteria, coffee shop, community centres, and the interviewer's car. The consent procedures, approved by both Georgia State University's and Emory University's Institutional Review Boards, were reviewed and signed prior to the collection of any data. The average length of time to complete the interview was 90 min, with a range from one to 2.5 h. The study participants received US$ 15 (US dollars) compensation for their time.

The in-depth interviews were organised around an interview guide that listed topics derived from the literature and our own past research. Among these topics were initial and continued ecstasy use, use patterns, types of users, the impact of set and setting, ecstasy market characteristics, and perceived social and health consequences. No direct questions were asked about defining recreational use or normalisation. The topics listed on the interview guide were not addressed in a specific order for all participants. Instead, the participants were allowed to guide the flow of the interview. If a topic did not naturally emerge, the interviewer would probe. Demographic information was collected using a close-ended format questionnaire.

Data Analysis

The qualitative data analysis was guided by a modified grounded theory approach (Charmaz, 1983; Glaser & Strauss, 1967; Sterk, Theall, & Elifson, 2000; Strauss & Corbin, 1998). The open-ended interviews were transcribed and the text imported into the qualitative analysis software MAXqda2. The interview transcripts were read and summary memos written, followed by a next reading during which first-level (open) codes were assigned. Inter-coder reliability was established by using multiple coders for the same transcript. The codes were then clustered into categories and descriptive and axial coding notes were included, explaining the decision-making processes followed by the team. Inductive and deductive questioning occurred throughout this process to identify similarities and differences in the data. Subsequently, the categories were clustered into themes allowing more abstraction and checking of negative cases. The salient themes that emerged in the context of the focus of this paper centered on recreational ecstasy use and normalisation.

Results
Sample Characteristics

Among the 112 study participants a majority were male (68 percent), white (54 percent), educated at least at the high school level (63 percent), and self-identified as middle class or higher (64 percent). Their median age was 20.7 years, with the youngest person being 18 and the oldest 25. When asked about their relationship status, approximately two-fifths (44 percent) indicated that they were not involved in a steady relationship. Almost one-half (49 percent) of the study participants lived independently, either by renting or by owning a residence.

When asked about their age of first ecstasy use, the median was 17 years. The oldest person was 24 when first trying ecstasy and the youngest was 11. Overall, the study participants had been using ecstasy for a median of 2.6 years, with the longest time of ecstasy use being 11 years and the shorted less than 1 year but at least 3 months. In terms of their use during the past 90 days prior to the interview, the median was 9 days. Four was the fewest number of days of use, which was the minimum requirement for enrollment. One study participant reported almost daily use (88 days) and this person was an outlier. Close to three-fourths (73.8 percent) of the study participants had friends who also used ecstasy. Poly drug use was common (Boeri, Sterk, Bahora, & Elifson, in press).

Recreational Ecstasy Use

When we asked the respondents to elaborate on their drug use trajectories, many indicated that they viewed the use of ecstasy as a recreational activity. They did not associate its use with symptoms of withdrawal or craving or serious negative health and social effects. When exploring dimensions of recreational use, we learned that it was less about the frequency of use or the length of time a person had been using ecstasy. Instead, the recreational nature of ecstasy use was largely captured by a user's ability to take the drug without interference with their everyday functioning in mainstream society. Good grades, employment, and healthy relationships were cited as examples of evidence. A 19-year-old white female explained:

> I do a lot of drugs, but I function well. I do well in school; I have healthy relationships. Most of the people that I'm around . . . they make good grades, they're good workers. They can keep jobs . . . they get along with their parents. If you just kind of keep it [ecstasy use] under control, then you can still just live your life normally.

Several study participants explained the unique nature of ecstasy, thereby highlighting that its high as well as its coming down were smooth. Consequently, they experienced less of an immediate desire for a next high, which in turn prevented binging. Instead, some reported taking a booster dose as a means to prolong the high. Ecstasy was described as a drug with some built-in control mechanism. However, some action on the part of the user remained necessary; for example, by only using ecstasy in certain settings or with certain people. A 19-year-old white college student discussed his approach to delineate his daily activities from his ecstasy use.

> I don't go out to get blazed every day of the week or get so screwed up on ecstasy everyday of the week that [I] don't know what's going on . . . I keep myself, for the majority, sober during the week . . . Any day that the world kind of slows down is a day that I can take to myself and have a good time for me. But as long as the world's, you know, moving about its business during the week, I want to make sure I can still be there too. I don't want to get to the point where I'm . . . so screwed up that I'm behind everybody else.

Others explained that by using ecstasy at set-aside times, such as weekend, holidays, or special occasions, contributed to it remaining enjoyable. They were unsupportive of an ecstasy habit that involved daily use. Among them were those who preferred no or limited use during the week or when working. They explained that the weekend and other times off from school or work were most carefree, therefore the best for an enjoyable ecstasy high. A 20-year-old female, who frequently used with her boyfriend, remarked:

> I go to school at night and I work in the mornings . . . he goes to work at night and he goes to school in the day. So it's kind of weird, like . . . that's kind of why we do it on special occasions like Fridays or like, Saturdays. Because we really, like, are so busy during the week [and] we just, basically, have our own time on the weekends.

Those who did report daily ecstasy use in the past 90 days tended to be a minority. In addition, they often also used other drugs such as heroin, cocaine or methamphetamine. Ecstasy was a drug they added to an already established drug repertoire. Compared with the effects, including the coming down and longing for the other drugs, ecstasy was perceived as harmless which in turn was associated with recreational.

The study participants referred to ecstasy as a means to relax and unwind independent of their frequency of use. A 19-year-old student athlete discussed this as follows:

> . . . if I want to get crazy pretty much ecstasy is one of my only options . . . I mean I'm not that crazy of a person. I don't have, like, a record or anything. But its [ecstasy's] something that I like to take. It's still enjoyable to me . . . It's something that I can take off my shoes and relax and enjoy others' company and have a good time.

One of the unique features mentioned by almost all study participants was that one of the effects of ecstasy use was an ability to easily connect to others. Some added it that it allowed them to be more open and less shy or withdrawn. Those who tended to use alone were an exception. Their reflections revealed that ecstasy allowed them to relax and be in touch with themselves. A number of them also indicated that ecstasy served as a form of self-medication similar to the prescribed medications they had for diagnosed mental health problems. One woman began using ecstasy immediately after having had a miscarriage and she continued to use it when feeling down because it helped her so well that first time.

Some study participants expressed concerns about persons who used ecstasy alone, commenting that solitary use was 'depressing' and a sign of a problematic and unregulated habit. A main component of the recreational use in the company of friends as that they would keep "each other in check." Some referred to ecstasy as solidifying their friendship. A 21-year-old white male explained:

> . . . it's different when you're with people you know because . . . like rolling with a group of your friends already enhances that friendship so much. Because you've got those memories of what was, you know, until you roll the next time, the happiest moment in your life and you're with these people . . . So it really, really strengthens the bond you have with your friends to roll with them. You've got a lot of memories there.

A young female elaborated on this thought comparing her ecstasy-using friends to family. She also explained that the connection established between friends while using ecstasy remained long after the high was over.

I think that relationship[s] you create with people around ecstasy are very, very influential or significant because it is so emotional. And I think it's hard to let go of people that you've met . . . because there's so much emotional background between two people when you share an experience on ecstasy.

Ecstasy Use and Mainstream Lives: Normalisation

As ecstasy use extended beyond raves and ravers, it became more widely available. According to a number of study participants, the increased availability or wider access allowed them to obtain the drug from a person they knew. In addition, we learned that the expansion of settings and the diversification of ecstasy users were viewed by many as a sign of normalisation. They explained that it made it more difficult to pinpoint or stereotype ecstasy users.

Availability and Accessibility of Ecstasy

None of the study participants indicated experiencing trouble obtaining ecstasy. The task of obtaining ecstasy was described as "effortless" or "like buying a bag of potato chips." Few worried about being detected as engaged in an illegal behavior when procuring ecstasy. Some declared it easier than being an under-aged person buying alcohol. The reality appeared to be that someone in the network of friends had ecstasy or that the group easily could get it through a dealer. Those dealers, whose market mainly was limited to raves in the early days, now could be found at local clubs or bars or at their private residence. One young male user described his experiences at a local club:

. . . there's always three of four people that as soon as I walk in I'm, like, alright, and I just walk around the outside of, like, around the inside of the club. And I always find it. It's easy. Fifteen minutes and [if] you can't find pills at the Globe, there's a problem. You're not looking.

A common theme among the study participants was the emerging popularity of ecstasy and the inability to "pigeonhole [ecstasy] into one specific demographic or another." A 24-year-old African-American male comments on this shift:

Well for one—more and more people are knowing about ecstasy because it's more common now, you know. And now since like everybody is doing it . . . it's kind of like almost getting like marijuana . . . cause so many have accepted it . . . Cause before it was kind of like, you know, I don't want to be stereotypical but it's like . . . you know only white people do this drug. I don't know if it was cause maybe they heard about it first, or maybe it happened in a certain, you know, area first and then it finally got around to this community or that community . . . but next thing you know, you're like in the club [and] everybody doing it.

This user, like others, held the view that the more aware individuals became about ecstasy, the more commonplace its use became in different contexts.

Social Accommodation of Recreational Ecstasy Use

The belief that ecstasy was analogous to other known substances perceived as harmless contributed to the reduced risk that the study participants associated with ecstasy use. Those who differentiated between soft and hard drugs, frequently placed ecstasy in the 'soft drug' category, alongside cigarettes, cannabis, alcohol, and LSD. A 21-year-old African American male explained why he ranked ecstasy directly above cannabis in relative harm, but beneath LSD, speed, crack, heroin, and cocaine:

Everybody takes ecstasy . . . and I haven't seen anyone die, fall out or whatever. So it's just like marijuana. It hit the scene and it ain't killing people so.

The majority of participants also asserted that it was nearly impossible to become addicted to or dependent on ecstasy. Typically, they based this belief on their own experiences as well as those experiences of their peers. Further justification was provided by the lack of experiencing withdrawal symptoms or craving. A substantial number of the study participants moreover believed that their ability to "take it or leave it" at will was indicative of ecstasy's inability to be addictive. A 21-year-old male explained, "I know that for me to survive every day I don't have to do ecstasy. . .because it's a choice. I want to do it. Not because I feel like I have to do it." Other study participants, as a result of their experimentation with other drugs, came to the same conclusion about ecstasy's addictiveness. Referencing her experiences of addiction with methamphetamine, this 21-year-old said:

I don't think it's addictive because I feel like I've experienced addiction with meth and that's a different kind of thing. It just kind of stops you from doing the things you want to do . . . Like with ecstasy when you come down, you're like, 'Wow that was really fun, that was really special, I'd like to do that again.' And when you come off of speed you're like, 'Yo, we need to get more high, we need to go buy anther bag.' so it's kind of debilitating and I don't think ecstasy really does you like that.

Few study participants considered ecstasy to be an addictive substance, indicating that it might create some mental dependence. Nevertheless, they went on to explain that ecstasy itself had limited addictive properties but that a person with limited willpower maybe could develop a habit.

Perception of Risk Regarding Recreational Ecstasy Use

When reflecting upon possible negative effects of ecstasy, some study participants recalled having heard or read about some long-term side effects associated with extended ecstasy use. However, none of them knew a person who had experienced dramatic or abnormal side effects. Negative reports were regarded skeptically and categorised as hearsay. A 20-year-old female who had been using ecstasy for approximately 2 years, replied:

I've watched, like, Dateline, not too long ago. And it they said—people really don't know, you know, like, really about it and never study, like, the long—term effects on it. Like, as far as, deaths, I never knew anybody who died of ecstasy. Or, you know, like OD'd, I never knew anybody like that. I heard of a girl . . . she didn't know that she was even taking it. So she was freaking out . . . that's the only thing. That's the only one, you know, the only person that I heard of, like, freaking out. Other than that, the people I do it with and other people I have done it with over the years and it's like, no, they haven't told me of had any bad effects. As far as, like, I haven't heard, they haven't told me anything.

This respondent, like many others, was cautious to embrace the validity of circulating information on ecstasy, relying on personal accounts of consequences. A doubtful 20-year-old female explained "I am starting to hear more about the news about ecstasy and the effect that is has on people. And then I am starting to see my friends . . . and its not happening to them, but it is happening to the people on the news." Having sought a variety of sources including internet chat rooms, telecast reports, and print media, users frequently referenced the ambiguity in reports on effects of ecstasy, confirming their general distrust of the media. Whether commenting that 'people don't really know about it' or that researchers had not studied long-term effects of the drug, they concluded that available knowledge was inconclusive at best. A 24-year-old male discussed his suspicion of the information about ecstasy's effect on the body, presented on television:

> . . . supposedly it like puts holes in your brain and does something to your spinal cord and stuff . . . I mean, I watch like a lot of Dateline, and you know they did something on Oprah about it. Or like in the paper, you know, they're always trying to do something to scare, you know? They're trying to show stuff to scare you to leave it alone.

The majority of study participants perceived any experienced negative side effects of ecstasy use to be minor and of little concern. Their main worry tended to be the potential of dehydration. This, however, was easily addressed by assuring the sufficient intake of fluids. Others described having experienced a temporary loss of perfect vision or hearing but, at the same time explained that this was because they truly become "emerged in the high." Few study participants who began using in the raves days mentioned that ecstasy has become "safer," noting that they have not heard recently of ecstasy being cut with heroin. Overall, little distinction was made between possible short or long-term effects of ecstasy use. In general the notion seemed to be that any short-term negative effects were minimal and that long-term effects were a public health scare tactic to keep people away from the drug. The general consensus appeared to be that any negative effects were overwritten by positive use experiences.

Discussion

The aim of this paper is to examine the meaning and culture of recreational ecstasy use among a sample of young ecstasy users in Atlanta, Georgia. In doing so, we sought to explore findings in the context of the 'normalisation' thesis, focusing on the social and contextual factors, as well as the influence of knowledge about possible consequences of ecstasy use, that contribute to users' perceptions of risk. This study gives further evidence to studies noting that the meaning of recreational drug use, namely ecstasy use, for adolescents and young adults has and is changing. In exploring how this process of normalisation is constructed in the lives of young adults, we hope to further consider the implication these data have on current treatment and policy models.

The majority of study participants viewed themselves as recreational ecstasy users, identifying their ability to maintain their daily activities, and function in mainstream society (Beck & Rosenbaum, 1994; Solowij, Hall, & Lee, 1992). By prioritising their responsibilities including employment, education, and family relationships, participants appeared to frame their consumption of ecstasy around these activities and believed their drug use to be another activity that fit into their leisure or recreational time. Accordingly, they did not identify with drug users who are often typified as reckless, irresponsible, or unable to negotiate their existence in mainstream society (Shildrick, 2002; Shiner & Newburn, 1997). Instead, participants' experiences were mirrored in the literature focusing on ecstasy, demonstrating its users to be conscientious and controlled in their patterns of use (Baggott, 2002; Gamble & George, 1997; Hansen et al., 2001; Panagopolous & Ricciardelli, 2005; van de Wijngaart et al., 1999). These findings present an overall cohesive picture of purposeful and conscientious consumption of ecstasy among young adults, providing corroborating evidence to studies proposing the emergence of a new type of drug user who is 'well-adjusted, responsible, and outgoing adolescent or young adult who uses drugs recreationally, very deliberately, and very strategically' (Duff, 2005; Parker, 1997, p. 25). In this study, we suggest that users' generally minimal level of concern appeared to stem partly from their perceptions of ecstasy's prevalence in their immediate and larger social networks, as well as easy accessibility, confirming aspects of Parker's normalisation thesis (Parker, 2005). Their repeated exposure and contact with individuals who used ecstasy served, in essence, to accommodate ecstasy's recreational use, and desensitise participants to the possibilities of ecstasy's negative consequences. Given the social nature of ecstasy consumption, further research needs to clarify the role peer networks can play in intervention and recovery services. Contributing to users' perception of ecstasy's risk was their mistrust of a great deal of mass media's messages about ecstasy's adverse effects, a trend that is confirmed in available literature (Eiserman et al., 2005; McElrath & McEvoy, 2002). Participants believed ecstasy unlikely to cause such long-term effects as brain damage or death, despite research linking ecstasy to hyperthermia, dehydration, depression, and impaired cognitive functioning (Hegadoren, Baker, & Bourin, 1999; Parrott, 2002; Parrott, Sisk, & Turner, 2000). Of information that was widely circulated, study participants categorised these accounts as rumors, thereby disparaging their credibility and accuracy. Given these findings, it is unsurprising that these young ecstasy users remained undeterred in their substance-using pattern, and believed ecstasy to be generally safe.

It can be argued that in a 'normalised drug culture', the actual risk of harm increases due to the presence of ill-informed, inexperienced users who are not able to easily access the knowledge informally held within a more entrenched illicit drug culture (Baxter, Bacon, Houseman, & Van Beek, 1994; Henderson, 1993; Masterson, 1993; Merchant & MacDonald, 1994). This research, combined with our own findings, alludes to the saliency of providing accurate and detailed information, specifically addressing acute adverse risks but also strategies to reduce negative experiences and moderate harmful patterns of drug use. By placing emphasis on a user's self-awareness in the myriad of settings of their consumption patterns, we provide tools to young adults weighing benefits against potential dangers (Parker & Egginton, 2002).

The limitations of this study need to be acknowledged. First, though this sample may be representative of young adult ecstasy users in the Atlanta area, we are unable to generalise our findings to wider populations in other cities and countries. The specific impact of drug legislation and law enforcement, as well as trends in drug availability may vary significantly across localities. Second, the cross-sectional design of this study limited our ability to draw causal conclusions between participants' beliefs and attitudes regarding ecstasy use and their changes in behavior, as well as perceptions of availability and risk. Finally, it is important to note that findings from this study are based upon self-reported data, which may be subject to recall and social desirability bias. Although a 90-day time frame was used to minimise recall bias, participants may have altered responses in attempts to create rapport with interviewers or out of fear in reporting illegal activities.

Despite these limitations, findings from the current study as well as previous work point to the need of re-examining current drug-intervention and education models and the theories that drive these policies for young adults. These policies should strive to consider accounts of youth and young adults' drug using experiences and the culture that encompasses it. With only their input can prevention and intervention strategies be better informed and equipped to reduce the harms associated with their drug use. Further, considering that in some cases users were not only aware of the risk involved in taking ecstasy, but also willing to forego the risk to participate in the drug-using behavior, services designed for young adults and adolescents, alike, should consider the willingness of these youth to accept such risks. In criminalising their drug using behaviors, and concentrating efforts on cessation, we neglect to engage a vast number of young ecstasy users who perceive their behavior as sensible, safe, and acceptable.

Acknowledgments

This research was supported by NIDA grant R01 DA014232 and the Emory Center for AIDS Research. The views presented in this paper are those of the authors and do not represent those of the funding agencies. The authors thank Johanna Boers and Miriam Boeri for their contributions to the research and the participants who made this study possible.

References

Baggott, M. J. (2002). Preventing problems in ecstasy users; reduce use to reduce harm. *Journal of Psychoactive Drugs, 34*(2), 145–162.

Baxter, T., Bacon, P., Houseman, M., & Van Beek, I. (1994). Targeting psychostimulant drug users—the rave safe project. *Paper presented at the 1994 Autumn School of Studies on Alcohol and Drugs.* Melbourne, St. Vincents Hospital.

Beck, J., & Rosenbaum, M. (1994). *Pursuit of ecstasy: The MDMA experience.* Albany, NY: State University of New York Press.

Boeri, M., Sterk, C., Bahora, M. & Elifson, K. (in press). Poly-drug use among ecstasy users: Separate, synergistic, and indiscriminate patterns. *Journal of Drug Issues.*

Boeri, M., Sterk, C., & Elifson, K. (2004). Rolling beyond raves: Ecstasy use outside the rave setting. *Journal of Drug Issues, 34*(4), 831–860.

Boys, A., Fountain, J., Marsden, J., Griffiths, P., Stillwell, G., & Strang, J. (2000). *Drugs decisions: A qualitative study of young people.* London: Health Education Authority.

Byrnes, J. (2003). Changing view on the nature and prevention of adolescent risk taking. In D. Romer (Ed.), *Reducing adolescent risk: Toward an integrated approach.* Thousand Oaks: Sage.

Carlson, R., McCaughan, J., Falck, R., Wang, J., Siegal, H., & Daniulaityte, R. (2004). Perceived adverse consequences associated with MDMA/Ecstasy use among young polydrug users in Ohio: Implications for intervention. *International Journal of Drug Policy, 15*(4), 265–274.

Chang, L. (2001). Neuroimaging studies in chronic effects of MDMA/Ecstasy use. In *NIDA Scientific Conference on MDMA/Ecstasy: Advances, challenges, and future directions* National Institute on Drug Abuse. Bethesda, MD, July.

Charmaz, K. (1983). The grounded theory method: An explication and interpretation. In R. M. Emerson (Ed.), *Contemporary field research: A collection of readings.* Prospect Heights, IL: Waveland Press.

Dew, B., Elifson, K., & Sterk, C. (2006). Treatment implications for young adult users of MDMA. *Journal of Addictions and Offender Counseling, 26*(2), 84–98.

Diemel, S., & Blanken, P. (1999). Tracking new trends in drug use. *Journal of Drug Issues, 29*(3), 529–548.

Duff, C. (2005). Party drugs and party people. *International Journal of Drug Policy, 16*(3), 161–170.

Eiserman, J., Diamond, S., & Schensul, J. (2005). Rollin' on E: A qualitative analysis of ecstasy use among inner city adolescents and young adults. *Journal of Ethnicity in Substance Abuse, 4*(2), 9–38.

Forsyth, A., Barnard, M., & McKeganey, N. (1997). Musical preference as an indicator of adolescent drug use. *Addiction, 92*(10), 1317.

Gamble, L., & George, M. (1997). 'Really useful knowledge': The boundaries, customs, and folklore governing recreational drug use in a sample of young people. In P. Erickson, D. Riley, Y. Cheung, & P. O'Hare (Eds.), *Harm reduction: A new direction for drug policies and programs.* Toronto: University of Toronto Press.

Gamma, A., Jerome, L., Liechti, M., & Sumnall, H. (2005). Is ecstasy perceived to be safe? A critical survey. *Drug and Alcohol Dependence, 77*(2), 185–193.

Glaser, B., & Strauss, A. (1967). *The discovery of grounded theory.* New York: Free Press.

Gross, S., Barrett, S., Shestowsky, J., & Pihl, R. (2002). Ecstasy and drug consumption patterns: A Canadian rave population study. *Canadian Journal of Psychiatry, 47*(6), 546–551.

Hammersley, R., Ditton, J., Smith, I., & Short, E. (1999). Patterns of ecstasy use by drug users. *British Journal of Criminology, 39*(4), 625–647.

Hammersley, R., Khan, F., & Ditton, J. (2002). *Ecstasy and the rise of the chemical generation.* New York: Routledge.

Hansen, D., Maycock, B., & Lower, T. (2001). 'Weddings, parties, anything. . .', a qualitative analysis of ecstasy use in Perth, Western Australia. *International Journal of Drug Policy, 12*(2), 181–199.

Hegadoren, K., Baker, G., & Bourin, M. (1999). 3, 4-Methylenedioxy analogues of amphetamine: Defining the risks to humans. *Neuroscience and Biobehavioral Reviews, 23*(4), 539–553.

Henderson, S. (1993). Fun, fashion, & fission. *International Journal of Drug Policy, 4,* 122–129.

Hitzler, R. (2002). Pill kick: The pursuit of "ecstasy" at techno-events. *Journal of Drug Issues, 32*(2), 459–466.

Johnston, L., O'Malley, P., & Bachman, J. (2001). *Monitoring the future National results on adolescent drug use: Overview of key findings.* Bethesda, MD: National Institute on Drug Abuse.

Lenton, S., Boys, A., & Norcross, K. (1997). Raves, drugs and experience: Drug use by a sample of people who attend raves in Western Australia. *Addiction, 92*(10), 1327–1337.

Masterson, A. (1993). Digital Hippies. *Revelation,* (December/January), 20–27.

McElrath, K., & McEvoy, K. (2002). Negative experiences on ecstasy: The role of drug, set, and setting. *Journal of Psychoactive Drugs, 34*(2), 199–207.

Measham, F., Newcombe, R., & Parker, H. (1994). The normalization of recreational drug use amongst young people in North-West England. *British Journal of Sociology, 45*(2), 287–312.

Measham, F., Parker, H., & Aldridge, J. (1998). The teenage transition: From adolescent recreational drug use to the young adult dance culture in Britain in the mid-1990s. *Journal of Drug Issues, 28*(1), 9–32.

Merchant, J., & MacDonald, R. (1994). Youth & the rave culture, ecstasy & health. *Youth and Policy, 45,* 16–38.

Millman, R., & Beeder, A. (1994). The new psychedelic culture: LSD, ecstasy, "rave" parties and the Grateful Dead. *Psychiatric Annals, 24*(3), 148.

Panagopolous, I., & Ricciardelli, L. (2005). Harm reduction and decision making among recreational ecstasy users. *International Journal of Drug Policy, 16*(1), 54–64.

Parker, H. (1997). Adolescent drug pathways in the 1990s. In J. Braggins (Ed.), *Tackling drugs together: One year on.* London: Institute for the Study and Treatment of Delinquency.

Parker, H. (2005). Normalization as a barometer: Recreational drug use and the consumption of leisure by younger Britons. *Addiction Research and Theory, 13*(3), 205–215.

Parker, H., & Egginton, R. (2002). Adolescent recreational alcohol and drugs careers gone wrong: Developing a strategy for reducing risks and harms. *International Journal of Drug Policy, 13,* 419–432.

Parker, H., Williams, L., & Aldridge, J. (2002). The Normalization of 'sensible' recreational drug use: Further evidence from the North West England longitudinal study. *Sociology, 36*(4), 941–964.

Parrott, A. (2002). Recreational Ecstasy/MDMA, the serotonin syndrome, and serotonergic neurotoxicity. *Pharmacology, Biochemistry, and Behavior, 71*(4), 837–844.

Parrott, A., Sisk, E., & Turner, J. (2000). Psychobiological problems in heavy ecstasy (MDMA) polydrug users. *Drug and Alcohol Dependence, 60*(1), 105–110.

Reid, L., Elifson, K., & Sterk, C. (2007). Ecstasy and gateway drugs: Initiating the use of ecstasy and other drugs. *Annals of Epidemiology, 17*(1), 74–80.

Riley, S., & Hayward, E. (2004). Patterns, trends, and meanings of drug use by dance-drug users in Edinburgh, Scotland. Drugs, Education. *Prevention and Policy, 11*(3), 243–262.

Riley, S., James, C., Gregory, D., Dingle, H., & Cadger, M. (2001). Patterns of recreational drug use at dance events in Edinburgh, Scotland. *Addiction, 96*(7), 1035–1048.

Schensul, J., Diamond, S., Disch, W., Bermudez, R., & Eiserman, J. (2005). The diffusion of ecstasy through urban youth networks. *Journal of Ethnicity in Substance Abuse, 4*(2), 39–71.

Scholey, A., Parrott, A., Buchanan, T., Hefferman, T., Ling, J., & Rodgers, J. (2004). Increased intensity of ecstasy and polydrug usage in the more experienced recreational Ecstasy/ MDMA users: A WWW study. *Addictive Behaviors, 29*(4), 743–752.

Schwartz, R., & Miller, N. (1997). MDMA (Ecstasy) and the rave. *American Academy of Pediatrics, 100*(4), 705–708.

Shewan, D., Dalgarno, P., & Reith, G. (2000). Perceived risk and risk reduction among ecstasy users: The role of drug, set, and setting. *International Journal of Drug Policy, 10*(6), 431–453.

Shildrick, T. (2002). Young people, illicit drug use, and the question of normalization. *Journal of Youth Studies, 5*(1), 35–50.

Shiner, M., & Newburn, T. (1997). Definitely, maybe not: The normalization of recreational drug use amongst young people. *Sociology, 31*(3), 1–19.

Sloan, J. (2000). It's all the rave: Flower power meets technoculture. *American Criminal Justice Society Today, 29*(1), 3–6.

Solowij, N., Hall, W., & Lee, N. (1992). Recreational MDMA use in Sydney: A Profile of ecstasy users and their experiences with the drug. *British Journal of Addiction, 87*(8), 1161–1172.

Spruit, I. P. (1999). Ecstasy use and policy responses in the Netherlands. *Journal of Drug Issues, 29*(3), 653–677.

Sterk, C., Theall, K., & Elifson, K. (2000). Women and drug treatment experiences: A generational comparison of mothers and daughters. *Journal of Drug Issues, 30*(4), 839–861.

Sterk, C., Theall, K., & Elifson, K. (2006). Young adult ecstasy use patterns: Quantities and combinations. *Journal of Drug Issues, 36*(1), 201–228.

Sterk, C., Theall, K., & Elifson, K. (2007). Individual action and community context: The health intervention project. *American Journal of Preventative Medicine, 32*(6), 177.

Strauss, A., & Corbin, J. (1998). *Basics of qualitative research: Techniques and procedures for developing grounded theory.* Thousand Oaks: Sage.

Theall, K., Elifson, K., & Sterk, C. (2006). Sex, touch, and HIV risk among ecstasy users. *AIDS and Behavior, 10*(2), 169–178.

Topp, L., Hando, J., Dillon, P., Roche, A., & Solowij, N. (1999). Ecstasy use in Australia: Patterns of use and associated harms. *Drug and Alcohol Dependence, 55*(1–2), 105–115.

van de Wijngaart, G., Braam, R., de Bruin, D., Fris, M., Maalaste, N., & Verbraeck, H. (1999). Ecstasy use at large-scale dance events in the Netherlands. *Journal of Drug Issues, 29,* 679–701.

Watters, J., & Biernacki, P. (1989). Targeted Sampling: Options for the study of hidden populations. *Social Problems, 36*(4), 416.

Critical Thinking

1. What is meant by normalization, and what role does it play in recreational ecstasy use? Provide an example of normalization.

2. Given what we know about the perceptions of ecstasy use among users, how should we approach prevention of ecstasy use?

MASUMA BAHORA Emory University, Rollins School of Public Health, Department of Behavioral Sciences and Health Education, 1518 Clifton Road N.E., Atlanta, GA 30322, USA. **CLAIRE E. STERK** *Geor*gia State University, Department of Sociology, Atlanta, GA, USA. and Corresponding author. Tel.: +1 404 727 9124; fax: +1 404 727 1369. E-mail address: csterk@emory.edu (C.E. Sterk). **KIRK W. ELIFSON** Emory University, Rollins School of Public Health, Department of Behavioral Sciences and Health Education, 1518 Clifton Road N.E., Atlanta, GA 30322, USA and Georgia State University, Department of Sociology, Atlanta, GA, USA.

From *International Journal of Drug Policy,* vol. 20, no. 1, January 2009. Copyright © 2009 by Elsevier Science Ltd. Reprinted by permission.

Examination of Over-the-Counter Drug Misuse Among Youth[1]

Erin J. Farley and Daniel J. O'Connell

Introduction

Potential harm from the intentional misuse of over-the-counter (OTC) medicines among youth has become an area of increased concern among medical practitioners and researchers (Bryner et al. 2006; Lessenger et al. 2008; Substance Abuse and Mental Health Services Administration (SAMHSA) 2006). Although the likelihood of death from overdose is rare, research has revealed an increase in dextromethorphan (a key ingredient in numerous cough and cold medicines) abuse cases reported to poison control centers (Bryner et al. 2006). Equally important is the suspicion that OTC use may be a stepping stone to other forms of drug misuse and abuse.

While OTC misuse has garnered increased media coverage, it has not yet attracted an equivalent interest among researchers. Further, it is possible that research to date has inappropriately specified the relationship between OTC and other drug misuse. Extant research has examined the relationship between OTC misuse and illicit drug use by utilizing a single construct, limiting the ability to completely flesh out the dimensions of this relationship between drug use. One area that needs further attention is if and how OTC misuse among youth is associated with other types of drug use. By combining all categories of drugs under a single construct, the nuances of how particular drugs relate to OTC use is diminished. This paper examines the current state of knowledge on OTC misuse by examining the prevalence of OTC misuse and its relationship with other types of drug use among a specific cohort to expand the current understanding of the problem.

Prevalence of OTC Misuse

OTC cough and cold medicines (e.g., Coricidin and Nyquil) can be easily purchased from pharmacies and drug stores. Adolescents typically ingest OTC medicines for the ingredient dextromethorphan (DXM). DXM is a synthetic drug related to opiates, which has the ability to produce effects similar to psychotropic drugs (Bobo et al. 2004; SAMHSA 2006). These effects include sensory enhancement, perceptual distortion, and hallucinations. DXM can be found in as many as 140 different cold and cough medications (Bobo et al. 2004; SAMHSA 2008). Misuse of these types of OTC drugs often involve youth seeking inexpensive and easily accessible substitute for other drugs that are more difficult to obtain.

Misuse of OTC drugs, especially in combination with other types of drugs, can lead to a variety of serious health problems, including confusion, blurred vision, slurred speech, loss of coordination, paranoia, high blood pressure, loss of consciousness, irregular heartbeat, seizure, panic attacks, brain damage, coma, and possibly death (Bobo et al. 2004; Food and Drug Administration 2005). Yet, there is a growing concern that youth who intentionally misuse OTC drugs misperceive that they are safe because these types of drugs are legal and prevalent (Johnston et al. 2006). If this misperception is contributing to the misuse of OTC drugs, the consequences can be serious. On the other hand, this same misperception also points towards potentially efficacious prevention programs focused on educating youth to the harm posed by these drugs.

Prevalence by Age

The abuse or misuse of OTC drugs appears to be mostly a problem among younger persons. A Drug Abuse Warning Network (DAWN) report revealed that 12,584 emergency department visits were associated with DXM use in 2004 (SAMHSA 2006). Among these, 44% (5,581) were associated with the nonmedical use of DXM products among patients aged 12 to 20. Findings from this report highlight that negative consequences associated with OTC misuse are more likely to occur among youth and young adults. For example, the rate of visits to the emergency department resulting from nonmedical use of DXM was 7.1 per 100,000 youths ages 12 to 20. For older age groups the rate was 2.6 visits or fewer per 100,000 (Bobo and Fulton 2004). In addition, a recent National Survey on Drug Use and Health (NSDUH) report highlighted OTC misuse as a significant problem among youth and young adults (SAMHSA 2008). According to this report, respondents age 12 to 17 years were more likely than those age 18 to 25 years to report past year misuse of OTCs (SAMHSA 2008).

One signal that OTC misuse is becoming of greater concern among researchers is the addition of an OTC measure ("to get high") by both the Monitoring the Future and the National Drug Use and Health in 2006 into their annual surveys. The 2007 Monitoring the Future (MTF) survey revealed that 4% of eighth graders, 5% of tenth graders and 6% of twelfth graders report past year use of OTCs to get high (Johnston et al., 2008). For eighth graders in particular, self-report misuse of OTCs was lower than past year marijuana (10%), inhalant (8%), and alcohol (32%) use. However, OTC misuse was higher than past year hallucinogen (2%), ecstasy (2%), Oxycontin (2%), Vicodin (3%), Ritalin (2%), and tranquilizer (2%) use.

Prevalence by Gender, Race, and Ethnicity

Extant research reveals significant gender differences in OTC misuse. A 2008 NSDUH report found an interaction of age and gender on self-report OTC misuse. While females age 12 to 17 years were more likely than males in the same age group to report past year OTC misuse, males age 18 to 25 years were more likely to report past year OTC misuse in comparison to females in the same age group (SAMSHA 2008). Other research has found significant gender differences in OTC misuse. For instance, both Steinman's (2006) analysis of 39,345 high school students from Ohio and Ford's (2009) examination of the 2006 National Survey on Drug Use and Health data (ages 12 to 17) revealed significant gender differences with females more likely to report OTC misuse than males (Ford 2009; Steinman 2006).

Research on racial and ethnic differences in OTC misuse is less clear. While Steinman's (2006) findings revealed Native Americans were more likely to report misuse, followed by white, "other/mixed," Hispanic, Asian, and African-American, the national survey conducted by SAMHSA (2008) revealed whites were more likely to report OTC misuse, followed by Hispanic and African-American. Misuse by Native Americans may be an additional area of concern, but the extant data indicate that whites and females are particularly at risk.

OTC Misuse Association with Prescription and Illicit Drugs

While the existing literature of OTC misuse is scant, there are key observations to be noted from research on the nonmedical use of prescription drugs (NMUPDs). Prior research on the NMUPDs has repeatedly highlighted the strong relationship between illicit prescription drug use and cigarette, alcohol, marijuana, and other drug use (Boyd et al. 2006; McCabe et al. 2004; McCabe et al. 2005; Simoni-Wastila et al. 2004). These findings suggest that nonmedical users of prescription drugs may not be a qualitatively different category of drug users, but are in fact part of well-established group of poly-drug users. It is unclear from available research whether the relationship between OTC and street drugs is the same as prescribed drugs.

Current research suggests there is reason to be concerned about the phenomena of youth mixing cough and cold medicines with other types of drugs. A 2006 DAWN report revealed that among those emergency department visits that involved DXM, 13% of 12 to 17 year old visits and 36% of 18 to 20 year old visits involved combinations of DXM and alcohol. In addition, Steinman's (2006) research on OTC misuse in Ohio high schools revealed OTC misuse was associated with alcohol, cigarette, marijuana, and other illicit drug use (e.g., cocaine, LSD, and ecstasy). Research by Ford (2009) also found a significant relationship between OTC misuse and binge drinking, marijuana use, prescription drug use, and other illicit drug use. Steinman (2006) emphasized the strong association between OTC misuse with alcohol and other illicit drugs suggesting that OTC misuse is not a "gateway" drug, but only one of a number of substance utilized by adolescents.

OTC as the Gateway?

The gateway drug concept suggests that there are lower tiered drugs that open the way towards other drugs, and that drug use itself is responsible for opening the gate (Kandel 1975; Kandel et al. 1975; Kandel et al. 2002). Other studies have attempted to refute this concept, suggesting that more serious drug users may in fact use harder drugs prior to drugs like marijuana (Mackesy-Amiti et al. 1997). Early teen drug use may largely be dictated by what drugs are available to adolescents, as well as a desire to alter one's consciousness. Access to most drugs, however, is not evenly distributed. Marijuana use by older youth may provide access to a small group of marijuana users, while another group might have access to prescription drugs, and another, access to drugs like cocaine. Unlike these other substances, almost all youth have access to OTC drugs.

While it has been shown empirically that "drug users use drugs," that is, using any substance increases the probability of using any other substance, this pattern may not be exclusively based on availability. In our modern consumer culture, adolescents are faced with multiple choices, and increasingly, the type of drug is one of them. Recognizing that the choice of drug is related to both availability and preference, it is important to understand the pattern of correlation between different drugs. Just as there are more choices in terms of which drugs, there are also more choices regarding where to obtain drugs. Those involved in traditional street drugs like marijuana and ecstasy are getting drugs from those who sell them, necessitating some link to a criminal element. Those using OTC drugs and prescription drugs can sidestep this path, which has important considerations for prevention policy.

The Current Study

This study intends to tease out the relationship between OTC misuse and the use of different types of drugs. Previous analyses have tended to lump "other illegal drugs" together in one category. If early teen usage is related to drug choice and availability, combining drugs may mask relationships that exist among individual drugs. The current study utilized a large enough sample to examine drugs both individually and in groups, and attempted to investigate which drugs are associated with OTC use.

The objective of the current study is twofold: First, the prevalence of OTC misuse among a sample of eighth grade public school students is examined, including gender and race differences in OTC misuse; Second, the relationship between OTC misuse and other substance use is examined to identify patterns of use, with a specific focus on whether estimating the effects of other illegal drugs individually provides more insight than using a single construct.

Methods

Data for the current study are from the 2005 Delaware School Survey. Data was collected by The Center for Drug and Alcohol Studies (CDAS) at the University of Delaware. CDAS has conducted an annual survey of eighth grade public school students since 1995 (the annual survey also measures fifth and eleventh graders). In order to ensure confidentiality and foster honesty, survey administrators are University personnel and not teachers. Passive parental and active student consent is solicited before administrating the survey. The purpose of the survey is to track prevalence rates of drug use among Delaware public school students.

A single question, "how often do you use OTC drugs (cough & cold meds, Nyquil) to get high?" measured eighth grade self-reports of OTC misuse. Response options included "never," "before, but not in past year," "a few times in past year," "once or twice a month," "once or twice a week," and "almost everyday." This measure was recoded into a dichotomous variable (0 = not in past year, 1 = in past year).

Other substance questions included past year cigarette, alcohol, and marijuana use. Binge drinking was also measured and defined as three drinks at a time in the last two weeks. Other drug use (with the intent of getting high) questions included: uppers (speed, meth, crank, diet pills), sedatives (tranquilizers, barbiturates, Xanax), heroin, inhalants, ecstasy, hallucinogens, pain relievers, stimulants (Ritalin, Adderall, Cylert etc.), albuterol, and crack/cocaine. All drug measures were recoded into dichotomous variables (0 = not in past year, 1 = in past year).

First, univariate and bivariate analyses were utilized to examine the prevalence of OTC use and the relationship with other substances; second a series of logistic regressions were used to demonstrate the difference between using a single construct "other illicit drug use" differs from utilizing each drug measure individually.

Results

A total of 7,815 eighth graders completed the 2005 survey (50% female and 50% male). The racial and ethnic distribution of students sampled consisted of 53% (3,975) white, 28% (2,065) black, 8% (632) Puerto Rican or Mexican, 2.6% (198) Asian, 1.9% (142) American Indian/Native Alaskan,

and 6.8% (509) "Other." With Steinman's (2006) findings that Native Americans reported the highest levels of OTC misuse, we conducted a crosstabulation as an initial examination into racial variation. While American Indians/Native Alaskans represented only 2.5% of the students reporting OTC misuse in the past year, this represented 13% of American Indians/Native Alaskans students, this being the highest rate of use in comparison to the other racial categories. This finding lends support to Steinman's (2006) findings. Due to small cell counts the race categories for Puerto Rican, Mexican, Asian, American Indian/Native Alaskan and "other" were collapsed into one encompassing "other" category. Subsequent crosstabulation analysis revealed no significant variation between White, Black and "other" students. As a result, the race variable was collapsed into white and nonwhite (0 = white, 1 = non-white) for use in the multivariate models.

The past year OTC misuse prevalence in eighth grade Delaware sample was 10% (n = 704). Table 1 displays the breakdown of student self-reports: 86% of eighth graders reported never misusing OTCs, 9% report past year use, and 4% report misusing OTC in the past month.

Table 2 demonstrates a significant difference between male and female past year misuse of OTC drugs but no significant difference between white and nonwhite students.

Crosstabulations of OTC and other drugs are presented in Table 3. The percent of people using OTC drugs is given for those who used and did not use each substance in the past year. For example, the first substance column alcohol is interpreted

Table 1   Eighth Grade Self-Reports of OTC Abuse to Get High

	Percentage
Never	86%
Before, but not in past year	5%
Few times in past year	5%
Once or twice a month	3%
Once or twice a week	1%
Almost everyday	0%*

*Note: Less than one-half of one percent.

Table 2   Crosstabulation of OTC Abuse by Gender and Race

	Past Year OTC Abuse
Gender*	
Male	8%
Female	12%
Race	
White	10%
NonWhite	10%

*Note: Significant at the .001 level.

as 5.6% of those who did not use alcohol in the past year used OTC drugs, while 15.1% of those who did use alcohol used OTC drugs. The distribution is not uniform across drug types. There is a clear distribution of the type of adolescents most likely to be misusing OTC drugs. There appear to be four steps in the distribution in Table 3. First, youth who do not report using a given substance remain below 10% across all substances. Second, those youth who used alcohol and marijuana used OTC drugs at the lowest rate among users, hovering between 15% and 22% (Binge drinkers). Third, those using the more traditional street drugs such as ecstasy, hallucinogens, inhalants, heroin and cocaine formed a middle tier, reporting OTC use on

the 25% to 30% range. Fourth and final, there is a group of persons using prescription drugs who are more likely to use OTC drugs as well. Those youths who used sedatives, amphetamines, pain relievers and stimulants were substantially more likely to use OTC drugs, with all categories reporting over 40% OTC users and 56% of those who use pain relievers using OTC drugs as well. In order to further investigate how these relationships function, we next employed regression techniques to control for the effect of other drugs.

The multivariate analyses begin in Table 4, with findings from the initial logistic regression (Model 1). This model tested the traditional means of measuring the effects of other illicit drugs by utilizing a single construct. Of the 7 variables, three did not reach significance (nonwhite, past year binge drinking and past year marijuana use). The odds of females misusing OTC drugs are 1.6 times greater (OR = 1.603, p = .000) than their male counterparts, holding all other variables constant. The odds of past year cigarette users misusing OTC drugs is 1.4 times greater (OR = 1.385, p =.011) than nonusers. The odds of past year alcohol users misusing OTC drugs is 1.8 times greater (OR = 1.779, p =.000) than nonusers. Using the single construct other illicit drugs category produced the largest effect, returning an odds ratio of 7.7 (OR = 7.685, p = .000), indicating that youth who reported using any of the other drugs reported in Table 3 increased the odds of using OTC drugs in the past year by 7.7 times.

The suggestion is that combining all other drugs into one construct misses variation among individual drugs. In order to tease out this concept, a logistic regression analysis examining the effect of other illicit drugs measured individually is presented as Model 2 in Tables 4A (Model 1)and 4B (Model 2). When compared to Model 1, there are no major differences

Table 3　Percent of OTC Use or Nonuse of Other Substances

	Did Not Use Drug	Used Drug
Alcohol	5.6%	15.1%
Binge Drink	8.1%	22%
Marijuana	7.8%	17.3%
Ecstasy	9.3%	31.0%
Hallucinogen	9.2%	31.0%
Sedatives	9.0%	48.3%
Albuterol	7.8%	28.2%
Amphetamines	8.9%	44.0%
Inhalants	8.3%	35.2%
Pain Relievers	7.1%	56.2%
Ritalin	8.8%	45.8%
Heroin	9.4%	25.4%
Crack/Cocaine	9.1%	32.5%

Table 4A　Reduced Logistic Regression Predicting Past Year OTC Misuse (Model 1)

	B	S.E.	Wald	Sig.	OR	95% CI
Constant	−.316	.108	1122.595	.000	.027	
Female	.472	.092	26.451	.000	1.603	1.339, 1.918
NonWhite	.085	.091	.806	.354	1.088	.910, 1.301
Past Year Cigarette Use	.325	.128	6.446	.011	1.385	1.077, 1.780
Past Year Alcohol Use	.576	.108	28.653	.000	1.779	1.441, 2.197
Binge Drinking	.180	.132	1.859	.173	.197	.924, 1.549
Past Year Marijuana Use	−.144	.129	1.259	.262	.866	.673, 1.114
Other Illegal Drug Use	2.039	.094	469.024	.000	7.685	6.390, 9.243
Past Year Ecstasy	-	-	-	-	-	-
Past Year Hallucinogens	-	-	-	-	-	-
Past Year Albuterol	-	-	-	-	-	-
Past Year Sedatives	-	-	-	-	-	-
Past Year Amphetamines	-	-	-	-	-	-
Past Year Inhalants	-	-	-	-	-	-
Past Year Pain Relievers	-	-	-	-	-	-
Past Year Ritalin	-	-	-	-	-	-
Past Year Heroin	-	-	-	-	-	-
Past Year Crack/Cocaine	-	-	-	-	-	-

in the effects of the lower tiered drugs on OTC misuse, when other variables were accounted for. The exceptions to this are the smokeable substances, cigarettes and marijuana, both of which lose significance in Model 2.

The odds of females misusing OTC drugs remained approximately 1.5 times greater (OR = 1.497, p = .000) than their male counterparts, holding all other variables constant. Modest effects were again found for cigarettes smokers (OR = 1.333, p < .05) and alcohol users (OR = 1.766, p = .000). The largest effects, however, were among users of pain relievers. The odds of students who reported past year use of illicit pain relievers reporting OTC drug misuse were over 9 times more likely than those who did not report pain reliever use (OR = 9.920, p = .000). Similarly, albuterol (or other asthma medicine) misusers were 4 times more likely to report OTC misuse in comparison to nonusers (OR = 4.071, p = .000). In addition, inhalant misusers were approximately twice as likely to report OTC misuse (OR = 2.302, p = .000). Similar effects were found for cocaine use (OR = 2.560, p < .01), and Ritalin use to get high (OR = 1.964, p < .01). Finally, heroin use significantly declined among those students who reported past year OTC drug misuse (OR = .321, p < .05).

Discussion and Conclusion

This study questioned whether combining all drugs into one construct is an appropriate measure in the current drug environment in which youth have more choices in terms of type of drug and routes of acquiring the drugs. While the current study replicates the findings of prior research indicating that OTC use is correlated with other drug use, the study demonstrated that this relationship is by no means uniform, and that combining drugs other than marijuana and alcohol into a single "other drug" construct misses the nuanced variation between drugs.

The objective of this study was to examine the relationship between past year OTC misuse and other drug types including other illicit drugs and the NMUPDs. Bivariate analyses revealed that nonmedical users of prescription drugs were more likely to use OTC drugs, and users of drugs like alcohol and marijuana were least likely to misuse OTC drugs. Our full model (Tables 4A and 4B) revealed that modeling drugs individually and allowing them to essentially "fight it out" in a regression analysis showed that past year nonmedical use of pain relievers and albuterol were by far the strongest predictors of OTC misuse.

Unlike Steinman's (2006) findings which led him to explore answers to the question of why is OTC misuse associated with more serious drug use, our findings lead us to ask the question, why is OTC misuse significantly associated with the NMUPDs? The significant association between OTC misuse and the NMUPDs (i.e., pain relievers, albuterol, and Ritalin) may be due to the similar accessibility or mode of acquisition for the two types of drugs. For example, both OTC drugs and prescription drugs may be easily accessible from friends at school, at home in the medicine cabinet, or, in the case of OTC drugs, from their local drug store. Acquiring OTC or prescription drugs does not require contact with a traditional

Table 4B Full Logistic Regression Predicting Past Year OTC Misuse (Model 2)

	B	S.E.	Wald	Sig.	OR	95% CI
Constant	−3.502	.110	1008.918	.000	.030	
Female	.403	.098	16.794	.000	1.497	1.234, 1.816
NonWhite	.141	.098	2.058	.151	1.151	.959, 1.395
Past Year Cigarette Use	.297	.141	4.139	.042	1.333	1.011, 1.757
Past Year Alcohol Use	.569	.113	25.248	.000	1.766	1.415, 2.205
Binge Drinking	.154	.150	1.059	.303	1.167	.870, 1.565
Past Year Marijuana Use	−.107	.141	.573	.449	.899	.682, 1.185
Other Illegal Drug Use	-	-	-	-	-	-
Past Year Ecstasy	−.307	.396	.600	.439	.736	.338, 1.600
Past Year Hallucinogens	−.533	.365	1.916	.166	.587	.276, 1.248
Past Year Albuterol	1.404	.122	132.464	.000	4.071	3.205, 5.170
Past Year Sedatives	.290	.320	.821	.365	1.336	.714, 2.499
Past Year Amphetamines	.138	.311	.197	.657	1.148	.624, 2.113
Past Year Inhalants	.834	.172	23.449	.000	2.302	1.643, 3.227
Past Year Pain Relievers	2.295	.148	239.336	.000	9.920	7.418, 13.267
Past Year Ritalin	.675	.244	7.662	.006	1.964	1.218, 3.169
Past Year Heroin	−1.137	.536	4.505	.034	.321	.112, .917
Past Year Crack/Cocaine	.940	.344	7.487	.006	2.560	1.306, 5.019

drug dealer which some students do not have access to and others might find discomforting.

The widespread and growing prevalence of OTC misuse is partially facilitated by its easy accessibility and the perception that OTC drugs are not as harmful as more traditional drugs. The relationship between these OTC and NMUPD may be due to the misperception that OTC and prescription drugs are safer than other types of drugs.

One relationship which appears counterintuitive to the finding that OTC use is more prominently associated with the NMUPD is the significant relationship between OTC misuse and crack/cocaine use. Not only did crack/cocaine use have a larger effect on OTC misuse than cigarette use, alcohol use, inhalant use, and illicit Ritalin use, crack/cocaine use is also a notable step into more serious types of drug use. One possible explanation is that crack/cocaine users often use some type of depressant to "take the edge off." It may thus be that some youth who are using crack/cocaine are also using OTC drugs to ease the "crash" from crack/cocaine. Further research is needed to explore the dimensions of this relationship.

What appears to emerge from this study is that misusers of OTC drugs are more likely to be using pills (sedatives, stimulants, pain relievers) and asthma drugs to get high than they are the traditional marijuana, cocaine, and hallucinogens of earlier eras (See Table 2). MTF data have already shown the new drug users are more likely to initiate use through prescription drugs rather than marijuana (Mackesy-Amiti et al. 1997). That finding, coupled with those above lead us to question whether there may be a shift in adolescent drug use on the horizon or even occurring currently.

A general awareness about the misuse potential of OTC drugs among adolescents already exists. This awareness can be seen in the recent movement to place OTC drugs behind cashier counters and also limiting the number of OTC drugs an individual can buy at one time. The findings from this analysis help to further our understanding of OTC misuse among youth.

Research limitations need to be acknowledged. The data utilized for the current analysis was cross-sectional data and limits our ability to examine directionality of drug misuse. The sample was drawn from a single state, thus limiting its generalizability. In addition, no survey data is available for students who were absent the day the survey was administered. Further, the OTC measure utilized represented one general question about OTC drug misuse instead of a list of OTC drugs by type. This general OTC measure limits our ability to interpret differences in misuse by type of OTC drug.

Based on the findings from this study, the authors emphasize continued education for adolescents on the dangers of misusing OTC drugs. Combating misuse should involve educating parents about the dangers of the drugs in their house and the potential for misuse, especially among youth who may not already be known for misusing or abusing drugs. OTC drug use occurs among inexperienced drug users and traditional signs of drug use among youth may not be successful in identifying youth who are abusing OTC drugs.

References

Bobo, William V. and Robert B. Fulton. 2004. "Commentary on: Severe Manifestations of Coricidin Intoxication." *American Journal of Emergency Medicine* 22: 624–625.

Boyd, Carol J., Sean E. McCabe, and Christian J. Teter. 2006. "Medical and Nonmedical Use of Prescription Pain Medication by Youth in a Detroit-Area Public School District." *Drug and Alcohol Dependence* 81: 37–45.

Bryner, Jodi K., Uerica K. Wang, Jenny W. Hui, Merlin Bedodo, Conan MacDougall, and Ilene B. Anderson. 2006. "Dextromethorphan Abuse in Adolescence: An Increasing Trend: 1999–2004." *Archives of Pediatrics & Adolescent Medicine* 160:1217–1222.

Food and Drug Administration. 2005. "FDA Warns Against Abuse of Dextromethorphan (DXM). (Talk Paper T05–23). Rockville, MD: National Press Office. (Also available at http://www.fda/gov/bbs/topics/answers/2005/ans01360.html.)

Ford, Jason A. 2009. "Misuse of Over-the-Counter Cough or Cold Medications Among Adolescents: Prevalence and Correlates in a National Sample." *Journal of Adolescent Health* 44: 505–507.

Johnston, Lloyd D., Patrick M. O'Malley, Jerald G. Bachman, and John E. Schulenberg. 2006. National press release, Teen drug use continues down in 2006, particularly among older teens; but use of prescription-type drugs remains high. University of Michigan News Service, Ann Arbor.

Johnston, Lloyd D., Patrick M. O'Malley, Jerald G. Bachman, and John E. Schulenberg. 2008. "Monitoring the Future National Results on Adolescent Drug Use, Overview of Key Findings, 2007." (*NIH Publication No. 08-6418*). Bethesda, MD: National Institution on Drug Use.

Kandel, Denise and Richard Faust. 1975. "Sequence and Stages in Patterns of Adolescent Drug Use." *Archives of General Psychiatry* 32: 923–932.

Kandel, Denise. 1975. "Stages in Adolescent Involvement in Drug Use." *Science* 190: 912–914.

Kandel, D. and K. Yamaguchi. 2002. "Stages of Drug Involvement in the US Population." Pp. 65–89 in *Stages and Pathways of Drug Involvement: Examining the Gateway Hypothesis,* edited by Denise B. Kandel. New York, Cambridge University Press.

Lessenger, James E. and Steven D. Feinberg. 2008. "Abuse of Prescription and Over-the-Counter Medications." *Journal of the American Board of Family Medicine* 21: 45–54.

Mackesy-Amiti, Mary Ellen, Michael Fendrich, and Paul J. Goldstein. 1997. "Sequence of Drug Use Among Serious Drug Users: Typical vs Atypical Progression." *Drug and Alcohol Dependence* 45: 185–96.

McCabe, Sean E., Carol J. Boyd, and Christian J. Teter. 2005. "Illicit Use of Opioid Analgesics by High School Seniors." *Journal of Substance Abuse Treatment* 28: 225–230.

McCabe, Sean E., Christian J. Teter, and Carol J. Boyd. 2004. "The Use, Misuse, and Diversion of Prescription Stimulants Among Middle and High School Students." *Substance Use and Misuse* 39: 1095–1116.

Steinman, Kenneth J. 2006. "High School Students' Misuse of Over-The-Counter Drugs: A Population-Based Survey in an Urban Area." *Journal of Adolescent Health* 38: 445–447.

Substance Abuse and Mental Health Services Administration (SAMHSA). 2006. The New Dawn Report: Emergency

Department visits Involving Dextromethorphan. Office of Applied Studies. Rockville, MD.

Substance Abuse and Mental Health Services Administration (SAMHSA). 2008. "The NSDUH Report: Misuse of Over-the-Counter Cough and Cold Medications among Persons Aged 12 to 25." Office of Applied Studies. Rockville, MD.

Simoni-Wastila, Linda, Grant Ritter, and Gail Strickler. 2004. "Gender and Other Factors Associated with Nonmedical use of Abusable Prescription Drugs." *Substance Use and Misuse* 39: 1–23.

Note

1. Original study supported by Delaware Health and Human Services, Division of Substance Abuse and Mental Health, through the Substance Abuse Prevention and Treatment Block Grant from the Substance Abuse and Mental Health Services Administration (SAMHSA), U.S. Department of Health and Human Services. Support for this study also received from The Delaware Legislature through the Delaware Health Fund.

Critical Thinking

1. Discuss the factors that contribute to the prevalence of over-the-counter drug misuse by teens.

2. Are their gender differences in misuse of over-the-counter misuse of drugs? If so, why do you think this is? If not, why not?

Self-Control, Opportunity, and Substance Use

We examine the effect of self-control and opportunity on adolescent substance use. When theorizing about the role of opportunity, we believe the "sanction potential" of a given situation should be considered. Our results suggest the effect of self-control on substance use does not depend on the availability of substances in the home (high sanction potential), but friends' substance use (low sanction potential) conditions the effect of self-control on adolescents' smoking, drinking, and marijuana use. Therefore, adolescents with low self-control are more likely to use substances only when they are presented with attractive opportunities that are unlikely to lead to sanctions.

SCOTT A. DESMOND, ALAN S. BRUCE, AND MELISSA J. STACER

Introduction

In *A General Theory of Crime,* Michael Gottfredson and Travis Hirschi (1990:117) present a theory designed to explain "all crime, at all times." Central to Gottfredson and Hirschi's theory is the concept of self-control, defined as a personality characteristic that regulates people's ability to resist opportunities for simple activities believed to provide immediate rewards. Gottfredson and Hirschi (1990:89) reason that crime is attractive to individuals with low self-control because it is simple, requires little skill or effort, and brings immediate gratification ("money without work, sex without courtship, revenge without court delays"). In Gottfredson and Hirschi's theory, behavior is determined by the interaction of self-control and the opportunity to engage in simple acts that promise immediate pleasures. All other things being equal, when a criminal opportunity arises, the person with low self-control is more likely to engage in crime than the individual with high self-control. Although controversial, considerable evidence supports Gottfredson and Hirschi's claims about the role of self-control in criminality, regardless of how self-control has been measured (Bolin 2004; Goode 2008a; Hay and Forrest 2008; Pratt and Cullen 2000; Smith 2004).

While researchers have examined the role of self-control as a cause of crime, opportunity has received considerably less attention (Hay and Forrest 2008; Seipel and Eifler 2010; Smith 2004). We believe opportunity is an important, and often overlooked, component of Gottfredson and Hirschi's theory. People with more criminal opportunities will be more likely to engage in crime, regardless of their level of self-control, while individuals with low self-control *and* opportunity for crime will have even greater criminal involvement. Given the role of opportunity in Gottfredson and Hirschi's theory, we examine both the direct effects of self-control and opportunity, and the interaction effect of these variables, on adolescent smoking, drinking, and marijuana use.[1]

Opportunities differ in their likelihood of punishment, or their sanction potential. We believe it is the sanction potential of a situation that determines when an offender will take advantage of an opportunity for crime. We also believe the sanction potential of some situations is inherently high and, accordingly, will always be unsuitable opportunities characterized by less crime. Therefore, crime is less likely to occur in some situations regardless of a person's level of self-control. In this article, we argue that obtaining substances (cigarettes, alcohol, and marijuana) from the home is an unattractive opportunity with high sanction potential, whereas getting substances from friends is an enticing opportunity with low sanction potential. We hypothesize that the effect of self-control on substance use will vary according to the availability of opportunities with low sanction potential (friends' substance use), but will not depend on the availability of opportunities with high sanction potential (substances in the home), as even adolescents with low self-control will find these opportunities unattractive.

Self-Control Theory

In developing self-control theory, Gottfredson and Hirschi (1990) adopt a classical perspective from which, they assert, there is no need to explain motivation, as we are all naturally motivated to engage in behavior that enhances our pleasure and/or reduces pain. Gottfredson and Hirschi assert that crime is inherently pleasurable. Therefore, criminal behavior depends on a person's ability to control the natural motivation to engage in activities that increase pleasure and/or reduce pain when suitable opportunities arises. The goal of their theory is to explain why some people control their pursuit of pleasure and/or reduction of pain while others do not.

Central to Gottfredson and Hirschi's theory is the "nature of crime," from which they determine the underlying trait believed to cause criminal activity. From their analysis of research on different types of crime, Gottfredson and Hirschi assert there are no important differences between offenses. Since all crimes share common properties, there is no need to develop offense specific explanations. Gottfredson and Hirschi (1990:89) argue that all crimes provide "*immediate* gratification of desires, . . . *easy or simple* gratification of desires, . . . are *exciting, risky, or thrilling,* . . . provide *few or meager long-term benefits,* . . . [and] require *little skill or planning.*" These properties constitute the nature of crime.

Based on the nature of crime, Gottfredson and Hirschi deduce the characteristics of "criminality," an individual trait determined by level of self-control. People with low self-control have greater criminality than those with high self-control and, given equal opportunity, are much more likely to offend because they are less able to resist the opportunity to increase their pleasure and/or reduce pain. Low self-control predisposes people to engage in a variety of criminal and non-criminal acts, while those with high self-control are less likely in all situations to engage in crime or analogous behaviors.

From the nature of crime Gottfredson and Hirschi deduce several dimensions of low self-control. Because crime easily provides instant gratification, those low in self-control prefer physical acts that bring immediate results. Preference for instant gratification means those low in self-control are also more likely to engage in non-criminal acts that bring immediate results, such as drinking and gambling. Because crime is exciting and risky, those low in self-control tend to act spontaneously, rather than considering the long-term implications of their behavior. Because a quick reduction in pain or discomfort is often the objective of crime, those low in self-control will prefer simple and immediate problem resolution. Gottfredson and Hirschi (1990:90) conclude "people who lack self-control will tend to be impulsive, insensitive, physical (as opposed to mental), risk-taking, short-sighted, and nonverbal, and they will tend therefore to engage in criminal and analogous acts." Because these properties are inherent in the nature of criminal acts, people with low self-control are attracted to crime.

In contrast to self-control, Gottfredson and Hirschi (1990) do not develop the role of opportunity in their theory (Simpson and Geis 2008). Given the brief discussion of opportunity provided by Gottfredson and Hirschi (1990), researchers have operationalized opportunity in a variety of ways with mixed results. One general approach to measuring opportunity has been to ask people about perceived opportunities for deviance (Bolin 2004; De Li 2004; Grasmick et al. 1993; Longshore 1998; Tittle and Botchkovar 2005a). In his prospective test of self-control and opportunity, Longshore (1998:106) measured opportunity as the perception an offense was "easy to do and you were pretty sure nobody who might do something about it would quickly find out." Additional studies have measured opportunity as the perception of how difficult it would be to get cigarettes, alcohol, and marijuana (De Li 2004) and the

likelihood of getting caught for cheating (Bolin 2004). These studies generally show that perceived opportunity has a significant effect on deviance, although Bolin (2004) found no direct relationship between opportunity and academic dishonesty. Each study that tested for an interaction between self-control and opportunity also found some support for the hypothesis that opportunity conditions the effect of self-control on deviance (De Li 2004; Grasmick et al. 1993; Longshore 1998; Tittle and Botchkovar 2005a). That is, low self-control has a stronger effect on deviant behavior when the individual also perceives there are opportunities to commit deviant acts.

A second, and more frequently used, approach has been to use variables that approximate opportunity. For example, in their examination of the interaction between self-control and opportunity on crimes of force and fraud, Longshore and Turner (1998) measured opportunity with two proxy variables. First, gender was used as an indicator of opportunity on the grounds that males have more opportunities for crime than females and, second, subjects were asked "how many of their current friends engage in crime other than illicit drug use" (Longshore and Turner 1998:88). For each measure of opportunity, Longshore and Turner (1998) found the relationship between self-control and crimes involving fraud was contingent on opportunity, but this was not the case for crimes requiring force. LaGrange and Silverman (1999) measured opportunity as supervision by mothers and fathers, whether or not the adolescent had a curfew, unsupervised time spent with friends, and time spent driving around in a car. Although having a curfew was not significantly related to any form of delinquency (general, property, violent, or drug), parental supervision, time spent with friends, and driving around in a car all had significant effects on multiple forms of delinquency. There were also many significant interactions between self-control, measured in more than one way, and the different measures of opportunity, especially for drug offenses (LaGrange and Silverman 1999). Cochran et al. (1998) measured opportunity as the number of credit hours students were enrolled in college. Opportunity had a significant direct effect on academic dishonesty and also conditioned the effect of self-control on academic dishonesty (see, also, Cochran et al. 2006).

Opportunity has most often been approximated using routine activities, especially "risky lifestyles" and evenings spent away from home. Forde and Kennedy (1997) measured opportunity as evening activities, such as the number of nights per month spent at bars, restaurants, sporting events, movies, visiting friends, going to work, and attending class, while Baron et al. (2007) operationalized opportunity as the number of months in the last year a person was homeless. Neither measure of risky lifestyles was strongly related to crime. Burton et al. (1998) found that evenings spent away from home did not have a significant effect on self-reported crime, but the interaction between opportunity and low self-control had a significant effect for girls. In another study, evenings spent away from home was significantly related to imprudent behaviors, such as drinking, smoking, and using drugs, but not crime (Burton et al. 1999). In general, as a measure of opportunity, evenings spent away from home tends to have an effect on substance use (i.e., imprudent behaviors), but is not significantly related to crime.

Sanction Potential and Opportunity

Given the importance of opportunity to their theory, Gottfredson and Hirschi have been accused of failing to provide an adequate definition of opportunity (Grasmick et al. 1993). Building on the classical perspective, however, we believe that Gottfredson and Hirschi (1990; 2003) do articulate their conception of opportunity. Drawing on the work of Bentham, Gottfredson and Hirschi suggest classical theorists have long recognized the influence of consequences on behavioral restraint and note that, although classical theorists focused on the importance of legal sanctions, this perspective is entirely consistent with the influence of informal social control mechanisms. "Put another way, in Bentham's view, the restraining power of legal sanctions in large part stems from their correlation to social sanctions" (Gottfredson and Hirschi 1990:85).

Gottfredson and Hirschi (2003) further clarify their conception of opportunity in their discussion of the deterrent effect of criminal justice policies. They argue it is the offender's *perception* of the certainty of punishment related to a situation that reduces the likelihood of crime. In particular, Gottfredson and Hirschi (2003:13) note that increasing the severity of sanctions for crime has little deterrent effect, while increasing the certainty of sanctions may help reduce crime, so "certainty becomes an opportunity factor as we have defined it." Furthermore, according to Gottfredson and Hirschi (2003:13) "(b)ecause immediate costs and benefits dominate the thinking of individuals with low self-control, even they will tend to be intimidated by the prospects of rapid reaction by the criminal justice system." Thus, the authors contend the sanction potential of a situation, defined as the would-be offender's *perception* of the certainty of punishment, is central to criminal opportunity and a key variable in determining whether a person will engage in crime.

There are a variety of sanctions that may accompany different offenses. Hirschi and Gottfredson (2001:88) classify the potential sanctions that might follow behaviors as: *physical* (the natural consequences of acts, such as injuries from fighting or death from drug use); *moral* or *social* (which are imposed by parents, friends, teachers, etc., such as shame or a reputation as untrustworthy); *political* or *legal* (formal sanctions for law breaking imposed by the government, such as fines or imprisonment); and *religious* (which are "imposed by supernatural authorities" and apply both "now and in the hereafter"). While the type of sanction may vary depending on the offense (e.g., alcohol use may lead to hangovers and blackouts, while robbery may lead to physical injury), self-control theory does not recognize the unique effect of any particular type of sanction, instead proposing that the person with low self-control will fail to be restrained by any form of sanction. We focus, however, on moral or social sanctions, which we think are central to conceptualizing opportunity for crime.

Consistent with Gottfredson and Hirschi (1990; 2003), in conceptualizing opportunity we believe it is important to focus on situational characteristics, the importance of which have long been recognized. For example, in their critique of subcultural explanations for delinquency Briar and Piliavin (1965:36) note that, "Because delinquent behavior is typically episodic, purposive, and confined to certain situations, we assume that the motives for such behavior are frequently episodic, oriented to short-term ends, and confined to certain situations." Emphasizing situational characteristics as the proximate cause of crime is consistent with the evidence that youthful offending is near universal. In other words, when presented with the "right" opportunity, nearly all juveniles engage in delinquency. The question then becomes what constitutes the right opportunity?

In conceptualizing opportunity for crime, Cohen and Felson's (1979) routine activities perspective is instructive. Cohen and Felson do not focus on offender characteristics, but on the convergence of factors allowing crime to occur at a given time. Crime is thus rooted in the properties of situations, rather than individuals. Cohen and Felson (1979:590) believe the three components necessary for crime are (1) a motivated offender who is a person with both criminal inclinations and the ability to carry out those inclinations," (2) a "suitable target for the offender," and (3) the "absence of guardians capable of preventing violations." As with Gottfredson and Hirschi, Cohen and Felson assume natural motivation for crime and they do not attribute motivation to more general life circumstances (e.g., poverty, unemployment). While Cohen and Felson (1979:589) initially focused on predatory crimes involving direct physical contact between at least one offender and at least one person or object which that offender attempts to take or damage," the range of their perspective has been widened to include acts that do not bring direct harm to a victim (Felson 2002).

Clearly it is the coexistence of these three elements in space and time that results in criminality, but only suitable targets and the absence of capable guardians require our attention, as motivated offenders are ever-present. We believe suitable targets and the absence of capable guardians are *the essential* elements for determining when a criminal opportunity exists. That is, it is important to identify *both the physical characteristics* that constitute a suitable target (e.g., small, portable items are more suitable targets than large, bulky items), *and the sanction potential of a situation,* based on an offender's perception of whether capable guardians are likely to interfere with the potential pleasure to be gained from a target by imposing sanctions.

Situations differ in their likelihood of punishment, or their sanction potential. We believe the sanction potential of situations has been neglected in discussions of opportunity and it is sanction potential that determines when an offender will take advantage of a physically suitable opportunity for crime. We also believe the sanction potential of some situations is inherently high and, accordingly, will always be unsuitable opportunities characterized by less crime. That is, the sanction potential of a situation is determined by a person's assessment of a situation, but some situations are so familiar that sanction potential is inherent to the situation. Therefore, crime is less likely to occur in some situations regardless of the level of self-control possessed by those who are present.

Some may argue our concept of sanction potential is inconsistent with Gottfredson and Hirschi's theory because those low in self-control, by definition, are unable to determine sanction potential. Piquero and Tibbetts (1996:448), for example, argued that individuals with low self-control "are more likely not to perceive shame and sanctions as important because these are long-term outcomes, whereas they perceive pleasure as a short-term result of committing an offense." Contrary to their expectations, however, the results of their study suggested that self-control had no effect on the perceived costs and risks of offending. That is, people with low self-control perceived the costs and risks of offending, such as the chances of arrest or the probability others would discover their crimes, to be the same as people with high self-control.[2]

Additional research also suggests that self-control does not influence offenders' perceptions of the sanction potential of a situation. For example, Wright et al. (2004:196) found that even criminally prone individuals may view crime as risky and costly, which provides "empirical support for the theoretical position that all persons consider the consequences of their behavior and that even those who are high in criminal propensity and impulsivity are capable of foresight." Similarly, Tittle and Botchkovar (2005b) found that fear of sanctions did not mediate the effect of self-control on criminal behavior. Although Nagin and Paternoster (1993:483) did find a significant effect for self-control on perceived sanctions, they also reported that self-control had only a weak effect, explaining less than 10% of the variance in perceived sanctions. In summary, although people who are low in self-control may be "more present-oriented than most, all individuals discount future consequences to some extent, and all to some degree are responsive to situational contingencies" (Wright et al. 2004:207).[3]

In summary, we believe opportunity is determined by the sanction potential actors associate with situations in which crime can occur. From our perspective opportunity is contingent on the sanction potential, both formal (e.g., criminal justice system) and informal (e.g., parental sanction), of a given situation.[4] Drawing on the earlier discussion, we formulated the following hypotheses:

H₁ Adolescents with low self-control will be more likely to use substances than adolescents with high self-control.

H₂ Adolescents with more opportunities for substance use will be more likely to use substances than adolescents with fewer opportunities.

H₃ The effect of self-control on substance use will *not* vary with opportunity when the sanction potential in a situation is high.

H₄ The effect of self-control on substance use *will* vary with opportunity when the sanction potential in a situation is low.

Previous research generally supports our hypothesis that the effect of self-control on substance use will depend on the sanction potential of available opportunities. Research using perceptual measures of opportunity, such as the perceived likelihood of being caught, which most clearly assesses the sanction potential of an opportunity, indicates that opportunity has a direct effect on deviant behavior *and* also interacts with self-control (De Li 2004; Grasmick et al. 1993; Longshore 1998). Therefore, when people perceive that a situation is unlikely to

lead to sanctions they are more likely to engage in crime and this is especially true for people with low self-control. Furthermore, many of the studies that have approximated opportunity have used items that we would argue are low in sanction potential, such as gender, parental supervision, and unsupervised time with friends. In general, although many studies that approximate opportunity did not test for an interaction between self-control and opportunity, these studies also suggest that individuals who are low in self-control are particularly likely to engage in crime when the sanction potential of an opportunity is low.

Methods
Data
We used data from the National Longitudinal Study of Adolescent Health (Add Health). The primary sampling frame for Add Health was a list of high schools. Schools were stratified by region of the country, urbanicity, percent white, size, and school type (public, private, and parochial) and a sample of 80 high schools was selected with unequal probability. Fifty-two middle schools that supplied students to the high schools were also included in the sample, for a total of 132 schools.

After students were stratified by sex and grade (7th–12th), approximately 200 students were randomly selected from each school. Students with disabilities, identical and fraternal twins, and racial minorities with at least one college educated parent were also over-sampled. Adolescents, and one of their parents, were interviewed between April and December of 1995. A second interview with the adolescents was completed approximately one year later.[5] In order to establish the appropriate temporal order between variables, all of the independent variables we used are taken from the first in-home survey completed by the adolescents and the parent survey, while the dependent variables are taken from the second wave. For all of the analyses, we corrected for the unequal probability of selection and the clustering of students within schools (for a thorough discussion of the Add Health sample design effects, and how corrections are made, see Chantala and Tabor 1999).

Substance Use
We used three measures of substance use: smoking, drinking, and marijuana use. First, adolescents were asked, "During the past 30 days, on how many days did you smoke cigarettes" (0 to 30 days)? Second, adolescents were asked, "Over the past 12 months, on how many days have you gotten drunk or very, very high' on alcohol?" The responses for this question ranged from "never" to "everyday or almost everyday." Finally, marijuana use was measured using an item that asked adolescents how many times in the last year they had used marijuana. The response format for this item also ranged from "never" to "everyday or almost everyday."

Opportunity
While Osgood et al. (1996:639) allude to the importance of "situational contingencies," such as "being in stores for

shoplifting, being with a potential partner for precocious sexuality, and being in a position of financial trust for embezzlement," they do not dwell on these as central to understanding criminal opportunity. In contrast, we believe these mundane characteristics of situations are important for understanding the opportunity to use substances. Although it may seem obvious, an essential ingredient for adolescent substance use, such as smoking, drinking, and using marijuana, is having access to the substances themselves. If adolescents have no opportunity to obtain drugs and/or alcohol, substance use cannot take place. Previous research suggests that friends are the most common source for adolescents to get cigarettes, alcohol, and drugs, followed by parents and siblings (Harrison et al. 2000; Wolfson et al. 1997). Commercial outlets tend not to be important sources of substances until adolescents become regular users (Harrison et al. 2000). For example, in a recent study (Harrison et al. 2000) almost half of adolescent drinkers reported getting alcohol from underage and overage friends, while 25% reported their parents or older siblings provided them with alcohol, and 28% took alcohol from parents or older siblings without their knowledge (similar percentages were reported for cigarettes). By comparison, only 18% of adolescent drinkers indicated they got alcohol from stores. Importantly, adolescents who smoke, drink, and use drugs often share these substances with their friends. For example, Wolfson et al. (1997) report that almost 70% of adolescents who smoked in the past 30 days provided cigarettes to another adolescent during that period.

Given that adolescents most commonly acquire substances from friends and family, we operationalized opportunity for substance use with items that tap each of these sources. First, we measured opportunity for substance use with three questions that asked if cigarettes, alcohol, and drugs were easily available" in adolescents' homes. Second, since adolescents' friends may provide access to cigarettes, alcohol, and marijuana, especially if they use these substances themselves, we used three items that asked adolescents how many of their three closest friends "smoke at least one cigarette a day," "drink alcohol at least once a month," and "use marijuana at least once a month" (0 = no friends to 3 = three friends).[6] For each dependent variable we used separate measures of opportunity that coincide with smoking, drinking, and marijuana use. For example, when smoking was used as the dependent variable, we used cigarettes available in the home and friends' smoking as the measures of opportunity. In contrast, when alcohol use was the dependent variable, we used alcohol available in the home and friends' alcohol use to measure opportunity.

Although having cigarettes, alcohol, and drugs in the home may present adolescents with an opportunity to use these substances, parents often monitor and guard substances in the home to prevent their use by children. Therefore, although having substances in the home may provide some opportunity, we believe the threat of detection and punishment by parents makes these opportunities less attractive. In other words, acquiring cigarettes, alcohol, and marijuana from parents has a *high sanction potential*. On the other hand, it is much more difficult for parents to monitor their children, and their friends, when they are away from home. Most underage smoking, drinking, and drug use

goes undetected. Therefore, acquiring cigarettes, alcohol, and marijuana from friends has a *low sanction potential*. Based on our hypotheses, there should be a significant interaction between self-control and friends' substance use (low sanction potential), but there should not be a significant interaction between self-control and substances in the home (high sanction potential).

Self-Control

Previous research has measured self-control using both behavioral and attitudinal (or cognitive) items. In general, both behavioral and attitudinal measures of self-control are significantly related to delinquency and substance use (Pratt and Cullen 2000). Since each of these approaches has its own limitations, we used both behavioral and attitudinal measures to create our measure of self-control.

Overall, we used eleven items to construct a measure of self-control (alpha = .703). Since we added the items together to form our measure of self-control, and all of the items are measured using a similar response format (0—4), each item in the index is weighted equally. First, following previous research that has used the Add Health data to study self-control, we used the same five items used by Perrone et al. (2004). Adolescents were asked how often they had difficulty getting along with their teachers, paying attention in school, and getting homework done. Perrone et al. (2004) argue these items capture important dimensions of self-control, such as temper, impulsivity, and preference for physical activities. Adolescents were also asked how often they had trouble keeping their minds on what they were doing. This item taps the preference for simple tasks dimension of self-control. The last item, which, according to Perrone et al. (2004), indicates how self-centered adolescents are, asked adolescents to indicate their level of agreement with the statement "You feel you are doing everything just about right."

In addition to the items used by Perrone et al. (2004), we added six items related to how adolescents make decisions and solve problems. In general, these items indicate whether adolescents make decisions cautiously or impulsively without much thought. The items were: "When you get what you want, it's usually because you worked hard for it," "When making decisions, you usually go with your gut feeling without thinking too much about the consequences of each alternative" (reverse coded), When you have problems to solve, one of the first things you do is get as many facts about the problem as possible," "When you are attempting to find a solution to a problem, you usually try to think of as many different ways to approach the problem as possible," "When making decisions, you generally use a systematic method for judging and comparing alternatives," and "After carrying out a solution to a problem, you usually try to analyze what went right and what went wrong."[7] Given how we have constructed our measure, *higher* scores on the index indicate *lower* levels of self-control.[8]

Interaction Effects

In order to test whether or not the effect of self-control on substance use depends on opportunity, we created two interaction terms. The first set of interaction terms was created by multiplying self-control and substances (i.e., cigarettes, alcohol, and drugs) easily available in the home. The second set of interaction terms was created by multiplying self-control and friends' smoking, drinking, and marijuana use.[9]

Control Variables

Previous research suggests that sex, age, race, and social class are significantly related to adolescent substance abuse. First, males are more likely to engage in substance use than females (Blum et al. 2000; Hoffmann 2002). Second, age is also significantly related to substance use, with older adolescents being more likely to use substances than younger adolescents (Challier et al. 2000; Hoffmann and Johnson 1998). Third, research on the relationship between race and substance use is somewhat mixed, although most studies indicate white youth are more likely than minorities to smoke, drink, and use marijuana (Blum et al. 2000). Finally, social class is also significantly related to adolescent substance use. Adolescents from lower socioeconomic status homes are more likely to smoke and drink (Blum et al. 2000; Ennett et al. 2001; Goodman and Huang 2002). The evidence for marijuana use is inconclusive, with some research indicating that lower socioeconomic status is related to higher levels of adolescent marijuana use (Hanson and Chen 2007) and others finding no relationship (Challier et al. 2000; Hoffmann and Johnson 1998).

Since previous research suggests that sex, age, race, and social class are significantly related to substance use among adolescents, we controlled for the effects of these variables in our analysis. Sex was coded as a dichotomous variable (1 = male and 0 = female). Age is a continuous measure that was computed by subtracting the interview date from the adolescent's date of birth. Race was coded as a set of dummy variables; white youth were used as the contrast category. We also included a measure for Hispanic ethnicity (1 = Hispanic, 0 = non-Hispanic). Social class was measured using two items: welfare status and parents' education. First, parents were asked if they or a member of their household had received Supplemental Security Income (SSI), Aid to Families with Dependent Children (AFDC), food stamps, and/or a housing subsidy in the last month. Welfare was coded one if the respondent received *any* form of welfare and zero if he/she did not receive public assistance. Second, because many of the adolescents live in single-parent homes, parent's education was based on the parent with the highest level of education (parent's education is listed as missing when no father or mother is present).

Previous research also suggests that family structure and process are significantly related to adolescent substance use. Adolescents who reside in single-parent homes are more likely to smoke, drink, and use marijuana (Blum et al. 2000; Hoffmann and Johnson 1998). Adolescents who report higher levels of attachment to their parents, and whose parents report higher levels of attachment to them, are less likely to engage in substance use (Chapple et al. 2005; Dornbusch et al. 2001; Hoffmann 2002; Kostelecky 2005; Miller and Volk 2002; van der Vorst et al. 2006). Therefore, in the analysis we included measures of family structure, parent's attachment to child, and child's attachment to parents.

Family structure was measured using a dichotomous variable, coded one if the adolescent lived with both biological parents and zero otherwise. Six items were combined to form a measure of parent's "attachment to child" (alpha = .731). Parents were asked "How often would it be true for you to make each of the following statements" about their sons or daughters: "You get along well with him/her," you and your child "make decisions about his/her life together," "You just do not understand him/her" (reverse coded), "You feel you can really trust him/her," and "(He/she) interferes with your activities" (reverse coded). For the final item, parents were asked if they agreed or disagreed with the statement "Overall, you are satisfied with your relationship with" your child. As part of the Add Health in-home survey, adolescents were asked a large number of questions about their relationships with their mothers and fathers. We used the following five items to compute a measure of "attachment to mother" (alpha = .941) and "attachment to father" (alpha =.980): "How close do you feel to your mom/dad," "How much do you think he/she cares about you," "Most of the time your mother/father is warm and loving toward you," "You are satisfied with the way your mother/father and you communicate with each other," and "Overall, you are satisfied with your relationship with your mother/father." When both parents were present in the home, the attachment to parents scale was computed by taking the average of the attachment to mother and attachment to father scales. In single parent homes, attachment to parents is the score for the parent who is present.

In addition to family processes, school experiences are also significantly related to adolescent substance use, with higher attachment to school and higher academic achievement related to lower levels of adolescent substance use (Dornbusch et al. 2001; Henry and Slater 2007; Kostelecky 2005). Therefore, we controlled for the effects of grades and school attachment in our analyses. Adolescents' grades were measured using a computed grade point average (A = 4) based on the grades they received in English or language arts, math, history or social studies, and science (alpha = .982). We used five items to construct a "school attachment" index (alpha = .761). Adolescents were asked to agree or disagree with the following statements: "You feel close to people at your school," "You feel like you are part of your school," "You are happy to be at your school," "The teachers at your school treat students fairly," and "You feel safe in your school." Descriptive statistics for all variables are depicted in Table 1.

Results

Table 2 depicts the OLS regression results for smoking.[10] For model 1 (column 1), we included all of the control variables, plus our two measures of opportunity, cigarettes in the home and friends' smoking, and our measure of self-control. With regard to opportunity, adolescents are more likely to smoke when cigarettes are easily available in their homes and when more of their friends smoke. Also, the lower adolescents' level of self-control the more likely they are to smoke. Thus, both opportunity and self-control have significant direct effects on smoking.

Table 1 Descriptive Statistics for Independent and Dependent Variables

Independent variables	Mean	Standard deviation	Range
Sex	.50	.50	0–1
Age	16.16	1.73	11–21
White	.50	.50	0–1
African American	.21	.41	0–1
Asian	.06	.24	0–1
Other Race	.05	.22	0–1
Hispanic	.17	.38	0–1
Welfare	.19	.39	0–1
Parent Education	13.73	2.69	0–18
Biological Family	.51	.50	0–1
Attachment to Child	12.76	2.55	0–18
Attachment to Parents	16.67	3.11	0–20
Grades	2.68	.87	0–4
School Attachment	13.42	3.76	0–20
Cigarettes in Home	.31	.46	0–1
Alcohol in Home	.29	.45	0–1
Drugs in Home	.03	.18	0–1
Friends Smoke	.82	1.06	0–3
Friends Drink	1.11	1.17	0–3
Friends Use Marijuana	.63	1.00	0–3
Self Control	13.22	5.13	0–44
Dependent variables			
Smoking (Wave 2)	5.13	10.32	0–30
Drinking (Wave 2)	.68	1.31	0–6
Marijuana Use (Wave 2)	.61	1.23	0–6

Table 2 OLS Regression Coefficients for the Effects of Opportunity and Self-Control on Smoking

	Model 1	Model 2	Model 3	Model 4
Sex	−.672* (.267)	−.669* (.266)	−.662* (.265)	−.661* (.265)
Age	.454** (.092)	.454** (.092)	.473** (.092)	.473** (.092)
African American	−4.227** (.320)	−4.213** (.318)	−4.223** (.320)	−1.215** (.319)
Asian	−1.422** (.422)	−1.434** (.421)	−1.475** (.423)	−1.480** (.422)
Other Race	−.175 (.560)	−.191 (.559)	−.183 (.565)	−.192 (.565)
Hispanic	−1.998** (.413)	−2.00** (.413)	−1.992** (.414)	−1.995** (.414)
Welfare	−.349 (.351)	−.344 (.349)	−.329 (.356)	−.328 (.355)
Parent Education	.038 (.047)	.037 (.047)	.032 (.047)	.032 (.047)
Biological Family	−.491 (.321)	−.498 (.321)	−.512 (.320)	−.515 (.320)
Attachment to Child	−.415** (.067)	−.414** (.067)	−.417** (.066)	−.417** (.066)
Attachment to Parents	−.026 (.052)	−.028 (.053)	−.026 (.052)	−.027 (.053)
Grades	−1.066** (.182)	−1.063** (.183)	−1.063** (.181)	−1.061** (.181)
School Attachment	−.119** (.038)	−.119** (.038)	−.114** (.038)	−.114** (.038)
Cigarettes in Home	1.072** (.254)	.183 (.546)	1.072** (.253)	.553 (.558)
Friends Smoke	4.140** (.214)	4.136** (.214)	2.883** (.435)	2.937** (.442)
Self-Control	.142** (.030)	.117** (.032)	.063* (.031)	.052 (.032)
Interaction Effects				
SC × Cigarettes in Home		.066 (.044)		.039 (.044)
SC × Friends Smoke			.086** (.026)	.082** (.026)
R-Squared	.312	.312	.314	.314

*p < .05; **p < .01.
Adjusted standard errors in parentheses.

For model 2, we added an interaction term between self-control and cigarettes in the home. As hypothesized, the interaction is not significant, which suggestions the effect of self-control on smoking does not depend on the availability of cigarettes in the home. With the addition of the interaction term, self-control has a significant effect on smoking. With an interaction term in the model, this coefficient represents the relationship between self-control and smoking when cigarettes in the home is equal to zero (i.e., when cigarettes are *not* easily available). In other words, even when cigarettes are not easily available in the home, adolescents with low self-control are still significantly more likely to smoke. Conversely, when the interaction effect is added, the simple effect of cigarettes in the home is not significant. This coefficient represents the relationship between cigarettes in the home and smoking when self-control is equal to zero. Recall that, for our measure of self-control, higher scores equal *lower* self-control. Thus, a score of zero indicates very high levels of self-control. Since the coefficient for cigarettes in the home is not significant, for adolescents with high self-control, having cigarettes easily available in the home does not lead to an increase in smoking (i.e., when adolescents have high self-control, this type of opportunity has no effect on their smoking).[11]

For model 3, we added an interaction term between self-control and friends' smoking. Unlike the results for self-control and cigarettes in the home, the interaction is significant. Thus, the effect of self-control on smoking depends on the number of friends who smoke. Figure 1 illustrates the interaction between self-control and friends' smoking. Moving from left to right, it is clear that adolescents smoke more often when they have friends who smoke. Exposure to friends who smoke, however, has a stronger effect on adolescents with low self-control. For example, for adolescents who have three smoking friends, those with high self-control smoked, on average, 13.5 days in the last month. Adolescents with low self-control, on the other hand, smoked 19.9 days in the last month. Unlike the results for cigarettes in the home, then, it appears that adolescents with high self-control are better able to avoid the temptation to smoke when presented with the opportunity to do so by their peers.

Returning to Table 2 (model 3), with the addition of the interaction term, self-control has a significant effect on smoking. This coefficient represents the relationship between self-control and smoking when an adolescent has no friends who smoke. Thus, when adolescents have no friends who smoke, self-control still has an effect on smoking. Conversely, when the interaction effect is added, the simple effect of friends' smoking is also significant. This coefficient represents the relationship between friends' smoking and adolescents' smoking when self-control is very high (i.e., self-control is equal to zero). This suggests that, for adolescents with high levels of self-control, having friends who smoke still leads to an increase in smoking.

Finally, for model 4 we included both interactions (self-control by cigarettes in the home and self-control by friends' smoking) in the same model. Consistent with our hypotheses, the interaction between self-control and friends' smoking is significant, while the interaction between self-control and cigarettes in the home is not. Therefore, the effect of self-control on substance use varies with opportunity when the sanction potential in a situation is low (friends' smoking), but does not vary with opportunity when the sanction potential in a situation is high (cigarettes in the home).

Table 3 depicts the results for alcohol use. For model 1 (column 1), the results are very similar to the results for smoking. Both opportunity and self-control have significant effects on drinking. Adolescents are more likely to drink when alcohol is easily available in their homes and when more of their friends drink. Also, the lower adolescents' level of self-control the more likely they are to drink.

For model 2, we added the interaction term for self-control and alcohol in the home. Similar to the results for smoking, the interaction is not significant. The effect of self-control on drinking does not depend on the availability of alcohol in the home. With the addition of the interaction term, self-control still has a significant effect on drinking. Therefore, consistent with the results for smoking, even when alcohol is not easily available in the home, adolescents with low self-control are still significantly more likely to drink. When the interaction effect is added, the effect of alcohol in the home is not significant. Thus,

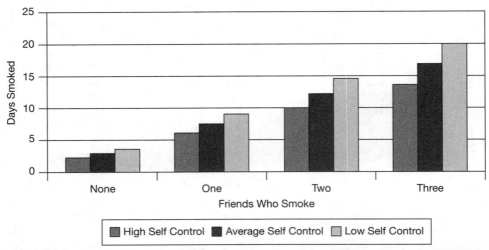

Figure 1 Interaction of Self-Control and Delinquent Friends on Smoking. (Color figure available online.)

Table 3 OLS Regression Coefficients for the Effects of Opportunity and Self-Control on Alcohol Use

	Model 1		Model 2		Model 3		Model 4	
Sex	.108**	(.035)	.108**	(.035)	.110**	(.035)	.110**	(.035)
Age	.079**	(.011)	.080**	(.011)	.082**	(.011)	.082**	(.011)
African American	−.313**	(.051)	−.314**	(.051)	−.315**	(.050)	−.315**	(.050)
Asian	−.300**	(.104)	−.300**	(.104)	−.305**	(.105)	−.305**	(.105)
Other Race	−.023	(.084)	−.024	(.084)	−.026	(.085)	−.026	(.085)
Hispanic	−.008	(.058)	−.008	(.058)	−.012	(.058)	−.012	(.058)
Welfare	−.105*	(.046)	−.105*	(.046)	−.107*	(.045)	−.107*	(.045)
Parent Education	.009	(.008)	.009	(.008)	.008	(.008)	.008	(.008)
Biological Family	−.023	(.037)	−.023	(.037)	−.025	(.037)	−.025	(.037)
Attachment to Child	−.018*	(.008)	−.018*	(.008)	−.018*	(.008)	−.018*	(.008)
Attachment to Parents	−.014*	(.007)	−.014*	(.007)	−.014*	(.007)	−.014*	(.007)
Grades	−.032	(.024)	−.032	(.024)	−.032	(.023)	−.032	(.023)
School Attachment	.001	(.005)	.001	(.005)	.002	(.005)	.002	(.005)
Alcohol in Home	.107*	(.043)	.070	(.089)	.110*	(.043)	.102	(.091)
Friends Drink	.410**	(.021)	.410**	(.021)	.260**	(.048)	.260**	(.049)
Self-Control	.020**	(.004)	.019**	(.004)	.008	(.004)	.008	(.004)
Interaction Effects								
SC × Alcohol in Home			.003	(.007)			.001	(.007)
SC × Friends Drink					.011**	(.003)	.011**	(.003)
R-Squared	.212		.212		.214		.214	

*p < .05; **p < .01.
Adjusted standard errors in parentheses.

when adolescents have high self-control, this type of opportunity has no effect on their drinking.

For model 3, we added the interaction term between self-control and friends' drinking. Consistent with the results for smoking, the interaction effect for self-control and friends' drinking is significant. Since the interaction effect for drinking follows the same pattern as the interaction for smoking, in order to conserve space we do not include a separate figure for drinking (instead, refer to Figure 1). The effect of friends' drinking is stronger for adolescents with low self-control. With the addition of the interaction term, self-control does not have a significant effect on drinking (although it is very close, $p = .069$). Thus, when adolescents have no friends who drink, adolescents with low self-control are not more likely to drink. This may suggest the importance of friends as a source of alcohol. When the interaction effect is added, the effect of friends' drinking is significant. This coefficient represents the relationship between friends' drinking and adolescents' drinking when self-control is very high. For adolescents with high levels of self-control having friends who drink still contributes to an increase in drinking.

Similar to the results for smoking, when both interactions are included in the same model (model 4), the interaction between self-control and friends' alcohol use is significant, but the interaction between self-control and alcohol in the home is not. Therefore, the results for alcohol use also suggest the effect of self-control on substance use varies when the sanction

potential in a situation is low, but does not vary when the sanction potential in a situation is high.

Table 4 depicts the results for marijuana use. Similar to the results for both smoking and drinking, both opportunity and self-control have significant effects on adolescent marijuana use. For model 1 (column 1), adolescents are not more likely to use marijuana when drugs are easily available in the home, but they are more likely to use marijuana when more of their friends use marijuana. Self-control is also significantly related to marijuana use. The lower adolescents' level of self-control the more likely they are to use marijuana.

For model 2, we added the interaction term for self-control and drugs in the home. Similar to the results for smoking and drinking, the interaction is not significant. Also comparable to the results for both smoking and drinking, when the interaction term is added to the model, self-control is significantly related to marijuana use, but the availability of drugs in the home is not. Thus, even when drugs are not easily available in the home (i.e., drugs in the home equals zero), adolescents with low self-control are still more likely to use marijuana. Conversely, for adolescents with high levels of self-control, having drugs easily available in the home does not lead to an increase in marijuana use. Thus, consistent with the results for drinking and smoking, when adolescents have high self-control, the easy availability of substances in the home has no effect on substance use.

For model 3, we added the interaction term between self-control and friends' marijuana use. The interaction is

Table 4 OLS Regression Coefficients for the Effects of Opportunity and Self-Control on Marijuana Use

	Model 1		Model 2		Model 3		Model 4	
Sex	.041	(.033)	.041	(.033)	.042	(.033)	.042	(.033)
Age	.019*	(.009)	.019*	(.009)	.021*	(.009)	.021*	(.009)
African American	−.216**	(.038)	−.216**	(.038)	−.213**	(.037)	−.213**	(.037)
Asian	−.207**	(.050)	−.207**	(.050)	−.207**	(.049)	−.207**	(.049)
Other Race	.021	(.069)	.021	(.068)	.024	(.068)	.024	(.068)
Hispanic	.070	(.052)	.070	(.052)	.072	(.052)	.072	(.052)
Welfare	−.069	(.048)	−.069	(.048)	−.069	(.049)	−.068	(.049)
Parent Education	.028**	(.005)	.028**	(.005)	.028**	(.005)	.027**	(.005)
Biological Family	−.131**	(.031)	−.131**	(.031)	−.133**	(.031)	−.132**	(.031)
Attachment to Child	−.029**	(.008)	−.029**	(.008)	−.029**	(.008)	−.029**	(.008)
Attachment to Parents	−.019**	(.006)	−.019**	(.006)	−.019**	(.006)	−.019**	(.006)
Grades	−.035	(.018)	−.035	(.018)	−.035	(.018)	−.035	(.018)
School Attachment	−.008	(.004)	−.008	(.004)	−.008	(.004)	−.008	(.004)
Drugs in Home	.072	(.074)	.080	(.112)	.064	(.073)	.115	(.115)
Friends Marijuana Use	.603**	(.028)	.603**	(.028)	.443**	(.068)	.441**	(.068)
Self-Control	.019**	(.003)	.019**	(.003)	.012**	(.003)	.012**	(.003)
Interaction Effects								
SC × Drugs in Home			−.001	(.011)			−.004	(.010)
SC × Friends Marijuana					.010*	(.005)	.011*	(.005)
R-Squared	.301		.301		.303		.303	

*p < .05; **p < .01.
Adjusted standard errors in parentheses.

significant. Consistent with the results for smoking and drinking, the effect of self-control on marijuana use depends on the number of friends who use marijuana. The pattern for marijuana use is the same as the results for smoking and drinking (refer to Figure 1). Adolescents are more likely to smoke marijuana when they have marijuana-smoking friends. Also, having friends who use marijuana has a stronger effect on adolescents with low self-control. Therefore, similar to the results for smoking and drinking, it appears that adolescents with low self-control are less able to avoid the opportunity to use marijuana when they are exposed to marijuana using friends, whereas adolescents with high self-control are better able to avoid this temptation.

Returning to Table 4 (model 3), with the addition of the interaction term, self-control still has a significant effect on marijuana use. Thus, even when adolescents have no friends who use marijuana, self-control still has a significant effect on marijuana use. Also, when the interaction effect is added, the effect of friends' marijuana use is also significant. Thus, adolescents are more likely to smoke marijuana when they have marijuana-smoking friends, even if they have high levels of self-control.

Similar to the results for smoking and alcohol use, and consistent with our hypotheses, the effect of self-control on substance use varies when the sanction potential in a situation is low, but does not vary when the sanction potential in a situation is high. That is, when both interactions are included in

the same model (model 4), the interaction between self-control and friends' marijuana use is significant, but the interaction between self-control and drugs in the home is not.

Conclusion

Since the publication of Gottfredson and Hirschi's (1990) *A General Theory of Crime,* a considerable number of studies have examined the effect of self-control on crime and analogous behaviors. For the most part, research suggests that self-control is consistently related to delinquency and substance use (Pratt and Cullen 2000). However, very few studies have examined the effect of opportunity, an important part of Gottfredson and Hirschi's theory, in conjunction with self-control. In order to address this important gap in the literature, we conceptualized opportunity from a classical perspective as the sanction potential in a situation and used two measures of opportunity with different sanction potentials, the availability of substances in the home (high sanction potential) and friends' substance use (low sanction potential), to examine the effects of self-control and opportunity on substance use.

The results of our study provide fairly strong support for Gottfredson and Hirschi's theory. First, for all three measures of substance use, smoking, drinking, and marijuana use, *both* opportunity and self-control had significant effects. When cigarettes and alcohol are easily available in the home, adolescents are more likely to use these substances. Furthermore, the more adolescents' friends use substances, the more likely they are to smoke, drink, and use marijuana. Finally, the lower adolescents' self-control, the more likely they are to smoke, drink, and use marijuana.

In addition to the direct effects of opportunity and self-control on substance use, we also found consistent evidence that the effect of self-control depends on the opportunities that are available for adolescents to use substances, although it is important to recognize the sanction potential that accompanies such opportunities. Whereas the easy availability of cigarettes, alcohol, and drugs in the home did not condition the effect of self-control on substance use, for all three measures of substance use, the interaction effect between self-control and friends' substance use is significant, which suggests that friends' substance use has a stronger effect on adolescents who have low self-control.

The results of our study suggest the relationship between self-control, "opportunity, and substance use may depend a great deal on the sanction potential of an opportunity. As Smith (2004:549) argues, opportunity is circumscribed by the potential of bringing immediate benefits, the ease of committing the act, and the absence of a high risk of detection." In other words, depending on the exact circumstances, opportunities may range anywhere from excellent (low sanction potential) to poor (high sanction potential). In some cases, the opportunity to use substances may be so great that even adolescents with high self-control find their capacity to resist temptation overwhelmed. In other cases, a minimal opportunity to use substances could be present, but the circumstances are so unfavorable they can be resisted even by adolescents with low self-control.

Our results illustrate such a relationship. We argue that friends' substance use represents a good opportunity with a low potential for sanctions. If friends smoke, drink, and/or use marijuana, then adolescents have access to the essential ingredients for substance use. Furthermore, if adolescents are getting substances from their friends, then avoiding detection by parents, teachers, and other adults may not be particularly difficult. Thus, when the interaction between self-control and friends' substance use was included in the models, for each measure of substance use the simple effect of friends' substance use remained significant. Therefore, even when adolescents have high levels of self-control, having friends who smoke, drink, and use marijuana still leads to an increase in substance use. In some cases, then, the opportunity to use substances may be so great that even adolescents with very high levels of self-control are unable to resist the temptation to smoke, drink, and use marijuana.

In contrast, we argue the availability of substances in the home represents a poor opportunity with a high potential for sanctions. If parents smoke, then adolescents might be able to steal an occasional cigarette, or even an entire pack. Depending on how carefully parents keep track of their cigarettes, however, getting cigarettes from parents might be quite difficult and adolescents risk detection. Getting alcohol and, especially, drugs from parents is probably even more difficult. Parents might, for example, secure alcohol in a locked liquor cabinet or monitor the contents of liquor bottles by marking the label to indicate how full the bottle was the last time it was used. It is very likely that parents who use drugs hide their drugs, and their use, from adolescents. Thus, when the interaction between self-control and substances in the home was included in the models, for each measure of substance use the simple effect of substances in the home was not significant. Therefore, when adolescents have high levels of self-control, the availability of substances in the home has no effect on adolescents' substance use. In some cases, then, if circumstances provide only a minimal opportunity, adolescents with very high levels of self-control are able to resist using substances. In fact, if an opportunity exists, but it is so unfavorable, even those with *moderate* or *low* levels of self-control might choose not to engage in substance use. If the degree of difficulty is sufficiently high and the possibility for detection is great, even fairly impulsive criminals may not perceive a viable opportunity.

Although we feel our study helps to increase our understanding of how the combination of low self-control and opportunity can lead to substance use, our study does suffer from a number of limitations. In particular, the concept of opportunity is not well defined in criminology. Gottfredson and Hirschi (2003:8) have defined opportunity as "sets of circumstances favorable to crime," but such a definition could include an endless number of situations. We have argued that when substances are "easily available in the home," this constitutes a measure of opportunity, but such a generic survey question could include a wide variety of circumstances. Since the items we use to measure the availability of substances in the home are dichotomous, an additional limitation of our study, we are unable to determine the particular characteristics of situations that make substance use more attractive.

Also, we have argued that friends' substance use represents a form of opportunity, but it is difficult to disentangle the effects of opportunity from other theoretical mechanisms, such as social learning, that might be at work. The significant interaction between self-control and friends' smoking could mean that adolescents with low self-control are less able to resist smoking when they are presented with the opportunity. Others have argued, however, that friends influence behavior because the peer group models, imitates, or reinforces deviant behavior" (Chapple 2005:92). Meldrum et al. (2009), for example, examined the compatibility of self-control and social learning theory. Similar to our study, the authors found a significant interaction between self-control and peers, but they attributed the effect of peers to social learning, rather than opportunity.

Although the effect of peers can be interpreted in several different ways, previous research on self-control and peers provides some support for our argument that peers represent a form of opportunity. Chapple (2005) found that adolescents who are low in self-control are more likely to have delinquent friends (see, also, McGloin and Shermer 2009), and part of the effect of self-control on delinquency was mediated by associating with delinquent peers. Chapple (2005:102) argues that the effect of peers could be the result of opportunity, as "the delinquent peer group may provide increased opportunities for crime or exert situational pushes towards delinquency net of the self-control of the members comprising these groups."

Also, McGloin and Shermer (2009) found that, independent of whether or not peers are delinquent, adolescents who are low in self-control tend to spend more time hanging out with friends. In turn, time spent with peers has also been conceptualized as a measure of opportunity that contributes to delinquency (Haynie and Osgood 2005).

"With regard to opportunity, part of the problem is that opportunity is a wickedly difficult construct to operationalize" (Simpson and Geis 2008:59). Although our measures of opportunity, substances easily available in the home and friends' substance use, may overlap with other theoretical mechanisms, the same can probably be said for just about every proxy measure of opportunity. For example, Hay and Forrest (2008) operationalize opportunity as time away from home unsupervised, time spent with peers, and adults being absent from the home after school, but note these measures overlap with parental supervision and peer association. The authors conclude the problem of conceptual overlap "is perhaps especially notable in attempts to measure opportunity, because this concept is embedded and interdependent with other concepts, largely because a role of opportunity is implicit in many theories" (Hay and Forrest 2008:1052).

Overall, our results are consistent with Gottfredson and Hirschi's assertion that self-control plays an important role in adolescent substance use. Our results also illustrate the vital role of opportunity, conceived as the sanction potential of situations, in adolescent substance use. A more thorough understanding of crime and delinquency, however, requires greater attention to the role of opportunity, as it is clear opportunities greatly vary in their sanction potential.

Notes

1. Although Gottfredson and Hirschi (1990) originally discussed the role of opportunity in their theory, following the publication of *A General Theory of Crime* they have consistently denied the importance of opportunity. For example, Gottfredson and Hirschi (2003:9) argue that "self-control can be measured and the theory assessed without undue concern for differences in opportunities to commit criminal, deviant, or reckless acts." Although Gottfredson and Hirschi have argued that opportunity is of little consequence, others argue that opportunity is an important part of self-control theory. For example, Goode (2008b:11) argues that "the criminally inclined do *not* commit crime under any and all circumstances; they commit crime only after assessing their odds of success and failure, and that assessment takes place within the context of opportunity."

2. Although self-control does not seem to influence perceptions about the risks and costs of crime, there is some evidence that people who are low in self-control are more likely to believe that crimes will be rewarding or pleasurable (Piquero and Tibbetts 1996) and to perceive sanctions as unfair (Piquero et al. 2004).

3. Previous research generally shows that self-control does not have a significant effect on perceptions of the certainty and severity of sanctions. A related issue is whether or not self-control conditions the effect of sanctions on deviant behavior. That is, do sanctions have the same effect on people with high and low self-control? Research on this point has been very

mixed. Nagin and Paternoster (1994) found that sanctions have a stronger effect on those high in self-control, while Wright et al. (2004) found that sanctions have a stronger effect on those low in self-control (see, also, Tittle and Botchkovar 2005b) and Cochran et al. (2008) found the effect of perceived sanctions did not vary by level of self-control.

4. We argue that opportunities differ in terms of their sanction potential, or the probability that offenders will be sanctioned for engaging in deviant behavior. Similarly, borrowing from rational choice theory, in a recent article Seipel and Eifler (2010) argue that opportunities vary according to their costs. That is, opportunities with a "high risk of being caught are costly and therefore unfavorable opportunities," whereas "opportunities linked to a low risk of being caught . . . are less costly and therefore favorable opportunities" (Seipel and Eifler 2010:173). Similar to our argument that adolescents with low self-control will be tempted most by opportunities with low sanction potential, Seipel and Eifler (2010) argue that personality traits, like self-control, are most relevant in low-cost situations. In contrast, Seipel and Eifler (2010) argue that in high-cost situations rational choice or utility is more important.

5. Not all of the adolescents included in the first wave of Add Health were included in subsequent waves. The vast majority of adolescents who were seniors in high school at Wave 1 were not re-interviewed at Wave 2. Also, some adolescents who were eligible for Wave 2 could not be located or were unable or unwilling to be interviewed again. In total, 13,568 adolescents were included in both Wave 1 and Wave 2. Analysis of non-response suggests that sample attrition introduces very little bias in estimates of smoking, drinking, and marijuana use, which we use for our dependent variables (Kalsbeek et al. 2001). Furthermore, the sample weights included in Add Health adjust for nonresponse at Wave 2.

6. We are not the first to argue that delinquent or substance using peers represent a measure of opportunity (see, for example, Longshore and Turner 1998; Warr 2001). As Warr (2001:79) argues, "opportunity is not only temporally and spatially structured, but socially structured as well, and opportunities for crime have as much to do with relations among offenders as with those between offenders and victims."

7. Gottfredson and Hirschi (1990:89) argue that self-control consists of multiple elements, including immediate gratification, simple gratification, thrill seeking, few long term benefits, little skill or planning, and insensitivity, many of which we tap with the items included in our measure of self-control. Contrary to Gottfredson and Hirschi (1990), but consistent with previous research, when we conducted a factor analysis the self-control items did not load on a single factor. Not surprisingly, the behavioral items tended to group together on one factor, while the problem solving items tended to group together on another. Despite the results of the factor analysis, following Gottfredson and Hirschi, and much previous research, we combine the items into a single measure of self-control.

8. Although it may seem odd to code the measure of self-control so that *higher* scores on the index indicate *lower* levels of self-control, for the analysis of interaction terms, coding self-control in this way makes the interpretation of the simple effects more meaningful.

9. Unstandardized interaction terms often cause problems with multicollinearity (Aiken and West 1991). In order to check our results, we replicated the analysis using standardized (or

"centered") interactions. Standardizing the interactions eliminated any problems with multicollinearity. The pattern of results for the standardized interactions was the same as the results using the unstandardized interactions (reported in the text).

10. The items we use to measure substance use are not normally distributed. Although ordinary least squares (OLS) regression does not assume a normally distributed dependent variable (Allison 1999a:130), when the dependent variable is positively skewed two assumptions of OLS regression may be violated: non-normally distributed errors and heteroscedasticity. It is unlikely either of these problems influences our results. First, Allison (1999a:130) notes that non-normally distributed errors are not a concern with samples over 200 (see also Fox 1991). Second, using robust standard errors, which we have done, helps address heteroscedasticity (Allison 1999a:127).

We also rely on OLS regression because testing interaction terms with a nonlinear model (e.g., logistic regression, ordered logistic regression, negative binomial, logit and probit models) creates statistical problems that can lead to faulty conclusions (Ai and Norton 2003; Allison 1999b; Norton et al. 2004). In particular, with nonlinear models interaction terms will often "reverse" direction. In fact, when we replicated the analysis for smoking using a negative binomial regression, compared to the OLS results the interaction terms were completely opposite (the same thing happened when we replicated the analysis for drinking and marijuana use with tobit regression). After closely inspecting the data (i.e., a series of crosstabs), we determined the OLS results are correct. That is, the direction of the OLS interaction terms fit the pattern that is found in the data, whereas the results for alternative models do not. Therefore, although some might argue an alternative method should be used for the analysis, we think OLS is a more trustworthy method.

11. When interaction terms are *standardized,* "b1 is the predicted effect of X on Y when Z equals its sample mean" (Jaccard and Turrisi 2003:25), but we used *unstandardized* interaction terms (i.e., we did not center the independent variables before creating the product term). Thus, "in the product-term model . . . the coefficient for X estimates the effect of X on Y when Z is at a specific value, namely, when Z = 0" and, conversely, "the coefficient for Z estimates the effect of Z on Y when X is at a specific value, namely, when X = 0" (Jaccard and Turrisi 2003:24).

In *some* cases, a score of zero on an independent variable either does not exist or is not meaningful, in which case it is inappropriate to interpret the simple effects. All of the variables we used to create the product terms, however, have meaningful zero points. For availability of substances in the home, which is a dummy variable, zero indicates substances are not easily available in the home. For friends' substance use, zero indicates an adolescent has no friends who use a particular substance. For self-control, zero indicates adolescents with very high self-control.

References

Ai, Chunrong and Edward C. Norton. 2003. "Interaction Terms in Logit and Probit Models." *Economics Letters* 80:123–129.

Aiken, Leona S. and Stephen, G. West. 1991. *Multiple Regression: Testing and Interpreting Interactions.* Newbury Park, CA: Sage.

Allison, Paul D. 1999a. *Multiple Regression: A Primer.* Thousand Oaks, CA: Pine Forge Press.

———. 1999b. "Comparing Logit and Probit Coefficients Across Groups." *Sociological Methods and Research* 28:186–208.

Baron, Stephen W., David R. Forde, and Fiona M. Kay. 2007. "Self-Control, Risky Lifestyle, and Situation: The Role of Opportunity and Context in the General Theory." *Journal of Criminal Justice* 35:119–136.

Blum, Robert W., Trisha Beuhring, Marcia L. Shew, Linda H. Bearinger, Renee E. Sieving, and Michael D. Resnick. 2000. "The Effects of Race/Ethnicity, Income, and Family Structure on Adolescent Risk Behaviors." *American Journal of Public Health* 90:1879–1884.

Bolin, Aaron U. 2004. "Self-Control, Perceived Opportunity, and Attitudes as Predictors of Academic Dishonesty." *Journal of Psychology* 138:101–114.

Briar, Scott and Irving Piliavin. 1965. "Delinquency, Situational Inducements, and Commitment to Conformity." *Social Problems* 13:35–45.

Burton, Velmer S., Jr., Francis T. Cullen, T. David Evans, Leanne F. Alarid, and R. Gregory Dunaway. 1998. "Gender, Self-Control, and Crime." *Journal of Research in Crime and Delinquency* 35:123–147.

Burton, Velmer S., Jr., T. David Evans, Francis T. Cullen, Kathleen M. Olivares, and R. Gregory Dunaway. 1999. "Age, Self-Control, and Adults' Offending Behaviors: A Research Note Assessing *A General Theory of Crime.*" *Journal of Criminal Justice* 27:45–54.

Challier, Bruno, Nearkasen Chau, Rosemay Predine, Marie Choquet, and Bernard Legras. 2000. "Associations of Family Environment and Individual Factors with Tobacco, Alcohol and Illicit Drug Use in Adolescents." *European Journal of Epidemiology* 16:33–42.

Chantala, Kim and Joyce, Tabor. 1999. *Strategies to Perform a Design-Based Analysis using the Add Health Data.* Carolina Population Center, University of North Carolina at Chapel Hill.

Chapple, Constance L. 2005. "Self-Control, Peer Relations, and Delinquency." *Justice Quarterly* 22:89–106.

Chapple, Constance L., Trina L. Hope, and Scott W. Whiteford. 2005. "The Direct and Indirect Effects of Parental Bonds, Parental Drug Use, and Self-Control on Adolescent Substance Use." *Journal of Child and Adolescent Substance Abuse* 14:17–38.

Cochran, John K., Peter B. Wood, Christine S. Sellers, Wendy Wilkerson, and Mitchell B. Chamlin. 1998. "Academic Dishonesty and Low Self-Control: An Empirical Test of a General Theory of Crime." *Deviant Behavior* 19:227–255.

Cochran, John K., Valentina Aleksa, and Mitchell B. Chamlin. 2006. "Self-Restraint: A Study on the Capacity and Desire for Self-Control." *Western Criminology Review* 7:27–40.

Cochran, John K., Valentina Aleksa, and Beth A. Sanders. 2008. "Are Persons Low in Self-Control Rational and Deterrable?" *Deviant Behavior* 29:461–483.

Cohen, Lawrence E. and Marcus Felson. 1979. "Social Change and Crime Rate Trends: A Routine Activity Approach." *American Sociological Review* 44:588–608.

De Li, Spencer. 2004. "The Impacts of Self-Control and Social Bonds on Juvenile Delinquency in a National Sample of Midadolescents." *Deviant Behavior* 25:351–373.

Dornbusch, Sanford M., Kristan Glasgow Erickson, Jennifer Laird, and Carol A. Wong. 2001. "The Relation of Family and School Attachment to Adolescent Deviance in Diverse Groups and Communities." *Journal of Adolescent Research* 16:396–422.

Ennett, Susan T., Karl E. Bauman, Vangie A. Foshee, Michael Pemberton, and Katherine A. Hicks. 2001. "Parent-Child Communication about Adolescent Tobacco and Alcohol Use: What Do Parents Say and Does It Affect Youth Behavior?" *Journal of Marriage and the Family* 63:48–62.

Felson, Marcus. 2002. *Crime and Everyday Life.* Thousand Oaks, CA: Sage.

Forde, David R. and Leslie W. Kennedy. 1997. "Risky Lifestyles, Routine Activities, and the General Theory of Crime." *Justice Quarterly* 14:265–294.

Fox, John. 1991. *Regression Diagnostics.* Newbury Park, CA: Sage Publications.

Goode, Erich. 2008a. ed. *Out of Control: Assessing the General Theory of Crime.* Stanford, CA: Stanford Social Sciences.

———. 2008b "Out of Control?: An Introduction to the General Theory of Crime." Pp. 3–25 in *Out of Control: Assessing the General Theory of Crime,* edited by Erich Goode. Stanford, CA: Stanford Social Sciences.

Goodman, Elizabeth and Bin Huang. 2002. "Socioeconomic Status, Depressive Symptoms, and Adolescent Substance Use." *Archives of Pediatrics and Adolescent Medicine* 156:448–453.

Gottfredson, Michael R. and Travis Hirschi. 1990. *A General Theory of Crime.* Stanford, CA: Stanford University Press.

Gottfredson, Michael R. and Travis Hirschi. 2003. "Self-Control and Opportunity." Pp. 5–19 in *Control Theories of Crime and Delinquency,* edited by Chester L. Britt and Michael R. Gottfredson. New Brunswick, NJ: Transaction Publishers.

Grasmick, Harold G., Charles R. Tittle, Robert J. Bursik, Jr., and Bruce J. Arneklev. 1993. "Testing the Core Empirical Implications of Gottfredson and Hirschi's General Theory of Crime." *Journal of Research in Crime and Delinquency* 30:5–29.

Hanson, Margaret D. and Edith Chen. 2007. "Socioeconomic Status and Health Behaviors in Adolescence: A Review of the Literature." *Journal of Behavioral Medicine* 30:263–285.

Harrison, Patricia A., Jayne A. Fulkerson, and Eunkyung Park. 2000. "The Relative Importance of Social Versus Commercial Sources in Youth Access to Tobacco, Alcohol, and Other Drugs." *Preventive Medicine* 31:39–48.

Hay, Carter and Walter Forrest. 2008. "Self-Control Theory and the Concept of Opportunity: The Case for a More Systematic Union." *Criminology* 46:1039–1072.

Haynie, Dana L. and D. Wayne Osgood. 2005. "Reconsidering Peers and Delinquency: How do Peers Matter?" *Social Forces* 84:1109–1130.

Henry, Kimberly L. and Michael D. Slater. 2007. "The Contextual Effect of School Attachment on Young Adolescents' Alcohol Use." *Journal of School Health* 77:67–74.

Hirschi, Travis and Michael R. Gottfredson. 2001. "Self-Control Theory." Pp. 81–96 in *Explaining Criminals and Crime,* edited by Raymond Paternoster and Ronet Bachman. New York: Oxford University Press.

Hoffmann, John P. 2002. "The Community Context of Family Structure and Adolescent Drug Use." *Journal of Marriage and the Family* 64:314–330.

Hoffmann, John P. and Robert A. Johnson. 1998. "A National Portrait of Family Structure and Adolescent Drug Use." *Journal of Marriage and the Family* 60:633–645.

Jaccard, James and Robert Turrisi. 2003. *Interaction Effects in Multiple Regression.* 2nd edition. Thousand Oaks, CA: Sage Publications.

Kalsbeek, William D., Carolyn B, Morris, and Benjamin J., Vaughn. 2001. *Effects of Nonresponse on the Mean Squared Error of Estimates from a Longitudinal Study.* Carolina Population Center, University of North Carolina at Chapel Hill.

Kostelecky, Kyle L. 2005. "Parental Attachment, Academic Achievement, Life Events, and Their Relationship to Alcohol and Drug Use During Adolescence." *Journal of Adolescence* 28:665–669.

LaGrange, Teresa C. and Robert A. Silverman. 1999. "Low Self-Control and Opportunity: Testing the General Theory of Crime as an Explanation for Gender Differences in Delinquency." *Criminology* 37:41–72.

Longshore, Douglas. 1998. "Self-Control and Criminal Opportunity: A Prospective Test of the General Theory of Crime." *Social Problems!* 45:102–113.

Longshore, Douglas and Susan Turner. 1998. "Self-Control and Criminal Opportunity: Cross-Sectional Test of the General Theory of Crime. " *Criminal Justice and Behavior* 25:81–98.

McGloin, Jean Marie and Lauren O'Neil Shermer. 2009. "Self-Control and Deviant Peer Network Structure." *Journal of Research in Crime and Delinquency* 46:35–72.

Meldrum, Ryan C., Jacob T. N. Young, and Frank M. Weerman. 2009. "Reconsidering the Effect of Self-Control and Delinquent Peers: Implications of Measurement for Theoretical Significance." *Journal of Research in Crime and Delinquency* 46:353–376.

Miller, Todd Q. and Robert J. Volk. 2002. "Family Relationships and Adolescent Cigarette Smoking: Results from a National Longitudinal Survey." *Journal of Drug Issues* 32:945–973.

Nagin, Daniel S. and Raymond Paternoster. 1993. "Enduring Individual Differences and Rational Choice Theories of Crime." *Law and Society Review* 27:467–496.

Norton, Edward C., Hua Wang, and Chunrong Ai. 2004. "Computing Interaction Effects and Standard Errors in Logit and Probit Models." *The Stata Journal* 4:154–167.

Osgood, D. Wayne, Janet K. Wilson, Patrick M. O'Malley, Jerald G. Bachman, and Lloyd D. Johnston. 1996. "Routine Activities and Individual Deviant Behavior." *American Sociological Review* 61:635–655.

Perrone, Dina, Christopher J. Sullivan, Travis C. Pratt, and Satenik Margaryan. 2004. "Parental Efficacy, Self-Control, and Delinquency: A Test of a General Theory of Crime on a Nationally Representative Sample of Youth." *International Journal of Offender Therapy and Comparative Criminology* 48:298–312.

Piquero, Alex R., Zenta Gomez-Smith, and Lynn Langston. 2004. "Discerning Unfairness Where Others May Not: Low Self-Control and Unfair Sanction Perceptions." *Criminology* 42:699–733.

Piquero, Alex R. and Stephen Tibbetts. 1996. "Specifying the Direct and Indirect Effects of Low Self-Control and Situational Factors in Of fenders' Decision Making: Toward a More Complete Model of Rational Offending." *Justice Quarterly* 13:481–510.

Pratt, Travis C. and Francis T. Cullen. 2000. "The Empirical Status of Gottfredson and Hirschi's General Theory of Crime: A Meta-Analysis." *Criminology* 38:931–964.

Seipel, Christian and Stefanie Eifler. 2010. "Opportunities, Rational Choice, and Self-Control: On the Interaction of Person and Situation in a General Theory of Crime." *Crime and Delinquency* 56:167–197.

Simpson, Sally S. and Gilbert Geis. 2008. "The Undeveloped Concept of Opportunity." Pp. 49–60 in *Out of Control: Assessing the General Theory of Crime,* edited by Erich Goode. Stanford, CA: Stanford Social Sciences.

Smith, Tony R. 2004. "Low Self-Control, Staged Opportunity, and Subsequent Fraudulent Behavior." *Criminal Justice and Behavior* 31:542–563.

Tittle, Charles R. and Ekaterina V. Botchkovar. 2005a. "The Generality and Hegemony of Self-Control Theory: A Comparison of Russian and U.S. Adults." *Social Science Research* 34:703–731.

Tittle, Charles R. and Ekaterina V. Botchkovar. 2005b. "Self-Control, Criminal Motivation, and Deterrence: An Investigation Using Russian Respondents." *Criminology* 43:307–353.

van der Vorst, Haske, Rutger C. M. E. Engels, Wim Meeus, and Maja Dekovic. 2006. "The Impact of Alcohol-Specific Rules, Parental Norms about Early Drinking and Parental Alcohol Use on Adolescents' Drinking Behavior." *Journal of Child Psychology and Psychiatry* 47:1299–1306.

Warr, Mark. 2001. "Crime and Opportunity: A Theoretical Essay." Pp. 65–94 in *The Process and Structure of Crime: Criminal Events and Crime Analysis,* edited by Robert F. Meier, Leslie Kennedy and Vincent F. Sacco. New Brunswick, NJ: Transaction Publishers.

Wolfson, Mark, Jean L. Forster, Ami J. Claxton, and David M. Murray. 1997. "Adolescent Smokers' Provision of Tobacco to Other Adolescents." *American Journal of Public Health* 87:649–651.

Wright, Bradley R. E., Avshalom Caspi, Terrie E. Moffitt, and Ray Paternoster. 2004. "Does the Perceived Risk of Punishment Deter Criminally Prone Individuals? Rational Choice, Self-Control, and Crime." *Journal of Research in Crime and Delinquency* 41:180–213.

Critical Thinking

1. Analyze the role of self-control on substance use

2. How do opportunity and self control work together to inhibit or contribute to substance use?

3. According to Desmond, Bruce and Stacer, what sanctions are most effective in inhibiting substance abuse?

Scott A. Desmond is a Visiting Assistant Professor in the School of Public and Environmental Affairs at Indiana University Purdue University-Indianapolis. Although his research focuses primarily on adolescent religious development, and how adolescent religiosity influences juvenile delinquency, he also studies how neighborhood characteristics and self-control contribute to crime, delinquency, and substance use. **Alan S. Bruce** is Associate Professor of Sociology and Director of the Criminal Justice Program at Quinnipiac University in Connecticut. His research and teaching interests include youth crime, crime theory, and crime and media. **Melissa J. Stacer** is an Assistant Professor of Criminal Justice Studies at the University of Southern Indiana. She received her PhD. from Purdue University in 2010. Her research interests include the social world of prisons, problems of prison inmates, and the impact of the federalization of crime on prison populations.

Received 9 August 2010; accepted 1 March 2011.

This research uses data from the National Longitudinal Study of Adolescent Health (Add Health), a program project designed by J. Richard Udry, Peter S. Bearman, and Kathleen Mullan Harris, and funded by a grant P01-HD31921 from the Eunice Kennedy Shriver National Institute of Child Health and Human Development, with cooperative funding from 17 other agencies. Special acknowledgment is due Ronald R. Rindfuss and Barbara Entwisle for assistance in the original design. Persons interested in obtaining data files from Add Health should contact Add Health, Carolina Population Center, 123 W. Franklin Street, Chapel Hill, NC 27516-2524 (addhealth@unc.edu). No direct support was received from grant P01-HD31921 for this analysis.

Address correspondence to Scott A. Desmond, School of Public and Environmental Affairs, Indiana University Purdue University-Indianapolis, 801 West Michigan Street, Indianapolis, IN 46202, USA. E-mail: Sadesmon@iupui.edu

---

UNIT 3

The Major Drugs of Use and Abuse

Unit Selections

14. **Marijuana and Medical Marijuana,** John Birchard
15. **'Bath Salt' Poisonings Rise as Legislative Ban Tied Up,** Donna Leinwand Leger
16. **Inhalant Abuse,** *National Institute on Drug Abuse Report*
17. **"Spice" and "K2" Herbal Highs: A Case Series and Systematic Review of the Clinical Effects and Biopsychosocial Implications of Synthetic Cannabinoid Use in Humans,** Erik W. Gunderson, et al.
18. **Monitoring the Future: National Results on Adolescent Drug Abuse, Overview of Key Findings 2011,** Lloyd D. Johnston, et al.
19. **Transcending the Medical Frontiers: Exploring the Future of Psychedelic Drug Research,** David Jay Brown

Learning Outcomes

After reading this Unit, you should be able to:

- Discuss the key factors in the debate to legalize marijuana.

- Discuss the dangers and public health challenges created by the new drug, bath salts.

- Discuss the influences that help perpetuate the problem of binge drinking on college campuses.

- Discuss the methods the United States and its allies intend to employ to disrupt heroin production in Afghanistan and Colombia.

- List and discuss the distinct features associated with the spread of methamphetamine use across the United States.

Student Website

www.mhhe.com/cls

Internet References

The American Journal of Psychiatry
http://ajp.psychiatryonline.org/cgi/content/abstract/155/8/1016

Multidisciplinary Association for Psychedelic Studies (MAPS)
www.maps.org

National Institute on Drug Abuse
www.drugabuse.gov

Office of Applied Studies
www.oas.samhsa.gov

QuitNet
www.quitnet.org

Streetdrugs.org
www.streetdrugs.org

The following articles discuss those drugs that have evolved historically to become the most popular drugs of choice. Although pharmacological modifications emerge periodically to enhance or alter the effects produced by certain drugs or the manner in which various drugs are used, basic pharmacological properties of the drugs remain unchanged. Crack is still cocaine, ice is still methamphetamine, and black tar is still heroin. In addition, all tobacco products supply the drug nicotine, coffee and a plethora of energy drinks provide caffeine, and alcoholic beverages provide the drug ethyl alcohol. All these drugs influence the way we act, think, and feel about ourselves and the world around us. They also produce markedly different effects within the body and within the mind.

To understand why certain drugs remain popular over time, and why new drugs become popular, one must be knowledgeable about the effects produced by individual drugs. Why people use drugs is a bigger question than why people use tobacco. However, understanding why certain people use tobacco, or cocaine, or marijuana, or alcohol is one way to construct a framework from which to tackle the larger question of why people use drugs in general. One of the most complex relationships is the one between Americans and their use of alcohol. More than 76 million Americans have experienced alcoholism in their families.

The most recent surveys of alcohol use estimate that 127 million Americans currently use alcohol. The use of alcohol is a powerful influence that serves to shape our national consciousness about drugs. The relationship between the use of alcohol and tobacco and alcohol and illicit drugs provides long-standing statistical relationships. The majority of Americans, however, believe that alcohol is used responsibly by most people who use it, even though approximately 10 percent of users are believed to be suffering from various stages of alcoholism.

Understanding why people initially turn to the nonmedical use of drugs is a huge question that is debated and discussed in a voluminous body of literature. One important reason why the major drugs of use and abuse, such as alcohol, nicotine, cocaine, heroin, marijuana, amphetamines, and a variety of prescription, designer, over-the-counter, and herbal drugs, retain their popularity is because they produce certain physical and psychological effects that humans crave. They temporarily restrain our inhibitions; reduce our fears; alleviate mental and physical suffering; produce energy, confidence, and exhilaration; and allow us to relax. Tired, take a pill; have a headache, take a pill; need to lose weight, take a pill; need to increase athletic performance, the options seem almost limitless. There is a drug for everything. Some drugs even, albeit artificially, suggest a greater capacity to transcend, redefine, and seek out new levels of consciousness. And they do it upon demand. People initially use a specific drug, or class of drugs, to obtain the desirable effects historically associated with the use of that drug.

Heroin and opiate-related drugs such as Oxycontin and Vicodin produce, in most people, a euphoric, dreamy state of well-being. The abuse of these prescription painkillers is one of the fastest growing (and alarming) drug trends. Methamphetamine and related stimulant drugs produce euphoria, energy,

© Lisa Zador/Getty Images

confidence, and exhilaration. Alcohol produces a loss of inhibitions and a state of well-being. Nicotine and marijuana typically serve as relaxants. Ecstasy and other "club drugs" produce stimulant as well as relaxant effects. Various over-the-counter and herbal drugs attempt to replicate the effects of more potent and often prohibited or prescribed drugs. Although effects and side effects may vary from user to user, a general pattern of effects is predictable from most major drugs of use and their analogs. Varying the dosage and altering the manner of ingestion is one way to alter the drug's effects. Some drugs, such as LSD and certain types of designer drugs, produce effects on the user that are less predictable and more sensitive to variations in dosage level and to the user's physical and psychological makeup.

Although all major drugs of use and abuse have specific reinforcing properties perpetuating their continued use, they also produce undesirable side effects that regular drug users attempt to mitigate. Most often, users attempt to mitigate these effects with the use of other drugs. Cocaine, methamphetamine, heroin, and alcohol have long been used to mitigate each other's side effects. A good example is the classic "speedball" of heroin and cocaine. When they are combined, cocaine accelerates and intensifies the euphoric state of the heroin, while the heroin softens the comedown from cocaine. Add to this the almost limitless combinations of prescription drugs, mixed and traded at "pharming" parties, and an entirely new dimension for altering drugs' physiological effects emerges. Additionally, other powerful influences on drug taking, such as advertising for alcohol, tobacco, and certain prescription drugs, significantly impact the public's drug-related consciousness. The alcohol industry, for example, dissects numerous layers of society to specifically market alcoholic beverages to subpopulations of Americans, including youth. The same influences exist with tobacco advertising. What is the message in Philip Morris's advertisements about its attempts to mitigate smoking by youth? Approximately 500,000 Americans die each year from tobacco-related illness. Add to the mix advertising by prescription-drug companies for innumerable human maladies and one soon realizes the enormity of the association between business and drug taking. Subsequently, any discussion of major drugs could begin and end with alcohol, tobacco, and prescription drugs.

Marijuana and Medical Marijuana

JOHN BIRCHARD

Marijuana, whose botanical name is cannabis, has been used by humans for thousands of years. It was classified as an illegal drug by many countries in the 20th century. But over the past two decades, there has been a growing movement to legalize it, primarily for medical purposes.

Medical marijuana use has surged in the 15 states and the District of Columbia that allow its use. But states and cities are also wrestling with the question of what medical marijuana is, or should be.

The Montana House of Representatives voted in February 2011 to repeal the state's six-year-old medical marijuana law. The 63-to-37 vote, largely along party lines in the Republican-controlled chamber, pushed Montana to the front lines of a national debate about social policy, economics and health regarding medical marijuana use

Montana's House speaker, Mike Milburn, a Republican and sponsor of the repeal bill, who said he thought that the arguments about medical use had been a pretext for encouraging recreational use and creating a path to full legalization. He said he feared gang drug wars in Montana's cities and debilitation of its youth. If the legislation is passed by the Montana Senate, it would face an uncertain fate on the desk of Gov. Brian Schweitzer, a Democrat, who has said he believes the laws need to be tightened, but he has not taken a position on repeal.

New Mexico's Republican governor, Susana Martinez, has also expressed interest in repeal in 2011. Colorado was formulating some of the most detailed rules in the nation for growing and selling. Lawmakers in New Jersey have jousted with the governor over regulation.

In November 2010, Californians defeated Proposition 19, a ballot measure that would have legalized possession and growing of marijuana outright, and taxed and regulated its use. California already reduced its penalty for possession, putting those caught with small amounts of the drug on the same level as those caught speeding on the freeway.

Advocates for Proposition 19 had said that if legalized California could raise $1.4 billion in taxes and save precious law enforcement and prison resources. Attorney General Eric Holder had insisted that the federal government would continue to enforce its laws against marijuana in California even if they conflict with state law.

Currently 15 states allow the use of marijuana for pain relief, nausea and loss of appetite by people with AIDS, cancer and other debilitating diseases. Those laws, however, are at odds with federal law. The federal government continues to oppose any decriminalization of the drug. And while the Obama administration has signaled some leeway when it comes to medical marijuana, raids on dispensaries and growers by law enforcement agencies are still common—even in California, where the industry effectively began in 1996, with the passage of the landmark Proposition 215, which legalized medical marijuana.

Rules vary widely in the states that permit medical marijuana. Some states require sellers to prove nonprofit status—often as a collective or cooperative—and all states require that patients have a recommendation from a physician. But even those in favor of medical marijuana believe that the system is ripe for abuse or even unintentional lawbreaking.

Although party line positions defined the issue in Montana, with Republicans mostly lined up in favor of restriction or repeal, there is widespread agreement among legislators and residents that medical marijuana has become something very different than it was originally envisioned to be.

Sixty-two percent of voters approved the use of medical marijuana in a Montana referendum in 2004. But the real explosion of growth came only in 2010, after the federal Department of Justice said in late 2009 that medical marijuana would not be a law enforcement priority. Since then, the numbers of patients have quadrupled to more than 27,000—in a state of only about 975,000 people—and millions of dollars have been invested in businesses that grow or supply the product.

With a growing number of Americans favoring legalization—a Gallup poll released in October 2010 found a record 46 percent approving of legalization—perhaps no ballot measure in the country was more closely watched than Proposition 19 in California.

The California ballot measure would have allowed anyone over 21 to buy, possess, use or cultivate marijuana. It would have barred personal possession of more than one ounce as well as smoking the drug in public or around minors.

Some civil rights activists favored the legalization of the drug on the grounds that marijuana arrests are wildly disproportionate in their racial impact and adversely affect minorities.

But the measure was strongly opposed by law enforcement, which said it would actually end up costing the state in increased public health and safety expenses.

As more and more states allow medical use of the drug, marijuana's supporters are pushing hard to burnish the image of marijuana by franchising dispensaries and building brands; establishing consulting, lobbying and law firms; setting up trade shows and a seminar circuit; and constructing a range of other marijuana-related businesses.

In July 2010, the Department of Veterans Affairs announced that it will formally allow patients treated at its hospitals and clinics to use medical marijuana in states where it is legal, a policy clarification that veterans had sought for several years.

The department directive resolves the conflict in veterans facilities between federal law, which outlaws marijuana, and the 14 states that allow medicinal use of the drug, effectively deferring to the states.

Marijuana is the only major drug for which the federal government controls the only legal research supply and for which the government requires a special scientific review. The University of Mississippi has the nation's only federally approved marijuana plantation. If researchers wish to investigate marijuana, they must apply to the National Institute on Drug Abuse to use the Mississippi marijuana and must get approvals from a special Public Health Service panel, the Drug Enforcement Administration and the Food and Drug Administration.

Critical Thinking

1. Fifteen states allow the use of medical marijuana. Why have these states chosen to allow marijuana for pain relief?

2. Provide a discussion of the primary issues inherent in states' legalization of marijuana.

'Bath Salt' Poisonings Rise as Legislative Ban Tied Up

As the number of accidental poisonings explodes and parents recount horror stories of crazed teenagers high on synthetic marijuana and "bath salts," federal attempts to outlaw the chemicals have stalled.

DONNA LEINWAND LEGER

The House has passed legislation that would outlaw "bath salts" and other chemical concoctions, sold at convenience stores and on the Internet as legal highs—and implicated in deaths and accidental poisonings around the country. But the legislation is stuck in the Senate, where Sen. Rand Paul, R-Ky., is keeping it from reaching a floor vote.

As the Senate dukes it out, the clock is running on the Drug Enforcement Administration's year-long emergency bans, and casualties are growing.

The number of calls to poison control centers nationwide involving "bath salts" soared in 2011, to 6,138 from 304 in 2010. The drugs come in powder and crystal form, which resemble conventional bath salts. Users looking for a high will snort or eat the powder.

Poison control centers fielded nearly 7,000 calls about synthetic marijuana in 2011, up from 2,906 in 2010.

"It is poison," said Republican Sen. Chuck Grassley of Iowa, a sponsor of a bill to outlaw synthetic marijuana. "People are spraying chemicals on a pile of plant clippings, putting that in an envelope and selling it to kids."

Dozens of teens and young adults have been hospitalized in recent months—and some have died—after smoking, snorting or swallowing the chemicals, which mimic the highs associated with popular illegal drugs such as marijuana, cocaine and Ecstasy.

Users have arrived in hospital emergency rooms gravely ill, and occasionally violent, with puzzling symptoms that confound doctors, said Debbie Carr, executive director of the American Association of Poison Control Centers. Carr said the unusual spike in cases "caused national alarm."

- In Blaine, Minn., a 22-year-old man pleaded guilty to murder last month and faces 20 years in prison after he shared 2 C-E, a synthetic hallucinogen he purchased on the Internet, with friends at a party. One teenager who tried the drug died.

- In Casper, Wyo., last month, public health officials warned people to avoid the synthetic drugs after three people who smoked or swallowed "blueberry spice" went into kidney failure and at least a dozen others needed medical help. "We are viewing use of this drug as a potentially life-threatening situation," said Tracy Murphy, state epidemiologist with the Wyoming Department of Health.

- In Bowling Green, Ky., Ashley Stillwell, a recent high school graduate, took a hit of a synthetic marijuana known as 7H while hanging out at a hookah bar with friends last year and was hospitalized, her mother, Amy Stillwell, said. "Within three minutes, she was paralyzed," her mother said.

The teen could hear her friends talking about her, including discussing how they could dispose of her body in a river should she die, Amy Stillwell said.

When she finally recovered enough to call her parents, they took her to the hospital, where she complained that her heart felt as if it was beating out of her chest. A drug screen didn't detect anything, so doctors called poison control to figure out how to treat her.

DEA Administrator Michelle Leonhart has used the agency's emergency powers to temporarily outlaw the substances while the FDA conducts the scientific and medical studies needed to include the chemicals under the Controlled Substances Act, making them the equivalent of marijuana, cocaine and other illicit drugs.

A year-long ban on three synthetic stimulants used to make "bath salts" expires Oct. 21. The ban on synthetic marijuana expires in September.

Leonhart believes the chemicals pose "an imminent danger" to the public, said Special Agent Gary Boggs of the DEA's Office of Diversion Control.

Manufacturers of the mixtures evade federal FDA regulations by printing a warning on the labels that says they are not for human consumption, Boggs said.

"What that means is that people are taking things that are manufactured under unregulated and unlicensed conditions," he said. "These aren't really bath salts. These things are made in basements and garages and warehouses."

At least 39 states have taken steps to ban synthetic marijuana, and 34 states have outlawed baths salts. The latest laws ban broad classes of the chemicals to prevent chemists from tweaking formulas to make them fall outside the ban. A permanent federal ban would allow the agents to act against people who import the drugs, sell them on the Internet and ship them across state lines.

Paul, a libertarian who says criminal justice is the purview of the states, placed a hold on the federal legislation that prevents the Senate from debating it. "He's a doctor. He understands these compounds are dangerous," said Paul spokeswoman Moira Bagley. "Our state has already made it illegal. It would be great to do that in all the states."

Sen. Amy Klobuchar, D-Minn., a former prosecutor who proposed legislation to ban the synthetic hallucinogens, said she and several other senators are trying to persuade Paul to lift his block and allow debate on the Senate floor.

"We've had many instances in our state of people who nearly died," Klobuchar said. "These synthetic drugs are often worse than the illegal drugs they claim to be."

Critical Thinking

1. What makes bath salts harder to regulate than other illegal drugs, and how might issues of regulation be addressed?

2. Discuss the effects of bath salts on the human body.

3. What do you predict the future of synthetic drugs will be and why?

Inhalant Abuse

What Are Inhalents?

Inhalants are volatile substances that produce chemical vapors that can be inhaled to induce a psychoactive, or mind-altering, effect. Although other abused substances can be inhaled, the term "inhalants" is used to describe a variety of substances whose main common characteristic is that they are rarely, if ever, taken by any route other than inhalation. This definition encompasses a broad range of chemicals that may have different pharmacological effects and are found in hundreds of different products. As a result, precise categorization of inhalants is difficult. One classification system lists four general categories of inhalants—volatile solvents, aerosols, gases, and nitrites—based on the forms in which they are often found in household, industrial, and medical products.

Volatile solvents are liquids that vaporize at room temperature. They are found in a multitude of inexpensive, easily available products used for common household and industrial purposes. These include paint thinners and removers, dry-cleaning fluids, degreasers, gasoline, glues, correction fluids, and felt-tip markers.

Aerosols are sprays that contain propellants and solvents. They include spray paints, deodorant and hair sprays, vegetable oil sprays for cooking, and fabric protector sprays.

Gases include medical anesthetics as well as gases used in household or commercial products. Medical anesthetics include ether, chloroform, halothane, and nitrous oxide (commonly called "laughing gas"). Nitrous oxide is the most abused of these gases and can be found in whipped cream dispensers and products that boost octane levels in racing cars. Other household or commercial products containing gases include butane lighters, propane tanks, and refrigerants.

Nitrites often are considered a special class of inhalants. Unlike most other inhalants, which act directly on the central nervous system (CNS), nitrites act primarily to dilate blood vessels and relax the muscles. While other inhalants are used to alter mood, nitrites are used primarily as sexual enhancers. Nitrites include cyclohexyl nitrite, isoamyl (amyl) nitrite, and isobutyl (butyl) nitrite and are commonly known as "poppers" or "snappers." Amyl nitrite is used in certain diagnostic procedures and was prescribed in the past to treat some patients for heart pain. Nitrites now are prohibited by the Consumer Product Safety Commission but can still be found, sold in small bottles labeled as "video head cleaner," "room odorizer," "leather cleaner," or "liquid aroma."

Generally, inhalant abusers will abuse any available substance. However, effects produced by individual inhalants vary,

From the Director:

Although many parents are appropriately concerned about illicit drugs such as marijuana, cocaine, and LSD, they often ignore the dangers posed to their children from common household products that contain volatile solvents or aerosols. Products such as glues, nail polish remover, lighter fluid, spray paints, deodorant and hair sprays, whipped cream canisters, and cleaning fluids are widely available yet far from innocuous. Many young people inhale the vapors from these sources in search of quick intoxication without being aware that using inhalants, even once, can have serious health consequences.

National surveys indicate that nearly 21.7 million Americans aged 12 and older have used inhalants at least once in their lives. NIDA's Monitoring the Future (MTF) survey reveals that 13.1 percent of 8th-graders have used inhalants. Parents and children need to know that even sporadic or single episodes of inhalant abuse can be extremely dangerous. Inhalants can disrupt heart rhythms and cause death from cardiac arrest, or lower oxygen levels enough to cause suffocation. Regular abuse of these substances can result in serious harm to vital organs, including the brain, heart, kidneys, and liver.

Through scientific research, we have learned much about the nature and extent of inhalant abuse, its pharmacology, and its consequences. This research has brought the picture of inhalant abuse in the Nation into focus and pointed to the dangers and the warning signs for parents, educators, and clinicians. We hope this compilation of the latest scientific information will help alert readers to inhalant abuse and its harmful effects and aid efforts to deal with this problem effectively.

Nora D. Volkow, M.D.
Director
National Institute on Drug Abuse

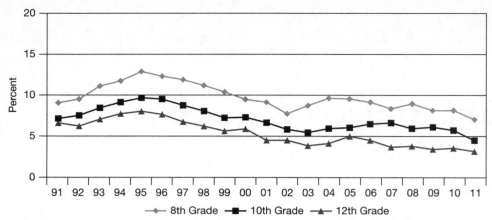

Past-Year Inhalant Use Among 8th-, 10th-, and 12th-Graders, 1991–2011.

Source: University of Michigan, 2011 Monitoring the Future Study

and some users will go out of their way to obtain their favorite inhalant. For example, in certain parts of the country, "Texas shoeshine," a shoe-shining spray containing the chemical toluene, is a local favorite.

What Is the Scope of Inhalant Abuse?

According to the 2010 National Survey on Drug Use and Health (NSDUH), there were 793,000 persons aged 12 or older who had used inhalants for the first time within the past 12 months; 68.4 percent were under the age of 18. In fact, inhalants—particularly volatile solvents, gases, and aerosols—are often the easiest and first options for abuse among young children who use drugs. NIDA's annual MTF survey of 8th-, 10th-, and 12th-graders consistently reports the highest rates of current, past-year, and lifetime inhalant use among 8th-graders.

Inhalant use has decreased significantly among 8th-, 10th-, and 12th-graders compared to its peak years in the mid-1990s (see figure). According to the 2011 MTF survey, past-year use was reported as 7.0, 4.5, and 3.2 percent, for 8th-, 10th-, and 12th-graders, respectively. Data compiled by the National Capital Poison Center also show a decrease in the prevalence of inhalant cases reported to U.S. poison control centers—down 33 percent from 1993 to 2008. The prevalence was highest among children aged 12 to 17, peaking among 14-year-olds.

Demographic differences in inhalant use have been identified at different ages. The MTF survey indicates that in 2011, 8.6 percent of 8th-grade females reported using inhalants in the past year, compared with 5.5 percent of 8th-grade males.

In terms of ethnicity, Hispanics have the highest rates of past-year use among 8th- and 10th-graders, compared to both Blacks and Whites.

People from both urban and rural settings abuse inhalants. Further, research on factors contributing to inhalant abuse suggests that adverse socioeconomic conditions, a history of

childhood abuse, poor grades, and school dropout are associated with inhalant abuse.

How Are Inhalants Used?

Inhalants can be breathed in through the nose or the mouth in a variety of ways, such as—

- "sniffing" or "snorting" fumes from containers;
- spraying aerosols directly into the nose or mouth;
- "bagging"—sniffing or inhaling fumes from substances sprayed or deposited inside a plastic or paper bag;
- "huffing" from an inhalant-soaked rag stuffed in the mouth; and
- inhaling from balloons filled with nitrous oxide.

Inhaled chemicals are absorbed rapidly into the bloodstream through the lungs and are quickly distributed to the brain and other organs. Within seconds of inhalation, the user experiences intoxication along with other effects similar to those produced by alcohol. Alcohol-like effects may include slurred speech; the inability to coordinate movements; euphoria; and dizziness. In addition, users may experience lightheadedness, hallucinations, and delusions.

Because intoxication lasts only a few minutes, abusers frequently seek to prolong the high by inhaling repeatedly over the course of several hours, which is a very dangerous practice. With successive inhalations, abusers can suffer loss of consciousness and possibly even death. At the least, they will feel less inhibited and less in control. After heavy use of inhalants, abusers may feel drowsy for several hours and experience a lingering headache.

Most inhalants produce a rapid high that resembles alcohol intoxication, with initial excitation then drowsiness, disinhibition, lightheadedness, and agitation.

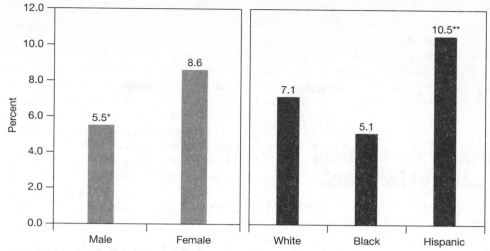

Gender and Race/Ethnicity Differences in Past-Year Inhalant Use Among 8th-Graders, 2011.
Level of significance of difference between Male and Female = .05
** *Level of significance of difference between Whites and Hispanics and Blacks and Hispanics = .001*
Source: University of Michigan, 2011 Monitoring the Future Study

How Do Inhalants Produce Their Effects?

Many brain systems may be involved in the anesthetic, intoxicating, and reinforcing effects of different inhalants. Nearly all abused inhalants (other than nitrites) produce a pleasurable effect by depressing the CNS. Nitrites, in contrast, dilate and relax blood vessels rather than act as anesthetic agents.

Evidence from animal studies suggests that a number of commonly abused volatile solvents and anesthetic gases have neurobehavioral effects and mechanisms of action similar to those produced by CNS depressants, which include alcohol and medications such as sedatives and anesthetics.

A 2007 animal study indicates that toluene, a solvent found in many commonly abused inhalants—including model airplane glue, paint sprays, and paint and nail polish removers—activates the brain's dopamine system. The dopamine system has been shown to play a role in the rewarding effects of nearly all drugs of abuse.

What Are the Short- and Long-Term Effects of Inhalant Use?

Although the chemical substances found in inhalants may produce various pharmacological effects, most inhalants produce a rapid high that resembles alcohol intoxication, with initial excitation followed by drowsiness, disinhibition, lightheadedness, and agitation. If sufficient amounts are inhaled, nearly all solvents and gases produce anesthesia—a loss of sensation—and can lead to unconsciousness.

The chemicals found in solvents, aerosol sprays, and gases can produce a variety of additional effects during or shortly after use. These effects are related to inhalant intoxication and may include belligerence, apathy, impaired judgment, and impaired functioning in work or social situations; nausea and vomiting are other common side effects. Exposure to high doses can cause confusion and delirium. In addition, inhalant abusers may experience dizziness, drowsiness, slurred speech, lethargy, depressed reflexes, general muscle weakness, and stupor. For example, research shows that toluene can produce headache, euphoria, giddy feelings, and the inability to coordinate movements.

Inhaled nitrites dilate blood vessels, increase heart rate, and produce a sensation of heat and excitement that can last for several minutes. Other effects can include flush, dizziness, and headache.

A strong need to continue using inhalants has been reported by many individuals, particularly those who have abused inhalants for prolonged periods over many days.

How Can Inhalant Abuse Be Recognized?

Early identification and intervention are the best ways to stop inhalant abuse before it causes serious health consequences. Parents, educators, family physicians, and other health care practitioners should be alert to the following signs:

- Chemical odors on breath or clothing
- Paint or other stains on face, hands, or clothes
- Hidden empty spray paint or solvent containers, and chemical-soaked rags or clothing
- Drunk or disoriented appearance
- Slurred speech
- Nausea or loss of appetite
- Inattentiveness, lack of coordination, irritability, and depression

Compulsive use and a mild withdrawal syndrome can occur with long-term inhalant abuse. A recent survey of 43,000 American adults suggests that inhalant users, on average, initiate use of cigarettes, alcohol, and almost all other drugs at younger ages and display a higher lifetime prevalence of substance use disorders, including abuse of prescription drugs, when compared with substance abusers without a history of inhalant use.

What Are the Other Medical Consequences of Inhalant Abuse?

Inhalant abusers risk an array of other devastating medical consequences. The highly concentrated chemicals in solvents or aerosol sprays can induce irregular and rapid heart rhythms and lead to fatal heart failure within minutes of a session of prolonged sniffing. This syndrome, known as "sudden sniffing death," can result from a single session of inhalant use by an otherwise healthy young person. Sudden sniffing death is associated particularly with the abuse of butane, propane, and chemicals in aerosols. Inhalant abuse also can cause death by—

- **asphyxiation**—from repeated inhalations that lead to high concentrations of inhaled fumes, which displace available oxygen in the lungs;
- **suffocation**—from blocking air from entering the lungs when inhaling fumes from a plastic bag placed over the head;
- **convulsions or seizures**—from abnormal electrical discharges in the brain;
- **coma**—from the brain shutting down all but the most vital functions;
- **choking**—from inhalation of vomit after inhalant use; or
- **fatal injury**—from accidents, including motor vehicle fatalities, suffered while intoxicated.

Based on independent studies performed over a 10-year period in three different states, the number of inhalant-related fatalities in the United States is approximately 100–200 per year.

Animal and human research shows that most inhalants are extremely toxic. Perhaps the most significant toxic effect of chronic exposure to inhalants is widespread and long-lasting damage to the brain and other parts of the nervous system. For example, chronic abuse of volatile solvents, such as toluene or naphthalene (the volatile ingredient in mothballs), damages the protective sheath around certain nerve fibers in the brain and peripheral nervous system. This extensive destruction of nerve fibers is clinically similar to that seen with neurological diseases such as multiple sclerosis.

The neurotoxic effects of prolonged inhalant abuse include neurological syndromes that reflect damage to parts of the brain involved in controlling cognition, movement, vision, and hearing. Cognitive abnormalities can range from mild impairment to severe dementia.

Inhalants also are highly toxic to other organs. Chronic exposure can produce significant damage to the heart, lungs, liver, and kidneys. Although some inhalant-induced damage to the nervous and other organ systems may be at least partially reversible when inhalant abuse is stopped, many syndromes caused by repeated or prolonged abuse are irreversible.

Abuse of inhalants during pregnancy also may place infants and children at increased risk of developmental harm. Animal studies designed to simulate human patterns of inhalant abuse suggest that prenatal exposure to toluene can result in reduced birth weights, occasional skeletal abnormalities, delayed neurobehavioral development, and altered regulation of metabolism and body composition in males, as well as food intake and weight gain in both sexes. A number of case reports note

---

Hazards of Chemicals Found in Commonly Abused Inhalants

amyl nitrite, butyl nitrite
("poppers,""video head cleaner")
sudden sniffing death syndrome, suppressed immunologic function, injury to red blood cells (interfering with oxygen supply to vital tissues)

benzene
(found in gasoline)
bone marrow injury, impaired immunologic function, increased risk of leukemia, reproductive system toxicity

butane, propane
(found in lighter fluid, hair and paint sprays)
sudden sniffing death syndrome via cardiac effects, serious burn injuries (because of flammability)

freon
(used as a refrigerant and aerosol propellant)
sudden sniffing death syndrome, respiratory obstruction and death (from sudden cooling/cold injury to airways), liver damage

methylene chloride
(found in paint thinners and removers, degreasers)
reduction of oxygen-carrying capacity of blood, changes to the heart muscle and heartbeat

nitrous oxide *("laughing gas")*, **hexane**
death from lack of oxygen to the brain, altered perception and motor coordination, loss of sensation, limb spasms, blackouts caused by blood pressure changes, depression of heart muscle functioning

toluene
(found in gasoline, paint thinners and removers, correction fluid)
brain damage (loss of brain tissue mass, impaired cognition, gait disturbance, loss of coordination, loss of equilibrium, limb spasms, hearing and vision loss), liver and kidney damage

trichloroethylene
(found in spot removers, degreasers)
sudden sniffing death syndrome, cirrhosis of the liver, reproductive complications, hearing and vision damage

Glossary

Anesthetic: An agent that causes insensitivity to pain and is used for surgeries and other medical procedures.

Central nervous system: The brain and spinal cord.

Dementia: A condition of deteriorated mental function.

Dopamine: A brain chemical, classified as a neurotransmitter, found in regions of the brain that regulate movement, emotion, motivation, and pleasure.

Naphthalene: Volatile, active ingredient in mothballs.

Toxic: Causing temporary or permanent effects that are detrimental to the functioning of a body organ or group of organs.

Withdrawal: Symptoms that occur after chronic use of a drug is reduced abruptly or stopped.

abnormalities in newborns of mothers who chronically abuse solvents, and there is evidence of subsequent developmental impairment in some of these children. However, no well-controlled prospective study of the effects of prenatal exposure to inhalants in humans has been conducted, and it is not possible to link prenatal exposure to a particular chemical to a specific birth defect or developmental problem.

Finally, a 2008 survey of over 13,000 high school students has identified an association between disordered eating (defined as a positive response to one or more of three questions about engaging in inappropriate behaviors for weight control during the past 30 days) and inhalant use among both male and female students.

What Are the Unique Risk Associated With Nitrates Abuse?

Nitrites are abused mainly by older adolescents and adults. Typically, individuals who abuse nitrites are seeking to enhance sexual function and pleasure. Research shows that abuse of these drugs in this context is associated with unsafe sexual practices that greatly increase the risk of contracting and spreading infectious diseases such as HIV/AIDS and hepatitis.

Animal research raises the possibility that there may also be a link between abuse of nitrites and the development and progression of infectious diseases and tumors. The research indicates that inhaling nitrites depletes many cells in the immune system and impairs mechanisms that fight infectious diseases. A study found that even a relatively small number of exposures to butyl nitrite can produce dramatic increases in tumor incidence and growth rate in animals.

References

Bowen, S.E.; Batis, J.C.; Paez-Martinez, N.; and Cruz, S.L. The last decade of solvent research in animal models of abuse: Mechanistic and behavioral studies. *Neurotoxicol Teratol* 28(6):636–647, 2006.

Bowen, S.E.; Daniel, J.; and Balster, R.L. Deaths associated with inhalant abuse in Virginia from 1987 to 1996. *Drug Alcohol Depend* 53(3):239–245, 1999.

Bowen, S.E.; Wiley, J.L.; Evans, E.B.; Tokarz, M.E.; and Balster, R.L. Functional observational battery comparing effects of ethanol, 1,1,1-trichloroethane, ether, and flurothyl. *Neurotoxicol Teratol* 18(5):577–585, 1996.

Fung, H.L., and Tran, D.C. Effects of inhalant nitrites on VEGF expression: A feasible link to Kaposi's sarcoma? *J Neuroimmune Pharmacol* 1(3):317–322, 2006.

Hall, M.T.; Edwards, J.D.; and Howard, M.O. Accidental deaths due to inhalant misuse in North Carolina: 2000–2008. *Subst Use Misuse* 45(9):1330–1339, 2010.

Institute for Social Research. *Monitoring the Future, 2011* (Study Results). Ann Arbor, MI: University of Michigan, 2012. Data retrieved 7/19/2012 from www.monitoringthefuture.org.

Jarosz, P.A.; Fata, E.; Bowen, S.E.; Jen, K.L.; and Coscina, D.V. Effects of abuse pattern of gestational toluene exposure on metabolism, feeding and body composition. *Physiol Behav* 93(4–5):984–993, 2008.

Jones, H.E., and Balster, R.L. Inhalant abuse in pregnancy. *Obstet Gynecol Clin North Am* 25(1):153–167, 1998.

Lubman, D.I.; Yücel, M.; and Lawrence, A.J. Inhalant abuse among adolescents: Neurobiological considerations. *Br J Pharmacol* 154(2):316–326, 2008.

Marsolek, M.R.; White, N.C.; and Litovitz, T.L. Inhalant abuse: Monitoring trends by using poison control data, 1993–2008. *Pediatrics* 125(5):906–913, 2010.

Maxwell, J.C. Deaths related to the inhalation of volatile substances in Texas: 1988–1998. *Am J Drug Alcohol Abuse* 27(4):689–697, 2001.

Mimiaga, M.J.; Reisner, S.L.; Vanderwarker, R.; Gaucher, M.J.; O'Connor, C.A.; Medeiros, M.S.; and Safren, S.A. Polysubstance use and HIV/STD risk behavior among Massachusetts men who have sex with men accessing Department of Public Health mobile van services: Implications for intervention development. *AIDS Patient Care STDS* 22(9):745–751, 2008.

Pisetsky, E.M.; Chao, Y.M.; Dierker, L.C.; May, A.M.; and Striegel-Moore, R.H. Disordered eating and substance use in high-school students: Results from the Youth Risk Behavior Surveillance System. *Int J Eat Disord* 41(5):464–470, 2008.

Riegel, A.C.; Zapata, A.; Shippenberg, T.S.; and French, E.D. The abused inhalant toluene increases dopamine release in the nucleus accumbens by directly stimulating ventral tegmental area neurons. *Neuropsychopharmacology* 32(7):1558–1569, 2007.

Sakai, J.T.; Hall, S.K.; Mikulich-Gilbertson, S.K.; and Crowley, T.J. Inhalant use, abuse, and dependence among adolescent patients: Commonly comorbid problems. *J Am Acad Child Adolesc Psychiatry* 43(9):1080–1088, 2004.

Schepis, T.S., and Krishnan-Sarin, S. Characterizing adolescent prescription misusers: A population-based study. *J Am Acad Child Adolesc Psychiatry* 47(7):745–754, 2008.

Sharp, C.W., and Rosenberg, N. Inhalant-related disorders. In: Tasman, A., Kay, J., and Lieberman, J.A., eds. *Psychiatry, Vol. 1.* Philadelphia, PA: W.B. Saunders, 1997. pp. 835–852.

Sharp, C.W., and Rosenberg, N.L. Inhalants. In: Lowinson, J.H., Ruiz, P., Millman, R.B., and Langrod, J.G., eds. *Substance Abuse: A Comprehensive Textbook (3d ed.).* Baltimore, MD: Williams & Wilkins, 1996. pp. 246–264.

Soderberg, L.S. Increased tumor growth in mice exposed to inhaled isobutyl nitrite. *Toxicol Lett* 104(1–2):35–41, 1999.

Substance Abuse and Mental Health Services Administration, Office of Applied Studies. Results from the *2010 National Survey on Drug Use and Health: Summary of National Findings.* HHS Pub. No. (SMA) 11–4658, Rockville, MD: SAMHSA, 2011.

Weintraub, E.; Gandhi, D.; and Robinson, C. Medical complications due to mothball abuse. *South Med J* 93(4):427–429, 2000.

Woody, G.E.; Donnell, D.; Seage, G.R.; Metzgera, D.; Michael, M.; Kobling, B.A.; Buchbinderh, S.; Grossd, M.; Stoneh, B.; and Judsoni, F.N. Noninjection substance use correlates with risky sex among men having sex with men: Data from *HIV/NET. Drug Alcohol Depend* 53(3):197–205, 1999.

Wu, L.T.; Howard, M.O.; and Pilowsky, D.J. Substance use disorders among inhalant users: Results from the national epidemiologic survey on alcohol and related conditions. *Addict Behav* 33(7):968–973, 2008.

Critical Thinking

1. Discuss the implications of the rates of inhalant use among United States youth.

2. What are the unique dangers of inhalant abuse?

3. How might schools and families address the risks of inhalant use in young adolescents?

From *National Institute on Drug Abuse Research Report,* July 2012. Published 2012 by National Institute on Drug Abuse/National Institutes of Health.

"Spice" and "K2" Herbal Highs: A Case Series and Systematic Review of the Clinical Effects and Biopsychosocial Implications of Synthetic Cannabinoid Use in Humans

Cannabis, the most commonly used illicit substance, exerts its primary psychoactive effect via delta-9 tetrahydrocannabinol (Δ^9-THC) agonism of cannabinoid receptor type 1 (CB1). Some users develop a cannabis use disorder and physical dependence manifested by withdrawal symptoms during abstinence. Hence, there is growing public health concern about increasing use of a new generation of synthetic cannabinoid (SC) agonists (eg, JWH-018, CP 47,497) marketed as natural herbal incense mixtures under brand names such as "Spice" and "K2." Anecdotal reports suggest overlapping effects with marijuana when the mixtures are smoked, however, systematic evaluation of SC-related psychoactive properties and adverse effects is lacking. We conducted a systematic review of published reports on SC clinical effects in humans. Most highlight potential toxicity such as acute anxiety and psychosis. In addition, we carefully document three cases in which experienced marijuana users meeting criteria for cannabis dependence with physiologic dependence smoked SC products regularly. The SC mixture effects were reportedly similar to marijuana and well tolerated. The individuals all reported that SC product use effectively alleviated cannabis withdrawal. Biopsychosocial factors associated with SC initiation and usage by the cases help to shed light on psychopharmacologic, clinical, and public health aspects of SC product consumption. (*Am J Addict* 20 12:21:320–326)

ERIK W. GUNDERSON, MD, ET AL.

Introduction

Cannabis is the most commonly used illicit substance in the world.[1] Initiation often occurs among young individuals (ie, < 18 years old), and although most users do not develop problems related to their use, a substantial minority meet criteria for a cannabis use disorder.[2] In some cases, these disorders are associated with an abstinence syndrome upon cessation of drug use (for review, see Budney et al. 2004).[3] Cannabis withdrawal symptoms such as irritability, anxiety, sleep disruptions, aches and pains, among others can be quite unpleasant.[3] A growing database demonstrates that administration of delta-9 tetrahydrocannabinol (Δ^9-THC), the major psychoactive component of cannabis, attenuates cannabis withdrawal symptoms.[4] This observation underscores the pharmacological specificity of the cannabis abstinence syndrome.[4]

Recently, a new generation of synthetic cannabinoid (SC) agonists has been reported to be used recreationally, especially by teens and young adults.[5,6] The products are marketed as natural herbal incense or potpourri under various brand names such as "Spice" or "K2," and have been sold legally in "head shops," convenience stores, and through the Internet to those seeking the "cannabis high." The poorly labeled contents have been found to include a mixture of psychoactively inert herbs and aromatic extracts sprayed with SC compounds.[7–9] The compound that has generated the most interest, JWH-018, was developed by chemist John W. Huffman (JWH) at Clemson University, USA.[7] Other cannabinomimetic compounds detected in Spice-type products in the United States, Europe, and Japan include SCs developed for research purposes such as CP 47,497 and cannabicyclohexanol, which were originally synthesized by Pfizer, as well as JWH-073, JWH-250, HU-210, and the fatty acid, oleamide.[5,9–14]

Although anecdotal reports indicate that smoked inhalation of SC-containing mixtures produces psychoactive effects overlapping with those of cannabis,[7,10,15] SC compounds have not been systematically studied in humans. Thus, the veracity of these claims is uncertain. Indeed, there is concern that SCs may exert deleterious effects on human health. Relative to Δ^9-THC, the synthetic compounds are more potent and efficacious agonists,[5,16] which could lead to greater cannabinomimetic toxicity.[7] Marijuana, the most frequently used cannabis agent, contains over 60 identified natural cannabinoids that may modulate Δ^9-THC-related effects, including negative ones.[16,17] Anecdotal case reports and increasing calls to poison control centers suggest potential adverse effects of SC exposure such as anxiety, tachycardia, and psychosis, which coupled with the abuse potential of the substances, recently led to Drug Enforcement Agency (DEA) control of several SCs under the Controlled Substances Act.[18] However, to date no systematic epidemiologic surveillance or comprehensive pharmacological assessment has taken place in humans to inform questions about the pharmacological effects and tolerability of these compounds.

In this report, we present the cases of three SC users who came to our attention during clinical care or participation in a human laboratory study examining medication development for cannabis use disorders. All patients met criteria for cannabis dependence and reported that SC use alleviated symptoms of cannabis withdrawal. To our knowledge, this is the first report to provide suggestive evidence that SC can mitigate symptoms associated with the cannabis abstinence syndrome and further demonstrate the pharmacological specificity of cannabis withdrawal. In addition, given the emerging public health issue of SCs, we systematically reviewed the existing literature on SC agonist-containing herbal blends to examine potential clinical effects and biopsychosocial correlates of initiation and usage. These issues are discussed in the context of the cases to shed light on clinical and public health concerns regarding use of SC products.

Methods

The three consecutive cases were identified between August 2010 and September 2010 at the University of Virginia (UVA) in Charlottesville. Case 1 was evaluated in primary care and Cases 2 and Case 3 were assessed during participation in an inpatient residential laboratory study examining medication development for cannabis dependence (NCT01204723). All three patients underwent a clinical interview by a physician (EWG) and were determined to meet DSM-IV-TR criteria for cannabis dependence (with physiological dependence). The findings are reported using an age estimate and without identifying information to protect case identity.

In conducting the literature review, English language studies were identified from the MEDLINE (PubMed) and PsychINFO databases through May 14, 2011 using medical subject headings "cannabinoids," "humans," and "Receptor, Cannabinoid, CB1/agonists." Additional text words were also searched including, "Spice cannabinoid," "K2," "synthetic," "JWH-018,"

"CP 47,497," "JWH-250," and "JWH-073." Only peer-reviewed publications that involved SC product or compound administration in humans were considered for the review. Two reviewers (EWG and ASJ) conducted an initial review of titles and abstracts of the electronic searches followed by more detailed assessment of relevant articles and examination of bibliographies of related reviews to find other sources. For studies presenting findings with the same or overlapping cohort, the most comprehensive sample was selected so as not to present duplicate data. The available studies presenting clinical effects of SC compounds were summarized qualitatively and findings discussed in the context of the current case series. Given the lack of peer-reviewed published information on this topic, an Internet search with Google was performed using similar terms to obtain governmental, poison control, health system, and media news releases and reports. The UVA Institutional Review Board exempted the case series from review.

Results

Nine articles (summarized in Table 1) reported SC effects in humans, including five case reports of toxicity,[19–23] a semistructured patient interview among inpatients on a forensic and rehabilitative psychiatric unit,[24] and three human toxicology laboratory studies evaluating SC detection in serum and urine samples.[10,25,26] Although two of the three laboratory studies administered commercial SC product samples in a laboratory setting,[10,25] they did not systematically report clinical effects with subjective psychoactive or psychomotor/cognitive performance measurements. Four studies confirmed specific SC compound ingestion through either testing of the commercial product that was smoked or through detection in serum/urine samples.[10,23,25,26] JWH-018 was in all four samples, along with CP 47,497 (two samples), and JWH-073 (one sample).

The nine studies suggest a cannabis-like effect after smoking SC products, including alteration in mood, perception, conjunctival injection, xerostomia, and increased pulse. Use may be complicated by more severe adverse effects including acute anxiety and psychotic reactions, particularly in those with an underlying biologic vulnerability.[19–21,24] Other associated effects reported in these studies, as well as in calls to Poison Control Centers[27,28] and National Drug Intelligence Center surveillance,[6] include hypertension, hyperventilation, diaphoresis, numbness and tingling, nausea, vomiting, tremors, muscle twitching, and seizures. Most acute effects dissipate approximately 2 hours postingestion; however, it remains unclear whether there are more prolonged residual effects of consumption.

Case Presentations

Case 1 is an approximately 30-year-old male with a 10-year history of marijuana use. He reported numerous unsuccessful attempts to discontinue marijuana use in the past year, in part, because of physical dependence. On the initial day of abstinence, he experienced typical withdrawal symptoms including irritability, dysphoria, poor sleep, and anxiety.[29] He reported smoking approximately 1–2 g/day of low-grade,

Table 1 A systematic review of published studies reporting clinical effects of synthetic cannabinoids in humans

Reference	N	Product (SC)	Amount smoked	Study type	Patient characteristic	Effects
Zimmerman et al., 2009[18]	1	Spice Gold (JWH-018, CP 47,497)	3 g/day (chronic use)	Case report	20 M with untreated ADHD	DSM-IV/ICD-10 dependence with tolerance and withdrawal that started on Day 2 of abstinence with: cognitive impairment; craving; diaphoresis; nausea; diarrhea; tremor; headache; internal unrest; insomnia; nightmares; depressed mood; palpitations; mild sustained hypertension and tachycardia (blood pressure 140/85–90 and pulse 95–100).
Müller et al., 2010[20]	1	Spice (JWH-018, CP 47,497)	3g	Case report	25 M prior cannabis-induced psychosis	Psychosis with paranoid and imperative voice hallucinations; anxiety.
Müller et al., 2010[21]	1	Spice (JWH-018, CP 47,497)	400 m	Case report	21 M with treated ADHD	Panic attack; anxiety; blurred vision; unsteady gait; fear; diaphoresis; irritability; weakness; palpitations; tachycardia. The panic attack lasted approximately 2 hours. Persistent anxiety resolved after lorazepam.
Vearrier and Oster-houdt, 2010[22]	1	JWH-018 "Pure" product purchased online	One "bong hit"	Case report	17 F	Agitation; visual hallucinations; anxiety; tachycardia (pulse 120), mild blood pressure increase (135/85); occasional muscle fasciculations; hypokalemia (2.9 mEq/L). Given lorazepam and effects resolved after 2 hours.
Schneir et al., 2011[23]	2	Banana Cream Nuke (JWH-018, JWH-073)*	0.5 g	Case report	20F, 22F	Anxiety; disoriented; injected conjunctiva; tachycardia (pulse 126 in one case); palpitations and a few beats of lateral gaze nystagmus (one case.) Effects resolved after 2 hours.
Every-Palmer, 2011[24]	15	Aroma (JWH-018; oleamide)	Not reported	Semi-structured interview	Mean age 34 years, all male with prior psychotic illness	All used as a cannabis substitute. Adverse effects included: psychosis (69%); anxiety (15%); tolerance (23%). None reported physical dependence. Acute effects lasted about 2 hours, with the psychotic reaction lasting 2 days to several weeks.
Auwärter et al., 2009[10]	2	Spice Diamond (JWH-018; CP 47,497 derivative)*	0.3 g	Human lab toxicology study	Investigator self-experiment	Performance and subjective effects measurements not reported, however, noted effects were: altered mood/perception; injected conjunctiva; increased pulse; xerostomia. Acute effects lasted about 6 hours, with mild, nonspecified residual next-day effects.
Teske et al.; 2010[25]	2	Smoke (JWH-018, 2.9% potency)*	100–150 g (50 µg per kg)	Human lab toxicology study	33 F, 47 M	Sedation; "sickness," xerostomia; hot flushes; burning eyes; "thought disruption;" increased pulse, no change in BP followed by residual tiredness lasting 6–12 hours.
Sobolevsky et al., 2010[26]	3	Tropical Synergy (JWH-018, CP 49,497)*	1g	Human lab toxicology study[†]	Mean age 22 ± 1 year (2 male, 1 female)	Anxiety; paranoia; hallucinations; short-term memory defect; impaired sense of time; injected conjunctiva; tachycardia.

SC = synthetic cannabinoid(s) confirmed or suspected of being in the brand name product based on regional product testing. *Confirmed SC compound based on direct testing of the product consumed or by urine/serum analysis. [†] Uncontrolled administration outside of the laboratory. Urinary metabolites were assessed in forensic samples seized by police during acute drug intoxication.

seeded marijuana with an approximate street price of $25 per 7 g. He initiated Spice in June 2010 to find a replacement for marijuana given concern about possible court-mandated drug testing. He had heard anecdotes and read online that Spice use resulted in a marijuana-like high but was undetected by commercially available urine toxicological screens. He was also motivated to avoid marijuana abstinence symptoms. During initial use, he purchased a 3 g bag of Spice, which he mixed in a 50:50 ratio with marijuana. For approximately 3–4 days, he smoked the mixture, and then transitioned to pure Spice. With this approach, he did not experience any marijuana withdrawal symptoms and also noted that Spice-only use resulted in similar psychoactive effects as marijuana. Other SC brands included Spice Diamond, XXX, K2, K2-Blond, Black Box, and Smoke 'n' Skulls (price range $30–40 per 3g).

Despite ongoing concern about court-mandated toxicology testing, he continued marijuana use because of excessive cost of the SC products relative to marijuana, which for him at the time was free and unlimited in supply. Between July 2010 and August 2010, he smoked approximately 3 g of SC products every other week. He no longer used the 50:50 crossover approach and started abruptly transitioning between marijuana and SC products. Three grams of SC products would last approximately 3–4 days, then he would switch back to marijuana. He did not report withdrawal symptoms during abrupt transition between marijuana and SC products. Around September 2010, he lost access to free unlimited marijuana and subsequently increased SC product use to 3 g or more per week. He only smoked SC products in a "bowl" and described the psychotropic effects as similar to marijuana regarding onset and duration of action. However, he felt that the SC mixtures were twice as potent by weight compared to the low quality marijuana he usually smoked. The only adverse effect he reported from SC use was a productive cough that did not occur with marijuana. He denied constitutional complaints and pulmonary exam was clear.

Case 2 is an approximately 25-year-old male with an 8-year history of marijuana use. His typically smoked blunts (a mixture of marijuana and tobacco), consuming an ounce per week of mid-grade marijuana with few seeds and costing approximately $50 per 7g. If he did not smoke marijuana, he experienced a withdrawal syndrome beginning on the initial day of abstinence that primarily manifested as irritability. Unlike Case 1, he was not attempting to decrease or stop marijuana use. He initiated SC product use in May 2010 seeking a novel high. He initially smoked various SC products during consecutive weekends ($40/3 g over 2–3 days). Brands included Spice Gold, Zombie, 2010, Bee Stinger, and Black Mamba. He smoked only by flavored blunt either alone or combined with marijuana. He noted no irritability of marijuana withdrawal during days in which he smoked only SC products without concurrent marijuana use. He described the "same feeling" as marijuana, with equally rapid onset, possibly shorter duration, but an "extreme high" that he likened to high quality marijuana. He reported no adverse effects other than dislike of SC product taste, which was the reason for smoking by flavored blunt. Initially, he used Spice regularly for 2–3 months to "try all the kinds," noting that the herbal products are marketed like a drug dealer markets numerous marijuana strains. In July 2010, he decreased regular use to 3 g every 2–3 months as the novelty wore off and as he became concerned about nonspecific anecdotes of potential harm.

Case 3 is an approximately 20-year-old male with a 4-year history of marijuana use. He typically smoked at least 7 g/week ($50) of mid-grade marijuana via blunt or bowl. He was not attempting to decrease or stop marijuana use and experienced a withdrawal syndrome beginning on the initial day of abstinence that included irritability and cravings. He initiated SC product use in May 2010. During the initial months, he smoked SC products primarily mixed with marijuana to get a "combined effect," noting greater "elevation" compared to either substance alone. He had only smoked SC products in a blunt. From May–August 2010 he spent approximately $25–30 every 2 days on SC products but cut back in September solely because of cost. Brands included those mentioned above and also Blueberry ($30–40/3g). Around October it became more difficult to obtain marijuana because of lack of marijuana selling contacts in his new rural residence. He noted that SC product use alleviated the irritability and cravings of marijuana abstinence. Avoidance of marijuana withdrawal became the primary motivator for current use of SC products, which were readily available. In addition, when smoking SC products alone, he described similar high quality as marijuana but of shorter duration of action and faster onset. He did not report any adverse effects of SC product use.

Discussion

The case series illustrates several pharmacological, clinical, and public health issues surrounding recent increased usage of SC-containing herbal products. All patients were regular marijuana smokers meeting DSM-IV-TR cannabis dependence criteria. Use of SC products alone or in combination with marijuana resulted in similar subjective effects as marijuana alone (eg, euphoria). Variation between cases in the degree, onset, and duration of high from SC products could reflect differences in baseline tolerance and also varying amounts and types of SC compounds in the herbal preparations.[9,13] Notably, all three individuals reported physical dependence on marijuana and experienced an attenuation or a lack of marijuana-related withdrawal by smoking SC preparations, which is consistent with evidence demonstrating Δ^9-THC administration substantially assuages withdrawal symptoms.[29,30] To our knowledge, these are the first reported cases suggesting cross-tolerance in which SC products substitute for marijuana to relieve withdrawal. Given the pharmacological specificity of marijuana withdrawal and that THC mediates its effect by CB1 neuronal activation, the cases provide novel *in vivo* suggestion of SC bioactivity via CB1 receptor agonism in humans. Of course, given the uncontrolled nature of case reports, carefully controlled studies of SC in humans are needed to confirm these results and further characterize the psychopharmacological effects.

Given the considerable overlapping effects of SC products and marijuana observed in this case series here, an important implication is that clinicians who treat cannabis use disorders should also assess patients for use of SC products. Development of urine toxicology assays for SC metabolites is under way,[26] but unfortunately routine laboratory testing for SCs is not readily available. Because of a distinct molecular structure that is different from THC metabolites, SC use will be undetected by laboratory assays for marijuana use even in heavy users.[10,19] Case 1 initiated SC use because of concern that court-mandated toxicology testing would detect his marijuana use. Such rationale for SC usage is reported among other populations in the United States[6] and Europe[5] and raises concern about clinical monitoring.

Demographically, the cases are young adults with recent SC product initiation, which reflects the burgeoning US trend indicated by an alarming rise in calls to poison control centers nationally[27] and observation by law enforcement officials.[6] Although a detailed review of poison control cases and adverse effects has yet to be published, there were 2,304 calls from 49 states and the District of Columbia as of November 22, 2010 according to the American Association of Poison Control Centers' National Poison Data System (NPDS).[27] In contrast, only 13 calls were received for all of 2009.[31] This represents a nearly 200-fold increase in calls to poison control from 2009 to 2010, potentially reflecting growing use. In comparison, there were 4,009 case mentions of marijuana during calls to poison control centers in 2008, of which 1,020 were single exposures to marijuana alone.[32] Unfortunately, the lack of prevalence data on SC product use precludes speculation about relative toxicity compared to marijuana.

SC product use was psychoactively well tolerated by the three cases in contrast to anecdotal reports collated in Table 1 suggesting potential acute anxiety reactions, agitation, psychosis, paranoia, and cognitive impairment.[6,15,19,20,22,24,27,28] Other reported associated effects have included nausea, hyperventilation, diaphoresis, pallor, headache, numbness, seizures, muscle twitching, and autonomic hyperactivity. Some of these adverse effects are incongruent with those typically associated with acute effects of Δ^9-THC (eg, hypertension, hyperventilation, nausea, vomiting, seizures) and rather than a direct result of SC agonism, could be secondary to an acute anxiety reaction or cross contamination from concomitant use of other drugs as well. The only reported adverse effect among our cases was medical in nature and included acute onset of productive cough during periods of SC product use. Similar pulmonary complaints are associated with chronic marijuana use.[33] However, the pulmonary risk of SC inhalation along with burned unidentified plant materials in the herbal mixtures remains unknown. This has led to recommendation for vaporization as a preferable delivery method of the volatile SCs without concomitant burned plant material.[34,35] Although numerous "legal weed" vaporizers are listed for sale online, vaporization of SC preparations has not been tested in a controlled research environment. Further study remains needed to examine potential adverse health effects of SC use.

The cases provide insight into potential biopsychosocial correlates of initiation and persistent use, such as the use of SC products concurrently with marijuana by Case 3 to maximize the high, whereas Case 2 decreased use over time because of concern about health risk. Case 2 also noted the impact of marketing that drew him in initially to try numerous brands. The herbal product marketing approach includes conspicuous packaging with psychedelic art, catchy names, and diverse branding. Cost and accessibility of SC product and marijuana were a common consideration for all cases. Specific brand-name products (eg, Spice) and SC compounds have undergone increased prohibition

during the last 2 years across much of Europe where the Spice phenomenon began several years earlier than the United States. In the United States, approximately 15 states enacted prohibitory policy regarding either brand-name products or specific SC ingredients. In addition, the DEA recently placed five SCs under temporary control on March 1, 2011 (JWH-018, JWH-073, JWH-200, CP 47,497, and cannabi-cyclohexanol), which will federally prohibit sale and possession for at least 1 year.[18]

Efforts to control SC consumption in Europe and the United States are understandable given our lack of empirical knowledge about the effects of these products in humans. Yet the products remain accessible in Europe via the Internet where they are sold without age restriction and with limited or no control.[36-39] In addition, with over a hundred potential SCs to choose from,[5] manufacturers have already demonstrated remarkable flexibility to alter the psychoactive components to evade regulation.[11,13] Importantly the DEA and US Department of Health and Human Services are mandated to study whether SCs merit permanent control,[18] which hopefully will generate epidemiologic and public health data on usage and access. Because available evidence on SC effects remains largely anecdotal, further study is also clearly needed to understand the psychopharmacology and health effects.

References

1. New York: United Nations Office on Drugs and Crime (UNODC). *UNODC, World Drug Report—2009.* New York: United Nations Office on Drugs and Crime; 2009.

2. Substance Abuse and Mental Health Services Administration. Results from the 2008 National Survey on Drug Use and Health: National Findings (Office of Applied Studies, NSDUH Series H-36, HHS Publication No. SMA 09–4434). Rockville, MD; 2009.

3. Budney AJ, Moore BA, Vandrey RG, et al. The time course and significance of cannabis withdrawal. *J Abnorm Psychol.* 2003;112:393–402.

4. Hart CL. Increasing treatment options for cannabis dependence: A review of potential pharmacotherapies. *Drug Alcohol Depend.* 2005;80:147–159.

5. European Monitoring Centre for Drugs and Drug Addiction. Action on new drugs briefing paper: Understanding the 'spice' phenomenon. 2009. Available at: www.emcdda.europa.eu/drug-situation/new-drugs. Accessed May 16, 2011.

6. U.S. Department of Justice, National Drug Intelligence Center. Drug alert watch: Use of synthetic cannabinoid products by teens and young adults increasing. EWS Report 000006. May 18, 2010. Available at: www.justice.gov/ndic/pubs41/41193/sw0006p.pdf. Accessed May 16, 2011.

7. Advisory Council on the Misuse of Drugs (ACMD). Consideration of the major cannabinoid agonists. 2009. Available at: drugs.homeoffice.gov.uk/drugs-laws/acmd. Accessed May 16, 2011.

8. Hillebrand J, Olszewski D, Sedefov R. Legal highs on the Internet. *Subst Use Misuse.* 2010;45:330–340.

9. Uchiyama N, Kikura-Hanajiri R, Ogata J, et al. Chemical analysis of synthetic cannabinoids as designer drugs in herbal products. *Forensic Sci Int.* 2010;198:31–38.

10. Auwarter V 'Spice' and other herbal blends: Harmless incense or cannabinoid designer drugs? *J Mass Spectrom.* 2009;44:832–837.

11. Lindigkeit R, Boehme A, Eiserloh I, et al. Spice: A never ending story?*Forensic Scilnt.* 2009;191:58–63.

12. Emanuel CEJ, Ellison B, Banks CE. Spice up your life: Screening the illegal components of 'Spice' herbal products. *Anal Meth.* 2010;2:614–616.

13. Dresen S, Ferreiros N, Putz M, et al. Monitoring of herbal mixtures potentially containing synthetic cannabinoids as psychoactive compounds. *J Mass Spectrom.* 2010; 45:1186–1194.

14. United States Drug Enforcement Agency. Office of Forensic Sciences. Intelligence alert: "Spice"—Plant material(s) laced with synthetic cannabinoids or cannabinoid mimicking compounds. *Microgram Bulletin.* 2009;42:23–24. Retrieved from: www.justice.gov/dea/programs/forensicsci/microgram/mg0309/mg0309.html. Accessed May 16, 2011.

15. Psychonaut Web Mapping Research Group. *Spice Report.* London, UK: Institute of Psychiatry, King's College London; 2009. Available at: 194.83.136.209/documents/reports/Spice.pdf. Accessed May 16, 2011.

16. Pertwee RG. The diverse CB1 and CB2 receptor pharmacology of three plant cannabinoids: Δ^9-tetrahydrocannabinol, cannabidiol and Δ^9-tetrahydrocannabivarin. *Brit J Pharmacol.* 2007;153:199–215.

17. O'Brien C. Drug addiction and drug abuse. In: Bruton LL, Lazo JS, Parker KL, eds. *Goodman and Gillman's The Pharmacological Basis of Therapeutics,* 11th edn. New York, NY: The McGraw-Hill Company, Inc.; 2006:621–642.

18. U.S. Drug Enforcement Agency. Chemicals used in "Spice" and "K2" type products now under federal control and regulation. News Release Number: 202-307-7977, March 1, 2011. Available at: www.justice.gov/dea/pubs/pressrel/pr030111.html. Accessed May 16, 2011.

19. Zimmermann US, Winkelmann PR, Pilhatsch M, et al. Withdrawal phenomena and dependence syndrome after the consumption of "Spice Gold". *Dtsch Arztebl Int.* 2009;106:464–467.

20. Müller H, Sperling W, Köhrmann M, et al. The synthetic cannabinoid Spice as a trigger for an acute exacerbation of cannabis induced recurrent psychotic episodes. *Schizophr Res.* 2010;108:309–310.

21. Müller H, Huttner HB, Köhrmann M, et al. Panic attack after Spice abuse in a patient with ADHD. *Pharmacopsychiatry.* 2010;43:152–153.

22. Vearrier D, Osterhoudt KC. A teenager with agitation: Higher than she should have climbed. *Pediatr Emerg Care.* 2010;26:462–465.

23. Schneir AB, Cullen J, Ly BT. "Spice" girls: Synthetic cannabinoid intoxication. *J Emerg Med.* 2011;40:296–299.

24. Every-Palmer S. Synthetic cannabinoid JWH-018 and psychosis: An explorative study. *Drug Alcohol Depend.* 2011;117:152–157.

25. Teske J, Weller JP, Fleguth A, et al. Sensitive and rapid quantification of the cannabinoid receptor agonist naphthalen-1-yl-(1-pentylindol-3-yl)methanone (JWH-018) in human serum by liquid chromatography-tandem mass spectrometry. *J Chromatogr B Analyt Technol Biomed Life Sci.* 2010;878:2659–2663.

26. Sobolevsky T, Prasolov I, Rodchenkov G. Detection of JWH-018 metabolites in smoking mixture post-administration urine. *Forensic Sci Int.* 2010;200:141–147.

27. Wehrman J. Fake marijuana spurs more than 2000 calls to U.S. poison centers this year alone. *AAPCC.* November 22, 2010. Available at: www.aapcc.org/dnn/Portals/0/Nov22revisedk2release.pdf. Accessed May 16, 2011.

28. Scalzo A. Epi-X The Epidemic Information Exchange. K2 Synthetic Marijuana Use Among Teenagers—Missouri, 2010. Available at www.iowa.gov/odcp/docs/Spice/K2Marijuana.pdf. Accessed March 6, 2012.

29. Haney M. The marijuana withdrawal syndrome: Diagnosis and treatment. *Curr Psychiatry Rep.* 2005;7:360–366.

30. Haney M, Hart CL, Vosburg SK, et al. Marijuana withdrawal in humans: Effects of oral THC or divalproex. *Neuropsychopharmacology.* 2004;29:158–170.

31. Pawaolski J. Pot substitutes lack controls. *The Olympian.* 2010. Available at: www.theolympian.com/2010/08/01/1322064/pot-substitutes-lack-controls.html Accessed May 16, 2011

32. Bronstein AC, Spyker DA, Cantilena LR, et al. 2008 Annual report of the American Association of Poison Control Centers' National Poison Data System (NPDS): 26th Annual Report. *Clin Toxicol.* 2009;47:911–1084. Available at: www.aapcc.org/dnn/Portals/0/2008annualreport.pdf. Accessed May 16, 2011.

33. Tetrault JM, Crothers K, Moore BA, et al. Effects of marijuana smoking on pulmonary function and respiratory complications: A systematic review. *Arch Intern Med.* 2007;167:221–228.

34. "K2 controversy continues." Drug News. *CelebStoner.* 2010 Feb 17. Available at: www.celebstoner.com/201002183796/news/drug-news/k2-controversy-continues.html. Accessed May 16, 2011.

35. Hazekamp A, Ruhaak R, Zuurman L, et al. Evaluation of a vaporizing device (Volcano) for the pulmonary administration of tetra-hydrocannabinol. *J Pharm Sci.* 2006;95:1308–1317.

36. Schmidt M, Sharma A, Schifano F, Feinmann C. "Legal highs" on the net-Evaluation of UK based Websites, products and product information. *Forensic Sci Int.* 2011;206:92–97.

37. Griffiths P. How globalization and market innovation challenge how we think about and respond to drug use: 'Spice' a case study. *Addiction.* 2010;105:951–953.

38. Vardakou I, Pistos C, Spiliopoulou CH. Spice drugs as a new trend: Mode of action, identification and legislation. *Toxicol Lett.* 2010;197:157–162.

39. Dargan PI, Hudson S, Ramsey J, Wood DM. The impact of changes in UK classification of the synthetic cannibinoid receptor agonists in 'Spice'. *Int J Drug Policy.* 2011;22:274–277.

Critical Thinking

1. Discuss some of the cannabis withdrawal symptoms and how synthetic marijuana is used during the withdrawal phase.

2. Describe what synthetic marijuana is and its appeal to users.

3. Discuss the public health issues associated with synthetic marijuana.

Received January 17, 2011; revised February 22, 2011; accepted May 27, 2011.

Address correspondence to Dr. Gunderson, University of Virginia Health System, Box 800623, Charlottesville, VA 22908. E-mail: erikgunderson@virginia.edu.

This project was supported by grants K23 DA02000 (Dr. Gunderson) and R01 DA027131 (Dr. Haughey) from the National Institute on Drug Abuse, Bethesda, MD.

We also gratefully acknowledge the patient and research participant interviewees.

Monitoring the Future: National Results on Adolescent Drug Use, Overview of Key Findings 2011

LLOYD D. JOHNSTON, PHD, ET AL.
The University of Michigan Institute for Social Research

Introduction

Monitoring the Future (MTF) is a long-term study of American adolescents, college students, and adults through age 50. It has been conducted annually by the University of Michigan's Institute for Social Research since its inception in 1975 and is supported under a series of investigator-initiated, competing research grants from the National Institute on Drug Abuse.

The need for a study such as MTF is clear. Substance use by American young people has proven to be a rapidly changing phenomenon, requiring frequent assessments and reassessments. Since the mid-1960s, when it burgeoned in the general youth population, illicit drug use has remained a major concern for the nation. Smoking, drinking, and illicit drug use are leading causes of morbidity and mortality, during adolescence as well as later in life. How vigorously the nation responds to teenage substance use, how accurately it identifies the emerging substance abuse problems, and how well it comes to understand the effectiveness of policy and intervention efforts largely depend on the ongoing collection of valid and reliable data. Monitoring the Future is uniquely designed to generate such data in order to provide an accurate picture of what is happening in this domain and why, and the study has served that function well for the past 37 years. Policy discussions in the media, in government, education, public health institutions, and elsewhere have been informed by the ready availability of extensive and consistently accurate information from the study relating to a large number of substances. Similarly, the work of organizations and agencies providing prevention and treatment services is informed by MTF.

The 2011 the MTF survey encompassed about 46,700 8th-, 10th-, and 12th-grade students in 400 secondary schools nationwide. The first published results are presented in this report. Recent trends in the use of licit and illicit drugs are emphasized, as well as trends in the levels of perceived risk and personal disapproval associated with each drug. This study has shown these beliefs and attitudes to be particularly important in explaining trends in use. In addition, trends in the perceived availability of each drug are presented.

A synopsis of the design and methods used in the study and an overview of the key results from the 2011 survey follow this introductory section. These are followed by a separate section for each individual drug class, providing figures that show trends in the overall proportions of students at each grade level (a) using the drug, (b) seeing a "great risk" associated with its use (perceived risk), (c) disapproving of its use (disapproval), and (d) saying they could get it "fairly easily" or "very easily" if they wanted to (perceived availability). For 12th graders, annual data are available since 1975, and for 8th and 10th graders, since 1991, the first year they were included in the study.

The tables at the end of this report provide the statistics underlying the figures; in addition, they present data on lifetime, annual, 30-day, and (for selected drugs) daily prevalence.[1] For the sake of brevity, we present these prevalence statistics here only for the 1991–2011 interval, but statistics on 12th graders are available for earlier years in other MTF publications. For each prevalence period, the tables indicate which of the most recent one-year changes (between 2010 and 2011) are statistically significant. The graphic depictions of multiyear trends often indicate gradual, continuing change that may not reach significance in a given one-year interval.

A much more extensive analysis of the study's findings on secondary school students may be found in *Volume I*, the second monograph in this series, which will be published later in 2012.[2] *Volume I* contains a more complete description of the study's methodology as well as an appendix explaining how to test the significance of differences between groups and of trends over time. The most recent such volume is always available on the MTF website, www.monitoringthefuture.org, listed under Publications.

MTF's findings on American college students and adults through age 50 are not covered in this early *Overview* report because the data from those populations become available later in the year. These findings will be covered in *Volume II*, the third monograph in this annual series, which will be published later in 2012.[3] A fourth monograph, *HIV/AIDS; Risk and Protective*

Behaviors Among Young Adults, dealing with national trends in HIV/AIDS-related risk and protective behaviors among young adults 21 to 30 years old, was added to the series in 2009.[4] For the publication years prior to 2010, the volumes in these annual series are available from the NIDA Drug Publications Research Dissemination Center at 877-NIDA-NIH (877-643-2644); or by e-mail at drugpubs.drugabuse.gov. Beginning with the 2010 publication date, the volumes are available electronically at the MTF website. Further information on the study, including its latest press releases, a listing of all publications, and the text of many of them may be found at www.monitoringthefuture.org.

Study Design and Methods

Monitoring the Future's main data collection involves a series of large, annual surveys of nationally representative samples of public and private secondary school students throughout the coterminous United States. Every year since 1975 a national sample of 12th graders has been surveyed. In 1991 the study was expanded to include comparable, independent national samples of 8th and 10th graders. The year 2011 marked the 37th national survey of 12th graders and the 21st national survey of 8th and 10th graders.

Sample Sizes

The 2011 sample sizes were about 16,500, 15,400, and 14,900 in 8th, 10th, and 12th grades, respectively. In all, about 46,700 students in 400 secondary schools participated. Because multiple questionnaire forms are administered at each grade level to increase coverage of attitudinal and behavioral domains relevant to substance use, and because not all questions are contained in all forms, the number of cases upon which a particular statistic is based may be less than the total sample size. The tables here contain notes on the number of forms used for each statistic if less than the total sample is used.

Field Procedures

University of Michigan staff members administer the questionnaires to students, usually in their classrooms during a regular class period. Participation is voluntary. Parents are notified well in advance of the survey administration and are provided the opportunity to decline their child's participation. Questionnaires are self-completed and are formatted for optical scanning.

In 8th and 10th grades the questionnaires are completely anonymous, and in 12th grade they are confidential (name and address information is gathered to permit the longitudinal follow-up surveys of random subsamples of participants after high school). Extensive, carefully designed procedures are followed to protect the confidentiality of the participants and their data. All procedures are reviewed and approved on an annual basis by the University of Michigan's Institutional Review Board (IRB) for compliance with federal guidelines for the treatment of human subjects.

Measures

A standard set of three questions is used to determine *usage* levels for the various drugs (except for cigarettes and smokeless tobacco). For example, we ask, "On how many occasions (if any) have you used marijuana . . . (a) . . . in your lifetime? (b) . . . during the past 12 months? (c) . . . during the last 30 days?" Each of the three questions is answered on the same answer scale: 0, 1–2, 3–5, 6–9, 10–19, 20–39, and 40 or more occasions.

For the psychotherapeutic drugs (amphetamines, sedatives [barbiturates], tranquilizers, and narcotics other than heroin), respondents are instructed to include only use ". . . on your own—that is, without a doctor telling you to take them." A similar qualification is used in the question on use of anabolic steroids, OxyContin, Vicodin and several other drugs.

For cigarettes, respondents are asked two questions about use. First they are asked, "Have you ever smoked cigarettes?" The answer categories are "never," "once or twice," and so on. The second question asks, "How frequently have you smoked cigarettes during the past 30 days?" The answer categories are "not at all," "less than one cigarette per day," "one to five cigarettes per day," "about one-half pack per day," etc.

Smokeless tobacco questions parallel those for cigarettes.

Alcohol use is measured using the three questions illustrated above for marijuana. A parallel set of three questions asks about the frequency of being drunk. A different question asks, for the prior two-week period, "How many times (if any) have you had five or more drinks in a row?"

Perceived risk is measured by a question asking, "How much do you think people risk harming themselves (physically or in other ways), if they . . ." ". . . try marijuana once or twice," for example. The answer categories are "no risk," "slight risk," "moderate risk," "great risk," and "can't say, drug unfamiliar."

Disapproval is measured by the question "Do YOU disapprove of people doing each of the following?" followed by "trying marijuana once or twice," for example. Answer categories are "don't disapprove," "disapprove," and "strongly disapprove." In the 8th-and 10th-grade questionnaires, a fourth category—"can't say, drug unfamiliar"—is provided and included in the calculations.

Perceived availability is measured by the question "How difficult do you think it would be for you to get each of the following types of drugs, if you wanted some?" Answer categories are "probably impossible," "very difficult," "fairly difficult," "fairly easy," and "very easy." For 8th and 10th graders, an additional answer category—"can't say, drug unfamiliar"—is offered and included in the calculations.

Summary of Key Findings

One important finding of the MTF study is that cohort effects—lasting differences between different cohorts entering secondary school—have emerged, beginning with increases in drug use during the early 1990s. Such cohort effects mean that usage rates (and sometimes attitudes and beliefs about various drugs) reach peaks and valleys in different years for different grades. We have seen such cohort effects for cigarette smoking throughout most of the life of the study, but they were much less evident for illicit drugs until the mid-1990s. Since then, 8th graders have tended to be the first to show turnarounds in illicit drug use, and have generally shown the greatest proportional declines from recent peak levels of use, attained for the most part during the 1990s, while the proportional declines have generally been smallest among 12th graders.

In 2008, we introduced a set of tables providing an overview of drug use trends for the *three grades combined*. While there are important differences by grade, this approach gives a more succinct summary of the general nature of historical trends over the last several years.

A number of interesting findings emerged from the 2011 survey, relating in particular to the three substances most widely used by adolescents—cigarettes, alcohol, and marijuana. We begin by discussing marijuana and two other illegal drugs of concern, then return to cigarettes and alcohol.

Marijuana use, which had been rising among teens for the past three years, continued to rise in 2011 in all prevalence periods for 10th and 12th graders. The recent rise in use stands in stark contrast to the long, gradual decline that had been occurring over the preceding decade. (Among 8th graders there was some decrease in annual prevalence in 2011 although annual prevalence has been rising overall since 2004.). It is relevant that perceived risk for marijuana has been falling for the past five years, and disapproval declined for the past three to four years. (The decline in perceived risk in particular may be related to the increased public discussions concerning medical marijuana.) Of particular importance, *daily marijuana use* increased significantly in all three grades in 2010, rising further in all three grades in 2011, though the one-year increase was not statistically significant. Daily use now stands at 1.3%, 3.6%, and 6.6% in grades 8, 10, and 12. That means that roughly one in fifteen high school seniors today is a current daily, or near-daily, marijuana user.

Synthetic marijuana

Which goes by such names as Spice and K-2, is an herbal drug mixture that usually contains designer chemicals that fall into the cannibinoid family. Until March of 2011 these drugs were not scheduled by the Drug Enforcement Administration, so they were readily available on the internet and in head shops, gas stations, etc. The DEA did schedule them under its emergency authority for one year, beginning March 1, 2011, making their possession and sale no longer legal. MTF first addressed the use of synthetic marijuana in its 2011 survey, asking 12th graders about use in the prior 12 months, which would have covered a considerable period of time prior to the drugs being scheduled. Some 11.4% indicated use in the prior 12 months. Next year's survey results should reflect any effects of the scheduling by the DEA.

Ecstasy

After a decline of several years in perceived risk and disapproval of ecstasy use—which we had been warning could presage a rebound in use— ecstasy use does now appear to be rebounding, primarily among the older teens.

Alcohol use, including *binge drinking,* continued its longer term decline among teens, reaching historically low levels in 2011 in all three grades under study. Use has been in a long-term pattern of decline since about 1980, with the interruption of a few years in the early 1990s during which alcohol use increased along with the use of cigarettes and almost all illicit drugs. Among 12th graders in 1981, 41% reported having five or more drinks in a row on at least one occasion in the two weeks prior to the survey (sometimes called binge drinking). This statistic fell to 28% by 1992, prior to the rebound in the 1990s, but has now fallen even further, reaching 22% in 2011—a decline of nearly one half since 1981.

Cigarettes

After decelerating considerably in recent years, the long-term decline in *cigarette* use, which began in the mid-1990s, appeared to come to a halt in the lower grades in 2010. Indeed, both 8th and 10th graders showed evidence of a slight increase in smoking in 2010, though the increases did not reach statistical significance. Perceived risk and subsequently disapproval had both leveled off some years ago. In 2011, however, the decline in teen smoking resumed in the lower grades (there was a significant drop in use among the 10th graders) and also continued among 12th graders. Perceived risk and disapproval rose in all three grades, significantly for both among 10th graders. Availability also dropped significantly among 8th and 10th graders but more than half of the 8th graders and nearly three quarters of the 10th graders still say it would be "fairly easy" or "very easy" for them to get cigarettes if they wanted some.

Use of any illicit drug

Because marijuana is by far the most prevalent drug included in the *any illicit drug* use index, an increase in prevalence occurred for that index in 2011, as well as for marijuana for the two upper grades. The proportions using *any illicit drug other than marijuana* had been declining gradually since about 2001, but no further decline occurred in 2010 and only slight (non-significant) declines occurred in 2011 for 8th and 10th graders; the 2011 levels are similar to the 2008 levels.

Other Drugs Declining in Use

Several other drugs showed signs of decreased use in 2011. These include: *inhalants, cocaine powder, crack cocaine,* the narcotic drug *Vicodin,* the amphetamine *Adderall, sedatives, tranquilizers,* and *over-the-counter cough and cold medicines* used to get high.

Inhalants

The annual prevalence of inhalant use fell in all grades in 2011 (significantly so in 8th and 10th grades), continuing modest declines occurring since the mid-2000s. This is surprising in light of the fact that perceived risk for inhalant use fell considerably among 8th and 10th graders from 2001 through 2008 before leveling, which we have interpreted as generational forgetting of the risks of inhalant use. Usually, when this occurs, there is a resurgence in use; but for whatever reason, such a resurgence has not yet occurred. (Twelfth graders are not asked about perceived risk for this drug.)

Powdered cocaine use continued gradual declines in 8th and 10th grades in 2011, while use among 12th graders leveled. All three grades are at their lowest levels of use since recent peak years. Use of *crack* continued to decline in 2011 with a significant decline among 12th graders. In 2011 *Vicodin,* the most widely used of the narcotic drugs, continued to decline among 8th graders, declined significantly among 10th graders but showed no further decline among 12th graders. Use of *Adderall,* the most widely used amphetamine and a drug used in the treatment of ADHD, declined in the lower grades and there was no further change among 12th graders. *Sedative* (barbiturates) use, which is reported only for 12th graders, continued its slow, non-significant decline in 2011. *Tranquilizer* use declined significantly for 8th graders but only slightly for 10th graders. There was no further change among 12th graders, but they remain at their lowest point in 12 years. The misuse of *over-the-counter (OTC) cough and cold medicines* to get high dropped some for 8th graders, increased a bit for 10th graders and dropped significantly for 12th graders. These OTC drugs usually contain the cough suppresant dextromethorphan, which can have hallucinogenic effects when taken in large quantities.

Drugs Holding Steady in 2011

Use of drugs in several categories held fairly steady in 2011. These included an index of the use of *any illicit drug other than marijuana, LSD, hallucinogens other than LSD, salvia, heroin* used with and without a needle, *narcotics other than heroin, OxyContin* specifically, *amphetamines* (and *Ritalin* specifically), several so-called "club drugs" (*Rohypnol, GHB,* and *Ketamine), methamphetamine, crystal methamphetamine, Provigil* (a stay-awake drug), and *anabolic steroids.* Use of most of these drugs is well below their recent peak levels attained in the past 15 years. Two exceptions are "any prescription drug" and salvia. While the proportion of students using any illicit drug has increased in the upper grades this year, due primarily to the rise in marijuana use, the proportion using any of the other illicit drugs held steady and may have even declined slightly in the lower grades. One group of drugs that is not down much from peak levels is *narcotics other than heroin;* their continued high rate of use is a disturbing finding.

The *psychotherapeutic drugs* now make up a larger part of the overall U.S. drug problem than was true 10–15 years ago, in part because use increased for many prescription drugs over that period, and in part because use of a number of street drugs has declined substantially since the mid-1990s. It seems likely that young people are less concerned about the dangers of using these prescription drugs outside of medical regimen, likely because they are widely used for legitimate purposes. (Indeed, the low levels of perceived risk for sedatives and amphetamines observed among 12th graders illustrate this point.) Also, prescription psychotherapeutic drugs are now being advertised directly to the consumer, which implies both that they are widely used and safe to use. Fortunately, the use of most of these drugs has either leveled or begun to decline in the past few years. The proportion of 12th graders misusing *any* of these prescription drugs (i.e., amphetamines, sedatives, tranquilizers, or narcotics other than heroin) in the prior year has leveled at 15.2%—about where it has been since 2008 and down slightly from 17.1% in 2005.

Implications for Prevention

The wide divergence in historical trajectories of the various drugs over time helps to illustrate that, to a considerable degree, the determinants of use are often specific to each drug. These determinants include both perceived benefits and perceived adverse outcomes that young people come to associate with each drug.

Unfortunately, word of the supposed benefits of using a drug usually spreads much faster than information about the adverse consequences. Supposed benefits take only rumor and a few testimonials, the spread of which have been hastened and expanded greatly by the media and Internet. It usually takes much longer for the evidence of adverse consequences (e.g., death, disease, overdose, addiction) to cumulate and then be disseminated. Thus, when a new drug comes onto the scene, it has a considerable grace period during which its benefits are alleged and its consequences are not yet known. We believe that ecstasy illustrated this dynamic. Synthetic marijuana and so-called "bath salts" are two more recent examples where evidence of adverse outcomes is only beginning to catch up to the push that these drugs have received through the Internet and the media.

To a considerable degree, prevention must occur drug by drug, because people will not necessarily generalize the adverse consequences of one drug to the use of others. Many beliefs and attitudes held by young people are drug specific. The figures in this *Overview* on perceived risk and disapproval for the various drugs—attitudes and beliefs that we have shown to be important in explaining many drug trends over the years— amply illustrate this assertion. These attitudes and beliefs are at quite different levels for the various drugs and, more importantly, often trend quite differently over time.

"Generational Forgetting" Helps Keep the Drug Epidemic Going

Another point worth keeping in mind is that there tends to be a continuous flow of new drugs onto the scene and of older ones being rediscovered by young people. Many drugs have made a comeback years after they first fell from popularity, often because knowledge among youth of their adverse consequences faded as generational replacement took place. We call this process "generational forgetting." Examples include LSD and methamphetamine, two drugs used widely in the 1960s that made a comeback in the 1990s after their initial popularity faded as a result of their adverse consequences becoming widely recognized during periods of high use. Heroin, cocaine, PCP, and crack are some others that have followed a similar pattern. At present, *LSD, inhalants,* and *ecstasy* are all showing some effects of generational forgetting—that is, perceived risk has declined appreciably for those drugs—which puts future cohorts at greater risk of having a resurgence in use. In the case of LSD, perceived risk among 8th graders has declined appreciably and more are saying that they are not familiar with the drug. It would appear that a resurgence in availability (which declined very sharply after about 2001, most likely due to the FDA closing a major lab in 2000) could generate another increase in use.

As for newly emerging drugs, examples include nitrite inhalants and PCP in the 1970s; crack and crystal methamphetamine in the 1980s; Rohypnol, GHB, and ecstasy in the 1990s; dextromethorphan, salvia and synthetic marijuana in the 2000s, and "bath salts" more recently. The frequent introduction of new drugs (or new forms or new modes of administration of older drugs, as illustrated by crack, crystal methamphetamine, and noninjected heroin) helps keep this nation's drug problem alive. Because of the lag times described previously, the forces of containment are always playing catch-up with the forces of encouragement and exploitation. Organized efforts to reduce the grace period experienced by new drugs would seem to be among the most promising responses for minimizing the damage they will cause. Such efforts regarding ecstasy by the National Institute on Drug Abuse and others appeared to pay off.

Cigarettes and Alcohol

The findings concerning use of the licit drugs—cigarettes and alcohol—remain a basis for considerable concern.

Cigarettes.

Four in every ten American young people (40%) have tried cigarettes by 12th grade, and nearly one in five (19%) 12th graders is a current smoker. (These proportions would be higher if high school dropouts were included in the study's coverage.) Even as early as 8th grade, nearly one in five (18%) has tried cigarettes, and 1 in 16 (6%) has already become a current smoker. Fortunately, there has been some real improvement in these statistics since the mid- to late 1990s, following a dramatic increase in adolescent smoking earlier in the 1990s. Some of the improvement was simply regaining lost ground; however, in 2011, cigarette use reached the lowest levels recorded in the life of the MTF study, going back over 36 years in the case of 12th graders and 20 years in the case of 8th and 10th graders.

Thirty-day prevalence of cigarette use reached a peak in 1996 at grades 8 and 10, capping a rapid climb from the 1991 levels (when data were first gathered on these grades). Between 1996 and 2011, current smoking fell considerably in these grades (by 71% and 61%, respectively). However, the decline in use had decelerated in recent years, and in 2010 there was evidence of some increase in smoking rates among 8th and 10th graders (though not statistically significant). In 2011 use decreased among 8th graders and decreased significantly for 10th graders. For 12th graders, peak use occurred a year later, in 1997, and has since shown a more modest decline, dropping to 19.2% by 2010 and then to 18.7% in 2011. Because of the strong cohort effect that we have consistently observed for cigarette smoking, we expect use at 12th grade to continue to show declines, as the lighter using cohorts of 8th and 10th graders become 12th graders. Overall increases in perceived risk and disapproval appear to have contributed to the downturn. Perceived risk increased substantially and steadily in all

grades from 1995 through 2004, after which it leveled in 8th and 10th grades; however, it continued rising in 12th grade until 2006, after which it leveled and then declined some in 2008. Disapproval of smoking had been rising steadily in all grades since 1996. After 2004, the rise decelerated in the lower grades through 2006—again, reflecting a cohort effect in this attitude. All three grades showed an increase in perceived risk and in disapproval in 2011. (The increases for both measures were significant for 10th graders.)

It seems likely that some of the attitudinal change surrounding cigarettes is attributable to the adverse publicity suffered by the tobacco industry in the 1990s, as well as a reduction in cigarette advertising and an increase in antismoking advertising reaching children.

Various other attitudes toward smoking became more unfavorable during that interval, as well, though some have since leveled off. For example, among 8th graders, the proportions saying that they "prefer to date people who don't smoke" rose from 71% in 1996 to 81% by 2004, about where it remains in 2011. Similar changes occurred in 10th and 12th grades, as well. Thus, at the present time, smoking is likely to make an adolescent less attractive to the great majority of potential romantic partners. However, most of the negative connotations of smoking and smokers have leveled off in the past few years. In addition to changes in attitudes and beliefs about smoking, price likely also played an important role in the decline in use. Cigarette prices rose appreciably in the late 1990s and early 2000s as cigarette companies tried to cover the costs of the tobacco settlement, and as many states increased excise taxes on cigarettes.

Smokeless tobacco use had also been in decline for some years, continuing into the early 2000s, but the decline ended in all grades by about 2007. Indeed, the 30-day prevalence rates for smokeless tobacco were down by about half from peak levels, but all grades showed an increase in use from about 1997 through 2009, before leveling in 2011. Appreciable increases in both perceived risk and disapproval in prior years likely contributed to the decline in use, but then they both showed a small reversal for a couple of years. In 2011 both measures increased at all grades except for perceived risk among 8th graders.

Alcohol remains the most widely used drug by today's teenagers. Despite recent declining rates, seven out of every ten students (70%) have consumed alcohol (more than just a few sips) by the end of high school, and one third (33%) has done so by 8th grade. In fact, half (51%) of 12th graders and more than one sixth (15%) of 8th graders in 2011 report having been drunk at least once in their life.

Alcohol use began a substantial decline in the 1980s. To a considerable degree, alcohol trends have tended to parallel the trends in illicit drug use. These include a modest increase in binge drinking (defined as having five or more drinks in a row at least once in the past two weeks) in the early and mid-1990s, though it was a proportionally smaller increase than was seen for cigarettes and most of the illicit drugs. Fortunately, binge drinking rates leveled off eight to eleven years ago, just about when the illicit drug rates began to turn around, and in 2002 a drop in drinking and drunkenness resumed in all grades.

Gradual declines continued into 2011, and we are now seeing the study's lowest rates of teen drinking and drunkeness in all three grades.

The longer term trend data available for 12th graders show that alcohol usage rates, and binge drinking in particular, are now substantially below peak levels measured in the early 1980s.

Any Illicit Drug

Monitoring the Future routinely reports three different indexes of illicit drug use—"any illicit drug," "any illicit drug other than marijuana," and "any illicit drug including inhalants." In this section we discuss only the first two.

In order to make comparisons over time, we have kept the definitions of these indexes constant. Levels are little affected by the inclusion of newer substances, primarily because most individuals using them are also using the more prevalent drugs included in the indexes. The major exception has been inhalants, the use of which is quite prevalent in the lower grades, so in 1991 a special index was added that includes inhalants.

Trends in Use

In the late 20th century, young Americans reached extraordinarily high levels of illicit drug use by U.S. as well as international standards. In 1975, when MTF began, the majority of young people (55%) had used an illicit drug by the time they left high school. This figure rose to two thirds (66%) in 1981 before a long and gradual decline to 41% in 1992—the low point. After 1992 the proportion rose considerably, reaching a recent high point of 55% in 1999; it then declined gradually to 47% in 2007 through 2009, before rising to 50% in 2011 as marijuana use has been rising again.

Trends for annual, as opposed to lifetime, prevalence appear in the second (upper right) panel. They are quite parallel to those for lifetime prevalence, but at a lower level. Among 8th graders, a gradual and continuing fall off occurred after 1996. Peak rates since 1991 were reached in 1997 in the two upper grades and declined little for several years. Between 2001 and 2007 all three grades showed declines, but annual use rates in all three grades have risen since then except for 8th grade in 2011. Because marijuana is much more prevalent than any other illicit drug, trends in its use tend to drive the index of any illicit drug use. Thus we also report an index that excludes marijuana, and shows the proportions of students who use the other, so-called "harder" illicit drugs. The proportions who have used any illicit drug other than marijuana in their lifetime are shown in the third panel (lower left). In 1975 over one third (36%) of 12th graders had tried some illicit drug other than marijuana. This figure rose to 43% by 1981, then declined for a long period to a low of 25% in 1992. Some increase followed in the 1990s as the use of a number of drugs rose steadily, and it reached 30% by 1997. (In 2001 it was 31%, but this apparent upward shift in the estimate was an artifact due to a change in the question wording for "other hallucinogens" and tranquilizers.[5]) Lifetime prevalence among 12th graders then fell slightly, to 25% in 2011. The fourth panel presents the *annual* prevalence data for any illicit drug other than marijuana, which shows a pattern of change over the past few years similar to the index of any illicit drug use, but with much less pronounced change since 1991. It leveled in all three grades in 2010 and then dropped slightly in the two lower grades in 2011.

Overall, these data reveal that, while use of individual drugs (other than marijuana) may fluctuate widely, the proportion using *any* of them is much more stable. In other words, the proportion of students prone to using such drugs and willing to cross the normative barriers to such use changes more gradually. The usage rate for each individual drug, on the other hand, reflects many more rapidly changing determinants specific to that drug: how widely its psychoactive potential is recognized, how favorable the reports of its supposed benefits are, how risky its use is seen to be, how acceptable it is in the peer group, how accessible it is, and so on.

Marijuana

Marijuana has been the most widely used illicit drug throughout MTF's 37 year history. It can be taken orally, mixed with food, and smoked in a concentrated form as hashish—the use of which is much more common in Europe. The great majority of consumption in the U.S. involves smoking it in rolled cigarettes ("joints"), in pipes or water pipes, or in hollowed-out cigars ("blunts").

Trends in Use

Annual marijuana prevalence peaked among 12th graders in 1979 at 51%, following a rise that began during the 1960s. Then use declined fairly steadily for 13 years, bottoming at 22% in 1992—a decline of more than half. The 1990s, however, saw a resurgence of use. After a considerable increase (one that actually began among 8th graders a year earlier than among 10th and 12th graders), annual prevalence rates peaked in 1996 at 8th grade and in 1997 at 10th and 12th grades. After these peak years, use declined among all three grades through 2006, 2007, or 2008; since then there has been an upturn in use in all three grades, indicating another possible resurgence in use although in 2011 there was some decline in use among 8th graders. In 2010 there was a significant increase in *daily use* in all three grades, followed by a nonsignificant increase in 2011 reaching 1.3%, 3.6%, and 6.6% in grades 8, 10, and 12, respectively. The rate for 12th graders is the highest rate since 1981, when it was 7.0%.

Perceived Risk

The proportion of students seeing great risk from using marijuana regularly fell during the rise in use in the 1970s, and again during the subsequent rise in the 1990s. Indeed, at 10th and 12th grades, perceived risk declined a year before use rose in the upturn of the 1990s, making perceived risk a leading indicator of change in use. (The same may have happened at 8th grade as well, but we lack data starting early enough to know.) The decline in perceived risk halted in 1996 in 8th and 10th grades; the increases in use ended a year or two later, again making perceived risk a leading indicator. From 1996 to

2000, perceived risk held fairly steady and the decline in use in the upper grades stalled. After some decline prior to 2002, perceived risk increased in all grades through 2004 as use decreased. Perceived risk fell after 2004 and 2005 in 8th and 12th grades respectively, (and since 2008 in 10th grade) presaging the more recent increase in use. In 2011 perceived risk continued to decline in grades 10 and 12 and leveled in grade 8.

Disapproval

Personal disapproval of trying marijuana use fell considerably among 8th graders between 1991 and 1996 and among 10th and 12th graders between 1992 and 1997—by 17, 21, and 19 percentage points, respectively, over those intervals of increasing use. After that there was some modest increase in disapproval among 8th graders, but not much among 10th and 12th graders until 2004, when the lower grades showed increases. From 2003 to 2007 (2008 in the case of 10th graders) disapproval increased in all three grades, but has declined some since then as use rose.

Availability

Ever since the MTF study began in 1975, between 81% and 90% of 12th graders each year have said that they could get marijuana fairly easily or very easily if they wanted some. It has been considerably less accessible to younger adolescents. Still, in 2011 38% of 8th graders, 68% of 10th graders, and 82% of 12th graders reported it as being fairly or very easy to get. It thus seems clear that marijuana has remained a highly accessible drug.

Inhalants

Inhalants are any gases or fumes that can be inhaled for the purpose of getting high. These include many household products—the sale and possession of which is legal—including glue, nail polish remover, gasoline, solvents, butane, and propellants used in certain commercial products such as whipped cream dispensers. Unlike nearly all other classes of drugs, their use is most common among younger adolescents and tends to decline as youth grow older. The use of inhalants at an early age may reflect the fact that many inhalants are cheap, readily available (often in the home), and legal to buy and possess. The decline in use with age likely reflects their coming to be seen as "kids' drugs," in addition to the fact that a number of other drugs become available to older adolescents, who are also more able to afford them.

Trends in Use

According to the long-term data from 12th graders, inhalant use (excluding the use of nitrite inhalants) rose gradually from 1976 to 1987, which was somewhat unusual as most other forms of illicit drug use were in decline during the 1980s. Use rose among 8th and 10th graders from 1991, when data were first gathered on them, through 1995; it rose among 12th graders from 1992 to 1995. All grades then exhibited a fairly steady and substantial decline in use through 2001 or 2002. After 2001 the grades diverged somewhat in their trends: 8th graders showed a

significant increase in use for two years, followed by a decline from 2004 to 2007; 10th graders showed an increase after 2002 but some decline since 2007 including a significant decrease in 2011; 12th graders showed some increase from 2003 to 2005, but a decline since then.

Perceived Risk

Only 8th and 10th graders have been asked questions about the degree of risk they associate with inhalant use. Relatively low proportions think that there is a "great risk" in using an inhalant once or twice. However, significant increases in this belief were observed between 1995 and 1996 in both 8th and 10th grades, probably due to an anti-inhalant advertising initiative launched by The Partnership for a Drug-Free America at that time. That increase in perceived risk marked the beginning of a long and important decline in inhalant use, and no other drugs showed a turnaround in use at that point. However, the degree of risk associated with inhalant use declined steadily between 2001 and 2008 among both 8th and 10th graders, perhaps explaining the turnaround in use in 2003 among 8th graders and in 2004 in the upper grades. The hazards of inhalant use were communicated during the mid-1990s; but a generational forgetting of those hazards has likely been taking place, as replacement cohorts who were too young to get that earlier message have entered adolescence. The decline in perceived risk is worrisome, though the decline did halt as of 2008, and perceived risk has not changed much since then. In this case, the decline in perceived risk (between 2002 and 2008) did not translated into a surge in use.

Disapproval

Over 80% of students say that they would disapprove of even trying an inhalant. There was a very gradual upward drift in this attitude among 8th and 10th graders from 1995 through about 2001, with a gradual fall off since then among 8th graders. Among 10th graders there was some decrease after 2004 but the decline halted after 2007.

Availability

Respondents have not been asked about the availability of inhalants. It seems reasonable to assume that these substances are universally available to young people in these age ranges.

LSD

For some years, LSD was the most widely used drug within the larger class of hallucinogens. This is no longer true, due to sharp decreases in its use combined with an increasing use of psilocybin.

Trends in Use

Annual prevalence of LSD use among 12th graders has been below 10% since MTF began. Use declined some for the first 10 years among 12th graders, likely continuing a decline that had begun before 1975. Use was fairly level in the latter half of the 1980s but, as was true for a number of other drugs, rose in all three grades between 1991 and 1996. Between 1996 and

2006 or so, use declined in all three grades, with particularly sharp declines between 2001 and 2003. Since then use has remained at historically low levels.

Perceived Risk

We think it likely that perceived risk for LSD use increased during the early 1970s, before MTF began, as concerns grew about possible neurological and genetic effects (most of which were never scientifically confirmed) as well as "bad trips" and "flashbacks." However, there was some decline in perceived risk in the late 1970s, after which it remained fairly level among 12th graders through most of the 1980s. A substantial decline occurred in all grades in the early 1990s, as use rose. Since about 2000, perceived risk has declined steadily and substantially among 8th graders, declined considerably among 10th graders before leveling in 2011, but held fairly steady among 12th graders through 2009 before dropping a bit. The decline in the lower grades suggests that younger teens are less knowledgeable about this drug's effects than their predecessors—through what we have called "generational forgetting"—making them vulnerable to a resurgence in use.

The decline of LSD use in recent years, despite a fall in perceived risk, suggests that some factors other than a change in underlying attitudes and beliefs were contributing to the downturn—prior to 2001 some displacement by ecstasy may have been a factor, while more recently a decline in availability (discussed below) likely is a factor.

Disapproval

Disapproval of LSD use was quite high among 12th graders through most of the 1980s, but began to decline after 1991 along with perceived risk. All three grades exhibited a decline in disapproval through 1996, with disapproval of experimentation dropping 11 percentage points between 1991 and 1996 among 12th graders. After 1996 a slight increase in disapproval emerged among 12th graders, accompanied by a leveling among 10th graders and some further decline among 8th graders. Since 2001, disapproval of LSD use has diverged among the three grades, declining considerably among 8th graders, declining less among 10th graders, and increasing significantly among 12th graders. Note, however, that the percentages of 8th and 10th graders who respond with "can't say, drug unfamiliar" increased over the years (a finding consistent with the notion that generational forgetting has been occurring); thus the base for disapproval has shrunk, suggesting that the real decline of disapproval among the younger students is less than it appears here. Regardless of these diverging trends, use fell sharply in all grades before leveling in 2004, with little change since then.

Availability

Reported availability of LSD by 12th graders fell considerably from 1975 to 1979, declined a bit further until 1986, and then began a substantial rise, reaching a peak in 1995. LSD availability also rose somewhat among 8th and 10th graders in the early 1990s, reaching a peak in 1995 or 1996. Since those peak years, there has been considerable fall off in availability in all three grades, including a significant decrease for 10th graders in 2011—quite possibly in part because fewer students have LSD-using friends from whom they could gain access. There was also very likely a decrease in supply due to the closing of a major LSD-producing lab by the Drug Enforcement Administration in 2000. It is clear that attitudinal changes cannot explain the recent declines in use.

Cocaine

Cocaine was used almost exclusively in powder form for some years, though "freebasing" emerged for a while. Then the early 1980s brought the advent of crack cocaine. Our original questions did not distinguish among different forms of cocaine or modes of administration. Since 1987, though, we have asked separate questions about the use of crack and "cocaine other than crack," which has consisted almost entirely of powder cocaine use. Data on overall cocaine use are presented in the figures in this section, and results for crack alone are presented in the next section.

Trends in Use

There have been some important changes in the levels of overall cocaine use over the life of MTF. Use among 12th graders originally burgeoned in the late 1970s and remained fairly stable through the first half of the 1980s before starting a precipitous decline after 1986. Annual prevalence among 12th graders dropped by about three quarters between 1986 and 1992. Between 1992 and 1999, use reversed course again and doubled before declining by 2000. Use also rose among 8th and 10th graders after 1992 before reaching recent peak levels in 1998 and 1999. Over the last decade, use declined in all three grades; 12th-grade use stands at an historical low at just 2.9% in 2011, with use by 8th and 10th graders still lower.

Perceived Risk

General questions about the dangers of cocaine have been asked only of 12th graders. The results tell a fascinating story. They show that perceived risk for experimental use fell in the latter half of the 1970s (when use was rising), stayed level in the first half of the 1980s (when use was level), and then jumped very sharply in a single year (by 14 percentage points between 1986 and 1987), just when the substantial decline in use began. The year 1986 was marked by a national media frenzy over crack cocaine and also by the widely publicized cocaine-related death of Len Bias, a National Basketball Association first-round draft pick. Bias' death was originally reported as resulting from his first experience with cocaine. Though that was later proven to be incorrect, the message had already "taken." We believe that this event helped to persuade many young people that use of cocaine at any level is dangerous, no matter how healthy the individual. Perceived risk continued to rise through 1991 as the fall in use continued. From 1991 to 2000, perceived risk declined modestly. Perceived risk has leveled in recent years at far higher levels than existed prior to 1987, and there is as yet little evidence of generational forgetting of cocaine's risks—at least among the 12th graders.

Disapproval

Questions about disapproval of cocaine have been asked only of 12th graders. Disapproval of cocaine use by 12th graders followed a cross-time pattern similar to that for perceived risk, although its seven-percentage-point jump in 1987 was not quite as pronounced. There was some decline from 1991 to 1997, followed by a period of stability. In recent years there has been a slight drift upwards in disapproval.

Availability

The proportion of 12th graders saying that it would be "fairly easy" or "very easy" for them to get cocaine if they wanted some was 33% in 1977, rose to 48% by 1980 as use rose, and held fairly level through 1982; then, after a one-year drop, it increased steadily to 59% by 1989 (in a period of rapidly *declining* use). Perceived availability then fell back to about 47% by 1994. After 2007 it dropped significantly and stands at 31% in 2011. Note that the pattern of change does not map well onto the pattern of actual use, suggesting that changes in overall availability have not been a major determinant of use—particularly during the sharp decline in use in the late 1980s. The advent of crack cocaine in the early 1980s, however, provided a lower cost form of cocaine, thus reducing the prior social class differences in use.

Crack

Several indirect indicators suggest that crack use grew rapidly in the period 1983–1986, beginning before we had direct measures of its use. In 1986 a single usage question was included in one of the five 12th-grade questionnaire forms, asking those who indicated any cocaine use in the prior 12 months if they had used crack. After that, we introduced into several questionnaire forms three questions about crack use covering our usual three prevalence periods.

Trends in Use

Clearly crack use rose rapidly in the early 1980s, judging by the 4% prevalence reached in 1986; but, after 1986 there was a precipitous drop in crack use among 12th graders—a drop that continued through 1991. After 1991 for 8th and 10th graders (when data were first available) and after 1993 for 12th graders, all three grades showed a slow, steady increase in use through 1998. Since then, annual prevalence dropped by roughly six tenths in all three grades. As with many drugs, the decline at 12th grade lagged behind those in the lower grades due to a cohort effect.

Perceived Risk

By the time we added questions about the perceived risk of using crack in 1987, crack was already seen by 12th graders as one of the most dangerous illicit drugs: 57% saw a great

risk in even trying it. This compared to 54% for heroin, for example. (See the previous section on cocaine for a discussion of changes in perceived risk in 1986.) Perceived risk for crack rose still higher through 1990, reaching 64% of 12th graders who said they thought there was a great risk in taking crack once or twice. (Use was dropping during that interval.) After 1990 some fall off in perceived risk began, well before crack use began to increase in 1994. Thus, here again, perceived risk was a leading indicator. Between 1991 and 1998 there was a considerable fall off in this belief in grades 8 and 10, as use rose quite steadily. Perceived risk leveled in 2000 in grades 8 and 12 and a year later in grade 10. We think that the declines in perceived risk for crack and cocaine during the 1990s may well reflect an example of generational forgetting, wherein the class cohorts that were in adolescence when the adverse consequences were most obvious (i.e., in the mid1980s) were replaced by newer cohorts who had heard much less about the dangers of this drug as they were growing up; nevertheless, it is still seen as a relatively dangerous drug.

Disapproval

Disapproval of crack use was not included in the MTF study until 1990, by which time it was also at a very high level, with 92% of 12th graders saying that they disapproved of even trying it. Disapproval of crack use declined slightly but steadily in all three grades from 1991 through about 1997. After a brief period of stability, disapproval increased some, but is now level.

Availability

Crack availability did not change dramatically across most of the interval for which data are available. Eighth and 10th graders reported some modest increase in availability in the early 1990s. This was followed by a slow, steady decrease from 1995 through 2004 in 8th grade (followed by a leveling) and sharper drops among 10th and 12th graders beginning in 1999 and 2000, respectively. Since 2007, availability has declined, particularly in the upper grades.

Amphetamines

Amphetamines, a class of psychotherapeutic stimulants, had a relatively high prevalence of use in the youth population for many years. The behavior reported here excludes any use under medical supervision. Amphetamines are controlled substances—they cannot be bought or sold without a doctor's prescription—but some are diverted from legitimate channels, and some are manufactured and/or imported illegally.

> **Note**
>
> The distinction between crack cocaine and other forms of cocaine (mostly powder) was made several years after the study's inception.

Trends in Use

The use of amphetamines rose in the last half of the 1970s, reaching a peak in 1981—two years after marijuana use peaked. We believe that the usage rate reached among 12th graders in 1981 (annual prevalence of 26%) may have been an exaggeration of true amphetamine use because "look-alikes" were in common use at that time. After 1981 a long and steady decline in 12th graders' use of amphetamines began, and ended in 1992.

As with many other illicit drugs, amphetamines made a comeback in the 1990s. Use peaked in the lower two grades by 1996. Since then, use declined steadily in 8th grade and sporadically in 10th grade. Only after 2002 did it begin to decline in 12th grade. The decline in 8th grade paused in 2008, but has since continued. In 10th grade there was a pause in the decline in 2009 and 2010, but the decline resumed in 2011. In 12th grade there has been a reversal of the decline since 2009. Since the recent peaks in use, annual prevalence is down by about six tenths in 8th grade, by about half in 10th grade, and by about one fourth in 12th grade.

Perceived Risk

Only 12th graders are asked about the amount of risk they associate with amphetamine use. For a few years, changes in perceived risk were not correlated with changes in usage levels (at the aggregate level). Specifically, in the interval 1981–1986, risk was quite stable even though use fell considerably, likely as a result of some displacement by cocaine. There was, however, a decrease in risk during the period 1975–1981 (when use was rising), some increase in perceived risk in 1986–1991 (when use was falling), and some decline in perceived risk from 1991 to 1995 (in advance of use rising again). Perceived risk has generally been rising in recent years, very likely contributing to the decline in use that was occurring among 12th graders after 2002; but it appears to have leveled since 2007. In 2011 the examples of specific amphetamines provided in the text of the questions on perceived risk, disapproval, and availability were updated with the inclusion of Adderall and Ritalin. This led to some discontinuities in the trend lines in 2011.

Disapproval

Disapproval of amphetamine use is asked in 12th grade only. Relatively high proportions of 12th graders have disapproved of even trying amphetamines throughout the life of the study. Disapproval did not change in the late 1970s despite an increase in use. From 1981 to 1992, disapproval rose gradually from 71% to 87% as perceived risk rose and use steadily declined. In the mid-1990s it declined along with perceived risk, but it has increased fairly steadily since 1996, again along with perceived risk.

Availability

When the MTF study started in 1975, amphetamines had a high level of reported availability. The level fell by about 10 percentage points by 1977, drifted up a bit through 1980, jumped sharply in 1981, and then began a long, gradual decline through 1991. There was a modest increase in availability at all three grade levels in the early 1990s, as use rose, followed by a long-term decline after that. Some further decline occurred in all grades in 2009 and 2010, but a comparison for 2011 is not possible due to the necessary question change.

Methamphetamine and Crystal Methamphetamine (Ice)

One subclass of amphetamines is called methamphetamine ("speed"). This subclass has been around for a long time and gave rise to the phrase "speed kills" in the 1960s. Probably because of the reputation it got at that time as a particularly dangerous drug, it was not popular for some years, so we did not include a full set of questions about its use in MTF's early questionnaires. One form of methamphetamine, crystal methamphetamine or "ice," grew in popularity in the 1980s. It comes in crystallized form, as the name implies, and the chunks can be heated and the fumes inhaled, much like crack.

Trends in Use

For most of the life of the study, the only question about methamphetamine use has been contained in a single 12th-grade questionnaire form. Respondents who indicated using any type of amphetamines in the prior 12 months were asked in a sequel question to indicate on a prespecified list the types they had used during that period. Methamphetamine was one type on the list, and data exist on its use since 1976. In 1976, annual prevalence on this measure was 1.9%; it then roughly doubled to 3.7% by 1981 (the peak year), before declining for over a decade all the way down to 0.4% by 1992. Use then rose again in the 1990s, as did use of a number of drugs, reaching 1.3% by 1998. In other words, it has followed a cross-time trajectory fairly similar to that for amphetamines as a whole.

In 1990, in the 12th-grade questionnaires only, we introduced our usual set of three questions for *crystal methamphetamine,* measuring lifetime, annual, and 30-day use. Among 12th graders in 1990, 1.3% indicated any use in the prior year; use then climbed to 3.0% by 1998, and has generally been declining since. This variable is charted on the first facing panel.

Responding to the growing concern about methamphetamine use in general—not just crystal methamphetamine use—we added a full set of three questions about the use of any methamphetamine to the 1999 questionnaires for all three grade levels.

These questions yield a somewhat higher annual prevalence for 12th graders: 4.3% in 2000, compared to the sum of the methamphetamine and crystal methamphetamine answers in the other, branching question format, which totaled 2.8%. It would appear, then, that the long-term method we had been using for tracking methamphetamine use probably yielded an understatement of the absolute prevalence level, perhaps because some proportion of methamphetamine users did not correctly categorize themselves initially as amphetamine users (even though methamphetamine was given as one of the examples of amphetamines). We think it likely that the shape of the trend curve was not distorted, however.

The newer questions for methamphetamine show annual prevalence rates in 2011 of 0.8%, 1.4%, and 1.4% for 8th, 10th, and 12th graders, respectively. All of these levels are down considerably from the first measurement taken in 1999, when they were 3.2%, 4.6%, and 4.7%. So, despite growing public concern about the methamphetamine problem in the United States, use actually has shown a fairly steady decline over the past 12 years, at least among secondary school students. (A similar decline in methamphetamine use did not begin to appear among college students and young adults until after 2004, likely reflecting a cohort effect.)

Other Measures

No questions have yet been added to the study on perceived risk, disapproval, or availability with regard to overall methamphetamine use.

Clearly the perceived risk of crystal methamphetamine use has risen considerably since 2003, very likely explaining much of the decline in use since then. Perceived availability has been falling in all three grades since 2006, perhaps in part because there are many fewer users.

Heroin

For many decades, heroin—a derivative of opium— was administered primarily by injection into a vein. However, in the 1990s the purity of available heroin reached very high levels, making other modes of administration (such as snorting and smoking) practical alternatives. Thus, in 1995 we introduced questions that asked separately about using heroin with and without a needle in order to determine whether noninjection use explained the upsurge in heroin use we were observing.

Trends in Use

The annual prevalence of heroin use among 12th graders fell by half between 1975 and 1979, from 1.0% to 0.5%. The rate then held amazingly steady until 1994. Use rose in the mid and late 1990s, along with the use of most drugs; it reached peak levels in 1996 among 8th graders (1.6%), in 1997 among 10th graders (1.4%), and in 2000 among 12th graders (1.5%). Since those peak levels, use has declined, with annual prevalence in all three grades fluctuating between 0.7% and 0.9% from 2005 through 2011.

Because the questions about use with and without a needle were not introduced until the 1995 survey, they did not encompass much of the period of increasing heroin use. Responses to the new questions showed that by then about equal proportions of all 8th-grade users were taking heroin by each method of ingestion, and some—nearly a third of users—were using both means. At 10th grade a somewhat higher proportion of all users took heroin without a needle, and at 12th grade the proportion was even higher. Much of the remaining increase in overall heroin use beyond 1995 occurred in the proportions using it without injecting, which we strongly suspect was true in the immediately preceding period of increase as well. Likewise,

most of the decrease in use since the recent peak levels has been due to decreasing use of heroin without a needle. Use with a needle has fluctuated less over time, though in 2010 12th graders showed a significant increase to 0.7%, about where it remained in 2011 (0.6%).

Perceived Risk

Students have long seen heroin to be one of the most dangerous drugs, which no doubt helps to account both for the consistently high level of personal disapproval of use and the quite low prevalence of use. Nevertheless, there have been some changes in perceived risk levels over the years. Between 1975 and 1986, perceived risk gradually declined, even though use dropped and then stabilized in that interval. Then there was a big spike in 1987 (the same year that perceived risk for cocaine jumped dramatically), where it held for four years. In 1992, perceived risk dropped to a lower plateau again, presaging an increase in use a year or two later. Perceived risk then rose again in the latter half of the 1990s, and use leveled off and subsequently declined. Based on the short interval for which we have such data from 8th and 10th graders, the tables at the end of this report illustrate that perceived risk of use without a needle rose in the lower grades between 1995 and 1997, foretelling an end to the increase in use. Note that perceived risk has served as a leading indicator of use for this drug as well as a number of others. During the 2000s, perceived risk has been relatively stable in all three grades along with use.

Disapproval

There has been little fluctuation in the very high disapproval levels for heroin use over the years, and the small changes that have occurred have been generally consistent with changes in perceived risk and use.

Availability

The proportion of 12th-grade students saying they could get heroin fairly easily if they wanted some remained around 20% through the mid-1980s; it then increased considerably from 1986 to 1992 before stabilizing at about 35% from 1992 through 1998. At the lower grade levels, reported availability has been markedly lower. Availability has declined gradually since the late 1990s in all three grades.

Other Narcotic Drugs, Including OxyContin and Vicodin

There are a number of narcotic drugs other than heroin—all controlled substances. Many are analgesics that can be prescribed by physicians and dentists for pain. Like heroin, many are derived from opium, but there are also a number of synthetic analogues in use today, including OxyContin and Vicodin.

Throughout the life of the MTF study, we have asked about the use of any narcotic drug other than heroin without specifying which one. Examples of drugs in the class are provided in the question stem. In one of the six 12th-grade questionnaire forms, however, respondents indicating that they had used any narcotic in the past 12 months were then asked to check which of a fairly long list of such drugs they used. Table E-4 in *Volume I* of this annual monograph series provides trends in their annual prevalence data. In the late 1970s, opium and codeine were among the narcotics most widely used. In recent years Vicodin, codeine, Percocet, and OxyContin have been the most prevalent.

Trends in Use

Use is reported only for 12th graders, because we considered the data from 8th and 10th graders to be of questionable validity. 12th graders' use of narcotics other than heroin generally trended down from about 1977 through 1992, dropping considerably. After 1992 use rose rather steeply, with annual prevalence nearly tripling from 3.3% in 1992 to 9.5% in 2004, before leveling. (In 2002 the question was revised to add Vicodin, OxyContin, and Percocet to the examples given, which clearly had the effect of increasing reported prevalence. So the extent of the increase over the full time span likely is exaggerated, but probably not by much, because these drugs came onto the scene later, during the rise. They simply were not being fully reported by the late 1990s.)

OxyContin use increased some in all grades from 2002 (when it was first measured) through 2011, though the trend lines have been irregular. Annual prevalence in 2011 was 1.8%, 3.9%, and 4.9% in grades 8, 10, and 12, respectively. Use of Vicodin, on the other hand, remained fairly steady at somewhat higher levels since 2002, though use among 10th and 12th graders has declined sharply since 2009. In 2011 annual prevalence rates were 2.1%, 5.9%, and 8.1% in grades 8, 10, and 12.

Availability

Questions were asked about the availability of other narcotics, taken as a class. Perceived availability increased gradually among 12th graders from 1978 through 1989, even as reported use was dropping. Among 12th graders, perceived availability rose gradually from 1991 through 2001, as use rose more sharply. In contrast, perceived availability has declined among 8th and 10th graders since the late 1990s. (A change in question wording in 2010 to include OxyContin and Vicodin as examples presumably accounts for the considerable jump in reported availability.) Availability declined further in all three grades in 2011.

Tranquilizers

Tranquilizers are psychotherapeutic drugs that are legally sold only by prescription, like amphetamines. They are central nervous depressants and, for the most part, comprise benzodiazepines (minor tranquilizers), although some nonbenzodiazepines have been introduced. Respondents are instructed to exclude any medically prescribed use from their answers. At present, Valium and Xanax are the two tranquilizers most commonly used by students. In 2001 the examples given in the tranquilizer question were modified to reflect changes in the drugs in common use—Miltown was dropped and Xanax was added.

Trends in Use

During the late 1970s and all of the 1980s, tranquilizers fell steadily from popularity, with 12th graders' use declining by three fourths over the 15-year interval between 1977 and 1992. Their use then increased, as happened with many other drugs during the 1990s. Annual prevalence more than doubled among 12th graders, rising steadily through 2002, before leveling. Use also rose steadily among 10th graders, but began to decline some in 2002. Use peaked much earlier among 8th graders, in 1996, and then declined slightly for two years. Tranquilizer use has remained relatively stable since then among 8th graders, at considerably lower levels than the upper two grades, though they did show a significant decline in 2011. From 2002 to 2005 there was some decline among 10th graders, followed by a leveling, while among 12th graders there was a very gradual decline from 2002 through 2007, before leveling. This staggered pattern of change suggests that a cohort effect has been at work. At present the prevalence of use of these prescription-type drugs is modestly lower than their recent peak levels, with annual prevalence rates of 2.0%, 4.5%, and 5.6% in grades 8, 10, and 12, respectively.

Perceived Risk and Disapproval

Data have not been collected on perceived risk and disapproval primarily due to questionnaire space limitations.

Availability

As the number of 12th graders reporting non-medically prescribed tranquilizer use fell dramatically during the 1970s and 1980s, so did the proportion saying that tranquilizers would be fairly or very easy to get. Whether declining use caused the decline in availability or vice versa is unclear. However, 12th graders' perceived availability has continued to fall since then, even as use rebounded in the 1990s; it is now down by more than three fourths over the life of the study—from 72% in 1975 to 17% by 2011. Availability has fallen fairly continuously since 1991 in the lower grades as well, though not as sharply.

Sedatives (Barbiturates)

Like tranquilizers, sedatives are prescription-controlled psychotherapeutic drugs that act as central nervous system depressants. They are used to assist sleep and relieve anxiety.

Though for many years respondents have been asked specifically about their use of barbiturate sedatives, they likely have been including other classes of sedatives in their answers. In 2004 the question on use was revised to say "sedatives/barbiturates"—a change that appeared to have no impact on reported levels of use. Respondents are told for what purposes sedatives are prescribed and are instructed to exclude from their answers any use under medical supervision. Usage data are reported only for 12th graders because we believe that 8th- and 10th-grade students tend to overreport use, perhaps including in their answers their use of nonprescription sleep aids or other over-the-counter drugs.

Trends in Use

As with tranquilizers, the use of sedatives (barbiturates) fell steadily among 12th graders from the mid-1970s through the early 1990s. From 1975 to 1992 annual prevalence fell by three fourths, from 10.7% to 2.8%. As with many other drugs, a gradual, long-term resurgence in sedative use occurred after 1992, and use continued to rise steadily through 2005, well beyond the point where the use of many illegal drugs began falling. Use has declined some since 2005, and by 2011 the annual prevalence rate is down by about four tenths from its recent peak. The sedative methaqualone has been included in the MTF study from the very beginning, and has never been as popular as barbiturates; use rates have generally been declining since 1975, reaching an annual prevalence of just 0.5% in 2007, about where it has remained since.

Perceived Risk

Trying sedatives (barbiturates) was never seen by most students as very dangerous. But then perceived risk shifted up some through 1991 while use was still falling. It dropped back some through 1995, as use was increasing, and then remained relatively stable for a few years. Perceived risk has generally been at quite low levels, which may help to explain why the use of this class of psychotherapeutic drugs (and likely others) has stayed at relatively high levels in the first half of the decade of the 2000s. However, it began to rise a bit after 2000, foretelling the decline in use that began after 2005. When the term "sedatives" was changed to "sedatives/barbiturates" in 2004, the trend line shifted down slightly, but perceived risk has continued to climb some. As perceived risk has risen, use has declined some.

Disapproval

Like many illicit drugs other than marijuana, sedative (barbiturate) use has received the disapproval of most high school seniors since 1975, with some variation in disapproval rates that have moved consistently with usage patterns. The necessary change in question wording in 2004 appeared to lessen disapproval slightly. There has been some modest increase in disapproval since 2000.

Availability

The perceived availability of sedatives (barbiturates) has generally been declining during most of the life of the study, except for one upward shift that occurred in 1981—a year in which look-alike drugs became more widespread. (The necessary change in question text in 2004 appears to have had the effect of increasing reported availability among 12th graders but not among those in the lower grades.)

Ecstasy (MDMA) and Other "Club Drugs"

There are a number of "club drugs," so labeled because they have been popular at night clubs and "raves." They include LSD, MDMA ("ecstasy"), methamphetamine, GHB (gammahydroxybutyrate), ketamine ("special K"), and Rohypnol. Because previous sections in this *Overview* have dealt with LSD and methamphetamine, they will not be discussed further here.

Rohypnol and GHB, both of which can induce amnesia while under the influence, have also been labeled "date rape drugs." The annual prevalence of GHB use in 2011 was 0.6%, 0.5%, and 1.4% in grades 8, 10, and 12, respectively, and the annual prevalence of ketamine use was 0.8%, 1.2%, and 1.7%, respectively. Both have shown considerable drops since their recent peak levels of use. There are no questions on risk, disapproval, or availability for GHB, ketamine, or Rohypnol.

Trends in Ecstasy Use

Ecstasy (3,4-methylenedioxymethamphetamine or MDMA) is used more for its mildly hallucinogenic properties than for its stimulant properties. Questions on ecstasy use were added to the high school surveys in 1996 (and have been asked of college students and adults since 1989).

Annual prevalence of ecstasy use in 10th and 12th grades in 1996 was 4.6%—considerably higher than among college students and young adults at that time—but it fell in both grades over the next two years. Use then rose sharply in both grades from 1999 to 2001, bringing annual prevalence up to 6.2% among 10th graders and 9.2% among 12th graders. From 2000 to 2001, use also began to rise among 8th graders, to 3.5%. In 2002, use decreased sharply—by about one fifth—in all three grades, followed by an even sharper decline in 2003. The drops continued in 2004, but decelerated considerably. By 2005 the decline had halted among 8th and 10th graders, but it continued for another year among 12th graders. For two or three years there was some rebound in use among 10th and 12th graders, raising the concern that a new epidemic of ecstasy use may be developing; however, after 2007 the trend lines leveled off in all grades until annual prevalence increased significantly in the lower grades between 2009 and 2010 (from 1.3% to 2.4% in 8th grade and from 3.7% to 4.7% in 10th grade), but then declined in 2011 in both grades. Use among 12th graders did increase in 2011.

Perceived Risk of Ecstasy Use

There was little change in 12th graders' perceived risk of ecstasy use until 2001, when it jumped by eight percentage points, and then by another seven percentage points in 2002. Significant increases occurred again in 2003 for all grades. This very sharp rise likely explains the turnaround in use that we had predicted in advance. However, since 2004, we have seen a troubling drop in perceived risk, first among 8th and 10th graders, then among 12th graders. This shift corresponded to the increase in use in the upper two grades, and then in all three grades, suggesting that there may be a generational forgetting of the dangers of ecstasy use resulting from generational replacement. The decline in perceived risk continued into 2010 in the upper grades, and then into 2011 in 8th and 12th grades.

Disapproval of Ecstasy Use

Disapproval of ecstasy use had been declining slightly after 1998, but increased significantly in all three grades in 2002, perhaps because of the rise in perceived risk. The significant increases in disapproval continued through 2003 for 8th graders, 2004 for 10th graders, and 2006 for 12th graders, suggesting some cohort effect. After those peaks, disapproval dropped sharply among 8th graders before leveling, dropped by less among 10th graders before leveling, and did not drop among 12th graders until 2010—suggesting a cohort effect. We previously stated that the erosion in perceived risk and disapproval—which has been sharpest among 8th graders—left these age groups more vulnerable to a possible rebound in ecstasy use: some rebound appears to have occurred.

Availability of Ecstasy

The figure shows a dramatic rise in 12th graders' perceived availability of ecstasy after 1991, particularly between 1999 and 2001, consistent with informal reports about growing importation of the drug. Perceived availability then declined considerably in all grades after 2001 but has been fairly level since 2009.

Alcohol

Alcoholic beverages have been among the most widely used psychoactive substances by American young people for a very long time. In 2011 the proportions of 8th, 10th, and 12th graders who reported drinking an alcoholic beverage in the 30-day period prior to the survey were 13%, 27%, and 40%, respectively. A number of measures of alcohol use are presented in the tables at the end of this report. Here we focus on episodic heavy or "binge" drinking (i.e., having five or more drinks in a row during the prior two-week interval at least once)—the pattern of alcohol consumption that is probably of greatest concern from a public health perspective. But it is important to mention that in 2011 all measures of alcohol use—lifetime, annual, 30-day, and binge drinking in the prior two weeks—reached historic lows over the life of the study, following a long period of gradual declines.

Trends in Use

Among 12th graders, binge drinking peaked at about the same time as overall illicit drug use, in 1979. It held steady for a few years before declining substantially from 41% in 1983 to a low of 28% in 1992 (also the low point of any illicit drug use). This was a drop of almost one third in binge drinking. Although illicit drug use rose by considerable proportions in the 1990s, binge drinking rose by only a small fraction, followed by some decline in binge drinking at all three grades. By 2011, proportional declines since the recent peaks reached in the 1990s are 52%, 39%, and 31% for grades 8, 10, and 12, respectively.

It should be noted that there is no evidence of any displacement effect in the aggregate between alcohol and marijuana—a hypothesis frequently heard. The two drugs have moved much more in parallel over the years than in opposite directions, at least until the past four years, during which time alcohol continued to decline while marijuana reversed course and rose.

Moreover, these two behaviors have consistently been positively correlated at the individual level.

Perceived Risk

Throughout most of the life of the MTF study, the majority of 12th graders have not viewed binge drinking on weekends as carrying a great risk.

However, an increase from 36% to 49% occurred between 1982 and 1992. There then followed a decline to 43% by 1997 as use rose, before it stabilized. Since 2003, perceived risk has risen some in all grades including in 2011. These changes are consistent with changes in actual binge drinking. We believe that the public service advertising campaigns in the 1980s against drunk driving, as well as those that urged use of designated drivers when drinking, may have contributed to the increase in perceived risk of binge drinking generally. As we have published elsewhere, drunk driving by 12th graders declined during that period by an even larger proportion than binge drinking.[6] Also, we have demonstrated that increases in the minimum drinking age during the 1980s were followed by reductions in drinking and increases in perceived risk associated with drinking.

Disapproval

Disapproval of weekend binge drinking moved fairly parallel with perceived risk, suggesting that such drinking (and very likely the drunk-driving behavior associated with it) became increasingly unacceptable in the peer group. Note that the rates of disapproval and perceived risk for binge drinking are higher in the lower grades than in 12th grade. As with perceived risk, disapproval has increased appreciably in all grades, though it has leveled some in recent years.

Availability

Perceived availability of alcohol, which until 1999 was asked only of 8th and 10th graders, was very high and mostly steady in the 1990s. Since 1996, however, there have been significant declines in 8th and 10th grades. For 12th grade, availability has declined only modestly with 89% still saying that it would be fairly easy or very easy for them to get alcohol. It appears that states, communities, and parents have been successful at reducing access to alcohol among the younger students, however.

Cigarettes

Cigarette smoking is the leading cause of preventable disease and mortality in the United States, and is usually initiated in adolescence. That makes what happens in adolescence particularly important.

Trends in Use

Differences in smoking rates between various birth cohorts (or, in this case, school class cohorts) tend to stay with those cohorts throughout the life cycle. This means that it is critical to prevent smoking very early. It also means that the trends in a given historical period may differ across various grade levels as changes in use occurring earlier in adolescence work their way up the age spectrum (i.e., "cohort effects").

Among 12th graders, 30-day prevalence of smoking reached a peak in 1976, at 39%. (The peak likely occurred considerably earlier at lower grade levels as these same class cohorts passed through them in previous years.) There was about a one quarter drop in 12th-grade 30-day prevalence between 1976 and 1981, when the rate reached 29%, and remained there until 1992 (28%). In the 1990s, smoking began to rise sharply, after 1991 among 8th and 10th graders and 1992 among 12th graders. Over the next four to five years, smoking rates increased by about one half in the lower two grades and by almost one third in grade 12—very substantial increases to which MTF drew public attention. Smoking peaked in 1996 for 8th and 10th graders and in 1997 for 12th graders before beginning a fairly steady and substantial decline that continued through 2004 for 8th and 10th graders (12th graders increased a bit in 2004). Between the peak levels in the mid-1990s and 2004, 30-day prevalence of smoking declined by 56% in 8th grade, 47% in 10th, and 32% in 12th. It is noteworthy, however, that this important decline in adolescent smoking decelerated sharply after about 2002. There was some further decline after 2004 in all grades, but the declines appeared to end in the lower two grades in 2010. In 2011, however, declines occurred in all three grades, with the decline in 10th grade reaching statistical significance.

Perceived Risk

Among 12th graders, the proportion seeing great risk in pack-a-day smoking rose before and during the first period of decline in use in the late 1970s. It leveled in 1980 (before use leveled), declined a bit in 1982, but then started to rise again gradually for five years. (It is possible that cigarette advertising effectively offset the influence of rising perceptions of risk during that period.) Perceived risk fell some in the early 1990s at all three grade levels as use increased sharply. Since then, there has generally been an increase (though not entirely consistently) in perceived risk. All three grades showed an increase in 2011, when use showed a decline. For all three grades, the 2011 levels of perceived risk are the highest ever observed. Note the differences in the extent of perceived risk among grade levels. There is a clear age effect, and by the time most youngsters fully appreciate the hazards of smoking, many of their classmates have already initiated the behavior.

Disapproval

Disapproval rates for smoking have been fairly high throughout the study and, unlike perceived risk, are higher in the lower grade levels. Among 12th graders, there was a gradual increase in disapproval of smoking from 1976 to 1986, some erosion over the following five years, and then steeper erosion from the early 1990s through 1997. After 1997, disapproval rose for some years in all three grades, but leveled in grade 12 after 2006 and in the lower grades after 2007. We measure a number of other smoking-related attitudes; these became increasingly negative for some years, but leveled off three to four years ago

(see Table 3 in the 2011 MTF press release on teen smoking, www.monitoringthefuture.org/press.html).

Availability

When the question was first introduced in 1992, availability of cigarettes was reported to be very high by 8th graders (78% saying fairly or very easy to get) and 10th graders (89%). (We do not ask the question of 12th graders, for whom we assume accessibility to be nearly universal.) Since 1996, availability has declined considerably, especially among 8th graders. Some 52% of 8th graders and 74% of 10th graders now say that cigarettes would be easy to get, reflecting declines since 1992 of 26 and 16 percentage points, respectively.

Smokeless and Other Forms of Tobacco

Traditionally, smokeless tobacco has come in two forms: "snuff" and "chew." Snuff is finely ground tobacco usually sold in tins, either loose or in packets. It is held in the mouth between the lip or cheek and the gums. Chew is a leafy form of tobacco, usually sold in pouches. It too is held in the mouth and may, as the name implies, be chewed. In both cases, nicotine is absorbed by the mucous membranes of the mouth. These forms are sometimes called "spit" tobacco because users expectorate the tobacco juices and saliva (stimulated by the tobacco) that accumulate in the mouth. "Snus" (rhymes with goose) is a relatively new variation on smokeless tobacco, as are some other dissolvable tobacco products. Given that snus appears to be gaining in popularity, items regarding the use of snus and dissolvable tobacco were added to the 2011 surveys. *Annual* prevalence among 12th graders were found to be 7.9% for snus and only 1.5% for dissolvable tobacco.

Trends in Use

The use of smokeless tobacco by teens had been decreasing gradually, and 30-day prevalence is now only about half of recent peak levels in the mid-1990s. Among 8th graders, 30-day prevalence dropped from a 1994 peak of 7.7% to a low of 3.2% in 2007. It stands at 3.5% in 2011. Tenth graders' use was down from a 1994 peak of 10.5% to 4.9% in 2004, but has risen some to 6.6% in 2011; and 12th graders' use decreased from a 1995 peak of 12.2% to 6.1% in 2006, before leveling and then rising to 8.3% in 2011. While use had been rising, it did not continue to rise in 2011. Thirty-day prevalence of *daily* use of smokeless tobacco fell gradually, but appreciably, for some years. Daily usage rates in 2011 are 0.8%, 1.7%, and 3.1% in grades 8, 10, and 12, respectively—down substantially from peak levels recorded in the 1990s but, again, the declines in daily use have halted and begun to reverse.

It should be noted that smokeless tobacco use among American young people is almost exclusively a male behavior. For example, among males the 30-day prevalence rates in 2011 are 4.9%, 11.5%, and 14.2% in grades 8, 10, and 12, respectively, versus 1.9%, 1.9%, and 1.8%, respectively, among females.

The respective current daily use rates for males are 1.5%, 3.3%, and 6.0% compared to 0.2%, 0.2%, and 0.0% for females.

Perceived Risk

The most recent low point in the level of perceived risk for smokeless tobacco was 1995 in all three grades. For a decade following 1995 there was a gradual but substantial increase in proportions saying that there is a great risk in using smokeless tobacco regularly. It thus appears that one important reason for the appreciable declines in smokeless tobacco use during the latter half of the 1990s was that an increasing proportion of young people were persuaded of the dangers of using it. But the increases in perceived risk ended by 2004, and it declined some in grades 10 and 12 for a couple of years, before leveling. The decline could be due to generational forgetting of the dangers of use, the increased marketing of snus and other smokeless products, and/or public statements about smokeless tobacco use being relatively less dangerous than cigarette smoking.

Disapproval

Only 8th and 10th graders are asked about their personal disapproval of using smokeless tobacco regularly. The most recent low points for disapproval in both grades were 1995 and 1996. After 1996, disapproval rose among 8th graders from 74% to 82% in 2005, about where it remains in 2011 (83%), and from 71% to 82% in 2008 among 10th graders, with a significant decline since 2008 to 79% in 2010. It is 80% in 2011.

Availability

There are no questions on perceived availability of smokeless tobacco.

Hookahs and Small Cigars

Twelfth graders were first asked about smoking small cigars and smoking tobacco using hookahs (waterpipes) in 2010. The *past year* prevalence rate in 2011 was 18.5% for hookah smoking (up from 17.1% in 2010) and 19.5% for small cigars (down significantly from 23.1% in 2010).

Steroids

Unlike all other drugs discussed in this *Overview,* anabolic steroids are not usually taken for their psychoactive effects but rather for muscle and strength development. However, they are similar to most other drugs studied here in two respects: they can have adverse consequences for the user, and they are controlled substances for which there is an illicit market. Questions about steroid use were added to MTF questionnaires beginning in 1989. Respondents are asked: "Steroids, or anabolic steroids, are sometimes prescribed by doctors to promote healing from certain types of injuries. Some athletes, and others, have used them to try to increase muscle development. On how many occasions (if any) have you taken steroids on your own—that is, without a doctor telling you to take them . . . ?" In 2006 the question text was changed slightly in some questionnaire forms—the phrase "to promote healing from certain types of injuries" was replaced by "to treat certain conditions."

The resulting data did not show any effect from this rewording. In 2007 the remaining forms were changed in the same manner.

Trends in Use

Anabolic steroids are used predominately by males; therefore, data based on all respondents can mask the higher rates and larger fluctuations that occur among males. (For example, in 2011, annual prevalence rates were 1.0%, 1.4%, and 1.8% for boys in grades 8, 10, and 12, compared with 0.4%, 0.4%, and 0.5% for girls.) Between 1991 and 1998, the overall annual prevalence rate was fairly stable among 8th and 10th graders, ranging between 0.9% and 1.2%. In 1999, however, use jumped from 1.2% to 1.7% in both 8th and 10th grades. (Almost all of that increase occurred among boys increasing from 1.6% in 1998 to 2.5% in 1999 in 8th grade and from 1.9% to 2.8% in 10th grade. Thus, rates among boys increased by about 50% in a single year.) Among all 8th graders, steroid use has declined by about half to 0.7% in 2011. Among 10th graders, use continued to increase, reaching 2.2% in 2002, but then declined by more than half to 0.9% by 2011. In 12th grade there was a different trend story. With data going back to 1989, we can see that steroid use first fell from 1.9% overall in 1989 to 1.1% in 1992—the low point. From 1992 to 1999 there was a more gradual increase in use, reaching 1.7% in 2000. In 2001, use rose significantly among 12th graders to 2.4% (possibly reflecting a cohort effect with the younger, heavier-using cohorts getting older). Their use decreased significantly in 2005 to 1.5%, where it remained in 2010, before falling slightly more to 1.2% in 2011. Use is now down from recent peak levels by 56%, 59%, and 52% among 8th, 10th, and 12th graders, respectively. (The use of androstenedione—a steroid precursor—has also declined sharply since 2001.)

Perceived Risk

Perceived risk and disapproval were asked of 8th and 10th graders for only a few years. All grades seemed to have a peak in perceived risk around 1993. The longer term data from 12th graders show a ten percentage-point drop between 1998 and 2000, and an additional three percentage-point drop by 2003 (to 55%, the lowest point ever). A change this sharp is quite unusual and highly significant, suggesting that some particular event or events in 1998—quite possibly publicity about use of performance-enhancing substances by famous athletes, in particular use of androstenedione by a famous home-run-hitting baseball player—made steroids seem less risky. It seems likely that perceived risk dropped substantially in the lower grades as well, and the sharp upturn in their use that year would be consistent with such a change. By 2011, perceived risk for 12th graders was up to 61%.

Disapproval

Disapproval of steroid use has been quite high for some years. Between 1998 and 2003 there was a modest decrease, though not as dramatic as the drop in perceived risk. From 2003 to 2008, disapproval rose some—as perceived risk rose and use declined— then leveled.

Availability

Perceived availability of steroids was relatively high and increased with grade level; but it has declined appreciably at all grades in recent years. Some steroids were previously sold over-the-counter, but now a number have been scheduled by the DEA. Androstenedione was classified as a Schedule III controlled substance in 2005.

Subgroup Differences

Understanding the important subgroup variations in substance use among the nation's youth allows for more informed considerations of substance use etiology and prevention. In this section, we present a brief overview of some of the major demographic subgroup differences.

Space does not permit a full discussion or documentation of the many subgroup differences on the host of drugs covered in this report. However, *Volume I* in this monograph series—including the one published in 2011 and the one forthcoming in 2012— contains an extensive appendix (Appendix D) with tables giving the subgroup prevalence levels and trends for all of the classes of drugs discussed here. Chapters 4 and 5 in *Volume I* also present a more in-depth discussion and interpretation of those subgroup differences. Comparisons are made by gender, college plans, region of the country, community size, socioeonomic level (as measured by educational level of the parents), and race/ethnicity. In addition, Monitoring the Future Occasional Paper 74—to be succeeded by Occasional Paper 77 (forthcoming)—is available on the MTF Web site (www.monitoringthefuture.org), and provides in chart form the many subgroup trends for all drugs. The reader will probably find the graphic presentations in these occasional papers much easier to comprehend than the tabular material.

Gender

Generally, we have found males to have somewhat higher rates of illicit drug use than females (especially higher rates of *frequent* use), and much higher rates of smokeless tobacco and steroid use. Males have generally had higher rates of heavy drinking; however, in their 30-day prevalence of alcohol use at 8th grade, girls overtook the boys in 2002 and have had higher rates since. At 10th grade, girls caught up to the boys by 2005, but boys have had higher use for the past three years. The genders have had roughly equivalent rates of cigarette smoking in recent years among 8th and 10th graders, at least until the last few years as use by males has begun to exceed that by females. Among 12th graders, the two genders have reversed order twice during the life of the study, but since 1991 males have had slightly higher smoking rates. These gender differences appear to emerge as students grow older. In 8th grade, females actually have higher rates of use for some drugs. Usage rates for the various substances generally tend to move much in parallel across time for both genders, although the absolute differences tend to be largest in the historical periods in which overall prevalence rates are highest.

College Plans

While in high school, those students who are *not* college-bound (a decreasing proportion of the total youth population) are considerably more likely to be at risk for using illicit drugs, drinking heavily, and particularly smoking cigarettes. Again, these differences are largest in periods of highest prevalence. In the lower grades, it was the college-bound who had a greater increase in cigarette smoking in the early to mid-1990s than did their non-college-bound peers.

Region of the Country

The differences associated with region of the country are sufficiently varied and complex that we cannot do justice to them here. In the past, though, the Northeast and West tended to have the highest proportions of students using any illicit drug, and the South the lowest (although these rankings do not apply to many of the specific drugs and do not apply to all grades today). In particular, the cocaine epidemic of the early 1980s was much more pronounced in the West and Northeast than in the other two regions, although the differences decreased as the overall epidemic subsided. While the South and West have generally had lower rates of drinking among students than the Northeast and the Midwest, those differences have narrowed somewhat in recent years. Cigarette smoking rates have generally been lowest in the West. The upsurge of ecstasy use in 1999 occurred primarily in the Northeast, but that drug's newfound popularity then spread to the three other regions of the country.

Population Density

There have not been very large or consistent differences in overall illicit drug use associated with population density since MTF began, helping to demonstrate just how ubiquitous the illicit drug phenomenon has been in this country. Crack and heroin use have generally not been concentrated in urban areas, as is commonly believed, meaning that no parents should assume that their children are immune to these threats simply because they do not live in a city.

Socioeconomic Level

The average level of education of the student's parents, as reported by the student, is used as a proxy for socioeconomic status of the family. For many drugs the differences in use by socioeconomic class are very small, and the trends have been highly parallel. One very interesting difference occurred for cocaine, the use of which was *positively* associated with socioeconomic level in the early 1980s. However, with the advent of crack, which offered cocaine at a lower price, that association nearly disappeared by 1986. Cigarette smoking showed a similar narrowing of class differences, but this time it was a large *negative* association with socioeconomic level that diminished considerably between roughly 1985 and 1993. In more recent years, that negative association has re-emerged in the lower grades as use declined faster among students from more educated families. We believe that the removal of the Joe Camel ad campaign may have played a role in this. Rates of binge drinking are roughly equivalent across the social classes in the upper grades, a pattern that has existed for some time among 12th graders. But, among 10th graders, a negative correlation between social class and binge drinking has begun to develop in the past few years.

Race/Ethnicity

Among the most dramatic and interesting subgroup differences are those found among the three largest racial/ethnic groups—Whites, African Americans, and Hispanics. African-American students have substantially lower rates of use of most licit and illicit drugs than do Whites at all three grade levels. These include any illicit drug use, most of the specific illicit drugs, alcohol, and cigarettes. In fact, African Americans' use of cigarettes has been dramatically lower than Whites' use—a difference that emerged largely during the life of the study (i.e., since 1975).

Hispanic students have rates of use that tend to place them between the other two groups in 12th grade— usually closer to the rates for Whites than for African Americans. Hispanics do have the highest reported rates of use for some drugs in 12th grade—*inhalants, cocaine, crack,* and *crystal methamphetamine.* In 8th grade, they tend to come out highest of the three racial/ethnic groups on nearly all classes of drugs. One possible explanation for this change in ranking between 8th and 12th grade may lie in the considerably higher school dropout rates of Hispanic youth: more of the drug-prone segment of that ethnic group may leave school before 12th grade compared to the other two racial/ethnic groups. Another explanation could be that Hispanics are more precocious in their initiation of these types of behaviors.

Again, we refer the reader to Occasional Paper 77 (forthcoming) at www.monitoringthefuture.org for a much more complete picture of these complex subgroup differences and how they have changed over the years.

Sponsored by—The National Institute on Drug Abuse, National Institutes of Health

This publication was written by the principal investigators and staff of the Monitoring the Future project at the Institute for Social Research, the University of Michigan, under Research Grant No. 3 R01 DA 01411 from the National Institute on Drug Abuse.

The findings and conclusions in this report are those of the authors and do not necessarily represent the views of the sponsor.

Recommended Citation—Johnston, L. D., O'Malley, P. M., Bachman, J. G., & Schulenberg, J. E. (2012). *Monitoring the Future national results on adolescent drug use: Overview of key findings, 2011.* Ann Arbor: Institute for Social Research, The University of Michigan.

Institute for Social Research
The University of Michigan
Ann Arbor, Michigan
Printed February 2012

Notes

1. Prevalence refers to the proportion or percentage of the sample reporting use of the given substance on one or more occasions in a given time interval—e.g., lifetime, past 12 months, or past 30 days. For most drugs, the prevalence of daily use refers to reported use on 20 or more occasions in the past 30 days, except for cigarettes and smokeless tobacco, for which actual daily use is measured, and for binge drinking, defined as having 5+ drinks on at least one occasion in the prior two weeks.

2. The most recent publication in this series is Johnston, L. D., O'Malley, P. M., Bachman, J. G., & Schulenberg, J. E. (2011). *Monitoring the Future national survey results on drug use, 1975—2010: Volume I, Secondary school students.* Ann Arbor: Institute for Social Research, The University of Michigan, 744 pp.

3. The most recent publication in this series is: Johnston, L. D., O'Malley, P. M., Bachman, J. G., & Schulenberg, J. E. (2011). *Monitoring the Future national survey results on drug use, 1975–2010: Volume II, College students & adults ages 19–50.* Ann Arbor: Institute for Social Research, The University of Michigan, 312 pp.

4. The most recent publication in this series is: Johnston, L. D., O'Malley, P. M., Bachman, J. G., & Schulenberg, J. E. (2010). *HIV/AIDS: Risk and protective behaviors among American young adults, 2004–2008* (NIH Publication No. 10-7586). Bethesda, MD: National Institute on Drug Abuse, 52 pp.

5. The term "psychedelics" was replaced with "hallucinogens," and "shrooms" was added to the list of examples, resulting in somewhat more respondents indicating use of this class of drugs. For tranquilizers, Xanax was added to the list of examples given, slightly raising the reported prevalence of use.

6. O'Malley, P.M. & Johnston, L.D. (2003). Unsafe driving by high school seniors: National trends from 1976 to 2001 in tickets and accidents after use of alcohol, marijuana, and other illegal drugs. *Journal of Studies on Alcohol, 64,* 305–312.

Critical Thinking

1. Discuss the changes in adolescent drug use since the 1990s.

2. What drug use do these authors find to be in decline? Why do you think that is?

3. Discuss implications for youth drug use prevention.

From *University of Michigan, Institute for Social Research*, February 2012, pp. 1–45. Copyright © 2012 by National Institute on Drug Abuse. Reprinted by permission.

Transcending the Medical Frontiers: Exploring the Future of Psychedelic Drug Research

DAVID JAY BROWN

When I was in graduate school studying behavioral neuroscience I wanted nothing more than to be able to conduct psychedelic drug research. However, in the mid-1980s, this was impossible to do at any academic institution on Earth. There wasn't a single government on the entire planet that legally allowed clinical research with psychedelic drugs. However, this worldwide research ban started to recede in the early 1990s, and we're currently witnessing a renaissance of medical research into psychedelic drugs.

Working with the Multidisciplinary Association for Psychedelic Studies (MAPS) for the past four years as their guest editor has been an extremely exciting and tremendously fruitful endeavor for me. It's a great joy to see how MDMA can help people suffering from posttraumatic stress disorder (PTSD), how LSD can help advanced-stage cancer patients come to peace with the dying process, and how ibogaine can help opiate addicts overcome their addiction. There appears to be enormous potential for the development of psychedelic drugs into effective treatments for a whole range of difficult-to-treat psychiatric disorders.

However, as thrilled as I am by all the new clinical studies exploring the medical potential of psychedelic drugs, I still long for the day when our best minds and resources can be applied to the study of these extraordinary substances with an eye that looks beyond their medical applications, toward their ability to enhance human potential and explore new realities.

This article explores these possibilities. But first, let's take a look at how we got to be where we are.

A Brief History of Time-Dilation Studies

Contemporary Western psychedelic drug research began in 1897, when the German chemist Arthur Heffter first isolated mescaline, the primary psychoactive compound in the peyote cactus. In 1943 Swiss chemist Albert Hofmann discovered the hallucinogenic effects of LSD (lysergic acid diethylamide) at Sandoz Pharmaceuticals in Basel while studying ergot, a fungus that grows on rye. Then, 15 years later, in 1958, he was the first to isolate psilocybin and psilocin—the psychoactive components of the Mexican "magic mushroom," Psilocybe mexicana.

Before 1972, nearly 700 studies with LSD and other psychedelic drugs were conducted. This research suggested that LSD has remarkable medical potential. LSD-assisted psychotherapy was shown to safely reduce the anxiety of terminal cancer patients, alcoholism, and the symptoms of many difficult-to-treat psychiatric illnesses.

Between 1972 and 1990 there were no human studies with psychedelic drugs. Their disappearance was the result of a political backlash that followed the promotion of these drugs by the 1960s counterculture. This reaction not only made these substances illegal for personal use, but also made it extremely difficult for researchers to get government approval to study them.

The New Wave of Psychedelic Drug Research

The political climate began to change in 1990, with the approval of Rick Strassman's DMT study at the University of New Mexico. According to public policy expert and MAPS president Rick Doblin this change occurred because, "open-minded regulators at the FDA decided to put science before politics when it came to psychedelic and medical marijuana research. FDA openness to research is really the key factor. Also, senior researchers who were influenced by psychedelics in the sixties now are speaking up before they retire and have earned credibility."

The past 18 years have seen a bold resurgence of psychedelic drug research, as scientists all over the world have come to recognize the long-underappreciated potential of these drugs. In the past few years, a growing number of studies using human volunteers have begun to explore the possible therapeutic benefits of drugs such as LSD, psilocybin, DMT, MDMA, ibogaine and ketamine.

Current studies are focusing on psychedelic treatments for cluster headaches, PTSD, depression, obsessive-compulsive disorder (OCD), severe anxiety in terminal cancer patients, alcoholism, and opiate addiction. The results so far look quite promising, and more studies are being planned by MAPS and other private psychedelic research organizations, with the eventual goal of turning MDMA, LSD, psilocybin, and other psychedelics into legally available prescription drugs.

As excited as I am that psychedelic drugs are finally being studied for their medical and healing potential, I'm eagerly anticipating the day when psychedelic drug research can really take off, and move beyond its therapeutic applications in medicine. I look forward to the day when researchers can explore the potential of psychedelics as advanced learning tools, relationship builders, creativity enhancers, pleasure magnifiers, vehicles for self-improvement, reliable catalysts for spiritual or mystical experiences, a stimulus for telepathy and other psychic abilities, windows into other dimensions, and for their ability to possibly shed light on the reality of parallel universes and nonhuman entity contact.

Let's take a look at some of these exciting possibilities.

The Science of Pleasure

Almost all medical research to date has been focused on curing diseases and treating illnesses, while little attention has been paid to increasing human potential, let alone to the enhancement of pleasure. However, one can envision a time in the not-too-distant future when we will have cured all of our most challenging physical ailments and have more time and resources on our hands to explore post-survival activities. It's likely that we'll then focus our research efforts on discovering new ways to improve our physical and mental performance.

A science devoted purely to enhancing pleasure might come next, and psychedelics could play a major role in this new field. Maverick physicist Nick Herbert's "Pleasure Dome" project seeks to explore this possibility, and although this is little more than an idea at this point, it may be the first step toward turning the enhancement of pleasure into a true science.

According to surveys done by the U.S. National Institute of Drug Abuse, the number one reason why people do LSD is because "it's fun." Tim Leary helped to popularize the use of LSD with the help of the word "ecstasy," and sex expert Annie Sprinkle has been outspoken about the ecstatic possibilities available from combining sex and psychedelics. Countless psychedelic trip reports have described long periods of appreciating extraordinary beauty and savoring ecstatic bliss, experiences that were many orders of magnitude more intense than the subjects previously thought possible.

With all the current research emphasis on the medical applications and therapeutic potential of psychedelics, the unspoken and obvious truth about these extraordinary substances is that, when done properly, they're generally safe and healthy ways to have an enormous amount of fun. There's good reason why, they're so popular recreationally, despite their illegality.

When psychedelic research begins to integrate with applied neuroscience and advanced nanotechnology in the future, we can begin to establish a serious science of pleasure and fun. Most likely this would begin with a study of sensory enhancement

and time dilation, which are two of the primary effects that psychedelics reliably produce.

Perhaps one day our brightest researchers and best resources will be devoted to finding new ways to enhance sexual, auditory, visual, olfactory, gustatory, and tactile sensations, and create undreamed of new pleasures and truly unearthly delights. Scientific studies could explore ways to improve sexual performance and enhance sensory sensitivity, elongate and intensify our orgasms, enlarge the spectrum of our perceptions, and deepen every dimension of our experience. Massage therapy, Tantra, music, culinary crafting, and other pleasure-producing techniques could be systematically explored with psychedelics, and universities could have applied research centers devoted to the study of ecstasy, tickling, and laughter.

The neurochemistry of aesthetic appreciation, happiness, humor, euphoria, and bliss could be carefully explored with an eye toward improvement. Serious research and development could be used to create new drugs, and integrate neurochemically heightened states with enhanced environments, such as technologically advanced amusement parks and extraordinary virtual realities. In this area of research, it seems that psychedelics may prove to be extremely useful, and countless new psychedelic drugs are just waiting to be discovered.

In addition to enhancing pleasure, psychedelics also stimulate the imagination in extraordinary ways.

Creativity Problem-Solving

A number of early studies suggest that psychedelic drugs may stimulate creativity and improve problem-solving abilities. In 1955, Louis Berlin investigated the effects of mescaline and LSD on the painting abilities of four nationally recognized graphic artists. Although the study showed that there was some impairment of technical ability among the artists, a panel of independent art critics judged the experimental paintings as having "greater aesthetic value" than the artists' usual work.

In 1959, Los Angeles psychiatrist Oscar Janiger asked sixty prominent artists to paint a Native American doll before taking LSD and then again while under its influence. A panel of independent art critics and historians then evaluated these 120 paintings. As with Berlin's study, there was a general agreement by the judges that the craftsmanship of the LSD paintings suffered; however, many received higher marks for imagination than the pre-LSD paintings.

In 1965, at San Francisco State College, James Fadiman and Willis Harman administered mescaline to professional workers in various fields to explore its creative problem-solving abilities. The subjects were instructed to bring a professional problem requiring a creative solution to their sessions. After some psychological preparation, subjects worked individually on their problem throughout their mescaline session. The creative output of each subject was evaluated by psychological tests, subjective reports, and the eventual industrial or commercial validation and acceptance of the finished product or final solution. Virtually all subjects produced solutions judged highly creative and satisfactory by these standards.

In addition to the scientific studies that have been conducted there are also a number of compelling anecdotal examples that suggest a link between creativity and psychedelic drugs. For example, architect Kyosho Izumi's LSD-inspired design of the ideal psychiatric hospital won him a commendation for outstanding achievement from the American Psychiatric Association, and Apple cofounder Steve Jobs attributes some of the insights which lead to the development of the personal computer to his use of LSD. Additionally, a number of renowned scientists have personally attributed their breakthrough scientific insights to their use of psychedelic drugs—including Nobel Prize winners Francis Crick and Kary Mullis.

There hasn't been a formal creativity study with psychedelics since 1965, although there are countless anecdotal reports of artists, writers, musicians, filmmakers, and other people who attribute a portion of their creativity and inspiration to their use of psychedelics. This is an area that is more than ripe for study. Anecdotal reports suggest that very low doses of LSD—threshold level doses, around 20 micrograms—are especially effective as creativity enhancers. For example, Francis Crick was reported to be using low doses of LSD when he discovered the double-helix structure of the DNA molecule.

I'd love to see a whole series of new studies exploring how cannabis, LSD, psilocybin, and mescaline can enhance the imagination, improve problem-solving abilities, and stimulate creativity. As advances in robotics automates more of our activities, I suspect that creativity will eventually become the most valuable commodity of all. Much of the creativity in Hollywood and Silicon Valley is already fueled by psychedelics and research into how these extraordinary tools could enhance creativity even more effectively may become a booming enterprise in the not-too-distant future.

However, creativity isn't the only valuable psychological ability that psychedelics appear to enhance.

ESP Psychic Phenomena

Few people are aware that there have been numerous, carefully controlled scientific experiments with telepathy, psychokinesis, remote viewing, and other types of psychic phenomena, which have consistently produced compelling, statistically significant results that conventional science is at a loss to explain. Even most scientists are currently unaware of the vast abundance of compelling scientific evidence for psychic phenomena, which has resulted from over a century of parapsychological research. Hundreds of carefully controlled studies—in which psi researchers continuously redesigned experiments to address the comments from their critics—have produced results that demonstrate small, but statistically significant effects for psi phenomena, such as telepathy, precognition, and psychokinesis.

According to Dean Radin, a meta-analysis of this research demonstrates that the positive results from these studies are significant with odds in the order of many billions to one. Princeton University, the Stanford Research Institute, Duke University, the Institute of Noetic Science, the U.S. and Russian governments, and many other respectable institutions, have spent years researching these mysterious phenomena, and conventional science is at a loss to explain the results. This research is summarized in Radin's remarkable book *The Conscious Universe.*

Just as fascinating as the research into psychic phenomena is the controversy that surrounds it. In my own experience researching the possibility of telepathy in animals, and other unexplained phenomena with British biologist Rupert Sheldrake, I discovered that many people are eager to share personal anecdotes about psychic events in their life—such as remarkable coincidences, uncanny premonitions, precognitive dreams, and seemingly telepathic communications. In these cases, the scientific studies simply confirm life experiences. Yet many scientists that I've spoken with haven't reviewed the evidence and remain doubtful that there is any reality to psychic phenomenon. However, surveys conducted by British biologist Rupert Sheldrake and myself reveal that around 78% of the population has had unexplainable "psychic" experiences, and the scientific evidence supports the validity of these experiences.

It's also interesting to note that many people have reported experiencing meaningful psychic experiences with psychedelics—not to mention a wide range of paranormal events and synchronicities, which seem extremely difficult to explain by means of conventional reasoning.

A questionnaire study conducted by psychologist Charles Tart, PhD. of 150 experienced marijuana users found that 76% believed in extrasensory perception (ESP), with frequent reports of experiences while intoxicated that were interpreted as psychic. Psychiatrist Stanislav Grof, M.D., and psychologist Stanley Krippner, PhD., have collected numerous anecdotes about psychic phenomena that were reported by people under the influence of psychedelics, and several small scientific studies have looked at how LSD, psilocybin, and mescaline might effect telepathy and remote viewing.

For example, according to psychologist Jean Millay, PhD., in 1997, students at the University of Amsterdam in the Netherlands did research to establish whether the use of psilocybin could influence remote viewing. This was a small experiment, with only 12 test-subjects, but the results of the study indicated that those subjects who were under the influence of psilocybin achieved a success rate of 58.3 percent, which was statistically significant.

A great review article by Krippner and psychologist David Luke, PhD. that summarizes all of the psychedelic research into psychic phenomena can be found in the Spring, 2011 MAPS Bulletin that I edited about psychedelics and the mind/body connection.

When I conducted the California-based research for two of Sheldrake's books about unexplained phenomena in science, *Dogs That Know When Their Owners Are Coming Home* and *The Sense of Being Stared At*, one of the experiments that I ran involved testing blindfolded subjects to see if they could sense being stared at from behind. One of the subjects that I worked with reported an unusually high number of correct trials while under the influence of MDMA. I'd love to run a whole study to see if MDMA-sensitized subjects are more aware of when they're being stared at.

It is especially common for people to report experiences with telepathy, clairvoyance, precognition, remote viewing, and psychokinesis while using ayahuasca, the potent hallucinogenic jungle juice from the Amazon. There have only been several studies with ayahuasca which demonstrate health benefits, but this is an area that is just crying out to be explored carefully and in depth. Future studies could examine ayahuasca's potential and accuracy as a catalyst for psychic phenomena, and all of the traditional studies that have been done with psychic phenomena, which generated positive results, could be redone with subjects dosed with different psychedelics to see if test scores can be improved.

Increasing our psychic abilities may open up the human mind to new, unimagined possibilities–and if you think that harnessing telepathic and clairvoyant abilities is pretty wild, then hold on to your hats for what's likely to come next.

Higher Dimensions and Nonhuman Entity Contact

A primary ingredient in ayahuasca is DMT, and users claim that this remarkable substance has the extraordinary power to open up an interdimensional portal into another universe. Some of the most fascinating psychedelic research has been done with this incredible compound.

DMT is a mystery. One of the strangest puzzles in all of nature—in the same league as questions like "What existed before the Big Bang?" and "How did life begin?"—revolves around the fact that the unusually powerful psychedelic DMT is naturally found in the human body, as well as in many species of animals and plants, and nobody knows what it does, or what function it might serve, in any of these places.

Because natural DMT levels tend to rise while we're asleep at night, it has been suggested that it may have a role in dreaming. But this is pure speculation, and even if true, it may do much more. Because of its endogenous status and unusually potent effects, many people have considered DMT to be the quintessential psychedelic. DMT has effects of such strength and magnitude that it easily dwarfs the titanic quality of even the most powerful LSD trips, and it appears to transport one into an entirely new world—a world that seems more bizarre than our wildest imaginings, yet, somehow, is also strangely familiar.

Psychiatric researcher Rick Strassman, PhD., who conducted a five year study with DMT at the University of New Mexico, has suggested that naturally elevated DMT levels in the brain may be responsible for such unexplained mental phenomena as spontaneous mystical experiences, near-death experiences, nonhuman entity contact, and schizophrenia. Strassman and others have even gone so far as to speculate about the possibility that elevated DMT levels in the brain might be responsible for ushering the soul into the body before birth, and out of the body after death.

But perhaps what's most interesting about DMT is that, with great consistency, it appears to allow human beings to communicate with other intelligent life forms. When I interviewed Strassman, I asked him if he thought that there was an objective reality to the worlds visited by people when they're under the influence of DMT, and if he thought that the entities that so many people have encountered on DMT actually have an independent existence or not. Rick replied:

> I myself think so. My colleagues think I've gone woolly brained over this, but I think it's as good a working hypothesis as any other. I tried all other hypotheses with our volunteers, and with myself. The "this is your brain on drugs" model; the Freudian "this is your unconscious playing out repressed wishes and fears;" the Jungian "these are archetypal images symbolizing your unmet potential;" the "this is a dream;" etc. Volunteers had powerful objections to all of these explanatory models—and they were a very sophisticated group of volunteers, with decades of psychotherapy, spiritual practice, and previous psychedelic experiences. I tried a thought-experiment, asking myself, "What if these were real worlds and real entities? Where would they reside, and why would they care to interact with us?" This led me to some interesting speculations about parallel universes, dark matter, etc. All because we can't prove these ideas right now (lacking the proper technology) doesn't mean they should be dismissed out of hand as incorrect.

A 2006 scientific paper by computer scientist Marko A. Rodriguez called "A Methodology for Studying Various Interpretations of the N,N-dimethyltryptamine-Induced Alternate Reality" explores how to possibly determine if the entities experienced by people on DMT are indeed independently existing intelligent beings or just projections of our hallucinating brains. Rodriguez suggests a test that involves asking the entities to perform a complex mathematical task involving prime numbers to verify their independent existence. While it seems like a long shot that this method could lead to fruitful results, I think that any serious speculation about establishing communication channels with these mysterious beings is constructive.

Strassman's work could represent the very beginning of a scientific field that systematically explores the possibility of communicating with higher dimensional entities, and this might prove to be a more fruitful endeavor for establishing extraterrestrial contact than the SETI project. What they can teach us, we can only imagine.

My own experiences with DMT lead me to suspect that Strassman's studies would have yielded far more fruitful results had the subjects been dosed with harmaline prior to receiving their DMT injections. Harmaline is an MAO-inhibiting enzyme that is found in a number of plants. It's found in the famous South American vine known as Banisteriopsis cappi, which composes half of the mixture in the sacred hallucinogenic jungle juice ayahuasca, which has been used for healing purposes by indigenous peoples in the Amazon basin for thousands of years. Harmaline is widely known as the chemical that allows the DMT in other plants, like Psychotria viridis, to become orally active.

Orally consumed DMT is destroyed in the stomach by an enzyme called monoamine oxidase (MAO), which harmaline inhibits. However, it does much more than just make the DMT orally active. I've discovered that drinking a tea made from

Syrian rue seeds–which also contain harmaline–two hours prior to smoking DMT dramatically alters the experience. Harmaline has interesting psychoactive properties of its own that are somewhat psychedelic, and it slows down the speed of the DMT experience considerably, rendering it more comprehensible, less frightening, and easier to understand. For thousands of years indigenous peoples in the Amazon jungles combined harmaline and DMT, and this long history has cultivated a powerful synergism between how the two molecules react in our body.

In future studies harmaline could be used in conjunction with DMT, to more accurately simulate the ayahuasca experience that strikes such a powerful primordial chord in our species. This would allow for the experience to become much more comprehensible, and last for a greater duration of time, which would allow for more ability to examine the phenomenon of nonhuman entity communication.

Some readers may have noticed that this article has loosely followed a Christian theological progression, from the ego death and bodily resurrection of the medical studies with psychedelics, to the paradisiacal pleasures of Heaven, where we discovered our godlike powers and met with the angels. Ultimately, it appears, this research will lead us to the source of divinity itself.

The Study of Divine Intelligence

Perhaps the most vital function of psychedelics is their ability to reliably produce spiritual or mystical experiences. These transpersonal experiences of inseparability often result in an increased sense of ecological awareness, a greater sense of interconnection, a transcendence of the fear of death, a sense of the sacred or divine, and identification with something much larger than one's body or personal life.

Many people suspect that this experience lies at the heart of the healing potential of psychedelics—and they believe that making this experience available to people is essential for the survival of our species. I agree that we need a compassionate vision of our interconnection with the biosphere to guide our technological evolution and without it we might destroy ourselves.

In his book *The Physics of Immortality*, physicist Frank Tipler introduces the idea that if a conscious designing intelligence is genuinely a part of this universe, then ultimately religion—or the study of this designer intelligence—will become a branch of physics. Psychedelic drug research may offer one pathway toward establishing this future science.

Recent studies by Roland Griffiths and colleagues at Johns Hopkins have confirmed that psilocybin can indeed cause religious experiences that are indistinguishable from religious experiences reported by mystics throughout the ages—and that substantial health benefits can result from these experiences.

These new studies echo the findings of an earlier study done in 1962 by Walter Pahnke of the Harvard Divinity School, and it's certainly not news to anyone who has had a full-blown psychedelic experience. R.U. Sirius responded to this seemingly redundant research by saying that "Wow! Scientists Discover Ass Not Elbow!" Nonetheless, this may represent the beginning of a whole new field of academic inquiry, which explores those realms that have been previously declared off-limits to science.

It appears that the integration of science and spirituality could be the next event horizon—our next adventure as a species. Our future evolution may depend on it. Without a transpersonal perspective of interconnection to guide our evolutionary direction, we seem to be firmly set on a path toward inevitable self-destruction. I personally believe psychedelics can help us get back on track, and help us heal the damage that we've done to ourselves and to the Earth. This is why I believe so strongly in psychedelic drug research.

There isn't much time left before our biosphere starts to unravel, and we may only have a small window of opportunity to save our fragile world. I think that MAPS—and sister organizations, like the Beckley Foundation and the Heffter Research Institute—are industrialized society's best hope for transforming the planet's ancient shamanic plants into the respectable scientific medicines of tomorrows and, in so doing, bring psychedelic therapy to all who need it. This may not only help to heal a number of difficult-to-treat medical disorders and increase ecological harmony on the planet, but it may also open up a doorway to untold and unimagined new worlds of possibility.

Critical Thinking

1. Discuss the benefits and the challenges in the use of psychedelic drugs.

2. Provide an argument for or against legalizing psychedelics for medical reasons.

UNIT 4

Other Trends in Drug Use

Unit Selections

20. **Adolescent Painkiller Use May Increase Risk of Addiction,** Heroin Use, Alcoholism and Drug Abuse Weekly
21. **'Legal Highs' Prevalence Makes Ban Policy 'Ridiculous',** Mark Townsend
22. **Alcoholism Isn't What It Used To Be,** NIAA Spectrum

Learning Outcomes

After reading this Unit, you should be able to:

- Explain why some drug-related trends are more specific to certain subpopulations of Americans than others.

- Describe the significance of socioeconomic status in influencing drug trends.

- Determine the influences that have contributed to the dramatic spread of prescription drug abuse in the United States.

- Determine what alcoholism and heavy drinking are.

- Explain the factors that cause drug-related trends to change.

Student Website
www.mhhe.com/cls

Internet References

Drug Story.org
    www.drugstory.org/drug_stats/druguse_stats.asp
Marijuana as a Medicine
    http://mojo.calyx.net/~olsen
Monitoring the Future
    www.monitoringthefuture.org
Prescription Drug Abuse
    www.prescription-drug-abuse.org
Prescriptions Drug Use and Abuse
    www.fda.gov/fdac/features/2001/501_drug.htm
SAMHSA
    www.drugabusestatistics.samhsa.gov/trends.htm
United States Drug Trends
    www.usdrugtrends.com

Rarely do drug-related patterns and trends lend themselves to precise definition. Identification, measurement, and prediction of the consequence of these trends is an inexact science, to say the least. It is, nevertheless, a very important process. One of the most valuable uses of drug-related trend analysis is the identification of subpopulations whose vulnerability to certain drug phenomena is greater than that of the wider population. These identifications may forewarn of the implications for the general population. Trend analysis may produce specific information that may otherwise be lost or obscured by general statistical indications. For example, tobacco is probably the most prominent of gateway drugs, with repeated findings pointing to the correlation between the initial use of tobacco and the use of other drugs.

The analysis of specific trends related to drug use is very important, as it provides a threshold from which educators, health-care professionals, parents, and policymakers may respond to significant drug-related health threats and issues. Over 20 million Americans report the use of illegal drugs. The current rate of illicit drug use is similar to the rates of the past three years. Marijuana remains as the most commonly used illicit drug with more than 14 million current users. Historically, popular depressant and stimulant drugs—such as alcohol, tobacco, heroin, and cocaine—produce statistics that identify the most visible and sometimes the most constant use patterns. Other drugs such as marijuana, LSD, ecstasy, and other "club drugs" often produce patterns widely interpreted to be associated with cultural phenomena such as youth attitudes, popular music trends, and political climate.

Two other continuing trends are those that involve the abuse of prescription drugs and those that involve the use of methamphetamine. Americans are abusing prescription drugs more than ever before with the most frequently mentioned offenders being oxycodone and hydrocodone. Currently, more than 5 million persons use prescription pain relievers for nonmedical reasons. Of those who used pain relievers for nonmedical reasons, 56 percent obtained them for free from a friend or relative. As more and more drugs get prescribed within the population, a steady trend, more and more drugs become easily accessible. The National Institute of Drug Abuse reports that 20 percent of the U.S. population over 12 has used prescription drugs for nonmedical reasons. Currently, prescription drug abuse among youth ranks second behind only marijuana. The good news is that drug use by youth has declined or leveled off in several important categories such as those associated with marijuana, alcohol, and methamphetamine. And although methamphetamine use is down, it is reported by local and state officials in the West and Midwest as the number one illegal-drug problem.

Although the federal government has modified its survey methods to more accurately identify the number of meth users, many worry that the meth problem is still understated and greatly outweighs those problems associated with other illegal drugs in the West, Southwest, and Midwest. Information concerning drug-use patterns and trends obtained from a number of different investigative methods is available from a variety of sources. On the national level, the more prominent sources are the Substance Abuse and Mental Health Services Administration, the National Institute on Drug Abuse, the Drug Abuse Warning Network, the national Centers for Disease Control, the Justice Department, the Office of National Drug Control Policy, the surgeon general, and the DEA. On the

© Ingram Publishing

state level, various justice departments, including attorney generals' offices, the courts, state departments of social services, state universities and colleges, and public health offices maintain data and conduct research. On local levels, criminal justice agencies, social service departments, public hospitals, and health departments provide information. On a private level, various research institutes and universities, professional organizations such as the American Medical Association and the American Cancer Society, hospitals, and treatment centers, as well as private corporations, are tracking drug-related trends. Surveys abound with no apparent lack of available data. As a result, the need for examination of research methods and findings for reliability and accuracy is self-evident. The articles in this unit provide information about some drug-related trends occurring within certain subpopulations of Americans. While reading the articles, it is interesting to consider how the trends and patterns described are dispersed through various subpopulations of Americans and specific geographical areas. Additionally, much information about drugs and drug trends can be located quickly by referring to the list of websites in the front section of this book.

Adolescent Painkiller Use May Increase Risk of Addiction, Heroin Use

Prescription opiate abuse is not only increasing among adolescents, but it predisposes them to becoming addicted as adults, according to animal research published earlier this month. Furthermore, clinicians report that prescription opiates are now a "gateway" drug that leads to heroin, with adolescent units, typically devoted to alcohol and marijuana, now treating more and more patients for opiate addiction.

"We're terrified," said Mary Jeanne Kreek, MD, professor and head of laboratory at the Laboratory of the Biology of Addictive Diseases at The Rockefeller University in New York City. "We don't know where prescription opiate illicit use is going to go, and we don't know how many will become addicted." Kreek, who with lead author Yong Zhang, PhD, and others conducted the study comparing the effects of oxycodone on adolescent and adult mice, spoke to *ADAW* last week about the effects of prescription opiates on the developing brain.

Adolescents may start using prescription opiates for the same reasons they start using any drug of abuse, said Kreek: risk-taking, impulsivity, and peer pressure. But that initial use could progress to addiction, because of the drug's effects on the dopamine system, she said. With heroin, as many as one in three who ever use it become addicted. In addition, once tried even once, opiates can be alluring to adolescents. "Opiates have what a lot of young people are looking for today—an escape from life's problems," she said.

The Mouse Study

The mouse study found that the lowest dose of oxydocone led to increased dopamine levels in adolescent mice, but not in adult mice. When the adolescent mice were re-exposed to oxycodone as adults, they had higher levels of dopamine than adults who were exposed to the same amount but had not been exposed as adolescents.

In addition, the adolescent mice self-administered smaller amounts of oxycodone, and less frequently, than adult mice did.

These findings suggest that adolescent mice are more sensitive to the oxycodone. Kreek hypothesized that this is because of the state of the adolescent brain, which has rapidly increasing dopamine receptors.

The number of dopamine receptors in the mouse brain increases exponentially from birth to early adolescence, and remain at a plateau at mid-adolescence (the equivalent of age 13 to 16 years) and then begin to decline until adulthood. It is this rapid development of dopamine receptors which might be the key to adolescent sensitivity to drugs.

Epidemiological studies have already proven that the earlier adolescents initiate use of alcohol or cigarettes, the greater the likelihood that they will be dependent as adults. When use is initiated as adults, the chance of subsequent dependence plummets.

"Adolescence is when we are forming our memories, our cues, and learning," said Kreek. "You don't want to batter a brain that's learning, and I look at drug abuse as battering a brain."

Gateway to Heroin

Kreek's study suggests that human adolescents are more sensitive to prescription opiates, said Joseph Frascella, PhD, director of the division of clinical neuroscience at the National Institute on Drug Abuse (NIDA), which funded the study. "We know that the earlier kids get involved in drugs, the more likely they are to have careers in drugs," Frascella told *ADAW*.

"In a sense this is a gateway theory at work—if you start with one drug, does it lead you down the path to another, like heroin," said Frascella. "I really don't think we know the answer to this yet. It could be that the kids who are willing to do these heavy drugs have some kind of brain vulnerability."

But even if science is still studying the reasons behind adolescent use of opiates, treatment providers see the effects. In Buffalo, N.Y., providers are reporting increased numbers of young people coming in with prescription opiate dependency and with heroin addiction. "When we opened in 1990, the three major gateway drugs were marijuana, alcohol, and nicotine," said Dick Gallagher, executive director of Alcohol and Drug Dependency Services, Inc., a 210-bed treatment facility for adolescents and young adults. "Now, there are four gateway drugs, and one is prescription opiates," he said.

Buffalo is a case in point because heroin is less expensive than prescription opiates there, because both are popular among young people there, and because the treatment system is coping with so much opiate dependency among adolescents, according to treatment providers.

"Ten years ago we would see five people a month in trouble with prescription opiates," said Robert B. Whitney, M.D., attending physician in the division of chemical dependency at Erie County Medical Center in Buffalo, where there are 700 out-patient slots and 400 beds for addiction treatment. "Now we see more than five a day."

And prescription opiates are a gateway for heroin use, Whitney told *ADAW*. "There's a limit to how much Oxycontin or hydrocodone they can get just to maintain themselves," he said. "They find that with heroin, they may get better management of their withdrawal."

Whitney described a typical pathway to heroin, with prescription drugs as the gateway. The user starts with oral opiates, moving to crushing and snorting them, to snorting heroin. These people say "at least I'm not using a needle," said Whitney. However, eventually many find that snorting the heroin gets too expensive or they can't maintain their addiction, and they move to intravenous use.

"There's a pattern of kids that have utilized the painkillers, and want to go on to the next level," Gallagher said. Heroin is less expensive than prescription opiates, and it's accessible, he said.

The Adolescent and Pain

What if an adolescent takes a prescription opiate for pain—does the Kreek study imply that this adolescent will be at greater risk for later addiction? "That's an excellent question," said NIDA's Frascella. "The data seem to suggest that if you take a medication for pain, there's a different response than if you take it just to get high."

Kreek agreed. "We do know that persons in severe pain have a different neurobiological substrate," she said.

However, Kreek warned that opiates are overprescribed for acute pain. "I'm not talking about cancer and chronic pain," she said. But it's not necessary for someone to get two weeks' supply of painkillers when they only need 48 hours' worth, she

said. "We can talk to the patient in two days and see if we've misjudged," she said. "But in general you can step down to a much lighter drug."

And Whitney in Buffalo related a story of a patient who three years ago at the age of 15 was in a car accident and went home from the hospital with a legitimate prescription for hydrocodone. "Within a month she was taking not only what they gave her but what she could get from her friends," he said. This girl—initially a patient in his hospital due to a car accident—became his patient due to heroin addiction.

"For sure prescription opiates are a gateway drug," said Whitney. "They're getting the heroin problem into a population that we did not see using opiates at all before." This population of young people requires long-term treatment.

Gallagher agreed, saying that for the adolescents, treatment for opiate addiction must be go on for months. "Don't think you can treat these kids in 28 days unless you have intensive support after," he said.

The Kreek study of mice lends credence to what the treatment providers are reporting. "If you want to make the jump to humans—which we shouldn't do, but we do—our findings suggest that recovery [from opiate addiction] is very slow," Kreek told *ADAW*, adding that the findings also show chemically that adolescent brains do have special vulnerabilities to opiates.

Resources

"Behavioral and Neurochemical Changes Induced by Oxycodone Differ Between Adolescent and Adult Mice" is published in the current issue of *Neuropsychopharmacology*. For the full text, go to http://www.nature.com/npp/journal/vaop/ncurrent/full/npp2008134a.html.

Critical Thinking

1. Adolescents are more susceptible to addiction while abusing prescription drugs. What are the reasons for this, and why is it important in relation to age and drug abuse?

2. How can parents address this?

Article 21

'Legal Highs' Prevalence Makes Ban Policy 'Ridiculous'

Prohibition approach is 'irrational' say experts as one new synthetic psychoactive substance appears every week.

MARK TOWNSEND

'Legal highs' such as mephedrone and naphyrone have been banned, but experts believe UK drugs policy is irrational.

New "legal highs" are being discovered at the rate of one a week, outstripping attempts to control their availability and exposing what some experts claim is the "ridiculous and irrational" government policy of prohibition.

Officials monitoring the European *drugs* market identified 20 new synthetic psychoactive substances in the first four months of this year, according to Paolo Deluca, co-principal investigator at the Psychonaut Research Project, an EU-funded organisation based at King's College London, which studies trends in drug use. He said officials at the European Monitoring Centre for Drugs and Drug Addiction (EMCDDA), an early-warning unit, had detected 20 new substances for sale by May this year. In 2010 the agency had noted 41 new psychoactive substances, a record number, many of which were synthetic cathinone derivatives that can imitate the effects of cocaine, ecstasy or amphetamines.

Deluca said that, given the plethora of new substances, the government's attempts to ban legal highs is not a "feasible" solution. "It's also becoming very difficult to know exactly how many new compounds there are, because you have all these brand names and when you test the batch they are different from the following one." The UK, according to his reasearch, remains Europe's largest market for legal highs and synthetic compounds.

Campaigners at the Transform *Drugs Policy* Foundation (TDPF), a charity, said the unprecedented speed at which new drugs are appearing highlights the government's "unsustainable" strategy of banning each one, as well as a basic lack of understanding of how the drugs market functions.

Last year the government unveiled plans to introduce temporary 12-month bans on "legal highs", while the Advisory Council on the Misuse of Drugs considered a possible permanent ban. So far two substances have received a complete ban– *mephedrone,* the former legal high known as "meow meow", and naphyrone, otherwise known as "NRG1". Another two, phenazepam and Ivory Wave, have also received an import ban, which means the UK Border Agency can seize and destroy shipments following safety concerns.

The government's continued emphasis on banning illegal compounds flies in the face of growing calls for a fresh approach to tackling drugs. Earlier this year prominent public figures, including former heads of MI5 and the Crown Prosecution Service, said the "war on drugs" had failed and should be abandoned in favour of evidence-based policies that treat addiction as a health problem and avoid criminalising users.

Steve Rolles, senior policy analyst at TDPF, said attempts to ban one new substance after another was "like a cat chasing its tail". He added: "Each time they ban one, another emerges. It seems to show a blindness to the basic market dynamic, effectively creating a void for backstreet chemists to create another product." The group is one of many urging the government to adopt a regulatory position between total prohibition or an "internet-free-for all".

Deluca cites the case of mephedrone, which despite being banned last year remains as popular as cocaine among teenagers and young adults, according to official figures released in July. Home Office data from the British Crime Survey estimate that around 300,000 16- to 24-year-olds used mephedrone in the previous 12 months, a similar level of popularity to the use of cocaine among the same age bracket. Deluca added: "The legality of the compounds will not stop potential users, only the quality."

The EMCDDA favours generic bans that would cover entire groups of structurally related synthetic compounds, or chemical families, therefore removing the need to ban individual substances as they appear on the market. Deluca said: "It is impossible to implement a ban for every single new compound."

Rolles said legal highs should be investigated and regulated using the same model as conventional pharmaceuticals. "It's just ridiculous, irrational really. If you're not looking at the regulatory options, then you're not following an evidence-based approach–you are following a political mandate."

Critical Thinking

1. How often are new psychoactive drugs being produced?

2. How many new psychoactive drugs were produced in the year 2010?

3. How many Britons used mephedrone in the year 2010?

Alcoholism Isn't What It Used To Be

"NIAAA's goal now and for the foreseeable future is to develop and disseminate research-based resources for each stage of the alcohol use disorder continuum, from primary prevention to disease management," according to acting NIAAA director Ken Warren, PhD.

The realization dawned gradually as researchers analyzed data from NIAAA's 2001–2002 National Epidemiologic Survey on Alcohol and Related Conditions (NESARC). In most persons affected, alcohol dependence (commonly known as alcoholism) looks less like Nicolas Cage in *Leaving Las Vegas* than it does your party-hardy college roommate or that hard-driving colleague in the next cubicle.

"We knew from the 1991–1992 National Longitudinal Alcohol Epidemiologic Study that alcohol dependence is most prevalent among younger adults aged 18 to 29," says Bridget Grant, PhD, chief of NIAAA's Laboratory Epidemiology and Biometry. "However, it was not until we examined the NESARC data that we pinpointed age 22 as the mean age of alcohol dependence onset." Subsequent analysis by Ralph Hingson, Sc.D., director, Division of Epidemiology and Prevention Research, showed that nearly half of people who become alcohol dependent do so by age 21 and two-thirds by age 25.

The NESARC surveyed more than 43,000 individuals representative of the U.S. adult population using questions based on criteria in the *Diagnostic and Statistical Manual of Mental Disorders, Fourth Edition* (DSM-IV) of the American Psychiatric Association (APA). Published in 1994, DSM-IV recognizes alcohol dependence by preoccupation with drinking, impaired control over drinking, compulsive drinking, drinking despite physical or psychological problems caused or made worse by drinking, and tolerance and/or withdrawal symptoms.

Meanwhile, findings continue to accumulate to challenge past perceptions of the nature, course, and outcome of alcoholism. Among those findings:

- Many heavy drinkers do not have alcohol dependence. For example, even in people who have 5 or more drinks a day (the equivalent of a bottle of wine) the rate of developing dependence is less than 7 percent per year.
- Most persons who develop alcohol dependence have mild to moderate disorder, in which they primarily experience impaired control. For example, they set limits and go over them or find it difficult to quit or cut down.

In general, these people do not have severe alcohol-related relationship, health, vocational or legal problems.

- About 70 percent of affected persons have a single episode of less than 4 years. The remainder experience an average of five episodes. Thus, it appears that there are two forms of alcohol dependence: time-limited, and recurrent or chronic.
- Although 22 is the average age when alcohol dependence begins, the onset varies from the mid-teens to middle age.
- Twenty years after onset of alcohol dependence, about three-fourths of individuals are in full recovery; more than half of those who have fully recovered drink at low-risk levels without symptoms of alcohol dependence.
- About 75 percent of persons who recover from alcohol dependence do so without seeking any kind of help, including specialty alcohol (rehab) programs and AA. Only 13 percent of people with alcohol dependence ever receive specialty alcohol treatment.

"These and other recent findings turn on its head much of what we thought we knew about alcoholism," according to Mark Willenbring, MD, director of NIAAA's Division of Treatment and Recovery Research. "As is so often true in medicine, researchers have studied the patients seen in hospitals and clinics most intensively. This can greatly skew understanding of a disorder, especially in the alcohol field, where most people neither seek nor receive treatment and those who seek it do so well into the course of disease. Longitudinal, general population studies such as the NESARC permit us to see the entire disease continuum from before onset to late-stage disease."

To Willenbring, these realizations call for a public health approach that targets at-risk drinkers and persons with mild alcohol disorder to prevent or arrest problems before they progress. NIAAA is addressing this need with tools to expand risk awareness (http://rethinkingdrinking.niaaa.nih.gov) and inform secondary prevention and primary care screening (www.niaaa.nih.gov/guide).

New criteria to guide clinicians in diagnosis and treatment await decisions by the DSM-V committee, expected about 2012. Both Dr. Grant and Howard Moss, MD, associate director for clinical and translational research, represent NIAAA on that committee.

"NIAAA's goal now and for the foreseeable future is to develop and disseminate research-based resources for each stage of the alcohol use disorder continuum, from primary prevention to disease management," according to acting NIAAA director Ken Warren, PhD.

Critical Thinking

1. What age group is alcohol dependence most prevalent in?
2. Are all heavy drinkers alcoholic and/or alcohol dependent?
3. What is the average age when alcohol dependence begins?

From *NIAA Spectrum,* vol. 4, no. 2, June 2012. Copyright © 2012 by National Institute on Alcohol Abuse and Alcoholism (NIAAA). Reprinted by permission.

UNIT 5

Measuring the Social Costs of Drugs

Unit Selections

23. **Drugs 'R' Us,** Stanton Peele
24. **OxyContin Abuse Spreads from Appalachia across United States,** Bill Estep, Dori Hjalmarson, and Halimah Abdullah
25. **My Mother-in Law's One High Day,** Marie Myung-Ok Lee

Learning Outcomes

After reading this Unit, you should be able to:

- Identify where one looks to identify the social costs associated with drug abuse.

- Understand the ubiquitous nature of drug use in the U.S.

- Explain how the spread of OxyContin use in the United States has impacted the country.

- Understand whether marijuana has any medical efficacy.

- Explain what you believe is the greatest drug-related threat currently facing the United States.

Student Website

www.mhhe.com/cls

Internet References

BMJ.com a Publishing Group
  http://bmj.bmjjournals.com/cgi/content/abridged/326/7383/242/a
Drug Enforcement Administration
  www.usdoj.gov/dea
Drug Policy Alliance
  www.drugpolicy.org/database/index.html
Drug Use Cost to the Economy
  www.ccm-drugtest.com/ntl_effcts1.htm
European Monitoring Center for Drugs and Addiction
  www.emcdda.europa.eu/html.cfm/index1357EN.html
National Drug Control Policy
  www.ncjrs.org/ondcppubs/publications/policy/ndcs00/chap2_10.html
The November Coalition
  www.november.org
TRAC DEA Site
  http://trac.syr.edu/tracdea/index.html
United Nations Chronicle—Online Edition
  www.un.org/Pubs/chronicle/1998/issue2/0298p7.html

The most devastating effect of drug abuse in America is the magnitude with which it affects the way we live. Much of its influence is not measurable. What is the cost of a son or daughter lost, a parent imprisoned, a life lived in a constant state of fear? The emotional costs alone are incomprehensible. The social legacy of this country's drug crisis could easily be the subject of this entire book. The purpose here, however, can only be a cursory portrayal of drugs' tremendous costs. More than one U.S. president has stated that drug use threatens our national security and personal well-being. The financial costs of maintaining the federal apparatus devoted to drug interdiction, enforcement, and treatment are staggering. Although yearly expenditures vary due to changes in political influence, strategy, and tactics, examples of the tremendous effects of drugs on government and the economy abound. The federal budget for drug control exceeds $14 billion and includes almost $1.5 billion dedicated to drug fighting in Mexico and Central America under the Merida Initiative. Mexican criminal syndicates and paramilitaries who control trafficking across the U.S. southern border threaten the virtual sovereignty of the Mexican government. Many argue that the situation in Mexico is as dangerous to the United States as the current situation in Afghanistan.

Since 9/11, the restructuring of federal, state, and local law enforcement apparatus in response to terrorism has significantly influenced the nature and extent of drug trafficking in the United States. Huge transnational investigative, intelligence, and enforcement coalitions have formed between the United States and its allies in the war against terrorism. One significant impact of these coalitions has been a tightening of border access and a decreased availability of international trafficking routes. Although drugs are believed to still pour in from Mexico, drug shortages, increased street prices, and a decrease in purity are occurring. Powder heroin is not widely available in the West, and many major U.S. cities are reporting major street declines in the availability of cocaine.

Still, drugs exist, in association with terrorism, as the business of the criminal justice system. Approximately 80 percent of the people behind bars in the country had a problem with drugs or alcohol prior to their incarceration—more of its citizens than almost any other comparable society, and the financial costs are staggering. Doing drugs and serving time produces an inescapable nexus, and it doesn't end with prison. Almost 29 percent of persons on supervised parole or probation abuse drugs. Some argue that these numbers represent the fact that Americans have come to rely on the criminal justice system in an unprecedented way to solve problems of drug abuse. Regardless of the way one chooses to view various relationships, the resulting picture is numbing.

In addition to the highly visible criminal justice-related costs, numerous other institutions are affected. Housing, welfare, education, and health care provide excellent examples of critical institutions struggling to overcome the strain of drug-related impacts. In addition, annual loss of productivity in the workplace exceeds well over a $160 billion per year. Alcoholism alone causes 500 million lost workdays each year. Add to this demographic shifts caused by people fleeing drug-impacted

neighborhoods, schools, and businesses, and one soon realizes that there is no victimless public or private institution. Last year, almost 4 million Americans received some kind of treatment related to the abuse of alcohol or other drugs. Almost 23 million Americans need treatment for an illicit drug or alcohol problem. Fetal Alcohol Syndrome is the leading cause of mental retardation in the United States, and still, survey data continue to report that over 11 percent of pregnant women drink alcohol. Add to this injured, drug-related accident and crime victims, along with demands produced by a growing population of intravenous drug users infected with AIDS, and a frighteningly-overwhelmed health-care system comes to the fore. Health-care costs from drug-related ills are staggering. Drug abuse continues to cost the economy more than $13 billion annually in health-care costs alone. Approximately 71 million Americans over 12 are current users of a tobacco product.

It should be emphasized that the social costs exacted by drug use infiltrate every aspect of public and private life. The implications for thousands of families struggling with the adverse effects of drug-related woes may prove the greatest and most tragic of social costs. Children who lack emotional support, self-esteem, role models, a safe and secure environment, economic opportunity, and an education because of a parent on drugs suggest costs that are difficult to comprehend or measure. In some jurisdictions in California and Oregon, as many as 50 percent of child welfare placements are precipitated by methamphetamine abuse.

When reading Unit 5 of this book, consider the diversity of costs associated with the abuse of both legal and illegal drugs. As you read the following articles, consider the historical progressions of social costs produced by drug abuse over the past century. How are the problems of the past replicating themselves and how have science, medicine, and social policy changed in an attempt to mitigate these impacts? Ample evidence informs us that there is no single approach to mitigate the diverse nature of drug-related social impacts. Further, some of the most astounding scientific discoveries about how addiction develops remain mysterious when compared to the reality of the lives of millions who find drugs an end in themselves. Some have argued that the roots of drug-related problems today seem even more elusive, complicated, and desperate. Good progress has been made in treating drug addiction, but only moderate progress has been made in preventing it in the first place. What are the disproportionate ways in which some populations of Americans are harmed by drugs? Are there epidemics within epidemics? How is drug abuse expressed within different populations of Americans? How do the implications for Native American families and culture differ from those for other racial and ethnic groups? What are the reasons for these disparities and how should they be addressed?

Drugs 'R' Us

Drugs are a part of our lives in ways we can't come to grips with.

STANTON PEELE

What do these New York Times headlines appearing in the last month have in common?

June 10: Candidates in Mexico Signal a New Tack in the Drug War

Candidates for the Mexican presidency indicate they are no longer willing to suffer the domestic losses required to staunch the flow of drugs into the United States.

June 9: Risky Rise of the Good-Grade Pill

Use of A.D.H.D. stimulants like Adderall by high school and college students is an accepted method for enhancing school performance. The alternate Times title for this article: Seeking Academic Edge, Teenagers Abuse Stimulants.

June 9: Parents Created This Problem, and Must Address It

Parental pressures on children have generated the "widespread abuse of stimulants like Ritalin and Adderall by teenagers and college students."

June 8: Global Soccer: Unrelenting Pressure to Mask the Pain

Use of painkillers is commonplace among World Cup soccer players.

June 8: Prescription Drug Overdoses Plague New Mexico

"For years now, New Mexico has wrestled with high rates of poverty, drunken-driving deaths and substance abuse—particularly heroin addiction, which has been passed down through generations in the state's northern, rural reaches. But over the past few years, a new affliction has hammered New Mexico: prescription drug overdoses."

June 4: In Hockey Enforcer's Descent, a Flood of Prescription Drugs

"In his final three seasons playing in the National Hockey League, before dying last year at 28 of an accidental overdose of narcotic painkillers and alcohol, Derek Boogaard received more than 100 prescriptions for thousands of pills from more than a dozen team doctors."

May 11: Diagnosing the D.S.M.

The American Psychiatric Association's new diagnostic manual (D.S.M.-5) is "proceeding with other suggestions that could potentially expand the boundaries of psychiatry to define as mentally ill tens of millions of people now considered normal."

May 11: Addiction Diagnoses May Rise Under Guideline Changes

The D.S.M.'s expansion of the definition of addiction indicates that more people will be treated for it. "'The ties between the D.S.M. panel members and the pharmaceutical industry are so extensive that there is the real risk of corrupting the public health mission of the manual,' said Dr. Lisa Cosgrove, a fellow at the Edmond J. Safra Center for Ethics at Harvard, who published a study in March that said two-thirds of the manual's advisory task force members reported ties to the pharmaceutical industry or other financial conflicts of interest."

Five things are going on here:

1. Privileged students and their parents seek every advantage they can to get ahead in life, including use of stimulant prescription drugs thought to enhance academic performance.
2. America's endless taste for illicit substances has overhwelmed the resources of Mexico and other Latin American countries, despite—or because of—all of our pressure on these countries to stem the flow of drugs into the U.S.
3. Athletes rely on drugs to deal with the everpresent pain that can sideline them and their careers, often leading to permanent injuries and drug dependence.
4. In poorer, rural regions, and not only these, prescription medications have replaced illicit substances as the primary source of drug abuse.
5. The medicalization and pharmaceuticalization of mental, emotional, and addiction problems is expanding, perhaps beyond our ability to grasp.

American life is suffused with drugs—there is no escaping them. Remember when Congress held hearings on steroid use by major-league baseball players, and the players fell into two groups—those who admitted their use of steroids and those who lied and denied it? Such drug use by baseball players (and football players, cyclsts, boxers, track athletes, et al.), like students' use of amphetamines, is for the purpose of performance enhancement. At the same time, the model of humans as fundamentally flawed and requiring constant administration of drugs to remedy their deficits is so integral to our thinking that we can't begin to question it. And, of course, the recreational use of drugs continues apace.

We can bemoan this new reality, but we can't reverse it. We need a new strategy to deal with the ubiquity of drugs in our lives. If people can't manage such experiences, it is hard to see how they can cope in the 21st Century. Nor will our society be able to function without a reconceptualization of drug use.

Critical Thinking

1. What drugs are high school and college students using to enhance their academic performance?

2. How prevalent is prescription drug abuse in professional hockey?

3. The American Psychiatric Association is expected to expand diagnostic criteria for addictive disorders in 2013. What effect, if any do you think this will have?

OxyContin Abuse Spreads from Appalachia across United States

BILL ESTEP, DORI HJALMARSON, AND HALIMAH ABDULLAH

Shawn Clusky has seen every side of Kentucky's battle with pain pill addiction over the past 10 years.

Clusky first tried OxyContin at age 17 with his school buddies, shortly after the high-powered narcotic painkiller went on the market. He was an occasional user and seller until about age 21, when he became fully addicted.

When he was 25, he got arrested at a Lexington gas station for selling $15,000 worth of pills. Clusky received probation, but was still using until he was sent to the WestCare rehabilitation center in eastern Kentucky.

He now works there as a counselor.

"A lot of times people believe a drug addict comes from poverty," he said. Not true. "Nine out of 10 of the guys I partied with came from millionaire families; their parents didn't use, they had good families."

Ten years ago, Kentucky learned it had a major drug problem.

OxyContin, a powerful prescription painkiller, was being abused at alarming rates in the Appalachian areas of eastern and southern Kentucky: A decade later, the level of pain pill abuse throughout the state and across the country is at epic levels, officials say.

Despite some successes—including several high-profile drug arrests across the country, increased treatment programs and the adoption of prescription drug monitoring programs in 43 states—the problem is now so entrenched that the cheap flights and van rentals drug traffickers use to travel from Florida to Kentucky and other states to peddle "hillbilly heroin" are nicknamed the "OxyContin Express."

The sheer scope of the problem is a key reason.

Kentucky often ranks at or near the top in U.S. measures of the level of prescription pain pill abuse.

According to a study by the Substance Abuse and Mental Health Services Administration, there was a fourfold increase nationally in treatment admissions for prescription pain pill abuse during the past decade. The increase spans every age, gender, race, ethnicity, education, employment level and region.

The study also shows a tripling of pain pill abuse among patients who needed treatment for dependence on opioids—prescription narcotics.

The rate of overdose-related deaths more than doubled among men and tripled among women in Kentucky from 2000 to 2009, according the state Cabinet for Health and Family Services.

Nearly every family in eastern Kentucky has been touched by prescription-drug addiction and death.

In the late 1990s, it was easier to find OxyContin—pure oxycodone with a time release—in Kentucky. The pill's maker, Purdue Pharma, was selling it "hand over fist" to doctors in eastern Kentucky, rich with coal mine injuries and government health care cards, Clusky said.

Clusky said a high school friend who worked at a pharmacy would steal the pills for his friends, so "It didn't cost any of us anything."

When many of the eastern Kentucky pill sources dried up after law enforcement raids in 2001, Clusky said, the trade moved to Mexico, where oxycodone could be bought for pennies over the counter and sold for as much as $100 a pill in the rural U.S. Clusky began making trips to Nuevo Laredo, driving back home with thousands of pills. By this time, heroin was his drug of choice. He often traveled to larger cities, where heroin could be found more cheaply.

"Five hundred dollars worth of heroin would last me a week. Five hundred dollars worth of oxy would last me one day," Clusky said.

Clusky lived part time in Ohio, sometimes making three doctor-shopping trips a day from Lexington to Dayton. He did a few stints in rehab, at one point trying methadone and Suboxone to treat his opiate addiction. It didn't work.

"I was as useless to society on methadone as I was on heroin," he said.

Nationally, prescription drug abuse has become a front-burner issue. There are more recovery options available now than a decade ago, but many states still don't have enough treatment available for all who need it.

Though Kentucky was no stranger to the abuse of prescription drugs long before federal regulators approved OxyContin in 1996, so many people in rural areas, including Appalachia, started abusing OxyContin in the late 1990s, it earned the nickname "hillbilly heroin."

Many chronic pain sufferers said the drug helped them immensely.

But abusers figured out they could crush a pill and snort or inject it, destroying the time-release function to get a whopping 12 hours' worth of the drug in one rush.

OxyContin quickly became the drug of choice in eastern Kentucky.

"You could leave a bag of cocaine on the street and no one would touch it, but leave one OxyContin in the back of an armored car and they'll blow it up to get at it," U.S. Attorney Joseph Famularo said at the February 2001 news conference announcing the first major roundup involving the drug.

By 2002, a quarter of the overdose deaths in the nation linked to OxyContin were in eastern Kentucky, authorities said.

Police, regulators and elected officials charged that Purdue Pharma, the Connecticut-based maker of OxyContin, marketed the drug too aggressively, feeding an oversupply and diversion onto the illicit market.

Purdue Pharma denied that, but the company and three top officials ultimately pleaded guilty in 2007 to misleading the public about the drug's risk of addiction and paid $634.5 million in fines.

Authorities had begun pushing back long before that against growing abuse of OxyContin and other prescription drugs, but addicts and traffickers kept finding ways to get pills.

"Law enforcement adjusts, and the criminals adjust," said Frank Rapier, the head of the Appalachia High Intensity Drug Trafficking Area, which includes 68 counties in Kentucky, Tennessee and West Virginia.

Kentucky Rep. Hal Rogers' voice grows tight with frustration whenever he talks about the prescription drug epidemic that's gripped Appalachia for more than a decade.

"Crook doctors operating these pill mills" in Florida are running rampant and are fueling the flow of illegally obtained prescription drugs to states such as Kentucky, Rogers, the chairman of the House Appropriations Committee, told Attorney General Eric Holder during a recent hearing. "My people are dying."

The White House "has got to act," Rogers said. "We've got more people dying of prescription drug overdoses than car accidents."

The Obama administration counters that it's the first to publicly call the prescription drug abuse problem an epidemic, has stepped up drug arrests and has directed millions in funding to state monitoring programs. The administration says it also has focused efforts on the Appalachia High Intensity Drug Trafficking Area, which includes 68 counties in Kentucky, Tennessee and West Virginia.

In the meantime, Rogers hopes legislation he's co-sponsoring with Rep. Vern Buchanan, a Florida Republican, calling for a tougher federal crackdown on so-called "pill mills"—pain clinics that dispense prescription drugs—will help stem the flow of drugs across state lines.

The measure includes provisions to support state-based prescription drug monitoring programs; to use the money from seized illicit operations for drug treatment; to strengthen prescription standards for certain addictive pain drugs; and to toughen prison terms and fines for pill mill operators.

The bill comes on the heels of Florida Republican Gov. Rick Scott's calls to repeal a monitoring program modeled after Kentucky's and designed to stem interstate prescription drug trafficking—a move lawmakers from Florida and Kentucky and White House officials oppose.

Scott has cited concerns about costs and patient privacy rights. He's turned down a $1 million donation by Purdue Pharma to help pay for a prescription database.

(Estep and Hjalmarson, of the Lexington Herald-Leader, reported from Lexington. Abdullah reported from Washington.)

Critical Thinking

1. What kind of drug is oxycontin? Why is it prescribed?
2. Nationally, how much did oxycontin use increase between 2000–2009?
3. What state ranks at or near the top for prescription painkiller abuse?

My Mother-in-Law's One High Day

MARIE MYUNG-OK LEE

When my mother-in-law was in the final, harrowing throes of pancreatic cancer, she had only one good day, and that was the day she smoked pot.

So I was heartened when, at the end of last month, the governors of Washington and Rhode Island petitioned the Obama administration to classify marijuana as a drug that could be prescribed and distributed for medical use. While medical marijuana is legal in 16 states, it is still outlawed under federal law.

My husband and I often thought of recommending marijuana to his mother. She was always nauseated from the chemotherapy drugs and could barely eat for weeks. She existed in a Percocet and morphine haze, constantly fretting that the sedation kept her from saying all the things she wanted to say to us, but unable to face the pain without it. And this was a woman who had such a high tolerance for pain, coupled with a distaste for drugs, that she insisted her dentist not use Novocain and gave birth to her two children without anesthesia. But despite marijuana's power to relieve pain and nausea without loss of consciousness, we were afraid she would find even the suggestion of it scandalous. This was 1997, and my mother-in-law was a very proper, law-abiding woman, a graduate of Bryn Mawr College in the 1950s. She'd never even smoked a cigarette.

But then an older family friend who worked in an AIDS hospice came bearing what he said was very good quality marijuana. To our surprise, she said she'd consider it. My husband and I—though we knew nothing about marijuana paraphernalia—were dispatched to find a bong, as the friend suggested water-processing might make the smoking easier for her. We found ourselves in a head shop in one of the seedier neighborhoods in New Haven, where my husband went to graduate school, listening attentively to the clerk as he went over the finer points of bong taxonomy, finally just choosing one in her favorite color, lilac.

She had us take her out on the flagstone patio because she refused to smoke in her meticulously kept-up house. Then she looked about nervously, as if expecting the police to jump out of the bushes. She found it awkward and strange to smoke a bong, but after a few tries managed to get in two and a half hits.

And then she said she wanted to go out to eat.

For the past month, we'd been trying to get her to eat anything: fresh-squeezed carrot juice made in a special juicer, Korean rice gruel that I simmered for hours, soups, oatmeal, endless cans of Ensure. Sometimes she'd request some particular dish and we'd eagerly procure it, only to have her refuse it or fall back asleep before taking a bite. But this time she sat down at her favorite restaurant and ordered a gorgeous meal: whitefish poached with lemon, hot buttered rolls, salad—and ate every bite.

Then she wanted to go to Kimball's, a local ice cream place famous for cones topped with softball-size scoops. The family had been regular customers starting all the way back when my husband and his brother were children, but they hadn't been there since her illness. My husband and I shared a small cone, which we could not finish, and looked on in awe as my mother-in-law ordered a large and, queenishly spurning any requests for a taste, polished the whole thing off—cone and all—and declared herself satisfied.

We were of course raring to make the magic happen again, but it never did. The pot just frightened her too much. She was scared her friend would be arrested for interstate drug trafficking, that my husband and I would be mugged in New Haven; she was afraid she'd become addicted or (à la "Reefer Madness") go insane. It was difficult watching her reject something that had so clearly alleviated her nausea and pain and—let's admit it—lightened her mood in the face of the terrible fact that cancer had invaded nearly every essential organ. And it was even worse to watch her pumped, instead, full of narcotics that made her feel horrible. The Percocet gave her a painfully dry mouth, but even ice chips made her heave. We were reduced to swabbing her lips with little sponges dipped in water, and waiting out her agony.

My husband and I have dredged up the memory of that one good day many times since, how she smiled and joked, for the last time seeming a little like her old self.

After the funeral, saying goodbye to all the family and friends, supervising the removal of the hospital bed, bedpans and related paraphernalia, one of the last things my husband and I did, under the watchful eyes of the hospice nurse, was destroy her remaining Percocets. We opened the multiple bottles and knelt in front of the toilet to perform this secular water rite, wishing there had been other days, other ways, a softer way for her to leave us.

Marie Myung-Ok Lee, the author of the novel "Somebody's Daughter," teaches writing at Brown University.

Critical Thinking

1. How many states have "legalized" marijuana?
2. What have the Governors of Washington and Rhode Island petitioned the Federal government to do regarding marijuana?
3. What kind of drug is Percocet? What is it used for?

UNIT 6

Creating and Sustaining Effective Drug Control Policy

Unit Selections

26. **Do the United States and Mexico Really Want the Drug War To Succeed?** Robert Joe Stout
27. **Engaging Communities to Prevent Underage Drinking,** Abigail A. Fagan, J. David Hawkins, and Richard F. Catalano
28. **Do No Harm: Sensible Goals for International Drug Policy,** Peter Reuter
29. **Convergence or Divergence? Recent Developments in Drug Policies in Canada and the United States,** Clayton J. Mosher
30. **Legalize drugs—All of them!** Vanessa Baird
31. **Former ONDCP Senior Advisor on Marijuana and Harm Reduction**
32. **Portugal's Drug Policy Pays Off; US Eyes Lessons,** Barry Hatton and Martha Mendoza

Learning Outcomes

After reading this Unit, you should be able to:

- Explain United States history of drug policy.
- Explain how drug policy shapes public opinion of drug-related events.
- Explain the role of community in affecting drug use patterns.
- Discuss the problems and issues surrounding the legal use of alcohol different from those surrounding the illegal use of heroin, cocaine, or methamphetamines.
- Describe your opinions on the legalization of medical marijuana, and whether you believe its legalization will result in its being overprescribed.
- Determine to what degree you would argue that the current problems with drug abuse exist because of current drug policies or in spite of them.

Student Website

www.mhhe.com/cls

Internet References

Drug Policy Alliance
www.drugpolicy.org

DrugText
www.drugtext.org

Effective Drug Policy: Why Journey's End Is Legalisations
www.drugscope.org.uk/wip/23/pdfs/journey.pdf

Harm Reduction Coalition
www.harmreduction.org

The Higher Education Center for Alcohol and Other Drug Prevention
www.edc.org/hec/pubs/policy.htm

The National Organization on Fetal Alcohol Syndrome (NOFAS)
www.nofas.org

National NORML Homepage
www.norml.org

Transform Drug Policy Foundation
www.tdpf.org.uk

The drug problem consistently competes with all major public policy issues, including the wars in Iraq and Afghanistan, the economy, education, and foreign policy. Drug abuse is a serious national medical issue with profound social and legal consequences. Formulating and implementing effective drug control policy is a troublesome task. Some would argue that the consequences of policy failures have been worse than the problems that the policies were attempting to address. Others would argue that although the world of shaping drug policy is an imperfect one, the process has worked generally as well as could be expected. The majority of Americans believe that failures and breakdowns in the fight against drug abuse have occurred in spite of various drug policies, not because of them. Although the last few years have produced softening attitudes and alternatives for adjudicating cases of simple possession and use, the get-tough, stay-tough enforcement policies directed at illegal drug trafficking remain firmly in place and widely supported. Policy formulation is not a process of aimless wandering.

Various levels of government have responsibility for responding to problems of drug abuse. At the center of most policy debate is the premise that the manufacture, possession, use, and distribution of psychoactive drugs without government authorization is illegal. The federal posture of prohibition is an important emphasis on state and local policymaking. Federal drug policy is, however, significantly linked to state-by-state data, which suggests that illicit drug, alcohol, and tobacco use vary substantially among states and regions. The current federal drug strategy began in 2001 and set the goals of reducing drug use by young persons by 25 percent over five years. In 2008, President Bush announced that drug use by the population in this age group was down by 24 percent. President Obama has continued the basic strategic constructs of the Bush policy. Core priorities of the overall plan continue to be to stop drug use before it starts, heal America's drug users, and disrupt the illegal market. These three core goals are re-enforced by objectives outlined in a policy statement produced by the White House Office of Drug Control Policy. All three goals reflect budget expenditures related to meeting goals of the overall policy. The current drug control policy, in terms of budget allocations, continues to provide for over $1.5 billion to prevent use before it starts, largely through education campaigns, which encourage a cultural shift away from drugs, and more than $3.4 billion to heal America's users. Each year produces modifications to the plan as a result of analysis of trends and strategy impacts. Allocations for interdiction, largely a result of the attempt to secure the borders and frustrate alliances between drug traffickers and terrorists, remain the most significant component of the budget at $10 billion dollars.

One exception to prevailing views that generally support drug prohibition is the softening of attitudes regarding criminal sanctions that historically applied to cases of simple possession and use of drugs. There is much public consensus that incarcerating persons for these offenses is unjustified unless they are related to other criminal conduct. The federal funding of drug court programs remains a priority with more than $38 million dedicated to state and local operation. Drug courts provide alternatives to

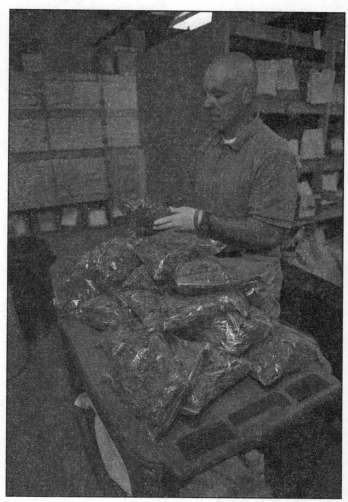

© Aaron Roeth Photography

incarceration by using the coercive power of the court to force abstinence and alter behavior through a process of escalating sanctions, mandatory drug testing, and outpatient programs. Successful rehabilitation accompanies the re-entry to society as a citizen, not a felon. The drug court program exists as one important example of policy directed at treating users and deterring them from further involvement in the criminal justice system. Drug courts are now in place in all 50 states.

The majority of Americans express the view that legalizing, and in some cases even decriminalizing, dangerous drugs is a bad idea. The fear of increased crime, increased drug use, and the potential threat to children are the most often stated reasons. Citing the devastating consequences of alcohol and tobacco use, most Americans question society's ability to use any addictive, mind-altering drug responsibly. Currently, the public favors supply reduction, demand reduction, and an increased emphasis on prevention, treatment, and rehabilitation as effective strategies in combating the drug problem. Shaping public policy is a critical function that greatly relies upon public input. The policymaking apparatus is influenced by public opinion, and public opinion is in turn influenced by public policy. When the president refers to drugs as threats to national security, the impact on public opinion is tremendous. Currently, record amounts of opium are being produced in Afghanistan, and the implications for its providing support for the Taliban and terrorism are clear. Opium production in Southwest Asia, an entrenched staple in the region's overall economic product, continues as a priority of U.S. national security. The resulting implications for sustaining enforcement-oriented U.S. drug policy are also clear; and in the minds of most Americans, they are absolutely necessary. The U.S. Department of State alone will receive $336 million for alternative crop production, diplomacy, interdiction, and enforcement.

Although the prevailing characteristic of most current drug policy still reflects a punitive, "get tough" approach to control, an added emphasis on treating and rehabilitating offenders is visible in policy changes occurring over the past 10 years. Correctional systems are reflecting with greater consistency the view that drug treatment made available to inmates is a critical component of rehabilitation. The California Department of Corrections, the largest in the nation, was recently renamed the California Department of Corrections and Rehabilitation. A prisoner with a history of drug abuse, who receives no drug treatment while in custody, is finally being recognized as a virtual guarantee to reoffend. In 2006, the National Institute of Drug Abuse published the first federal guidelines for administering drug treatment to criminal justice populations.

Another complicated aspect of creating national as well as local drug policy is consideration of the growing body of research on the subject. The past 20 years have produced numerous public and private investigations, surveys, and conclusions relative to the dynamics of drug use in U.S. society. Although an historical assessment of the influence of research on policy produces indirect relationships, policy decisions of the last few years can be directly related to evidence-based research findings and not just political views. One example is the consistently increasing commitment to treatment. This commitment comes as a direct result of research related to progress achieved in treating and rehabilitating users. Treatment, in terms of dollars spent, can compete with all other components of drug control policy.

One important issue affecting and sometimes complicating the research/policymaking relationship is that the policymaking community, at all levels of government, is largely composed of persons of diverse backgrounds, professional capacities, and political interests. Some are elected officials, others are civil servants, and many are private citizens from the medical, educational, and research communities. In some cases, such as with alcohol and tobacco, powerful industry players assert a tremendous influence on policy. As you read on, consider the new research-related applications for drug policy, such as those related to the rehabilitation of incarcerated drug offenders.

Do the United States and Mexico Really Want the Drug War To Succeed?

ROBERT JOE STOUT

Until 1914 laudanum and morphine were legally sold and distributed in the United States, heroin was prescribed as a cough medicine, and coca and cocaine were mixed with wine and cola drinks. Although most of the opium came from the Orient, Chinese settlers on Mexico's west coast, particularly in the state of Sinaloa, began cultivating adormidera (opium gum) during the 1870s and gradually developed an export trade.

Even after the use of opium-based products was declared illegal in the United States the exportations from Sinaloa continued; prosecution of offenders, if it happened at all, was benign. The adormidera crossed into the United States through places like Tijuana, a dusty little frontier town until the mid-twentieth century; San Luis Rio Colorado, across the border from Yuma, Arizona; Nogales, also on the Arizona border; and Ojinaga, across the Rio Grande River from Presidio in Texas's isolated Big Bend country. Customs agents on both sides of the border, but particularly in Mexico, cooperated with the exporters and the flow of drugs, though not large by 1960s or '70s standards, went through virtually unimpeded.

The majority of those involved were locals who spent the cash they acquired in the areas in which they operated. They hired local residents for construction, transportation, ranching, and other sidelines in which they invested their earnings. As far as most of their neighbors were concerned they were good citizens whose business was no better or worse from that of any other.

Prohibition changed this genial and basically cooperative landscape. Large amounts of liquor were harder to conceal than adormidera or marijuana, making it necessary for exporters to bribe–or form partnerships–with those in charge of customs. Politicians ranging from local councilmen to state governors became involved, forcing the local exporters either to join them or evade them as well as evade law enforcement.

The end of Prohibition wounded but did not slay the golden calf of liquor exportation. The politically connected entrepreneurs that controlled the aduanas (customs inspection stations) also controlled prostitution and a percentage of drug exportations. They financed the construction and operation of luxurious night clubs, gourmet restaurants, and gambling activities that attracted large numbers of U.S. residents. Both politically

affiliated and independent drug exporters invested in these enterprises as Tijuana, Ciudad Juárez, and other border cities became brightly lit tourist meccas surrounded by desolate slums packed with new arrivals, deportees, addicts, beggars, and petty criminals.

By 1948 the volume of Sinaloa adormidera crossing the border triggered harsh recriminations from representatives of the U.S. federal government. Mexico's Attorney General responded with equally acerbic suggestions that officials north of the border deal with those who were purchasing the drugs since the market attracting the exports was in the United States. Mexican federal and state law enforcement did arrest a few farmers and mulas (mules, i.e., those hired to transport contraband) but did not prosecute any leading political or business figures.

Despite cinema and television depictions of drug runners as gun-toting, Pancho Villa-like gangsters, the truth was that many well-attired and well-educated governors, bankers, and businessmen considered the business of growing and exporting adormidera as natural (and as profitable) as growing cotton or corn. The income from drug exportations filtered through the economies of the states involved and was attributed to "sale of agricultural products" if the source was questioned.

As marijuana and cocaine use increased exponentially during the 1960s in the United States, Sinaloa drug exporters expanded into other areas, particularly Tamaulipas in northeastern Mexico, where they clashed with exporters who had greater access to delivery points across the border. They also competed for connections with the major Colombian "cartels."

By the 1970s importing Colombian cocaine and getting it into the United States had become an increasingly complex business. The socalled "cartels" or drug corporations included accountants, lawyers, chemists, legislators, and entire corps of police departmentalized into individual functions which included marketing, investment, press relations, and militarized units, most of which were led by experienced former Mexican Army and Navy officers. (The term "cartel" is erroneous since the drug organizations have nothing to do with medieval trade unions; instead they function like private corporations.)

As these organizations grew they brought more elements of Mexican society into their operations, particularly for laundering profits and transporting drugs. Tourists and businessmen and women–well-dressed, affable, polite–crossed the border with false-bottomed luggage filled with cocaine. Soccer balls and balloons contained packets of powder. Brassieres that made small-breasted women seem much more amply endowed were padded with cocaine sewed into the garments. According to retired U.S. Air Force journalist James McGee, importers in El Paso brought thousands of colorful Mexican piñatas across the border–piñatas that never were retailed but ripped open and discarded after the cocaine packed inside them had been removed.

As happens with most corporations, junior operatives (executives) began to break away and form smaller organizations of their own. Murders and assassinations between rival bands increased as they vied for portions of the lucrative trade. Breakaway groups unable to chisel a large enough portion for themselves branched into people smuggling, counterfeiting, business shakedowns, prostitution, auto theft, and kidnapping. Others paid their bribes and expenses with "merchandise" (i.e., cocaine or heroin) or, unable to push it into the United States, increased distribution in Mexico, where profits were lower but easier to obtain. Gradually–first along the frontier with the United States, then in cities throughout the country–more and more Mexican nationals, especially those under thirty years of age, became habitual drug users.

Gradually the principal criminal organizations gobbled up smaller local operatives. ("Join us or join those in the cemetery," was the ultimatum usually given.) The smaller criminal bands paid monthly "quotas" to be allowed to operate. The dominant corporations paid quotas to government officials, business executives, and military commanders, while also purchasing legitimate businesses like major sports franchises and investing in the stock market.

The financial fluidity of these rapidly expanding corporations enabled them to establish "nations within the nation" that were functionally self-governing and absorbed or supplanted many social and communal activities. The kingpin was Juan García-Ábrego; his so-called "Cartel del Golfo" transferred thousands of tons of cocaine that had been flown from Colombia to clandestine landing strips in Quintana Roo and the Yucatán for smuggling into the United States.

When Mexican authorities arrested and extradited García-Ábrego to the United States in 1996 his organization foundered and its new leaders temporarily allied themselves with the Sinaloa group. Such "marriages" and subsequent breakups occurred frequently throughout the 1980s and '90s depending upon arrests, betrayals, governmental changes, and business opportunities. But although the names and faces changed the business continued unabated.

In many aspects (investment, trade, communication, transportation, defense) the "nations within the nation" that the drug corporations formed paralleled the structure of Mexico's federal government. Many who operated within the corporate systems functioned in similar capacities within federal and state law enforcement and financial entities. The capos contributed to local and regional political campaigns, thus assuring themselves of being able to extract needed favors and permissions

from the many officeholders in their debt. According to a retired state employee named Pedro Enrique Martinez who chauffeured a number of Sinaloa politicians:

The capos (drug lords) realized it wasn't cost effective to have to keep bribing those who held higher offices so they started recruiting young local candidates, helping finance them to win elections. Soon every city, every municipio (county), every state bureaucracy was infiltrated. Sometimes the capos would go years and not require anything then one day they'd say "We need this bill passed" or "We need this shipment to go through" and they'd get what they wanted.

What the leader of the so-called "Sinaloa cartel" Joaquin ("El Chapo") Guzman wanted, he informed the government of Mexican president Felipe Calderón, was to be allowed to run his business without interference from the military. Some members of the bureaucracy and Senate and House of Deputies quietly supported this concept, harking back to the presidency of the PRI's Carlos Salinas de Gortari between 1988 and 1994, when drug exportations enriched participating politicians without arousing bloody criminal confrontations. Nonetheless, Calderón and his administration remained committed to U.S. financed policies of militarized action.

Although Calderón and his inner circle were loath to admit it the militarization provoked greater violence and bloodshed without diminishing the flow of drugs northward (and rapidly increasing narcotics use and addiction in Mexico). As proof of the success of the military operations Calderón cited increases in the street price of cocaine in the United States, but he did not mention how much those increases stimulated importers and producers to greater activity.

Addiction and crime associated with drug users became a major problem in the United States but the vast majority of users–like the vast majority of persons who buy and use alcoholic beverages–are not addicts. Bankers, politicians, athletes, university professors, insurance salespersons, construction workers, and thousands of others indulge only on weekends or at parties or as sexual provokers. They purchase the cocaine and marijuana from other athletes, salespersons, or bankers who have regular suppliers, most of whom they have being doing business with for years. All are far removed from street warfare between mafiosos and armed military and they are a primary reason that the "War on Drugs" has not reduced the demand for cocaine, marijuana, and other narcotics in the United States.

In her "Americas Program" column on September 3, 2009, entitled "Drug War Doublespeak," Laura Carlsen insisted: "Drug-war doublespeak pervades and defines the United States-Mexico relationship today. The discourse aims not to win the war on drugs, but to assure funding and public support for the military model of combating illegal drug trafficking, despite the losses and overwhelming evidence that current strategies are not working."

According to Mexican national security specialist Ghaleb Krame the narcotraficantes developed a sophisticated counter-intelligence system and utilized highly mobile guerrilla groups that constantly changed their bases and personnel while the Mexican army, bogged down by traditional channels of protocol and information, was unable to effectively counter these maneuvers. As a consequence the Mexican government expanded its dependence on paramilitaries to do what the police and military could not do legally.

Undercover operations are not confined to infiltrating and investigating drug corporation activities but like the brigadasblancas of the 1960s and '70s guara sucia ("dirty war") they disrupted social protest movements and sequestered and sometimes tortured those defending ecological, communal, or union rights. Human rights advocates and journalists like Miguel Badillo insist that the "War on Drugs" is "a simulation whose real objective is to stomp out growing social discontent" in the country.

Other forces primarily formed of former military and police personnel became private "armies" contracted by individual entrepreneurs. They escort dignitaries and their families, guard business and industrial sites, and–like the drug organization paramilitaries–serve as armed couriers. As a Oaxaca self-employed contractor, Ali Jiménez, told me, "It's come to the point that the government lets these guys (entrepreneurs) surround themselves with gunmen since nobody can trust the police and there's no public security." A former Chihuahua journalist who left the profession because of death threats told me, "The War on Drugs is like a football [soccer] game without coaches or referees, soldiers and narcos charging this way and that, doing more harm to the spectators than to each other."

The drug corporations have infiltrated all levels of government and their payrolls include thousands of lookouts, messengers, farmers, and truck drivers. However, the federal government and the inexperienced Mexican military seem to lack cohesive intelligence reports or effective plans for doing anything more than random searches and seizures. Often they respond to misleading or false information they acquire from informants, many of whom are paid by the drug organizations to finger competitors or businesses whose only connection with the mafiosos is having failed to pay adequate protection money.

Drug corporations like the "Cartel del Golfo" were even able to seduce high-ranking members of Mexico's top organized crime-fighting agency, SIEDO (Sub-Prosecutor General of Special Investigations into Organized Crime). The PGR (Prosecutor General of the Republic, Mexico's Attorney General's office), which had its own problems with infiltrators in its ranks, investigated high-ranking SIEDO functionaries in 2008– investigations that were hampered because SIEDO informants, some of whom were receiving more than $450,000 a month, informed the "Cartel del Golfo" of every step that the PGR was taking. Finally, through a former Cartel del Golfo member who testified against the organization as a protected witness, the PGR arrested Sub-Prosecutor Noé Ramírez-Mandujano and Miguel Colorado, SIEDO's Coordinator of Intelligence, for their connections with organized crime.

The drug corporations retaliated. In May 2007 gunmen assassinated José Lugo, Mexico's coordinator of information of the Center for Planning and Analysis to Combat Organized Crime. Others ambushed and shot Edgar Millán, acting head of Mexico's federal police, later that same year. In November 2008 a drug organization hit squad abducted and executed Army General Mauro Tello a few days after he assumed the post of anti-drug czar in Cancun, Quintana Roo. In 2009 they executed government-protected witness Edgar Enrique Bayardo-del Villar while he was breakfasting in a Mexico City *Starbucks*.

Although Calderón's government tried to squelch rumors that the fatal crash of a Lear jet carrying Government Secretary Juan Camilo Mouriño was not the result of pilot error, journalists and commentators throughout the country insisted that government version was a cover up and the aircraft had been sabotaged by El Chapo Guzman's corporation in retaliation for the arrest and imprisoning of one of his top aides.

As competition among the major drug organizations increased, with assassinations of rival leaders commonplace, the militarized "Zetas" emerged as an elite armed force, first aligned with the Beltrán-Leyva Gulf Cartel, but later an independent corporation functioning on both Mexico's northern and southern borders. The Zetas were tightly disciplined (their leaders were deserters from Mexico's Special Forces and many had been trained by the U.S. School of the Americas and/ or the Kaibilies in Guatemala) and brazenly recruited active duty militaries.

Although the Zetas occasionally openly confronted police and military units they focused primarily on intimidating and extracting quotas from growers and transporters as well as those engaged in legitimate businesses, including cattle ranchers, merchants, local entrepreneurs, bar and nightclub owners, farmers, polleros (people smugglers), and truckers. They dealt harshly with those who tried to circumvent or reduce these obligations–kidnapping, torturing, and often decapitating those who were delinquent in their payments.

By 2008 Mexico had committed some 50,000 troops to the "War on Drugs." Because the Mexican military had been a peacetime force primarily involving garrison duty (and, since 1994, containment controls around the Zapatista autonomous communities in Chiapas) it offered relatively few benefits and minimal salaries to enlisted personnel. Recruiting was focused on marginal residents of city slums where life was hazardous, and in poverty-wracked rural areas that offered no other hopes of employment. Theoretically recruits needed to have completed junior high school to enter the military but proof seldom was required and criminal behavior, if confined to misdemeanors, often was overlooked.

These poverty-bred soldiers, many just out of basic training, adhere to medieval practices of supplementing their meager salaries with what they acquire during cateos (searches and seizures of property) and shakedowns. Victims accuse soldiers of stealing money and stripping personnel property from persons stopped at highway checkpoints. Federal authorities derail prosecution of soldiers accused of abuses by insisting that those levying the charges "are politically motivated" and that the accusations are exaggerated or falsified.

The drug corporations also recruit from marginal areas. Although they promise "guns, money, cars, and women" to potential deserters many of the hundreds of thousands they hire do not carry weapons and primarily act as lookouts, messengers, decoys, and money handlers. Like many legitimate corporations the drug organizations have established salary scales, usually beginning with the equivalent of US$800 per month, a figure that doubles after a set number of months or year of service. (Schoolteachers in southern Mexico receive the equivalent of $800–$1,100 per month and most workers are paid less, thus vaulting a newly recruited drug corporation lookout or messenger into the upper 10 percent of money earners in his or her community.)

To tens of thousands of young people employment with a drug corporation "at least offers something," as a seventeen-year-old high school dropout told me after a friend offered to connect him with a recruiter. Al]azeera quoted a drug organization member: "I could never go back to making ten dollars a day. At least here I get paid and I have some opportunity to rise up. In other jobs I will always be at the bottom." That most of these newly recruited members have no criminal records and intermingle with the general population created an environment "like those old science-fiction movies about androids, you never know who's on your side and who isn't," as an editor from a Mexican daily exclaimed during a Mexico City news conference.

Drug-associated killings became so frequent that by 2008 Mexican newspapers like La Jornada grouped daily execution and assassination reports under a single back page headline. During the first eight months of 2009 they reported an average of twenty-one killings a day. By 2010 the average number of drug-associated deaths averaged nearly forty a day.

Because President Calderón needed–or thought he needed (or his ultra-conservative National Action Party thought that he needed)–the support of governors alleged to have connections with various drug organizations he shunted aside revelations about their narco-business contacts. Prosecution of commerce in cocaine, marijuana, and other drugs occurred in a patchwork pattern, with political alliances given priority over enforcement. Many governors, high-ranking politicians, business impresarios, and generals remained immune even when military raids or PGR investigations targeted their agencies.

Only when "the structure of power that those controlling the politics of the nation have maintained as accomplices and members of this series of criminal organizations has collapsed" will real solutions to the internal warfare among the "nations within a nation" be possible, Guillermo Garduño- *Valero,* a specialist in national security analysis from Mexico's Metropolitan University (UAM), told La Jornada. The drug corporations have become so powerful politically, he argued, that both the federal and state governments have become subservient to them and the occasional arrests and assaults on organization leaders have little or no impact on the lucrative trade.

Both the governments of Mexico and the United States have demonstrated a need to justify military actions and to portray the "War on Drugs" as a battle between good and evil with no gray areas in between. To make the rhetoric effective it has been necessary to villainize the perpetrators of the "evil" and to ignore the dominant reasons that the evil exists: unabated drug consumption in the United States. Also overlooked has been drug associated violence in the United States, particularly in city ghettos where gang warfare involving drug distribution has existed since the 1960s.

Until late in the twentieth century heroin and cocaine addiction in Mexico was not considered a major problem. Narcotics filtered to Mexican buyers as a spin off from smuggling, but most production and distribution was focused on getting the narcotics to consumers north of the border who would pay ten or more times what the drugs sold for in Mexico. Governmental sources in both countries consistently denied that U.S. military intervention into Mexican territory was being planned; nevertheless several governors of states on the U.S. side of the border have requested permanent military "protection," including armed patrols and battle-ready commandos.

Many of the groups that distribute narcotics in the United States are linked to specific Mexican corporations just as U.S. auto, livestock, cosmetics, and computer exporters are linked with importers in Mexico. Gangs in the United States clash primarily over obtaining drugs for street sales, but the majority of imported narcotics passes into the hands of white-collar distributors with regular clients who can afford the prices established for purchasing cocaine and other drugs.

Although many journalists and editors would like to deny it, newspapers and television which rely financially on readers, viewers, and advertisers profit more from graphic reports about beheadings, drug raids, and highspeed chases than they do from features about controlled or casual use of narcotics. Attitudes towards drug use in both countries run a gamut between "drugs are a sin" to "I enjoy them, why not?" That they can be detrimental to one's health, just as the consumption of alcoholic beverages, cigarette smoking, overeating, driving a car at excessive speeds, or longterm exposure to direct sunlight can be detrimental, is grounded in fact.

Unfortunately facts and politics do not go hand in glove. Nor do facts and marketing. Newspaper wire services and television reports designed to stimulate interest and sell sponsors' products (and/or comply with ownership political biases) influence public opinion and public opinion influences the decisions of legislators and Congressmen. As Laura Carlson insists: "These claims and others like them, although unsubstantiated, accumulate into a critical mass to push a public consensus on implementing dangerous and delusional policies. . . . Like the model it mimics–the Bush war on terror–the drug war in Mexico is being mounted on the back of hype, half-truths, omissions and outright falsehoods."

Unfortunately, major questions that need to be answered are shunted aside by policymakers on both sides of the border and preference is given to partisan stances that have less to do with the drug trade or the war against it than they have to do with maintaining economic and political power. Neither government seems capable of asking: Can Mexico really afford to end the production and exportation of heroin, cocaine, marijuana, amphetamines, and designer drugs without its U.S. dependent economy collapsing?

In many respects, the drug organizations operating in Mexico exemplify what "free enterprise" is about: developing and marketing a product that satisfies willing consumers. Their armed components make their competition deadlier than competitors in other industries, but their methods of operation duplicate those of legitimate corporations: they seek (or buy) government support, network a well-organized retail trade, and invest their profits in condominiums, the stock market, and high-visibility consumer items. Their corporate structures, divided into distinct operations and with well-defined chains of command, enable them to replace any executive who is arrested or killed without that materially affecting production or sales.

The money they bring into Mexico, unlike money brought in by legitimate corporations, does not require government investment and consequently is untaxed and unreported (which prevents it from benefiting the nearly 80 percent of the population with inadequate and/or poverty level incomes). Nevertheless, what the mafiosos spend on purchases, construction, and salaries circulates throughout the economy. The owner of a Michoacán taquería reflected the viewpoint of many Mexican residents: "They have lana [literally wool, but popularly used to describe money], they eat well; I now have five locations instead of just one."

Proposals to decriminalize the possession of small amounts of marijuana, as various states in the United States have done, came under discussion during the early years of President Vicente Fox's administration but evoked a vehemently negative response, particularly from the Catholic Church hierarchy and those influenced by Church doctrine. Calderón's PAN government seemed more inclined to reinstitute the Salinas de Gortari era of tacit coordination with a single dominant drug corporation, a process that could not be discussed openly and would involve purging local, state, and federal governments of alignments with everyone except the chosen affiliate (which many sources in Mexico insist is El Chapo's "Sinaloa Cartel").

As long as the assassinations, beheadings, cáteos, and the majority of the corruption of government official remain south of the border the United States can maintain its pro-military stance, send money and arms to Mexico's conservative government, and focus on more demanding issues. Mexico, in contrast, rejecting any form of legalization, remains bound to its U.S. appeasing commitment to continue a bloody confrontation that seems to have no end.

Although legalization would re-channel importation and sales and make addiction, overdoses, and side effects a public health problem instead of strictly a law-enforcement concern, drug-related crimes would continue to exist, just as alcohol-related crimes continued to make headlines and fill jails after the repeal of Prohibition. Taxes on importation and sales could finance rehabilitation and other government programs;

corporations handling importation and sales could be effectively audited but social, ethical, and religious conflicts over morality and behavior would continue.

Nor would legalization magically resolve the economic issues that gave rise to the complex business of drug exportation and use, and it would have to occur in both Mexico and the United States to be effective. Restricting or controlling the financing of drug operations would not be possible without breaking up the distribution and investment chains that involve not only the two governments, but also entrepreneurs and legalized businesses. But it can hardly be denied that legalization is a necessary first step toward any decent, or even tolerable, outcome.

The nationalism exhibited by the governments of both the United States and Mexico has impeded dealing rationally with drug cultivation and distribution. Coupled with the lack of accurate information–and/ or falsification of the information available–it has created a paradigm where the solution has preceded analysis and wrenched fact and fiction into a definition that fits the solution, rather than the solution being the culmination of analysis. In much the same way that trying to solve the "illegal immigration problem" by constructing walls and making arrests puts the cart (solution) before the horse (employers), trying to curb the importation of cocaine, marijuana, heroin, and other drugs by militarized procedures is doomed to fail because it does not recognize or deal with the undiminished demand for the products involved.

Critical Thinking

1. What do believe were the most important turning points in the history of United States drug policy?

2. What do believe were the most important turning points in the history of Mexican drug policy?

3. Discuss the current barriers to resolution for the shared United States-Mexico drug war.

ROBERT JOE STOUT (mexicoconamor@yahoo.com) lives in Oaxaca, Mexico, and his articles and essays have appeared recently in America, Conscience, The American Scholar, and Monthly Review. His most recent book is *Why Immigrants Come to America* (Praeger Publishers, 2007). Copyright Monthly Review Press Jan 2012

From *Monthly Review*, vol. 63, no. 8, January 2012, pp. 34–44. Copyright © 2012 by Monthly Review Foundation. Reprinted by permission.

Engaging Communities to Prevent Underage Drinking

ABIGAIL A. FAGAN, PHD., J. DAVID HAWKINS, PHD., AND RICHARD F. CATALANO, PHD

Community-based efforts offer broad potential for achieving population-level reductions in alcohol misuse among youth and young adults. A common feature of successful community strategies is reliance on local coalitions to select and fully implement preventive interventions that have been shown to be effective in changing factors that influence risk of youth engaging in alcohol use, including both proximal influences and structural and/or environmental factors related to alcohol use. Inclusion of a universal, school-based prevention curriculum in the larger community-based effort is associated with the reduction of alcohol use by youth younger than 18 years of age and can help reach large numbers of youth with effective alcohol misuse prevention.

Research has identified multiple risk factors that increase the likelihood of alcohol use among youth and young adults. These conditions or experiences include individual characteristics (e.g., displaying aggression at a young age or believing that alcohol use is not harmful), peer influences (e.g., having friends who use alcohol or who believe that alcohol use is acceptable), family experiences (e.g., heavy alcohol use by parents or siblings, or inadequate parental supervision), school factors (e.g., academic failure, or having a low commitment to school or education), and neighborhood experiences (e.g., availability of alcohol to youth, or community norms that are permissive of youth alcohol use) (Durlak 1998; Hawkins et al. 1992; Pentz 1998). Protective or promotive factors that ameliorate the negative influences of risk factors or directly reduce the likelihood of alcohol use among young people also exist in all areas of people's lives. They include, for example, being attached to others who do not abuse alcohol, having a resilient temperament, or holding clear standards against the use of alcohol before one is of legal age (Pollard et al. 1999; Werner 1993).

Prevention efforts aimed at reducing rates of alcohol use typically do so by seeking to minimize the target population's exposure to harmful risk factors and/or enhance protective/promotive factors (Coie et al. 1993; Munoz et al. 1996). Focusing prevention efforts on youth offers particularly great potential, because the early onset of drinking has been associated with an increased likelihood of alcohol dependence later in life (Hingson et al. 2006). Although many prevention efforts have been found to reduce tobacco, alcohol, and other drug use (Hawkins et al. 1995; National Research Council and Institute of Medicine 2009; Spoth et al. 2008), these strategies often are limited by addressing risk and protective factors in just one socialization domain. Thus, most of these efforts focus only on the most direct (i.e., proximal) causes of alcohol use, such as the availability of alcohol or peer or family influences, rather than targeting the complex contexts in which youth and young adults live. This narrow focus may reduce the overall impact and long-term effectiveness of alcohol-abuse prevention strategies, both because multiple factors affect alcohol use and because the effectiveness of any intervention likely is compromised if the environment in which people live is unfavorable to or does not support intervention goals and activities (Flay 2000; Wagenaar and Perry 1994).

One at least equally promising strategy for affecting rates of alcohol use, abuse, and dependence (not just among youth and young adults) centers on community-based efforts. Such approaches rely on multiple strategies intended to change a variety of factors that place individuals at risk for engaging in alcohol misuse (Pentz 1998; Wandersman and Florin 2003). Most of these efforts seek to alter not only proximal influences, but also the long-term, structural, and environmental influences associated with alcohol abuse and dependence, which increases their potential to make a significant and long-lasting impact (Wagenaar et al. 1994). By saturating the environment with prevention strategies and messages, community-based efforts aim to reach many individuals, which may allow them to achieve population-level reductions in alcohol misuse.

Another potential advantage of community-based strategies is their reliance on members of the local community to plan, implement, and monitor prevention activities, usually via coalitions made up of stakeholders from diverse organizations and backgrounds. By actively involving the community in the prevention effort, these approaches may enhance community buy-in for prevention activities and may help to ensure that services are a good fit with local needs, resources, and norms (Hawkins et al. 2002; Stevenson and Mitchell, 2003; Wandersman et al. 2003; Woolf 2008). The levels of risk and protective/promotive factors vary across communities, and measures most needed in one community to reduce youth alcohol use may not be needed in another community (Hawkins et al. 2002; Reiss and Price 1996). Thus, prevention efforts that are based upon assessing local needs (i.e., risk and protective/ promotive factors faced by those in the community) and implementing prevention strategies that are best suited to address these needs may be more effective than implementing a single prevention program across many communities. Community mobilization also may allow for effective pooling of information and resources across agencies and individuals, minimizing duplication of services, and potentially offering more cost-effective services that can be implemented better and are more likely to be sustained.

After defining what exactly community mobilization implies, this article explores what community-based strategies work to reduce alcohol use and misuse among youth and the role of school-based interventions in the context of community-level efforts. Finally, the article looks at the challenges associated with the successful implementation of community-based programs to prevent youth alcohol use.

What Is Community Mobilization to Prevent Alcohol Misuse?

Existing community-based alcohol abuse prevention efforts are tailored to local circumstances, which makes it difficult to identify the specific components that define this type of approach. Nonetheless, community mobilization efforts have in common the goal of reducing alcohol misuse by changing the larger environment, using approaches that are owned and operated by the local community (Wandersman et al. 2003). Most programs rely on coalitions of community stakeholders to collaboratively plan and coordinate prevention activities. In some cases, coalitions focus on implementing, in a coordinated fashion, multiple, discrete prevention programs and practices that seek to decrease elevated risk factors and enhance depressed protective/promotive factors related to alcohol use (Hawkins et al. 2002). Other efforts specifically focus on transforming the environment via changes in local ordinances, norms, and policies related to alcohol. These latter efforts target a more limited number of risk factors, particularly community norms and laws related to alcohol use, the availability of alcohol, and individual attitudes favorable to alcohol use (Pentz 2000). Some community-based efforts rely on a combination of these strategies.

What Community-Based Strategies Work to Reduce Alcohol Misuse Among Youth?

The findings presented in this article are based upon a comprehensive review of evaluations conducted in the United States that involved the implementation of a substantial, community-based prevention initiative aimed at reducing alcohol and other drug (AOD) use among minors (i.e., adolescents and young adults age 20 or younger). Projects were included in the review if they met the following criteria:

- They were evaluated using a well-conducted quasi-experimental or true experimental design that involved, at a minimum, one intervention group (implementing the strategy) and one comparison group.
- Data on alcohol use outcomes were collected at least twice during the research project (e.g., before and after the intervention was conducted).
- There were no significant threats to the validity and reliability of the study, as determined by the first two authors of this review.

Although many studies were reviewed, only nine community-based initiatives demonstrated reduced rates of alcohol use or alcohol availability among youth and young adults according to the above criteria (see the table). It is notable that several of these strategies affected not only alcohol use but also the use of tobacco and, in some cases, other illicit drugs. The table briefly describes each program, the population in which the intervention was evaluated, and the program's significant effects in reducing AOD use.

The findings allow the following conclusions. First, a common feature of successful community-based prevention approaches is reliance on local coalitions to select effective preventive interventions and implement them with fidelity. Second, the inclusion of a universal, school-based drug prevention curriculum as part of the larger community initiative is associated with reductions in alcohol use among middle- and high-school students. Third, environmental strategies focused on changing local laws, norms, and policies related to alcohol access and use do not appear to reduce alcohol use among adolescents younger than age 18 when implemented independently of other community-based strategies. However, they have been part of successful multicomponent interventions and, when implemented on their own, have reduced the availability of alcohol in communities and lowered the rate of drunk-driving arrests among young adults.

Reliance on Community Coalitions

All of the community-based initiatives listed in the table relied on local coalitions to plan and implement prevention activities. This observation indicates that to be successful, community efforts must ensure the presence of active, broad-based groups of individuals who believe it is possible to prevent youth AOD use and who are willing to engage in collaborative prevention activities. Although coalitions vary in their structures, sizes, goals, and activities, a defining feature of such groups is their focus on facilitating desired changes through collaborative action. Although the specific members of a coalition may vary depending on the focus of the group, coalitions usually seek to be broad based and to unite diverse stakeholders and key leaders from key agencies and sectors of the community. For example, coalitions focused on preventing alcohol use by youth may include representatives

Table Community Mobilization Strategies With Evidence of Effectiveness in Reducing the Use and/or Availability of Alcohol for Minors

Study	Description	Study Population	Significant Effects
Kentucky Incentives for Prevention (Collins et al. 2007)	Coalition-based prevention strategy targeting risk and protective factors related to drug use with effective programs conducted in schools and other community agencies	19 coalitions in Kentucky; 25,032 students in grades 8 and 10	Reduced smoking, drinking and binge drinking among 10th graders
Communities That Care (CTC) (Hawkins et al. 2009)	Coalition-based prevention strategy targeting elevated risk and depressed protective factors related to drug use with effective programs conducted in schools and other community agencies for peer review	24 communities in 7 States; 4,407 students in grade 5	Reduced the initiation of smokeless tobacco, smoking, and alcohol Reduced past-month use of smokeless tobacco, alcohol, and binge drinking
Midwestern Prevention Project (Pentz et al. 1989)	Combines coalition-led community mobilization strategies with the implementation of school-based prevention curricula	42 schools in Kansas City; 5,065 students in grades 6 and 7	Reduced past-month smoking and drinking
Project SixTeen (Biglan et al. 2000)	Combines coalition-led community mobilization strategies with the implementation of school-based prevention curricula	16 communities in Oregon; 4,438 students in grades 7 and 9	Reduced smoking, drinking, and marijuana use
Project Northland (Perry et al. 2002)	Combines coalition-led community mobilization strategies with the implementation of school-based prevention curricula	24 school districts in Minnesota; 2,953 students in grade 6	Reduced binge drinking and alcohol sales to minors
Native American Project (Schinke et al. 2000)	Combines coalition-led community mobilization strategies with the implementation of school-based prevention curricula	27 tribal and public schools in the Midwest; 1,396 students in grades 3–5	Reduced smokeless tobacco, alcohol, and marijuana use
DARE Plus (Perry, Komro, Veblen-Mortenson et al. 2003)	Combines coalition-led community mobilization strategies with the implementation of school-based prevention curricula	24 schools in Minnesota; 7,261 students in grade 7	Reduced past-year and past-month smoking and drinking for boys and having ever been drunk for girls
Communities Mobilizing for Change on Alcohol (Wagenaar et al. 2000a, b)	Coalition-led activities seeking changes to community policies, practices, and norms related to alcohol use	15 school districts in Minnesota and Wisconsin; 4,506 students in grade 12, and 3,095 18- to 20-year-olds	Reduced the provision of alcohol to minors and arrests for drunk driving reported by 18- to 20-year-olds
Community Trials Project (Grube 1997; Holder et al. 2000)	Coalition-led activities seeking changes to community policies, practices, and norms related to alcohol use	6 communities in California and South Carolina	Reduced heavy drinking among adults, alcohol sales to minors, and alcohol-related car crashes

from law enforcement, local government, schools, health and human service agencies, youth service groups, business, religious groups, youth, and parents. The coalitions typically are formed around a common vision that inspires and motivates their actions. By working together to bring about change, they allow intervention approaches to be tailored to local needs, as identified by coalition members. They also increase political alliances, foster communication among community members, and coordinate human and financial resources (Hawkins et al. 2002; Pentz 2000; Wandersman et al. 2003).

Although coalitions are a common element of effective community-based prevention, not all coalition efforts have produced significant changes in alcohol use. Some coalition initiatives have failed to reduce rates of AOD use among youth and adolescents, even when they were well funded and members were well intentioned and willing to make changes. Evaluations of two coalition efforts—the Fighting Back (Hallfors and Godette 2002) and Community Partnership (Yin et al. 1997) initiatives—found that both failed to bring about changes in youth AOD use. The evaluations indicated that the coalitions involved in these projects had insufficient guidance in how to enact prevention strategies, varied widely in the nature and amount of prevention services provided, and largely relied on locally created prevention strategies that likely had not been previously evaluated for effectiveness in reducing AOD use. These studies suggest that the mere presence of an active, well-intentioned coalition is not enough to prevent AOD use. In other words, simply gathering local stakeholders and asking them to collaborate to do their best to solve local drug problems or prevent underage drinking does not produce desired changes.

Instead, the evidence suggests that in order to be successful, coalitions must ensure the following (Hallfors et al. 2002):

- They must have clearly defined, focused, and manageable goals;
- They must have adequate planning time;
- Prevention decisions must be based on empirical data about what needs to change in the community and on evidence from scientifically valid studies of what has worked to address those needs;
- They must implement prevention policies, practices, and programs that have been tested and shown to be effective; and
- They must carefully monitor prevention activities to ensure implementation quality.

One prevention system that exemplifies these principles is Communities That Care (CTC), which has been found to reduce the initiation and prevalence of youth alcohol use community-wide (Feinberg et al. 2007; Hawkins et al. 2009). CTC provides proactive training and technical assistance to community coalitions to ensure that they select and implement prevention strategies that previously have been demonstrated to be effective in reducing youth AOD use. The CTC model involves a structured and guided intervention process involving five phases in which coalitions (1) assess community readiness to undertake collaborative prevention efforts, (2) form a diverse and representative prevention coalition, (3) use epidemiologic data to assess prevention needs, (4) select evidence-based prevention policies and programs that target these needs, and (5) implement the new policies and programs with monitoring to ensure fidelity and evaluation to ensure that goals are being met. The coalitions are structured, ideally with a chair person, cochairs, and workgroups; employ at least a half-time coordinator; and are broad based. The prevention activities chosen and implemented can take place in a variety of settings and may target individual, family, school, peer, and/or community risk and protective/promotive factors related to youth AOD use. They are selected by the community coalitions from a menu of options that only includes policies and programs that have been shown in at least one study using a high-quality research design to significantly change risk and protective factors and reduce rates of AOD use (Hawkins and Catalano 1992; Hawkins et al. 2002).

Several evaluations of the CTC coalition model have been conducted, including a randomized trial involving 24 communities in 7 States that were randomly assigned to either implement the CTC system (n = 12) or serve as control communities (n = 12) (Hawkins et al. 2008). The intervention sites received training in the CTC model, proactive and intensive technical assistance, and funding for 5 years to plan and implement their chosen prevention strategies. This study found that after 4 years of the intervention, students in the CTC communities had lower rates of AOD use compared with students in control communities. They were less likely to initiate cigarette, alcohol, and smokeless tobacco use as well as delinquent behavior by the eighth grade. In addition, eighth-grade students in the intervention communities reported significantly lower rates of drinking, binge drinking, and smokeless tobacco use in the past month, as well as delinquent behavior in the past year, compared with students in the control communities (Hawkins et al. 2009).

These results indicate that when local community coalitions are provided with proactive training and technical assistance, have clear goals and guidelines, and ensure effective implementation of prevention strategies that have prior evidence of effectiveness, they have the potential to significantly reduce alcohol and tobacco use as well as delinquent behavior community-wide. Moreover, the findings indicate that coalitions may enact a variety of prevention policies and programs targeting a range of different risk and protective factors and still be successful, as long as their efforts focus on using methods that have been demonstrated to be effective and ensure that prevention activities are carefully implemented, monitored, and coordinated.

Inclusion of School-Based Curricula in Community-Based Efforts

Implementation of universal, school-based drug prevention curricula as part of the larger community effort appears to predict reduced rates of AOD use among middle- and high-school students. All of the initiatives listed in the table that were effective in preventing or reducing alcohol use among those younger than age 18 involved the implementation of a school-based curriculum. Although neither the CTC prevention system nor the Kentucky Incentives for Prevention initiative (Collins et al. 2007) requires the use of school-based curricula, all of the coalitions involved in the randomized CTC evaluation (Hawkins et al. 2009), and all but one of the 19 coalitions evaluated in Kentucky, implemented a school curriculum to target particular risk factors whose influence in the community was considered too high or protective factors whose influence was considered too low by local coalitions.

The other community-based prevention initiatives listed in the table that reduced alcohol use among those younger than age 18 involved implementation of a particular school curriculum offered to students in conjunction with coalition-led efforts to change community-level risk factors related to drug use. The latter efforts typically attempted to change community norms and local ordinances related to alcohol use and availability. An evaluation of the Project Northland Program in Minnesota (Perry et al. 2002), for example, demonstrated reduced rates of alcohol use in communities that implemented a multi-year school curriculum and modified local policies and practices associated with youth alcohol use. The school program focused on altering student views regarding the acceptability of alcohol use, improving student skills in refusing drug offers, and fostering parent/ child communication about alcohol use through homework assignments and information mailed to parents. Environmentally focused strategies included increased identification checks by retail liquor establishments and legal consequences for selling alcohol to minors. The evaluation of Project Northland found that after receiving services in both middle and high school, students in the intervention communities had lower rates of binge drinking (i.e., drinking five or more alcoholic beverages on one occasion) compared with students in control communities. In addition, retail establishments were less likely to sell alcohol to minors in intervention than in control communities (Perry et al. 2002).

A similar combination of activities was advocated in the Midwestern Prevention Project (MPP). This program involved the implementation of a 2-year middle-school curriculum to promote students' drug resistance skills, along with parent education, media campaigns to reinforce antidrug messages throughout the community, and local policy changes to reduce demand and supply of drugs. When implemented in schools in Kansas City, the MPP demonstrated reductions in past-month smoking and alcohol use for students receiving the intervention compared with students in control schools (Pentz et al. 1989).

In Project SixTeen, small communities in Oregon implemented a five-session, school-based program aimed at reducing youth tobacco use, along with media campaigns and responsible beverage training for alcohol retail outlets. The evaluation showed a significant reduction in past-week smoking and marijuana use for seventh- and ninth-grade students in intervention communities compared with control communities; similarly, alcohol use was reduced among ninth graders (Biglan et al. 2000).

These studies indicate that the inclusion of school-based prevention programs in comprehensive, coalition-led, community-based initiatives can contribute to reductions in alcohol use among adolescents. Currently, most schools in the United States provide some type of drug-prevention programming to students. However, not all school districts implement strategies that have evidence of effectiveness, even though the Safe and Drug-Free School (SDFS) legislation mandates the use of effective substance-use prevention curricula. Inclusion of school-based programs in larger community prevention initiatives provides multiple advantages, including the ability to reach a large proportion of the youth population and thus increase the potential of achieving community-level changes in desired outcomes. Community coalitions can help school districts fulfill the SDFS mandate by helping them identify and adopt effective strategies and by helping to ensure that the new programs are well suited to addressing the needs of local students. In addition, coalitions can partner with schools to find the needed resources to initiate and sustain new effective prevention strategies and can help oversee the implementation of new strategies to ensure quality. To promote successful partnerships, coalitions should ensure that school personnel, including administrators (e.g., superintendents and principals) and staff (e.g., teachers and counselors), are actively involved in the decisionmaking process and prevention efforts from the beginning of the initiative (Fagan et al. 2009).

Targeting Environmental Risk Factors for Substance Use

The initiatives just described combined the implementation of school curricula with community mobilization efforts that target environmental risk factors in order to reduce the availability of and demand for alcohol. Such efforts include changes in community-level policies, practices, and norms, such as increasing alcohol pricing, creating drug-free zones, limiting alcohol sales in venues easily accessible to youth, requiring keg registrations, and increasing the use or severity of community laws related to alcohol use by minors or adults (Pentz 2000; Wagenaar et al. 1994). Changes in community practices also may involve responsible beverage service training—that is, educating merchants about the negative consequences of providing alcohol to minors or serving intoxicated patrons, encouraging identification checks, and ensuring that merchants who violate rules are appropriately sanctioned (Holder 2000). Media campaigns may also be used in conjunction with these activities to educate the public about the negative effects of alcohol use, increase support for drug prevention, and counter norms favorable to alcohol use. Such media campaigns increase public awareness by saturating the community with print, radio, and television advertisements; mailing informational fliers to businesses or homes; or holding community forums to discuss alcohol-use issues.

Evidence is mixed regarding the effectiveness of these types of environmentally focused prevention strategies. As discussed in the previous section, when offered in conjunction with school-based prevention curricula, these prevention strategies seem to be effective in reducing rates of adolescent alcohol use. However, efforts that focus exclusively on changing environmental risk factors at the local level, without also targeting more proximal risk factors related to alcohol use, have not been associated with reductions in alcohol use among youth under age 18. An evaluation of Communities Mobilizing for Change on Alcohol (CMCA) found no statistically significant changes (i.e., p<.05 using two-tailed test of significance) in alcohol or drug use among 12th-grade students or 18- to 20-year-olds in communities implementing CMCA compared with those in control communities (Wagenaar et al. 2000b). In this project, community coalitions coordinated a variety of activities aimed at limiting alcohol sales to minors, increasing enforcement of underage drinking laws, and changing alcohol policies at community events, as well as increasing public attention about problems associated with underage drinking. Although rates of alcohol use by youth were not significantly changed by the intervention, the evaluation did show that 18- to 20-year-olds from intervention sites were significantly less likely to provide alcohol to minors (Wagenaar et al. 2000a,b).

The Community Trials Project used similar environmentally focused prevention strategies to reduce alcohol use and related risky behaviors. A quasi-experimental evaluation of this program in six communities indicated significantly fewer alcohol-related automobile crashes in intervention communities than in control communities (Holder et al. 2000). Among adults (those age 18 or older), a greater proportion of those in communities implementing the program reported having one or more drinks in the past year versus those in comparison communities. However, among those who reported any drinking, adults in intervention sites had lower rates of self-reported heavy drinking and drunk driving (Holder et al. 2000). Although there were fewer sales to minors by alcohol sales establishments in intervention versus comparison sites (Grube 1997), none of the evaluations of the Community Trials Project have found significant reductions in drinking among youth under age 18 in intervention versus comparison sites.

The available evidence indicates that these types of community-based, environmentally focused strategies are effective in reducing alcohol use among those under age 18 only when offered in conjunction with effective school curricula. However, few evaluations have been conducted of community-based prevention efforts that rely solely on changing community policies, practices, and norms, and more research is needed to assess the impact of environmental strategies when used independently and when combined with other types of prevention strategies.

Challenges Associated With Community Mobilization Efforts

There is much public support for community mobilization efforts that seek to reduce substance use, particularly by youth and young adults, and many communities have coalitions in place to coordinate local prevention strategies. However, implementing, evaluating, and sustaining such efforts can be challenging. For example, it often is difficult to recruit, engage, and ensure collaboration among community members from diverse backgrounds who may have different skills, needs, resources, and ideas about what is needed to prevent AOD use (Merzel and D'Afflitti 2003; Quinby et al. 2008; Stith et al. 2006). Furthermore, compared with single prevention programs, community-level strategies likely are costlier to implement and evaluate because they entail more components and require longer-term interventions to achieve community-wide outcomes (Merzel et al. 2003). It also can be difficult to define community boundaries, gain support for participation in a research study from key leaders and stakeholders, and measure processes and outcomes that may vary across communities (Stith et al. 2006; Wandersman et al. 2003). Finally, community-based prevention strategies are intended to be owned and operated by the community, which can create tension between local practitioners and scientists who may differ in their ideas about what is most needed to prevent alcohol misuse (Holder et al. 1997; Hyndman et al. 1992; Merzel et al. 2003).

The many challenges related to the implementation of community-based prevention efforts likely are responsible for the relatively small number of interventions that have demonstrated evidence of success (see the table). In addition, evaluations of some community prevention programs have failed to demonstrate significant effects on alcohol use, sometimes because of problems related to program implementation and intensity. For example, the initial evaluation of Project Northland in Minnesota indicated that the original 3-year intervention, which was implemented in middle schools, was insufficient to lead to

sustained effects on alcohol use. Therefore, additional services were added in high schools, which reduced rates of alcohol use through grade 12 (Perry et al. 2002). A replication of this extended program in Chicago, Illinois, however, failed to produce positive effects, which led the evaluators to recommend that in lower-income, urban populations, where problems other than youth alcohol use (e.g., gangs, violence, and housing) may take precedence, longer-term and more intense community-based strategies may be needed to bring about change (Komro et al. 2008).

The Project Northland replication in Chicago and other evaluations have noted that implementation challenges, such as difficulties in engaging community members in the initiative and challenges in moving from planning to action, may compromise the ability of community-based efforts to produce significant effects. On the other hand, evaluations of the CTC prevention system have shown that communities can successfully mobilize volunteers, create high-functioning and goal-driven coalitions, and ensure high-quality implementation of prevention strategies that target salient risk and protective factors (Quinby et al. 2008). One factor that increases the likelihood of success is the provision of proactive and high-quality training and technical assistance from system developers to the community coalitions (Feinberg et al. 2008). In the absence of such training and technical assistance, common implementation challenges are likely to threaten implementation and the likelihood of realizing desired reductions in youth alcohol use.

Research also has indicated that communities that rely on prevention-focused coalitions, as in the CTC model, can successfully sustain the implementation of tested and effective programs, despite the human and financial costs associated with these efforts. An evaluation of 110 CTC coalitions in Pennsylvania (Feinberg et al. 2008) indicated that nearly all coalitions (91 percent), which still were operating after the State discontinued funding for CTC activities, continued to implement effective programs. In fact, on average, the coalitions were able to fund their program and coalition activities at levels exceeding those initially provided by the State. Funding success was positively associated with having a well-functioning coalition, adhering to the CTC model, and planning for sustainability. These findings reinforce the importance of utilizing broad-based coalitions to plan, implement, and sustain prevention activities in communities.

Identifying the cost-effectiveness of community-based prevention initiatives also is important. Although the review presented here identified nine community-based strategies with evidence of effectiveness in reducing alcohol use and availability among minors, only two of these interventions have been rigorously evaluated for cost-effectiveness. In both cases, the analyses demonstrated fiscal savings. According to the Washington State Institute for Public Policy (Aos et al. 2004), every dollar spent on Project Northland in Minnesota resulted in savings of $2.45 in later treatment, morbidity, mortality, and criminal justice costs; similarly, the MPP produced savings of $1.27 per dollar spent. Because cost is a major factor influencing community decisions to adopt new programs, information on financial benefits may help to increase the dissemination of community-based prevention strategies, their long-term sustainability, and ultimately their potential to substantially reduce rates of alcohol use among young people.

In summary, this review clearly has shown that community-based efforts can reduce alcohol use and misuse among youth. A common feature of successful community strategies is reliance on local coalitions to select and fully implement preventive interventions that have prior evidence of effectiveness in changing risk and protective or promotive factors related to alcohol use. Inclusion of a universal, school-based prevention curriculum in the larger community-based effort is associated with lower rates of drinking, binge drinking, and other drug use by those younger than 18. Focusing community-based prevention efforts on youth offers particularly great potential, because it not only lowers rates of alcohol use among minors but also reduces the likelihood of alcohol misuse and dependence later in life (Hingson et al. 2006).

References

Aos, S.; Lieb, R.; Mayfield, J.; et al. Benefits and Costs of Prevention and Early Intervention Programs for Youth. Olympia, WA: Washington State Institute for Public Policy, 2004.

Biglan, A.; Ary, D.V.; Smolkowski, K.; et al. A randomised controlled trial of a community intervention to prevent adolescent tobacco use. Tobacco Control 9:24–32, 2000. PMID: 10691755

Coie, J.D.; Watt, N.F.; West, S.G.; et al. The science of prevention: A conceptual framework and some directions for a national research program. American Psychologist 48:1013–1022, 1993. PMID: 8256874

Collins, D.; Johnson, K.; and Becker, B.J. A meta-analysis of direct and mediating effects of community coalitions that implemented science-based substance abuse prevention interventions. Substance Use and Misuse 42:985–1007, 2007. PMID: 17613959

Durlak, J.A. Common risk and protective factors in successful prevention programs. American Journal of Orthopsychiatry 68:512–520, 1998. PMID: 9809111

Fagan, A.A.; Brooke-Weiss, B.; Cady, R.; and Hawkins, J.D. If at first you don't succeed . . . keep trying: Strategies to enhance coalition/school partnerships to implement school-based prevention programming. Australian & New Zealand Journal of Criminology 42:387–405, 2009. PMID: 20582326

Feinberg, M.E.; Bontempo, D.E.; and Greenberg, M.T. Predictors and level of sustainability of community prevention coalitions. American Journal of Preventive Medicine 34:495–501, 2008. PMID: 18471585

Feinberg, M.E.; Greenberg, M.T.; Osgood, D.W.; et al. Effects of the Communities That Care model in Pennsylvania on youth risk and problem behaviors. Prevention Science 8:261–270, 2007. PMID: 17713856

Feinberg, M.E.; Ridenour, T.A.; and Greenberg, M.T. The longitudinal effect of technical assistance dosage on the functioning of Communities That Care prevention boards in Pennsylvania. Journal of Primary Prevention 29:145–165, 2008. PMID: 18365313

Flay, B.R. Approaches to substance use prevention utilizing school curriculum plus social environment change. Addictive Behaviors 25:861–885, 2000. PMID: 11125776

Grube, J.W. Preventing sales of alcohol to minors: Results from a community trial. Addiction 92(Suppl 2):S251–S260, 1997. PMID: 9231448

Hallfors, D., and Godette, D. Will the "principles of effectiveness" improve prevention practice? Early findings from a diffusion study. Health Education Research 17:461–470, 2002.

Hallfors, D.; Cho, H.; Livert, D.; and Kadushin, C. Fighting back against substance use: Are community coalitions winning? American Journal of Preventive Medicine 23:237–245, 2002. PMID: 12406477

Hawkins, J.D., and Catalano, R.F. Communities That Care: Action for Drug Abuse Prevention. San Francisco, CA: Jossey-Bass, 1992.

Hawkins, J.D.; Arthur, M.W.; and Catalano, R.F. Preventing substance abuse. In: Tonry, M., and Farrington, D.P. (Eds.) Crime and Justice: A Review of Research. Building a Safer Society: Strategic Approaches to Crime Prevention. Volume 19. Chicago, IL: University of Chicago Press, 1995, pp. 343–427.

Hawkins, J.D.; Catalano, R.F.; and Arthur, M.W. Promoting science-based prevention in communities. Addictive Behaviors 27: 951–976, 2002. PMID: 12369478

Hawkins, J.D.; Catalano, R.F.; Arthur, M.W.; et al. Testing Communities That Care: The rationale, design and behavioral baseline equivalence of the Community Youth Development Study. Prevention Science 9:178–190, 2008. PMID: 18516681

Hawkins, J.D.; Catalano, R.F.; and Miller, J.Y. Risk and protective factors for alcohol and other drug problems in adolescence and early adulthood: Implications for substance abuse prevention. Psychological Bulletin 112:64–105, 1992. PMID : 1529040

Hawkins, J.D.; Oesterle, S.; Brown, E.C.; et al. Results of a type 2 translational research trial to prevent adolescent drug use and delinquency: A test of Communities That Care. Archives of Pediatrics & Adolescent Medicine 163:789–798, 2009. PMID: 19736331

Hingson, R.W.; Heeren, T.; and Winter, M.R. Age at drinking onset and alcohol dependence: Age at onset, duration, and severity. Archives of Pediatrics & Adolescent Medicine 160:739–746, 2006. PMID: 16818840

Holder, H.D. Community prevention of alcohol problems. Addictive Behaviors 25:843–859, 2000. PMID: 11125775

Holder, H.D.; Gruenewald, P.J.; Ponicki, W.R.; et al. Effect of community-based interventions on high-risk drinking and alcohol-related injuries. JAMA: Journal of the American Medical Association 284:2341–2347, 2000. PMID: 11066184

Holder, H.D.; Saltz, R.F.; Grube, J.W.; et al. Summing up: Lessons from a comprehensive community prevention trial. Addiction 92(Suppl 2):S293–S301, 1997. PMID: 9231452

Hyndman, B.; Giesbrecht, N.; Bernardi, D.R.; et al. Preventing substance abuse through multicomponent community action research projects: Lessons learned from past experiences and challenges for future initiatives. Contemporary Drug Problems 19:133–164, 1992.

Komro, K.A.; Perry, C.L.; Veblen-Mortenson, S.; et al. Outcomes from a randomized controlled trial of a multi-component alcohol use preventive intervention for urban youth: Project Northland Chicago. Addiction 103:606–618, 2008. PMID: 18261193

Merzel, C., and D'Afflitti, J. Reconsidering community-based health promotion: Promise, performance, and potential. American Journal of Public Health 93:557–574, 2003. PMID: 12660197

Munoz, R.F.; Mrazek, P.J.; and Haggerty, R.J. Institute of Medicine report on prevention of mental disorders: Summary and commentary. American Psychologist 51:1116–1122, 1996. PMID: 8937259

National Research Council and Institute of Medicine. Preventing Mental, Emotional, and Behavioral Disorders Among Young People: Progress and Possibilities. Committee on the Prevention of Mental Disorders and Substance Abuse Among Children, Youth, and Young Adults: Research Advances and Promising Interventions. Washington, DC: Board on Children, Youth, and Families, Division of Behavioral and Social Sciences and Education, National Academies Press, 2009.

Pentz, M.A. Preventing drug abuse through the community: Multicomponent programs make the difference. In: Sloboda, Z., and Hansen, W.B. (Eds.) Putting Research to Work for the Community. NIDA Research Monograph. Rockville, MD: National Institute on Drug Abuse, 1998, pp. 73–86.

Pentz, M.A. Institutionalizing community-based prevention through policy change. Journal of Community Psychology 28:257–270, 2000.

Pentz, M.A.; Dwyer, J.H.; MacKinnon, D.P.; et al. A multicommunity trial for primary prevention of adolescent drug abuse: Effects on drug use prevalence. JAMA: Journal of the American Medical Association 261:3259–3266, 1989. PMID: 2785610

Perry, C.L.; Komro, K.; Veblen-Mortenson, S.; et al. A randomized controlled trial of the middle and junior high school D.A.R.E. and D.A.R.E. Plus programs. Archives of Pediatrics & Adolescent Medicine 157:178–184, 2003. PMID: 12580689

Perry, C.L.; Williams, C.L.; Komro, K.A.; et al. Project Northland: Long-term outcomes of community action to reduce adolescent alcohol use. Health Education Research 17:117–132, 2002. PMID: 11888042

Pollard, J.A.; Hawkins, J.D.; and Arthur, M.W. Risk and protection: Are both necessary to understand diverse behavioral outcomes in adolescence? Social Work Research 23:145–158, 1999.

Quinby, R.; Fagan, A.A.; Hanson, K.; et al. Installing the Communities That Care prevention system: Implementation progress and fidelity in a randomized controlled trial. Journal of Community Psychology 36:313–332, 2008.

Reiss, D., and Price, R.H. National research agenda for prevention research: The National Institute of Mental Health report. American Psychologist 51:1109–1115, 1996. PMID: 8937258

Schinke, S.P.; Tepavac, L.; and Cole, K.C. Preventing substance use among Native American youth: Three-year results. Addictive Behaviors 25:387–397, 2000. PMID: 10890292

Spoth, R.L.; Greenberg, M.T.; and Turrisi, R. Preventive interventions addressing underage drinking: State of the evidence and steps towards public health impact. Pediatrics 121(Suppl 4):S311–S336, 2008. PMID: 18381496

Stevenson, J.F., and Mitchell, R.E. Community-level collaboration for substance abuse prevention. Journal of Primary Prevention 23:371–404, 2003.

Stith, S.; Pruitt, I.; Dees, J.E.; et al. Implementing community-based prevention programming: A review of the literature. Journal of Primary Prevention 27:599–617, 2006. PMID: 17051431

Wagenaar, A.C., and Perry, C.L. Community strategies for the reduction of youth drinking: Theory and application. Journal of Research on Adolescence 4:319–345, 1994

Wagenaar, A.C.; Murray, D.M.; and Toomey, T.L. Communities Mobilizing for Change on Alcohol (CMCA): Effects of a randomized trial on arrests and traffic crashes. Addiction 95:209–217, 2000a. PMID: 10723849

Wagenaar, A.C.; Murray, D.M.; Gehan, J.P.; et al. Communities Mobilizing for Change on Alcohol: Outcomes from a randomized community trial. Journal of Studies on Alcohol 61:85–94, 2000b. PMID: 10627101

Wandersman, A., and Florin, P. Community intervention and effective prevention. American Psychologist 58:441–448, 2003. PMID: 12971190

Werner, E.E. Risk, resilience, and recovery: Perspectives from the Kauai longitudinal study. Development and Psychopathology 5:503–515, 1993.

Woolf, S.H. The power of prevention and what it requires. JAMA: Journal of the American Medical Association 299:2437–2439, 2008. PMID: 18505953

Yin, R.K.; Kaftarian, S.J.; Yu, P.; and Jansen, M.A. Outcomes from CSAP's Community Partnership Program: Findings from the national cross-site evaluation. Evaluation and Program Planning 20:345–355, 1997.

Critical Thinking

1. Describe one common feature in successful community strategies that address substance abuse.

2. Discuss the most salient risk factors for adolescent alcohol abuse.

3. Analyze what works for prevention of adolescent alcohol abuse.

ABIGAIL A. FAGAN, PhD, is an assistant professor in the Department of Criminology and Criminal Justice, University of South Carolina, Columbia, South Carolina. **J. DAVID HAWKINS, PhD,** is Endowed Professor of Prevention, and **RICHARD F. CATALANO, PhD,** is Bartley Dobb Professor for the Study and Prevention of Violence and director of the Social Development Research Group, School of Social Work, University of Washington, Seattle, Washington.

Acknowledgments—This work was supported by a research grant from the National Institute on Drug Abuse (R01 DA015183–03), with co-funding from the National Cancer Institute, the National Institute of Child Health and Human Development, the National Institute of Mental Health, the Center for Substance Abuse Prevention, and the National Institute on Alcohol Abuse and Alcoholism. The content of this paper is solely the responsibility of the authors and does not necessarily represent the official views of the funding agencies.

Financial Disclosure—The authors declare that they have no competing financial interests.

From *Alcohol Research and Health,* vol. 34, no. 2, 2011, pp. 167–174. Copyright © 2011 by National Institute on Alcohol Abuse and Alcoholism (NIAAA). Reprinted by permission.

Do No Harm

Sensible Goals for International Drug Policy

PETER REUTER

D rug policy has been an inconvenient issue for the national security apparatus of the United States, whether run by a Democratic or Republican administration. Even after 35 years of some sort of domestic "war on drugs", forcefully articulated by every President since Ronald Reagan, the international dimension of the issue remains distasteful to diplomats. It often involves dealing with law enforcement in corrupt countries and complicates many a U.S. Ambassador's life. The contending lobbies that care about it are loud, moralistic and well informed. If that were not enough, most of our principal allies, particularly in Europe, think there is a certain madness in the American belief that international interventions against the drug trade can accomplish much good.

Mere inconvenience is an insufficient reason to abandon a policy, of course, but in this case there are stronger arguments for change. The Obama Administration has an opportunity before it, for both history and argument show that U.S. international efforts to control drug production and trafficking cannot do much more than affect where and how coca and opium poppies are grown. The quantity produced is minimally affected, since suppression of production in one country almost invariably leads to expansion in another.

More important, control efforts often cause damage. Not only are such programs as spraying poppy and coca fields themselves harmful, but forcing the drug trade to move from one country to another may hurt the new producer country more than it helps the old one. Hence, the U.S. government should no longer push for "global containment", as the policy has been defined. Rather, it should focus attention and resources on supporting the few states both willing and able to do something about production or trafficking in their countries. Unfortunately, Afghanistan, the center of attention right now, is not one of those countries.

American Bull in the China Shop

The United States has been the principal driver of international drug control efforts since 1909, when it convened a meeting of the International Opium Commission (primarily aimed at helping China cut its opium consumption). The United States then pushed for the creation of a web of prohibitionist international treaties under the auspices first of the League of Nations and then the United Nations. Its voice is the dominant one at the annual meetings of the UN Commission on Narcotic Drugs. In that forum it has stood firm against any softening of existing policies. Most prominently, the United States has denounced in recent years "harm reduction" interventions such as needle-distribution programs aimed at reducing the spread of HIV.

Nor does it hesitate to scold even its closest neighbors for deviating from its hard-line, prohibitionist stance. In 2003, U.S. drug czar John Walters accused Canada of poisoning American youth when Ottawa proposed decriminalizing marijuana possession, a policy similar to that of a dozen U.S. states. The United States has even proven willing to barter specific foreign policy interests to influence other nations' drug policies. In the Clinton Administration senior State Department officials told Australia that trade negotiations would be dragged out if Canberra went ahead with a planned experiment in which the most troubled heroin addicts might be supplied with the drug (a program now routine in Switzerland and the Netherlands). Though not a lot of money (by the standards of the overall U.S. drug policy budget) is spent on overseas drug control, Plan Colombia ($5 billion since 2001) is by far the largest U.S. foreign assistance program in Latin America, making Colombia the fourth largest recipient of U.S. aid.

These interventions have real consequences for U.S. foreign policy. Tensions with NATO allies in Afghanistan have been exacerbated by disagreements over how aggressively to act against opium production. Plan Colombia, which funds the civil rights-abusing Colombian military, causes much unease among neighboring countries. From 1986 until 2001, relations with Mexico were roiled by Mexican indignation at the U.S. annual "certification", in which the world's largest drug consumer decided whether its neighbors had done enough to reduce its own importation of drugs.

What these policies and programs seem not to have done is to reduce either the American or the global drug problems. That is not the consequence of badly designed programs or administrative incompetence, though there are plenty of both. Rather, it is a result of the fact that international programs like eradication or interdiction simply cannot make much of a difference because they aim at the wrong part of the problem: production and trafficking in source countries. The right part of the problem to aim at is demand in importing countries, including our own. But, of course, that is a difficult and uncertain task, and even successful programs take a long time to have much effect.[1]

It would not be wise to close up shop altogether. After all, there are some connections between the illicit drug trade and terrorist financing that Americans would be foolish to ignore, and there may occasionally be promising opportunities to help specific countries.

But we should adopt more limited, common sense goals for U.S. international drug policy.

Heroin and Cocaine

Today's mass market in illegal heroin is a new phenomenon. Before 1965, the drug was a niche product and one of declining popularity in the United States. Poppies were refined into opium and mostly consumed in Asia. However, between 1965 and 1995 heroin epidemics erupted in many rich industrialized countries from Australia to Norway. The loosening of social and economic controls in China in the late 1980s and the break-up of the Soviet Union in the early 1990s added a few more countries to the list of those with heroin problems. Iran, Pakistan, Thailand and other traditional opium producers also became heroin-consuming countries, partly as a consequence of Western pressures to crack down on opium distribution. Heroin use can't be found everywhere in the world these days, but it is certainly no longer just a niche problem. So serious is the challenge that there have even been times when the United States, Iran and Russia have quietly made common cause to deal with it.

While heroin use was spreading, heroin production became more concentrated. By the 1980s, Afghanistan and Burma had come to dominate production, accounting for more than 90 percent of the total each year. Since 2002, Afghanistan has been the dominant producer: In 2007, with a new record output, it produced roughly 93 percent of the world total, about 8,000 tons. (Before the Taliban banned opium production in 2000, production had only once exceeded 4,000 tons.)

Why do Afghanistan and Burma dominate? It's not because either is particularly well suited in terms of land or climate. Opium has been produced in many countries; Australia and France are two big producers for the contemporary legal market, while Thailand and Macedonia were major producers in the past. So what accounts for the current situation?

Afghanistan was not historically a large opium producer, but three major events combined to change that. The overthrow of the Shah in 1979 led to the installation of an Iranian regime much more concerned with drugs as a moral issue. The Islamic Republic promptly cracked down on opium production in Iran. Willing to execute producers and growers after only minimal due process, Iran quickly eliminated domestic opium poppy cultivation. However, it was much less successful in reducing demand, and the result was a new market for Afghan exports. This happened at roughly the same time that the Soviet Union invaded Afghanistan, which eroded central government authority and led to the rise of warlords for whom opium production was a major source of income. The civil war that broke out following the exit of the Soviet troops exacerbated the situation and made Afghanistan still more attractive for opium growing and heroin refining.

For Burma the shaping events took place over an even longer period. Those events relate partly to the political history of China. When the Communists took the Chinese Mainland in 1949, some Kuomintang army units retreated south into up-country Burma. Now forced to support themselves, they put their military and organization skills to work in the opium industry. Then, in the 1970s, the Burmese Communist Party, cut off from Chinese government finance as China attempted to improve relationships with its neighbors, turned to the heroin trade as a way to finance its activities. Thus Chinese anti-communists and Burmese communists alike helped raise Burma's heroin production profile—proof of how deeply the drug trade is embedded in larger geopoliti-

cal processes. Drug production cannot be treated as just another industry, responding primarily to economic influences. The Burmese and Afghan cases also illustrate how easily the location of production can shift. There are many corrupt and poor countries available for production if for some reason Afghanistan should cut its production.

Cocaine lacks the global reach of heroin; it's still mostly a rich nation's drug (though, of course, not mostly rich people in those nations use it). What seemed in the 1980s a uniquely American problem has now spread to Europe. Britain and Spain clearly have substantial cocaine problems and others are vulnerable as well. Eastern Europe is also catching up in heretofore Western vices as its productivity and politics approach Western levels.

The production story here is straightforward. Bolivia, Colombia and Peru are the only commercial producers of cocaine for the illegal market. Whereas in the 1980s Colombia was the third most important producer of coca leaves, for the past ten years it has accounted for about two thirds of the total, as well as the vast majority of refining. The shift of coca growing from Peru and Bolivia to Colombia is probably the result both of massive rural flight in Colombia and tougher policies in the other two countries. The violent conflict in Colombia's established rural areas has forced farmers to frontiers within the country where there is little infrastructure for legitimate agriculture, and coca growing is very attractive in part because these areas are difficult to monitor or police. Despite a massive eradication campaign, production levels for the Andes as a whole have been fairly stable over the past decade.

Ties to Terrorism

That U.S. policies over several decades now have not appreciably affected the overall level of heroin and cocaine on the market is a cause for some frustration. One reason it vexes U.S. policymakers is that illegal drugs are funding some terrorist organizations—though it would be counterproductive to exaggerate the extent of this funding. In 2003, the Office of National Drug Control Policy attracted considerable derision with its Super Bowl ads tying drug use to the promotion of international terrorism. Since most U.S. drug use is limited to marijuana, much of it produced domestically or in Canada, the connection seemed flimsy. The ads disappeared quickly.

That said, the problem is not imaginary. Before it banned opium production in 2000, the Taliban taxed it, though no more than it taxed other agricultural products. Since it didn't provide much in the way of government services, the estimated $30 million the Taliban got from opium taxes was the second largest source of revenue, after its taxation of consumer goods smuggled into Pakistan. Al-Qaeda's sources of revenue are a matter of mystery, at least in the unclassified literature, but it certainly has earned some money from trafficking opium or heroin over the years. Nowadays its involvement in protecting (i.e., taxing) opium production in Afghanistan may be an important activity. Secretary of Defense Robert Gates has asserted that al-Qaeda receives $80–100 million annually from the heroin trade. (Like all such figures, this one has no known provenance and should be treated with some skepticism.)

Many other terrorist groups have known ties to drug trafficking. The FARC in Colombia taxes coca growing, the Kurdistan People's Party in Turkey has some connection to drug traffickers among the Kurdish diaspora in Europe, and the Tamil Tigers have been caught smuggling heroin. None of these groups are particularly important in the global drug trade, but the trade may be particularly important to them.

For policymakers the relevant question is whether attacking the drug trade is an efficient method for cutting terrorist finance. Given the fact that there are few successful examples of policies that generate large-scale reductions in drug revenues, the answer is generally no. While there might be specific opportunities in which, say, moving the drug trade from one route to another could help reduce the flow of funds to terrorists, in general these criminal problems are hardly twins joined at the hip. The drug trade is just one of many illegal activities for which terrorist organizations have some useful organizational assets. In short, we would not cripple terrorist financing even if we were successful in international drug policy efforts. But this is merely an academic point, for experience shows us why we cannot be successful.

Cutting Drug Exports

The United States has pushed three types of programs to cut source country production: eradication, alternative development and in-country enforcement. Eradication, usually involving aerial spraying, aims literally to limit the quantity of the drug available in the United States, raise the costs of those drugs, or otherwise discourage farmers from producing them. Alternative development is the soft version of the same basic idea. It encourages farmers growing coca or poppies to switch to legitimate crops by increasing earnings from these other products—for example, by introducing new and more productive strains of traditional crops, better transportation to get the crops to market or some form of marketing scheme. Finally, the United States pushes other countries to pursue traffickers and refiners more vigorously. None of the three methods has worked all that well.

Few countries are willing to allow aerial eradication, which may cause environmental damage. It is also politically unattractive because it targets peasant farmers, who are among the poorest citizens even when growing coca or poppy. Colombia and Mexico, neither one traditional producers of drugs, have been the producer countries most willing to allow spraying. Most others allow only manual eradication, a slow and cumbersome method.

The fundamental problem of source-country interventions aimed at producers of coca and poppy is easily described. These programs have always had a peculiar glamor and occupy a large share of the headlines about drug policy. But the fact that the actual production costs of coca or opium account for a trivial share of the retail price of cocaine or heroin dooms source-country interventions as ways of controlling the problem.

It costs approximately $300 to purchase enough coca leaves to produce a kilogram of cocaine, which retails for about $100,000 in the United States when sold in one-gram, two-thirds pure units for $70 per unit. The modest share of the agricultural costs associated with cocaine production is easily explained: Production involves cheap land and labor in poor countries, and it requires no expensive specialized inputs. (Even Bolivia, the smallest of the three producer countries, has more than 500,000 square miles of territory—much of it opaque to surveillance.) Assume that eradication efforts lead to a doubling of the price of coca leaf, so that cocaine refiners now must pay $600 for enough leaf to produce one kilogram of cocaine. Even if the full cost increase is passed along, the change in retail price will still be negligible. Indeed,

leaf prices have varied enormously over the past decade, while the retail price of cocaine has fallen almost throughout the same period. If retail prices do not rise, then total consumption in the United States will not decline as a consequence of eradication. In this scenario, there will be no reduction in total production—just more land torn up in more places to plant an environmentally damaging crop.

There is, of course, a less harsh option for policy in the source country: alternative development. Offer the farmers the opportunity to earn more money growing pineapples than coca, and they will move to the legal crop, the argument goes.

Quite aside from the time and money it takes to implement a successful alternative-crop program, the argument, alas, is subject to the same economic illogic as that for eradication. It assumes that the price of coca leaf will not increase enough to tempt the peasants back to coca growing. But as long as the price of leaf is so small compared to the street price of cocaine in Chicago, refiners will offer a high enough price to get back the land and labor needed to meet the needs of the cocaine market. Peasants will be better off than before the alternative development, but only because they will make more money growing coca. Mexican peasants are substantially better off than those in Bolivia, but that has not kept them out of the drug business. Indeed, the same can be said for Kentucky corn farmers, who are prominent in the marijuana trade in the United States.

Three Countries, Three Problems

For the United States the international drug problem is dominated by three countries: Afghanistan, Colombia and Mexico. Each presents a different problem, both to the United States and to the producing country. But all three show why the elimination/interdiction approach to source country supply doesn't work.

The United States is trying to create an effective democratic state in Afghanistan and is demonstrably failing. Further, despite the presence of 60,000 NATO and U.S. troops, Afghanistan's output of opium has increased massively over the seven years since the Taliban fell. That has provided important funding for the Taliban and al-Qaeda as well as for warlords independent of the central government. It has also worsened the country's deep-seated corruption. According to the former coordinator of U.S. counter-narcotics efforts in Afghanistan, there was much conflict within the Bush Administration about pursuing aggressive counter-narcotics efforts. Insiders argued over whether these efforts were needed to establish a strong state or, on the contrary, whether they would threaten the very existence of the Karzai government.[2]

The drug hawks have usually won the rhetorical battles, but they have lost the programmatic wars. In October 2008, Defense Secretary Gates declared that the U.S. military will go after traffickers and warlords but will not eradicate farmers' poppy fields. Given the relative invisibility of trafficking, this is effectively a truce. But better a truce than a "war" against poppies that cannot be won and might be counterproductive politically if it were won.

Colombia, unlike Afghanistan, is a principal producer of drugs for the United States, most prominently cocaine but also heroin. The United States has tried to strengthen a Colombian government long beleaguered by guerrilla conflict, and in this it has succeeded reasonably well. But the primary goal of its assistance has been to reduce the flow of Colombian-produced cocaine into the United States, and in that task it has largely failed.

Mexico, occasionally described as a natural smuggling platform for the United States, has been the principal drug transshipment country into the United States for two decades. The bulk of America's imports of cocaine, heroin, marijuana and methamphetamine all come through Mexico. In the past two years the level of violence associated with the U.S.-destined drug trade has skyrocketed. More than 5,000 people were killed in drug-related violence in 2008; that included systematic terror killings of innocent individuals, honest police and reporters. This has happened partly because of changes in the trade itself and partly as a consequence of government efforts to control the violence. The new U.S. program to help Mexico—$400 million for training police and military—may ostensibly be aimed at cutting down the flow of drugs to the United States, but such low levels of funding are not likely to achieve much. The money is more properly viewed as reparations: Mexico is suffering from the consequences of our continued appetite for illegal drugs, so the United States has an obligation to help ameliorate those problems regardless of whether it cuts U.S. drug imports.

Strategic Consequences of the Balloon Effect

There is almost universal skepticism that international efforts by rich countries can reduce global production of cocaine and heroin. It is hard to find anyone outside of the State Department, the White House or Congress who argues otherwise. But efforts to curb production in specific places have had some effect. We noted previously that targeting Bolivian and Peruvian smuggling into Colombia helped make Colombia the dominant producer of coca. The Chinese government since about 1998 has pushed the United Wa State Army to successfully (and brutally) cut Burma's production of heroin. Spraying in Mexico in the 1970s shifted opium production from a five-state region in the north to a much more dispersed set of states around the country.

Interdiction can also affect the routing of the trade. In the early 1980s then-Vice President George H.W. Bush led the South Florida Task Force that successfully reduced smuggling through the Caribbean. The traffic then shifted to Mexico, but the effort did help several Caribbean governments. Similarly, more heroin may now be flowing through Pakistan because the Iranian government has intensified its border control.

In recent years this kind of interaction has been most conspicuous with respect to cocaine trafficking. The Netherlands Antilles is conveniently located for Colombian traffickers shipping to Europe, as there are many direct flights from Curaçao to Amsterdam's Schiphol airport, one of the busiest in Europe. In response to evidence of growing cocaine trafficking to Amsterdam, the Dutch government implemented a 100 percent search policy for airline passengers from Curaçao in March 2004. Whereas cocaine seizures in the Netherlands Antilles had not exceeded 1.3 tons before 2003, in 2004 they reached nine tons, a remarkable figure for a jurisdiction with fewer than 200,000 inhabitants. (The United States seizes only about 150 tons per year.) Shipments through Schiphol airport have since fallen sharply.

Probably as a consequence, new trafficking routes have opened up from South America to Europe via West Africa. For example, Guinea-Bissau is impoverished and small, it has no military or police capacity to deal with smugglers, and its government is easily corrupted. Smugglers have begun using landing strips there for large shipments. In 2007, there was one seizure of three-quarters of a ton, and it is believed that an even larger quantity from that shipment made it out of the country.

Ghana, a larger nation but one with fragile institutions, has also seen a sudden influx of cocaine traffickers. In 2005, flights from Accra accounted for more seized cocaine at London's Heathrow airport than from flights from any other city. There are now regular reports of multi-kilo seizures of the drug either in Ghana itself or at airports receiving flights from Ghana.

Assuming that Ghana and Guinea-Bissau are serving as trafficking platforms at least in part because of the effective crackdown on an existing route through Curaçao, is the world better off? Certainly the Netherlands has helped itself. One can hardly be critical of a country making a strong effort to minimize its involvement in the drug trade. However, one can reasonably ask whether, in making these decisions, the Netherlands should take into account the likely effects of its actions on other, more vulnerable countries.

This analysis also applies to Afghanistan, assuming that it will for the foreseeable future be the most attractive location for opium production. The U.S. government continues to press the Karzai Administration to begin eradication activities in the areas it controls. At the same time, the United States emphasizes the importance of opium production to the Taliban. If farmers in government-controlled areas are forced out of business, it is likely that more of the growing activity, and probably more refining as well, will shift to areas controlled by the Taliban. The result may be to increase Taliban strength, both politically and financially—obviously not a result we would ever intend.

Awkward Choices

International drug policy will not be high on the Obama Administration's list of priorities, given that the U.S. drug problem itself is gradually declining. It has indeed not been a major issue for the Bush Administration. Congress was fairly passive on the issue during the past eight years, but those members who have been vocal have all been drug hawks, passionately arguing that this nation has a moral obligation to fight one of the great scourges of modern times on a worldwide scale. The public is apparently indifferent, seeing the drug problem as one for which every measure (tough enforcement, prevention or more treatment slots) is fairly hopeless. This, in turn, has not encouraged liberal members of Congress to take on the issue.

Drug policy is one of many areas of international policy in which the Obama Administration would benefit from adopting a more humble attitude. The arrogance with which U.S. delegations at the annual Commission on Narcotic Drugs lecture the rest of the world would be laughable if it weren't for the fact that many nations are still cowed by the sheer scale of U.S. efforts. There is no evidence that the United States knows how to help reduce the world's drug problems or to affect the ease with which cocaine, heroin and methamphetamine are procured and trafficked. Moreover, the harm that some of our interventions cause is more apparent than their benefits. For example, spraying coca fields in Colombia clearly has adverse environmental consequences if only because it spreads production further, and it also probably sharpens conflict between the Colombian government and its citizens. Pressing the Karzai government to spray poppy fields increases tensions with our allies. Our attack on drug policy initiatives in other countries exacerbates the U.S. reputation for bullying and disinterestedness in true multilateral collaboration.

Doing less about a problem is rarely an attractive policy recommendation. But for international drug policy it is the only recommendation one can make with confidence. It is perhaps true, as Simone Weil once said, that "it is better to fail than to succeed in doing harm."

Notes

1. See, for example, Jonathan Caulkins and Peter Reuter, "Re-orienting Drug Policy", *Issues in Science and Technology* (Fall 2006); David Boyum and Peter Reuter, *An Analytic Assessment of U.S. Drug Policy* (American Enterprise Institute Press, 2005); and Mark A.R. Kleiman, "Dopey, Boozy, Smoky—and Stupid", *The American Interest* (January/February 2007).

2. Thomas Schweich, "Is Afghanistan a Narco-State?" *New York Times Magazine*, July 27, 2008.

Reference

Reuter, Peter. (2009, March/April). The American Interest: Do No Harm. *Sensible Goads for International Drug Policy,* Vol. IV. No. 4, 46-52.

Critical Thinking

1. Should we continue with our current international drug policy? Why?

2. Some argue that current strategies to counter global drug issues are not working. What suggestions would you make?

PETER REUTER is a professor of public policy and criminology at the University of Maryland. He is co-author (with Letizia Paoli and Victoria Greenfield) of the forthcoming *The World Heroin Market: Can Supply Be Cut?* (Oxford University Press).

Convergence or Divergence? Recent Developments in Drug Policies in Canada and the United States

Clayton J. Mosher

In a recent publication in the Association for Canadian Studies in the United States occasional paper series, Paul Gecelovsky (2007) wrote about marijuana as an "irritant" in Canada–US relations, suggesting that the alleged widespread cultivation of marijuana, particularly in British Columbia, and importation of the product to the US, is becoming a serious issue. Similarly, an article in *Time* magazine referred to the Canada–US cross-border traffic in illegal drugs as "one of the knottiest areas of disagreement between the US and its northern neighbor"[1] (Bergman et al. 2004). Eagles (2006) further notes that legislative proposals to decriminalize possession of small amounts of marijuana by the federal Liberal government in the early 2000s (the bill died with the defeat of Paul Martin's minority government in 2006) and the opening of safe injection sites for heroin addicts in Vancouver "contributed to the popular impression that Canadians were out of step with their more conservative neighbor to the south" (821). However, Eagles (correctly) predicted that "the election of [Stephen] Harper will mark the beginning of a new, less contentious era in Canadian–American relations" (2006, 822).

Drawing on official government data and publications from both Canada and the United States, as well as a variety of media sources, this article presents a comparison of drug laws in the two countries, with a particular focus on recent attempts by US officials to influence Canadian drug policies. Consistent with the themes of the 2010 Enders Symposium, I argue that the United States has much to learn from an examination of some of the more recent harm reduction drug policies that have been adopted in Canada (although it is important to note that, as discussed in more detail below, there are indications that, under the Conservative government of Stephen Harper, Canada is reversing its course on some of these policies). At the same time, Canada can benefit from a detailed consideration of the stringent drug policies adopted in the United States in the last three decades, which have led to significant increases in rates of incarceration and gross racial disparities in the United States' criminal justice system (Alexander 2010; Mosher and Akins 2007). In addition to the fact that drug policies represent

an important component of bilateral relations between the two countries, drug markets are increasingly global, and the United States and Canada are prominent participants (primarily from the demand side) in these global drug markets.

In order to contextualize the discussion that follows, I begin with a brief consideration of drug laws and their consequences (especially with respect to rates of incarceration and racial disparities in sentencing) in the United States. This is followed by a discussion of Canadian drug policies, with a focus on the relaxed stance towards marijuana and more specific harm reduction policies enacted in the 2000s. These developments resulted in reactions on the part of several US officials—in particular then-drug czar John Walters—who openly expressed their concerns. The article concludes with a discussion of recent changes in Canadian drug policies enacted under Harper's conservative government.

Drug laws, crime, and sentencing: United States

The first federal law banning psychoactive substances in the United States was the Harrison Narcotics Act, passed in 1914; marijuana was banned at the federal level in 1937, with the passage of the Marijuana Tax Act (Mosher and Akins 2007). Since that time, there have been a series of "drug wars" in the United States, and drug law enforcement has been a major component of the US criminal justice system.

The most recent drug war in the United States was initiated under the Reagan administration in the 1980s and continued through the 1990s and 2000s. In the last 35 years, there has been a tremendous increase in the number of drug arrests in the US. Adult drug arrests increased from 322,000 in 1970 to 1,663,582 in 2009, and drug arrests comprised more than 12 percent of the total arrests in the US in that year (Federal Bureau of Investigation 2010). Despite the rhetoric on the part of some US government and law enforcement officials that the war on drugs is focused on those who traffic in illegal substances, arrests for possession of drugs were approximately four times higher than arrest for trafficking (Federal Bureau of Investigation 2010). And despite the additional rhetoric that the US drug war is concentrated on "hard" drugs, 858,408 individuals were arrested for marijuana possession in 2009, constituting close to 52 percent of all drug arrests in that year; 92 percent of these arrests were for simple possession of the drug. Although self-report surveys and other measures indicate that marijuana use in the US has remained relatively constant over the last few decades (Mosher and Akins 2007), arrests for marijuana have increased significantly since the late 1980s, while arrests for cocaine and heroin have declined significantly. These data may indicate that the increased focus on marijuana has come at the expense of enforcing laws against hard drugs such as heroin, cocaine, and methamphetamine.

With respect to the sentencing of drug offenders in the Unites States, in 2002 (the most recent year for which such data are available), drug offenders constituted 32 percent of felons convicted in state courts, and of the approximately 340,000 felony drug offense cases in that year, 66 percent resulted in sentences of incarceration. Examined in a different way, in 2001, individuals convicted of drug offenses constituted 20.4 percent of all adults serving time in state prisons and 55 percent of federal prison inmates (Harrison and Beck 2005). Between 1980 and 2001, the number of individuals in state and federal prisons for drug offenses increased by approximately 1300 percent. The United States currently has more people incarcerated for drug offenses than the countries of the European Union have for all offenses combined, despite the fact that the European Union has 100 million more citizens (Wood et al. 2003).

John Walters, who served as "drug czar" under President George W. Bush, tried to silence critics of US marijuana laws through claims that it was a myth that large numbers of Americans had been incarcerated for marijuana offenses. However, in 1999, calculations based on Bureau of Justice Statistics indicate that 59,300 prisoners (3.3 percent of the total incarcerated population in that year) were convicted of violations of marijuana laws. Schlosser (2003) further notes that the number of marijuana offenders sent to federal prisons in 1999 was greater than the number of offenders sent to such prisons for methamphetamine, crack, or powder cocaine offenses, which are supposedly more dangerous drugs. In fact, under California's "Three Strikes and You're Out" law, more people have been sent to prison for possession of marijuana than for all violent offenses *combined*.

An additional important characteristic of US drug laws is their contribution to racial inequality in the criminal justice system (and larger society) (Alexander 2010). It is estimated that of all users of illegal drugs in the United States, 13 percent are African American. However, 38 percent of those arrested, 59 percent of those incarcerated, and fully 75 percent of those incarcerated for drug offenses are African American (Harkavy 2005). It is important to stress that the higher arrest rates for African Americans are *not* the result of higher rates of illegal drug use by blacks—blacks use illegal drugs in roughly the same proportion as whites (Mosher and Akins 2007). Instead, these disparities are the result of law enforcement's emphasis on inner-city areas where drug use and trafficking are more likely to take place in the open, and where African Americans are disproportionately concentrated (Alexander 2010).

These racial disparities in drug law enforcement and sentencing are also a result of the fact that the United States has enacted several laws in the last 30 years which facilitate law enforcement in focusing their efforts in these inner-city areas. The United States has a long history of racist drug (and other) laws (Alexander 2010; Brecher 1972; Musto 1999), but in the current context, the most significant law is the 1986 Federal Anti-Drug Abuse Act, which, among other things, created a distinction between crack and powder cocaine. Under this legislation, a first-time offender convicted of possession of 5.01 grams of crack cocaine was subject to a mandatory minimum penalty of five years imprisonment (Wilkins, Newton, and Steer 1993). For powder cocaine, however, the five-year minimum sentence did not apply until an individual possessed more than 500 grams of the substance. It is important to stress that crack and powder cocaine are essentially the same drugs pharmacologically and have the same effects and consequences (Hatsukami and Fischman 1996). Since this federal law was passed in 1986, close to 90 percent of those prosecuted under the crack cocaine provisions have been African American (Alexander 2010), despite the fact that numerically there are far more white crack users than African American crack users.

While US drug laws over the past three decades have been quite severe and have contributed to unprecedented levels of incarceration and gross racial disparities, there are signs that these laws may soften somewhat under the administration of Barack Obama. Obama admitted to smoking marijuana, and unlike his Democrat predecessor, Bill Clinton, did not include the proviso that he "did not inhale"—in fact, when he was asked if he inhaled marijuana, his response was "that was the point" (as quoted in Seelye 2006). Obama also admitted to "doing a little blow" before entering politics, and in a 2008 with *Rolling Stone* magazine, indicated that he believed in shifting the paradigm with respect to drugs to more of a public health approach. "I would start with criminal, nonviolent, first-time drug offenders. The notion that we are imposing felonies on them or sending them to prison . . . instead of thinking about ways, like drug courts, that can get them back on track in their lives . . . it doesn't make sense" (as quoted in Wenner 2008).

Although not solely the result of Obama's efforts, a sign that the US is moving in the direction of somewhat less stringent drug policies was the passage of the Fair Sentencing Act, which went into effect in July 2010. While still not entirely fair (in that it maintained a distinction between crack and powder cocaine), and although it was not retroactive and therefore did not apply to the tens of thousands of offenders currently imprisoned for violations of the law (Fields 2010), this legislation reduced the disparity in sentences for crack and powder cocaine offenses from 100 to 18 to one (*Los Angeles Times* July 31, 2010) by raising the minimum quantity of crack cocaine necessary to trigger a five-year sentence from five grams to 28.

Some proponents of more liberal drug laws in the US were encouraged when Obama appointed Gil Kerlikowske as his drug czar. Kerlikowske was chief of police in Seattle, Washington, when a ballot initiative required police to make marijuana possession their lowest law enforcement priority. In reaction to an announcement that then-drug czar John Walters would travel to Seattle to discuss drug issues, Kerlikowske noted that while he would be willing to converse with Walters:

> *The one thing that is pretty clear here is that there's a strong recognition that the drug issues and the drug problems are not just a law enforcement or criminal justice problem. . . . Just arresting the same people, putting handcuffs on the same people makes no sense. (as quoted in Pope 2003)*

While there is thus little doubt that Kerlikowske is unlikely to support the stringent stance towards drugs characteristic of his predecessor Walters, and while Kerlikowske seems rhetorically committed to devoting a larger share of the federal government's drug control budget to prevention and treatment, up to this point at least, there appears to be no significant change in the US federal government's approach to drugs. For example, in response to California's 2010 Proposition 19 legalization of marijuana ballot measure (which did not pass), Attorney General Eric Holder stated that the federal government would continue to vigorously enforce marijuana laws (Wood 2010).

At the level of state governments, however, there are indications that crime policies in general, and drug policies in particular, are becoming somewhat more lenient. On average in the US, spending on corrections constitutes approximately 7 percent of state budgets, and several states are spending more on corrections than on higher education (Pew n.d.). In the past decade, a number of states have modified or repealed mandatory minimum sentencing options for drug and other offenses, allowed for earlier parole for offenders, and increased support for alternatives to incarceration such as drug courts.

For example, in 2000, California voters approved Proposition 36—the Substance Abuse and Crime Prevention Act—which mandated that first- or second-time nonviolent drug possession offenders be offered drug treatment instead of incarceration (Appel, Bakces, and Robbins 2004). In 2002, Washington State passed legislation to decrease the amount of time drug offenders were incarcerated and increase substance abuse treatment for such offenders (Washington State Institute for Public Policy 2008). Similarly, in April of 2009, the state of New York, whose 1973 Rockefeller drug laws were among the most severe in the United States, changed its laws to eliminate mandatory prison terms for most drug offenders, reduce sentence length, expand access to drug treatment, and provide for alternatives to incarceration (Sayegh 2010). While these and similar developments in several other states indicate a softening of drug laws, it is important to stress that the changes have been primarily motivated by fiscal concerns related to the costs of incarcerating a large number of individuals, as opposed to a "coddling" of offenders.

Drug laws, crime, and sentencing: Canada

Similar to the United States, Canada has a long history of stringent drug policies with a criminal justice system focus. In fact, Canada's first drug legislation, the Opium and Narcotic Drug Act, was passed in 1908, pre-dating the US Harrison Narcotics Act by six years (Mosher 1999). Similarly, although federal legislation addressing marijuana was not enacted in the US until 1937, Canada added cannabis to its Narcotic Control Act in 1923.

Canada's 1961 revised Narcotic Control Act allowed for a maximum of seven years imprisonment for possession of certain drugs, including marijuana, and life imprisonment for most trafficking offenses (Fischer et al. 2003). While recommendations to decriminalize marijuana were made by the LeDain Commission in 1973 (Canada 1973), the Canadian law dealing with marijuana was not substantially changed until 1996. Under the Controlled Drug and Substances Act passed in that year, individuals found in possession of 30 grams of marijuana or one gram of hashish or less were subject to maximum penalties of a $1000 fine and six months imprisonment for first offenses, with double those amounts for repeat offenders (Fischer et al. 2003).

In 2007, there were over 100,000 "drug incidents" reported by police in Canada, translating to a rate of 305 per 100,000 population, the highest rate in 30 years (Dauvergne 2009). Earlier (in 2003) the rate of drug offenses in Canada declined by 7 percent, largely due to reductions in the number of arrests for cannabis possession offenses. At that time, legislation to decriminalize possession of small amounts of cannabis was introduced in the House of Commons and the constitutionality of marijuana laws was challenged in a number of court decisions. While the proposed legislation did not pass, Dauvergne (2009) suggests that the decrease in arrests may have been related to the lack of clarity surrounding the legal status of cannabis at that time.

Similar to the situation in the United States, the majority (62 percent) of drug arrests in Canada involve cannabis, and of those, three-quarters were for possession (Dauvergne 2009). In fact, the per capita arrest rate for marijuana offenses in Canada is actually higher than in the United States (Fischer et al. 2003). In addition, offenses related to the production of cannabis were eight times higher in 2007 compared to 30 years earlier (Dauvergne 2009). The second largest category of drug offenses in Canada involve cocaine, at approximately 25 percent of all police-reported incidents, with half of those cases involving possession, and half involving trafficking.

It is important to note that there are significant provincial/territorial and city variations in drug incident rates in Canada. The 2007, rates were highest in the Northwest Territories at more than 1000 per 100,000 population; in the same year, British Columbia's rate of 654 per 100,000 was more than double the rate of the province of Saskatchewan (Dauvergne 2009). Although the most recently available data are from 2002, among Canadian census metropolitan areas, the highest rate of drug-related incidents was in Thunder Bay (at 571 per 100,000) followed by the British Columbia cities of Vancouver and Victoria (Statistics Canada 2004). There is also considerable variation across the country with respect to the processing of drug-related incidents by law enforcement authorities. In the year 2000, for example, only 17 percent of all incidents of marijuana possession in the province of British Columbia led to a formal charge, compared to 71 percent in Ontario (Skelton 2001). Finally, there is also variation with respect to law enforcement responses to drug offenses between cities in the same province. Police in Victoria, issue charges against marijuana users they apprehend at a rate that is eight times higher than the rate in Vancouver. Interestingly, despite its reputation as "Vansterdam," police in Vancouver charged only 74 people with possession of marijuana in 1999 (Skelton 2001).

A key difference between Canada and the United States in responding to drug offenses is manifested in sentencing practices. While, as noted above, sentences for drug offenses in the US have been quite severe, in Canada in 2007, 43 percent of all drug-related adult court cases, and 51 percent of all drug-related juvenile cases, were stayed, withdrawn, or dismissed (Dauvergne 2009). Fifty-five percent of adult cases and 48 percent of youth cases resulted in a finding of guilt—44 percent of adults convicted of drug offenses received fines, while 28 percent received sentences of probation. Also for adults, just over half of those convicted of trafficking were sentenced to custody, with an average sentence of 278 days. For adults convicted of possession, 16 percent were sentenced to custody, with an average of 19 days (Dauvergne 2009). Clearly, at the level of sentencing, the US is much more severe in its response to drug offenders.

A move toward harm reduction in Canada

In the early 2000s, there were indications that Canada was moving towards drug policies based on harm reduction principles. In 2002, for example, a special committee of the Canadian Senate recommended the legalization of cannabis possession and use (Canada 2002). Under the model proposed by the Senate committee, cannabis would have been treated similarly to alcohol, with use and access to supply regulated and only specific situations of harm—for example, driving under the influence of marijuana—being subject to criminal penalties. The Senate committee also recommended expunging the criminal records for the roughly 600,000 Canadians previously convicted of marijuana possession.

While not accepting the Senate committee's recommendation to legalize marijuana, the Canadian federal government proposed legislation in 2003 that mandated a maximum $400 fine for adults and $250 for individuals under the age of 18 for possession of 15 grams or less of marijuana (Russo 2004). In reference to the proposed changes in cannabis laws, then-Prime Minister Jean Chretien told a reporter from the *Winnipeg Free Press,* "I don't know what is [*sic*] marijuana. Perhaps I will try it when it will no longer be criminal. I will have my money in one hand and a joint in the other hand" (as quoted in

Drug Policy Alliance 2003). Although the proposed law was not passed before Chretien resigned from the leadership of the Liberal Party, incoming Prime Minister Paul Martin indicated his intention to change the marijuana laws when he commented that it achieves "absolutely nothing to give a criminal record to young people caught with small amounts [of marijuana]" (as quoted in J. Brown 2003). Dana Hanson, President of the Canadian Medical Association, similarly agreed that those caught with marijuana should not be subject to terms of incarceration or criminal records (Smith 2002). And, in a case that overturned a lower court conviction for a marijuana growing operation, British Columbia Court of Appeal Justice Mary Southin commented, "In my years on the bench. I have sat on over 40 cases which had something to do with this substance [marijuana] which appears to be of no greater danger to society than alcohol." She further noted that marijuana laws made "criminals of those who are no better or worse, morally or physically, than people who like a martini" (as quoted in Hall 2003). Even the conservative *National Post* newspaper recommended the "full legalization" of marijuana:

> It makes little sense to criminalize otherwise law-abiding Canadians simply because they indulge in a substance that is less dangerous or addictive than either alcohol or tobacco. The idea that smoking marijuana should be the subject of social opprobrium has become a joke. ("Ending Reefer Madness" 2004)

More recently, a report published by the conservative Fraser Institute (Easton 2004) examining marijuana growing operations in British Columbia recommended the legalization of marijuana. Going further, a report by the British Columbia Progress Board, examining crime and the operations of the criminal justice system in BC, recommended that the province "Lobby the federal government to legalize the drug trade, perhaps limiting access to the products to adults in the same way that tobacco and alcohol is limited, and in the same vein, treating drug addictions as health rather than criminal justice problems" (Gordon and Kinney 2006).

With respect to the related issue of medical marijuana, regulations that came into effect in Canada in 2001 allowed certain individuals with chronic or terminal illnesses to apply for federal government permission to use the substance. Included in the list of those allowed to apply to use medical marijuana were people who were determined by medical authorities to have less than one year to live and those suffering from AIDS, cancer, multiple sclerosis, spinal cord injuries, and severe arthritis or epilepsy, among other conditions (Kennedy 2002). In addition, in March of 2002, the Canadian government announced plans to make government-certified medical marijuana available in pharmacies ("Canada plans" 2004), making Canada only the second country in the world (after the Netherlands) to enact such legislation. Canada also followed a number of European countries in the late 1990s in legalizing hemp production, allowing approximately 250 farmers to grow close to 6000 acres of the substance. Despite the fact that hemp has a very low THC content, and, as an agricultural economist from

North Dakota noted, "you'd croak from inhalation before you'd get high on hemp" (as quoted in Cauchon 1998), then-US drug czar Barry McCaffrey asserted that the move to grow hemp in Canada was a "subterfuge" for attempts to legalize marijuana.

There were also indications in the early 2000s that in some jurisdictions at least, marijuana had been de facto decriminalized in Canada. For example, between 2002 and 2005, the city of Vancouver was home to three marijuana cafes, including establishments named "Blount Brothers," and "New Amsterdam" (Mackie 2003), both of which were located in the downtown core of the city. Although the proprietors of these establishments claimed that they only sold marijuana seeds (as opposed to prepared marijuana), the "Da Kine Smoke and Beverage Shop" apparently was filling gram bags of marijuana from "football sized bags of marijuana" and doing "about $30,000 [in marijuana sales] a day" (Hainsworth 2004). And in 2004, Vancouver achieved what some might see as a dubious distinction when it was chosen by *High Times* magazine as the best place in the world for marijuana smokers to visit, surpassing even Amsterdam (Matas 2002a). Similarly, in Winnipeg, Manitoba, a "cannabis church cafe" was opened in 2002 in one of the busiest sections of the city. The purpose of this establishment was allegedly to "worship" cannabis—individuals who frequented it would be allowed to smoke marijuana as a religious sacrament (Foss 2002). Although perhaps overstated, the *New York Times* noted "pot smoking is pervasive in Canada, especially in British Columbia. . . . Marijuana is so prevalent in Vancouver that the city has been compared to Amsterdam as a pot smoker's paradise" ("There's a funny smell" 2002). And as a result of the country's comparative tolerance of marijuana, Canada also attracted a number of "pot refugees"—by some counts, there were more than 100 expatriate US citizens who sought asylum in Canada from the US war on drugs (Campbell 2002).

In addition to the developments with marijuana discussed above, some Canadian jurisdictions have adopted harm reduction policies in order to address problems related to intravenous drug use. Vancouver has an estimated 12,000 intravenous drug users in population of 1.3 million, and more than 4500 of these live in a 12-block section of the city known as the Downtown Eastside. This area has a drug overdose rate that is five times higher than any other Canadian city and the highest HIV infection rate of any jurisdiction in the Western world. More than 1000 drug users died in this area over the course of a decade, with 416 overdose deaths in 1998 alone (Glionna 2003). In response to this situation, beginning with Mayor Philip Owen in the late 1990s and continuing with Mayor Larry Campbell, a former Royal Canadian Mounted Police drug squad officer, Vancouver implemented a "four pillars" approach to drug issues—focusing on treatment, prevention, enforcement, and harm reduction—and established a safe injection facility (known as "Insite") for intravenous drug users (Mulgrew 2007).

An evaluation of this facility's first year of operation found that there were approximately 600 visits a day, and although there were more than 1000 overdose cases, none were fatal. The study found that the site led to reductions in the number of people injecting drugs in public in the downtown eastside of Vancouver, as well as fewer discarded syringes and less injection-related litter in the area (British Columbia Center for Excellence in HIV/AIDS 2004; see also Wood et al. 2007). Participation in Vancouver's safe injection facility was also associated with a 30 percent increase of entry into drug detoxification programs (Strathdee and Pollini 2007) and a study published in the *Canadian Medical Association Journal* estimated that Insite would save the province of British Columbia $14 million and prevent 1000 HIV infections over a 10-year period (Bayoumi and Zaric 2008). Boyd et al. (2008) conclude:

> *In sum, there is no compelling evidence to suggest that Insite has had a negative impact on public order, and, more specifically, there is no evidence to suggest that Insite has had any significant impact on the spatial distribution of criminal activity within the neighborhood. There is clear evidence, however, that a clear majority of our sample of people who live and/or work in the neighborhood view Insite as making a positive contribution to public order. (viii)*

In addition to the Vancouver safe injection site, a special Canadian House of Commons committee on drug issues supported the creation of federally approved safe injection sites for hardcore users of heroin or cocaine, the expansion of methadone maintenance, and needle exchange programs (MacCharles 2002). In response to the recommendations of this House of Commons report, Canada initiated a heroin maintenance study in 2003, the first to be implemented in North America. Under this program, which was to be launched in the major metropolitan cities of Vancouver, Toronto, and Montreal, 70 heroin addicts in each city would receive free heroin and would be able to inject the drug up to three times per day at a drug treatment center. Addicts would also receive counseling at the end of the first year and were to be weaned off heroin or offered methadone withdrawal and counseling for an additional year (Carey 2003). In addition, in 2005, the city of Toronto passed a measure that allowed for crack cocaine users to be given pipes and proposed a study to determine whether sites where addicts could use drugs should be set up in the city (Spears 2005).

While the policies described above thus signal a move toward harm reduction policies, it is important to note that there was by no means a consensus in Canada with respect to these policies. The head of the Canadian Police Association referred to the Canadian Senate committee's report recommending the legalization of marijuana as a "back to school gift for drug pushers" (as quoted in Lunman 2002), and the Canadian Council of Chief Executives, representing 150 multinational companies, expressed concern that marijuana decriminalization would increase on-the-job injuries, absenteeism, and lead to poor job performance (Fife 2004). Similarly, Randy White, a member of the (now defunct) right-wing Canadian Alliance Party, who served on the House of Commons committee on drug issues, referred to that committee's harm reduction proposals as "harm extension" (MacCharles 2002). More specifically, White, who was part of the committee that visited drug injection facilities in European cities, commented, "There was no checking of the quality of the drugs used. Surrounding the facilities, I saw human carnage for blocks, as well as a substantial gathering of addicts and pushers in areas where trafficking and using were reluctantly permitted" (as quoted in Benzie and Hume 2002).

United States' reaction to Canadian drug policy developments

While internal dissent over Canada's recent drug policies is to be expected, an arguably more disturbing development has been evidenced in numerous commentaries by US government officials regarding these policies. Historically speaking, Canada and the US have agreed more than disagreed on drug-related policies—as Giffin et al. (1991, as cited in Thomas 2003) comment, "Close cooperation between Canada and the United States on drug control is necessitated to some degree by their long border, but there is also evidence that their relationship on this issue is based as much on political objectives as on functional necessity."

But in recent years, there have been direct attempts on the part of US officials to influence Canadian drug policies. Of particular concern on the part of these US officials has been the alleged increased exports of Canadian marijuana, including "BC Bud," "Quebec Gold," and "Winnipeg Wheelchair," (the latter so-named because of its reported debilitating effects on users) to the United States (Nickerson 2003). Referring to (unsubstantiated) US Drug Enforcement Administration estimates indicating that "BC Bud" had 25 percent THC content, drug czar Walters asserted, "Canada is exporting to us the crack of marijuana" (as quoted in Bergman et al. 2004).

In an interview on the "Canada AM" morning news program, Walters reiterated many of the myths (see Zimmer and Morgan 1997) in criticizing Canada's marijuana policies:

> There is no question that marijuana is a dependency-producing substance today. Some people seem to be living with the view of the reefer madness '70s. The issue for the US is that Canada has become a major supplier of certain drugs. We're worried about the common health of our citizens.... We have major supply coming in from Canada that's growing and we need to get on top of it. (as quoted in Lunman and McCarthy 2002)

Similarly, in a visit to Vancouver, Walters claimed that marijuana posed a greater danger to the United States than heroin, cocaine, or amphetamines, and argued that allowing the use of marijuana for medical purposes was not supported by science (Matas 2002b). He also asserted, "We know that marijuana is a harmful drug, particularly for young people. We also know that if you make more available, you'll get more use. More use leads to more addiction and more problems" (as quoted in D. Brown 2002). In reference to the proposals to reduce penalties for marijuana possession, Walters claimed (without providing any supporting evidence), "No country anywhere has reduced penalties without getting more drug addiction and trafficking

and the consequences of all that" (as quoted in Kraus 2003). Going further, although he had earlier emphasized that "Canada is a sovereign nation, of course" (as quoted in D. Brown 2002), in reference to the previously mentioned "marijuana refugees" who had moved to Canada from the United States, Walters said, "If Canada wants to become the locus of that kind of activity, they're likely to pay a price" (as quoted in Bailey 2003). In addition to Walters' threats, the Chairman of the United States Congressional Drug Policy Committee warned that the decriminalization of marijuana in Canada would lead the US to tighten border controls, thereby disrupting trade between the two countries (Clark 2002). Similarly, the US ambassador to Canada, Paul Celluci, cautioned that young people trying to enter the US from Canada would become the targets of increased scrutiny by border officials if the country did not dispel the perception that it was relaxing the penalties for marijuana use (Russo 2004).

Shortly after the Canadian Senate committee issued its discussion paper on cannabis, one of the top US advisors on drug policy, Colonel Robert Maginnis, interviewed by a Canadian reporter, commented that the US was planning "[t]o antagonize government leaders and grass roots leaders [in Canada] because you insist on having a radical drug policy that we will not ignore in the long term, then it is going to have adverse consequences and I hope we would be able to rectify it before it comes to blows" (as quoted in Thomas 2003, 33).

Not to be outdone, in a 2007 interview on MSNBC's "Tucker Carlson Show," Congressman Mark Souder, the ranking Republican on the House of Representatives subcommittee responsible for federal drug policy, claimed that smoking marijuana was not much different from smoking crack cocaine. When asked by Carlson why the US federal government was directing its efforts towards marijuana rather than more dangerous drugs, Souder responded:

> The content of BC Bud, Quebec Gold and this marijuana that's currently on the streets isn't like the Cheech and Chong marijuana. It's more like cocaine. In other words, the THC of the ditchweed and what was happening when I was in college in the late '60s and early '70s had a THC content of four to eight percent, maybe as high as 12. Now we're looking at 20, 30, 40 percent. And the kick and the addiction you get, the destruction in your brain cells, is more like coke or crack than it is like the old time marijuana. (as quoted in Piper 2007)

In the same interview, Souder also asserted that most marijuana users were polydrug users, and that there were several thousand deaths associated with marijuana use in any given year, both of which are gross distortions of the truth.

Walters' and others' claims regarding Canadian marijuana being imported to the US need to be considered in light of actual data—it is notable that estimates suggest that no more than 5 percent of the marijuana consumed in the United States is produced in Canada (Sabbag 2005). In 2002, the US Customs Service seized more than 867,000 pounds of marijuana entering the country from Mexico. In the same year, approximately

22,000 pounds of marijuana entering the country from Canada were seized. While it is certainly true that differences in enforcement emphasis and the relative success of customs officials in seizing drugs on the two borders must be taken into account, it seems unlikely that these factors alone would explain the 40:1 ratio of Mexican to Canadian marijuana intercepted at the respective borders.

Walters is also apparently less concerned about the widespread cultivation of marijuana in states such as California, where cannabis was estimated to be the state's most lucrative cash crop with a value of $1.4 billion in the early 1990s—almost twice the value of the next most lucrative crop—cotton (Pollan 1997). Richard Cowan, the editor and publisher of marijuananews.com commented, "They grow more pot in California than in all of Canada" (as quoted in Sabbag 2005). Walters' musings about Canada's proposed relaxed penalties for marijuana possession also seem rather curious in light of the fact that 11 states in the US have virtually eliminated all criminal penalties associated with possession and use of the substance (MacCoun and Reuter 2001).

In the summer of 2005, Walters was also influential in the arrest (and request for extradition to the United States) of Marc Emery, who operated a marijuana seed and shipping business (and the previously mentioned Blount Brothers café) in Vancouver. Emery, who listed his occupation as "marijuana seed vendor," and who also broadcast "Pot TV" on the Internet, had been arrested at least 21 times for marijuana-related offenses in Canada but was usually penalized only with small fines or short jail sentences (Struck 2006). However, Emery and two of his employees were eventually indicted by a Seattle-based grand jury on drug and money laundering charges. There were indications that Walters' actions might have been motivated by a previous interaction with Emery—while delivering a speech in Vancouver criticizing Canada's drug laws, Walters was subjected to taunts and heckling from Emery and other marijuana activists. Emery noted, "He [Walters] just had a total slow burn. . . . I'm sure I've never been forgiven for that" (as quoted in Lewis 2005). However, Karen Tandy of the US Drug Enforcement Administration emphasized larger goals in commenting on Emery's arrest:

> Today's arrest of Marc Scott Emery, publisher of Cannabis Culture magazine and the founder of a marijuana legalization group, is a significant blow not only to the marijuana trafficking trade in the US and Canada, but also to the marijuana legalization movement . . . hundreds of thousands of Emery's illicit profits are known to have been channeled to marijuana legalization groups active in the US and Canada. (as quoted in Lewis 2005)

One Canadian commentator claimed that the Emery case "mocks our independence as a country. . . . Canadian police grew so frustrated that neither prosecutors nor the courts would lock up Emery and throw away the key, they urged their US counterparts to do the dirty work" (Mulgrew 2008). The same commentator added, "If Emery has been breaking the law and must be jailed, our Justice Department should charge him and

prosecute him in Canada. It's time for [Justice Minister] Rob Nicholson to step in and say, sorry, Uncle Sam, not today, not ever." The US Attorney who prosecuted the Emery case claimed that Emery was "adding fuel to the fire" of the "growing problem of violence surrounding marijuana grow [operations]," (as quoted in Inwood 2010) and he was eventually sentenced to five years in prison by Seattle District Court judge Ricardo Martinez.

In addition to criticizing Canada's proposed marijuana policies and blaming the country for importation of marijuana to the US, Walters also referred to the above-mentioned safe injection site[2] for intravenous drug users in Vancouver as "state sponsored suicide" (Novack 2003). He further argued:

> The very name is a lie. There are no safe injection sites. It is reprehensible to allow people and encourage people to continue suffering. That is why we [the United States] don't make this choice and I don't believe we ever will. (as quoted in D. Brown 2003)

Walters' comments prompted then-Vancouver Mayor Larry Campbell to retort: "I think all you have to do is look at your [United States] prison system and your law enforcement to see if the drug war is being won in the States. It's an unmitigated disaster and they know it, but they can't back out of it" (as quoted in Novack 2003).

Walters and the US Drug Enforcement Administration have also criticized Canada for being a primary source of ephedrine, used to manufacture methamphetamine. A 2003 US report listed Canada and the Netherlands among a group of countries identified as "offenders" in the international drug trade, the former largely for failing to control its exports of pseudoephedrine (Koring and Sallot 2003). While it is certainly true that ephedrine has been imported to the US from Canada, this criticism also seems to be somewhat misplaced. A former agent with the Canadian Security Intelligence Service commented:

> The US has been trying to make us a scapegoat for a long time. As far as I'm concerned, it's just a big political game. They're trying to pass the buck, but the fact is, it stops with them. Now it's drugs. Before, they accused us of bringing in terrorists. And that was bogus too. The September 11 hijackers didn't come through Canada. They came through the front door. (as quoted in Koring and Sallot 2003)

Recent developments in Canadian drug legislation under the Harper Government

Stephen Harper's federal Conservative Party obtained a minority victory in the 2006 Canadian federal election and was re-elected with a stronger minority in 2008.[3] Harper, a former member of the right-wing Reform Party, and former president of the National Citizens' coalition, an organization that one commentator referred to as "the most virulently right-wing and anti-government organization in the country" (Dobbin 2006), has taken a hard line on crime policies in general and drug policies in particular. An article in *The Economist* (2009) noted that one-third of the bills introduced in the Canadian House of Commons in 2009 dealt with some aspect of the criminal justice system; a later article in *Maclean's* titled "Jailhouse Nation," (2010) outlined the changes in Canadian crime policies under Harper. In 2008, the "Tackling Violent Crime" bill came into effect, which, among other things, mandated longer sentences for gun-related crimes, and an increased use of indefinite sentences for repeat violent or sexual offenders; the "Truth in Sentencing" Act eliminated a provision whereby prisoners received a two-for-one credit for time they served prior to being convicted.

With respect to drug policies, Bill C-26 imposed mandatory minimum sentences for growing marijuana, and included "aggravating factors" such as if the offense was committed at or near a school, that would increase sentences in drug-related cases (Mulgrew 2007). The bill also reduced funding for the previously mentioned harm reduction programs. With respect to the supervised injection site, Prime Minister Harper stated, "If you remain a drug addict, I don't care how much harm you reduce, you are going to have a short and miserable life" (as quoted in Hunter 2009). Former Federal Health Minister Tony Clement hinted that the federal government would discontinue the site, asking the question:

> Do safe injection sites contribute to lowering drug abuse and fighting addiction? Right now the only thing the research to date has proven conclusively is that drug addicts need more help to get off drugs. . . . given the need for more facts, I am unable to approve the current request to extend the Vancouver site for another three and a half years. (as quoted in Garmaise 2006)

But as Garmaise (2006) pointed out, the primary purpose of the safe injection facility was never to get people to stop using drugs—instead, it was designed to reduce the harms from injection drug use by reducing public disorder, overdoses, deaths, emergency room visits, and needle sharing. The research reviewed above suggests that Insite has been fairly successful with respect to these measures.

In November of 2007, the Harper government proposed changes to the Controlled Substances Act which would: (1) allow for a one-year mandatory minimum sentence for drug trafficking if a weapon or violence was involved; (2) provide a two-year mandatory minimum sentence for dealing hard drugs (cocaine, heroin, or methamphetamines) near a school or in other areas frequented by young people; (3) enact a two-year minimum penalty for marijuana grow operations of more than 500 plants; and (4) increase the maximum penalty for marijuana cultivation from seven to 14 years (Fitzpatrick and Foot 2007).

After a "Senate and Commons tug of war" in 2010, the Senate finally passed a drug sentencing bill that provided mandatory six-month terms of incarceration for growing five or more marijuana plants with intent to sell, and one-year sentences if marijuana trafficking was linked to organized crime or weapons (Tibbetts 2010). This theme of getting tougher on drug crimes

was further emphasized in the Harper government's 2010 "National Drug Strategy" (Canada 2010), which potentially provided close to an additional $170 million over a five-year period for law enforcement efforts to "help locate, investigate, and shut down organizations involved in the production and distribution of illicit drugs." In comparison, the new drug strategy would devote only $30 million in new funding to drug prevention efforts and $100 million for drug treatment over the same five-year period. The policies enacted, and attitudes towards drug problems expressed, by the Harper government signal a retreat from the harm reduction principles established in the early 2000s.

These "get tough on drug" strategies on the part of the Harper government need to be considered in the context of the attitudes of the Canadian public towards drug issues. While the government's stance on mandatory sentences for large-scale drug dealers was supported by the majority surveyed, 57 percent of Canadians believed it would be wrong to eliminate harm reduction programs (the percentage opposed in British Columbia was 64 percent) and 53 percent supported the legalization of marijuana (AngusReidStrategies 2008).

Conclusion

From the 1980s to the mid-2000s, US and Canadian drug policies appeared to be changing in opposite directions. Over this period, the United States enacted several laws that facilitated law enforcement officials in making large numbers of drug arrests and provided mandatory minimum sentences for drug-related offenses. These policies contributed to unprecedented levels of incarceration in the US and gross racial disparities in the criminal justice system. In Canada over the same period, relaxed stances towards marijuana and the implementation of harm reduction policies seemed to portend a move away from the "drug war mentality of our closest neighbor" and toward the "harm reduction focus of some European states" (MacRae 2003, 67). However, US government officials did not view these developments favorably and openly expressed their concern.

Given the recent changes in Canadian drug policies under the Harper administration and the apparent softening of US drug policies under the Obama administration, Thomas (2003) comment that "[t]he historical congruence between US and Canadian drug control policies seems to be breaking down" (32) seems rather prescient. Of course, Thomas was correct—but for the wrong reason—these comments were made in the context of indications that Canada's drug policies were becoming less severe, while US policies were becoming more severe. While it is impossible to predict the future directions of drug policies in the two countries, in the current context it appears that US policies are becoming less severe while Canadian policies become more severe.

Notes

1. Although not addressed in this article, another controversial aspect of the cross-border traffic in drugs involves Americans purchasing reduced price generic and prescription drugs, either through physically crossing the border, or though electronic

purchase via Canadian-based Internet pharmacies (Coates 2006; Mosher and Akins 2007).

2. The United States has maintained a ban on federal funding for safe injection sites for nearly two decades, and for a short time in 1988, even prohibited the use of federal funds to evaluate needle exchange programs (Strathdee and Pollini 2007).

3. With the election of the majority Conservative government in the summer of 2011, it is likely that much of the proposed crime and drug legislation will pass.

References

Alexander, M. 2010. *The New Jim Crow.* New York: The New Press.

AngusReidStrategies. May 12, 2008. "Canadians want federal government to retain harm reduction programs." Retrieved December 18, 2010, from www.angus-reid.com.

Appel, J., G. Bakces and J. Robbins. 2004. "California's Proposition 36: A success ripe for refinement and replication." *Criminology and Public Policy,* 4, 1001–9.

Bailey, E. February 2, 2003. "The drug war refugees." *Los Angeles Times.* Retrieved from www.latimes.com.

Bayoumi, A., and G. Zaric. 2008. "The cost effectiveness of Vancouver's supervised injection facility." *Canadian Medical Association Journal* 179, 1143–51.

Benzie, R., and M. Hume. December 10, 2002. "Clement vows to block drug injection sites." *National Post.* Retrieved from www.canada.com/nationalpost.

Bergman, B., L. Blue, C. Daniels, D. Jones, and E. Shannon. August 23, 2004. "This bud's for the US" *Time.*

Boyd, N., B. Kinney, C. McLean, J. Heidt, and I. Otter. 2008. *Final Report: Public Order and Supervised Injection Facilities:* Vancouver's SIS.

Brecher, E. 1972. *Licit and Illicit Drugs.* Boston: Little, Brown.

British Columbia Center for Excellence in HIV/AIDS. 2004. *Evaluation of the supervised injection site.* Vancouver, BC: Author.

Brown, D. September 5, 2002. "Canadian panel backs legalizing marijuana." *Washington Post.* Retrieved from www.washingtonpost.com.

Brown, D. August 2, 2003. "With injection sites, Canadian drug policy seeks a fix." *Washington Post.* Retrieved from www.washingtonpost.com.

Brown, J. December 18, 2003. "Martin to roll out his own pot bill." *Canadian Press.* Retrieved from www.cp.org.

Campbell, D. July, 20, 2002. "US cannabis refugees cross border." *Guardian.* Retrieved from www.guardian.co.uk.

Canada. 1973. *Commission of inquiry into the non-medical use of drugs.* Ottawa: Queen's Printer.

Canada. 2002. *Report of the senate special committee on illegal drugs.* Ottawa: Queen's Printer.

Canada. 2010. *National Anti-Drug Strategy.* Retrieved October 20, 2010, from www.nationaldrugstrategy.gc.ca.

(no author?) "Canada plans to offer medical marijuana in B.C. pharmacies, but move won't heal government pot program's woes, activist says." March 26, 2004. *Drug War Chronicle.* Retrieved March 26, 2004, from www.stopthedrugwar.org.

Carey, E. October 22, 2003. "Heroin addicts to get drug for free." *Toronto Star.* Retrieved from www.thestar.com.

Cauchon, D. October 7, 1998. "Canadian hemp isn't going to pot." *USA Today.* Retrieved from www.usatoday.com.

Cauchon, D. April 13, 1999. "Zero tolerance policy lacks flexibility." *USA Today.* Retrieved April 13, 2009, from: www.usatoday.com.

Clark, C. October 2, 2002. "US warns against liberalizing laws on pot." *Globe and Mail.* Retrieved from www.theglobeandmail.com.

Coates, K. 2006. "Convergence and Divergence in the Canadian and American West." in K. Froschauer, N. Fabbi, and S. Pell (eds.) *Convergence and Divergence in North America: Canada and the United States.* Burnaby, BC: Center for Canadian Studies, Simon Fraser University, 39–43.

Dauvergne, M. 2009. *Trends in Police-reported Drug Offenses in Canada.* Ottawa: Statistics Canada.

Dobbin, M. 2006. "Will the real Stephen Harper please stand up?" Retrieved October 15, 2007, from www.canadians.org/wordwarriors/2006-jan-10.html.

Drug Policy Alliance. October 3, 2003. "Chretien waiting to inhale." Retrieved from www.drugpolicy.org

Eagles, M. 2006. "Canadian-American relations in a turbulent era." *Political Science and Politics,* 37, 821–24.

Easton, S. 2004. *Marijuana Growth in B.C.* Fraser Institute. Retrieved August 15, 2004, from www.fraserinstitute.org.

The Economist. May 28, 2009. "British Columbia or Colombia?" Retrieved June 15, 2009, from www.economist.com.

Ending Reefer Madness. August 13, 2004. *National Post.* Retrieved from www.canada.com/nationalpost.

Federal Bureau of Investigation. 2010. *Crime in the United States.* Washington, D.C.: US Department of Justice.

Fields, G. December 22, 2010. "Crack sentences still tough." *Wall Street Journal.* Retrieved from online.wsj.com.

Fife, R. November 22, 2004. "CEOs fear reefer madness." *National Post.* Retrieved from www.canada.com/nationalpost

Fischer, B., K. Ala-Leppilampi, E. Single, and A. Robins. 2003. "Cannabis law reform in Canada: Is the 'saga of promise and retreat' coming to an end?" *Canadian Journal of Criminology and Criminal Justice,* 45, 265–98.

Fitzpatrick, M., and R. Foot. November 20, 2007. "New legislation would impose minimum sentences for drug crimes." *Vancouver Sun.* Retrieved from www.canada.com.

Foss, K. March 30, 2002. "Holy smoke: Cannabis church café set to open." *Globe and Mail.* Retrieved from www.theglobeandmail.com.

Garmaise, D. 2006. "Supervised injection facility granted limited-time extension." *HIV/AIDS Policy Law Review,* 11, 21–23.

Gecelovsky, P. 2007. "Canadian cannabis: Marijuana as an irritant/problem in Canada–US relations." *ACSUS Occasional Papers Series* 1,1. Retrieved August 15, 2007, from www.acsus.org/public/pdfs.

Glionna, J. June 1, 2003. "Light and darkness in Canada." *Los Angeles Times.* Retrieved from www.latimes.com.

Gordon, R., and J. Kinney, J. 2006. *Reducing crime and improving criminal justice in British Columbia: Recommendations for change.* BC Progress Board. Retrieved January 15, 2007, from www.bcprogressboard.com.

Hainsworth, J. September 10, 2004. "Café continues to sell pot after raid." *Vancouver Sun.* Retrieved from www.vancouversun.com.

Hall, N. June 21, 2003. "Pot growers no worse than martini drinkers, judge says." *Vancouver Sun.* Retrieved from www.vancouversun.com.

Harkavy, W. January 4, 2005. "The numbers behind the bling." *The Village Voice.* Retrieved from www.villagevoice.com.

Harrison, P., and A. Beck. 2005. *Prisoners in the United States.* Washington, DC: US Department of Justice.

Hatsukami D., and M. Fischman. 1996. "Crack cocaine and cocaine hydrochloride. Are the differences myth or reality?" *Journal of the American Medical Association, 276,* 1580–8.

Hunter, J. June 1, 2009. "Trial to give free heroin to hard core addicts." *Globe and Mail.* Retrieved from www.theglobeandmail.com.

Inwood, D. September 18, 2010. "'Prince of pot' Marc Emery sentenced to 5 years in prison by US judge." *Vancouver Province.* Retrieved from www.theprovince.com.

Kennedy, M. May 8, 2002. "Medical marijuana is bad weed." *Saskatoon Star Phoenix.* Retrieved from www.canada.com/saskatoonstarphoenix.

Kennedy, P. August 1, 2005. Pot activist is scared, fiancée says. *Globe and Mail.* Retrieved from www.theglobeandmail.com.

Koring, P., and J. Sallott. January 31, 2003. "US faults Canada for letting drugs across border." *Globe and Mail.* Retrieved January 31, 2003, from www.theglobeandmail.com.

Kraus, C. May 18, 2003. Canada parts with US on drug policies. *New York Times.* Retrieved from www.nytimes.com.

Lewis, P. October 25, 2005. "B.C.'s 'prince of pot' fights extradition." *Seattle Times.* Retrieved, from www.seattletimes.com.

Los Angeles Times. July 31, 2010. "The fair sentencing act of 2010: It's about time." Retrieved October 15, 2010, from www.latimes.com.

Lunman, K. September 5, 2002. "Senators want pot legalized." *Globe and Mail.* Retrieved from www.theglobeandmail.com.

Lunman, K., and S. McCarthy. December 9, 2002. "Drug czar talks about tightening border." *Globe and Mail.* Retrieved, from www.theglobeandmail.com.

MacCharles, T. December 9, 2002. "Safe sites urged for hard drug users." *Toronto Star.* Retrieved from www.thestar.com.

Maclean's. September 7, 2010. "Jailhouse nation." Retrieved October 15, 2010, from www2.macleans.ca.

MacCoun, R., and P. Reuter. 2001. *Drug War Heresies.* Cambridge, UK: Cambridge University Press.

Mackie, J. January 21, 2003. "B.C.—A pot friendly, pot-profitable province." *Vancouver Sun.* Retrieved from www.vancouversun.com.

MacRae, B. 2003. "Drug Policy in Canada: War if necessary but not necessarily war." *Perspectives on Canadian Drug Policy, Volume I.* John Howard Society, 43–76.

Matas, R. June 29, 2002a. "Magazine picks Vancouver as pot lover's paradise." *Globe and Mail.* Retrieved from www.theglobeandmail.com.

Matas, R. November 22, 2002b. "Stop marijuana trade, US drug czar urges." *Globe and Mail.* Retrieved November 22, 2002, from www.theglobeandmail.com.

Mosher, C. 1999. "Imperialism, Irrationality, and Illegality—The first 90 years of Canadian drug policy." *New Scholars/New Visions in Canadian Studies,* 3(3), 1–40.

Mosher, C., and S. Akins. 2007. *Drugs and Drug Policy—The Control of Consciousness Alteration.* Thousand Oaks, CA: Sage Publications.

Mulgrew, I. October 10, 2007. "City drug policy at odds with Harper's announced plans." *Vancouver Sun.* Retrieved from www.canada.com.

Mulgrew, I. January 14, 2008. "Marc Emery agrees to five years in Canadian prison." *Vancouver Sun.* Retrieved from www.vancouversun.com.

Musto, D. 1999. *The American Disease.* New Haven, CT: Yale University Press.

Nickerson, C. May 10, 2003. "Ottawa's marijuana plan irks US." *Boston Globe.* Retrieved from www.boston.com.

Novack, K. July 7, 2003. "Shooting up legally up north." *Time.* Retrieved July 8, 2003, from www.time.com.

Pew. (n.d.) *Public Safety Performance Project.* Retrieved October 1, 2010, from www.pewcenteronthestates.org.

Piper, B. February 12, 2007. "What is Congressman Souder smoking? *Huffington Post.* Retrieved from www.huffingtonpost.com.

Pope, C. June 27, 2003. "White House to tap Seattle in drug war." *Seattle Post-Intelligencer.* Retrieved from www.seattlepi.com.

Powell, B. March 25, 1998. "Cannabis Café on a roll in B.C." *Toronto Star.* Retrieved, from www.thestar.com.

Russo, R. January 21, 2004. "Tougher pot penalties might prevent increased border scrutiny: Celucci." *Vancouver Sun.* Retrieved from www.vancouversun.com.

Sabbag, R. July 2005. "High in the Canadian Rockies." *Playboy.* Retrieved July 15, 2005, from www.playboy.com.

Sayegh, G. 2010. "After the Rockefeller drug laws: A new direction in New York and the nation." Retrieved October 16, 2010, from www.drugpolicy.org.

Schlosser, E. 2003. *Reefer Madness.* Boston: Houghton Mifflin.

Seelye, K. October 24, 2006. "Barack Obama, asked about drug history, admits he inhaled." *New York Times.* Retrieved October 24, 2010, from www.nytimes.com.

Skelton, C. May 26, 2001. "Vancouver: The next Amsterdam." *Vancouver Sun.* Retrieved from www.vancouversun.com.

Smith, G. September 13, 2002. "Canada's pot policy under fire from US." *Globe and Mail.* Retrieved from www.theglobeandmail.com.

Spears, J. December 15, 2005. "Addicts get crack pipes in new drug strategy." *Toronto Star.* Retrieved from www.thestar.com.

Statistics Canada. 2004. Trends in drug offenses and the role of alcohol and drugs in crime. Ottawa: Author.

Strathdee, S., and R. Pollini. 2007. "A 21st century Lazarus: The role of safer injection sites in harm reduction and recovery." *Addiction, 102,* 848–9.

Struck, D. March 18, 2006. "High crimes, or a tokin' figure?" *Washington Post.* Retrieved from www.washingtonpost.com.

(Author?) "There's a funny smell in the air." July 21, 2002. *New York Times.* Retrieved from www.nytimes.com.

Thomas, G. 2003. "Balance in theory but not in practice: Exploring the continued emphasis on supply reduction in Canada's national drug control strategy." *Perspectives on Canadian Drug Policy, Volume II.* John Howard Society, 26–41.

Tibbetts, J. November 26, 2010. "Senate passes bill with mandatory sentencing for growing five pot plants." *Vancouver Sun.* Retrieved November 28, 2010, from www.vancouversun.com.

Washington State Institute for Public Policy. 2008. *Drug Offender Sentencing Grid: Preliminary Report.* Accessed October 17, 2010, from, www.wsipp.wa.gov.

Wenner, J. June 25, 2008. "A conversation with Barack Obama." *Rolling Stone.* Retrieved October 15, 2010, from www.rollingstone.com.

Wilkins, W., P. Newton, and J. Steer. 1993. "Comparing sentencing policies in a 'war on drugs' era." *Wake Forest Law Review, 28,* 305–27.

Wood, D. October 15, 2010. "Marijuana in California: Prop. 19 won't stop federal drug enforcement." *Christian Science Monitor.* Retrieved from www.csmonitor.com.

Wood, E., et al. 2003. "The health care and fiscal costs of the illicit drug use epidemic: The impact of conventional drug control strategies, and the potential of a comprehensive approach." *B.C. Medical Journal* 45(3), 128–34.

Wood, E., M. Tyndall, R, Zhang, J. Montaner and T. Kerr. 2007. "Rate of detoxification service use and its impact among a cohort of supervised injection facility users." *Addiction* 102, 916–919.

Zimmer, L., and J. Morgan 1997. *Marijuana Myths, Marijuana Facts.* New York: The Lindesmith Center.

Critical Thinking

1. What can the United States learn from the drug policies of Canada?

2. What can Canada learn from the drug policies of the United States?

3. How does each county's administration impact the future of drug policy?

Legalize Drugs—all of Them!

Are we at the beginning of a revolution? asks.

VANESSA BAIRD

W e were sitting in a café drinking cola. My two companions, drug enforcement soldiers, kept their guns resting across their knees. Fingers not quite on triggers but close enough for rapid response. They were smiling.

The woman running the café was not. Her face was closed, expressionless. Through the open window we could hear the almost constant sound of light aircraft taking off and landing somewhere in the thick greenery of Peru's Upper Huallaga Valley. When, earlier, I had innocently asked a local mayor whether such planes were carrying drugs, he had smiled and equally innocently replied: 'They are air taxis. That's how people get about here.'

Later I went out with soldiers on patrol. Running through the jungle, we spotted coca plants being grown between generous banana leaves. Finally we came upon a lab for making coca paste. It was a simple affair—two big piles of coca leaves, a trough made out of wood and plastic sheeting, and some cans of kerosene.

'It's been abandoned,' remarked one of the soldiers. He didn't seem surprised or disappointed. 'Will they be back?' I asked.

'Probably not. They won't use this one again if they know we have been here. They will make another lab somewhere else. It's easy.'

This was 27 years ago, early days in the 'war on drugs'. And already then it seemed hopeless.

Steps to showdown

'They used to laugh at us,' says Danny Kushlick of Transform, a British drug policy reform group.

Today he and his colleagues are regularly called upon to make the case for ending the prohibitionist policy that has dominated the world since the UN Single Convention on Narcotic Drugs was put in place in 1961.

They have been researching other possibilities, including an idea that until recently was pretty much taboo—making all drugs legal.

The list of high-profile figures supporting the cause for reform is growing by the minute, and ranges from Nobel laureate economists and police chiefs to stand-up comedians and drug activists.

Serving politicians have tended to be cautious, fearing voter backlash. Before coming to power, both Barack Obama and David Cameron indicated that they were in favour of reform, including some degree of legalization. Once in high office, they fell silent. Mexico's former leader Vicente Fox, now a leading advocate of 'legalization all the way', waited until he was safely out of office.

But today, even incumbent leaders are sticking their heads above the parapet. 'That's something new,' says Kushlick.

In the past few months, President Juan Manuel Santos of Colombia, for example, has initiated a global taskforce for a total rethink of drug policy. Costa Rica's Laura Chinchilla has said the consumption of drugs should be a matter of health, not law. Guatemalan President Otto Pérez Molina is calling for legalization of the use and sale of drugs. While in Uruguay, President José Mujica has proposed a groundbreaking law that would enable the state to sell marijuana to its people and derive tax revenue from it. 'Someone has to be first,' he commented.

Uruguayan President José Mujica has proposed a law that would enable the state to sell marijuana and derive tax revenue from it. 'Someone has to be first,' he says

The US is not immune to the whiff of drug revolution. In November three states—Washington, Oregon and Colorado—will vote on legalization of marijuana for adult recreational use. This would directly contravene both federal law and the UN Convention. 'We're heading for a showdown,' says Sanho Tree of the Institute for Policy Studies in Washington. 'It's hard to talk about tipping points but I think we are close to one with regard to cannabis. This is a clear sign that people are looking for a different paradigm.'

War on drugs

From a country like Mexico, where ever-deepening drug-related violence claims 33 lives a day, the global 'war on drugs' declared by President Nixon 40 years ago can be seen for what it is—a colossal failure. Costing more than a trillion dollars, this 'war' has involved hundreds of thousands of military personnel, customs officers, enforcement agents, crop eradicators, police and prison staff. But still the illegal narcotics trade flourishes—worth about $320 billion a year—and drug use keeps growing.

Drugs have little intrinsic value. It's prohibition that gives an astronomical 'price support' to traffickers. The profits are extreme and so are the violence and corruption needed to protect them

Worse, the war on drugs has unleashed a deadly set of 'unintended consequences'.

It's 'like trying to put out an electrical fire by dousing it with water,' says Sanho Tree.

Crackdowns on drug cartels have increased the huge profits bestowed by illegality. Violence has surged as rival groups jockey to fill the vacuum left when a major cartel has been hammered by government forces.

The global war is militarizing societies and tearing up democratic rights. It also enables illegal drug money to flow into the coffers of Al Qaeda, the Taliban, and the Colombian FARC, ELN, AUC and others.[1,2] Meanwhile, punishing drug users and sellers has filled prisons and increased addiction.

Something needs to be done.

'It is the biggest, most complex challenge facing us today,' says Mauricio Rodríguez, Colombian ambassador in London and a close ally of President Santos, whose proposed taskforce of global experts is already at work under the auspices of the Inter-American Drug Abuse Control Commission (CICAD), expected to report within 12 months.

Colombians know better than most the cost of the war on drugs. They have been on the frontline of the US-designed Plan Colombia, a $7 billion anti-narcotics and military aid drive also used to tackle leftwing insurgency. In 2002 the conflict was claiming some 28,000 Colombian lives a year.[3]

Today, violence is down by about a third and coca production has declined by 58 per cent. 'But any improvements in Colombia have meant serious deterioration in other parts of Latin America and the world,' says Rodríguez. 'Production has gone to Peru and Bolivia and traffic has gone mostly to Central America, West Africa, and islands of the Caribbean.'

This is the so-called balloon effect, where action taken in one place simply pushes the illegal drug problem into another.

Latin Americans, the ambassador says, are fed up with drug-related violence. 'Why do we have to pay such a price for a problem that is essentially not ours? We are not big consumers; it's unfair that tens of thousands of Mexicans or Colombians or Guatemalans have to lose their lives because of consumption in the US. Who is really responsible? The consumers are and so are those who have created this model of illegality. Either consuming nations need to reduce their consumption or they need to help us to change this model.'

The damage done?

Many people in those major consuming nations would agree. In recent months opinion polls have shown remarkable upswings in people supporting legalization of some drugs at least. A survey in Colorado showed 61 per cent of the population supported legalization of cannabis. Polls in Britain, Australia and Canada show similar seismic shifts in public attitude.

The number of people who have never tried an illegal recreational drug is dwindling and with it the hysteria that surrounds narcotics. Psychoactive—mind-altering—substances have always been a part of human experience. And other animal experience too, if you count elephants bingeing on fermenting fruit and goats getting high on coffee beans.

The effects of different drugs and their wider impacts vary enormously. But for many people, current legal classification of drugs seems divorced from the reality they know, especially in relation to cannabis or 'party drugs' like ecstasy.

There is also a growing awareness that some legal drugs—alcohol and tobacco, for example—are much more harmful than many currently illegal ones. Some illicit substances have medically therapeutic benefits, such as cannabis (to alleviate the symptoms of multiple sclerosis) and ecstasy or magic mushrooms (for treating post-traumatic stress disorder), that cannot be properly researched or exploited by medical professionals and patients.

But what about the hard stuff?

Heroin and crack cocaine are high on the scientific list of harmful illegal drugs. The 27 million 'problem drug users' in the world tend to be addicted to these or related substances. The proliferation of drugs like krokodil (a cheaper heroin derivative that gets its name from the skin damage it causes and its flesh-devouring tendencies) in Russia compounds fear of drugs and what they can do.

Andria Efthimiou-Mordaunt is a Harm Reduction activist and former heroin addict living in London. She sees addiction as a disease to be treated. She also thinks that legal regulation and control is the only way to go. 'I don't say it fearlessly though, because I think that, at least temporarily, there will be an increase in drug use. But I don't think that will be sustained.'

In 2001, Portugal embarked on one of the most daring and progressive actions in recent times: it effectively decriminalized the personal use of all drugs, including the hard ones.

The results were interesting. Drug use carried on increasing but at a slower rate than in Spain or France. But, significantly, addiction to hard drugs fell by half, from an estimated 100,000 addicts before decriminalization to 40,000 in 2011. Opiate-related deaths and HIV infection were also down—the latter by 17 per cent.[4,5] This is partly because Portugal coupled decriminalization with a well-funded public health programme to help people get off drugs.

Counter-intuitive as it may seem, the evidence suggests that criminalization does not deter use—but decriminalization does.

It makes perfect sense to Andria Efthimiou-Mordaunt. 'I have now heard thousands of stories of people who have become dependent on heroin, cocaine and so on. Most of us were most interested because these drugs were forbidden.

'Also we were a bit vulnerable, didn't have much love for ourselves, and therefore we put ourselves in danger. We don't care that it's a crime and we could go to jail. We just want to use this drug that we have found is comforting or exciting or pleasurable.'

She explains: 'People aren't wilfully creating havoc: they are doing something that they find will assist them in their lives, even if it's temporary and it gets them into all sorts of other problems. But for the majority of us, it is clear that the prohibitive punitive system has actually been the cause of most of our other problems—like poverty, homelessness, sex work, shoplifting, dealing.'

These problems in turn intensify the need for the drug and make it harder to stop.

'What saddens me is that some of the people who are most punitive and intolerant are those who are directly affected. One of our arguments needs to be that just because you are legalizing the drug does not mean that you are promoting it. You can say: look, we are not changing the laws because we want everyone to take these substances, but because they're currently bloody dangerous because of where you get them from.'

There are many good models for reducing harm, through a combination of *de facto* decriminalization and supportive treatment. 'In Switzerland they found that people would come off heroin faster because there was nothing to fight against any more; they still had their addictions but once the other bits of their lives had been sorted to some degree, there wasn't this huge monster that needed to be medicated every day.'

In Vancouver, Canada, the response to a high level of drug deaths was the creation of a 'consumption room' where users can safely inject legal or illegal drugs. They call it 'the demilitarized zone'. Similar initiatives have been developed in Australia, Spain, Germany, Portugal and the Netherlands.

Decriminalize or legalize?

So why not go down the Portuguese route and decriminalize the use of all drugs?

It is, to varying degrees, already happening in practice in around 25 countries, mainly in Europe and Latin America, where people found in possession may simply have their drugs confiscated but will not be prosecuted.[5]

However, decriminalization does not deal with the supply side—and the deadly nexus of money and violence.

Drugs have little intrinsic value. It's prohibition that gives an astronomical 'price support' to traffickers. The profits are extreme and so are the violence and corruption needed to protect them. Hence the grotesquely cruel methods used by the gangs, making simple decapitation a blessing.

Only legalization and regulation can break the hold of the criminals. Legal drugs could be taxed. The corrupt network of tax-evading banks and front companies that support the industry by laundering drug money would have to start paying their way. 'The war on drugs I would like to see is the war on laundering drug money,' says ambassador Rodríguez. And some of the criminals might even be caught. It's worth remembering that only when the prohibition of alcohol ended in the US was Al Capone finally apprehended—on a charge of tax evasion in 1933.

Making drugs legal has many potential benefits. It could interrupt the flow of money to warlords, corrupt officials and the Taliban that is ensuring continuing instability in Afghanistan and other parts of the world. This is highlighted in a recent study by the former MI6 director of operations Nigel Inkster and Virginia Comolli, a research analyst at the International Institute of Strategic Studies.[6]

It could dramatically reduce prison populations. The billions the world spends on the global war on drugs could instead go towards health, addiction treatment and prevention, and other socially useful things. It would lower the risk of death by overdose because the strength and quality of drugs would be marked and controlled.

But one of the biggest impacts would be on HIV/AIDS. Contrary to global trends, infection through injecting drug use is on the rise and now accounts for a third of all new HIV infections outside sub-Saharan Africa. Punitive policies are fuelling the AIDS pandemic in the US, Thailand, China and especially the former soviet states. In Russia violent police attacks on drug users are commonplace, opiate substitutes are outlawed, and needle exchange programmes non-existent. 'Refusing to reduce HIV infection and protect people who have a drug problem is criminal,' said entrepreneur Richard Branson at the launch of a hard-hitting report by the Global Commission on Drugs, a collection of ex-drug tsars, former leaders and experts who are calling upon current world leaders to decriminalize drug use and to invest in harm reduction.[7]

In a world where drug taking was not a crime, addicts would be less likely to go underground, less likely to share needles and more likely to test for HIV. Millions of new HIV infections could be averted.

Other human rights abuses generated by prohibition could be reduced, such as capital punishment in Iran. This is mainly used against people found in possession of drugs and is effectively being funded by Britain, Ireland and others through a UN anti-drug smuggling programme.[8]

Finally, legalization would provide a decent living, without fear, for thousands of poppy and coca farmers in some of the world's poorest countries.

What next?

What happens in the US, the world's premier drugs consumer and also the most ardent guardian of the UN Convention, is critical. In the lead-up to November's elections, President Obama is in ultra-cautious mode. He has said he is 'critical' of legalization but is prepared to consider whether Washington policies are 'doing more harm than good in certain places'.

To Take It Further . . .

Action and Resources

Organizations

International

The Global Commission on Drug Policy
globalcommissionondrugs.org
International Drug Policy Consortium idpc.net
International Centre for Science in Drug Policy icsdp.org
Transnational Institute tni.org
International HIV/AIDS Alliance aidsalliance.org
International Network of People who Use Drugs
(INPUD) inpud.net

Aotearoa/New Zealand

The Green Party greens.org.nz/druglawreform
Legalise marijuana legalise.org.nz

Australia

Australian Drug Law Reform Foundation adlrf.org.au
Families of Drug Users fds.org.au
Family and Friends for Drug Law Reform ffdlr.org.au

Britain

Transform drug policy foundation tdpf.org.uk
The Beckley Foundation reformdrugpolicy.com
Harm Reduction International ihra.net
The Independent Scientific Committee on Drugs
drugscience.org.uk

Canada

Canadian Harm Reduction Network
canadianharmreduction.com

Canadian Drug Policy Coalition drugpolicy.ca
Canadian Foundation for Drug Policy cfdp.ca

US

Drug Policy Alliance drugpolicy.org
Law Enforcement Against Prohibition (LEAP) leap.cc
Drug Reform Co-ordination Network
stopthedrugwar.org
NORML norml.org
Drug Sense drugsense.org
Drug War Facts drugwarfacts.org

Books

Legalize by Max Rendall, 2011 (*Stacey International*)
After the War on Drugs: Blueprint for Regulation by
Steve Rolles/Transform, 2009 (download at tdpf.org.uk)
Fixing Drugs by Sue Pryce, 2012 (*Palgrave Macmillan*)
Drugs—without the hot air by David Nutt, 2012 (*UIT Cambridge*)
The Candy Machine by Tom Feiling, 2009 (*Penguin*)
Drug War in Mexico by Peter Watt and Roberto Zepeda,
2012 (*Zed*)
Seeds of Terror by Gretchen Peters, 2009 (*Oneworld*)
Drugs, Insecurity and Failed States by Nigel Inkster and
Virginia Cornolli, 2012 (IISS)

Reports

The Alternative World Drug Report, Transform, June
2012, nin.tl/Mbmuoa
The War on Drugs and HIV/AIDS, Global Commission
on Drugs, June 2012 nin.tl/M3ldEw
World Drug Report, UNODC, June 2012 nin.tl/Mbnqcd

The US drug warriors in Congress and in the military are entrenched and still have international clout, as Bolivia saw when it tried to legalize production of coca for traditional use.

In theory, the US can act against countries that depart from the UN Convention by blocking loans from financial institutions such as the IMF or the World Bank. But when there is a regional uprising, with one country after another saying they want to legalize, be it Belize or Uruguay or Argentina, it may get harder to do.

In the US itself Sanho Tree reckons that: 'Once we have a regulated model for cannabis, it will show voters that the sky didn't fall, life did not grind to a halt. That will help. On the hard drugs, examples from Europe of successful harm reduction programmes will show people in the US that another way is possible.'

But he adds that the main political work will be in public education. This is because drugs policy is, by its nature, counterintuitive; being tough is the opposite of being effective.

Prohibition is a simplistic solution to a complex problem that simply does not work. At no time or place in history has it ever

worked. Sue Pryce, an academic and mother of a drug addict, observes: 'There is an uncomfortable similarity between the drug addict and those who support drug prohibition. The addict comes to see a fix as the solution to life's problems; the prohibitionists have come to see prohibition as the fix for the drug problems which are also part of life itself.'[9]

Even if the world, or even a part of it, comes to accept that legalization is the way forward, the devil will be in the detail. Pricing, for example, is a tricky issue—too cheap and use may rocket; too expensive and the rationale for a criminal market is re-ignited.

Antonio Maria Costa, former UN drug tsar and a leading prohibitionist, warns that multinational corporations will muscle in if drugs are legalized. Steve Rolles from Transform, however, presents a model that involves considerable state control and a ban on advertising.[10]

In an ideal world the UN would replace the prohibitionist conventions with a new progressive policy that all countries could sign up to together. Perhaps President Santos' global taskforce process will produce a blueprint for such a policy. But it's questionable how radical it will be if it has to have US and Canadian approval. UN-watcher Damon Barrett of Harm Reduction International thinks that real change is more likely to come 'from below'. Social and harm reduction activists, public educators and just ordinary people opening their minds will be the key players in this revolution.

People have and always will take intoxicants that provide pleasure and harm. But there are ways in which we can make that activity safer, less damaging to individuals, to society, to the world.

It may sound paradoxical, but ridding ourselves of prohibition could be the best way of getting a grip.

1. Gretchen Peters, *Seeds of Terror: How heroin is bankrolling the Taliban and Al Qaeda,* Oneworld Publications, 2009. **2.** BBC nin.tl/OqjN6j **3.** *Los Angeles Times* nin.tl/MptbV8 **4.** *Forbes* nin.tl/OqkDQx **5.** Transform, 'The Alternative World Drugs Report', 2012 nin.tl/Oqp0Lf **6.** Nigel Inkster and Virginia Comolli *Drugs, Insecurity and Failed States: the Problems of Prohibition,* IISS, 2012 **7.** Global Commission on Drugs, 'The War on Drugs and HIV/AIDS', globalcommission-ondrugs.org **8.** Harm Reduction International, 'Partners in Crime', 2012 nin.tl/MpuQtS **9.** Sue Pryce, *Fixing Drugs: the Politics of Drug Prohibition,* Palgrave Macmillan, 2012. **10.** Intelligence Squared, 'It's time to end the war on drugs', nin.tl/OqvtG5

Critical Thinking

1. Analyze Baird's position on the war on drugs.
2. Describe the key arguments for legalizing drugs.
3. Discuss the comparisons Baird makes between the United States and other countries.

From *New Internationalist,* vol. 455, 2012, pp. 12–17. Copyright © 2012 by Reprinted by permission.

Former ONDCP Senior Advisor on Marijuana and Harm Reduction

This month's revelation in the National Survey on Drug use and Health that marijuana use is increasing among youth (see ADAW, Sept. 12) was not a surprise to Kevin Sabet, until last week senior advisor at the Office of National Drug Control Policy. "We saw the signs when I got to the ONDCP in 2009," Sabet told ADAW last week, his first in the private sector. "There was an erosion of concern, and increases in use," he said. "The baby boom generation is wrestling with discussing the subject with their children."

Sabet, who left his job to pursue a consulting career, talked to ADAW about the risks of the marijuana legalization, and some of the behind-the-scenes strategy for the anti-legalization movement.

"We need people strategically thinking about this," said Sabet, who thinks that one of the reasons for an increase by youth in marijuana use is the more widespread acceptance of medical marijuana. "It still astounds me that after 15 years of medical marijuana, we still don't know the precise effects," he said. "We still need to learn a lot more about the effect of medical marijuana dispensaries."

Under Sabet, the ONDCP was moving away from the "culture war" approach to marijuana prevention and towards a more research-based one, he told ADAW. "We have learned a lot about marijuana's ability to affect cognition, memory, and mental health," he said. "And we want to stress to people that whether marijuana is being offered as a cure for cancer or for state budget woes, they need to be wary of what it really does."

Marijuana is a "tricky subject," said Sabet. "It's something a lot of people would rather ignore—or they'd rather just tell people not to use marijuana." Instead, policymakers need to focus on the data and on the negative consequences of use, he said.

Credible communication is important, said Sabet. "Marijuana is still often linked with the fun times in the 1960s and not thought of as a serious drug compared to cocaine," he said. Also, against the backdrop of the overdose deaths caused by prescription opioids, it's easy to view marijuana as less dangerous, Sabet acknowledged. "But we need to be concerned with the short- and long-term effects," he said. "We're trying, but we have a history in this country of not communicating in a very credible way about the effects of marijuana."

One of the most serious long-term effects is poor educational out-comes for youth who smoke marijuana, said Sabet. "We need to communicate credible scientific messages to kids," said Sabet. "For example, we know that one in 10 people who ever start using marijuana will become dependent. If that use starts in adolescence, one in two will become dependent."

As for the idea that a legitimate marijuana marketplace—like the alcohol marketplace—could ever develop, Sabet dismisses this completely. "If we think we're going to have a responsible industry that's going to label correctly, not market to kids, that's a ridiculous notion," he said. "Look at the alcohol industry. It only makes money from high-consuming drinkers. If everyone drank responsibly, the alcohol industry would go out of business. The same thing is true with marijuana and any other drug."

Finally, Sabet said that targeting prevention at specific drugs won't work. "It sounds like a cliche, but it does need to be a comprehensive approach," he said.

Sabet also negotiated the use of "harm reduction" approaches by the administration: including Narcan to reverse overdoses, needle exchanges as part of a comprehensive approach to treatment, and good Samaritan laws allowing people to report overdoses without fear of criminal charges for drug possession for either the victim or the reporter. "There are a lot of well-intentioned harm reduction advocates," he said. Where he obviously parts ground with them is legalization of marijuana.

Critical Thinking

1. What does Sabet believe is one of the main problems in making progress on public education about marijuana? Do you agree or disagree and why?

2. Discuss the methods of harm reduction mentioned in this article.

3. Do you believe marijuana should be legalized, and why or why not?

From *Alcoholism & Drug Abuse Weekly*, vol. 23, no. 38, 2011, pp. 6–7. Copyright © 2011 by Wiley-Blackwell. Reprinted by permission.

Portugal's Drug Policy Pays Off; US Eyes Lessons

BARRY HATTON AND MARTHA MENDOZA

Lisbon, Portugal—These days, Casal Ventoso is an ordinary blue-collar community—mothers push baby strollers, men smoke outside cafes, buses chug up and down the cobbled main street.

Ten years ago, the Lisbon neighborhood was a hellhole, a "drug supermarket" where some 5,000 users lined up every day to buy heroin and sneak into a hillside honeycomb of derelict housing to shoot up. In dark, stinking corners, addicts—some with maggots squirming under track marks—staggered between the occasional corpse, scavenging used, bloody needles.

At that time, Portugal, like the junkies of Casal Ventoso, had hit rock bottom: An estimated 100,000 people—an astonishing 1 percent of its population—were addicted to illegal drugs. So, like anyone with little to lose, the Portuguese took a risky leap: They decriminalized the use of all drugs in a groundbreaking law in 2000.

Now, the United States, which has waged a 40-year, $1 trillion war on drugs, is looking for answers in tiny Portugal, which is reaping the benefits of what once looked like a dangerous gamble. White House drug czar Gil Kerlikowske visited Portugal in September to learn about its drug reforms, and other countries—including Norway, Denmark, Australia and Peru—have taken interest, too.

"The disasters that were predicted by critics didn't happen," said University of Kent professor Alex Stevens, who has studied Portugal's program. "The answer was simple: Provide treatment."

Drugs in Portugal are still illegal. But here's what Portugal did: It changed the law so that users are sent to counseling and sometimes treatment instead of criminal courts and prison. The switch from drugs as a criminal issue to a public health one was aimed at preventing users from going underground.

Other European countries treat drugs as a public health problem, too, but Portugal stands out as the only one that has written that approach into law. The result: More people tried drugs, but fewer ended up addicted.

Here's what happened between 2000 and 2008:

There were small increases in illicit drug use among adults, but decreases for adolescents and problem users such as drug addicts and prisoners.
Drug-related court cases dropped 66 percent.
Drug-related HIV cases dropped 75 percent. In 2002, 49 percent of people with AIDS were addicts; by 2008 that number fell to 28 percent.
The number of regular users held steady at less than 3 percent of the population for marijuana and less than 0.3 percent

for heroin and cocaine—figures that show decriminalization brought no surge in drug use.
The number of people treated for drug addiction rose 20 percent from 2001 to 2008.

Portuguese Prime Minister Jose Socrates, one of the chief architects of the new drug strategy, says he was inspired partly by his own experience of helping his brother beat an addiction.

"It was a very hard change to make at the time because the drug issue involves lots of prejudices," he said. "You just need to rid yourselves of prejudice and take an intelligent approach."

Officials have not yet worked out the cost of the program, but they expect no increase in spending, since most of the money was diverted from the justice system to the public health service.

In Portugal today, outreach health workers provide addicts with fresh needles, swabs, little dishes to cook up the injectable mixture, disinfectant and condoms. But anyone caught with even a small amount of drugs is automatically sent to what is known as a Dissuasion Committee for counseling. The committees include legal experts, psychologists and social workers.

Failure to turn up can result in fines, mandatory treatment or other sanctions. In serious cases, the panel recommends the user be sent to a treatment center.

Health workers also shepherd some addicts off the streets directly into treatment. That's what happened to 33-year-old Tiago, who is struggling to kick heroin at a Lisbon rehab facility.

Tiago, who requested that his first name only be used to protect his privacy, started taking heroin when he was 20. He shot up four or five times a day, sleeping for years in an abandoned car where, with his addicted girlfriend, he fathered a child he has never seen.

At the airy Lisbon treatment center where he now lives, Tiago plays table tennis, surfs the Internet and watches TV. He helps with cleaning and other odd jobs. And he's back to his normal weight after dropping to 50 kilograms (110 pounds) during his addiction.

After almost six months on methadone, each day trimming his intake, he brims with hope about his upcoming move to a home run by the Catholic church where recovered addicts are offered a fresh start.

"I just ask God that it'll be the first and last time—the first time I go to a home and the last time I go through detox," he said.

Portugal's program is widely seen as effective, but some say it has shortcomings.

Antonio Lourenco Martins is a former Portuguese Supreme Court judge who sat on a 1998 commission that drafted the new drug strategy and was one of two on the nine-member panel who voted against decriminalization. He admits the law has done some good, but complains that its approach is too soft.

Francisco Chaves, who runs a Lisbon treatment center, also recognizes that addicts might exploit goodwill.

"We know that (when there is) a lack of pressure, none of us change or are willing to change," Chaves said.

Worldwide, a record 93 countries offered alternatives to jail time for drug abuse in 2010, according to the International Harm Reduction Association. They range from needle exchanges in Cambodia to methadone treatment in Poland.

Vancouver, Canada, has North America's first legal drug consumption room—dubbed as "a safe, health-focused place where people inject drugs and connect to health care services." Brazil and Uruguay have eliminated jail time for people carrying small amounts of drugs for personal use.

Whether the alternative approaches work seems to depend on how they are carried out. In the Netherlands, where police ignore the peaceful consumption of illegal drugs, drug use and dealing are rising, according to the European Monitoring Centre for Drugs and Drug Addiction. Five Dutch cities are implementing new restrictions on marijuana cafes after a wave of drug-related gang violence.

However, in Switzerland, where addicts are supervised as they inject heroin, addiction has steadily declined. No one has died from an overdose there since the program began in 1994, according to medical studies. The program is also credited with reducing crime and improving addicts' health.

The Obama administration firmly opposes the legalization of drugs, saying it would increase access and promote acceptance, according to drug czar Kerlikowske. The United States is spending $74 billion this year on criminal and court proceedings for drug offenders, compared with $3.6 billion for treatment.

But even the United States has taken small steps toward Portugal's approach of more intervention and treatment programs, and Kerlikowske has called for an end to the "War on Drugs" rhetoric.

"Calling it a war really limits your resources," he said. "Looking at this as both a public safety problem and a public health problem seems to make a lot more sense."

There is no guarantee that Portugal's approach would work in the United States, which has a population 29 times larger than Portugal's 10.6 million.

Still, an increasing number of American cities are offering nonviolent drug offenders a chance to choose treatment over jail, and the approach appears to be working.

In San Francisco's gritty Tenderloin neighborhood, Tyrone Cooper, a 52-year-old lifelong drug addict, can't stop laughing at how a system that has put him in jail a dozen times now has him on the road to recovery.

"Instead of going to smoke crack, I went to a rehab meeting," he said. "Can you believe it? Me! A meeting! I mean, there were my boys, right there smoking crack, and Tyrone walked right past them. 'Sorry,' I told them, 'I gotta get to this meeting.'"

Cooper is one of hundreds of San Franciscans who landed in a court program this year where judges offered them a chance to go to rehab, get jobs, move into houses, find primary care physicians and even remove their tattoos. There is enough data now to show that these alternative courts reduce recidivism and save money.

Between 4 and 29 percent of drug court participants in the United States will get caught using drugs again, compared with 48 percent of those who go through traditional courts.

San Francisco's drug court saves the city $14,297 per offender, officials said. Expanding drug courts to all 1.5 million drug offenders in the U.S. would cost more than $13 billion annually, but would return more than $40 billion, according to a study by John Roman, a senior researcher at the Urban Institute's Justice Policy Center.

The first drug court opened in the U.S. 21 years ago. By 1999, there were 472; by 2005, 1,250.

This year, new drug courts opened every week around the U.S., as states faced budget crises exacerbated by the high rate of incarceration for drug offenses. There are now drug courts in every state, more than 2,400 serving 120,000 people.

Last year, New York lawmakers followed their counterparts across the U.S. who have tossed out tough, 40-year-old drug laws and mandatory sentences, giving judges unprecedented sentencing options. The U.S. Department of Health and Human Services is also training doctors to screen patients for potential addiction and reimbursing Medicare and Medicaid providers who do so.

Arizona recently became the 15th U.S. state to approve medical use of marijuana, following California's 2006 legislation.

In Portugal, the blight that once destroyed the Casal Ventoso neighborhood is a distant memory.

Americo Nave, a 39-year-old psychologist, remembers the chilling stories his colleagues brought back after the first team of health workers was sent into Casal Ventoso in the late 1990s. Some addicts had gangrene, and their arms had to be amputated.

Those days are past, though there are vestiges. About a dozen frail, mostly unkempt men recently gathered next to a bus stop to get new needles and swabs in small green plastic bags from health workers, as part of a twice-weekly program. Some ducked out of sight behind walls to shoot up, and one crouched behind trash cans, trying to shield his lighter flame from the wind.

A 37-year-old man who would only identify himself as Joao said he's been using heroin for 22 years. He has contracted Hepatitis C, and recalls picking up used, bloody needles from the sidewalk. Now he comes regularly to the needle exchange.

"These teams . . . have helped a lot of people," he said, struggling to concentrate as he draws on a cigarette.

The decayed housing that once hid addicts has long since been bulldozed. And this year, Lisbon's city council planted 600 trees and 16,500 bushes on the hillside.

This spring they're expected to bloom.

Critical Thinking

1. How do other European countries deal with drug use?

2. How is Portugal unique among European nations in its dealing with drugs?

3. Do you think that Portugal's drug policy could serve as a model to the United States? What parts could we implement here at home?

4. Which U.S. states have legalized marijuana use? Is there a trend here?

Mendoza reported from San Diego, California.

UNIT 7

Prevention, Treatment, and Education

Unit Selections

33. **Old Habits Die Hard for Ageing Addicts,** Matthew Ford
34. **Fetal Alcohol Spectrum Disorders: When Science, Medicine, Public Policy, and Laws Collide,** Kenneth R. Warren and Brenda G. Hewitt
35. **Addiction Diagnoses May Rise Under Guideline Changes,** Ian Urbina,
36. **An Addiction Vaccine, Tantalizingly Close,** Robert Benson
37. **Understanding Recovery Barriers: Youth Perceptions about Substance Use Relapse,** Rachel Gonzales, et al.
38. **High-Risk Offenders Participating in Court-Supervised Substance Abuse Treatment: Characteristics, Treatment Received, and Factors Associated with Recidivism,** Elizabeth Evans

Learning Outcomes

After reading this Unit, you should be able to:

- Explain how the drug problem can be impacted by targeting demand and not supply.

- Understand what harm reduction is in the context of drug policy and treatment and how harm reduction differs from the American model of criminalization and punishment for drug using behaviors.

- Discuss correctional systems' involvement in treating drug dependency of prisoners. Explain why this practice should exist or not.

Student Website
www.mhhe.com/cls

Internet References

American Council for Drug Education
www.acde.org
D.A.R.E.
www.dare-america.com
The Drug Reform Coordination Network (DRC)
www.drcnet.org
Drug Watch International
www.drugwatch.org
Hazelden
www.hazelden.org
Join Together
www.jointogether.org

KCI (Koch Crime Institute) The Anit-Meth Site
www.kci.org/meth_info/faq_meth.htm
Marijuana Policy Project
www.mpp.org
National Institute on Drug Abuse
www.nida.nih.gov/Infofacts/TreatMeth.html
Office of National Drug Control Policy (ONDCP)
www.whitehousedrugpolicy.gov
The Partnership for Drug-Free America
www.drugfree.org/#
United Nations International Drug Control Program (UNDCP)
www.undcp.org

There are no magic bullets for preventing drug abuse and treating drug-dependent persons. Currently, more than 22 million Americans are classified as drug dependent on illicit drugs and/or alcohol. Males continue to be twice as likely to be classified as drug dependent as females. Research continues to establish and strengthen the role of treatment as a critical component in the fight against drug abuse. Some drug treatment programs have been shown to dramatically reduce the costs associated with high-risk populations of users. For example, recidivism associated with drug-related criminal justice populations has been shown to decrease by 50 percent after treatment. Treatment is a critical component in the fight against drug abuse but it is not a panacea. Society cannot "treat" drug abuse away just as it cannot "arrest" it away.

Drug prevention and treatment philosophies subscribe to a multitude of modalities. Everything seems to work a little and nothing seems to work completely. The articles in this unit illustrate the diversity of methods utilized in prevention and treatment programs. Special emphasis is given to treating the drug problems of those who are under the supervision of the criminal justice system. All education, prevention, and treatment programs compete for local, state, and federal resources. Current treatment efforts at all public and private levels are struggling to meet the demands for service due to the impacts from the U.S. economic crisis of the past few years.

Education: One critical component of drug education is the ability to rapidly translate research findings into practice, and today's drug policy continues to emphasize this in its overall budget allocations. Funding for educational research and grants is generally strong with the trend being toward administering funds to local communities and schools to fund local proposals. For example, in 2011 more than $50 million was again made available to schools for research-based assistance for drug prevention and school safety programs. Another example is the refunding of the $120 million National Youth Media Campaign designed to help coach parents in processes of early recognition and intervention. Encouraging successful parenting is one primary emphasis in current federal drug policy. Other significant research efforts continue to support important education, prevention, and treatment programs such as The National Prevention Research Initiative, Interventions and Treatment for Current Drug Users Who Are Not Yet Addicted, the National Drug Abuse Treatment Clinical Trial Network, and Research Based Treatment Approaches for Drug Abusing Criminal Offenders. In 2011, federal research-related grants totaling almost $100 million were made available to local and state school jurisdictions.

Prevention: A primary strategy of drug prevention programs is to prevent and/or delay initial drug use. A secondary strategy is to discourage use by persons minimally involved with drugs. Both strategies include (1) educating users and potential users; (2) teaching adolescents how to resist peer pressure; (3) addressing problems associated with drug abuse such as teen pregnancy, failure in school, and lawbreaking; (4) creating community support and involvement for prevention activities; and (5) involving parents in deterring drug use by children. Prevention and education programs are administered through a variety of

© Design Pics/Steve Nagy

mechanisms, typically amidst controversy relative to what works best. Schools have been an important delivery apparatus. Funding for school prevention programs is an important emphasis within the efforts to reduce the demand for drugs. Subsequently, an increase in federal money was dedicated to expanding the number of high school programs that implement student drug testing. Drug testing in high schools, authorized by the Supreme Court in a 2002 court decision, has produced a positive and measurable deterrent to drug use. Despite its controversy, school drug testing is expanding as a positive way to reinforce actions of parents to educate and deter their children from use. The testing program provides for subsequent assessment, referral, and intervention process in situations where parents and educators deem it necessary.

In addition, in 2011, approximately $90 million in grant funds were again dedicated to support the federal Drug-Free Communities Program, which provides funds at the community level to anti-drug coalitions working to prevent substance abuse among young people and in local neighborhoods. There are currently more than 700 local community coalitions working under this program nationwide. Also, there are community-based drug prevention programs sponsored by civic organizations, church groups, and private corporations. All programs pursue funding through public grants and private endowments. Federal grants to local, state, and private programs are critical components to program solvency. The multifaceted nature of prevention programs makes them difficult to assess categorically. School programs that emphasize the development of skills to resist social and peer pressure generally produce varying degrees of positive results. Research continues to make more evident the need to focus prevention programs with specific populations in mind.

Treatment: Like prevention programs, drug treatment programs enlist a variety of methods to treat persons dependent upon legal and illegal drugs. There is no single-pronged approach to treatment for drug abuse. Treatment modality may differ radically from one user to the other. The user's background, physical and mental health, personal motivation, and support structure all have serious implications for treatment type. Lumping together the diverse needs of chemically dependent persons for purposes of applying a generic treatment process does not work. In addition, most persons needing and seeking treatment have problems with more than one drug—polydrug use. Current research also correlates drug use with serious mental illness (SMI). Current research by the federal Substance Abuse and Mental Health Services Administration (SAMHSA) reports that adults with a drug problem are three times more likely to suffer from a serious mental illness. The existing harmful drug use and mental health nexus is exacerbated by the fact that using certain powerful drugs such as methamphetamine push otherwise functioning persons into the dysfunctional realm of mental illness. Although treatment programs differ in methods, most provide a combination of key services. These include drug counseling, drug education, pharmacological therapy, psychotherapy, relapse prevention, and assistance with support structures. Treatment programs may be outpatient oriented or residential in nature. Residential programs require patients to live at the facility for a prescribed period of time. These residential programs, often described as therapeutic communities, emphasize the development of social, vocational, and educational skills. The current trend is to increase the availability of treatment programs. One key component of federal drug strategy is to continue to fund and expand the Access to Recovery treatment initiative that began in 2004. This program uses a voucher system to fund drug treatment for individuals otherwise unable to obtain it. This program, now operational in 14 states and one Native American community, allows dependent persons to personally choose care providers, including faith-based care providers. It is hoped that this program will encourage states to provide a wider array of treatment and recovery options. As one example, the state of Missouri has transformed all public drug treatment within the state to an "Access to Recovery-Like" program in which involved persons choose their providers and pay with state vouchers. It is hoped that this and similar programs will allow a more flexible delivery of services that will target large populations of dependent persons who are not reached through other treatment efforts.

Old Habits Die Hard for Ageing Addicts

The number of older drug users is rising. But what health and care challenges do they face as they age, and is the system prepared to deal with them?

Matthew Ford

Maggie Jones receives a regular dose of methadone from her GP and dreads the thought of having to go into a care home with her dependency.

"I know I'm lucky: I've got a great GP who will arrange things and make sure I get my methadone if I have to go into hospital. But the idea of being stuck in a bed somewhere and not having your [prescription], that's very scary.

"As for the thought of going into an old people's home, that's absolutely terrifying. Or what if you get infirm and get stuck at home and can't get to the chemist to get your prescription?

"Getting old is worrying for many people, I know that. But if you're an addict then there is this consuming fear of being powerless."

Jones (not her real name) is not alone in contemplating her dotage with a long-standing addiction. Although an early death is a reality for many addicts, methadone prescriptions and the success of harm-reduction programmes now mean that large numbers of people who began using drugs in the 1960s and 1970s are living longer. Figures from the National Treatment Agency for Substance Misuse show that there were more than 1,300 addicts over the age of 60 in treatment in England in 2009. In 1998, just 8 percent of drug users were aged 40-49, but by 2006, a quarter were in this age bracket. Caryl Beynon, reader in substance use epidemiology at the centre for public health, Liverpool John Moores University, calculates that there are now around 70,000-75,000 addicts aged over 40 in the UK.

Older drug users face a grim catalogue of serious health problems as they age. "What we are seeing is that users in their 40s frequently have many of the health issues of someone in their 60s or even 70s," says Beynon. "There is also some evidence that addicts are more prone to early onset dementia."

But public services are not geared up for older addicts. Society just does not expect older people to be addicts, and drugs remain firmly linked with youth behaviour. As a result, treatment is still focused on the needs of the young, but that will need to change. "There's definitely a gap in service provision for older users," says Michael Simpson, communications officer at the charity DrugScope.

Of particular concern are the health problems facing people who have been using intravenously for many years. "I've seen horrendous injuries that have gone untreated," says Erin O'Mara, editor of Black Poppy, a magazine for heroin users, whose co-founder, Chris Drouet, died of an overdose last year, aged 60.

"There are ulcers, amputations, repeated heart problems, abscesses, breaks that aren't healed properly. Often, when people do seek help, the care they get is so lackadaisical. Many people have said to me that medical staff treat addicts like scumbags, and so they just won't go to the doctor's," O'Mara adds.

Jones agrees that health issues are worse for those still using intravenously. "Drug use takes a hefty toll: they've got Hepatitis C, HIV, bronchial problems, depression."

Reluctance to seek treatment almost cost Andrew O'Malley, 48, a recovering addict, his hand. "It was badly infected in the bone, but I felt too ashamed to get treatment. Every day I was covering it up and trying to get along," he says. "In the end I went to hospital, but I've lost most of the movement in my hand."

Older addicts also find it harder to cope with pain than elderly people who do not take drugs. "Inadequate pain relief is a real concern," says Beynon. "If someone has been on opiates for years, their tolerance will be higher and they will need higher doses to achieve an analgesic effect. But some doctors don't realise that.

"Another big problem is that as people age they inevitably need to take more medicine, particularly if they have health issues. Helping addicts to keep track of complicated regimes can be hard. They just don't remember to take their pills."

There is also mounting evidence that overdoses can be more likely as users get older—despite the false confidence many might feel after surviving decades using a particular substance.

"General problems of ageing may well make it harder to fight an overdose, putting long-standing users at greater risk," says Simpson. In particular, emphysema, bronchitis and other lung problems—smoking cigarettes as well as illegal substances is common among addicts—can result in chronic obstructive pulmonary disease, which can in turn heighten the risk of overdose.

Some addicts and those who work with them believe that the culture of methadone prescriptions has exacerbated the problem, as for decades treatment has focused on stabilising addicts, leaving many "parked up" at home.

"They just sit there waiting for the dole to turn up," says Lewis Ward, 55, a service user involvement worker in Castleford, west Yorkshire, for the social enterprise Turning Point. He was addicted to heroin for 20 years until he quit five years ago. "Although I was always working, I know how they feel. I thought I couldn't give up for years and years because I was raising a family and I couldn't afford the six-month disruption of getting clean."

Under the coalition government's drug strategy, every addict should be helped off all drugs, including methadone. But there are concerns that it will be much harder for older users to get clean than younger addicts, who have not been using drugs for as long. "We need to be really sensitive about how we do this," says O'Mara. "It's very different dealing with a 20-year-old who might have been on heroin for a short time and someone who's been an addict for 30-40 years. A lot of people are thinking: 'I'm 60. How am I going to do this?'"

She also believes that there needs to be some acknowledgment that, for some, it will be too late to change. "Most people don't want to be an addict forever. But at the same time we need to recognise that for some people they just can't live any other way. They've been on opiates their whole lives and we can't just start poking them with a stick and saying: 'Get up. Get a job.'"

Ultimately, there will come a point for many ageing addicts when they can no longer look after themselves at home, and then there is huge uncertainty about what to do.

In Rotterdam, this apprehension is being allayed. Seniorepand is a semi-private medical foundation billed as the world's first retirement home for drug users. In the Netherlands, addicts receive free healthcare and methadone, and while residents at Seniorepand are encouraged to use fewer drugs, its aim is to provide a place for them to live out their last days in dignity.

Could such a facility work in the UK? "There are no plans to introduce similar specialist facilities in England," says Paul Hayes, chief executive of the National Treatment Agency for Substance Misuse.

But representatives of the care industry remain concerned that it is not fully prepared for rising numbers of addicts and that care homes for older people cannot at present meet drug users' needs.

"[Managing people with addictions] will be an enormous challenge," says Martin Green, chief executive of the English Community Care Home Association. Care homes are not paid to look after addicts and do not have the requisite expertise to manage people with significant drug or indeed alcohol problems.

"This is an issue that will increase in prevalence and the health and social care system needs to start planning for it. The government should acknowledge this issue and re-direct some of the money currently in rehab services to care providers," says Green.

But a spokesman for the Department of Health insists the system is ready: "Before a person is admitted to a care home, the local authority social services department should assess their health and personal care needs, including any addictions, and arrange care to meet those needs that fall within its eligibility criteria."

Either way, Jones is not reassured: "Can you imagine being an addict in a regular old people's home? You wouldn't be able to move without being glared at. It would be terrible.

"With the way things are I'd rather be dependent on drugs than other people," she says.

Critical Thinking

1. Why are addicts living longer?
2. What are some of the serious health problems that addicts confront as they are?
3. What is Seniorepand? What do they do?

Fetal Alcohol Spectrum Disorders: When Science, Medicine, Public Policy, and Laws Collide

KENNETH R. WARREN AND BRENDA G. HEWITT

Historically, alcohol has been used for different purposes, including as a part of religious observances, as a food, at times as a medicine, and its well-known use as a beverage, often in place of uncertain water sources [Vallee 1994, 1998]. It is alcohol's use as a beverage and to some extent as a medicine that has most often come into social and legal conflict, partly as interest in the effects of alcohol on the social fabric of society has waxed and waned and partly due to increasing scientific evidence of alcohol's benefits and risks. While the literature on alcohol's many uses over the millennia is fascinating and growing, we will limit our comments in this article to cyclic waxing and waning of concern for the effects of prenatal alcohol use, primarily focusing on changing views of alcohol's prenatal and antenatal effects.

Historical Reflections: What Did We Know and When Did We Know It?

As noted by Jones and Smith, "historical reports indicate that the observation of an adverse effect on the fetus of chronic maternal alcoholism is not new" [Jones et al., 1978]. As many authors have concluded, mention of adverse pregnancy outcomes associated with alcohol use has been noted by Aristotle, Plutarch, and Diogenes [Lemoine et al. 2003], in the Bible [Randall, 2001], in 18th Century England [Warner and Rosett, 1975], and in 19th century medical and temperance literature [Warner and Rosett, 1975]. For example, Aristotle's warning about the effects of drinking on progeny ("foolish, drunken, and harebrained women most often bring forth children like unto themselves, morose, and languid") is often cited as one of the earliest observations of alcohol's effect on pregnancy and pregnancy outcomes. Another often cited reference is Judges 13:7 in which an angel appears to Manoah and his wife and states "Behold, thou shall conceive, and bear a son, and now drink no wine or strong drink. . . ." The couple obeys the admonition and Manoah's wife bears a son, Sampson, who becomes renowned for his physical strength and wisdom. However, much of the literature on alcohol use and pregnancy begins within the 18th century and the "London Gin Epidemic" which is considered by many authors to be the genesis of the first medical warnings about the dire consequences of drinking during pregnancy.

London Gin Epidemic (~1720–1750)

The "London Gin Epidemic" occurred at a time when newer distillation technologies entered England from the Netherlands simultaneous with the ascent of William and Mary (from the same country) to the throne of England. Bans were placed on the importation of French wines, England experienced bumper crops of wheat, and taxes were lowered on gin (distilled from wheat) for the benefit of wealthy landowners. These conditions created what amounted to the "perfect storm" for the production, distribution, and consumption of "cheap, plentiful" gin [Warner and Rosett, 1975]. In his often quoted treatise on the excesses of gin drinking as the underlying cause of increased criminal behavior in 18th century London, the English author and magistrate, Henry Fielding, addressed a number of social, moral, and health ills he and other members of the upper social strata attributed to the excess drinking of gin. According to Fielding, "the consumption of [gin] is almost wholly confined to the lowest Order of the People [Fielding, 1751]." Among the ills he described were those inflicted on unborn children and future generations: . . . What must become of the Infant who is conceived in Gin? with the poisonous distillations of which it is nourished both in the Womb and the Breast [Fielding, 1751]." Other contemporaries of Fielding made similar observations. For example, customs administrator and noted economist Corbyn Morris observed that the significant death rate relative to births in London was particularly attributable to the enormous use of spirituous liquors . . . which render such as are born meager and sickly and unable to pass through the first stages of life [Morris, 1751]. William Hogarth's depiction of the horrors of gin drinking by the lower classes in his famous Gin Lane [1751] has been described by some authors (but not by all) as depicting the fetal alcohol syndrome [Rodin, 1981; Abel, 2001b].

By 1725 the damage that was attributed to alcohol was so great that the London College of Physicians presented its concerns about the medical and social problems occasioned by excessive alcohol use in a petition to the House of Commons. Among the concerns expressed was that

". . . the frequent use of several sorts of distilled Spirituous Liquors . . . [is] too often the cause of weak, feeble, distempered children, who must be instead of an advantage and strength, a charge to their Country." Whether prompted by fear of losing the common worker, fear for self and property, or medical concerns about alcohol's effects including those on pregnancy outcome, the observations made by influential Londoners, including Fielding, Morris, and Hogarth, are widely credited as contributing to the eventual repeal of laws that helped fuel the cheap production of gin and the "gin epidemic" [Coffey, 1966].

Not All Agree

Examples of historic knowledge of alcohol's effects on pregnancy such as those described above are presented in many articles on alcohol and pregnancy. The most comprehensive of the earliest reviews of historic observations was an excellent account from ancient times to the early 1970s [Warner and Rosett, 1975]. This article was subsequently criticized in a number of publications [Abel 1997, 1999, 2001a,b; Armstrong and Abel, 2000] for over interpretation and imputing the meaning of historical events to imply that the earlier centuries truly understood alcohol teratogenesis and had seen FAS. For example, while Warner and Rosett suggest that the entry in Judges is a recognition of the harm alcohol can cause during pregnancy, Abel notes that there are other explanations in the biblical text, for example, membership of Manoah in a sect that was abstinent (meaning that Samson should also be abstinent) to account for this admonition without invoking a knowledge of teratology [Abel, 1997]. We would also suggest that it may well have simply reflected an acknowledgement of warnings handed down from antiquity concerning the use of alcohol at the time of conception (by men and women) to prevent damage to the child or to the pregnancy. In this interpretation, both parents were judged capable of damaging a child due to alcohol use. As pointed out by Lemoine, "unfortunately, two errors have persisted throughout time . . . very often paternal alcoholism was blamed . . ."; and "exaggerations led to accusing alcohol for many unidentified physical and psychological anomalies" [Lemoine, 2003].

Alcohol, Medicine, and Politics: Temperance to Prohibition

"The abuse of alcohol is so mixed up with morals, science, and economics that it is impossible to disentangle the effects of the chemical substance itself from its associated social complexities" [Boycott, 1923].

"Our society's conceptions of disease are often weighted by moral valences as well as biological realities" [Armstrong, 1998].

That alcohol has an effect on pregnancy outcome is well documented in 19th and early 20th Century literature [Warner and Rosett, 1975]. However, scientific findings were interpreted through the lens of then contemporary public attitudes about alcohol, its linking to a wide variety of social ills by the temperance movement, and by a lack of basic scientific understanding, particularly with regard to the differences between heredity and prenatal effects [Katcher, 1993].

That alcohol has an effect on pregnancy outcome is well-documented in 19th and early 20th Century literature.

Reviewing 19th century scientific/medical literature, it is difficult to determine whether deficits in children are attributed to alcohol consumption in pregnancy, male and/or female alcohol use at the time of conception or before conception, damage to genetic factors (germ cells); toxic damage to the fetus from alcohol exposure in the womb; alcohol exposure post pregnancy through breast milk, or even the direct feeding of alcohol to the infant in place of breast milk.

One often cited reason for this difficulty is the involvement of a large number of physicians in the temperance movement (primarily in the United States and England) and the subsequent influence of this movement on medical views of alcohol's injurious effects on health in general and on pregnancy outcome in particular.

Another complicating factor with the early literature was a lack of modern (20th century) understanding of genetics, heredity, toxicity, and teratology. In the preMendel period, even knowledgeable physicians were unaware of the heredity principles of Mendelian genetics, and the distinction between genetic inheritance (DNA), damage to the "germ line" (sperm and ova), and direct toxic damage to developing tissues and organs. The Lamarckian view that traits acquired by either parent during his or her lifetime can be passed on to offspring (like inebriety or alcoholism) was not uncommon. Consistent with Lamarck, Robert MacNish of Glasgow wrote in 1835: "the children (of confirmed drunkards) are in general neither numerous nor healthy. From the general defect of vital power in the parental system, they are apt to be puny and emaciated" [MacNish, 1835]. Ironically, we now understand that some aspects of Lamarckian inheritance do indeed exist via mechanisms of epigenetics. This view was somewhat modified by WC Sullivan in his observations on 600 births to female prison inmates. Sullivan found 335 pregnancies ended in stillbirth or death to surviving children before age 2 and 80 women had three or more such infant deaths. He concluded that although inebriety could be transmitted by either parent to his or her offspring, "maternal inebriety is a condition peculiarly unfavorable to the vitality and to the normal development of the offspring a large part [of which] depends on the primary action of the poison" [Sullivan, 1899].

Between 1912 and 1920 Charles Stockard (Cornell University) conducted what for the time were very careful experiments on pregnancy outcomes in a guinea pig model. Both male and female guinea pigs were exposed to alcohol via an inhalation model before conception. Stockard found effects on growth and viability (liveborn, stillborn) in the offspring. These effects on viability persisted when the 1st generation offspring were mated with guinea pigs without a heritage of alcohol exposure but diminished with each subsequent generation. After four generations, the initial alcohol-exposed line had returned to the values of the control group [Stockard, 1918]. Stockard's findings appear very consistent with the 21st century understanding of epigenetics. MacDowell reproduced Stockard's results with rats finding reduced viability in the first generation and increased litters in the second generation [MacDowell and Vicari 1917; MacDowell, 1922]. He attributed the reduced viability in alcoholized rats to the effect of alcohol on "germplasm bearing factors detrimental to litter production" and "increased litters in the second generation to the elimination of the litters in the first generation that bore the less fertile germinal material" [MacDowell, 1922].

The following passage from an article appearing in the British Journal of Inebriety in 1923 sums up 19th and early 20th century thought on alcohol and pregnancy: "I think it is not an exaggeration to state that alcohol is a poison, and that the fetus of a chronic alcoholic mother is itself a chronic alcoholic, absorbing alcohol from the mother's blood and subsequently from her milk . . ." That is, they knew it did damage to the fetus if not exactly how. This knowledge appears to have been widely held among physicians and scientists during this time.

Nascent research progress that had begun during the heyday of early alcohol research came to an abrupt halt in 1919 with the passage of the Volstead Act and the ratification of the 18th Amendment to the U.S. Constitution prohibiting "the manufacture, sale, or transportation of intoxicating liquors . . . for beverage purposes" ushering in the era known as Prohibition. From the mid-1850s until Prohibition, many physicians were "temperance" advocates supporting total abstinence from alcohol use [Varma and Sharma, 1981]. By the time Prohibition became a reality, public opinion, largely stimulated by the temperance movement, had shifted from a view of inebriety as being an individual problem to one that found alcohol at the root of most health and social ills. With alcohol ostensibly no longer available, problems related to its use were viewed as less urgent. When Prohibition ended in the United States in 1933, temperance leaders and temperance tenets were by and large denounced. The country had swung away from the view of alcohol as villain to one that viewed alcoholism, rather than alcohol use, as the problem. A new era in alcohol science resulted, in which alcohol's harmful effects were minimized, and the study of alcoholism (once again an individual problem) became the prime scientific/ medical focus [Katcher, 1993].

Alcohol and Pregnancy Research: Postprohibition and Beyond

A clear cycle can be seen between the large attention to drinking during pregnancy that occurred during the late 19th and early 20th centuries, and the "forgetfulness" of the harmful consequences of alcohol use [Warner and Rosett, 1975]. The country that had seen Prohibition turn into one of the deadliest crime waves then known, wanted nothing to do with alcohol as a problem. Not only did the country repudiate the prohibition of alcohol, but also the large body of science that had been generated during the late 19th and early 20th centuries likely because much of it was associated with temperance movement "moralism." Many of the physicians and scientists who had been involved in generating much of this science were so integrally identified with the temperance movement that most of their research was dismissed as reflecting a no longer fashionable "moral" view of alcohol [Katcher, 1993]. This carried over in the 1940s as scientists began, once more, to address concerns about harmful alcohol use [Warner and Rosett, 1975]. These scientists made it perfectly clear that their problem was not with alcohol use in the main but in what has come to be known as chronic late stage alcohol dependence. In an interesting chapter-by chapter repudiation of late 19th and early 20th century temperance "science" on alcohol, Haggard and Jellinek sought to distance the neo-science of "chronic intolerance" (alcoholism) from the temperance-colored science published in the earlier century. They wanted the focus on alcoholism, not on alcohol. Writing in a 1942 book covering what was then known about the biological and psychological effects of alcohol, Haggard and Jellinek addressed the temperance view of alcohol's damage to the "germ" or the egg of the mother and/ or sperm of the father, thus affecting the physical/mental status of the child. According to Haggard and Jellinek, ascribing damage to the child as a result of drinking alcohol was a "belief, reflected in myth and custom . . ." that has "maintained itself up to present times." Thus, they approached alcohol not in terms of alcohol as a teratogen, but in terms of alcohol's effect on reproduction and associated organs. While acknowledging that the appearance of feeblemindedness, epilepsy, and mental disorders is more frequent among the offspring of abnormal drinkers, they stated unequivocally that this was not a direct effect of alcohol, but of "bad stock" or defects inherited by offspring "which predispose to alcoholism" [Haggard and Jellinek, 1942].

Even then, vestiges of the country's dislike of the temperance movement and Prohibition remained and Jellinek, often referenced as the father of the modern era of alcoholism research, and others who were at the head of alcohol's rediscovery as a researchable topic, did not believe that maternal alcohol use was detrimental to the fetus. In fact, Haggard and Jellinek wrote, "the fact is that no acceptable evidence has ever been offered to show that acute alcoholic intoxication has any effect whatsoever on the human germ or . . . in altering heredity" [Warner and Rosett, 1975]. They posited that the damaged children of alcoholic parents were the result of poor nutrition; alcohol exposure in the womb as the agent responsible for causing physical and mental abnormalities in children did not appear to be a possibility.

Modern Recognition of Alcohol as a Teratogen

We now know that alcohol, certainly when consumed at doses consistent with the lowest thresholds of legal intoxication (0.08% blood alcohol concentration), is an agent capable of causing not only a variety of health problems but also birth defects. Alcohol is a teratogen. Because of its common availability and usage, alcohol is more than just a teratogen; it is the most prominent behavioral teratogen in the world. Indeed, alcohol may be viewed as having introduced an entirely new discipline—that of behavioral teratology.

Because of its common availability and usage, alcohol is more than just a teratogen; it is the most prominent behavioral teratogen in the world.

FAS as a Modern Diagnosis

In 1970, Christine Ulleland, a medical student at the University of Washington, undertook a thesis project to study children hospitalized for failure to thrive. In reviewing the medical charts, she observed that a common element in the medical records was an indication of alcoholism in over 41% of the mothers noting, "these observations indicate that infants of alcoholic mothers are at high risk for pre- and postnatal growth and developmental failure," and suggesting that "greater attention should be given to alcoholic women during the child bearing years" [Ulleland, 1970].

When the prominent dysmorphologist, David Smith, and his associate, Kenneth Lyons Jones, examined a group of these children they immediately recognized the subtle, but important, pattern we now know as FAS. The physical and behavioral characteristics of these children were subsequently published [Jones et al., 1973], ushering in the modern era of research on fetal alcohol syndrome.

In their search for other evidence of the adverse effects of alcohol on fetal outcome, Jones and Smith discovered a paper published in 1968 in France, by Lemoine et al., [1968] describing virtually the identical physical and behavioral problems among 127 children of alcoholic mothers from Roubaix, France. The Lemoine paper had likely escaped attention because it appeared in a minor journal and was published in French [Warner and Rosett, 1975]. Subsequently, an earlier doctoral dissertation on the influence of parental alcoholic intoxication on the physical development of young babies by Jacqueline Rouquette, published in Paris in 1957, came to the attention of FAS researchers [Barrison et al., 1985]. In their second publication, David Smith introduced the name "fetal alcohol syndrome" to describe their clinical observations [Jones and Smith, 1973]. It was often the case that a new syndrome would be named after the scientists or physicians who first describe the condition (e.g., Williams's Syndrome). The authors chose to assign the name fetal alcohol syndrome (FAS) because they believed that the name would call attention to alcohol as a teratogen, alert women to the dangers of drinking in pregnancy, and aid in the elimination of this disorder. While the name FAS does garner attention in the medical community and public, some argue that the name FAS today may actually be more problematic due to the stigma associated with alcohol problems than if a neutral name like "Smith and Jones" or "Lemoine" syndrome had been applied.

No Immediate Acceptance

Despite the Lemoine and Jones and Smith reports, much skepticism as to whether alcohol could cause birth defects existed in the 1970s. For example, if it truly existed, why did we not know about it before in this era of modern medicine? How did we know that alcohol was indeed the agent rather than nutrition, other drug use, or the "deviant lifestyle" of the alcoholic woman?

The answer to these questions required the undertaking of animal and epidemiological research and a funding agency to support that research.

The National Institute on Alcohol Abuse and Alcoholism and FAS: The Story of a Science Success

In the late 1960s, a United States Senator, Harold E. Hughes, himself a recovering alcoholic, along with a group of influential recovering alcoholics with business and political acumen and ties, began advocating for legislation to create a federal focal point for alcoholism. At this time, medicine had little if any concern for alcoholics who were seen as morally deficient, or suffering from weak wills or character defects (shades of the earlier 19th/20th centuries temperance movement). Treatment for alcoholism was mainly accomplished through Alcoholics Anonymous, and to a much smaller extent within state mental health systems (a small center for the control and prevention of alcoholism in the National Institute of Mental Health was tasked with helping to create a federal alcoholism presence mainly within the existing federal and state mental health services system).

Many early alcohol investigators noted that alcohol research was as stigmatized as alcoholism itself [Lieber, 1988]. The National Institutes of Health supported very limited alcohol research; what was supported was often disguised as something else, e.g., using alcohol as a "probe" to study other types of liver disease. Indeed, a major epidemiological study of birth defects undertaken in the late 1960s did not ask any questions on alcohol use [Jones et al., 1974]. This attitude changed with the passage of the landmark Comprehensive Alcohol Abuse and Alcoholism Prevention, Treatment and Rehabilitation Act of 1970 (P.L. 91–616) which established the National Institute on Alcohol Abuse and Alcoholism (NIAAA) and provided national visibility and funds to understand, prevent, and treat alcoholism and problems related to alcoholism. NIAAA, with its newly minted research mandate, supported the research that helped to validate the existence of FAS and what we now recognize as the full spectrum of fetal alcohol spectrum disorders (FASD).

The 1970s alcohol and pregnancy research took two forms: animal research and human epidemiological research. Animal research established the nature of FAS teratogenesis by verifying that the same deficits reported by Lemoine and Jones and Smith could be seen in animals (rodents, dogs, and later primates); and that alcohol and not other confounding factors were responsible. Human epidemiological research prospectively examining the outcomes of children exposed to alcohol in pregnancy demonstrated the range of physical and behavioral deficits in children exposed to alcohol in pregnancy. By 1977, NIAAA sponsored the first international research conference on FAS. Though not an original intent of the meeting, those attending were so impressed with the findings to date that they collectively recommended that NIAAA issue the first government health advisory on FAS.

Warning the Public

Doing anything the first time in Government presents numerous challenges. In this instance, NIAAA was attempting to have the Federal Government put its imprimatur on a warning about drinking during pregnancy that ran counter to prevailing medical and social practices. Resistance from within the US Department of Health, Education and Welfare (now the US Department of Health and Human Services), NIAAA's administrative home, and from non-Federal groups and organizations was expected. Federal skepticism was overcome primarily due to the strength of the science, and the first governmental advisory about alcohol use during pregnancy was published by NIAAA in 1977 [Warren and Foudin, 2001]. Taking a "conservative approach" this first ever advisory stated that more than six drinks a day was dangerous and recommended a "2-Drink Limit" per day. Unlike today's warnings against any use until proven safe, implicit in this first warning was the notion that alcohol use is "safe" within the given guidelines until proven dangerous.

The response was as varied (and as vocal) as expected. For example, the recommendation in the advisory was supported by the American College of Pediatrics, but not immediately by the American College of Obstetrics and Gynecology. Some medical and patient advocacy organizations criticized NIAAA for going too far, and some for not going far enough, by not recommending abstinence during pregnancy. However, the 1977 Health Advisory did focus sufficient attention on the issue of alcohol and pregnancy that Senate hearings were held for the purpose of considering legislation requiring warning labels related to alcohol and pregnancy risks. The outcome of the hearings was the call for a Report to the President and Congress on *Health Hazards Associated with Alcohol and Methods to Inform the General Public of these Hazards* prepared jointly by the Departments of Health and Human Services and Treasury [US Department of Transportation and US Department of Health and Human Services, 1980]. The report did not immediately call for alcoholic beverage labeling but did recommend the issuance of a Surgeon General's Advisory on

Alcohol and Pregnancy that was subsequently issued in 1981 [FDA Drug Bulletin 1981]. Unlike the previous Advisory, the 1981 Advisory recommended that women who are pregnant or planning to become pregnant avoid alcohol. In 1988 Congress considered the issue of alcoholic beverage labeling as a means to warn of the dangers of alcohol exposure in the womb and enacted the Alcoholic Beverage Labeling Act of 1988 (Public Law 100690) which became effective in 1989. In 2005, the Surgeon General reissued an updated advisory on alcohol use and pregnancy that warned against FASD, the full spectrum of birth defects caused by prenatal alcohol exposure (US Surgeon General, 2005].

Conclusion: Promises of Current Research

Although today there is little disagreement about the existence of FASD, we are again embroiled in determinations that are as much about policy as medicine. What does a physician tell his/her patient who is either pregnant or may become pregnant? The US Surgeon General's Advisory on Alcohol and Pregnancy is clear. We do not know the dose at which we can unequivocally state that the fetus will not be harmed. It is therefore prudent advice to avoid all drinking during these time periods. Yet, there is not full agreement on this issue. Recently, for example, a medical ethicist likened this message to "medical paternalism" [Gavaghan, 2009]. As science continues to refine our knowledge of the consequences of exposure to alcohol during gestation, we are hopeful that public health policies and practice can reach closure on what advice will best serve pregnant women and their future offspring.

As concluded by Clarren and Smith, alcohol exposure during gestation "appears to be the most frequent known teratogenic cause of mental deficiency in the Western world" which "through accurate understanding . . . and widespread public awareness could be largely reduced and, ideally, eliminated" [Clarren and Smith, 1978]. This was the goal of the early pioneers in describing FAS and FASD, and it remains the goal of committed scientists, patients, and their families today.

References

Abel EL. 1997. Was the fetal alcohol syndrome recognized in the ancient Near East? Alcohol Alcohol 32:3–7.

Abel EL. 1999. Was the fetal alcohol syndrome recognized by the Greeks and Romans? Alcohol Alcohol 34:868–872.

Abel EL. 2001a. The gin epidemic: much ado about what? Alcohol Alcohol 36:401–405.

Abel EL. 2001b. Gin lane: did Hogarth know about fetal alcohol syndrome? Alcohol Alcohol 36:131–134.

Armstrong EM. 1998. Diagnosing moral disorder: the discovery and evolution of fetal alcohol syndrome. Soc Sci Med 47:2025–2042.

Armstrong EM, Abel EL. 2000. Fetal alcohol syndrome: the origins of a moral panic. Alcohol Alcohol 35:276–282.

Barrison IG, Waterson EJ, Murray-Lyon IM. 1985. Adverse effects of alcohol in pregnancy. Addiction 80:11–22.

Boycott AE. 1923. The action of alcohol on man. Lancet 202:1055–1056.

Clarren SK, Smith DW. 1978. The fetal alcohol syndrome. N Engl J Med 298:1063–1067.

Coffey T. 1966. Beer street—Gin lane—some views of 18th-century drinking. Quart J Stud Alcohol 27:669–692.

FDA Drug Bulletin. 1981. Surgeon general's advisory on alcohol and pregnancy. Washington, DC: FDA Drug Bulletin. p 9–10.

Fielding H. 1751. An enquiry into the causes of the late increase of robbers, etc.: with some proposals for remedying this growing evil. London: printed for A. Millar. 203 p.

Gavaghan C. 2009. "You can't handle the truth"; medical paternalism and prenatal alcohol use. J Med Ethics 35:300–303.

Haggard HW, Jellinek EM. 1942. Alcohol explored. Garden City: Doubleday, Doran and Company. 297 p.

Jones KL, Hanson JW, Smith DW. 1978. Palpebral fissure size in newborn infants. J Pediatr 92:787.

Jones KL, Smith DW. 1973. Recognition of the fetal alcohol syndrome in early infancy. Lancet 302:999–1001.

Jones K, Smith D, Streissguth A, et al. 1974. Outcome in offspring of chronic alcoholic women. Lancet 303:1076–1078.

Jones K, Smith D, Ulleland C, et al. 1973. Pattern of malformation in offspring of chronic alcoholic mothers. Lancet 301:1267–1271.

Katcher BS. 1993. The post-repeal eclipse in knowledge about the harmful effects of alcohol. Addiction 88:729–744.

Lemoine P. 2003. The history of alcoholic fetopathies (1997). J FAS Int 1:e2.

Lemoine P, Harousse H, Borteyru JP, et al. 1968. Children of alcoholic parents—anomalies in 127 cases. Arch Francaises De Pediatr 25: 830–832.

Lemoine P, Harousseau H, Borteyru JP, et al. 2003. Children of alcoholic parents—observed anomalies: discussion of 127 cases. Ther Drug Monit 25:132–136.

Lieber C. 1988. NIAAA and alcohol research: a researcher's view—National Institute on alcohol abuse and alcoholism. Perspectives on current research. Alcohol Health Res World 12:306–307.

MacDowell EC. 1922. The influence of alcohol on the fertility of white rats. Genetics 7:117–141.

MacDowell EC, Vicari EM. 1917. On the growth and fecundity of alcoholized rats. Proc Natl Acad Sci USA 3:577–579.

MacNish R. 1835. The anatomy of drunkenness. New York: D. Appleton. 227.

Morris C. 1751. Observation on the past growth and present state of the city of London. London.

Randall CL. 2001. Alcohol and pregnancy: highlights from three decades of research. J Stud Alcohol 62:554–561.

Rodin AE. 1981. Infants and Gin mania in 18th century London. JAMA 245:1237–1239.

Stockard CR, GNP. 1918. Further studies on the modification of the germ-cells in mammals: the effect of alcohol on treated guinea-pigs and their descendants. J Exp Zool 26: 119–226.

Sullivan WC. 1899. A note on the influence of maternal inebriety on the offspring. J Mental Sci 45:489–503.

Ulleland C. 1970. Offspring of alcoholic mothers. Pediatr Res 4:474.

US Department of Transportation, US Department of Health and Human Services. 1980. Report to the president and congress on health hazards associated with alcohol and methods to inform the general public of these hazards. Washington, DC.

US Surgeon General. 2005. Surgeon general's advisory on alcohol and pregnancy. Washington, DC: US Department of Health and Human Services.

Vallee BL. 1994. Alcohol in human history. EXS 71:1–8.

Vallee BL. 1998. Alcohol in the western world. Sci Am 278:80–85.

Varma SK, Sharma BB. 1981. Fetal alcohol syndrome. Prog Biochem Pharmacol 18: 122–129.

Warner RH, Rosett HL. 1975. The effects of drinking on offspring: an historical survey of the American and British literature. J Stud Alcohol 36:1395–1420.

Warren KR, Foudin LL. 2001. Alcohol-related birth defects—the past, present, and future. Alcohol Res Health 25:153–158.

Critical Thinking

1. To date, scientists have not been able to determine the dose level at which the fetus will be harmed by alcohol. What factors must a pregnant mother consider when deciding whether to drink during pregnancy?

2. What do you think is the best advice a doctor can give his or her patient concerning alcohol consumption during pregnancy?

3. How should policymakers approach this topic to reduce the incidence rate of FAS?

Addiction Diagnoses May Rise Under Guideline Changes

IAN URBINA

In what could prove to be one of their most far-reaching decisions, psychiatrists and other specialists who are rewriting the manual that serves as the nation's arbiter of mental illness have agreed to revise the definition of addiction, which could result in millions more people being diagnosed as addicts and pose huge consequences for health insurers and taxpayers.

The revision to the manual, known as the Diagnostic and Statistical Manual of Mental Disorders, or D.S.M., would expand the list of recognized symptoms for drug and alcohol addiction, while also reducing the number of symptoms required for a diagnosis, according to proposed changes posted on the website of the American Psychiatric Association, which produces the book.

In addition, the manual for the first time would include gambling as an addiction, and it might introduce a catchall category—"behavioral addiction—not otherwise specified"—that some public health experts warn would be too readily used by doctors, despite a dearth of research, to diagnose addictions to shopping, sex, using the Internet or playing video games.

Part medical guidebook, part legal reference, the manual has long been embraced by government and industry. It dictates whether insurers, including Medicare and Medicaid, will pay for treatment, and whether schools will expand financing for certain special-education services. Courts use it to assess whether a criminal defendant is mentally impaired, and pharmaceutical companies rely on it to guide their research.

The broader language involving addiction, which was debated this week at the association's annual conference, is intended to promote more accurate diagnoses, earlier intervention and better outcomes, the association said. "The biggest problem in all of psychiatry is untreated illness, and that has huge social costs," said Dr. James H. Scully Jr., chief executive of the group.

But the addiction revisions in the manual, scheduled for release in May 2013, have already provoked controversy similar to concerns previously raised about proposals on autism, depression and other conditions. Critics worry that changes to the definitions of these conditions would also sharply alter the number of people with diagnoses.

While the association says that the addiction definition changes would lead to health care savings in the long run, some economists say that 20 million substance abusers could be newly categorized as addicts, costing hundreds of millions of dollars in additional expenses.

"The chances of getting a diagnosis are going to be much greater, and this will artificially inflate the statistics considerably," said Thomas F. Babor, a psychiatric epidemiologist at the University of Connecticut who is an editor of the international journal Addiction. Many of those who get addiction diagnoses under the new guidelines would have only a mild problem, he said, and scarce resources for drug treatment in schools, prisons and health care settings would be misdirected.

"These sorts of diagnoses could be a real embarrassment," Dr. Babor added.

The scientific review panel of the psychiatric association has demanded more evidence to support the revisions on addiction, but several researchers involved with the manual have said that the panel is not likely to change its proposal significantly.

The controversies about the revisions have highlighted the outsize influence of the manual, which brings in more than $5 million annually to the association and is written by a group of 162 specialists in relative secrecy. Besieged from all sides, the association has received about 25,000 comments on the proposed changes from treatment centers, hospital representatives, government agencies, advocates for patient groups and researchers. The organization has declined to make these comments public.

While other medical specialties rely on similar diagnostic manuals, none have such influence. "The D.S.M. is distinct from all other diagnostic manuals because it has an enormous, perhaps too large, impact on society and millions of people's lives," said Dr. Allen J. Frances, a professor of psychiatry and behavioral sciences at Duke, who oversaw the writing of the current version of the manual and worked on previous editions. "Unlike many other fields, psychiatric illnesses have no clear biological gold standard for diagnosing them. They present in different ways, and illnesses often overlap with each other."

Dr. Frances has been one of the most outspoken critics of the new draft version, saying that overly broad and vaguely worded definitions will create more "false epidemics" and "medicalization of everyday behavior." Like some others, he has also questioned whether a private association, whose members stand to gain from treating more patients, should be writing the manual, rather than an independent group or a federal agency.

Under the new criteria, people who often drink more than intended and crave alcohol may be considered mild addicts. Under the old criteria, more serious symptoms, like repeatedly missing work or school, being arrested or driving under the influence, were required before a person could receive a diagnosis as an alcohol abuser.

Dr. George E. Woody, a professor of psychiatry at the University of Pennsylvania School of Medicine, said that by describing addiction as a spectrum, the manual would reflect more accurately the distinction between occasional drug users and full-blown addicts. Currently, only about 2 million of the nation's more than 22 million addicts get treatment, partly because many of them lack health insurance.

Dr. Keith Humphreys, a psychology professor at Stanford who specializes in health care policy and who served as a drug control policy adviser to the White House from 2009 to 2010, predicted that as many as 20 million people who were previously not recognized as having a substance abuse problem would probably be included under the new definition, with the biggest increase among people who are unhealthy users, rather than severe abusers, of drugs.

"This represents the single biggest expansion in the quality and quantity of addiction treatment this country has seen in 40 years," Dr. Humphreys said, adding that the new federal health care law may allow an additional 30 million people who abuse drugs or alcohol to gain insurance coverage and access to treatment. Some economists have said that the number could be much lower, though, because many insurers will avoid or limit coverage of addiction treatment.

The savings from early intervention usually show up within a year, Dr. Humphreys said, and most patients with a new diagnosis would get consultations with nurses, doctors or therapists, rather than expensive prescriptions for medicines typically reserved for more severe abusers.

Many scholars believe that the new manual will increase addiction rates. A study by Australian researchers found, for example, that about 60 percent more people would be considered addicted to alcohol under the new manual's standards. Association officials expressed doubt, however, that the expanded addiction definitions would sharply increase the number of new patients, and they said that identifying abusers sooner could prevent serious complications and expensive hospitalizations.

"We can treat them earlier," said Dr. Charles P. O'Brien, a professor of psychiatry at the University of Pennsylvania and the head of the group of researchers devising the manual's new addiction standards. "And we can stop them from getting to the point where they're going to need really expensive stuff like liver transplants."

Some critics of the new manual have said that it has been tainted by researchers' ties to pharmaceutical companies.

"The ties between the D.S.M. panel members and the pharmaceutical industry are so extensive that there is the real risk of corrupting the public health mission of the manual," said Dr. Lisa Cosgrove, a fellow at the Edmond J. Safra Center for Ethics at Harvard, who published a study in March that said two-thirds of the manual's advisory task force members reported ties to the pharmaceutical industry or other financial conflicts of interest.

Dr. Scully, the association's chief, said the group had required researchers involved with writing the manual to disclose more about financial conflicts of interest than was previously required.

Dr. O'Brien, who led the addiction working group, has been a consultant for several pharmaceutical companies, including Pfizer, GlaxoSmithKline and Sanofi-Aventis, all of which make drugs marketed to combat addiction.

He has also worked extensively as a paid consultant for Alkermes, a pharmaceutical company, studying a drug, Vivitrol, that combats alcohol and heroin addiction by preventing craving. He was the driving force behind adding "craving" to the new manual's list of recognized symptoms of addiction.

"I'm quite proud to have played a role, because I know that craving plays such an important role in addiction," Dr. O'Brien said, adding that he had never made any money from the sale of drugs that treat craving.

Dr. Howard B. Moss, associate director for clinical and translational research at the National Institute on Alcohol Abuse and Alcoholism, in Bethesda, Md., described opposition from many researchers to adding "craving" as a symptom of addiction. He added that he quit the group working on the addiction chapter partly out of frustration with what he described as a lack of scientific basis in the decision making.

"The more people diagnosed with cravings," Dr. Moss said, "the more sales of anticraving drugs like Vivitrol or naltrexone."

Critical Thinking

1. What exactly is the Diagnostic and Statistical Manual of Mental Disorders?

2. What is a "behavioral addiction?

3. Who is responsible for writing and publishing the DSM?

An Addiction Vaccine, Tantalizingly Close

ROBERT BENSON

Imagine a vaccine against smoking: People trying to quit would light up a cigarette and feel nothing. Or a vaccine against cocaine, one that would prevent addicts from enjoying the drug's high.

Though neither is imminent, both are on the drawing board, as are vaccines to combat other addictions. While scientists have historically focused their vaccination efforts on diseases like polio, smallpox and diphtheria—with great success—they are now at work on shots that could one day release people from the grip of substance abuse.

"We view this as an alternative or better way for some people," said Dr. Kim D. Janda, a professor at the Scripps Research Institute who has made this his life's work. "Just like with nicotine patches and the gum, all those things are just systems to get people off the drugs."

Dr. Janda, a gruff-talking chemist, has been trying for more than 25 years to create such a vaccine. Like shots against disease, these vaccines would work by spurring the immune system to produce antibodies that would shut down the narcotic before it could take root in the body, or in the brain.

Unlike preventive vaccines—like the familiar ones for mumps, measles and so on—this type of injection would be administered after someone had already succumbed to an addictive drug. For instance, cocaine addicts who had been vaccinated with one of Dr. Janda's formulations before they snorted cocaine reported feeling like they'd used "dirty coke," he said. "They felt like they were wasting their money."

It's a novel use for vaccines that has placed Dr. Janda, who is 54, in the vanguard of addiction treatment. Because addiction is now thought to cause physical changes in the brain, doctors increasingly advocate medical solutions to America's drug problem, leading to renewed interest in his work.

"It's very fashionable now," said Dr. Janda, seated in a black leather chair in his office. "When we started doing this 27 years ago, it wasn't."

In July, Dr. Janda's lab—25 researchers, most of graduate-school age—made headlines when it announced that it had produced a vaccine that blunted the effects of heroin in rats. Rodents given the vaccine didn't experience the pain-deadening effects of heroin and stopped helping themselves to the drug, presumably because it ceased to have any effect.

But as has often been the case in Dr. Janda's career, the breakthrough came on the heels of a setback: A Phase 2 clinical trial for a nicotine vaccine that was based largely on his work was declared a failure this summer when people receiving the drug quit smoking at the same rate as people receiving a placebo.

To this day, despite many promising breakthroughs, not one of Dr. Janda's vaccines has won approval from the Food and Drug Administration. For despite many successes in the lab—including promising animal tests—the vaccines have yet to produce consistent results in humans during clinical trials.

"It's like having the carrot right in front of the horse," he said. "The big problem plaguing these vaccines right now is difficulty predicting in humans how well it's going to work."

Or, he added, "maybe I'm just unlucky."

The scientific principle behind Dr. Janda's vaccines is, as he put it, "simplistically stupid." Much like vaccines against disease, they introduce a small amount of the foreign substance into the blood, causing the immune system to create antibodies that will attack that substance the next time it appears.

The difficulty is that molecules like cocaine, nicotine and methamphetamine are tiny—much smaller than disease molecules—so the immune system tends to ignore them. To overcome that, Dr. Janda attaches a hapten—which is either a bit of the drug itself, or a synthetic version of it—to a larger protein that acts as a platform. The last part of the vaccine is an adjuvant, a chemical cocktail that attracts the immune system's notice, effectively tricking it into making antibodies against a substance it usually wouldn't see.

"It's not like some magical premise," Dr. Janda said. "And the beauty of it is you're not messing with brain chemistry."

The contrast, he said, is to medications like Suboxone or methadone that are currently used to treat heroin addiction. In addition to blocking heroin's effects, the medications induce a mild high in many patients.

Dr. Janda says he has tried and failed to make vaccines against alcohol and marijuana abuse. In the case of alcohol, he said, ethanol molecules proved just too small to attach to the protein that would deliver the immunity. And in the case of marijuana, the main ingredient that produces the high—tetrahydrocannabinol, or THC—hides too well inside the body.

He has also tried formulating a vaccine against obesity. Rather than block a foreign substance, that vaccine would block the effects of a peptide hormone produced by the stomach called ghrelin that signals hunger in the brain. So far, a version of the vaccine has been shown to lower food intake in animals, though—again—it's unclear whether it will work in humans.

Even so, addicts and their families are clamoring to get into Dr. Janda's clinical trials. He says he gets e-mails every week from addicts asking to be included. He has had to turn away parents who showed up at his office with their drug-addicted children after reading about his work.

"What am I supposed to do, go in the lab and pull it out of the refrigerator and inject you?" he said. "I guess it's been so devastating in their families that they're looking for anything, and there's just nothing out there. It's really sad when you see these types of things."

Despite the disappointments, some scientists predict that Dr. Janda will succeed. No less an addiction expert than Dr. Nora Volkow, director of the National Institute on Drug Abuse, calls him a "visionary" who saw the opportunity to treat addiction with medicine decades before most. Indeed, one reason that her institute is a chief source of Dr. Janda's financing is Dr. Volkow's belief that his work will eventually produce a marketable vaccine.

"Now many people say, 'Yes, of course' " to the idea of treating drugs through vaccines, Dr. Volkow said. "But that took many years, and he traveled the road when there was a lot of skepticism."

Today, the scientists who are working to create vaccines against narcotics include Thomas Kosten at the Baylor College of Medicine and S. Michael Owens at the University of Arkansas. Dr. Kosten has had limited success with a cocaine vaccine, while Dr. Owens is focused on vaccines for methamphetamines.

All three researchers say they are hobbled by a lack of interest—read: financing—from pharmaceutical companies in vaccines for any drug other than nicotine, presumably because there is little money to be made in a shot given once every six months, and because such companies aren't eager to associate their brands with drug addicts.

And yet Dr. Janda's lifelong pursuit of vaccines against narcotics began not with some painful family struggle with addiction, but in a simple request in the 1980s from one of the Scripps Institute's former corporate partners.

"They were interested in the whole antibody area," he said. "They kind of approached me and said, 'Could you make antibodies to a drug of abuse?' So we embarked on this."

Dr. Janda spent many years trying to bring his own vaccines to market. In the '80s and '90s, he helped start some small pharmaceutical companies that patented and tested his work,

with varying degrees of success. One burned through $60 million of venture capital with nothing to show for it; another sold for $95 million in 1999, but "due to bad management and bad splits, I ended up with about enough money for a case of beer," he said—even more disappointing, perhaps, for a man with a taste for expensive bourbon.

These days, Dr. Janda prefers to publish his results in scientific journals and let others try to bring the vaccines to market.

He is quick to caution that taking away someone's ability to get high off of one drug hardly cures them of their addiction problems. There's nothing to stop a vaccinated cocaine addict, for example, from turning to methamphetamines.

Like any anti-addiction treatment, his vaccines are simply meant as "a crutch for people wanting to go into abstinence," Dr. Janda said. "The whole thing with addicts is you have to want to get off the drug, or it's not going to happen."

He is also wary of ethical issues posed by his work. Today, a recovering cocaine addict will pass a drug test just days after getting clean. But once vaccinated, that person could be tested for antibodies for up to six months, alerting employers to his struggles with addiction.

"Before a parent takes a kid into college, can she take him in for a round of vaccines against all drugs?" asked Jenny Treweek, a researcher at Janda Laboratories who is working on a vaccine for Rohypnol, otherwise known as the date-rape drug. "Some teenagers might have a real problem with that."

It's questions like that—and the desire to solve the molecular puzzle he's set up for himself—that motivate Dr. Janda to spend seven days a week in his lab, he said. He spends much of that time tweaking the components of his vaccines—trying different proteins or haptens, adjusting the adjuvants—hoping to hit precisely the right formula.

"If I vaccinated three people and they all got the same" immune response, he said, "then you would have a really straightforward shot how to move things forward."

But with nearly 30 years of tweaking already under his belt, he seems increasingly resigned to the idea that it might not be he who eventually moves it across the finish line.

"I figure I have eight or 10 years left," he said. "If something doesn't go in eight or 10 more years, then it's someone else's turn."

Critical Thinking

1. What is the difference between an addiction vaccine and medicines used to help someone withdrawal, such as suboxone or methadone?

2. Describe some of the hurdles in creating an addiction vaccine.

3. Discuss some possible problems with using an addiction vaccine.

Understanding Recovery Barriers: Youth Perceptions about Substance Use Relapse

Objective: To qualitatively explore how treatment-involved youth retrospectively contextualize relapse from substance use. *Methods:* Fourteen focus groups were conducted with 118 youth (78.3% male; 66.1% Latino) enrolled in participating substance abuse treatment programs (4 young adult and 10 adolescent) throughout Los Angeles County. Transcripts were analyzed for relapse perception themes. *Results:* Dominant relapse themes include emotional reasons (90%), life stressors (85%), cognitive factors (75%), socialization processes (65%), and environmental issues (55%). *Conclusions:* Youth perceptions about relapse during treatment should be used to better inform clinical approaches and shape early-intervention recovery agendas for substance-abusing youth.

RACHEL GONZALES, ET AL.

Substance use problems among youth under 25 represent one of the major prevention and treatment issues in the United States: nearly 70% of all youth mortality (ages 15–24) has been attributed to unintended injuries, homicide, and suicide,[1] all of which are highly correlated with substance use behaviors.[2,3] Moreover, statistics from general population US-based prevalence surveys, national treatment admission data, and juvenile justice drug offense cases support the extent of problem. National (US) survey studies show that illicit substance use and binge drinking trends for youth are up from previous years: 10.0% of 12-to 17-year-olds and 21.2% of 18-to 25- year-olds report past-month use of illicit substances, and past-month binge drinking rates were 8.8% and 41.7% for 12-to 17-and 18-to-25-year-olds, respectively.[4] Publicly funded treatment admissions are also high: 7.6% of admissions are under 18 and increase to 21.6% for those 18 to 25.[5] Substance use-related juvenile/criminal court cases are common as well: 44.2% of all cases ages 10–24 were for drug offenses, 15.1% for juveniles 10–17 years of age.[6]

Given such public health complexities, much of the attention regarding addressing substance use issues among youth has been directed at interrupting drug use through treatment settings, where the main goals are to "effectively reduce substance use behaviors and improve critical areas of life functioning that are expected to be positively influenced by treatment."[7] Large-scale treatment outcome studies with youth demonstrate that treatment (in general) produces positive changes in substance use and other psychosocial outcomes;[8–11] however, treatment benefits tend to diminish over time.[12] Substance use "relapse"

is of primary concern, which is typically about 65% in the first 90 days after treatment and increases to rates of about 85% during the post-year follow-up period.[11,13–20]

Relapse has been contextualized both as a "discrete outcome" or "a process."[21] Definitions of relapse also differ and typically have been either operationalized as "a return to any use" or "a return to original problematic use" before treatment.[22,23] There have been several attempts to establish specific conceptual models for relapse among adult populations.[23–33]

To date, conceptual models tend to categorize relapse using 4 major precursors/antecedents,[34,35] including the specific drug (agent), characteristics of the user (personal), characteristics of the user's social relationships/setting (interpersonal), and environmental (situational) factors. Relapse precursors that have received the most support include negative affective emotional states,[34,36,37] cognitive-behavioral factors including self-efficacy/confidence,[38] outcome expectancies,[39] urges/temptations,[40] coping,[41,42] and motivation/readiness to change.[34,44,45]

Interpersonal determinants include relationship conflict,[46–48] social pressures,[49] social support, and life stressors.[50–53] Environmental determinants include cue-situational exposures and geographic disadvantage, ie, high availability of drugs, crime and poverty.[27,54–57] Despite these findings, many studies conclude that relapse is often random, complex, and dynamic,[58–60] determined by an interaction of diverse physiological, individual, and situational factors,[32,61] and cannot be solely captured by a single process model.[62]

Research on substance use relapse among youth is less extensive. Existing youth-based studies have identified similar relapse determinants as are found among adult samples;[63-66] however, it is considered to be particularly more complex for several reasons: adolescents are still undergoing brain maturation and are in the midst of greater cognitive and social-emotional development processes;[67-69] have higher co-occurring mental health and psychosocial dysfunctions within family, school, and legal settings;[70-73] have greater influence from social agents/events;[74-76] have different clinical courses of substance use severity/diagnosis[77-80] and lower levels of treatment motivation.[80,81]

Although the literature is growing in the area of substance use relapse among youth populations, retrospective accounts of the relapse process are limited, and many substantive questions remain. This study employed a qualitative approach to examine the following research questions: (1) How do youth in treatment perceive their risk for substance use after treatment? (2) What are some major factors that are associated with relapse risk among treatment-involved youth? This study seeks to address these questions to identify some of the early warning signals indicating potential relapse for youth 24 years and younger to better inform clinical approaches to better meet the needs of substance-abusing youth as well as shape early-intervention recovery agendas.

Methods

A convenience sample of youth aged 12–24 was drawn from participating substance abuse treatment programs (10 adolescent specific and 4 adult) in diverse Los Angeles areas (San Gabriel Valley, North Hollywood, West Los Angeles, San Fernando Valley, and Antelope Valley). Unlike the adolescent-specific programs used, this sample does not include young adult-specific programs, but rather a select set of participating adult programs that had designated young adult groups to capture youth 18–24. Hence, due to the participating treatment sites availability of young adults, there are fewer young adults groups available. Research procedures were approved by the Institutional Review Board of the University of California Los Angeles.

Participants

One-hundred eighteen youth between 12 and 24 constitute the study sample: average age was 17.4 ± 2.9 years; 78.3% male; 66.1% Latino and 25.2% white (25.2%); 69.5% were in outpatient treatment; and most reported marijuana (40.9%) or methamphetamine (30.4%) as their primary substances of abuse. Sample characteristics are representative of youth based on wide-scale California treatment evalautions: average age of youth admissions is 17, 68% male, and 59% Latino.[84]

Procedure

A total of 14 focus groups were conducted with 118 youth in participating substance abuse treatment programs between September 2010 and December 2010. Focus groups were 90 minutes in length and digitally audio-recorded. Each participant received a $10 gift card for incentive. The principal investigator (PI) moderated each group using scripted questions.[34]

A research assistant (RA) trained in focus group procedures assisted with moderating the focus groups.

The scripted questions covered youth perceptions and attitudes around substance use behaviors, substance use relapse, and substance use recovery. The focus group leader (PI) used a standardized script to discuss the relapse concept and provide a common level of understanding of relapse. For this, participants were asked to think about life after treatment and consider the most common situations or reasons that caused them to relapse (defined as both (1) using any alcohol or drugs again and (2) reverting back to their pretreatment pattern of drug use). Using the following scenario: "Jane/John went through treatment for substance use problems. After treatment (within the next 3 months), he/she relapsed. Finish my statement: 'He/she relapsed because . . . ?'" After general responses to the relapse scenario were noted (ie, stress), specific reasons related to each response were assessed (ie, family, school, legal, etc). In addition to participating in the focus group discussion, all participants anonymously completed a demographic questionnaire collecting age, gender, race/ethnicity, primary substances used, and treatment history information for descriptive purposes.

Data Analysis

Audio recordings for 14 focus groups were transcribed by 2 research assistants and edited and re-reviewed by the research team for accuracy and fidelity. Transcripts were coded using a systematic set of procedures based on grounded theory[84] to inductively develop themes around relapse perceptions among youth. To ensure completeness and accuracy, 2 reviewers coded each transcript, and a third coder was used to resolve any discrepant coding by a consensus approach with the research team.[85] Using ATLAS.Ti, a qualitative statistical software program for content and text analysis,[86] focus group responses from all youth participants (N = 118; 92 adolescents and 24 young adults) were assessed to obtain overall percentages for each theme identified and unique responses per theme by age-group. Responses to the brief demographic questionnaire were quantitatively analyzed using SPSS, version 18; however, because of the assured anonymity, demographic questionnaire data could not be linked to focus group responses; hence, these results are presented descriptively. Overall, themes reported in results are based on analysis of open-ended responses to focus group scripted questions. Where appropriate, focus group (age) differences (ie, adolescent versus young adult) are reported.

Results

Table 1 provides 5 major themes that emerged in response to qualitative youth responses to the relapse scenario "He/She Relapsed Because . . ." This table is followed by examples of youth statements supporting each theme. It is important to note that some youth (from 10 adolescent focus groups, n = 92) did not even know what *relapse* meant (10%). For these youth, they were asked to consider responding to the questions based on the definitions of relapse used in the field [defined as (1) using any alcohol or drugs again or (2) reverting back to their pretreatment pattern of drug use].

Table 1 General Themes of Substance Use Relapse Among Youth 12–24 (N = 118)

	% Overall Group Response
Emotional Reasons	90%
Life Stressors	85%
Cognitive Factors	75%
Socialization Processes	65%
Environmental Issues	55%

Emotional Reasons

The dominant relapse theme for youth, including both adolescents (ages 12 through 17) and young adults (ages 18 through 24) was emotional reasons (90%), feeling unable to cope with negative emotions without drugs. Table 2 displays combined statements from youth supporting this theme.

Life Stressors

The second theme identified was life stressors (85%) for both adolescent and young adults as supported by statements such as "To take the stress away," "To get away from life stressors," "Because life and everything that comes with it–sucks." However, when questioned more deeply about the reasons for stress, responses greatly differed for adolescent and young adult participants worth noting. For adolescents (12–17), stress was referred to more so because of parents (criticizing, nagging, mistrust, conflict, put-downs, no faith/confidence in us, not being around), school (failing classes, getting in trouble), and peer pressure (fitting in); whereas older-aged youth (18–24) were more likely express stress in terms of realities of life that had to do with intimate relationships (commitment), financial

Table 2 Combined Qualitative Youth (12–24) Statements of "Emotional Reasons"

"To cope or take the edge off of problems"

"To feel better about all the drama in our life"

"To cope with negative feelings, anger, sadness, loneliness, guilt, fear, pain, and anxiety"

"To escape or just to get away from reality"

"They don't want to face their fears"

"They know there is a better feeling than being sober where life sucks"

"Because it helps you break those internal barriers"

responsibility (debt, employment issues) and housing stress (rent and bills). Table 3 displays statements from both youth groups supporting this theme.

Cognitive Factors

The third theme in response to "He/She Relapsed Because . . ." was cognitive (75%), with the dominant reasons for both adolescents and young adults alike being poor motivation, craving/urges, and low confidence. Table 4 displays combined statements from youth supporting this theme.

Socialization Processes

The fourth theme had to do with socialization processes (65%); however, responses regarding the type of social processes differed between adolescents and young adults. Specifically, adolescents were more likely to note peer pressure and media influence whereas young adults discussed issues related to social networks and social norms. Table 5 displays statements from both youth groups supporting this theme.

Table 3 Qualitative Statements of Life Stressors by Youth Group

Adolescents (12–17)

"Still, after treatment, parents continue to just criticize us all the time and put us down . . . we're no good, failures. They constantly complain and nag about how we do everything wrong. They don't trust us, where we go, who we talk to. Basically they have no faith or confidence in us."

"School is hard, all the homework, tests, and class things you have to keep up with . . . it never ends."

"Relapsing has to do with the stress of hanging out with your friends and fitting in." "Using starts as a social thing, and then after a while, it becomes all you do with your friends . . . You wouldn't know what else to do."

Young Adults (18–24)

"Well coming out of treatment you're on a pink cloud, telling everyone you're gonna do hella fi'ng well. . . . And then life kicks in . . . just reality is a bitch . . . the stress is overwhelming and makes me, feel like stuck. Cuz I've gotten myself in a hole and that makes me want to use you know."

"Relapse happens because relationships go bad, break-ups and being lonely, sex becomes an issue, or just commitment issues."

"Drugs and alcohol become an easy solution for fears about your financial and life stressors . . . having a job or a place to live."

Table 4 Combined Qualitative Youth (12–24) Statements of Cognitive Factors

Poor Motivation

"They weren't ready or willing to do what it takes to stay clean."

"There are some who choose to be here, but most are here because of parents or court-ordered, so they're gonna relapse because they have to want to stop on their own"

"Because motivation is the biggest issue for most of us–and it's not mere . . . everything told to us in treatment just comes in one ear and out the other"

"No more testing, they're finally out of treatment"

Cravings/Urges

"Having positive feelings that make you want to celebrate–have a drink or use"

"They had cravings because you are either in the presence of drugs or alcohol, drug or alcohol users, or at places where you used or bought drugs before"

"Because that's what typically happens after treatment–we all go back to craving or chasing that first high"

Low Confidence (Self-efficacy)

"Because they were scared to take on the challenge of quitting . . . they didn't have the strength to not use again"

"Not having confidence to manage their life on their own"

Environmental Issues

The final theme identified among both youth groups was environmental issues (55%), which included responses about access/availability and cues/triggers (55%). Table 6 displays statements from both youth groups supporting this theme.

Discussion

Considering the relapse ecology of youth, our data highlight 5 major reasons for youth relapse: negative emotions, stress, cognitive factors, socialization processes, and environmental issues. Although this study contributes a qualitative assessment of the relapse process among treatment-involved youth, there is still significant complexity in understanding the developmental pathways to relapse.

As supported by our results, such pathways are best conceptualized as multifactorial,[87,88] which fall into 3 general theoretical streams of influences: individual-level factors, socialization influences, and broader environmental influences. Specifically, individual-level influences included negative emotions, stress,

Table 5 Qualitative Statements of Socialization Processes by Youth Group

Adolescents (12–17)

PeerPressure

"Because my friends are negative influences . . . they keep asking–you want to get high"

"For me, it's not really about the place or situation–like a party, but about the people there–friends have a strong influence on what we do–they can turn any place into a bad place"

Media Influence

"Because they saw it glorified on TV or heard about how fun it is on the radio, so it reminds them of how it feels and how it's good, and how happy they will feel"

"I think because of the media influence. All types, TV, radio, film, internet, video games show alcohol, cigarettes, marijuana, prescription pills, other drugs, in a positive light and make using/drinking normal. So we start to believe it and think it's normal part of life"

Young Adults (12–24)

Social Networks

"They continued to want to party and connect with old drug use networks"

Social Norms

"Like seriously? Like if you've never tried pot. Like, I mean, you don't have to be a black tar heroin user, but I mean it's just what's in our social culture and expected"

"Because of the social standards or whatever you want to call them about using alcohol and drugs in our age group–young people just use a lot of drugs . . . and they think it's normal and being sober is not normal"

Table 6 Combined Qualitative Youth (12–24) Statements of Environmental Issues

Access/Availability

"We just have to walk down the street in our neighborhood . . . dope dealers and drugs are everywhere"

Cues/Triggers

"Just triggers–the day-to-day things we hear, see, do,"

"It's always around–in your face . . . and when you see it or smell it you're like damn, pass that–you might contemplate it little bit, but in the end, you just say, ok"

---

and cognitive factors; socialization influences included peer pressure, social network/social norms, and media influence; and broader environmental influences included access/availability and cues/triggers, which merit separate discussions for each. It is important to note that, as discussed in the introduction, these relapse determinants are fairly similar to relapse factors observed among adult samples;[63–66] however, such relapse processes have more emphasis around social-emotional and environmental development processes, rather than personal clinical orientations around substance use severity.

Negative Emotions

Research supports that the majority of youth with substance use problems also have one or more co-occurring problems such as depression, anxiety, traumatic stress, self-mutilation or suicidal thoughts, hyperactivity and conduct disorder, criminal or violent tendencies, etc. Prevailing beliefs under the psychoanalytic framework is that drug use is a symptom of an underlying psychological disorder.[89] Accordingly, substance use is a secondary condition caused by underlying mental disturbances, known as the self-medication model, whereby individuals use drugs to self-medicate or relieve symptoms of psychological distress.[90] Because relapse is likely to occur if these symptoms are not adequately addressed during treatment, a major goal of treatment programs is to include care and services (counseling interventions) that uncover and treat the underlying psychopathology feeding drug abuse behaviors.[91,92] Although treatment programs are working to effectively address such multiple problems simultaneously (eg, standardized assessment for other problems and provision/coordination of case management services),[16] extending these efforts beyond formal treatment is not a common practice.[95] It is possible that the positive outcomes observed in treatment could be better sustained if posttreatment recovery maintenance services (ie, continuing care models) included emotion regulation and coping skills for dealing with negative emotions.

Stress

Stress has been well established as a significant risk factor for relapse.[96–101] We found developmental differences in relapse-associated stress that support the conceptualization of stress

"as a relationship between an individual and his/her environment."[102] For adolescents, parental issues, peer pressure, and school problems were dominant stressors, whereas for young adults, stress was described more in terms of life circumstances, emerging adult responsibilities, and interpersonal romantic relationships that coincide with their current developmental period: "gaining greater independence" and "leaving the parent nest or family environment."[103] Many studies consistently show that parents, peers, and school serve as major socialization factors in predicting the initiation, maintenance, and exacerbation of substance abuse in adolescents; and the stress-related findings specific to young adults are similar to what is typically found with older adults in treatment, which is linked to pretreatment problems of legal issues, relationships, job loss, and financial debt.[104,105] From a clinical and recovery support perspective, these results highlight the importance of integrating stress management efforts into programs rather than simply focusing on parental, school, or employment problems specifically as is done in most programs.[76,106,107]

Cognitive Factors

Three important cognitive factors warrant further consideration in terms of understanding relapse among youth: motivation, cravings/urges, and confidence, ie, self-efficacy. As other studies have found, relapse or continued use of alcohol and drugs, is related to the fact that few youth with substance use problems are motivated to be in treatment as they rarely express desires to quit or any strong commitments to maintain abstinence.[81,108,109] Further, most youth presenting for treatment are not self-referred. Instead, they are coerced by a parent, juvenile justice system official (judge, probation or parole officer), school official, child welfare worker, or representative of some other community institution.[8,10] These findings highlight the need for relapse prevention models in both clinical and recovery support settings to take into account the extent to which youth are motivated or ready to change their substance use behaviors.[44,110] Future research on youth relapse needs to consider the potential differences in perceptions among youth mandated to treatment versus youth voluntarily in treatment. By ignoring motivation at treatment admission, assessments of outcomes become complicated and often limit interpretation of relapse prevention models.

Confidence (self-efficacy) was also cited as an important cognitive factor related to relapse as has been found in other studies.[111] However, the confidence expressed by youth had more to do with one's ability to abstain from drugs in the face of life stressors or internal/social cues/triggers, such as the stress of fitting in, rather than on peer pressure associated with being "forced" to use drugs. This result highlights the importance of integrating stress management skills (in addition to peer resistance skills) into youth relapse-prevention models. Lastly, an interesting area of research worthy of further inquiry has to do with continued substance use after treatment that is not related to one's primary drug of choice, particularly tobacco use. As others have noted, a major issue facing individuals in treatment (in general) is a drug-use recovery environment that far too often facilitates tobacco use.[112]

Socialization Processes

All youth support the view that relapse is a byproduct or function of socialization processes that influence developmental vulnerability for relapse. Although we observed differences in socialization processes between adolescent and young adults, the circumstances and extent to which relapse occurs is largely regulated by peer/social norms, customs, traditions, and standards.[113] In general, adolescents reported friendships and peer pressure along with media influence as important relapse triggers; whereas young adults tended to highlight social networks and social norms as dominant features of their social surrounding that influenced relapse.

Numerous studies have established that peer-group and social norm processes are strong influencers of drug use behaviors,[86,115,116] as they foster positive expectancies about drug use and create prosocial norms, and both serve to encourage drug use behavior.[117,118] It is important to point out that for most adolescents, cliques or friendship bonds are an important and a common feature during social/emotional development contributing to substance use risk behaviors.[114,115,120,121] However, as our data indicate, the peer/friendship clique might not be as important for young adults as they have "developed and matured" over time into a web of social relationships and social networks more associated with larger social processes operating.[122]

Moreover, although not as apparent for older youth, media depictions of drugs were noted as important determinants of relapse by many adolescents. Other research supports this view, such that the tobacco and alcohol industries alone spend billions of dollars each year aggressively marketing their products to adolescents through depicting images of glamour, success, and independence—all highly esteemed social values within American society.[123] Such marketing strategies have paid off as noted by several studies showing a positive impact on youth decisions to smoke or drink.[124,125] Overall, such socialization processes that youth experience are complex issues that create obstacles for those attempting to develop a drug-free recovery lifestyle (ie, break free from peer pressure and extant social norms that promote and normalize substance use).

Environmental Issues

As reflected by our data, environmental factors of access/availability and cues/triggers also play a critical role in facilitating relapse for youth. According to most, drugs are readily available and accessible to them. National survey data from Monitoring the Future highlight the importance of the positive relationship between perceived availability of drugs and trends in use among adolescent youth.[126]

To date, most attention on relapse determinants has been directed at individual-level factors, promoting the view that the responsibility for one's relapse ultimately falls on oneself and shifting attention away from larger environmental forces that also may be influencing relapse behavior. However, such environmental influences on relapse are important to consider as "the individual cannot be conceptualized as an autonomous actor making self-governing decisions in a social vacuum."[129]

For clinical and recovery support programs to be effective, they must also address such structural influences.

Limitations

The present study must be considered in light of its limitations. The accuracy of relapse descriptions or circumstances among this clinical sample must be questioned as they are retrospectively providing aggregate perceptions of relapse rather than any specific experiences. Also, the data were from a single time point, thereby limiting conclusions regarding the process of posttreatment relapse. Additionally, the results cannot be overgeneralized to treatment-involved youth in other treatment settings given the variability between the treatment sites used to conduct the qualitative work as well as the nature of the sample used (convenience). Finally, focus group thematic results are only presented descriptively. Although it may be that the general risk for substance use relapse among youth as a whole may be similar, with some general differences noted among age-groups, there may be important gender or other differences in relapse risk factors among treatment-involved youth that this study did not consider due to confidentiality limitations associated with anonymous data collection. Further research should find procedures to remedy such deficiencies.

Conclusion

This study contributes to the extant literature on relapse specific to youth populations. Results add clarity to the dynamic process of relapse in youth as they explicate the actual experiences and perceptions of treatment-involved youth. Overall, there is no single variable sufficient to predict relapse among youth alone. Although individual(personal)-level factors have been shown to account for much of the variance explaining proneness to youth initiation and maintenance of substance use,[84,108] there is still a wide array of social and environmental forces that contribute to the progression of substance use behavior.[128,129] Hence, the interrelations among key individual, socialization, and broader environmental variables are likely to be of increasing importance for understanding the developmental relapse trajectories of treatment-involved youth.

Furthermore, because treatment for substance use and related problems tends to be treated acutely and for a relatively short period (less than 3 months),[130] a systems issue to consider is the need for ongoing interventions (continuing care) to promote the necessary skills acquired during treatment, as they may not carry over or be sustainable posttreatment. It needs to be recognized that most treatment-involved youth are in a structured clinical environment and when it is removed they struggle with the loss of structure as they transition into a less unstructured world. In the transition they continue to experience co-occurring issues that can hijack emotions, be exposed to drug using friends, encounter repeated life stressors, face competing social norms that reinforce drug use, enter into a broader environment where drugs and alcohol are frequently available, and continue to be triggered or cued to drug use. To minimize adverse effects, continuing care models must be developed addressing such complex, interrelated issues.

References

1. Centers for Disease Control and Prevention. (2009) Youth Risk Behavior Survey. Available at: www.cdc.gov/yrbss. Accessed March 10, 2011.

2. American Academy of Pediatrics. Practicing adolescent medicine: Priority health behaviors in adolescents: Health promotion in the clinical setting. Adolescent Health Update. 3(2). 1991. Available at: www.aap.org. Accessed March 10, 2011

3. Robert Wood Johnson Foundation. Reclaiming Futures: Quick Facts. Retrieved Available at: www.reclaimingfutures.org/quickfacts.asp. Accessed February 12, 2004.

4. Substance Abuse and Mental Health Services Administration. (2010a). Results from the 2009 National Survey on Drug Use and Health: Volume I. Summary of National Findings (Office of Applied Studies, NSDUH Series H-38A, HHS Publication No. SMA 10-4586Findings). Rockville, MD. Available at: www. cdc.gov/nchs/data/hus/hus10.pdf#061

5. Substance Abuse and Mental Health Services Administration, Office of Applied Studies. Treatment Episode Data Set (TEDS). Rockville, MD: U.S. Department of Health and Human Services; 2010.

6. U.S. Department of Justice, Federal Bureau of Investigation. Crime in the United States. Available at: www2.fbi.gov/ucr/cius2008/data/table_38.html. Accessed September 16, 2009.

7. McLellan AT, Chalk M, Bartlett J. Outcomes, performance, and quality – What's the difference? *J Subst Abuse Treat.* 2007; 32:331–340.

8. Dennis ML. Global Appraisal of Individual Needs Manual: Administration, Scoring and Interpretation. Bloomington, IL: Lighthouse; 1998.

9. Brown SA, D'Amicio EJ, McCarthy DM, et al. Four-year outcomes from adolescent alcohol and drug treatment. *J Stud Alcohol.* 2001; 62:381–388.

10. Hser YI, Grella CE, Hubbard RL, et al. An evaluation of drug treatments for adolescents in 4 cities. *Arch Gen Psychiatry.* 2001; 58:689–695.

11. Winters KC, Stinchfield RD, Opland E, et al. The effectiveness of the Minnesota Model approach in the treatment of adolescent drug abusers. *Addiction.* 2000; 95:601–612.

12. Brown SA, Vik PW, Creamer VA. Characteristics of relapse following adolescent substance abuse treatment. *Addict Behav.* 1989; 14:291–300.

13. Brown SA, Mott M, Myers MG. Adolescent alcohol and drug treatment outcome. In Watson RR, ed. Drug and Alcohol Abuse Prevention. Totowa, NJ: Humana Press; 1990.

14. Brown SA, Gleghorn A, Schuckit MA, et al. Conduct disorder among adolescent alcohol and drug abusers. *J Stud Alcohol.* 1996; 57:314–324.

15. Williams RJ, Chang SY, Addiction Centre Adolescent Research Group. A comprehensive and comparative review of adolescent substance abuse treatment outcome. Clin Psychol: Sci Prac. 2000; 7:138–166.

16. Kaminer Y, Burleson JA, Burke RH. Efficacy of outpatient aftercare for adolescents with alcohol use disorders: a randomized controlled study. *J Am Acad Child Adolesc Psychiatry.* 2008; 47:1405–1412.

17. Brown S, Tapert S, Granholm E, et al. Neurocognitive functioning of adolescents: effects of protracted alcohol use. *Alcohol Clin Exp Res.* 2000; 24(2):164–171.

18. Lewis RA, Piercy FP, Sprenkle DH, et al. Family-based interventions for helping drug abusing adolescents. *J Adolesc Res.* 1990; 50:82–95.

19. Dennis M, Godley SH, Diamond G, et al. The Cannabis Youth Treatment (CYT) Study: main findings from two randomized trials. J Subst Abuse Treat. 2004; 27:197–213.

20. Cornelius JR, Maisto SA, Pollock NK, et al. Rapid relapse generally follows treatment for substance use disorders among adolescents. *Addict Behav.* 2003; 28:381–386.

21. Milkman H, Weiner SE, Sunderwirth S. Addiction relapse. *Adv Alcohol Subst Abuse.* 1984; 3:119–134.

22. Polivy J, Herman CP. If at first you don't succeed: false hopes of self-change. *Am Psychol.* 2002; 57(9):677–689.

23. Marlatt GA, Gordon JR. Determinants of relapse: Implications for the maintenance of behavior change. In P.O. Davidson & S.M. Davidson, eds, Behavioral Medicine: Changing Health Lifestyles. Elmsford, NY: Pergamon; 1980: 410–452.

24. Abrams DB, Niaura RS, Carey KB, et al. Understanding relapse and recovery in alcohol abuse. *Ann Behav Med.* 1986; 8:27–32.

25. Witkiewitz K, Marlatt GA. Relapse prevention for alcohol and drug problems: that was Zen, this is Tao. Am Psychologist. 2004; 59:224-235.

26. Davis JR, Tunks E. Environments and addiction: a proposed taxonomy. *Int J Addict* 1990; 25:805–826.

27. Tucker JA, Vuchinich RE, Gladsjo JA. Environmental influences on relapse in substance use disorders. *Int J Addict.* 1991; 25(7A/8A):017–1050.

28. Dielman TE, Butchart AT, Shope JT, et al. Environmental correlates of adolescent substance use and misuse: implications for prevention programs. *Int J Addict.* 1991; 25:855–880.

29. Rosenhow DJ, Niaura RS, Childress AR, et al. Cue reactivity in addictive behaviors: theoretical and treatment implications. *Int J Addict.* 1991; 25:957–994.

30. Simpson DD, Joe GW, Brown BS. Treatment retention and follow-up outcomes in the Drug Abuse Treatment Outcome Study (DATOS). *Psychol Addict Behav.* 1997; 11:294–307.

31. Gifford R, Hine DW. Substance misuse and the physical environment: the early action of a newly completed field. *Int J Addict.* 1991; 25:827–853.

32. Brownell KD, Marlatt GA, Lichtenstein E, et al. Understanding and preventing relapse. *Am Psychologist.* 1986; 41:765–785.

33. Marlatt GA, Baer JS, Quigley LA. Self-efficacy and addictive behaviour. In Banura A, ed, Self-efficacy in Changing Societies. New York, NY: Cambridge University Press; 1995: 289–315.

34. Miller WR, Westerberg VS, Harris RJ, et al. What predicts relapse? Prospective testing of antecedent models. *Addiction.* 2002; 91(12s1):155–172.

35. Miller WR, Carroll K. Rethinking Substance Abuse: What the Science Shows, and What We Should Do About it. New York, NY: Guilford Press; 2006.

36. De Leon G. Integrative recovery: a stage paradigm. *Subst Abuse.* 1996; 17:15–63.

37. Cornelius JR, Maisto SA, Wood DS, et al. Major depression associated with earlier alcohol relapse in treated teens with alcohol use disorder. *Addict Behav.* 2004; 29:1035–1038.

38. McKay JR, Rutherford MJ, Alterman AI, et al. An examination of the cocaine relapse process. *Drug Alcohol Depend.* 1995; 38:35–43.

39. Jones BT, Corbin W, Fromme K. A review of expectancy theory and alcohol consumption. *Addiction.* 2001; 96:57–72.

40. Niaura R. Cognitive social learning and related perspectives on drug craving. *Addiction.* 2000; 95:155–163.

41. Moos RH. Coping Responses Inventory. Odessa, FL: Psychological Assessment Resources; 1993.

42. Drummond DC, Litten RZ, Lowman C, et al. Craving research: future directions. *Addiction.* 2000; 95(Suppl 2):247–255.

43. Burke BL, Arkowitz H, Menchola M. The efficacy of motivational interviewing: a meta-analysis of controlled clinical trials. *J Consult Clin Psychol.* 2003; 71(5):843–861.

44. Simpson DD, Curry SJ. Drug abuse treatment outcome studies. *Psychol Addict Behav.* 1997; 11: 211–337.

45. Joe GW, Simpson DD, Sells SB. Treatment process and relapse to opioid use during methadone maintenance. *Am J Drug Alcohol Use.* 1994; 20:173–197.

46. Dobkin PL, Civita M, Paraherakis A, et al. The role of functional social support in treatment retention and outcomes among outpatient adult substance abusers. *Addiction.* 2002; 97(3):347–356.

47. Anderson KG, Frissell KC, Brown SA. Contexts of post-treatment use for substance abusing adolescents with comorbid psychopathology. *J Child Adolesc Subst Abuse.* 2007; 17:65–82.

48. Ulrich RS, Simons RF, Losito BD, et al. Stress recovery during exposure to natural and urban environments. *J Environment Psychol.* 1991; 11:201–230.

49. Ennett ST, Flewelling RL, Lindroth RC, et al. School and neighborhood characteristics associated with school rates of alcohol, cigarette, and marijuana use. *J Health Social Beh.* 1997; 38:55–71.

50. Anglin MD, Hser Y-I. Treatment of Drug Abuse Drugs & Crime, eds. M Tonry, JQ Wilson. Chicago, IL: The University of Chicago Press; 1990.

51. Beattie MC, Longabaugh R. General and alcohol specific social support following treatment. *Addict Behav.* 1999; 24(5):593–606.

52. Moos RH, Finney JW, Cronkite RC. Alcoholism Treatment: Context, Process and Outcome. New York, NY: Oxford University Press; 1990.

53. Lang MA, Belenko S. Predicting retention in a residential drug treatment alternative to prison program. *J Subst Abuse Treat.* 2000; 19:145–160.

54. De Leon G, Hawke J, Jainchill N, et al. Therapeutic communities enhancing retention in treatment using "senior professor" staff. *J Subst Abuse Treat.* 2000; 19:375–382.

55. Lillie-Blanton M, Anthony JC, Schuster CR. Probing the meaning of racial/ethnic group comparisons in crack cocaine smoking. *JAMA.* 1993; 269:993–997.

56. Agnew JA, Duncan JS. The Power of Place, Boston, MA: Unwin Hyman; 1989.

57. Boardman JD, Finch BK, Ellison CG, et al. Neighborhood disadvantage, stress, and drug use among adults. *J Health Soc Behav.* 2001; 42:151–165.

58. Buhringer G. Testing CBT mechanisms of action: humans behave in a more complex way than our treatment studies would predict. *Addiction.* 2000; 95(11):1715–1716.

59. Dononvan DM. Marlatt's classification of replase precipitants: is the emperor still wearing clothes? *Addiction.* 1996; 91(Suppl):131–137.

60. Longabaugh R, Rubin A, Stout RL, et al. The reliability of Marlatt's taxonomy for classifying relapses. *Addiction.* 1996; 91(Suppl):73–88.

61. Carroll KM. Relapse prevention as a psycho-social treatment: a review of controlled clinical trials. *Exp Clin Psychopharmacol.* 1996; 4:46–54.

62. Irvin JE, Bowers CA, Dunn ME, et al. Efficacy of relapse prevention: a meta-analytic review. *J Consult Clin Psychol.* 1999; 67(4):563–570.

63. Brown SA, D'Amico EA. Outcomes of alcohol treatment for adolescents. In Galanter M, ed. Recent Developments in Alcoholism, vol. 16. New York, NY: Kluwer Academic/Plenum; 2003: 289–312.

64. Myers RJ, Smith JE. Clincal Guide to Alcohol Treatment: The Community Reinforcement Approach. New York, NY: Guilford Press; 1995.

65. Brown SA, Vik PW, Craemer VA. Characteristics of relapse following adolescent substance abuse treatment. *Addict Behav.* 1989; 14:291–300.

66. Brown SA. Measuring youth outcomes from alcohol and drug treatment. *Addiction.* 2004; 99(Suppl 2):38–46.

67. Labouvie EW, Bates M. Reasons for alcohol use in young adulthood: validation of a three-dimensional measure. *J Stud Alcohol.* 2002; 63:145–155.

68. Millman RB, Botvin GJ. Substance use, abuse, and dependence. In: Levine M, Carey NB, Crocker AC, Gross RT, eds. Developmental-behavioral Pediatrics. New York, NY: W. B. Saunders; 1992:451–467.

69. McNeal RB, Hansen WB. Developmental patterns associated with the onset of drug use: changes in postulated mediators during adolescence. *J Drug Issues.* 1999; 29(2):381–400.

70. Jessor RS, Chase JD, Donovan JE. Psychosocial correlates of marijuana use and problem drinking in a national sample of adolescents. *Am J Public Health.* 1980; 70:604–613.

71. Grella CE, Hser Y, Joshi V, Rounds-Bryant J. Drug treatment outcomes for adolescents with comorbid mental and substance use disorders. *J Nerv Ment Dis.* 2001; 189:384–392.

72. Morral AR, McCaffrey DF, Ridgeway G. Effectiveness of community-based treatment for substance-abusing adolescents: 12-month outcomes of youths entering Phoenix Academy or alternative probation dispositions. *Addict Behav.* 2004; 18(3):257–268.

73. Stein JA, Newcombe MD, Bentler PM. An 8-year study of multiple influences on drug use and drug use consequences. *JPers Soc Psychol.* 1987; 53:1094–1105.

74. Oetting ER, Donnermyer JF. Primary socialization theory: the etiology of drug use and deviance I. *Subst Use Misuse.* 1998; 33(4):995–1026.

75. Jessor R. Risk behavior in adolescence: a psychosocial framework for understanding and action. *J Adolesc Health.* 1991; 12:597–605.

76. Sameroff AJ, Seifer R, Bartko WT. Environmental perspectives on adaptation during childhood and adolescence. In Luthar SS, Burak JA, Cicchetti D, et al., eds, Developmental Psychopathology: Perspectives on Adjustment, Risk, and Disorder. New York, NY: Cambridge University Press; 1997: 507–526.

77. Liddle H, Rowe C, eds. Treating Adolescent Substance Abuse: State of the Science. Cambridge, UK: Cambridge University Press; 2006.

78. Oetting ER. Primary socialization theory. Developmental stages, spirituality, government institutions, sensation seeking, and theoretical implications V. *Subst Use Misuse.* 1999; 34(7):947–82.

79. Waldron HB, Slesnick N, Brody JL, et al. Treatment outcomes for adolescent substance abuse at 4- and 7-month assessments. *J Consult Clin Psychol.* 2001; 69:802–813.

80. Maisto SA, Martin CS, Pollock NK, et al. Non-problem drinking outcomes in adolescents treated for alcohol use disorders. *Exp Clin Psychopharmacol.* 2002; 10:324–331.

81. Ramo, DE, Anderson KG, Tate SR, et al. Characteristics of relapse to substance use in comorbid adolescents. *Addict Behav.* 2005; 30:1811–1823.

82. Rawson RA, Gonzales R, 2009. CalOMS. Evaluation of the Substance Abuse Treatment System. Los Angeles: UCLA Integr. Subst. Abuse Progr. Available at: www.uclaisap.org/caloms/documents/CalOMSEvaluationReport.pdf. Accessed March 4, 2011.

83. Huba GJ. Bentler PM. A developmental theory of drug use: derivation and assessment of a causal modeling approach. In Baltes PB, Brim Jr OG Jr., eds, Lifespan Development and Behavior. New York: Academic Press, 1982; 4:47–203.

84. McNeal RB, Hansen WB. Developmental patterns associated with the onset of drug use: changes in postulated mediators during adolescence. *J Drug Issues*. 1999; 29(2):381–400.

85. Krueger RA. Moderating Focus Groups. Thousand Oaks, CA: Sage; 1998.

86. Miles MB, Huberman AM. Qualitative Data Analysis: An Expanded Sourcebook. 2nd ed. Thousand Oaks, CA: Sage; 1994.

87. Alexander BK. What can professional psychotherapists do about heroin addiction? *Medicine and Law.* 1986; 5(4):323–330.

88. Hawkins JD, Catalano RF, Miller JY. Risk and protective factors for alcohol and other drug problems in adolescence and early adulthood. Implications for substance abuse prevention. *Psychol Bull*. 1992; 112:64–105.

89. Khantzian EJ. The self-medication hypothesis of addictive disorders: focus on heroin and cocaine dependence. *Am J Psychiatry*. 1985; 142:1259–1264.

90. Hwang S. Utilizing qualitative data analysis software: a review of Atlas.ti. *Social Science Computer Review*. 2008; 26(4):519–527.

91. Aarons GA, Brown SA, Hough RL, et al. Prevalence of adolescent substance use disorders across five sectors of care. *J Am Acad Child Adolesc Psychi*. 2001; 40:419–426.

92. Kaminer Y, Napolitano C. Dial for therapy: aftercare for adolescent substance use disorders. J Am Academy Child Adolesc Psychiatry. 2004; 43:1171–1174.

93. Dennis ML, Titus JC, Diamond G, et al. The Cannabis Youth Treatment (CYT) experiment: Rationale, study design and analysis plans. *Addiction*. 2002; 97(Suppl 1):84–97.

94. Kaminer Y, Napolitano C. Dial for therapy: aftercare for adolescent substance use disorders. J Am Academy Child Adolesc Psychiatry. 2004; 43:1171–1174.

95. Godley MD, Kahn JH, Dennis ML, et al. The stability and impact of environmental factors on substance use and problems after adolescent outpatient treatment for cannabis abuse or dependence. *Psychol Addict Behav*. 2005; 19:62–70.

96. Preston KL, Epstein DH. Stress in the daily lives of cocaine and heroin users: relationship to mood, craving, relapse triggers, and cocaine use. (Published online ahead of print 12 February 2011). *Psychopharmacol (Berl)*. 2011. Available aat: www.springerlink.com/content/j82465x38 5448145/. Accessed March 6, 2011.

97. Goeders NE. The impact of stress on addiction. *European Neuropsychopharmacol*. 2003; 13:435–441.

98. Goeders NE. Stress and cocaine addiction. *J Pharmacol Exp Ther*. 2002; 301:785–789.

99. Sinha R, Fuse T, Aubin LR, et al. Psychological stress, drug-related cues and cocaine craving. *Psychopharmacol*. 2000; 152:140–148.

100. Sinha R. How does stress increase risk of drug abuse and relapse? *Psychopharmacol*. 2001; 158:343–359.

101. Wills TA. Stress, coping, tobacco and alcohol use in early adolescence. In: Shiffman S, Wills TA, eds. Coping and Substance Use. New York, NY: Academic Press; 1986.

102. Lazarus RS, Folkman S. Stress, Appraisal, and Coping. New York, NY: Springer; 1984.

103. Wilks J. The relative importance of parents and friends in adolescent decision making. *J Youth Adolescence*. 1986; 15:323–334.

104. Chassin L, Presson CC, Sherman SJ, et al. Changes in peer and parental influence during adolescence: longitudinal versus cross-sectional perspectives on smoking initiation. *Dev Psychol*. 1986; 22:327–334.

105. Whiston SC. The relationship among family interaction patterns and career indecision and career decision-making self-efficacy. *J Career Dev*. 1996; 23:137–149.

106. Jessor R, Donovan JE, Costa FM. Beyond Adolescence: Problem Behavior and Young Adult Development. New York, NY: Cambridge University Press; 1991.

107. King KM, Chassin L. Mediating and moderated effects of adolescent behavioral under control and parenting in the prediction of drug use disorders in emerging adulthood. *Psychol Addict Behav*. 2004; 18(3): 239–249.

108. Cornelius JR, Maisto SA, Pollock NK, et al. Rapid relapse generally follows treatment for substance use disorders among adolescents. *Addict Beh*. 2003; 28:381–386.

109. Chung T, Maisto SA. Review and reconsideration of relapse as a change point in clinical course in treated adolescents. Clin Psychol Rev. 2006; 26:149–161.

110. Godley SH, Godley MD, Dennis ML. The assertive aftercare protocol for adolescent substance abusers. In: Wagner E, Waldron H, eds. Innovations in Adolescent Substance Abuse Interventions. Elsevier Science; New York: 2001.

111. Bobo JK, Slade J, Hoffman AL. Nicotine addiction counseling for chemically dependent patients. *Psychiatr Svcs*. 1995; 46:945–947.

112. Burleson JA, Kaminer Y. Self-efficacy as a predictor of treatment outcome in adolescent substance use disorders. *Addict Behav*. 2005; 30:1751–1764.

113. Berkowitz AD. The Social Norms Approach: Theory, Research, and Annotated Bibliography. Newton, MA: Higher Education Center for Alcohol and Other Drug Prevention; 2001.

114. Dishion TJ. Cross-setting consistency in early adolescent psychopathology: deviant friendships and problem behavior sequelae. *J Pers*. 2000; 68(6):1109–1126.

115. Vandell DL. Parents, peer groups, and other socializing influences. *Dev Psychol*. 2000; 36(6):699–710.

116. Clapp JD, McDonnell AL. The relationship of perceptions of alcohol promotion and peer drinking norms to alcohol problems reported by college students. *J Coll Stud Dev*. 2000; 41:19–26.

117. Dishion TJ, Capaldi DM, Spracklen KM, Li F. Peer ecology of male adolescent drug use. *Dev Psychopathol*. 1995; 7:803–824.

118. Duncan TE, Duncan SC, Hops H. The effects of family cohesiveness and peer encouragement on the development of adolescent alcohol use: a cohort sequential approach to the analysis of longitudinal data. *J Stud Alcohol*. 1994; 55:588–599.

119. Hartup WW. The company they keep: Friendships and their developmental significance. *Child Dev*. 1996; 67:1–13.

120. Elliot D, Huizinga D, Ageton S. Explaining Delinquency and Drug Use. Newbury Park, California: Sage Publications, Inc; 1985.

121. Kandel DB. Processes of peer influence in adolescence: In: Silberstein, R.K., Eyferth, K. & Rudinger, G. (Eds.). Development as Action in Context: Problem Behavior and Normal Youth Development. New York, NY: Springer-Verlag; 1986:203–227.

122. Perry CL, Baranowski T, Parcel GS. How Individual, Environments, and Health Behavior Interact: Social Learning Theory. San Francisco: Jossey-Bass; 1997.

123. Arnett J. Adolescents' uses of media for self-socialization. *J Youth Adolesc*. 1995; 24(5):519–533.

124. Kelly K, Donohew L. Media and primary socialization theory. *Subst Use Misuse*. 1999; 34(7):1033–1045.

125. Moore DJ, Williams JD, Qualls WJ. Target marketing of tobacco and alcohol-related products to ethnic minority groups in the United States. *Ethn Dis*. 1996; 6(12):83–98.

126. Johnston LD, O'Malley PM, Bachman JG, et al. Monitoring the Future National Results on Adolescent Drug Use: Overview of Key Findings, 2005. (NIH Publication No. 06–5882). Bethesda, MD: National Institute on Drug Abuse: 2006.

127. Thombs DL, Wolcott BJ, Farkash LG. Social context, perceived norms and drinking behavior in young people. *J Subst Abuse.* 1997; 9:257–267.

128. Sussman S, Dent CW, Galaif ER. The Correlates of substance abuse and dependence among adolescents at high risk for drug abuse. *J Subst Abuse.* 1997; 9:241–255.

129. Oetting ER, Donnermyer JF, Deffenbacher JL. Primary socialization theory: the influence of the community on drug use and deviance III. *Subst Use Misuse.* 1998; 33(8): 1629–1665.

130. Becker SJ, Curry JF. Outpatient interventions for adolescent substance abuse: a quality of evidence review. *J Consult Clin Psychol.* 2008; 76:531–543.

Critical Thinking

1. Discuss the reasons youth report they relapse from drug treatment.

2. What is one limitation of the study described in this article?

3. Discuss possible approaches to reducing the barriers to youth treatment success.

Acknowledgments—The authors would like to thank the administrative and treatment staff at the participating treatment programs for their support. This study was supported by a grant provided by the National Institute on Drug Abuse (NIDA), grant number DA027754-01A1.

Rachel Gonzales, Research Psychologist; M. Douglas Anglin, Professor in Residence, Associate Director; Rebecca Beattie, Staff Research Associate; Chris Angelo Ong, Staff Research Associate, Integrated Substance Abuse Programs, University of California, Los Angeles, CA, Semel Institute for Neuroscience and Human Behavior, David Geffen School of Medicine at UCLA, Los Angeles, CA. Deborah C. Glik, Professor, School of Public Health, University of California, Los Angeles, CA.

Contact Dr Gonzales; rachelmg@ucla.edu

From *American Journal of Health Behavior,* vol. 36, no, 5, 2012, pp. 602–614. Copyright © 2012 by PNG Publications. Reprinted by permission.

High-Risk Offenders Participating in Court-Supervised Substance Abuse Treatment: Characteristics, Treatment Received, and Factors Associated with Recidivism

ELIZABETH EVANS, MA, DAVID HUANG, DrPH, AND YIH-ING HSER, PhD

Introduction

Since 2001, California's voter-initiated Substance Abuse and Crime Prevention Act, more commonly known as Proposition 36 (Prop 36), has been providing community-based treatment to eligible drug offenders. Under Prop 36, adults convicted of nonviolent drug possession offenses can choose to receive drug treatment in the community in lieu of incarceration. Offenders on probation or parole who commit nonviolent drug possession offenses or who violate drug-related conditions of probation or parole can also opt to receive treatment. The intent of the Prop 36 program is to preserve jail and prison beds for serious and violent offenders, enhance public safety by reducing drug-related crime, and improve public health by reducing drug abuse through proven and effective treatment strategies.[1] From a broader perspective, Prop 36 is one example of the trend in the USA and several other countries toward use of alternative sentencing policies to rehabilitate drug offenders in lieu of imprisonment, and lessons learned from California's experiences with treating high- and low-risk drug offenders have implications for other similar types of programs.

The Prop 36 program has resulted in taxpayer savings, primarily due to reduced use of incarceration, and savings are highest among offenders who complete drug treatment.[2] Despite these gains, however, California's state budget crisis worsened in recent years, and Prop 36 stakeholders have struggled to maintain the integrity of the program in the context of increasing fiscal constraints.[3] At the same time, legislators charged with deciding funding amounts for the continuation of Prop 36 have called for strategies for making the program more cost-effective.[4]

It was in this context that evaluation reports identified a subgroup of Prop 36 offenders that comprised only 25 percent of all offenders in the program but that accounted for 80 percent of the re-arrests and costs that occurred over the 30 months following program entry.[2] The new crimes committed by these "high-risk, high-cost" offenders are eroding the savings and other benefits reaped by the Prop 36 program thus far and risk undermining the public safety that the Prop 36 law intends to protect. High-risk, high-cost offenders have been primarily characterized as having five or more prior convictions at program entry, and compared to other Prop 36 offenders, more are male and younger, their arrest and conviction costs after Prop 36 program entry are 26 times higher, and their treatment completion rates are significantly lower.[2] Prop 36's high-risk offenders have been identified only recently as one area for targeting program improvement efforts, and it follows that relatively little is known about this subgroup. For example, no study has examined the impact of drug treatment "dose" or other program and offender-level factors, such as offender motivation level and urine testing during treatment, that prior research on Prop 36 has identified as being associated with outcomes.[5,6] Outside of the Prop 36 arena, the topic of high-risk drug offenders and how best to address their addiction and criminal behavior in community-based treatment settings has been the focus of research for some time.

Much of the research on drug treatment for offenders proposes that outcomes are enhanced when risk of criminal recidivism is factored into choosing the appropriate level of care and that it is most effective to intensify treatment based on criminogenic factors in addition to need for services.[7,8] Furthermore, although challenging at times,[9] an integrated approach that combines close judicial supervision with high-intensity treatment has been found to be particularly effective for high-risk offenders.[10–13] Among non-criminal justice samples, better outcomes for individuals with more severe substance abuse or psychiatric problems have also been associated with providing more intensive treatment.[14–17] However, in two major studies of alcoholics (i.e., Project MATCH and the

US Department of Veterans Affair Effectiveness Study), matching treatment to patient attributes was shown to only minimally enhance outcomes (see[18] for a summary of study findings) More recent analyses found that while treatment matching was beneficial but not essential to achieving good outcomes, mismatches had serious consequences, and this effect was magnified with multiple mismatches.[19] The potentially iatrogenic effects of treatment mismatching were also reported by a study of offenders which found that residential treatment decreased recidivism rates among higher risk offenders but increased recidivism rates among lower risk offenders.[20]

Aside from documenting the additive value of receipt of appropriate drug treatment intensity by risk level, the literature on treatment for offenders also highlights how there is no general consensus on how best to define "high risk." Risk classification has included the use of individual items such as history of involvement with the criminal justice system, diagnostic criteria for antisocial personality disorder, and history of prior drug abuse treatment,[12,13] as well as the use of risk screening tools that combine information on a variety of behaviors such as prior criminal and substance abuse history, psychological health, education level, and employment status.[7,8,20] Among Prop 36 offenders, five or more prior convictions was identified as a strong predictor of later recidivism, and research showed that average crime costs increased as the number of convictions prior to program entry increased.[2]

It has been recommended that high-risk offenders be made ineligible for Prop 36 program participation or, to better manage these offenders, more intense treatment and supervision is needed.[2] While it is clear that high-risk offenders are a costly component of the Prop 36 program and that strategies are needed to improve their outcomes, very little else is known about this group. Furthermore, analysis of an early cohort of Prop 36 offenders revealed that compared to clients referred to treatment through other means, Prop 36 offenders with severe drug problems were significantly less likely to be treated in a residential treatment setting, that is, high drug severity Prop 36 offenders tended to be "undertreated".[21] Although there is variation in the operation and performance of Prop 36 by county,[22] reports have confirmed that across California, Prop 36 resulted in an expansion of mostly outpatient treatment capacity,[23] that most Prop 36 offenders are treated in outpatient settings, and that very few Prop 36 offenders receive residential treatment,[24] a treatment setting that some research indicates more commonly provides wraparound services for offenders.[25] Public policy discussions on what to do with high-risk Prop 36 offenders—provide more intense supervision or make them ineligible for Prop 36 program participation—require information on whether some high-risk offenders can demonstrate successful outcomes after program participation and whether the provision of more intensive treatment can be effective with this population.

To better understand the characteristics of high-risk offenders in Prop 36, their treatment experiences, recidivism rates, and impact of providing more treatment on recidivism, the following research questions were examined: (1) How are high-risk offenders different from low-risk offenders in characteristics at assessment for treatment and in experiences during drug treatment? (2) What offender characteristics and treatment factors predict more re-arrests over 12 months and over 30 months after assessment for treatment? (3) Does offender risk level interact with the amount of treatment received to impact the number of re-arrests?

It was hypothesized that high-risk offenders would exhibit more severe problems at intake assessment than their low-risk counterparts and that few would receive intensive treatment. Also, it was expected that the re-arrest rate would be higher among high-risk offenders but that more treatment would decrease recidivism.

Methods
Data source
Data analyzed in this study were derived from "Treatment System Impact and Outcomes of Proposition 36 (TSI)," a NIDA-funded multisite prospective treatment outcome study designed to assess the impact of Prop 36 on California's drug treatment delivery system and evaluate the effectiveness of the services delivered. Thirty treatment assessment sites in five counties were selected for participation based on geographic location, population size, and diversity of Prop 36 implementation strategy (see[26] for additional information). County assessment center or treatment program staff collected data from all Prop 36 participants assessed for treatment in the selected counties. Of participants who had completed the intake assessment in 2004 ($n = 2,636$), a sample of 1,588 was randomly selected for telephone follow-up by UCLA-trained interviewers at 3 and 12 months post-intake. Participants were paid US $10 and $15, respectively. Additionally, administrative data were acquired on all participants on arrest histories from the California Department of Justice (DOJ) and on mental health services utilization from the California Department of Mental Health (DMH). Data linking procedures and quality of data linkage are described elsewhere.[27] The Institutional Review Boards at UCLA and at the California Health and Human Services Agency approved all study procedures.

Subjects and recruitment
Of the 1,588 targeted, 1,465 completed the 3-month follow-up interview (48 were incarcerated, 3 were deceased, 6 refused, and the remainder was not found or was unable to complete the interview) and 1,290 completed the 12-month follow-up interview (73 were incarcerated, 12 were deceased, 9 refused, and the remainder was not found or was unable to complete the interview). Excluding the deceased and incarcerated from the interview pool, the follow-up interview completion rates were 95 percent and 86 percent, respectively. Comparisons between those who did and did not complete the interview revealed no statistically significant differences in all variables examined (county, treatment modality, age, race/ethnicity, marital status, education, employment, lifetime arrest, and primary drug problem) except for gender. More females (30 percent vs. 20 percent) were in the follow-up completion group than in the noncompletion group.

Of the total sample, mean age was 36.8 years, 29.1 percent were women, 50.6 percent were White, 24.8 percent were Hispanic, 18.1 percent were African American, 6.3 percent were other race/ethnic group, mean years of education was 11.7, 51.4 percent reported methamphetamine as their primary drug, and more than one third was employed full- or part-time (38.6 percent).

This analysis focuses on 1,087 Prop 36 offenders in TSI who completed the 3-month follow-up interview and also had a criminal history record on file with the California DOJ. Examination of the 378 who were omitted from analysis [because of missing 3-month follow-up variables ($n = 6$) or a missing DOJ record ($n = 372$)] showed that this group was different from the 1,087 who were included in analysis on gender only; slightly more males were in the study sample than in the non-study sample (72 percent vs. 66 percent). Missing DOJ records may have resulted from several factors such as data entry error, record expungement, commission of probation or parole violations that made an offender eligible for the Prop 36 program but did not result in a new arrest, deliberate falsification of personal information, and inaccuracies in the personal identifiers needed to link data. Of note is that this study applied a deterministic method to link records, and a combination of personal identifiers (including offender name, Social Security number, and date of birth) served as the primary linking variables. Only those cases that completely fulfilled the matching criteria were treated as a match. For this reason, underlinkage of data was expected, but this concern was outweighed by the high certainty of linkage associated with the deterministic method and the corresponding level of confidence in resulting findings.

Eligibility for the Prop 36 program is determined based on the offender's current offense and past criminal history, with special attention paid to convictions that occurred during the 5-year period prior to the offender's current offense.[28] For example, not eligible are drug offenders with a prior serious or violent felony conviction, unless the associated prison time has been served and the individual has been living in the community for 5 years with no felony or violent misdemeanor conviction. If eligible, offenders are offered treatment in lieu of routine criminal justice processing, and offenders who choose to participate complete a treatment assessment. Assessment entails a systematic review of offender drug problem severity and other service needs followed by a decision regarding appropriate treatment placement. Offenders are required to report to their assigned treatment program promptly, typically within 3–7 days after assessment.

To replicate prior analyses,[2] DOJ conviction data were analyzed; offenders with five or more convictions in the 5 years prior to their Prop 36 treatment assessment date were coded as "high-risk" ($n = 78$) and offenders with fewer than five convictions coded as "low-risk" ($n = 1,009$). Convictions over the 5-year pre-period were examined by offense type. For both groups, most convictions were for drug-related offenses, but compared to low-risk offenders, high-risk offenders had significantly greater numbers of convictions ($p<0.001$) for all offense types, including drug offenses (e.g., drug possession or use; 2.6 vs. 0.9 convictions); property offenses (e.g., theft, burglary; 1.4 vs. 0.2 convictions); violent offenses (e.g., homicide, rape, robbery; 0.3 vs. <0.1 convictions); and other offenses (e.g., prostitution, vandalism; 1.6 vs. 0.4 convictions, data not shown). Analysis of lifetime adult conviction data revealed similar patterns, with significantly more high-risk offenders having been convicted of offenses related to drugs (97.4 percent vs. 86.6 percent), property (74.4 percent vs. 44.7 percent), violence (29.5 percent vs. 14.5 percent), and other crimes (88.5 percent vs. 56.8 percent, data not shown).

Instruments and measures
At assessment for treatment

The baseline assessment included the Addiction Severity Index (ASI), a semi-structured interview instrument that captures *demographic information* and also assesses *problem severity* in seven areas: alcohol and drug use, employment, family and social relationships, legal, psychological, and medical status.[29,30] A composite score can be computed for each scale to indicate severity in that area; scores range from 0 to 1, with higher scores indicating greater severity. Distinguished by excellent inter-rater and test–retest reliability as well as high discriminant and concurrent validity,[31,32] the ASI is widely used in the addictions field.[33]

Motivation for treatment was also measured at baseline using the Stages of Change Readiness and Treatment Eagerness Scale (SOCRATES) 8D, a 19-item questionnaire which assesses readiness for change among drug and alcohol abusers. Responses are captured using a 1–5 Likert scale. A variable was constructed by summing all responses to measure offenders' overall motivation for treatment. Scores ranged from 19 to 95, with higher scores indicating greater motivation for treatment. Data from a multisite clinical sample and a test–retest study provided support for the reliability of SOCRATES scales.[34]

County of residence was recorded at treatment assessment. In order to maintain the confidentiality and anonymity of participating counties, each was arbitrarily assigned a letter from A to E. Detailed information on county characteristics is provided elsewhere.[26]

During treatment

Treatment retention was defined by the number of days from admission to the last day of treatment. Statewide administrative data indicate that a majority of Prop 36 offenders receive more than 90 days of treatment.[22] Thus, a median split was conducted on all calendar days of treatment received to distinguish *longer treatment retention* ($\geq$113 days) from shorter treatment retention (<113 days).

The number of treatment services received was calculated from data collected by the Treatment Services Review (TSR). Administered at the 3-month follow-up interview, the TSR captured services received in the previous 3 months (either during or after treatment) in each of the seven domains of the ASI (e.g., alcohol and drug use, employment, family, etc.), including the number of professional services and discussion sessions received. The number of times an individual self-reported receipt of services in any domain (either in the program or through other sources) was summed (range = 0–1,407 services) and the mean number of treatment services received during the 3 months following assessment for treatment were calculated. Test–retest studies on the TSR indicated satisfactory reliability, and tests of concurrent validity showed the ability to discriminate different levels of treatment services and good correspondence with independent measures of treatment provided.[35]

Administrative records contained in the California Alcohol and Drug Data System (CADDS) were analyzed to determine *modality of care* (outpatient, residential, methadone maintenance) at treatment entry and *completion status* at treatment discharge.

Before and after treatment assessment

Mental health services utilization was calculated using administrative records acquired on all individuals from the California DMH Client and Service Information system. This database tracks services and psychiatric diagnoses for clients treated in community-based mental health facilities that receive DMH funds. Services received prior to the baseline assessment for Prop 36 treatment were analyzed.

Recidivism was calculated using DOJ administrative records on arrests. The recidivism rate and the number of re-arrests included all arrests that occurred in the 12 months and in the 30 months following the date each individual was assessed for treatment. The 12-month time period was chosen to examine patterns for an outcome time period that is typically used in related research, while the 30-month time period was utilized to replicate prior research on high-risk Prop 36 offenders.[2]

Statistical analyses

Statistical analyses were conducted to examine differences in characteristics between high-risk and low-risk Prop 36 offenders and to identify factors associated with the number of re-arrests (as recorded in DOJ records) 12 and 30 months after intake assessment.

To test differences among the high-risk and low-risk offenders, ANOVA on continuous measures and chi-square tests on categorical measures were conducted. Controlling for county variation (as a set of dummy variables) and adjusting for several demographic covariates (age, gender, race/ethnicity), multiple regression analyses were conducted to examine predictors of more re-arrests as recorded in DOJ records in the 12 and 30 months following the baseline interview date. Four separate models were run to examine predictors of re-arrest during the two time periods of interest and before and after inclusion of an interaction term indicating high/low-risk level $\times$ longer/shorter treatment retention (described below).

Selection of variables for inclusion in the multiple regression models was informed by the relevant literature as well as by the descriptive analysis of characteristics. When indicators of similar behaviors were correlated, only one indicator was chosen for inclusion. To check that no potential multicollinearity biases existed among the selected predictors, diagnostic analysis with variance inflation factor (VIF) was also conducted. The VIF values of the selected predictors were below 5, indicating no multicollinearity biases among the predictors. Predictors examined in the model included age, gender, race/ethnicity, county of residence, employment status at intake, primary drug type, motivation for treatment, treatment modality, urine testing, services received during treatment, and mental health services utilization prior to Prop 36 entry. In addition, high/low-risk level and longer/shorter treatment retention as well as their interaction [i.e., four strata were created ("high risk with longer treatment retention," "high risk with shorter treatment retention," "low risk with longer treatment retention," "low risk with shorter treatment retention") and included as an interaction term using "low risk with shorter treatment retention" as the reference group] were included as primary predictors in the multiple regression models. Unless otherwise stated, the significance level for all statistical tests was set at $p < 0.05$.

Results
Characteristics of high-risk offenders

At assessment for treatment, high-risk offenders were distinguishable from low-risk offenders on several characteristics. As shown in Table 1, compared to low-risk offenders, high-risk offenders were younger (33.4 vs. 37.3 years old), fewer were female (14.1% vs. 28.9%), more were taking psychiatric medication (17.8% vs. 10.2%), more had been incarcerated in the prior 30 days (65.3% vs. 49.7%), first arrest occurred at a younger age (18.5 vs. 20.9 years old), the number of arrests (13.0 vs. 8.9 arrests) and convictions

(8.4 vs. 4.7 convictions) accumulated over the lifetime was greater, and more had received mental health services (47.4% vs. 26.2%) according to services utilization data from the Department of Mental Health. There were no significant differences at intake between high-risk and low-risk offenders on the other variables that were examined, including race/ethnicity, education, marital status, employment status, homelessness, parole status, motivation level, severity of problems in all of the domains measured by the ASI composite scores, primary drug type, recent drug use and arrests and psychiatric problems, age at first primary drug use, years of primary drug use, receipt of prior treatment, number of prior treatments, and months incarcerated in lifetime. Of note is that about half of offenders in both groups reported no use of any drugs (excluding alcohol) in the 30 days prior to treatment assessment.

Treatment received and recidivism

As shown in Table 2, several measures of treatment received were examined, but only one measure indicated differences between high-risk and low-risk offenders. Fewer high-risk offenders were urine tested during treatment than low-risk offenders (70.1 percent vs. 82.6 percent). Except for this difference, the treatment experiences of offenders were similar regardless of risk classification. For both groups, most offenders were treated in an outpatient setting, average time in treatment was approximately 4.5 months—during this time between 129.2 and 137.9 services were received on average—less than half of offenders received a longer period of treatment, about one third completed treatment, and slightly more than half stayed in treatment for 90 or more days or completed treatment. To better understand the type of treatment received by offenders in the sample, services and retention data were analyzed by modality (data not shown). This analysis revealed that compared to offenders in outpatient treatment settings, offenders in residential treatment settings received almost twice as many services over a fewer number of days (an average of 212 services over 86 days for residential vs. an average of 121 services over 148 days for outpatient), and this was the case for both high-risk and low-risk offenders.

Also shown in Table 2, a similar proportion of high-risk and low-risk offenders were re-arrested in the 12 months (64.1% and 53.8%) and in the 30 months (78.2% and 69.6%) following intake assessment; however, the mean number of re-arrests that occurred was greater among high-risk offenders compared to low-risk offenders for both time periods (1.6 vs. 1.1 re-arrests over 12 months and 3.4 vs. 2.3 arrests over 30 months). Very few (<1%) re-arrests over 12 and 30 months were due to a probation or parole violation, but instead mostly reflected a new offense (drug-related offenses were most common, data not shown).

Offender and program factors associated with number of re-arrests

Shown in Table 3 are four models which were run to examine factors associated with the number of re-arrests over 12 months (models 1 and 2) and over 30 months (models 3 and 4) before (models 1 and 3) and after (models 2 and 4) inclusion of an interaction term indicating high/low-risk level $\times$ longer/shorter treatment retention as a predictor.

Table 1   Offender characteristics at assessment for treatment

Variables	High-risk ($\geq$5 prior convictions, $n=78$)	Low-risk (<5 prior convictions, $n=1,009$)	Test statistic, p value
Age, mean (SD)	33.4 (8.9)	37.3 (9.7)	$F(1,1085) = 11.43, p < 0.01$
Female (percent)	14.1	28.9	$\chi^2_1 = 0.88, p < 0.01$
Ethnicity (percent)			$\chi^2_3 = 0.49, p = 0.92$
White	53.9	50.9	
African American	18.0	19.1	
Hispanic	23.0	23.1	
Other	5.1	6.8	
Education, mean (SD)	11.8 (2.0)	11.8 (1.9)	$F(1,1055) = 0.01, p = 0.92$
Married (percent)	12.2	16.3	$\chi^2_1 = 0.88, p = 0.35$
Employed (full- or part-time, percent)	36.5	39.0	$\chi^2_1 = 0.18, p = 0.67$
Homeless (percent)	12.3	7.7	$\chi^2_1 = 1.70, p = 0.19$
Taking psychiatric medication	17.8	10.2	$\chi^2_1 = 4.10, p = 0.04$
On parole (percent)	15.6	11.0	$\chi^2_1 = 0.14, p = 0.70$
Motivation level, mean (SD)	77.5 (11.2)	77.3 (12.5)	$F(1,1071) = 0.03, p = 0.86$
ASI Composite Scores, mean (SD)			
Alcohol	0.09 (0.16)	0.10 (0.18)	$F(1,1040) = 0.02, p = 0.88$
Drug	0.14 (0.11)	0.13 (0.11)	$F(1,1017) = 0.40, p = 0.53$
Employment	0.77 (0.26)	0.71 (0.29)	$F(1,1059) = 2.94, p = 0.09$
Family	0.16 (0.22)	0.16 (0.20)	$F(1,1033) = 0.00, p = 0.98$
Legal	0.28 (0.22)	0.26 (0.18)	$F(1,1058) = 1.17, p = 0.28$
Medical	0.20 (0.29)	0.26 (0.34)	$F(1,1062) = 1.79, p = 0.18$
Psychiatric	0.19 (0.22)	0.18 (0.22)	$F(1,1040) = 0.20, p = 0.65$
Primary drug (percent)			$\chi^2_4 = 7.60, p < 0.11$
Methamphetamine	43.2	50.6	
Cocaine	17.6	12.5	
Marijuana	10.8	13.4	
Heroin	10.8	8.5	
Alcohol	14.9	7.2	
Past 30 days (percent)			
Used any drug (excludes alcohol)	54.1	48.5	$\chi^2_1 = 0.84, p = 0.36$
Arrested	50.7	43.7	$\chi^2_1 = 1.31, p = 0.25$
Incarcerated	65.3	49.7	$\chi^2_1 = 6.82, p < 0.01$
Had psychiatric problems	41.0	39.4	$\chi^2_1 = 0.07, p = 0.78$
Lifetime			
Age at first primary drug use, mean (SD)	18.9 (7.5)	20.5 (8.0)	$F(1,1057) = 2.86, p = 0.09$
Years of primary drug use, mean (SD)	17.4 (25.5)	22.2 (33.5)	$F(1,1036) = 1.42, p = 0.23$
Received prior drug treatment, percent	73.0	65.0	$\chi^2_1 = 1.95, p = 0.16$
No. of prior drug treatments, mean (SD)	0.40 (1.1)	0.50 (1.5)	$F(1,1060) = 1.40, p = 0.24$
Age at first arrest, mean (SD)	18.5 (5.3)	20.9 (7.9)	$F(1,1074) = 6.80, p < 0.01$
No. of arrests, mean (SD) (data source: DOJ)	13.0 (11.3)	8.9 (12.0)	$F(1,1060) = 7.81, p < 0.01$
No. of convictions, mean (SD) (data source: DOJ)	8.4 (3.7)	4.7 (3.7)	$F(1,1085) = 72.44, p < 0.01$
Months incarcerated, mean (SD)	29.9 (30.4)	26.4 (34.4)	$F(1,1057) = 0.76, p = 0.38$
Received mental health services (percent) (Data source: DMH)	47.4	26.2	$\chi^2_1 = 16.36, p < 0.01$

Data source: All variables were extracted from the baseline assessment interview unless stated otherwise

Table 2 Treatment received and recidivism

Variables	High-risk (≥ 5 prior convictions, $n=78$)	Low-risk (<5 prior convictions, $n=1,009$)	F test or chi-square
Treatment received			
Modality (percent) (data source: CADDS)			$\chi^2_2 = 2.75, p = 0.25$
Outpatient	73.1	78.8	
Residential	24.4	17.2	
Methadone maintenance	2.6	4.0	
Longer treatment retention (≥113 days, percent) (data source: CADDS and follow-up interview)	46.2	42.4	$\chi^2_1 = 0.41, p = 0.52$
No. of services received, mean (SD) (data source: follow-up interview)	129.2 (169.1)	137.9 (138.7)	$F(1,1079) = 0.28, p = 0.60$
Urine tested during treatment (percent) (data source: follow-up interview)	70.1	82.6	$\chi^2_1 = 7.40, p < 0.01$
No. of urine tests, mean (SD) (data source: follow-up interview)	5.8 (7.7)	7.0 (7.1)	$F(1,1079) = 1.77, p = 0.18$
Completed treatment (percent) (data source: CADDS)	31.3	39.3	$\chi^2_1 = 1.59, p = 0.21$
Recidivism over 12 months after assessment for treatment (data source: DOJ)			
Re-arrested (percent)	64.1	53.8	$\chi^2_1 = 3.08, p = 0.07$
No. of re-arrests, Mean (SD)	1.6 (1.8)	1.1 (1.6)	$F(1,1085) = 7.14, p < 0.01$
Recidivism over 30 months after assessment for treatment (data source: DOJ)			
Re-arrested (percent)	78.2	69.6	$\chi^2_1 = 2.58, p = 0.11$
No. of re-arrests, mean (SD)	3.4 (3.6)	2.3 (2.6)	$F(1,1085) = 12.45, p < 0.01$

As shown in model 3, high-risk offender classification was associated with more re-arrests over the 30 months following intake assessment (0.061). A similar association was evident over the 12-month time period (model 1), but this result was not statistically significant. White race/ethnicity (−0.069) and employment at intake (−0.072) were associated with a fewer number of re-arrests over the 12-month time period. These associations were evident for the 30-month time period, but were not statistically significant. Report of methamphetamine as the primary drug problem (vs. other drug types such as heroin and cocaine) was associated with a fewer number of arrests over 30 months, as was also evident (but did not reach statistical significance) over the 12-month time frame.

For both the 12- and 30-month time periods, the number of re-arrests was increased by residing in County E (vs. County A, 0.136 and 0.174) and decreased by older age (−0.126 and −0.163), being female (−0.076 and −0.092), residing in County D (vs. County A, −0.109 and −0.092), receipt of more services during treatment (−0.102 and −0.063), and longer treatment retention (−0.248 and −0.179).

A significant interaction effect between risk classification and treatment retention on the mean number of re-arrests was found for both the 12- and 30-month time periods (Figs. 1 and 2). When this interaction effect was included in multiple regression analyses (Table 3, models 2 and 4), additional significant predictors emerged. For both time periods, a shorter treatment length for high-risk offenders increased the number of re-arrests (0.067 and 0.099), whereas a longer treatment length decreased the number of re-arrests for both high-risk offenders (−0.109 and −0.074) and low-risk offenders (−0.223 and −0.158).

Discussion
Summary of findings
In summary, high-risk offenders were distinguishable from low-risk offenders (defined as having five or more and less than five convictions in the 5 years prior to the current offense, respectively) on several characteristics at assessment for treatment including younger age, male gender, prior contact with the mental health services system, and more frequent contact with the criminal justice system. Treatment received and the proportion of offenders who recidivated were mostly similar across groups, but fewer high-risk offenders were urine tested during treatment and high-risk offenders had more re-arrests over 12 and 30 months following intake assessment. Consistent with prior research, multiple regression analysis showed that high-risk classification was a significant predictor of more re-arrests over 30 months after intake (results for the association between high-risk classification and re-arrests over 12 months pointed in the same direction, but did not reach statistical significance). Significant predictors associated with fewer re-arrests over 12 months after intake included White race/ethnicity

Table 3 Multiple regression models predicting number of re-arrests over 12 and 30 months after assessment for treatment

Variables	Over 12 months		Over 30 months	
	Estimates			
	Model 1	Model 2	Model 3	Model 4
Age at intake	−0.126**	−0.130**	−0.163**	−0.168**
Female (vs. male)	−0.076*	−0.076*	−0.092**	−0.092**
White (vs. non-White)	−0.069*	−0.066*	−0.038	−0.035
Employed (vs. not employed) at intake	−0.072*	−0.069*	−0.061	−0.058
County B (vs. County A)	−0.005	−0.001	0.013	0.018
County C (vs. County A)	−0.016	−0.021	0.001	−0.004
County D (vs. County A)	−0.109**	−0.108**	−0.092**	−0.090*
County E (vs. County A)	0.136**	0.139**	0.174**	0.177**
Primary drug is methamphetamine (vs. all other drug types)	−0.019	−0.021	−0.068*	−0.070*
Motivation level	0.004	0.004	0.014	0.013
Treatment setting is residential (vs. methadone maintenance)	0.004	0.002	0.053	0.050
Treatment setting is outpatient (vs. methadone maintenance)	0.038	0.033	0.033	0.027
Received mental health services prior to intake	0.017	0.014	0.036	0.033
No. of urine tests received during treatment	−0.001	Less than −0.001	−0.018	−0.016
No. of services received during treatment	−0.102**	−0.105**	−0.063*	−0.066*
High-risk offender (vs. low-risk offender)	0.029	–	0.061*	–
Longer treatment retention [≥113 days vs. shorter treatment retention (<113 days)]	−0.248**	–	−0.179**	–
High-risk offender and longer treatment retention (vs. low-risk offender and shorter treatment retention)	–	−0.109**	–	−0.074*
Low-risk offender and longer treatment retention (vs. low-risk offender and shorter treatment retention)	–	−0.223**	–	−0.158**
High-risk offender and shorter treatment retention (vs. low-risk offender and shorter treatment retention)	–	0.067*	–	0.099**

Standardized betas are shown. R^2 was 0.16 for models 1, 3, and 4 and 0.17 for model 2
*$p < 0.05$;
**$p < 0.01$

and employment at intake. Regardless of the length of the outcome observation time period, the number of re-arrests was smaller with older age, being female, residing in a particular county, receipt of more services during treatment, and receipt of a longer length of treatment. Moreover, congruent with expectations, the interaction between risk classification and treatment length had a significant effect on the mean number of re-arrests. The number of re-arrests was greater with shorter treatment retention lengths for high-risk offenders and was smaller with longer treatment retention lengths for both low-risk and high-risk offenders.

Limitations

The present study has several limitations. Offender risk classification relied on a single indicator (number of prior convictions)—and it is not intended to serve as definitive criteria for classifying offenders in the future—but use of this indicator permitted constructive comparisons with existing Prop 36 evaluation reports. The treatment received measure primarily relied on one indicator (treatment retention), and potential effects associated with the quantity and quality of treatment services were omitted; however, other indicators of treatment received (treatment modality, urine testing, number of services received) were also examined and described. Also, for ethical and feasibility reasons, offenders were not randomly assigned to receive different lengths of treatment, as would have been the case with an experimental study design, and thus self-selection biases may have contributed to group differences that emerged; however, key factors that have been associated with outcomes were examined and included in the analyses. Another limitation is that group comparisons yielded a medium effect size, suggesting that some differences may not have reached

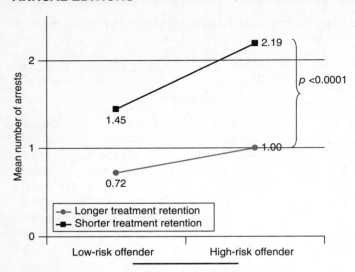

Figure 1 Interaction effect between risk level and treatment retention on re-arrests over 12 months after assessment for treatment

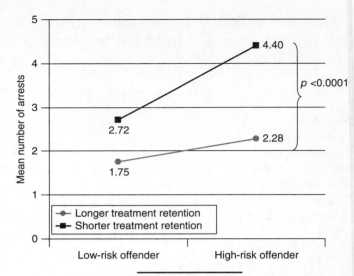

Figure 2 Interaction effect between risk level and treatment retention on re-arrests over 30 months after assessment for treatment

statistical significance because of low power. Findings were congruent with general trends, but replication of analyses with larger sample sizes is warranted. Also, information on periods of incarceration was not available, and thus, re-arrest data were not adjusted to account for possible group differences in time-at-risk periods. Similarly, re-arrest may be influenced by contextual differences in criminal justice policing, supervision practices, or other environmental factors. Except for inclusion of "county" in the models, data were not adjusted to account for potential contextual biases. Also, this study captured a relatively small proportion of the larger statewide population of Prop 36 offenders and focused on only one outcome measure (re-arrest). Findings may vary with analysis of a larger sample and inclusion of additional outcome indicators. The study utilized administrative data, a data source vulnerable to over- or underreporting of behaviors.[36,37] For example, measures of arrest and drug treatment/mental health services utilization that relied on administrative data did not capture events that may have occurred outside of California. Also omitted from the analysis were any events they may have occurred but did not come to the attention of the institution from which the data were acquired (e.g., utilization of health services in non-publicly funded settings; crimes for which there was no arrest). Finally, future research that aims to isolate causal factors related to outcomes would likely be strengthened by the application of propensity scoring or other approaches to adjust for differences in offender characteristics. Despite these and other limitations of administrative data, it is generally believed to be a valuable resource for the evaluation of substance abuse treatment outcomes.[27,36–38] The findings support and extend existing knowledge on drug treatment for offenders and new aspects of a unique and costly offender subgroup were documented.

Implications for Behavioral Health

The study findings pose several important implications for future program planning and research on court-supervised drug treatment

for offenders. Examining conviction history to assign offenders to a risk level is a clear-cut and pragmatic tool, yet the classification of offenders based on the number of convictions alone is problematic. The results showed that recidivism was associated with risk classification at intake, but it was also associated with individual demographic variables (i.e., age, sex, race/ethnicity, employment status), history of interactions with the mental health services system and criminal justice system, and county of residence. Using the number of convictions as the sole criteria for program exclusion/inclusion would not only overlook the range of personal characteristics, system interactions, and environmental factors that influence behavior but would also represent a significant change in current eligibility criteria which looks beyond conviction frequency to consider offense type and the timing of conviction occurrence in the life course.

Another study implication is that using recidivism as the only measure of program outcomes is problematic. Variation in Prop 36 program operations has been documented,[39] and community-level differences in program practices and approach likely impact criminal justice outcomes differentially. Also, differences between groups may appear in one behavioral domain but not in another. For example, for this study, separate analysis of self-reported use of any drug (excluding alcohol) in the 30 days prior to the 12-month follow-up interview indicated no significant differences in the proportion of high- and low-risk offenders who had used (about one quarter of both groups had used drugs). As has been done in other similar work,[40] future treatment outcomes research would be strengthened by the examination of a range of behaviors impacted by drug use, including not only recidivism but also employment, family and social relationships, and general health and well-being.

The intent to spend Prop 36 public resources efficiently is a valid reason for omitting high-risk offenders from the program, but it is also the case that by excluding those with more prior convictions, there is the risk of omitting individuals who are most in need of treatment. Prior research indicates that few offenders in prisons and jails have access to substance abuse services,[41] drug treatment programs have been shown to reduce criminal behavior,[42] and judicial mandates can provide an opportunity for substance-using offenders to access and benefit from needed treatment.[43] A significant added economic benefit is the cost savings that are consistently associated with substance use treatment.[44]

Risk classification based on conviction history might be best suited for use as a clinical tool for identifying offenders who are most in need of longer lengths of drug treatment. The findings indicated that the number of re-arrests was decreased by receipt of more services and longer lengths of treatment, and most notably, the results showed that the number of re-arrests was less when high-risk offenders received longer lengths of treatment. Also, although not a significant predictor of re-arrest, fewer high-risk offenders were urine tested during treatment. Undoubtedly, the provision of more treatment, especially high-intensity treatment, is expensive[14] and offenders may drop out of treatment prematurely, effectively choosing to receive less treatment. Yet it is also evident that a standardized risk assessment is not used by the Prop 36 program, as is the case in many community-based substance abuse treatment programs that treat drug-involved offenders,[45] and about one third of counties report that special strategies to manage Prop 36 high-risk offenders are not used.[2] So it may not be surprising to find that in the sample that was studied, Prop 36 treatment retention lengths were not significantly different by risk level and that similar proportions of high-risk and low-risk offenders received longer treatment stays. The provision of longer treatment to low-risk offenders was not shown to harm outcomes. But the overtreatment of some low-risk offenders, when there is an undertreatment of others who are in greater need, is wasteful of scarce resources and is an indication that there is room to improve efforts to retain high-risk offenders in treatment. Tools to engage and retain offenders in court-supervised community-based treatment have been identified and include a range of strategies such as the use of incentives and sanctions, adequate monitoring, participation in mutual self-help groups, and development of relapse prevention skills.[46]

In recent years, fiscal constraints have obliged many counties to shorten the expected length of treatment stay for Prop 36 offenders and, in some areas, to eliminate certain costlier modalities, such as residential treatment, from Prop 36 programming altogether. The data indicated that residential treatment often appears to be a setting where Prop 36 offenders receive more services in a shorter amount of time, a practice that can "intensify" the treatment experience but may not be as important for enhancing outcomes as the provision of a sufficient length of time in treatment. Some research indicates that a highly controlled environment may precipitate treatment dropout for some high-risk offenders.[47] Also, for many drug offenders, recovery from drug dependence is a lengthy process and the effects of treatment require adequate time to develop and sustain in order to have long-term impacts on overall health, quality of life, and social functioning.[48–50] In the absence of adequate residential treatment (for example due to limited residential treatment capacity or offender ineligibility), lengthened engagement with the type of treatment that is available (e.g., outpatient, self-help groups) may be warranted. More research is needed to understand how risk level may interact with treatment setting, as well as services received and level of supervision, to impact outcomes. Criminal justice mandated treatment clients face numerous obstacles to treatment compliance[51] and barriers to implementing client treatment matching exist,[52] but taken together, the information presented here indicates that more can be done to evaluate the risk level of Prop 36 offenders at program entry and that this information could be used to ensure that treatment, especially length of treatment, is better matched to need.

Finally, receipt of mental health services was one of the few client characteristics that differentiated high-risk offenders from low-risk offenders at assessment for treatment. Offenders diagnosed with both mental illness and drug dependence are particularly challenging to treat, and Prop 36 stakeholders have expressed concerns regarding their ability to effectively address the needs of these offenders.[53] Evidence-based treatment practices for individuals with co-occurring disorders can be difficult to implement within criminal justice settings.[54] Yet finding ways to integrate treatments for drug and mental health disorders (e.g., assessment of mental health needs, co-location of services, on-site service delivery, adequately trained mental health professionals) will likely improve outcomes. Also, no studies have been published on offenders with mental illness who participate in drug treatment through Prop 36. More research is needed to identify special needs and strategies for improving outcomes among this population.

In conclusion, alternative sentencing policies that focus on the rehabilitation of drug offenders in lieu of imprisonment appear to be gaining in popularity among the general public. In the past decade, more than 20 states have considered legislation that is similar to Prop 36.[55] In California, voters were recently given the opportunity to consider a new drug diversion option, the Nonviolent Offender Rehabilitation Act,[56] and the debate continues over whether to solve the state's overcrowded prison problem through early prisoner release programs that would presumably route significant numbers of drug offenders to community-based treatment programs. Stakeholders desire sentencing options that save taxpayer money and also perform better than incarceration in reducing recidivism and improving longer term outcomes. However, the effectiveness and financial benefits of such programs are in jeopardy when treatment lengths are inadequate. To improve outcomes among high-risk offenders who receive court-supervised treatment, efforts are needed to address psychiatric problems and criminal history and to ensure receipt of appropriate lengths of treatment. The findings may be useful for optimizing the effectiveness of criminal justice diversion programs for treating drug-addicted offenders.

References

1. California Department of Alcohol and Drug Programs. *Substance Abuse and Crime Prevention Act of 2000 (Prop. 36)*. 2008. Available at: www.adp.ca.gov/sacpa/prop36.shtml. Accessed October 8, 2009.
2. Hawken A. *High-risk and high-cost offenders in Proposition 36*. 2008. Available at: www.uclaisap.org/Prop36/html/reports. html. Accessed October 9, 2009.
3. California Department of Finance. *Governor's Budget 2008–2009*. 2008. Available at: www.ebudget.ca.gov/Enacted/ BudgetSummary/BSS/BSS.html. Accessed October 8, 2009.
4. Little Hoover Commission. *Addressing addiction: Improving and integrating California's substance abuse treatment system. A report to the California Legislature*. 2008. Available at: www. lhc.ca.gov/lhcdir/report190.html. Accessed October 8, 2009.
5. Evans E, Li L, Hser YI. Client and program factors associated with dropout from court mandated drug treatment. *Evaluation and Program Planning*, 2009; 32: 204–212.
6. Hser YI, Evans E, Teruya C, et al. Predictors of short-term treatment outcomes among California's Proposition 36 participants. *Evaluation and Program Planning*, 2007; 30: 187–196.

7. Taxman FS, Thanner M, Weisburd D. Risk, need, and responsivity (RNR): It all depends. *Crime & Delinquency,* 2006; 52: 28–51.

8. Thanner MH, Taxman FS. Responsivity: The value of providing intensive services to high-risk offenders. *Journal of Substance Abuse Treatment,* 2003; 24: 137–147.

9. Taxman FS, Bouffard J. Treatment inside the drug treatment court: The who, what, where, and how of treatment services. *Substance Use & Misuse,* 2002; 37: 1665–1688.

10. Marlowe DB. Integrating substance abuse treatment and criminal justice supervision. *Science and Practice Perspectives,* 2003; 2: 4–14.

11. Marlowe DB. Judicial supervision of drug-abusing offenders. *American Journal of Drug and Alcohol Abuse,* 2006; 29: 337–357.

12. Marlowe DB, Festinger DS, Dugosh KL, et al. Adapting judicial supervision to the risk level of drug offenders: Discharge and 6-month outcomes from a prospective matching study. *Drug and Alcohol Dependence,* 2007; 88: 4–13.

13. Marlowe DB, Festinger DS, Lee PA, et al. Matching judicial supervision to clients' risk status in drug court. *Crime & Delinquency,* 2006; 52: 52–76.

14. Chen S, Barnett PG, Sempel JM, et al. Outcomes and costs of matching the intensity of dual-diagnosis treatment to patients' symptom severity. Journal of Substance Abuse Treatment. 2006; 31: 95–105.

15. Thornton CC, Gottheil E, Weinstein SP, et al. Patient-treatment matching in substance abuse drug addiction severity. *Journal of Substance Abuse Treatment,* 1998; 15: 505–511.

16. Tiet QQ, Ilgen MA, Byrnes HF, et al. Treatment setting and baseline substance use severity interact to predict patients' outcomes. *Addiction,* 2007; 102: 432–440.

17. Timko C, Sempel JM. Short-term outcomes of matching dual diagnosis patients' symptom severity to treatment intensity. *Journal of Substance Abuse Treatment,* 2004; 26: 209–218.

18. Babor TF. Treatment for persons with substance use disorders: Mediators, moderators, and the need for a new research approach. International Journal of Methods in Psychiatric Research, 2008; 17: 45–49.

19. Karno MP, Longabaugh R. Does matching matter? Examining matches and mismatches between patient attributes and therapy techniques in alcoholism treatment. *Addiction,* 2007; 102: 587–596.

20. Lowenkamp CT, Latessa EJ. Increasing the effectiveness of correctional programming through the risk principle: Identifying offenders for residential placement. *Criminology & Public Policy,* 2005; 4: 263–290.

21. Farabee D, Hser Y, Anglin D, et al. Recidivism among an early cohort of California's Proposition 36 offenders. *Criminology & Public Policy,* 2004; 3: 563–584.

22. Urada D, Evans E, Yang J, et al. *Evaluation of the Substance Abuse and Crime Prevention Act 2009 Report.* 2009. Submitted to the California Department of Alcohol and Drug Programs. Los Angeles, CA: UCLA Integrated Substance Abuse Programs.

23. Hser YI, Teruya C, Brown AH, et al. Impact of California's Proposition 36 on the drug treatment system: Treatment capacity and displacement. *American Journal of Public Health,* 2007; 97: 104–109.

24. Urada D, Hawken A, Conner B, et al. (2008). *Evaluation of the Substance Abuse and Crime Prevention Act 2008 Report. 2008.* Available at: www.uclaisap.org/Prop36/html/reports.html. Accessed October 8, 2009.

25. Grella CE, Greenwell L, Prendergast M, et al. Organizational characteristics of drug abuse treatment programs for offenders. *Journal of Substance Abuse Treatment,* 2007; 32: 291–300.

26. Hser YI, Teruya C, Evans E, et al. Treating drug-abusing offenders: Initial findings from a five-county study on the

27. impact of California's Proposition 36 on the treatment system and patient outcomes. *Evaluation Review,* 2003; 27: 479–505.

27. Hser YI, Evans E. Cross-system data linkage for treatment outcome evaluation: Lessons learned from the California Treatment Outcome Project. *Evaluation and Program Planning,* 2008; 31: 125–135.

28. Longshore D, Urada D, Evans E et al. *Evaluation of the Substance Abuse and Crime Prevention Act: 2004 report.* 2005 Available at: www.uclaisap.org/Prop36/html/reports.html. Accessed October 9, 2009.

29. McLellan AT, Luborsky L, Woody GE, et al. An improved diagnostic evaluation instrument for substance abuse patients: The Addiction Severity Index. *Journal of Nervous and Mental Disease,* 1980; 168: 26–33.

30. McLellan AT, Kushner H, Metzger D, et al. The fifth edition of the Addiction Severity Index. *Journal of Substance Abuse Treatment,* 1992; 9: 199–213.

31. Bovasso GB, Alterman AI, Cacciola JS, et al. Predictive validity of the Addiction Severity Index's composite scores in the assessment of 2-year outcomes in a methadone maintenance population. *Psychology of Addictive Behaviors,* 2001; 15: 171–176.

32. Kosten TR, Rounsaville BJ, Kleber HD. Concurrent validity of the Addiction Severity Index. *Journal of Nervous and Mental Disease,* 1983; 171: 606–610.

33. McLellan AT, Cacciola JC, Alterman AI, Rikoon SH, Carise D. The Addiction Severity Index at 25: Origins, contributions and transitions. *American Journal of Addictions,* 2006; 15:113–24.

34. Miller WR, Tonigan JS. Assessing drinkers' motivation for change: The Stages of Change Readiness and Treatment Eagerness Scale (SOCRATES). *Psychology of Addictive Behaviors,* 1996; 10: 81–89.

35. McLellan AT, Alterman AI, Cacciola J, et al. A new measure of substance abuse treatment: Initial studies of the treatment services review. *Journal of Nervous and Mental Disease,* 1992; 180: 101–110.

36. McCarty D, McGuire TG, Harwood HJ, Field T. Using state information systems for drug abuse services research. *American Behavioral Scientist,* 1998; 41: 1090–106.

37. Saunders RC, Heflinger CA. Integrating data from multiple public sources: Opportunities and challenges for evaluators. *Evaluation: International Journal of Theory, Research, and Practice,* 2004; 10: 349–65.

38. Evans E, Grella C, Murphy D, Hser YI. Using administrative data for longitudinal substance abuse research. *Journal of Behavioral Health Services & Research,* 2010; 37: 252–271.

39. Evans E, Anglin MD, Urada D, Yang J. Promising practices for delivery of court-supervised substance abuse treatment: Perspectives from six high-performing California counties operating Proposition 36. *Evaluation and Program Planning,* 2011; 34:124–134.

40. Evans E, Li L, Urada D, Anglin M.D. Comparative effectiveness of California's Proposition 36 and drug court programs before and after propensity score matching. *Crime & Delinquency,* 2011 (in press).

41. Taxman FS, Perdoni ML, Harrison LD. Drug treatment services for adult offenders: The state of the state. *Journal of Substance Abuse Treatment,* 2007; 32: 239–254.

42. Holloway KR, Bennett TH, Farrington DP. The effectiveness of drug treatment programs in reducing criminal behavior: A meta-analysis. *Psicothema,* 2006; 18: 620–629.

43. Kelly JF, Finney JW, Moos R. Substance use disorder patients who are mandated to treatment: Characteristics, treatment process, and 1-and 5-year outcomes. *Journal of Substance Abuse Treatment,* 2005; 28: 213–223.

44. Ettner SL, Huang D, Evans E, Ash DR, Hardy M, Jourabchi M, Hser YI. Benefit-cost in the California Treatment Outcome Project: Does substance abuse treatment "pay for itself?" *Health Services Research,* 2006; 41: 192–213.

45. Friedmann PD, Taxman FS, Henderson CE. Evidence-based treatment practices for drug-involved adults in the criminal justice system. *Journal of Substance Abuse Treatment,* 2007; 32: 267–277.

46. Center for Substance Abuse Treatment. Substance Abuse Treatment for Adults in the Criminal Justice System. Improvement Protocol (TIP) Series 44. DHHS Publication No. (SMA) 05–4056. Rockville, MD: Substance Abuse and Mental Health Services Administration, 2005.

47. McKellar J, Kelly J, Harris A, et al. Pretreatment and during treatment risk factors for dropout among patients with substance use disorders. *Addictive Behaviors,* 2006; 31: 450–460.

48. Laudet AB. The road to recovery: Where are we going and how do we get there? Empirically driven conclusions and future directions for service development and research. *Substance Use & Misuse,* 2008; 43: 2001–2020.

49. Laudet AB, White W. What are your priorities right now? Identifying service needs across recovery stages to inform service development. *Journal of Substance Abuse Treatment,* 2010; 38:51–59.

50. McLellan AT. Have we evaluated addiction treatment correctly? Implications from a chronic care perspective. *Addiction,* 2002; 97: 249–252.

51. Sung HE, Belenko S, Feng L, et al. Predicting treatment noncompliance among criminal justice-mandated clients: A theoretical and empirical exploration. *Journal of Substance Abuse Treatment,* 2004; 26: 315–328.

52. Merkx MJ, Schippers GM, Koeter MJ, et al. Allocation of substance use disorder patients to appropriate levels of care: Feasibility of matching guidelines in routine practice in Dutch treatment centres. *Addiction,* 2007; 102: 466–474.

53. Hardy M, Teruya C, Longshore D, et al. Initial implementation of California's Substance Abuse and Crime Prevention Act: Findings from focus groups in ten counties. *Evaluation and Program Planning,* 2005; 28: 221–232.

54. Chandler RK, Peters RH, Field G, et al. Challenges in implementing evidence-based treatment practices for co-occurring disorders in the criminal justice system. *Behavioral Sciences & the Law,* 2004; 22: 431–448.

55. The Avisa Group. *Comparing California's Proposition 36 (SACPA) with similar legislation in other states and jurisdictions.* 2005 Available at: www.prop36.org/pdf/ComparisonProp36OtherStates.pdf. Accessed October 8, 2009.

56. California Secretary of State. *Voter information guide.* 2008. Available at: www.voterguide.sos.ca.gov/title-sum/prop5-title-sum.htm. Accessed October 8, 2009.

Critical Thinking

1. Discuss key differences between high and low risk drug offenders.

2. Discuss important treatment program factors for drug users at high risk for relapsing.

3. Discuss this study's implications for future court mandated treatment programs.

Acknowledgments—The study was supported in part by the National Institute on Drug Abuse (NIDA; grant no. R01DA15431 & P30DA016383). Also, Dr. Hser is supported by a Senior Scientist Award (K05DA017648) and Dr. Huang is supported by the National Institute of Mental Health (NIMH, grant no. R03MH084434-01A1 & R03MH084434-02). The content of this publication does not necessarily reflect the views or policies of NIDA or NIMH.

Address correspondence to Elizabeth Evans, MA, UCLA Integrated Substance Abuse Programs, Semel Institute for Neuroscience and Human Behavior, Department of Psychiatry and Biobehavioral Sciences, David Geffen School of Medicine, 1640 S. Sepulveda Blvd., 200, Los Angeles, CA 90025, USA. Phone: +1-310-2675315; Email: laevans@ucla.edu.

DAVID HUANG, DrPH, UCLA Integrated Substance Abuse Programs, Semel Institute for Neuroscience and Human Behavior, Department of Psychiatry and Biobehavioral Sciences, David Geffen School of Medicine, Los Angeles, CA, USA. Phone: +1-310-2675288; Email: yhuang@ucla.edu.

YIH-ING HSER, PhD, UCLA Integrated Substance Abuse Programs, Semel Institute for Neuroscience and Human Behavior, Department of Psychiatry and Biobehavioral Sciences, David Geffen School of Medicine, Los Angeles, CA, USA. Phone: +1-310-2675388; Email: yhser@ucla.edu.

Journal of Behavioral Health Services & Research, 2011. © 2011 National Council for Community Behavioral Healthcare.

Test-Your-Knowledge Form

We encourage you to photocopy and use this page as a tool to assess how the articles in *Annual Editions* expand on the information in your textbook. By reflecting on the articles you will gain enhanced text information. You can also access this useful form on a product's book support website at www.mhhe.com/cls

NAME: DATE:

_____

TITLE AND NUMBER OF ARTICLE:

_____

BRIEFLY STATE THE MAIN IDEA OF THIS ARTICLE:

_____

LIST THREE IMPORTANT FACTS THAT THE AUTHOR USES TO SUPPORT THE MAIN IDEA:

_____

WHAT INFORMATION OR IDEAS DISCUSSED IN THIS ARTICLE ARE ALSO DISCUSSED IN YOUR TEXTBOOK OR OTHER READINGS THAT YOU HAVE DONE? LIST THE TEXTBOOK CHAPTERS AND PAGE NUMBERS:

_____

LIST ANY EXAMPLES OF BIAS OR FAULTY REASONING THAT YOU FOUND IN THE ARTICLE:

_____

LIST ANY NEW TERMS/CONCEPTS THAT WERE DISCUSSED IN THE ARTICLE, AND WRITE A SHORT DEFINITION: